Talking ACT

Notes and Conversations on Acceptance and Commitment Therapy

Talking ACT

Notes and Conversations on Acceptance and Commitment Therapy

Edited by

David Chantry

CONTEXT PRESS
Reno, Nevada

Talking ACT: Notes and Conversations on Acceptance and Commitment Therapy

Paperback. pp. 342

Distributed by New Harbinger Publications, Inc.

Library of Congress Cataloging-in-Publication Data

Talking ACT : notes and conversations on acceptance and commitment
therapy / edited by David Chantry.
    p. cm.
 Includes index.
 ISBN-13: 978-1-878978-58-5 (pbk.)
 ISBN-10: 1-878978-58-6 (pbk.)
 1. Acceptance and commitment therapy--Miscellanea. I. Chantry, David
(David Keith), 1958- II. Title.

 RC569.5.A53T35 2007
 616.89'14--dc22

2007019113

© 2007 CONTEXT PRESS
933 Gear Street, Reno, NV 89503-2729

Printed in the United States of America

Table of Contents

Introduction

This book contains a selection of e-mails to the Acceptance and Commitment Therapy (ACT) listserv between July 2002 and August 2005. This period saw significant growth and development in the worldwide ACT community, with membership of the listserv increasing to around 700 members (now, in 2007 membership is topping 1,200).

This e-mail collection started life as a personal archive. Realizing that the listserv was an invaluable source of guidance on ACT, I began to keep what seemed to be the most useful material as a resource, purely for personal use. No formal selection criteria were adopted; however, given the non-availability of specialist ACT supervision in my home area, I looked in particular for posts that would support my own formative clinical practice. To this end the archive incorporated e-mails concerning the main principles of ACT, its application to particular presenting problems, ACT resources (for example, new metaphors and exercises), and clinical issues. Also included were posts describing the theoretical, scientific and philosophical roots of ACT, discussing new research findings, and comparing and contrasting ACT with other therapeutic approaches. However, my interest in these topics was not merely professional as, in common with many other list members, I came to recognise the personal relevance and application of the ACT work as elaborated and enriched in listserv community discussions.

As the collection grew, I was persuaded that it might be of value to others. With so many useful messages being sent to the listserv on a daily basis, bringing them into a publishable form seemed a worthwhile project. The major editorial problem, however, lay in deciding what to omit, given that space limitations allowed only a fraction of the 4400 or so e-mails during this period to be included. This inevitably meant leaving out very many interesting and thoughtful contributions. Posts containing substantial material from already-published sources (for example, ACT-relevant poems or long quotations) were also excluded in the final edit for copyright reasons.

One consequence of presenting a limited selection is that the book may not fully convey the collegiate, supportive nature of the ACT listserv community, where contributions, whether from novice or expert in ACT, are respectfully received and where the absence of hierarchy is a defining feature. ACT is a model of therapy, and it is also an approach that encourages people to work together for the common good. It is hoped that the humanity and goodwill of the ACT community will be sensed in these pages.

Readers may also sense the dynamic and informal nature of these e-mail communications. These are not comments meant for scholarly publication – they are loose, moment by moment conversations. In order to avoid risk of unfairness or harm to contributors, it is hoped that any reader wishing to quote from posts published here will be mindful of the context in which they were written, and that checks with the original authors will be made where appropriate. It should also be mentioned that, as some e-mails refer to real clinical cases, where appropriate, factual information has been altered in order to preserve client confidentiality.

A note on the composition of the book: each chapter contains a brief introduction to its subject-matter and an index. As many e-mails do not fit neatly into single-subject categories, readers will find plenty of overlap in the organization of the material, particularly as "threads" of e-mails (often containing a variety of topics) have, as far as possible, been kept together. The chapter indices show, in italics, entries for relevant e-mails found in other chapters. Each post or thread may be located via one or more index entries; however, the range of topics sometimes addressed in a single e-mail or thread has necessitated an indexing system that might be described as indicative rather than comprehensive.

By way of acknowledgements, first and foremost I would like to thank members of the ACT listserv, not only for their permissions to use their work, but also for sharing their knowledge and experience in the first place. I am especially grateful to members who were not afraid to raise the kind of issues that others of us might have been quietly thinking about; their questions and comments stimulated invaluable discussions to the benefit of the whole community. Similarly, at one time a "beginner's group" operated on the listserv, sharing their thoughts as they worked through the 1999 ACT book, section by section. Again, this generated much useful material that has been included here.

Many thanks also to Emily Neilan Rodrigues, manager at Context Press, for her kind patience and persistence (far beyond any call of duty!) in obtaining permissions from contributors, and in tackling the significant formatting challenges involved in preparing the manuscript for publication. Finally, I express my sincere appreciation to Steve Hayes for his encouragement and support in the creation of this book, my involvement in which has been a privilege.

David Chantry
Staffordshire, UK
May 2007

Note:

The ACT listserv (membership of which is restricted to professionals in relevant fields) can be joined at:
http://groups.yahoo.com/group/acceptanceandcommitmenttherapy/join

A listserv open to members of the public interested in ACT can be joined at:
http://groups.yahoo.com/group/ACT_for_the_Public/join

Key

The indices for each chapter show the main headings and sub-headings around which material in the chapter has been organized, with a chapter number-page number notation to indicate the location of each entry. In the following example, for instance, 1-34 refers to Chapter 1, page 34.

BEHAVIOR CHANGE
Behavioral health website (inc. re smoking, diabetes) [6-7-05] 1-34
EVIDENCE
Anxiety, social - ACT cf. CBT [4-26-05]... 1-34
CBT, ACT cf. [4-4-05]... 1-34
Defusion, helpfulness of - Milk, milk, milk exercise [1-23-04].. *3-107*
Hypotheses/ principles, testable [5-18-04] 1-35

Sub-headings are shown in italics when the relevant post or thread does not appear in the current chapter but in another chapter (because it also contains material relevant to that other chapter). In the example above, *3-107* indicates that the post/ thread can be found in Chapter 3, page 107 of the book.

All page numbers refer to the page on which the relevant post begins; for posts with multiple headings, the indexed heading/ sub-heading may sometimes be found on the subsequent page.

ACT cf.
    Motivational
    Interviewing [cont'd]
 	
CHOICE
    ACT concept of
    [5-29-05]
      Niklas Törneke
 	
    Cross Reference:
    See 4-160 for later
    posts in the thread:
    CHOICE
    ACT concept of
	This might be to say something that is obvious to all on this list but as talking about choice in an ACT context sometimes is misunderstood, I'll risk that.
	
	When we talk about choice in ACT this is not a philosophical or scientific statement, made as an argument for "free will." In ACT choice is a kind of common sense term or, even better, an experiential term.
	
	Human beings constantly act without being able to know (verbally) the actual causes of that behavior. We play games that we have learned, and in these games it is as if we really know why we did this and that. This is helpful, especially in social action. But it can also constitute a trap; that's why we target this in ACT, of course. As we act the actual causes of that behavior are forever hidden in history, so to speak. So what term are we to use for this "action without knowing the causes"? Choice. There is no better word for this actual experience.

Headings and sub-headings shown in bold type mark the start of a new topic. So in this example, the first heading/ sub-heading (ACT cf. Motivational Interviewing [cont'd]) is, as indicated, the continuation of a thread, whereas the second heading/ sub-heading in bold (**CHOICE ACT concept of**) denotes a new topic. Bold headings and sub-headings are also used to mark the continuation of a thread from another area of the book.

Where a post introduces at least one new topic, the date on which it was sent to the listserv is shown in bold (in this example, **[5-29-05]**). The author's name is also shown.

A *Cross Reference* indicates that the thread begins or continues in another area of the book, which again can be located via the chapter number-page number notation.

Chapter 1
<u>ACT: Basic and Applied</u>

This chapter presents material that introduces some of the key issues in Acceptance and Commitment Therapy, providing a backdrop for later, more specific chapters. For example, there are posts that describe the core principles and components of the therapy, including in particular what is called (somewhat tongue in cheek) the "Hexaflex" model. There are also posts that help to situate ACT as a new form of psychotherapy in its historical context, with its roots firmly in the traditions of empirical behavioral science, or that provide insight into the broader, strategic aims of the movement that comprises ACT and its theoretical base, Relational Frame Theory (RFT).

Another major theme of the chapter is evidence - including considerations as to how ACT, in common with other forms of psychotherapy, should properly be evaluated, as well as news and updates on individual studies of ACT processes, the application of ACT with particular populations and/or clinical problems, and the state of the ACT/RFT evidence base more generally. Posts in these latter categories, perhaps more than most other posts in this volume, may be considered as snapshots of the position as at the time they were written, particularly in view of the rapid pace of ACT/RFT research developments.

The chapter also includes posts touching on issues pertaining to mental health and the mental health establishment more generally, as well as on the application of ACT/RFT principles in contexts beyond the therapy room - namely, politics and the workplace.

Given the range of topics addressed in this chapter, there is inevitably a degree of overlap with material presented in later chapters.

ACT Age of [5-5-03] Steve Hayes	I came across a copy of the attached article today [Hayes, S. C. (1984). Making sense of spirituality. *Behaviorism, 12*, 99-110] which I just scanned in and cleaned up. I've asked Eric to post it on the website (contextualpsychology.org). I am sending it out to the list in part because in reading through it (esp. the references) I noticed that it documents ACT's age fairly precisely (periodically people do ask). Bottom line: ACT is 22. The article also foretells of deictic frames, perspective taking, acceptance, defusion, a relational definition of "verbal", etc. To age ACT: The article mentions the first controlled piece of ACT data ... a project on pain tolerance presented at AABT in November 1982. The data collection had to be running in Fall 1981 -- thus the 22 year figure. (Shockingly, these data did not come out until 1999 in *The Psychological Record, 49*, 33-47. How's that for speed of publication?)
ACT Agenda - not "killing the [emotion/ thought] messenger" EVIDENCE Process of change - consider context/ assumptions [7-6-05] Steve Hayes	Monica Pignotti wrote: > For those in abusive situations (e.g., battered spouses), anger could provide the necessary impetus the person needs to stop tolerating the situation and get out, if that is possible. "Killing" the anger in the name of "defusion" could be "killing the messenger." All emotions are messengers. Thoughts too. They say that something in your past and in the current situation has had this effect. Very important info, that. Defusion and acceptance, done properly, should not "kill" any emotion (or thought for that matter). If they are being used for that purpose you aren't doing ACT, that is for sure. I mostly see this kind of thing early on, when beginning ACT therapists are trying to shoe horn ACT into the usual treatment agenda. Acceptance and defusion allow us to FEEL what we feel, as we feel it, not as it (sort of) feels when we are trying not to feel it. Acceptance and defusion allow us to THINK what we think as we think it, not as we (sort of) think when the whole process of thinking disappears into the world structured by that process. Kelly's example of a hand over your eyes and a hand held out a foot away is a good one. In one case hands "look" dark and formless. In the other case hands have fingers. If it is being done true to ACT, acceptance and defusion are in the service of thinking and feeling more fully and more directly, and then linking all of that to a valued life path. We have some data in support of the acceptance/defusion link to a greater ability to feel. Note, for example, that alexithymia is a) one of the most pathological processes known, and b) is one of the highest correlates of ACT processes as measured by the AAQ. As far as the trauma evidence regarding emotional exposure: I have the same reaction to that as I do to the recent evidence that mindfulness meditation can be unhelpful with first time depressives. When seen from the point of view of ACT we need to think about all of the elements and we should be careful about how we apply existing evidence that comes from only some of these elements applied in a different context. It is too early to conclude that, for example, early emotional exposure is harmful in trauma work. It is so far, and that is a clear warning sign, but a lot of that work was done out of a traditional "reduce arousal" exposure model -- which is not an ACT model of exposure. Folks were trained to dig deep; to push; and all of that without fully creating a context in which that was a humane and loving and valued thing to do ... beyond "getting over" the pain. ACT is a different package with a different rationale. Suppose we did early intervention work that included values / a transcendence sense of self / and defusion in addition to opening up to various emotions. My guess is that the whole package might transform some of the effects of, say, contacting the present moment more fully and accepting emotions more fully ... even right after trauma. I still wouldn't "push" into any emotion unless it linked to moving ahead (remember the swamp metaphor) but my point is that we need to look at the existing evidence in its full context. You can't decontextualize it and make good sense of it. Methods and techniques that overlap with ACT methods and techniques may not functionally be the same methods and techniques -- the context is different. This line of thinking puts even more of a burden on us in ACT research and practice (and it is one reason that knowledge of the whole theory ultimately can be helpful). It means that we cannot as readily take things as a given and it means we have the difficult work of explaining to others what the contextual differences are, and then testing them empirically (hard, because often these are assumptive and not noticed within the mainstream. Assumptions? What assumptions?). If we learn that, say, perception of control predicts good anxiety outcomes we have to think "hmmm. But I wonder if we could solve that problem another way. Did they also measure the apparent NEED for control? Did they also measure the believability of thoughts being controlled, or the seeming behavior regulatory power of emotions being controlled? What

would happen if the need for control was targeted instead of just the degree of perceived control?" Furthermore, we need a theory so adequate that it even explains WHY folks get the effects they do, done outside of an ACT context. You need to account for ALL of the data. Given the lofty goals of ACT / RFT anything less is a cop out. That is a huge burden ... but a great goal.

I don't have time to post on it right now, but the work on metacognition and cognitive reappraisal (other threads of late) is an example. You have to unpack what is really being said; what is really known; the assumptions inside that work; and the language that makes linkage to ACT work initially difficult. The lingo is not the process -- personally I see no contradiction once you get into it. Same with perceived control. Etc.

Once the assumptions get brought to the fore it is possible to look at all of this. The field itself is doing that in some areas (e.g., acceptance and defusion), but not yet all of the areas ACT works with (e.g., workability/values is barely there yet).

The shift to the "third wave" comes from that process of seeing the fields' assumptions. ACT or no ACT it is having a huge effect on empirically supported treatments generally.

ACT
 	
    Aims of
 	
PAIN
 	
    Suffering, vs. - aims of ACT
 	
PRESENT MOMENT
 	
    Contact with - through defusion not language/ rules [3-11-03]
 	
      Steve Hayes
	ACT does seek to reduce suffering and trauma. And it seeks to increase vitality. It just doesn't seek to reduce pain or to produce a particular positive feeling. Suffering comes from a root word that denotes carrying or bearing (the same root as the word "ferry"). It's like we are carrying our pain in a sack, waiting for something to do with it. It is the "do with it" part we target.
	
	... The present moment shows up when we defuse from language. Pain contacted in the present moment from a defused, accepting place is not traumatic and there is no suffering. My sense is that experienced ACT folks often have more pain, not less. Try this: walking into your grocery store and really, really look at the people in there. Watch how they carry themselves. What you will see is an incredible amount of pain and suffering (and dignity; and maybe some joy). I sometimes find myself tearing up just walking around town. When I look around, the amount of pain (and courage) in human beings is simply staggering.
	
	Quite a number of ACT folks have told me that this just deepens over time. There is no sense of oppression in this ... it feels alive and real.
	
	I have no problem telling clients that we are working on reducing suffering -- we are. I just do not think we are working on reducing pain (although that might happen) ... and folks come in thinking that suffering and pain are one and the same thing. And if folks hear me saying that we are going to reduce pain, we will delay the process.
	
	There may be an issue here about the role of values that is worth mentioning. ACT has a radical acceptance agenda. The point is to show up. It is not FOR anything. Within the chessboard metaphor: we go board level because in some fundamental way we are conscious (spiritual?) beings, and showing up is simply an inherently validating or loving thing to do. From there we move, because that is what living creatures do (pretending that somewhere else is more important than here as they do the process of living). When we let go, we fall into no-thing -- and on the other side of that we take a breath (as if having that next breath is more important than not having it).
	
	This connects with my worry about too hard a push on the values end first: you cannot go into the void (into no-thing) as a planned sequence. Stated in a less airy fairy way: you cannot work to get into the present moment. A rule that is about the present moment, and that is occurring in the present moment, will nevertheless take you out of the present moment inside its relational network because reference itself "carries" you somewhere else, somewhen else (there is that same root again ... note that reference, relation, and suffering all have that same etymological root. Hmmmm). "Now" does not exist inside the functions of relational networks. Even if you say "now" as fast as you can, the "now" you are "talking about" is the now that was, not the now that is.
	
	What this means is that "I must let go" is as entangling and out of the present moment as "I must not have anxiety" when we allow these relational networks to structure the behavioral functions in the present moment. Paradox and confusion are the lions at the gate. At a deep level, I think the ACT message is something more like "believe in nothing, including this."
	
	As far as feeling GOOD -- the data coming in on ACT show increases in positive measures of all kinds. But that does not demand that we adopt feeling good as a goal. Feel what you feel, as it is, not as what it says it is. If you do that you may feel GOOD sometimes. Sometimes you won't. So what?

ACT
 	
    Applicability to range of clinical problems
	Eric Morris wrote:
	
	    You [Steve Hayes] wrote quite a while ago:
	
	        "The reason we do ACT in the ACT group at UNR is that the supervision group is part of a clinical program and ours is for training ACT. We filter clients on the way in; we modify what we do inside

BOOK **ACT Practical Guide** [1-31-04] Steve Hayes	the team with every case; we sometimes refer out. If there are no data supportive of ACT-focused processes in problems that are functionally of the kind we are treating, I'm nervous about why our team has the case and I'm looking either for a referral or a way to alter what we do to fit the case." I was wondering: so far in your research what sort of clinical problems have you found do not have ACT-focused processes (e.g., experiential avoidance) that lead you to refer on? You can't answer the question by diagnosis. The diagnostic system has little to do with functional processes, and the ACT functional processes seem to cut across the current taxonomy. There are *some* ACT data with most kinds of problems you'd want to name and so far I am unaware of any ACT research that has flat *struck out* with anything (does anyone else? Are there failures in the drawer anyone wants to fess up to? I am aware of a couple of "just as good as" results, and one "effective but not quite as good as" result when ACT was compared to an EST, but these do not seem like real strike outs since ACT was still effective in these cases). ACT is not yet an EST but it is reaching that level in some areas and the literature is moving amazingly fast. The state of the data is much better than the state of the literature because so much is done and being written up right now ... in two years it will be very different than it is now. As an example of the breadth, the ACT Practical Guide that Kirk and I are finishing up (Plenum/ Kluwer ... should be out in late 04) includes these chapters: Affective Disorders. (Robert D. Zettle); Anxiety Disorders. (Susan M. Orsillo, Lizabeth Roemer, Jennifer Block, Chad LeJeune, & James D. Herbert); Posttraumatic Stress Disorder. (Alethea A. Smith and Victoria M. Follette); Substance Use Disorders. (Kelly Wilson and others ...); The Seriously Mentally Ill. (Patricia Bach); Personality Disorders. (Kirk D. Strosahl); Children, Adolescents, and their Parents. (Amy R. Murrell, Lisa W. Coyne, & Kelly G. Wilson); Stress. (Frank Bond); Medical Settings. (Patricia Robinson, Jennifer Gregg, JoAnne Dahl, & Tobias Lundgren); Chronic Pain Patients. (Patricia Robinson, Rikard K. Wicksell, Gunnar L. Olsson); and ACT in Groups Format. (Robyn D. Walser and Jacqueline Pistorello). ACT always involves direct behavioral work as well ... so that should count as part of any sensible ACT protocol. Take panic. The five areas that are most strongly supported are psychoeducation, breathing training, situational exposure, interoceptive exposure, and work on catastrophizing cognitions. An ACT protocol can do all of that ... true it works on cognitions in a new way, but there are no data showing that cognitive restructuring per se (etc.) is necessary, and there is a growing body of support for defusion as a process and technology that targets these kinds of problems. And there are supportive data for ACT components facilitating effective situational and interoceptive exposure. And there are some outcome data. But when you get down to the level of the individual the issue is not syndromal: it is functional. That is the dirty little secret of the EST movement: it is a great idea that stands on the sand of our current (lousy) diagnostic system. Individually I'd personally take the view that the cases that don't fit ACT are cases that a) do not have a clear experiential avoidance / cognitive fusion / values side to them. Simple skills problems can sometimes look like that, for example. Bed wetting, say. b) are too easy for a relatively complicated technology like ACT. I would not use ACT for a simple phobia, for example ... unless acceptance / defusion/ values work was necessary to do exposure.
ACT **Basic questions re** [7-1-05] Steve Hayes	A lot of the emails the last few days are fairly basic. They are important questions but they are difficult to respond to. In essence what is being asked is "what is ACT at the level of theory and technology; how do we measure that; how can we test it; does it comport with RFT; couldn't it be explained otherwise?" Whew. Good questions but I understand the answers already posted that basically say "read" ... I know that must feel dismissive but these questions encompass almost the entire ACT / RFT literature and research agenda. I feel a sense of hopelessness (not the creative kind) as I start to respond. To answer them carefully here is to rewrite several thousand pages of existing material. Not possible. Answers just by way of orientation: What is ACT at the level of technology? Start with the list of core skills and competencies in the ACT Practical Guide; then read the books and

chapters that fit with this list. The new website will have most of them available for downloading ...

If you mean it research wise, look at adherence measures.

What is ACT at the level of theory?

If you mean applied theory at a fairly conceptual level: start with the ACT book; then read the ACT Practical Guide; then several of the major recent statements and some old ones like the JCCP 1996 paper on EA; look at the hexaflex model and unpack that.

If you mean it research wise go from there to look at the tests of components, correlational tests of processes said to comport with psychopathology, mediational tests of process-outcome relations, outcome tests with targeted comparison conditions, analogue studies, basic studies that construct the phenomena targeted, and basic studies that model the processes manipulated by ACT. Some of these areas have a reasonable amount of early data behind them (that review article I keep mentioning goes through them). The last two areas are weakest, which means we have a lot of work to do in the ACT - RFT link.

If you mean it in terms of basic processes, start with a good behavioral principles text, then read the RFT book; then read the ACT book; then read the articles referenced there. You will find you need to read on philosophy of science; contextualism; etc. as well.

Could it be explained otherwise: probably ... but in a grand sense of that answer, it is not our job. In a narrow sense it is and there you have to look at the research and the comparison conditions selected.

Do we have data beyond outcome that support the theory? Sure.

For example, if you focus just on acceptance and defusion we now have eight studies looking at whether changes in one or the other of these processes mediate outcomes in ACT. All eight say yes. This is very unusual, especially considering how underpowered these studies were. If you are not sure of that, look at the traditional CBT literature where mediational analyses are a tale of woe. If comparisons are used, most of these studies also say that alternative treatments are not mediated by these effects, suggesting that the effect is specific. To the extent that this is so, the outcomes found now DO provide support for the theory, beyond simply the looser pragmatic support of good outcomes per se. Just two of the six processes in the hexaflex have so far been examined enough really to say much, however, so we have a long way to go. And when you get that far you still have not shown that, say, defusion is best explained in Cfunc terms (etc. etc.) so the link to RFT is still a bit general. That's why these other areas of research mentioned above are needed.

We made a decision not to define ACT as a simple technology. That makes these questions both possible and difficult. But there is a model; there is a theory; there is a technology; and there are some data and at virtually all levels. And yeah, you have to read. A lot. And even then you will not find THE answer. You will find answers and you can begin writing the rest as a member of a group. It is precisely the fact that ACT is part of an open tradition that makes it available to the community to create protocols, create measures, tweak models, add principles, and otherwise expand a tradition.

We are in a slightly scary time, to be honest: far enough along to seem potentially important, and not far enough along to answer all the questions that are coming because a) it is a "we" thing, and b) writing the new answers requires a lot of group members, and c) data come sooo much more slowly than ideas.

If I defined treatment X as a protocol, then the answers are sooo easy:

1. What is x? The protocol.

2. What is the evidence for it? Read the results section.

3. What are the processes? First let's see if it works.

4. What are the components? Ditto.

5. What is the theory? My really neat sociospiritubioemotiobehavioral model I talked about on page 3.

6. Where did the theory come from? [list every major name you can think of]

7. What is the evidence for it? Read the results section.

8. How can I learn to do it? Come get certified. Bring cash.

9. Who can tell me if I really did it? The originators (bring more cash).

ACT is not going to go in that direction. That makes us more dangerous to the status quo. Who knows where the data will lead us if we allow it to take us to the most basic questions.

So here is the really hard answer. This is not flippant because this is exactly what I myself (and all of the other ACT contributors) do in written articles etc.

When a person says "what would ACT say about x?" the deepest answer often is "can you restate that this way: based on my understanding it seems that from an ACT perspective we should say ___ about x?" If the person can do it the next "answer" is "and what leads you to say that?" and if the person can do THAT the final answer is: "hmm. Interesting. Discuss."

When that is the process another small step forward is taken that might lead to new research, new methods, new principles and so on.

Sooo

Pick one issue (not everything at once). Can you restate it this way: based on my understanding it seems that from an ACT perspective we should say ___ about x?

ACT **Brief intervention - telephone counseling [8-27-04]** Steve Hayes	Matthew Smout wrote: Am talking to some telephone drug & alcohol counsellors soon about ACT. These counsellors will get a lot of one-off calls, most calls would be expected to be within 30 minutes duration, most callers would be in something like crisis mode. I have some general plans to introduce them to the ACT model of psychopathology, how the model might influence the line of questioning and things to reflect (e.g., values statements, appraisals of workability, orientation to present moment, response-ability), and highlight that good results have come from very brief ACT protocols. To your very good list (e.g., values statements, appraisals of workability, orientation to present moment, response-ability) I'd add normalization of pain and difficult thoughts; use of a defused style in the interaction; raising possibility of acceptance; focus on effective action. Patty Robinson's depression protocol had some interesting phone work that is ACT based. Context Press sells the therapist manual.
ACT **Contingency-shaped cf. rule-governed** **THERAPY** **"Markers" for intervention [2-28-03]** Patty Bach	Niklas Törneke wrote: I think there is an alternative to focusing on order of components. That is to discuss and identify "markers" for interventions in one direction or the other. These could be markers in client behavior in session, interpersonal markers, or maybe even markers in the therapist. I think this is already done to a degree but it could be developed more systematically. One potential problem I see with identifying client markers, or discriminations that are important for selecting or sequencing interventions, is that this is a largely rule-governed process. So much in ACT unabashedly acknowledges the difficulty and contradictions of even describing the therapy processes verbally, and emphasizes the importance of experiential, or contingency-shaped processes. Of course we might be able to specify some rules and markers - however, is there a point where, if we create a complete list of important therapist and client discriminations, it will no longer be ACT? Much of my current job involves training mental health staff in how to perform very basic behavioral interventions. Some feel dissatisfied with didactic training because it does not inform them what to do with client X. They inevitably bring up the gap between 'theory and practice,' which is an issue in disseminating empirically-validated treatment approaches. Being an effective therapist is largely contingency shaped. This is, of course, true in any kind of therapy, and I would argue that it is especially important in ACT and related approaches. One may read the ACT book and get a good idea of what ACT is about and how to do it in a rule-governed sense. However, as an explicitly experiential enterprise ACT is primarily contingency-shaped. My experience in ACT workshops is that the experiential components are valuable in part because trainees learn the value of them through the contingency-shaped process of experiencing the exercises and their 'consequences' themselves. This is at least as important as having a list of metaphors and exercises. A limitation of all manualized treatments is that a manual is rule governed, and to paraphrase a clinical question, we want to know 'what is the most effective intervention for this client with this problem at this time?' If we are doing therapy with 'individuals,' a large part of determining this will be contingency-shaped rather than rule-governed. This is, I think, especially relevant in ACT since the therapist is, in therapy, modeling ACT (Accept, Choose, Take Action). It can be a powerful intervention to say, "I'm not sure what to do right now." I wonder if adding "I'll look at my list, aha, this is the acceptance/control marker, let me check out page 47, and I'll be right back" would be as effective. At its heart ACT is about decreasing rule governance. I fear that too many rules for the therapist will make this less clear to both clients and would-be therapists. A cognitive therapist can get away with looking up a rule, because cognitive therapy is largely about replacing ineffective rules with other rules. ACT is about replacing ineffective behavior with effective behavior, which often means throwing out some of the rules altogether and seeing what happens and, perhaps, after some time spent allowing one's behavior to become contingency shaped, one might be able to create a rule that describes their own behavior. However, if the rule is too specific one is right back in the same hole where one started. I am deliberately over-stating this, and I believe it is an important consideration....

ACT
 	
    Contingency-shaped cf.
    rule-governed [cont'd]
 	
THERAPY
 	
    "Markers" for
    intervention [cont'd]
        Niklas Törneke
	... As for Pat's concern about the risks of relying too much on rule-governed behavior, this is an important concern; I think you are right in this. Markers could well be experiential, though. What to do in the presence of a specific marker has to be rule-governed, I guess. But I don't think the way to avoid the dangers of rules is to try to avoid rules. The key is to use them lightly, to hold them at a distance in your hand. For after all, there is no way a human being (not even an ACT therapist!) can avoid rule-governed behavior except for short, very short moments of time. Trying to do so would be ... guess what? Rule-governed behavior!

ACT
 	
    Contingency-shaped cf.
    rule-governed [cont'd]
 	
THERAPY
 	
    "Markers" for
    intervention [cont'd]
        Patty Bach
	Yes! The part about 'using rules loosely' is a difficult piece to learn and to train!
	
	I like your idea of 'experiential markers.' I agree that rules are not to be avoided and excessive reliance on them is. Rules are important in learning new behaviors, and they only take us so far. The novice/expert distinction in RGB (rule-governed behavior) comes to mind - that the novice relies heavily on RGB while increasing expertise is accompanied by less reliance on rules and increasing contingency-shaped behavior.
	
	I suspect that 'using rules loosely' is a difficult piece for both therapist and client to 'get' in ACT. I find it so easy to grasp tightly onto a new 'rule' before I realize that has happened and must again loosen my grip....

ACT
 	
    Contingency-shaped cf.
    rule-governed [cont'd]
 	
ACT cf.
 	
Functional Analytic
Psychotherapy [3-4-03]
        Steve Hayes
	On this issue of shaping and rules in relationships. A focus on shaping has always been in the ACT / RFT work. It emerged from our work on rule governance. That work is part of the deep background that created FAP in the first place (not my place to say that, but Bob has...). I think we do FAP inside of ACT (increasingly so) and basically always have.
	
	If folks are interested in how to do shaping that is effective without having to know the rule behind what you are shaping, check out this old article (done by myself and Nate Azrin's daughter Rachel): Azrin, R. D., & Hayes, S. C. (1984). The discrimination of interest within a heterosexual interaction: Training, generalization, and effects on social skills. *Behavior Therapy, 15*, 173-184. You can use it directly as a model for how to shape social discrimination skills in therapy. Indeed, Bill Follette's lab did some studies of that kind using it. Not sure if they published (anyone know?).
	
	As far as rules for ACT, we have used language to attack the excesses of language. I would be cautious about any rules. (Remember the ACT line: "do not believe this.") With my science hat on I have lots of rules. That is what is in the research articles. But rules for shaping is not itself shaping. When we do training in ACT we do it experientially....
	
	As a training matter I don't think you can or should distill ACT into a set of rules. A set of experiences: sure. A set of processes: absolutely.
	
	What life asks of people is this:
	
	Are you willing to experience your own experience, fully and without defense, as it is and not as what it says it is, AND do what moves you in the direction of your chosen values in this moment (and this moment, and this, and this ...). That question is asked of clients and therapists, over and over and over. Ya want a rule? Here it is: Answer yes.

ACT
 	
    Contingency-shaped cf.
    rule-governed [cont'd]
 	
Principles/ "Rules" - 28
statements [3-5-03]
 	
ACT cf.
 	
    Functional Analytic
    Psychotherapy [cont'd]
        Steve Hayes
	Jonathan Kanter wrote:
	
	   Is there a basic, shared set of valued actions of ACT therapists? I'm talking a real small set, five or less. Perhaps "don't believe any of this" is the first, or last one.
	
	Just a quick thing before I get to my main reason to post something:
	
	In reading my own earlier post it might have sounded that I did not think that FAP is a major innovation. I hope no one thought that, but just in case: it is. It is just that it is a sister technology and fellow traveler with deep connections conceptually, technically, and professionally (ask Barbara Kohlenberg). ACT and FAP are (and always have been) related. They are not competitors. As a result they combine so thoroughly that I think of ACT + FAP as "good ACT."
	
	As far as what Jonathan asks for:
	
	Here are the 28 rules we send around. I have not tried to rise to the challenge of distilling these to the shortest list possible (I did something like that a few days ago in a post and came up with: Love and Be) but I would think that someone on this list may have already done so or could readily do so. These 28 statements are obviously highly redundant. I suspect that one could get them down into the 5-10 range with an hour or two of thought and wordsmithing.

THE QUICK AND DIRTY ACT ANALYSIS OF PSYCHOLOGICAL PROBLEMS

Psychological problems are due to a lack of behavioral flexibility and effectiveness.

Narrowing of repertoires comes from history and habit, but particularly from cognitive fusion and its various effects.

Prime among these effects is the unnecessary avoidance and manipulation of private events.

"Conscious control" is a matter of verbally regulated behavior. It belongs primarily in the area of overt, purposive behavior, not automatic and elicited functions.

All verbal persons have the "self" needed as an ally for defusion and acceptance, but some have run from that too.

Clients are not broken, and in the areas of acceptance and defusion they have the basic psychological resources they need to acquire the needed skills.

The value of any action is its workability measured against the client's true values (those he/she would have if it were a choice).

Values specify the forms of effectiveness needed and thus the nature of the problem. Clinical work thus demands values clarification.

To take a new direction, we must let go of an old one. If a problem is chronic, the client's solutions are probably part of them.

When you see strange loops, inappropriate verbal rules are involved.

The bottom line issue is living well, and FEELING well, not feeling WELL.

THE ACT THERAPEUTIC POSTURE

Assume that dramatic, powerful change is always possible and possible quickly.

Whatever a client is experiencing is not the enemy. It is the fight against experiencing experiences that is harmful and traumatic.

You can't rescue human beings from the difficulty and challenge of growth.

Compassionately accept no reasons -- the issue is workability not reasonableness.

If the client is trapped, frustrated, confused, afraid, angry or anxious be glad -- this is exactly what needs to be worked on and it is here now. Turn the barrier into the opportunity.

If you yourself feel trapped, frustrated, confused, afraid, angry or anxious be glad: you are now in the same boat as the client and your work will be humanized by that.

In the area of acceptance, defusion, self, and values it is more important as a therapist to do as you say than to say what to do.

Don't argue. Don't persuade. The issue is the client's life and the client's experience, not your opinions and beliefs. Belief is not your friend. Your mind is not your friend. It is not your enemy either. Same goes for your clients.

You are in the same boat. Never protect yourself by moving "one up" on a client.

The issue is always function, not form or frequency. When in doubt ask yourself or the client "what is this in the service of?"

ACT THERAPEUTIC STEPS

Be passionately interested in what the client truly wants.

Compassionately confront unworkable agendas, always respecting the client's experience as the ultimate arbiter.

Support the client in feeling and thinking what they directly feel and think already -- as it is, not as what it says it is -- and to find a place from which that is possible.

Help the client move in a valued direction, with all of their history and automatic reactions.

Help the client detect traps, fusions, and strange loops, and to accept, defuse, and move in a valued direction in a committed way that builds larger and larger patterns of effective behavior.

Repeat, expand the scope of the work, and repeat again, until the client generalizes.

Don't believe a word you are saying ... or me either.

ACT	
Hexaflex model; what is ACT? **Applicability to range of clinical problems** [11-3-03] Steve Hayes	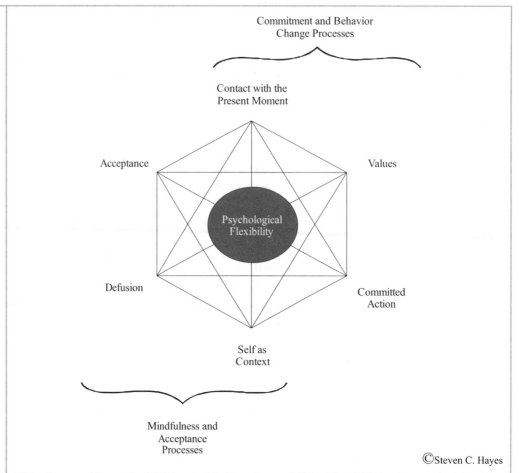 ©Steven C. Hayes We've been working on the ACT Practical Guide and on an ACT training initiative (more on both later) but in the context of all that I've been trying to get clearer about what ACT is anyway. We've consistently said (in the book and elsewhere) that ACT is an orientation / approach / or model of intervention based on a particular philosophy and theory but the details of that model are not all that clear. At the level of technology ACT is all over the map because every ACT protocol has to be fitted to the specific problem. With anxiety you add explicit exposure; with depression behavioral activation; with drug abuse sometimes we've added life skills; we almost always add some psychoeducation, etc., etc., etc. And you have to fit the protocol to the delivery system and vehicle. But since it seems clear now that ACT will apply to myriad problems and settings we will literally have scores of ACT protocols in the next 3-4 years. I see no limit yet to how far that can go. The cognitive therapists found a way to use the term "cognitive therapy" both as a generic term and as a name for certain technical protocols, which greatly aided their collective success since when one person did something helpful others could claim the evidence as relevant to them. I think it was because they could agree that CT was (to paraphrase Beck) the application of a cognitive model and techniques in the service of the modification of dysfunctional beliefs. A similar clarify in the ACT wing would allow folks to hang out under a common conceptual umbrella with a fair amount of technical diversity as the diversity of human problems will demand. We have a draft chapter trying to answer the "what is ACT?" question which will be in the *A Practical Guide to Acceptance and Commitment Therapy* book ...., but the basic model in that chapter is above. The complete Powerpoint "Hexaflex.ppt" can be found on the contextualpsychology.org website.
ACT **Introductory article** [2-2-05] Kevin Vowles	Joel Guarna wrote: Does anyone have a concise article giving an overview of ACT for clinicians who may or may not be familiar with behavior analysis, etc.? A good introductory article in my opinion is: Hayes, S. C., Masuda, A., & De Mey, H. (2003). Acceptance and Commitment Therapy and the third wave of behavior therapy. *Gedragstherapie (Dutch Journal of Behavior Therapy), 36*, 69-96.

ACT **Introductory article for non-specialist audience [7-26-05]** Tom Waltz	For those who were at Robert Zettle's ACT & depression workshop, he mentioned handing out a reading to clients early in therapy. It's a nice quick intro to ACT for a non-specialist audience. *A new leash on life*, by Martha Beck. August 2002. O, The Oprah Magazine.
ACT **Model of psychopathology, functional dimensional [1-25-05]** Steve Hayes	Francis De Groot wrote: Many ACT writings refer to a functional dimensional approach to assessment and diagnosis. Such an approach (comprehensive and clear, not simplifying) would be very welcome. Does this already exist, or is it still wishful thinking? The only functional dimension that seems to be referred to is experiential avoidance. What are the others? To get a good sense of the phenomena that could form the base of such a system, check out a book by Allison Harvey et al. called "cognitive behavioural processes across psychological disorders." They list quite a number of known "transdiagnostic" processes: selective attention, selective memory, overgeneral memory, avoidant encoding and retrieval, attributional errors, thought suppression, experiential avoidance, etc. and summarize the data on them. What is missing is a grand uniting theory -- it is all bits and pieces of empirical evidence. It is my sense that you can come pretty close to a transdiagnostic functional dimensional model of psychopathology by bringing in RFT and looking at how relational networks and direct contingencies interact. I think we are doing this implicitly in the ACT and RFT work but it will take more to pull it together. Playing around with it this morning: In addition to problems of direct contingency control (e.g., development of odd reinforcers etc.) you can cluster problems into problems of weak verbal development and regulation and problems of imbalanced or distorted verbal regulation. With these (see below) I think virtually all of the processes mentioned by Harvey could be pulled into a system. I'm just playing around but I mean for this to be an example of how we might begin to step up to the enormous challenge of psychopathology and assessment within the ACT / RFT tradition. It's hugely important that we do so. You will notice that almost all of these components cross over between ACT ideas and RFT ideas. We need both - but in the long run RFT may be more important. The first cluster is more common in child disorders and developmental problems: 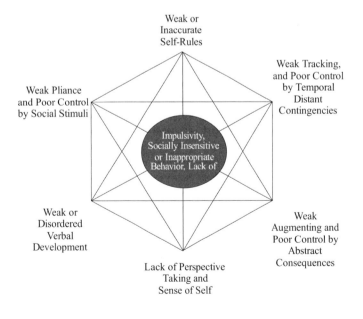

The second is more common of adult psychopathology:

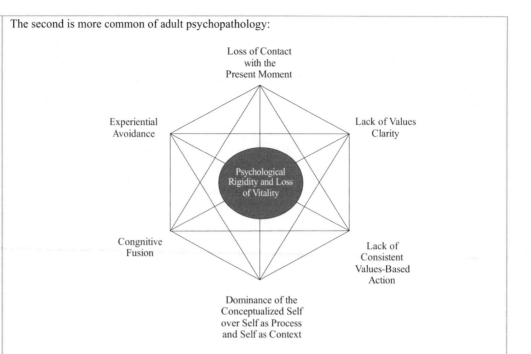

ACT	ACT Listserv Member wrote:
Naming conventions -protocols, studies etc. **MINDFULNESS** **ACT processes, equivalence of [1-8-04]** Steve Hayes	Being a Swedish talking person sometimes gets you in language problem. And now we've got one (a small one). Our paper on unemployed, on sick leave with depression (ACT group treatment) needs a title...

The issue of what to call ACT interventions (ACT based program; ACT intervention; ACT for x) is a generic one. This is a long message for a small question but the issue is bigger than the specific question.

ACT is an orientation / approach / strategy / or model of intervention based on a particular philosophy and theory. ACT interventions tend to focus on a set of major components within that model: defusion, acceptance, self as context, contact with the present moment, values, and committed action. (Mindfulness is not specifically listed ... it means many different things ... but in a general way it was part of the approach from the first day forward -- I believe however that acceptance, defusion, self as context, and contact with the present moment IS mindfulness at the level of process and mindfulness *techniques* are commonly used in several parts of the ACT protocol.)

However, every ACT protocol has to be fitted to the specific problem. With anxiety you add explicit exposure; with depression behavioral activation; with drug abuse sometimes we've added life skills; we almost always add some psychoeducation; with smoking we've added mindful smoking, smoke holding, targeted quit dates, etc. And you have to fit the protocol to the delivery system and vehicle. And you have to sequence components and give them greater or lesser emphasis.

Some of these elaborations just define "what is the committed action." Some of it is "how do you define acceptance in a specific instance" (or defusion, etc.). Some of it is about targeting problems. But since it seems clear now that ACT will apply to myriad problems and settings we will literally have scores of ACT protocols in the next 3-4 years. I see no limit yet to how far that can go. Concerns over naming conventions seem well placed.

We are already seeing:

- ACT being combined with things that already have a name (e.g., FAP);

- protocols named ACT - X where the "x" is the population, the method added, or the component emphasized;

- folks talking about the "traditional" ACT approach and then adding things;

- ACT components that have powerful effects on their own in some applied area.

There are risks of fractionation and incoherence in some of these options and naming conventions could foster or inhibit bad outcomes. To mention one I rather dislike: "traditional" ACT is really no such thing: from the very beginning ACT protocols have varied widely to fit the situation and population.

The cognitive therapists found a way to use the term "cognitive therapy" both as a generic term and as a name for certain techniques, which greatly aided their collective success since when one person did something helpful others could claim the evidence as relevant to them. Should ACT try to do the same? If so, how should we do this? If not, what should we do?

Kelly, Kirk, and I have puzzled over issues relevant to this and have a statement coming soon on the issue of the processes that define ACT but it does not speak to the naming conventions per se.

In the 1999 ACT book and on the website (in the protocols section) we say it this way:

> As such, [ACT] is not a specific set of techniques. ...ACT protocols are ... instances of a strategy. ACT protocols can vary from very short interventions done in minutes or hours, to those that take many sessions. When an ACT strategy is applied to a given problem it will include specific interventions designed to help with that specific difficulty, and thus every population will lead to different ACT protocols ... and there will be variation even with specific populations based on the creativity of the researcher/clinician and relative emphasis on various ACT/RFT-sensible processes. For all of these reasons and many more, the world ACT community has chosen not to ossify the treatment through processes of centralization, certification and the like, preferring to trust its development to open scientific processes. These include sharing of protocols, identification of processes of change, outcome research, basic research, and so on. Protocols cited or displayed here are not *the* ACT approach to any given problem, but *an* ACT approach in the eyes of the serious researchers who post them.

Usually at the end of an ACT workshop I ask people to feel free to take the approach to use it; combine it; take responsibility for its development -- and I know that most ACT trainers say similar things. I think the Sweden conference showed what wonderful things can happen when people are willing to step forward and take collective responsibility for the work. It is cool that many countries have their own ACT (and RFT) experts and these folks just have taken the work and moved it along. The number of ACT books is growing and many folks are involved beyond the "founders." If we foster the use of "ACT" to refer to the overall set, strategy, or approach, I think that process will build. I am aware that some will prefer to use something even more generic (e.g., "acceptance-based behavior therapy") but to do that you either have to stay narrow or expand "acceptance" (or mindfulness; or whatever) to mean also defusion, values, focus on the present moment, etc. By the time you do the latter you are either back to ACT or the "generic" term (e.g., acceptance) is now idiosyncratic again.

My own opinions on naming conventions are these:

In every case I've thought of, you get the right sense by thinking of how people use the term "cognitive therapy" and then just substitute "ACT." For example, people speak of "Cognitive therapy for depression" or "a cognitive therapy protocol for panic" -- ACT could be used in the same way. But folks would rarely name their protocols "Cognitive Therapy - Panic." They also rarely used "-based" in the names. It would be uncommon to see "a Cognitive Therapy-based protocol for panic" -- rather it is simply "a Cognitive Therapy protocol for panic" or even "Cognitive Therapy for panic." Qualifiers can come as adjectives however. "Group Cognitive Therapy" or "long term Cognitive Therapy" sounds normal. It feels quite reasonable to qualify ACT that way too. Of course if articles are used they should be general and not specific or limiting. Better not to say "*the* Acceptance and Commitment Therapy program for depression."

So far, the ACT protocols that have been tested seem to be following this common sense approach. Most are just calling themselves "an ACT treatment for x" or "ACT for x" or "[qualifier] ACT for x."

Where the term "-based" comes in is in the area of models. You can have specific ACT-based models (though generally they are really RFT-based models or even contextualistic models). Specific models are often quite idiosyncratic -- folks should name them any way they feel makes sense. If there is a specific model for how to apply ACT to a specific problem folks should name the model ... but the treatment is still ACT.

If the world ACT community followed this approach we'd build quite a range of ACT interventions. The advantage is coherence and visibility. The downside might be centralization but since the worldwide leadership of ACT is growing and open, that risk seems minimal ...

By the way: getting "a randomized controlled trial" into a title is a good thing but my experience tells me that it raises the bar in the review process.

ACT Naming conventions - protocols, studies etc. [cont'd] Matthew Smout	Regarding naming conventions for ACT studies, I guess it depends on what function we want to serve. Personally, I find the use of cognitive therapy as a generic term to cover a range of often quite different interventions quite frustrating because it is imprecise. I want to know the difference between a study that did cognitive therapy like Beck would do it, and one that did it like Marlatt & Gordon would do it. To me these interventions would look quite dissimilar, and in drug and alcohol it seems to matter - Beck's type of intervention hasn't fared so well, whereas Marlatt & Gordon's intervention has become the gold standard in many places. The use of a generic term 'cognitive therapy' masks the differences between approaches and allows practitioners of a less effective intervention to claim empirical support from a different approach of a similar name. I don't think this is a practice we should encourage.

I think we need to leave room for other people to own (and name) their own innovations too. It seems ACT practitioners have been sensitive to this with FAP (which would be unheard of in this country, I suspect). There has been an irritating tendency of cognitive therapy to subsume any innovations in technique or theory into its generic brand and lose the context that brought about the insight in the first place. One of the biggest barriers I faced introducing people to ACT was the tendency to try and see ACT as just cognitive therapy with different language - and I think they missed the point. Some of these clinicians may now include a mindfulness exercise in with their general approach to therapy. They could call what they do CBT, some might even call it ACT - but I don't think either term is appropriate - they are being eclectic, which is fine outside of research, but just confusing in a research context.

ACT has a distinct agenda. ACT therapists are looking for stuff and to guide clients through a process in a particular way that is separable from other therapy approaches. Just as a Beckian therapist might hunt for automatic thoughts, or a family therapist look for tension in interpersonal relationships, ACT therapists seek out emotional avoidance, fusion, and values. Not all interventions do this or do it consistently.

Now we can add life skills and psychoeducation and condition-specific stuff to this core agenda - but these things can be added to any other approach too. As we are still establishing the empirical basis for ACT we need to be clear about what is ACT (distinct from other psychotherapy approaches) and what is added to it, and be sensitive to detecting interactions between this material. E.g., if we incorporate psychoeducation into an ACT group, does that enhance, diminish or make no difference to the impact of the ACT group? If we have a 12-session intervention that includes life skills, problem-solving, psychoeducation, condition-specific info., and all of a sudden only about 50% of the time is actually ACT-specific stuff - do we have a 12-session ACT intervention? Or do we have ACT as a major component of an x disorder-management package?

My preference is that ACT be defined rather than nebulous, at the level of clinical processes (e.g., looking for emotional avoidance, defusing language, self, values clarification), rather than specific exercises (e.g., includes "milk milk" exercise) and acknowledges the techniques of other authors as adjuncts until the author indicates he/she sees it as an ACT strategy or until the technique has been used in several studies together with ACT (i.e., becomes common practice).

ACT Naming conventions - protocols, studies etc. [cont'd] Steve Hayes	I agree on the process issue. That was my major point. I agree on combinations too: an ACT/FAP combo should be called an ACT/FAP combo (I forgot to mention that in the post, but it is an obvious extension of the logic of my argument). What does not seem to make sense is to label the protocols in a way that suggests that ACT is not ACT whenever ACT is applied to something. We'd already have 20 "different" treatments if we did that and we are headed toward triple digits. We would also have the anomalous situation in which "ACT" has never been tested -- since I am unaware of any ACT protocol that has included only ACT in a technological sense. Does anyone do interventions without some psychoeducation? And when you come to behavior change and commitment, don't you have to include behavioral methods (specific goal setting; practice; self-monitoring; something?). The ACT model itself suggests that you should. What seems to make sense to me is to label the protocol (an ACT protocol for x); to label the model used to generate it; if there are processes/procedures that are not in ACT processes (e.g., not in the hexaflex set), to label them; and if there are combos with existing packages to label both. And assess the processes; assess the components; evaluate the additional processes and let that be the guide over time. Credit does not seem to be the issue -- the very examples you use from CT show that major folks have developed models and approaches and become famous for them while also positioning their approaches in such a way that, say, Beck helps Marlatt and vice versa. There are already more ACT books out or in press with senior authors not on the original ACT book than there are those from that list. And that ratio is growing. If there was anything obvious from Sweden it was this: ACT can be a pretty big playground. By the way, the downsides you note to the "cognitive therapy" example are not a 1 to 1 parallel to ACT, because the ACT model itself is more specific. Often "cognitive therapy" refers to a domain more than a specific model ... we could and should avoid that. And the key processes are often not even specified and assessed -- a bad idea. It is worth noting though that this problem could be worse with terms like "acceptance" or "mindfulness" used as an umbrella. Maybe the generic "acceptance-based behavior therapy" solution that Orsillo/Roemer are talking about will work but I worry that "acceptance" (or "mindfulness" for that matter) is too vague to serve us adequately over time (Sue/Liz know I think they are great regardless so this is no poke at them ... it is just an issue we all need to consider ...). Frankly, people will do what they want, and there are big problems in any use of labels (RFT helps explain why!). And long run, it doesn't matter. At the end of every workshop I do I tell people to do what they want re using and renaming all of this, but I also ask them to look at their values and to see if connecting with "ACT" serves those values or not. Right now, we barely are visible and we need a lot more work to get going. ACT is not yet even on an EST

	list. 10 years from now it will be a different situation. But I think we could be in for a rocky ride. ACT challenges the status quo, but some folks don't want to see that. If we don't push ahead, I'm afraid we are more likely to be pushed aside. There is room for diversity on this though. If folks feel otherwise after considering all the pros and cons, they should follow their heart. This is just how it seems to me right now ... Kel, Kirk, and I are perhaps in a weakened position to argue for using ACT as a term, for obvious reasons.
ACT Naming conventions - protocols, studies etc. [cont'd] Niklas Törneke	As for keeping ACT "on track," I think it is important to have a balance between stressing, on the one hand, its newness and, on the other, the continuity with behavior therapy (or clinical behavior analysis, behavioral psychotherapy) generally. In a simple way this can be done from this perspective: ACT can be seen as a development of two well-documented treatment strategies in this tradition, exposure and behavioral activation. At the same time it is easy to see that there is genuine newness, it is not only "the same old thing." 1. Exposure. An important point is to stress the "operant view" of exposure. This could be said as "exposure/response widening" (rather than prevention). The newness is clearest in defusion (deliteralization), that is in a special way of relating to private experience. Other therapies do some similar things (not typically BT, though) but the analysis and the understanding of this strategy is unique to ACT (RFT). 2. Behavioral activation. This is at the heart of most behavior therapy. As for newness, valuing and the experiential position of choice is central for ACT. This, also, can be found in part in other therapy traditions but once again the analysis of these phenomena is unique to ACT and opens up for a clearer and better way of doing this. How much better these new things are is of course an empirical question. My experience with my own clients is clear enough for me, but I realize that is not enough... As for the name Acceptance and Commitment Therapy, I must say I find it extremely well found. (It is hardly possible to translate into Swedish ... but I guess I must accept that as a minor problem...). One part of the name stresses the way to relate to your "inside" and the other how to move forward. These two things are a part of all good psychotherapy but I know of no other that points to this so clearly, even in the name. So I hope we will keep that name, at the same time as we uphold that we are a part of a long tradition that still stands. "ACT is all on its own" would be disaster, I think. But I have never heard any of "the seniors" say anything in that direction.
ACT **Third wave - Hayes' AABT Presidential address [12-30-02]** Steve Hayes	... I'm working on the Presidential address now. It is a lot different than the one I gave some years ago. I find myself telling a story that characterizes behavior therapy as compared to other forms of therapy in the early days; characterizes the two streams within behavior therapy in the early days (functional-contextualistic and mediational-mechanistic); and then characterizes the three waves of behavior therapy (traditional BT / traditional CT & CBT / and the current new wave). In essence I am arguing that the third wave resolves and recasts all of the earlier divisions: it is no longer possible to easily distinguish BT from, say, analytic, existential, or humanistic thinking on the basis of content or the issues considered - the distinction is one of approach; within the field of behavior therapy (meaning BT / CT / CBT / CBA / etc.) it is also no longer possible to distinguish subapproaches either on the basis of content or the issues considered - the third wave makes most of those distinctions unimportant; the meaningful distinction that is left within the tradition is philosophical, and I argue that almost all of the innovation in the third wave behavior therapies (using that term in its broadest meaning) seems contextualistic, functional, less syndromal, and more interested in normal human functioning. I note that this is both different than what went before and a reaffirmation of what went before. I give a few examples (e.g., mindfulness), and then I use ACT and RFT as a more detailed example of all of that. Finally, I describe the ACT approach, and some of the data in support of it. In essence, the piece is a declaration that the world of BT has permanently changed, and that ACT/ RFT is part of that change....
ACT **Third wave rap [2-20-05]** Steve Hayes	Daniel Moran wrote: I would like some help getting people interested in [ACT].... Are there available figures so that I can say ... "ACT is the fastest growing behavioral health trend according to X measurement...."? Something generally interesting... like for newspapers, deans, surgeons, and case managers that don't really care much about acceptance or mutual entailment. Re data for creating a readily accessible "progressivity story": I know of no statistical things. Well - I can think of a few but they are inside baseline type figures. Things like: ACT had more index items at last year's AABT convention than any other treatment.

	If I am creating a progressivity story I usually tell a variant of the 3rd wave rap. Something like this:
	"You've probably heard of cognitive behavior therapy. CBT is by far the most dominant wing of empirical clinical approaches: approaches based on data. Well, for about 25 years CBT focused on trying to get people to change what they think or feel in order to change what they do.
	They did a lot of other things too, but that was the focus. But now that's changing. It turns out that even though CBT works, the science is telling us that changing thought and feelings is not the reason it works. It seems to be related more to helping people change the role of thoughts and feelings in their lives -- so that they are less pushed and pulled by them. Newer forms of CBT, such as ACT, now target that process very directly. We teach people how to persist when that is needed, even though various thoughts and feelings say to stop / or how to change when that is needed, even though change is often frightening.
	These methods look a bit more like methods linked some of our spiritual and religious traditions -- learning to make room for discomfort when discomfort is part of doing something that is hard; learning to notice your own thoughts and not get all entangled with them - much as meditative traditions have long taught. But we've used our progress in understanding how human cognition works to develop ways to do this quickly and without all of the hoopla that sometimes accompanies these methods. And we've kept them linked to behavior change, whether it be in the workplace or in managing a disease, or in dealing with anxiety. Long run, we think the key issue is really one of helping people to live their values, and to be more flexible as they do that: to persist or change as that is needed. And so far the science both in terms of outcomes and processes of change, seems to show that we are making progress. This whole area is one of the hottest areas of empirical clinical psychology."
ACT **Use/ compatibility with other treatment approaches [6-22-05]** Patty Bach	Janet Sallabank wrote: I have a client who is seen by myself and another health worker... there is a conflict in what we are doing in that I am going ACT... around willingness to 'feel' and not avoid ... other health worker is going ... "let's find you a multitude of distractions so you don't 'feel' that way". ... having worked in a few interdisciplinary/ multi-modal treatment settings where there are no other ACT therapists and primarily providing psychotherapy to persons with serious mental illness, this is what I can offer from my experience: Share your treatment goals with other treatment providers. If you are in a position to do so and if others are receptive, educate staff about ACT and how it might be similar to and different from other treatment approaches used in the setting and/or (if applicable) if there is evidence for the utility of ACT with that problem/ population. Address 'coping skills' and the like as viable short-term strategies for application in some contexts that supplement ACT with its long-term implications ... If the client is responding positively to ACT, point out positive changes to other relevant staff - I suggest this from a context where I have worked with clients who may still be 'symptomatic,' e.g., hearing voices or describing delusional beliefs AND are moving in a valued direction by adhering to treatment, staying out of the hospital, changing problematic behavior patterns, seeking out or maintaining valued goals in spite of symptoms and associated distress - I suggest this not as advocating ACT per se and rather as advocating for the client where ACT seems to be working.
ACT **Workshops/ training/ research/ development- issues/criticisms [5-1-05]** Kelly Wilson	Niklas Törneke wrote: [I would like to know your thoughts and your experience on] the risk of presenting ACT in a way that could be misunderstood as a quick fix, as something like conversion. The risk is greater if you don't include basic behavioral principles in your training and especially if you train people without prior knowledge of this. Part of this is born of rightly held skepticism. Part of it is, IMO, psychology's longstanding discounting of profound experiences typically characterized as "religious" or "spiritual" experiences. Heavens! Strong engagement in religious activity is typically equivalent to pathology in academic psychology. I personally think that we ought to be deeply interested in these experiences. Another difficulty is the dominance of the bankrupt philosophy of science that we see in mainstream psychology. Nothing is "real" that can't be measured by independent observers. Of course, the same folks who say this, if asked: "Do you love your children?", would answer that they do. If you asked where is the independent measure of that? They might list a bunch of things, but you could easily make up an example that had all of the criteria, except love felt and they would say -- no, not that. Another funny anomaly is that these same folks, if they are huge football fans, and listened into the coach's motivational talk in the locker room, would be willing to look at the score board to say whether it "works." Generating that high motivation in clients (or therapists), on the other hand, is viewed with skepticism. If you go to the gym and get a great workout, you feel fantastic. Somehow we do not discount that. Why? It is equally true that if you leave the gym and do nothing else, the

	"buzz" will quickly fade. However, if the trip to the gym is part of an ongoing engagement in physically healthy activity--it lasts just fine. If you eat a great meal, if feels terrific. If you never eat again, the buzz fades. If you go to a workshop and behave genuinely with your fellow humans. If you let go of your defenses for a little while--long enough to see that you are one among your fellows, if you make a potent and genuine commitment, you feel alive, vital. And, if you let that be about what happens at the workshop and leave it there when you walk out the door, it will make little difference. The thing that happens at the workshops is that we erode the illusion of separation--it is very hard work. People get to show up with their fellows. *And* it can be the beginning of a practice. If one persists in the practice, the dividends are pretty clear, at least to this observer. It does require that we begin to organize a little world around ourselves that can support the practice. Seems worthwhile to me. To the skeptics, well, we will let the data, over time, do the convincing.
	The basic science piece is central to the ongoing integrity of the work. This is why we are making ongoing efforts to keep it in the mix--organizationally and in the workshops. It is also why I and others are working our butts off to produce students who can do the basic to applied science stretch.
ACT Workshops/ training/ research/ development - issues/criticisms [cont'd] Kelly Wilson	Monica Pignotti wrote [re Kelly Wilson's reference to 'profound experiences typically characterized as "religious" or "spiritual" experiences']: Over the past 30 years, my own experience tells me that I've seen people get this kind of "high" in workshops from all kinds of different techniques from tapping, walking on hot coals -- even from being humiliated by a trainer and having a catharsis of some sort -- it doesn't even seem to matter what the method is. I have no intention of inducing some kind of high in folks. If there is a "high" in there, it is a byproduct of showing up psychologically. As an outcome, I have no particular interest in any feeling. Even the feeling of vitality is no goal of mine. My goal is to live vitally and to create contexts in which it is possible. Feeling vital is a byproduct and as a felt state is a nice marker. Being able to discriminate it seems useful to me. It can sometimes signal that ever so transient shift from aversive to appetitive control. [MP] And what kind of real lasting effect does it have? As I said--the buzz is a byproduct. It is not the thing I seek. And, as you point out, there are lots of ways to get buzzed. Many are harmful (smoking crack). Some are delightful (seeing your child being born). The first is *for* the buzz. The latter is unlikely to be. But neither is much of an end in and of itself--unless one is in the business of marketing buzzes. Not me. Not ACT. [MP] From what I've seen, these effects tend to wear off or worse, induce dependence of the person on a particular group in a way that can for some people become addictive. The best protection against this is our ongoing commitment to science and the fact that as a group it is pretty tough to find any signs of dependence or hierarchy. No one tithes to the mighty ones. In fact it would be difficult to find a group in professional psychology that is working as hard as we are to keep the technology open and free as possible. Could things like the workshop be exploitive? Sure. But the culprit is not the enthusiasm. The culprit is the exploiter *and* the structure that allows exploitation to live. I would say that it is akin to having a very powerful therapeutic relationship with a client. A client could be more easily exploited given such a relationship, but again, it is not the relationship that is the problem. [MP] Your point that an ongoing commitment is required is well-taken. Yet I have to wonder what, if any, role, inducing a "high" in people plays in this. When I think of times when commitments have worked for me personally, they have nothing to do with any such experience (although I've had plenty such experiences). I agree. Most of the real work with commitments is gritty, difficult, day-to-day hard work. It is also the case though, in my opinion, that if you are upside-down with avoidance, to the point that you can't even see it (i.e., the human condition) and a context precipitates the part you are playing in your own misery, and in that context, you step up--well that can be a pretty powerful experience. However, the powerful feeling is really the booby prize--or, at best, a happy byproduct. The real prize is in the living. [MP] A third question is what impact such an experience would have on a future research-therapist in terms of enthusiasm, increased expectancy and allegiance effects. I worry more about lowering expectancies than raising them. If folks' enthusiasm is excessive, science and data collection are the corrective. I am very enthusiastic. People see that when I present. However, I always say that ultimately the data will tell the story. We are early on in the data collection trajectory in ACT. I would say, however, that we are doing a pretty good job of keeping our eye on outcome, process, and basic behavioral science data simultaneously. This is our ultimate protection against the effects of mere enthusiasm. [MP] What does generating this high degree of motivation and enthusiasm in research-therapists do to the research itself? How could someone on this kind of high compete with a plain old cognitive behavioral

therapist in terms of generating enthusiasm that could impact the outcome?

I think we mostly have too little enthusiasm in science. We have a correction for too much--the sobering facts given in our data set. What is the alternative? Doing therapies about which we are unenthusiastic? The data is in on that. Treatments about which we are unenthusiastic tend to lose. If it is the case that outcomes improve with enthusiasm, we need a science of enthusiasm--not less enthusiasm.

> [MP] It is one thing to be deeply interested in these experiences (and I agree that we should be -- I'm deeply interested myself in this). It is another matter, however, to be incorporating them into therapeutic processes. Is this helpful? Well maybe, I'm open to the possibility, but I am also very wary of the potential dangers and side effects of inducing such a religious/spiritual experience as part of the therapy.

Not sure that I know the side-effects to which you point. I don't think that I do induce spiritual or religious experiences--or advocate it. But then it depends on what is meant by spiritual. I am not religious myself in any obvious ways--though I am interested in some of the sensibilities. I differ though in that I want a science of those sensibilities. I *would* readily admit to attempting to work a conversion experience on people. However, it is not a conversion to some spiritual or religious practice. Instead it is a conversion from living a life that is dominantly under aversive control to one that is dominantly under appetitive control (and I do not mean hedonism). And, as you say, ultimately the effects, long-term and short, are an empirical matter. I am willing to let the data fall where they may. To sum up, I think our best protection against all sorts of problems you mention is to be found in an open scientific enterprise. I don't see any issues in here that can't be addressed by that.

> [MP] I'd also like to ask if you could clarify what you mean by the following statement: "The thing that happens at the workshops is that we erode the illusion of separation--it is very hard work."

As to "eroding the illusion of separation" I actually have a workshop on this at the Summer Institute. This email is already damned long, but the short version:

People seem to walk around with a profound sense of how different they are from their fellows. One thing that can happen in a group training or in a group treatment is that we begin to see that the perceived differences are mostly differences in form, not function. Hence my contention that the differences are illusory.

ACT Workshops/ training/ research/ development - issues/criticisms [cont'd] Steve Hayes	Monica Pignotti wrote: > If the therapist's own personal experience of ACT is important to the outcome [of research], this creates a more complicated situation since it wouldn't be possible to test it with "neutral" therapists. Training neutral people in ... ACT [is not very easy] since it is being claimed that the therapist's personal experience can make the treatment more effective. This would make the therapists participating in research a self-selected group. The claim is not that therapists' personal experiences make the therapy more effective (is that in writing somewhere?). The claim is that you are working against yourself when you try to establish acceptance / defusion and so on in patients while simultaneously doing the opposite in session when your own emotions and thoughts come up. You are then teaching through modeling things that contradict what you are trying to do through therapy. But that is just a normal adherence and competence issue. There is not a Rx out there that avoids issues of adherence and competence -- ACT is no different in broad terms. The difference is simply that so far we are not sure we can establish these processes simply through didactic instruction. By the time we overcome that, we might be able to get this technology directly to people through books, tapes, etc. and we are trying exactly that right now. Some ACT studies have been done in forms that eliminate the issue of therapist allegiance. We have taped interventions with clients, for example (e.g., Levitt et al. 2004). In one way ACT is actually more liberal. I would not care one bit if an ACT therapist disbelieved the entire ACT model ... heck, we actually TELL folks not to believe it --as long as they knew how to defuse from that thought and do the treatment. So we don't even need agreement and belief. All we need is skillful use of these processes. There are ACT therapists who've never done an ACT intensive workshop and some of these are in ACT research studies. So some of the data out there don't fit your worries. I'm not sure that is wise, actually, but my reservations come from the data we have (e.g., the Strosahl et al. 1998 effectiveness trial) that show that we can train more effective therapists using intensives, followed by core skills and competencies, follow by supervision with a manualized treatment regimen, followed by "do what you want." You might be able to train effectively through other means but you have to hold that as an empirical question until we know. As far as the problem of self-selection -- the solution is better effectiveness trials. Randomly assign therapists to ACT or non-ACT trainings and follow them all (once assigned they are in the dataset even if they drop out). Raimo Lappalainen is doing such a study right now. We are doing similar studies and we are already farther along than most. After all the same issue applies to CBT. No one ever talks about why they

	pick the therapists for their CBT studies, but if you've done these things you know that it is la la land to think that CBT studies are done in the main with any old therapist. They have to be good and they have to buy into the model enough to get the training and perform at a competent level.
	ACT is not just superficially associated with the human potential movement -- it borrows from it. That is true of the third wave generally (you'd be surprised to know how many major figures in CBT did some of those workshops etc. decades ago). The difference is that ACT is attempting to bring these sensibilities into empirically supported approaches and create a theory that makes sense of all of this, linked to basic processes.
	Meanwhile we continue to explore ways of getting these processes established without having to have that bottle neck of intensive workshops. I personally would hope we can eventually get virtually automated training methods and the intensives would be just a way to expand understanding and skill. For example, we recently submitted an STTR trying to get the funds to develop a software program that would train therapists to detect avoidance and fusion in their clients.
	Thankfully I think the data so far seem to show that you can get good progress even with ACT done badly. It's amazing really ... dangerous perhaps but amazing.
	But there is an underlying sense of danger in these questions that I would also like to confront. Inside many of the more cultish movements are effective processes: who can doubt that? I don't apologize for a second that ACT / RFT are taking the ones that seem important, studying them, understanding them, and using them.
	It is the process of researching these things in an open, horizontal, scientifically-oriented culture that makes them safe. Everything is open, known, and shared. We are working hard not just to validate these methods but to pull them at the joints; to weed out what is not needed; to link them to basic processes. You can go to the Summer Institute and learn about all the new training methods.
	Everyone is welcome. You don't need to sign anything to get in. You don't have to promise not to use what you learn. You don't have to swear to use ACT terminology. There are no secret levels of training; no fees to leaders; no unsubstantiated claims of special powers. There are methods, processes, and outcomes -- that's it. All open and being studied and anyone can be part of it, without control or criticism beyond that inside any scientific enterprise (e.g., even if folks came to try to blow up ACT they would be welcomed, and if they generated critical arguments and data "what are your data for that?" would be a fair criticism back; "why didn't you do this needed analysis?" would be fair; "who gave you permission to say that?" would not be fair).
	So, sure, these methods might be dangerous in the sense that anything that can produce real change is dangerous. You might be able to use them to create cults; teach sales people to trick unsuspecting consumers; and maybe these methods are -- to some degree -- inside cults (etc.) right now.
	That should make us hold on to our science values, but it should not push us to avoid the questions such processes raise precisely because it is that method of studying them that makes them safe and available to advance human progress.
	My primary evidence for the "who could doubt it" comment is that huge life changes happen around issues raised by cults / religions / etc. Calling them placebos doesn't change that comment one bit. Physical medicine can make that move because placebos are not their field -- behavioral health fields can't. A placebo effect, for psychology / psychiatry / social work etc. is a real effect that needs to be understood.
	I personally think there is more in these traditions than placebos though. I have not had direct exposure to Scientology, but some of Hubbard's ideas make sense in the context of exposure, for example. I see defusion and acceptance (and more) inside meditation. Acceptance is in Gestalt. etc.
	I don't have a list of things that need to be brought in from these traditions. I do what I think most ACT / RFT folks would do. As I bump into them I strip away the psychobabble theory part; look at the technology; think of processes of change that might be involved; try out the ones that seem worthwhile; try to test the processes they engage; and for key ones try to model them in the lab. ACT as we know it is built up from 20+ years of that process, in the hands of scores of people.
	I did not know that Perls was linked to Hubbard. Of more interest to me was that he was linked to a really brilliant behavior analyst: Ralph Hefferline. I've always thought of Gestalt therapy (minus the theory) as fairly behavior analytic.
	Then again I think of Zen in the same way.
ACT Workshops/ training/ research/ development - issues/criticisms [cont'd]	In my opinion you perform lots of functional analyses with clients when you practice ACT (especially in the first -creative hopelessness- part), only you do them implicitly. All those questions about workability, 'what's it in the service of?' etcetera, are questions asked while performing a functional analysis. I wonder if there's something against making these implicit analyses more explicit, e.g., by writing them out on a white board. I often do that at the beginning of therapy, using the TRAP model Jacobson et al. describe in

BEHAVIOR ANALYSIS **Functional analysis, explicit use of; TRAP model [5-1-05]** Nico van der Meijden	their book 'Depression in context': you write out a *T*rigger (a situation), the *R*eaction (thoughts and feelings) and the *A*voidance *P*atterns (behavioral and experiential avoidance behaviors). Then I spend a lot of time discussing the workability of the avoidance behaviors (advantages, disadvantages) and ultimately use the 'digging-in-a-hole' metaphor. My experience of writing out a functional analysis is quite positive; people often have a kind of AHA-reaction when they see it written out. Besides that, you implicitly teach clients to think functionally, how to make a functional analysis themselves and you already make a start with defusing thoughts by writing them out. I suppose there's nothing against doing this in workshops when you teach ACT to students who lack a behavioral background. ACT *is* ultimately a behavior therapy in my opinion.
	Kelly's remarks on religious and spiritual experience hits another chord. ACT heavily stimulates non-verbal knowledge by undermining the grip our verbal system has on our behavior. But what exactly is the nature of that non-verbal knowledge? I would say the stimulus functions of direct here-and-now contingencies that come to the fore when verbal dominance diminishes. But I've noticed that this non-verbal knowledge has acquired some metaphysical properties in some posts. Like: "I have this or that value conflict, what should I do?"; answer: "just open up to yourself and listen, you'll know." It struck me that this argument has the same structure as: "I have this or that value conflict, what should I do?"; "just open yourself to God, you'll know." Perhaps this is a way of letting spirituality in (I agree that operationalizing everything makes thinking arid), but I wonder if it also opens the back door to obscurantism when the ACT community grows further.
ACT Workshops/ training/ research/ development - issues/criticisms [cont'd] BEHAVIOR ANALYSIS Functional assessment - use of; TRAP model [cont'd] Steve Hayes	In stigma workshops with therapists we used that method in talking about the TRAP of FEAR Trigger, Response, Automatic Patterns of Fusion, Evaluation, Avoidance, and Reasons that we need to DEACTIVATE: Defuse Empathize Accept Choose Take action Integrated with your Values Acknowledging The Essence of ourselves and the human beings we work with This kind of thing can be helpful methinks. Cutesy perhaps, but helpful.
ACT Workshops/ training/ research/ development - issues/criticisms [cont'd] Steve Hayes	My personal opinion is that [disclosure] works best when individuals do the work, and then share as a manifestation of that (if they choose). This sequence works: open up to pain; take responsibility for it; connect with what it has been costing to hide it; choose otherwise; and THEN put it out there as a manifestation of moving on. It is almost always to the good ... One of the ways I've seen training create problems (thankfully in very small numbers) is when individuals try to reverse that order and trainers don't rein them in. I've done it / missed it / regretted it. It actually can work in that order (i.e., sharing can be the primary mode of doing the work) but it's more risky and I personally do not choose to do that except in advanced intensives (and even then ...). Furthermore, avoiding this is part of what makes it possible for ACT to go where the human potential movement cannot. The two other big ways to screw up that I'm well aware of are: getting permission from the whole group but missing that someone is just being silent; not detecting (usually larger group context) that someone is getting overwhelmed.
ACT/ RFT **Broader vision [6-19-05]** Steve Hayes	What is the purpose of ACT/RFT? What is the purpose of these listserves? Why are both ACT and (independently) RFT called a cult? How should we move forward from here? I've been pondering these questions for several months - I realize now that I have not so much been trying to find the answers, but to find the courage to say them out loud.... I'd like to try to say some things clearly. ACT will be on the list of empirically supported treatments soon enough, but that is not its primary purpose.

ACT is part of a larger effort to create a psychology more adequate to the challenges of the human condition. Its theory starts with the normal and explains human suffering in terms of a basic account of human language and cognition. As such there is no way to cordon off ACT and ACT concepts from the individual human lives of ACT therapists; from the culture in which we participate; and from the social and psychological concerns of human beings who make contact with the work. It is not so much that ACT or RFT provides an answer to such issues as it is that it opens the door to a psychology that could help do so. That is what the culture needs from us; that is what the work itself leads toward....

ACT is not just a technology - it is an approach or model of therapy. It is not just an approach or model of therapy, it is a set of principles, methods and practices of known and potential relevance to social, educational, and personal concerns such as prejudice, learning, organizations, child rearing, relationships, and effective living. It is not just a set of such principles, methods, and practices it is linked to a basic theory and research program in human cognition, with possible implications for education, attitude change, communication, and every other area involving the cognition of human beings. It is not just a theory and research program, it is part of an intellectual tradition, behavior analysis, that from its beginning aspired to construct a psychology that would apply to every area of human concern and that could be consciously used to better society. And it not just part of that tradition, it views that tradition from a particular philosophical stance.

I know this list is not about me, but it is about things I initiated and some few facts of personal history seem relevant here. I became a behavior analyst in the 1960's. I saw in it the possibility of bringing together science and application; science and art; science and human meaning; science and spirituality. The earliest and most important book in my development as a behaviorist was Walden II (Skinner's utopian novel). Those aspects have been and are part of ACT and RFT and contextualism, for good or ill.

Behavior analysis stumbled badly over human language and cognition. RFT provides a way forward. B. F. Skinner's original vision remains. The ACT / RFT tradition is destined to pick up the mantle of that vision: it seeks a comprehensive account that enables the prediction and influence of human activities of all kinds, up to and including new ways of arranging the world and our own lives. As Skinner said, Walden II is not an answer so much as a challenge to find such an answer in science. ACT / RFT are all about that vision. It is why they exist....

This is an open, scientific movement AND it aspires to a vision that has not been seen in scientific psychology since the heyday of version one of Skinnerian psychology....

ACT / RFT is about creating a scientific behavioral psychology that works, in every area of complex human behavior. That includes your home, these lists, my kids, your church, the government, business, marketing, and so on. We are seeking a psychology that applies to our lives not just to our clients; one that applies to these lists and the people on it. We are living, as Kelly says, one life....

We are seeking a psychology that can help keep (to take two topics that have come up recently) children from smoking, and wars of self-destruction from happening.... This work is DESIGNED to create a scientific psychology that can do such things. That does not mean we can - it means that is the vision. That is the beacon in the distance....

ACT/ RFT Broader vision [cont'd] **Public health/ prevention science, role in [6-24-05]** Tony Biglan	Steve's recent post on the aspirations of ACT/RFT prompts me to discuss a scientific framework that is relevant and perhaps essential to the ACT/RFT movement realizing the vision of a better society that has motivated so many behavior analysts (e.g., Biglan, 1993). If we are going to "create a psychology more adequate to the challenges of the human condition," we will be most effective in doing so if we do it in collaboration with other areas of the behavioral sciences that are pragmatic and committed to the improvement of human well-being. I am speaking specifically about the scientific practices that are characteristic of public health and prevention science (Kellam [with Koretz]). The key features of this framework are its focus on the incidence and prevalence of phenomena of interest (disease, problematic behavior, or desired behavior) and the identification and exploitation of *any* variables that affect the prevalence of the target. If 20 years from now ACT/RFT has contributed to improving the human condition, it will be because (at a minimum) the prevalence of people who engage in experiential avoidance has decreased and the prevalence of people who consciously specify their values and engage in committed action has increased. [In the remainder of this I will concentrate on experiential avoidance, but one could apply the same analysis to psychological flexibility.] The first step in a prevention science or public health analysis is to identify a disease or behavior that is problematic in terms of its prevalence and cost. As a practical matter, public health gives the greatest attention to the conditions that are both prevalent and costly. An infectious disease that kills people and is or could become widespread will get attention before a problem such as depression simply because it is more likely to kill more people. This principle of targeting problems on the basis of prevalence times cost provides an empirical framework for making choices about what a society (or a group of scientists) will target. There is now substantial empirical evidence about the incidence or prevalence and the cost of a wide

variety of aspects of human behavior including depression, anxiety disorders, child abuse, aggressive social behavior, tobacco, alcohol, and other drug use, marital discord, etc. From both a scientific and public policy perspective, decisions about what to target for study or for amelioration are typically driven by evidence about prevalence times cost.

(Incidentally, this framework does not require that one reify diagnostic labels. Depression, for example, might be thought of as a "thing," but it can just as usefully be seen as a loose collection of psychological tendencies. The important thing from this perspective is simply that one can reliably identify a "syndrome" and can show that it has a significant cost.)

This approach is applicable to ACT/RFT. There is evidence that experiential avoidance (EA) and committed action are patterns of behavior that are stable and that are related to a variety of psychological problems - all of which have been shown to have associated costs. (And by "cost" I refer to any type of undesired outcome - treatment expense, damage to property, harm to others, harm to self, etc.) The public health justification for studying and attempting to change experiential avoidance, therefore, is that it is prevalent and costly. If you write a proposal to NIH to study these patterns of behavior, you will have to justify doing so precisely in terms of their prevalence and cost.

Current evidence is not as strong as it could be regarding experiential avoidance. For example, to my knowledge there is not yet a study of this pattern of behavior in a population-based sample. Such a sampling procedure is important because it would allow you to estimate the prevalence of the problem in a population and to derive more precise estimates of its contribution to a host of problems. Such evidence would provide a strong basis for advocating for greater allocation of resources to research on this problem. Existing evidence is a strong basis for making the case for doing such a study. In particular, the possibility that EA contributes to diverse psychological and behavioral problems means that targeting it could have enormous benefit in preventing a wide variety of problems.

Public health, and especially prevention science, focus on using all available means to reduce the prevalence of a problem. This follows naturally from the goal of reducing the prevalence of costly problems. Treatment is the first practice that has generally been applied to most public health problems. But, for infectious diseases and most unhealthy behaviors, it was quickly realized that other means of preventing and ameliorating problems were available. In the case of infectious disease, quarantine and removal of pathogens were important (and were developed, by the way, before germ theory was empirically established). In the case of unhealthy behaviors such as smoking, it was soon realized that it is difficult to get people to stop using substances and so both preventive interventions targeting individuals and policies (such as reduction of access to alcohol) have been developed.

The implication for ACT/RFT is that treatment is only one of a number of things that could be done to address problematic patterns of EA (as well as commitment to valued action). As we become clearer about how EA gets established and how it can be prevented, we will probably find that there are a variety of things that can be done in families, schools, and other organizations to prevent the development of these patterns. In our work here at ORI, we are trying to develop research on the prevention of these patterns in middle schools because middle school is the period and place where so many problems get started.

This analysis has implications for the recent discussion of the nature of the ACT/RFT movement. However one characterizes that movement, its benefit for society can be measured in terms of the degree to which it contributes to affecting human well-being, and human well-being can, to a large extent, be measured in terms of the prevalence of positive and negative aspects of individual function.

But an analysis of how ACT/RFT might affect human well-being would be quite incomplete if it only examined how individuals would be affected. Individuals' behavior is influenced by their families, peer groups, schools, work organizations, neighborhoods, churches, etc. An analysis is needed of the way in which these groups and organizations influence processes such as experiential avoidance and the way in which interventions targeting these groups and organizations could affect processes such as EA.

Consider families. There is considerable research showing that processes such as coercion influence children's development of aggressive social behavior and although there is some evidence regarding the problematic cognitions of parents and children that are associated with the development of aggressive behavior, an analysis of relational processes is wholly lacking. It seems likely that coercive interactions, which have been carefully studied using direct observation, often involve EA. A parent yells or hits in response to the feelings that come up when the child says something mean. A child attacks a sibling after being called a name. Behavioral parenting skills training is sufficiently advanced that people like Matt Sanders in Australia is targeting entire populations with his parenting programs - using approaches that range from intensive clinical interventions to mass media. Research is needed on how ACT/RFT might enhance these interventions and alter the EA of children and parents alike.

Consider schools. They are the place where much of the socialization of children occurs and it is in adolescence that most psychological and behavior problems begin to escalate. There are a growing number of interventions that have been shown to prevent the development of problems ranging from anti-social behavior and substance use to depression (Biglan et al., 2004). None of this research has included attention to EA or other ACT-relevant processes. Although these studies are very encouraging there is enormous room for improving the size of their effects. It seems likely (to me, at least) that understanding the role of experiential avoidance and other relational processes (such as those involving the conceptualized self) in the development of problems among children and adolescents would pinpoint important targets for intervention that are not currently being addressed. ACT interventions targeting them could enhance the effectiveness of existing preventive interventions.

Moreover, dealing with schools and other organizations requires that we analyze the practices of those organizations - as organizations - not just the behavior of individuals in them (Biglan 1995, and [selection by consequences article]). Schools are highly bureaucratic organizations that resist change and it has proved difficult to influence them to adopt research-based instructional or behavior management practices. At the same time, burnout and depression among teachers are at high levels (Jurado, Gurpegui, Moreno, & de Dios Luna, 1998), stand in the way of innovation (Evers, Brouwers, & Tomic, 2002) and contribute to teachers' absenteeism (Bartoli, 2002) and leaving the profession (Hughes, 2001). There appears to be no evidence on whether EA is a critical process among teachers and other school staff, but existing evidence suggests that that is quite likely. We are just beginning to explore an ACT intervention for schools that is like the one that Bond and colleagues used in England and Steve and others used with drug abuse counselors. In general, a program of research on whether the ACT/RFT analysis of human functioning could guide more effective ways of helping schools adopt and implement effective practices to benefit both staff and students is a logical expansion of the ACT/RFT research agenda.

Lastly, consider work organizations generally. Frank Bond's work has shown that the ACT/RFT analysis has great promise for transforming work organizations. But I bet he would agree that we have only scratched the surface on what might happen if a thoroughgoing analysis were applied to work organizations. Might business ethics be improved? Would work conditions be improved? Would organizations become more innovative and productive, without sacrificing worker well-being? Would improvements in work organizations contribute to lowering the prevalence of psychological and behavioral problems?

In sum, if ACT/RFT research is going to contribute to widespread improvements in the well-being of human populations, its insights and research and intervention practices will need to be integrated within the public health perspective - not in the sense of losing any of its philosophical, methodological, conceptual, or intervention features--but in the sense that the public health perspective specifies what it means to have a widespread effect and points to the venues where ACT/RFT needs to work to achieve its maximum benefit.

(I realized in writing this last sentence, that historically Behavior Analysis has had trouble integrating with other disciplines, partly because of the hostility of those disciplines to BA and partly because of the fear among behavior analysts that they would abandon key features of the Skinnerian paradigm if they did. Perhaps this time we are clear enough and comfortable enough with what we are about that we can go out and work with people of varying views without fear of losing our souls. Steve has been a good model in that regard.)

...

References

Bartoli, P.V. (2002). Burnout and job performance among education professionals and paraprofessionals. *Dissertation Abstracts International: Section B: The Sciences and Engineering, 63*(4-B), 2049.

Biglan, A. (1993). Recapturing Skinner's legacy to behavior therapy. *Behavior Therapist, January*, 3-5.

Biglan, A. (2003). Selection by consequences. *Prevention Science, 4*(4), 213-232.

Biglan, A. (1995). *Changing cultural practices: A contextualist framework for intervention research.* Reno, NV: Context Press.

Biglan, A., Brennan, P.A., Foster, S.L., Holder, H.D., Miller, T.L., Cunningham, P.B., et al. (2004). *Helping adolescents at risk: Prevention of multiple problems of youth.* New York: Guilford.

Evers, W.J.G., Brouwers, A., & Tomic, W. (2002). Burnout and self-efficacy: A study on teachers' beliefs when implementing an innovative educational system in the Netherlands. *British Journal of Educational Psychology, 72*(2), 227-244.

Hughes, R.E. (2001). Deciding to leave but staying: Teacher burnout, precursors, and turnover. *International Journal of Human Resource Management, 12*(2), 288-298.

Jurado, D., Gurpegui, M., Moreno, O., & de Dios, L. J. (1998). School setting and teaching experience as risk factors for depressive symptoms in teachers. *European Psychiatry, 13*(2), 78-82.

| ACT/ RFT Broader vision [cont'd] | These are really important points. One idea we've been pursuing here at Nevada is to think about what is already in place to effect change and to see if we can help in these areas. |
| | So, for example, we are looking at the impact of ACT on learning. We seem to be finding that it makes it |

Public health/ prevention science, role in [cont'd] Steve Hayes	easier to learn new things. If that held up it would enable us to construct brief workshops that could be used to make education more impactful.
	We are looking at the impact of ACT on stigma toward clients. We seem to be finding that it reduces it. If that held up it would enable us to construct brief workshops that could be used to make diversity training for health care workers (required in many areas) better and more impactful.
	We are looking at the impact of ACT on racial prejudice. We just a couple of days ago looked at a pilot trial of comparing ACT versus educational lectures in a college class on racial issues. ACT produced significantly larger changes in planned positive behaviors. If that held up it would enable us to enter schools with better training materials / programs.
	There are hundreds of such entry points once you start looking for them. The point is not ACT uber alles -- it is finding ways to do a better job and then finding places in the system where knowledge of that kind might be used.

ACT/ RFT
 	
   Co-dependence of; "contextualist world" view
 	
RFT
 	
   Should clinicians learn? [5-1-03]
 	
   Steve Hayes
	... To me, ACT, RFT, contextualism, the new behavioral psychology that comes from all of them, are all one world. Thus the title of the Sweden conference. You can enter into that world and explore its neighborhoods but sooner or later you will realize that if you are in the applied side, you need the basic theory; if you are in the basic theory, you will realize you need application; in either area you will realize you need the philosophy. So initially, the view might be "ACT is its own world ... RFT is in there because the originators of ACT also worked on it." Later, however, questions will naturally arise ... that can only be addressed by having both.

	RFT is difficult to get ... but once you get it, it is simple. What is hard about it is its radical functionalism / contextualism. Guess what: that is what is hard about ACT too, and RFT and ACT both help each other because they are like key multiple exemplars from the same contextualistic space (itself an RFT-sensible idea). As we add other applied programs from that same space (e.g., prevention interventions; media; attitude change; education; etc.) I predict that we will find additional exemplars that people need to really get what this neighborhood is about. Learning RFT is not easy, I admit. I do believe, however, that is it not possible to be fully competent in ACT without some grasp of it ... because without it you inevitably divide the world differently, as based on lay or other language distinctions, and that in turn leaks into therapy....
	One problem with the "contextualistic world" view of the ACT / RFT relation needs to be admitted: if it is too much "in your face" it makes entry into that world seem too daunting. Also, if too few people's hands are on it, it looks too narcissistic. The latter problem is being relieved by the wonderful way that ACT / RFT is being taken over and owned by the whole world ACT / RFT community. I think this developmental process can't be forced ... but I see clear signs (the Sweden conference itself is one) that more folks are seeing the whole neighborhood. It is the whole neighborhood that makes what is happening here the sort of thing that could be of fundamental importance.

ACT/ RFT
 	
   Falsifiability of
 	
FUNCTIONAL CONTEXTUALISM
 	
   Truth, pragmatic, criterion - cf. falsifiability [6-22-05]
 	
   Steve Hayes
	Monica Pignotti wrote:
	
	   The way I see it, ACT as a way of life (vs. a specific empirically supported treatment for specific conditions) is not a falsifiable claim or concept, so that puts it outside the realm of science.... ACT is testable and falsifiable as an intervention with specific populations for specific conditions, but to say it is scientific as a way of life is, IMO, a major error ...

	Somewhere along the line the idea of falsifiability became the functional equivalent of "truly scientific." It is especially so in the EST wing of empirical clinical psychology, and especially by critics talking about other folks' ideas, not their own. But the assumptive nature of the criterion is usually denied -- as if this is a settled matter. It is not. Falsification is the criterion of a particular form of philosophy of science; most often it is linked to mechanistic, hypothetico-deductive formulations. There are scores of holes in it and ever since Kuhn it is on the wane in philosophy of science ... only psychologists seem not to have noticed.
	In fact you can "falsify" ACT and RFT if you want, and we've said in several places how to do it and we've actively sought evidence in these areas (e.g., early childhood RFT work; attempts to train relational operants), but within its own philosophy of science the truth criterion is prediction and influence with precision, scope, and depth. The logical flaw in workability is that ways of speaking can have positive impact in one situation but not in others, but you don't test the "others" so you can never know if a way of speaking is "really true." Thus, the only TRUE knowledge is knowing that something is not true. Voila -- falsification.
	The logical flaw in falsifiability is that all tests are based on auxilliaries and conditions which are themselves not tested. Thus, when tests do not work out, the auxilliaries and conditions can always be at fault (e.g., the concept is indeed still related to the outcome, I just did not measure it right). That is ALWAYS true, for reasons Godel showed: all analytic systems are based on assumptions outside the system. Add in the POWERFUL psychological effect of stating a hypothesis beforehand and it becomes an almost impossible move to resist. As a result, "falsification" is 99.9% empty rhetoric. It is hard to find good

	examples of it. It is mostly used to attack others; it is rarely applied to oneself.
	[In an article: Hayes, S.C. (2004). Falsification and the protective belt surrounding entity-postulating theories. *Applied & Preventive Psychology, 11*, 35-37] I whomp on one of the heroes of the EST wing of empirical clinical psychology, Paul Meehl, and try to show that his embrace of falsifiability was itself fundamentally flawed. He himself saw the fatal flaw but also denied it, creating an unresolvable contradiction. Lesser minds than he have gone on uncritically to accept his position and somehow to avoid seeing both the flaws and their implications. But Meehl himself actually did what I just said: he used to attack others; and would not apply it to oneself. What he did apply is a form of workability, but without the protections provided by the avoidance of hypothetical constructs. Read my critique and then read the Meehl original and see. I think it is right there: Meehl's pants are at his knees. Well, if one of the most brilliant minds of the 20th century can do this in one article, what do you think schmoos like us will do? Duh.
	Contextualism provides another way forward. 1. There is no "really true" anything. Speaking is just a humble human activity that can be useful in creating more effective behavior in and with the one world. In order words, if it is language, hold it lightly. 2. Stay in touch with more descriptive ways of speaking that lead direction to manipulable events throughout, so that every language step can be tested pragmatically. Avoid hypothetical constructs. If you use intervening variables do it very lightly and keep coming back to what you can actually change. 3. Go for precision, scope, and depth. The pragmatic filter is broadened and deepened, so it is harder to make truly upsetting forms of the logical errors possible in workability (or, to say it more offensively, you allow for "affirming the consequent" but you prevent pragmatically lethal forms of it by weaving a web of interconnected knowledge using these five concepts -- prediction; influence; precision; scope; depth -- and by keeping a firm grip on your unit of analysis -- for us, the act-in-context). In other words, if a way of speaking is very useful in reaching your analytic goals (in this case, prediction-and-influence of whole organisms interacting in and with a context considered both historically and situationally) then you "test" that analytic construction by ever-expanding circles of greater precision, scope, and depth.
	This is all exactly what is happening and has happened for 25 years with ACT / RFT. Note how the early literature in RFT examined the utility of thinking in terms of multiple stimulus relations; contextual control; relations among relations; development and so on. Now we are training relational frames; examining how they impact complex phenomena predicted to be due to relational frames; looking at natural phenomena such as IQ or a sense of perspective. And we are beginning to test the depth of the units through neurobiological measures; basic cognitive preparations. Over and over again it is an iterative, multiplicative process of seeking precision, seeking scope and depth while maintaining precision, refinement and more precision. Back and forth, with all three dimensions in view and constantly using both prediction and influence as metrics.
	The same thing happened with ACT. Small, very focused studies. Correlational evidence. Then broader studies. Then more refinement. Then mediational studies. Now we are seeing RFT preparations building up into ACT and ACT being dissembled down into RFT; we are seeing large scale studies, prevention, etc.
	The great benefit psychologically is that everything is held more lightly to begin with. There is nothing to be right about -- we are just talking for pragmatic purposes. Truth is always with a small "t." There are things to be effective about, but there the data decide and we can start small and work up.
	By the way, to a large degree this functional contextualism way of thinking this is all just behavior analysis reworked, but with a bit more philosophical tap dancing.
ACT/ RFT **Technical terms, need for [5-5-05]** Steve Hayes	Monica Pignotti wrote: I can see ... that the movement around ACT does in some ways have the appearance of a pseudoscience (especially the excessive use of jargon...). ... The unfamiliar terms that are unnecessary (and using them in contexts that are unnecessary) we can change. The use of technical terms when only technical terms will do we change only at our great risk. Let's remember what we are trying to do in the ACT / RFT community: create a more progressive science that will be more adequate to the challenges of human suffering and growth. ACT / RFT seems to me to be leading to a new contextualistic form of behavior analysis (whatever it will end up being called) and even that is not quite big enough. We are groping toward a pragmatic natural science of complex human behavior, including language and cognition. That does not exist on the planet. That is something that has never been done before. It will not be done without technical terms / principles / theories that will be really hard to understand. ACT / RFT is just a step in that direction. If it works the jargon problem will get a lot worse. We are not there yet -- but in the clinical fields we've gotten used to common sense accounts masquerading as science. That is not good for us as a field. Inside ACT is RFT and inside RFT is traditional Skinnerian behavior analysis and inside that is functional

	contextualism/radical behaviorism. We don't set it up so that everyone into ACT needs to learn all of that in order to do anything, but ultimately it all links. That is the strength of it ... and the challenge....
BEHAVIOR CHANGE **Behavioral health website (inc. re smoking, diabetes) [6-7-05]** Kirk Strosahl	... I am very active in the arena of integrating behavioral health and primary care services and providers. It turns out that ACT is developing a huge presence with medical problems such as pain, smoking, diabetes and other chronic conditions. Some of the most powerful demonstrations of ACT seem to be coming in these "non-traditional" areas of human behavior change. If you are among the many of those who are getting increasingly interested in the whole movement of integration of behavioral health and primary care services, I have just launched a new website exclusively devoted to that area. You can access it directly at [www.behavioral-health-integration.com]. It is very interactive, has a ton of free downloads (i.e., patient education materials, program tools, screening tools for primary care, synopses of the latest clinical trials in integrated care) and a forums section where you can dialogue with people working in primary care across the country. All of these things are free--we are just trying to create a nationwide wave of interest to reunite the mind and body! ...
EVIDENCE **Anxiety, social - ACT cf. CBT [4-26-05]** Joseph Cautilli	ACT has been studied with socially anxious students and found to be as effective as CBT: Block, J. A., & Wulfert, E. (2000). Acceptance or Change: Treating Socially Anxious College Students with ACT or CBGT. *The Behavior Analyst Today, 1*(2), 3-10.
EVIDENCE **Anxiety, social - emotion suppression/ acceptance [8-2-05]** Steve Hayes	... Todd Kashan and Michael Steger just landed a very cool study in Psychological Science (Woo hoo! Go, Todd, Go). If that ain't mainstreaming these issues I don't know what is. Here is the reference: Kashdan, T. B., & Steger. M. F. (in press). Expanding the topography of social anxiety: An experience sampling assessment of positive emotions and events, and emotion suppression. *Psychological Science.* In a 21-day experience sampling study, dispositional social anxiety, emotional suppression, and cognitive reappraisal was compared daily measures of social anxiety. Socially anxious individuals reported the lowest rate of positive events on days when they were more socially anxious and tended to suppress emotions, and the highest rate of positive events on days when they were less socially anxious and more accepting of emotional experiences. Irrespective of dispositional social anxiety, participants reported the most intense positive emotions on days when they were less socially anxious and more accepting of emotional experiences....
EVIDENCE **CBT, ACT cf.** **ACT cf.** **CBT – evidence [4-4-05]** Steve Hayes	Russ Harris wrote: ... in the two studies comparing ACT to CBT for depression, the results were equivalent.... Is there any data out there showing ACT is significantly superior to CBT, in the short term and/or long term? The two studies comparing ACT to CBT for depression were not equivalent. In one (Zettle & Hayes, 1986) ACT was superior (which was surprising because it was horribly underpowered; total N = 18). The data showed better Hamilton Rating Scale outcomes for ACT at post & 6 month follow-up. (See Zettle, R. D. & Hayes, S. C. (1986). Dysfunctional control by client verbal behavior: The context of reason giving. *The Analysis of Verbal Behavior, 4,* 30-38.) A second study (Zettle & Rains, 1986) done in group form it was equivalent, but the effect size for ACT was still up there (a *d* of .6 or so). The other completed outcome study is Ann Branstetter's end stage cancer study. ACT was superior. The other underway is the Drexel effectiveness study. At mid-point (presented at ABCT nee AABT) ACT was superior but we will have to wait to see how it turns out. There is another coming in Finland with similar outcomes (Lappalainen et al. (in press). *Behavior Modification.*). In component studies, ACT components (e.g., acceptance rationales and metaphors) generally work better than equivalent CBT components (e.g., see the Hayes et al. 1999 pain study in Psych Record; among several others). Bottom line: of the studies so far ACT generally seems to be working better. That is not common in Rx research. The Dodo bird verdict is the general outcome, as you know. Also, in all studies so far that have compared the two, ACT works through a different process. CBT works but usually not through its putative process. ACT works, but usually through its putative processes. I walked through this issue in my 3rd wave MS in BT. We don't need to trash CBT (we are part of CBT writ large and obviously there is overlap in many areas) but neither do we need to take the "it works so it's true" line. The traditional CBT model does not really work that well - the technology works but through unknown processes and a lot of what is working seems to be the BT components (which ACT also is happy to use) and components (like distancing) that ACT so far

	seems to do better.
	It will take a while to get truly definitive data to see if ACT works better (you need big studies to ask that question reliably which means they probably have to be funded studies). So far, however, if you had to choose I think a neutral observer would have to say that ACT is doing very well indeed in head to head comparisons. It's early. We shall see.
EVIDENCE **Hypotheses/ principles, testable [5-18-04]** Steve Hayes	Joseph Ciarrochi wrote: What would a list of ACT/RFT relevant ESP's [empirically supported principles of change] look like? Joe's question is a good one. I think there are at least a couple hundred testable hypotheses in ACT and RFT ... some of them have been relatively extensively tested and could conceivably already be what Rosen and Davison are talking about as "empirically supported principles." Others are extensions of the theory that haven't yet been fully tested. I wonder if it would be a good exercise to see if we could come up with 50-100 or so of these and put them on the ACT and RFT websites. Anyone willing to propose some? An exercise like this is deliciously risky (easy to be wrong if you do something like this) but I love that feature of it. Why not give folks something to shoot at? "Win" or "lose" the field would be better for it. In no particular order (I only spent about 20 minutes on this) here is a starter set. They shift from narrow hypotheses to broad ones; from ones that are absolutely central to ACT / RFT to ones that are more like implications. I did not try to tag these with folks who have advocated for them over the years ... many if not most of these associated originally with other folks. I also did not defend them ... if any aren't obvious (i.e., why would these fall out of ACT / RFT) I can walk through why they seem so ... I did this in a free form ... whatever occurred went down without much filtering ... pretty much in this order. I thought doing it that way might be itself useful ... (we really do have to write that "An RFT analysis of everything" paper!). A lot of the ones below are ACT related. I was just working on my ACT talk for tomorrow here in Australia and these things are on my mind at this moment ... if I had time I'd add a bunch of RFT ones to balance them (it is even easier to do this exercise with RFT ... and we even tried in the book) but I'm running out of time and energy to create balance tonight. A lot of them are also phrased in a form that focuses on action over context. I think they all are translatable to interactive and contextual language though, so I will just put them out in this form (though to test them fully you have to actually do that translation). I'm looking forward to what others come up with! A small sample of empirically supported or empirically testable ACT and RFT hypotheses and principles: ♦ Experiential avoidance is generally unhelpful to positive life outcomes ♦ Experiential avoidance produces its unhelpful effects in part through its repertoire narrowing and self-amplifying effects ♦ Experiential avoidance is based in part on cognitive fusion ♦ Response inflexibility is generally unhelpful to positive life outcomes ♦ Psychological persistence and change linked to valued outcomes will predict quality of life over time ♦ Health is more determined by the function of private events and other experiences than by their form ♦ Experiential avoidance is supported by market driven cultural developments and is resisted by the mystical and experiential aspects of our spiritual and religious traditions ♦ Training in response flexibility will be of general utility (e.g., focusing on the present moment in a flexible way, now maintaining a constant focus, now shifting from an internal to an external focus, contacting difficult experiences in a flexible and creative way) to persons who are suffering ♦ The positive effects of exposure are increased with emotional acceptance; reduced with experiential avoidance; increased in the context of cognitive defusion; fostered by response flexibility during exposure ♦ A transcendent sense of self will support acceptance / defusion / and psychological flexibility ♦ Relational frames initially require multiple exemplars to be established (though once a relational repertoire is well established other frames may be producible by earlier frames) ♦ Some forms of psychopathology will be positively correlated with verbal exposure and verbal repertoire ♦ Catching the process of thinking is helpful in reducing inflexible rule-governed behavior ♦ A sense of "free choice" is reduced in the context of cognitive fusion ♦ Brain functions associated with negative emotional arousal, literal reasoning, and fixed patterns of rule following of behavior (e.g., when exposed to or following difficult material) will be lower following acceptance and defusion training ♦ A sense of "free choice" is helpful to values clarification and adoption ♦ Excessive levels of reason giving can make treatment more difficult ♦ While helpful initially to the development of verbal regulation, high rates of pliance are associated with

	several forms of psychopathology, including anxiety and depression ♦ The measured stages of moral development suggested by RFT will be associated with higher rates of socially responsible behavioral ♦ Deictic frames are necessary for development of a transcendent sense of self ♦ In the area of psychopathology, our thoughts about our thoughts are more important than our thoughts ♦ The use of verbal framing strategies that are commonly used with external objects can be helpful in producing defusion with regarded to feelings and thoughts ♦ So called social fears and problems are usually based on psychological avoidance and fusion, not really on an external social focus ♦ Verbal problem solving and mental illness go together: you don't have much of the latter until you get the former ♦ Temporal and evaluative frames (Right and wrong / good and bad / past and future) are necessary before suicide is possible ♦ Augmentals are based on increasing or diminishing the sensory / perceptual functions of verbal events frames as occurring in the future. Thus impulsive behavior is promoted by an inability to defuse from those functions that are produced by impulsive behavior; conversely, persistence is promoted by focusing on those functions produced by persistence
EVIDENCE Hypotheses/ principles, testable [cont'd] Steve Hayes	[In clarification of the last-mentioned hypothesis] We've argued that one of the reasons for augmentation (temporary changes in the ability of events to function as consequences due to relational frames) is that some such rules bring the future into the present. Tasting the steak will function as a motivational events for working to get more steak ... if you "taste it" verbally the same thing happens ("wouldn't a nice cold beer go good right now?"). That can work in to the other way if the normal sensory/perceptual functions are disrupted via language (e.g., "think of donuts as flour fried in gear lube"). My point about impulsivity is that learning to produce functions via language can make impulsivity better or worse, depending on the functions produced. We have some early data on this ...
EVIDENCE **Normal population - avoidance/ acceptance/ defusion [5-5-05]** Steve Hayes	Monica Pignotti wrote: Steven Hayes commented that there was loads of data [about ACT helping "normal" people who do not have any specific psychological diagnosis with life issues], but I still think that sort of claim is way too general to even begin to support or refute… Regarding whether we have "loads of data" that experiential avoidance has costs and acceptance / defusion is helpful using normal subjects, the data below are all on the ACT website ... By my memory about 1000 of the participants in the following studies are normal folks. The AAQ does interesting things here (like predictive validity in improvements in overall quality of life ... John Forsyth's data). I'm pretty sure that is the kind of thing Frank was referring to with the phrase "all aspects of their life." I'm sure Frank is not claiming that every single problem is an acceptance problem; rather that psychological flexibility does relate to overall functioning: Hayes, S. C., Strosahl, K. D., Wilson, K. G., Bissett, R. T., Pistorello, J., Toarmino, D., Polusny, M., A., Dykstra, T. A., Batten, S. V., Bergan, J., Stewart, S. H., Zvolensky, M. J., Eifert, G. H., Bond, F. W., Forsyth J. P., Karekla, M., & McCurry, S. M. (2004). Measuring experiential avoidance: A preliminary test of a working model. *The Psychological Record, 54*, 553-578. Normal folks in a work environment: Bond, F. W., & Bunce, D. (2003). The role of acceptance and job control in mental health, job satisfaction, and work performance. *Journal of Applied Psychology, 88*, 1057-1067. Shows that AAQ predicts positive work outcomes (mental health, satisfaction, performance) even one year later, especially in combination with job control. Donaldson, E., & Bond, F.W. (2004). Psychological acceptance and emotional intelligence in relation to workplace well-being. *British Journal of Guidance and Counselling, 34*, 187-203. Study compared experiential avoidance (as measured by the AAQ) and emotional intelligence in terms of their ability to predict general mental health, physical well-being, and job satisfaction in workers (controlling for the effects of job control since this work organization variable is consistently associated with occupational health and performance). Results from 290 United Kingdom workers showed that emotional intelligence did not significantly predict any of the well-being outcomes, after accounting for acceptance and job control. Acceptance predicted general mental health and physical well-being but not job satisfaction. Job control was associated with job satisfaction only. Not controlling one's thoughts and feelings (as advocated by acceptance) may have greater benefits for mental well-being than attempting consciously to regulate them (as emotional intelligence suggests). Other studies with normal folk: Sloan, D. M. (2004). Emotion regulation in action: Emotional reactivity in experiential avoidance.

Behaviour Research and Therapy, 42, 1257-1270. Examined the relationship between emotional reactivity (self-report and physiological reactivity) to pleasant, unpleasant, and neutral emotion-eliciting stimuli and experiential avoidance as measured by the AAQ. Sixty-two participants were separated into high and low experiential avoiders. Results indicated that high EA participants reported greater emotional experience to both unpleasant and pleasant stimuli compared to low EA participants. In contrast to their heightened reports of emotion, high EA participants displayed attenuated heart rate reactivity to the unpleasant stimuli relative to the low EA participants. Findings were interpreted as reflecting an emotion regulation attempt by high EA participants when confronted with unpleasant emotion-evocative stimuli.

Karekla, M., Forsyth, J. P., & Kelly, M. M. (2004). Emotional avoidance and panicogenic responding to a biological challenge procedure. *Behavior Therapy, 35*, 725-746. Normal participants high or low on the AAQ were exposed to a CO2 challenge. High emotional avoiders reported more panic symptoms than low avoiders. No difference physiologically.

Greco, L. A., Heffner, M., Poe, S., Ritchie, S., Polak, M., & Lynch, S. K. (in press). Parental adjustment following pre-term birth: Contributions of experiential avoidance, child temperament, and perceived social support. *Behavior Therapy*. Experiential avoidance as measured by the AAQ correlated positively with post-discharge parental stress and traumatic stress symptoms surrounding preterm birth. Moreover, it partially mediated the association between stress during delivery and later traumatic stress symptoms. This process was not moderated by parent reports of child temperament or perceived social support, suggesting that experiential avoidance plays a mediating role irrespective of child characteristics or perceived support from family members and close friends.

Marcks, B. A., & Woods, D. W. (2005). A comparison of thought suppression to an acceptance-based technique in the management of personal intrusive thoughts: A controlled evaluation. *Behaviour Research and Therapy, 43*, 433-445. Two studies. Correlational study shows suppressing personally relevant intrusive thoughts is associated with more thoughts, more distress, greater urge to do something. Those who accept are less obsessional, depressed and anxious. Experimental study shows that instructions to suppress does not work and leads to increased level of distress; instructions of accept (using a couple of short metaphors drawn from the ACT book) decreases discomfort but not thought frequency.

Masuda, A., Hayes, S. C., Sackett, C. F., & Twohig, M. P. (2004). Cognitive defusion and self-relevant negative thoughts: Examining the impact of a ninety year old technique. *Behaviour Research and Therapy, 42*, 477-485. Shows in a series of time-series designs and a group study, that the "milk, milk, milk" defusion technique reduces distress and believability of negative self-referential thoughts.

Gutiérrez, O., Luciano, C., Rodríguez, M., & Fink, B. C. (2004). Comparison between an acceptance-based and a cognitive-control-based protocol for coping with pain. *Behavior Therapy, 35*, 767-784. Randomized study with analogue pain task showing greater tolerance for pain in the defusion and acceptance-based condition drawn from ACT as compared to a closely parallel cognitive-control based condition.

Hayes, S.C., Bissett, R., Korn, Z., Zettle, R. D., Rosenfarb, I., Cooper, L., & Grundt, A. (1999). The impact of acceptance versus control rationales on pain tolerance. *The Psychological Record, 49*, 33-47. Analog study. Shows that an acceptance rationale drawn from the ACT protocol produces more pain tolerance than a pain control rationale drawn from a CBT pain management package.

Eifert, G. H., & Heffner, M. (2003). The effects of acceptance versus control contexts on avoidance of panic-related symptoms. *Journal of Behavior Therapy and Experimental Psychiatry, 34,* 293-312. Randomized study comparing control versus acceptance during a CO2 challenge with anxious subjects. Acceptance oriented exercise (the finger trap) reduced avoidance, anxiety symptoms, and anxious cognitions as compared to breathing training.

Feldner, M. T., Zvolensky, M. J., Eifert, G. H., & Spira, A. P. (2003). Emotional avoidance: An experimental test of individual differences and response suppression during biological challenge. *Behaviour Research and Therapy, 41*, 403-411. High emotional avoidance subjects showed more anxiety in response to CO2, particularly when instructed to suppress their emotions.

Takahashi, M., Muto, T., Tada, M., & Sugiyama, M. (2002). Acceptance rationale and increasing pain tolerance: Acceptance-based and FEAR-based practice. *Japanese Journal of Behavior Therapy, 28*, 35-46. Small randomized trial that replicated Hayes, Bissett, Korn, Zettle, Rosenfarb, Cooper, & Grundt, 1999. An acceptance rationale plus two ACT defusion exercises (Leaves on the stream and Physicalizing) did significantly better than a match control focused intervention on pain tolerance, or a lecture on pain.

Keogh, E., Bond, F. W., Hanmer, R., & Tilston, J. (in press). Comparing acceptance and control-based coping instructions on the cold-pressor pain experiences of healthy men and women. *European Journal of Pain*. Simple acceptance-based coping instructions improved affective pain more than distraction but only for women.

Blackledge, J. T. (2004). *Using Acceptance and Commitment Therapy in the treatment of parents of autistic children*. Unpublished doctoral dissertation, University of Nevada, Reno. Pre - post study shows that ACT

	workshop helps parents cope with the stress of raising autistic children.
	Gregg, J. (2004). *Development of an acceptance-based treatment for the self-management of diabetes.* Unpublished doctoral dissertation, University of Nevada, Reno. RCT showing that six hour ACT workshop with patient education works better than patient education alone in producing changes in diabetes self-management and blood glucose (at 3 month follow-up). Mediational analyses show that ACT works through increased acceptance and defusion of diabetes related feelings and thoughts.
	I think there are about 1800 (my guesstimate ... I did not count them) normal folks in these 16 studies and the data are very, very consistent. If you add in the growing literature of distress tolerance, anxiety sensitivity, learned industriousness, mindfulness, alexithymia (which correlates very highly with the AAQ), ways of coping (e.g., emotion focused coping versus active coping), experiencing (I'm thinking here of the data on things like the Experiencing Scale), thought suppression, and emotional suppression, just to name the ones that are obviously related, it seems fair to say that we do indeed have "loads of data" that experiential avoidance defined the way we define it in ACT is generally harmful in normal populations. We also have some data that ACT methods are helpful in this regard. We have a review article that will walk through all of this in BRAT and Dermot recently published a short review in an Irish journal…
	That does not mean that we've answered all of the questions. Not close. But I was going after the idea that we had no data or very little data on the effect of experiential avoidance in normal populations, as if the ACT work has been limited to pathological populations and therefore it was premature to consider the relevance for normal folks. As Mike Kirkeberg said in response to one of the early messages in this thread "it sounds like what is being said is that ACT is true in a clinical one-on-one setting, but not necessarily true in the real world." Yipes. I hope not. ACT starts out with an analysis of the normal (in rejecting the assumption of healthy normality) and that rejection is based on a theory, RFT, that makes the most basic claims you can imagine and has evidence going all the way down to normal infants. The idea that this applies only to abnormal populations is a fairly direct challenge to the whole research program. It would be very disturbing if true. But it is not.
	The research program is still developing. We have a long way to go. But it is not so that we have very little data in normal populations. We have, well ... how shall I say it? Loads of data.
EVIDENCE Normal population - avoidance/ acceptance/ defusion [cont'd] Dermot Barnes-Holmes	... in a recent study we have found that a brief acceptance instruction failed to improve tolerance significantly on a shock task, but a brief distraction instruction actually reduced tolerance significantly (it's a non-significant reduction when you correct for multiple tests). In contrast, when we employed an acceptance instruction with a defusion exercise and relevant metaphor tolerance improved significantly, but a distraction condition with an appropriate exercise and metaphor did not. A placebo condition also produced no significant increase in tolerance. The entire experiment was automated with video-based delivery of intervention material etc.
	Anyway, these data seem to suggest that simply telling someone to accept is not much use, and simply telling someone to distract might actually reduce behavioral persistence (perhaps due to .. relational incoherence ..). A critical part of an acceptance intervention, therefore, at least in this type of analog pain study, is the defusion element, which seeks to transform the avoidance functions of the aversive stimulus. In effect, relational coherence between the intervention and the participant's experience on the task is not sufficient to increase tolerance -- if it does anything it serves to keep tolerance at about the same level from pre to post.
	It is also interesting that the distraction condition with exercises/metaphor increased tolerance (but not significantly) whereas distraction with no exercises/metaphor did not (and in fact reduced tolerance significantly if you don't correct for repeated tests). This might indicate that certain so-called distraction exercises actually possess some defusion functions….
EVIDENCE **Panic - emotion suppression/ acceptance [cont'd]** Jill Levitt *Cross Reference:* *See 2-65 for an earlier post in this thread*	Thanks, Steve, for noting our study on acceptance vs. suppression in patients with panic disorder. The reference is: Levitt, J. T., Brown, T.A., Orsillo, S. M., & Barlow, D. H. (2004). The effects of acceptance versus suppression of emotion on subjective and psycho physiological response to carbon dioxide challenge in patients with panic disorder. *Behavior Therapy, 35*, 747-766. Interestingly, we found significant differences between the acceptance group and the other two groups on subjective anxiety (e.g., average SUDS ratings during the CO_2 challenge) but not on self-report of panic symptoms or physiological measures. We also found that the acceptance group was significantly more willing to participate in a second CO_2 challenge than the suppression or no-instruction control groups. I think these findings are consistent with two of the goals of acceptance-based interventions: 1) to encourage patients to experience emotions fully, without judging or evaluating them, and 2) to increase patients' willingness to participate in important activities. The fact that SUDS ratings were different, but that symptom reports were not different suggests that acceptance participants experienced the same symptoms as other participants, but did not evaluate their symptoms as being as distressing as the other groups did. This is pretty interesting, because the acceptance intervention definitely did not contain any psyched. on panic (therefore it should not have directly reduced

	the appraisal of threat of panic symptoms).
	Of note, this was just a 10 minute intervention with patients with panic disorder prior to a 15 minute 5.5% CO_2 challenge.
	As Steve noted, I would expect that the more often one experiences symptoms fully, without judging or evaluating them, the less impact the symptoms have, the less they will actually come. But, since this was just a one-time evaluation, we do not have any data indicating that panic symptoms decreased in the long term.
	I am now working on submitting a grant to develop an acceptance-based tx for young adults (18-25) with panic disorder, so, I hope to be able to answer that question (in, say, 5-7 years from now!). I really see acceptance as the context which will facilitate exposure (both interoceptive exposure and situational exposure), and foster both better living, and symptom reduction.
EVIDENCE **Review article [6-7-05]** Steve Hayes	Jay Luoma, Frank Bond, Aki Masuda, Jason Lillis and I have just completed a review of the ACT literature (especially ACT processes) for BRAT.... It includes some new mediational analyses, it includes a meta-analysis of the AAQ data, and meta-analyses of ACT outcomes.... For the AAQ part we included anything available in printed form. For the process and outcome part we included all published controlled studies (including time series designs) and all randomized trials that were presented or in dissertation / thesis form.
EVIDENCE Review article [cont'd] Steve Hayes	Here is what is in the article: Quantitative characterization of the relative strength of ACT outcomes. Understanding processes of change is of no importance unless there is change to begin with. The between condition effect sizes for the ACT outcome literature (including all studies with a direct applied purpose and excluding non-clinical analogue studies) are frequent enough now to be worth summarizing. Summarizing across this early extant literature on the primary outcome variable targeted, and weighting average effect sizes by the number of cases that produced the effect, ACT has produced between condition effect sizes (using Cohen's d) of .74 at post (N = 629) and 1.17 at follow-up (N = 519). Average effect sizes for comparisons between ACT and active, well-specified treatments that were deliberately provided to affect the targeted problem were .58 at post (N = 381) and 1.41 at follow-up (N = 343); for comparisons with wait list, treatment as usual, or placebo treatments the effect sizes were .99 at post (N = 248) and .72 at follow-up (N = 176). Across the dataset, follow-ups, when they occurred, ranged from 8 to 52 weeks with a weighted average of 19.6 weeks. As these results apply to the ACT model per se it seems worth noting the few studies that have directly compared ACT and traditional CT or CBT (Block, 2002; Branstetter et al., 2004; Zettle & Hayes, 1986; Zettle & Rains, 1987). Between condition effect sizes were .73 at post (range: .49 to 1.23) and .83 (range: .79 to .92) at follow-up in favor of the ACT approach on primary outcome measures. The total number of participants in these four studies is still very small however (N = 96 and 39 at post and follow-up, respectively). On primary processes of change measures specified from an ACT model, the between condition effect sizes in these studies were 3.32 at post (N = 96) and .74 at follow-up (N = 39). These early data provide a possible indication that ACT and traditional CBT impact change processes differently and that ACT may contribute to clinical outcome, although no conclusions should be reached given the extremely preliminary nature of the data. Furthermore, although some of these trials have been conducted by Beck-trained clinicians (Zettle & Hayes, 1986; Zettle & Rains, 1987), these studies are also being conducted by researchers interested in ACT, so bias is possible. Larger scale studies and broader effectiveness trials than those currently conducted (Strosahl et al., 1998) will be needed to tease out these issues. Positive preliminary results from effectiveness studies that have randomly assigned patients in an outpatient clinic to ACT or to traditional CBT have recently been presented (e.g., Foreman & Herbert, 2004), so more evidence seems likely soon. Notice that across the entire ACT literature... the between group effect sizes are larger at follow-up than at post.
EVIDENCE **Studies (re GAD and psychosis) [3-16-05]** Steve Hayes	Interesting article that just came out: Roemer, L., Salters, K., Raffa, S. D., & Orsillo, S. M. (2005). Fear and avoidance of internal experiences in GAD: Preliminary tests of a conceptual model. *Cognitive Therapy and Research, 29,* 71-88. This is a nice piece showing that experiential avoidance (AAQ etc.) is associated with GAD symptoms in both clinical and non-clinical populations. Interesting article that just got accepted: Guadiano, B.A., & Herbert, J.D. (in press). Acute treatment of inpatients with psychotic symptoms using Acceptance and Commitment Therapy. *Behaviour Research and Therapy*. This study replicates the Bach and Hayes study with better measures and a better control condition. Good results esp. on measures of overt psychotic behavior (the BPRS). Part of what is amazing about this study is the dose is at times even smaller than the Bach & Hayes study and the N is smallish and yet the effects are so good. Mediational analyses

	also fit the ACT model and are described in more detail in Gaudiano, B. A., & Herbert, J. D. (in press). Believability of hallucinations as a potential mediator of their frequency and associated distress in psychotic inpatients. *Behavioural and Cognitive Psychotherapy*.
EVIDENCE **Trichotillomania -** **ACT/Habit Reversal** **(initial study) [7-27-03]** Doug Woods	... our lab did an initial study investigating the efficacy of a 7-session combined ACT/Habit Reversal treatment for adult trichotillomania. Outcomes were good. Even more exciting was the finding that pre-post decreases in AAQ scores correlated at something like .85 with improvement at follow-up....
	The work stemmed from the idea that there seemed to be two sets of controlling variables involved in trichotillomania (chronic hair pulling to the point of extensive hair loss). There seemed to be some habitual pulling controlled by direct contingencies, and there seemed to be some pulling involving the avoidance or control of private events. These two processes have been called non-focused and focused pulling. The initial combination of ACT and HR was based on this idea, and both interventions were included because people often exhibit both processes in their pulling. We have since gone back and collected data. We now know that AAQ (read experiential avoidance) is significantly correlated with TTM severity. The more avoidant the person, the more severe the pulling. We also know that the AAQ is more involved in predicting the antecedent urge to pull and the overall distress the person experiences about their condition. Finally, we know that experiential avoidance is only relevant in the focused process of pulling. It does not relate to the non-focused process....
EVIDENCE **Trichotillomania -** **ACT/Habit Reversal** **(RCT) [5-19-05]** Doug Woods	Steve asked me to post this information about a study that was just accepted at BRAT.
	Woods, D. W., Wetterneck, C. T., & Flessner, C. A. (in press). A controlled evaluation of Acceptance and Commitment Therapy plus habit reversal for trichotillomania. *Behaviour Research and Therapy*.
	Abstract: This randomized trial compared a combined Acceptance and Commitment Therapy/Habit Reversal Training (ACT/HRT) to a waitlist control in the treatment of adults with trichotillomania (TTM). Twenty-five participants (12 treatment and 13 waitlist) completed the trial. Results demonstrated a significant reduction in hair pulling severity, impairment ratings, and hairs pulled, along with significant reductions in experiential avoidance and both anxiety and depressive symptoms in the ACT/HRT group compared to the waitlist control. Reductions generally were maintained at a 3-month follow-up. Decreases in experiential avoidance and greater treatment compliance were significantly correlated with reductions in TTM severity, implying that targeting experiential avoidance may be useful in the treatment of TTM. Other implications and suggestions for future research are noted.
EVIDENCE **Update [7-26-04]** Steve Hayes	Francisco José Ruiz Jiménez wrote:
	Are there more recent RCTs about ACT evidence? I only know RCTs named on [the website].
	Ones not listed in the summary table you linked to:
	Gaudiano, B. A., & Herbert, J. D. (2004). Acute Treatment of Inpatients with Psychotic Symptoms using Acceptance and Commitment Therapy. Manuscript under review. This study replicates the Bach and Hayes study with better measures and a better control condition. Good results esp. on measures of overt psychotic behavior (the BPRS). Mediational analyses fit the ACT model.
	Gutiérrez, O., Luciano, C., Rodríguez, M., & Fink, B. C. (in press). Comparison between an acceptance-based and a cognitive-control-based protocol for coping with pain. *Behavior Therapy*. Randomized study with analogue pain task showing greater tolerance for pain in the defusion and acceptance-based condition drawn from ACT as compared to a closely parallel cognitive-control based condition.
	[By the way, there is a *very* tightly controlled replication of this being written up by a student of Ian Stewart ... several other Irish researchers involved as well. Great data.]
	Levitt, J. T., Brown, T. A., Orsillo, S. M., & Barlow, D. H. (in press). The effects of acceptance versus suppression of emotion on subjective and psychophysiological response to carbon dioxide challenge in patients with panic disorder. *Behavior Therapy*. Acceptance methods (drawn directly from the ACT book) did a better job than control strategies in promoting successful exposure in panic disordered patients.
	As yet unpublished dissertations:
	Block, J. A. (2002). *Acceptance or change of private experiences: A comparative analysis in college students with public speaking anxiety*. Doctoral dissertation. University at Albany, State University of New York. Small RCT on the treatment of social anxiety. Compared ACT to Cognitive Behavioral Group Therapy and to a no treatment control. Results indicated that ACT participants evidenced a significant increase in reported willingness to experience anxiety, a significant decrease in behavioral avoidance during public speaking, and a marginally decrease in anxiety during the exposure exercises as compared with the control group. Similar results were found for CBGT, but ACT found greater changes in behavioral avoidance.
	Folke, F., & Parling, T. (2004). *Acceptance and Commitment Therapy in group format for individuals who*

	are unemployed and on sick leave suffering from depression: A randomized controlled trial. Unpublished thesis, University of Uppsala, Uppsala, Sweden. RCT showing that ACT significantly reduces depression among workers on sick leave.
	Gregg, J. (2004). *Development of an acceptance-based treatment for the self-management of diabetes.* Unpublished doctoral dissertation, University of Nevada, Reno. RCT showing that six hour ACT workshop with patient education works better than patient education alone in producing changes in diabetes self-management and blood glucose (at 3 month follow-up). 75% non-Caucasian sample. Mediational analyses show self-management changes mediated by increased acceptance and defusion of diabetes related feelings and thoughts.
	Lundgren, A. T. (2004). *Development and evaluation of an integrative health model in the treatment of epilepsy: Two randomized controlled trials investigating the effects of a short term ACT intervention, yoga, and attention control therapy in India and South Africa.* Two small RCTs (N = 18; and N = 28) comparing a three session ACT protocol (two individual; one group) to two other conditions. As compared to yoga, significantly reduced seizures in the ACT condition; as compared to attention control, significantly reduced seizures and experiential avoidance, and significantly increased quality of life in the ACT condition.
	[by the way, this one is also relevant to the issue of ACT with non-Caucasians that was on the list a week or two ago … as is Jen Gregg's above]
	Those are the ones I know about, but I'm sure there are others.
EVIDENCE-BASED PRACTICE **Criteria; invalid claims** **FUNCTIONAL CONTEXTUALISM** **Contextualism cf. interest in context [8-5-05]** Steve Hayes	William Kordonski wrote: A friend of mine is a psychologist who does his clinical work based on state dependent learning. His position is according to him "evidenced based." Is SDL synonymous with the ACT contextual view? I suspect that contextualism includes SDL but covers more areas. SDL is a relatively narrow and specific empirical contextual effect. The other things you mention are clinical models and methods, or philosophies of science. Hard to compare them -- it would be like comparing the fact that grapes are sweet to a theory of digestion or to determinism. If a clinical approach is "evidence based" because it can be conceptually linked to an empirical finding, I can't think of a clinical approach that is not evidence based. Maybe space alien therapy. Contextualism is a philosophy of science, and shouldn't be confused merely with an interest in context. Contextualism is defined by its truth criteria, unit of analysis, and epistemological and ontological assumptions, not an appreciation of context per se. All robust approaches have some way of dealing with context or they would not be robust. Even very mechanistic theories deal with context -- they just do so mechanistically. ACT emphasizes context but it is a model and a set of methods linked to applied and basic theories. The range of contexts considered is far wider. There would be no reason not to include SDL in an analysis and set of methods when and if it was relevant, as one might include any behavioral concept from peak shift to establishing operations ...
EVIDENCE-BASED PRACTICE Criteria; invalid claims [cont'd] Steve Hayes	Monica Pignotti wrote: Even the proponents of "space alien" therapy have attempted to do this, by the way (see e.g., the late John Mack's (mis)interpretation of McNally's laboratory findings, www.centerchange.org/center/center_news.ask?id=217). … I tried to use the most ridiculous example I could and if even that can make it by this criterion (a claimed conceptual link to evidence) the point should be thoroughly made: it truly is a useless criterion for "evidence-based practice." I've seen the same from those who point to the correlational evidence that good therapeutic outcomes are linked to such things as the quality of the therapeutic relationship, the warmth of the therapist and so on and then leap from that to the idea that relationship-oriented therapy is the way to go and that this correlation makes all of this evidence-based. There are whole departments of fuzzy-headed thinkers trying to live out this self-delusion, confident in the belief that it will protect them from the heathen scientists at the gate. It won't. You still have to show that your relationship-oriented therapy (or whatever) manipulates those processes AND that they still have the same relationship to outcome AND that in well-controlled trials it changes both these processes and outcomes better than well-crafted comparisons. This perversion of the evidence-based practice movement will turn the term "evidence-based practice" into a joke. In fact, I already see lots of signs that this is happening. Yes, you need good theory to be scientifically progressive. Yes, that theory should be linked to and itself be supported by an empirical research program. But, no, that is not enough. Not nearly. Applied technologies have to themselves be tested both by good, controlled outcome studies AND good analyses of process of change linked to the theory. Anything short of that is scientifically inadequate.

| EVIDENCE-BASED PRACTICE

Criteria; invalid claims [cont'd]

Steve Hayes | William Kordonski wrote:

While we are on the topic of evidence-based therapy, I'd like to mention the Solution Therapy approach. I have no problem with using their techniques as I see them as compatible for the most part with ACT, but I wonder what list folk think about Scott Miller's assertions about outcome research. In short, as I remember it, Miller states that almost all the variance in successful therapy can be accounted for by the therapeutic relationship and accessing the client's own personal resources that they bring into therapy. As a matter of fact, according to Miller only about 5 to 10% of the positive outcomes is due to "techniques." Apparently, the techniques Miller presents e.g., the magic question or describing the perfect day do not count as techniques because they tap those personal resources.

It is a classic example of poor scientific thinking and I confess SFT was among the list of sinners I was thinking about when I posted that post [above]. The point about the *relationship* is factually wrong (the amount of variance accounted for is less; and even then it is largely in very behavioral areas that involve agreeing on goals etc.); and you cannot conveniently claim your techniques are not subject to the need for evaluation because they *mobilize personal resources* (what, and other folks' techniques do not?). Oh please.

The outcome data on Solution Focused Therapy is very poor, last time I checked. Huge marketing. Millions made for a select few gurus. Poor data. Why?

What little there is I have worried about ever since I was told by a person on this list who I respect deeply that some major SFT folks entered into a large outcome evaluation of SFT training with this person. The early data looked good, and they were happy to be part of it. The follow-up data look pretty bad and they pulled out of the evaluation study.

Ever since I heard this story from a person I trust I've personally been very cautious about SFT. If the story is true it is a terrible example of what not to do. Show me the good, controlled, replicated, transportable SFT data, or go home.

The correlational data provide no cover for interventions supposedly linked to them. Zero.

Are there useful techniques in SFT? I would guess so. I like the miracle question for example. I like a constructional approach. But the total package has all the earmarks of other "positive thinking" and purely motivational approaches: patients get excited; they believe; they are uplifted; they give you good data; they go home; it starts not to work; they blame themselves; they are worse than when they started. We've seen this pattern in other areas in the past. In fact, the ACT values components, without defusion and acceptance etc. have exactly this same danger. I was not surprised to hear that the initial data were good and the follow-up data were poor in that study above. Makes sense. That does not mean my guess is right. But YOU are taking the money for treatment and training and putting human lives at risk in the meantime so the onus is on YOU to show your therapy is helpful, not on ME to show that it is not. Correlational data provide no cover because therapy involved DOING something and as soon as you do something that thing -- whether you call it a "technique" or "enhancement of personal resources" -- has to be evaluated.

I reiterate: When you have Rx based on good correlational data you still have to show that your therapy manipulates those processes AND that they still have the same relationship to outcome when they are manipulated AND that in well-controlled trials changes in both these processes and outcomes linked to them are better than in well-crafted comparisons. You can't get out of this by claiming that your methods are not techniques, yet you want the money to train people in your non-techniques. It is self-interested BS.

It is ironic that the most fuzzy thinkers hide behind this ... and these are exactly the same folks who want their copyrights, secrecy pledges, big fees, and guild protections (or to pick an example from psych, their prescription pads).

If 95% of therapy outcomes is due to good relationships in the sense of warm fuzzies, hire warm people off the street and shut down our training programs. If you think you can produce them - and that you get better outcomes because you do - could we have some controlled evidence please? Is that so much to ask? |
| **EVIDENCE-BASED PRACTICE**

EST status; disorder/ syndrome vs. functional process [11-24-02]

Kirk Strosahl | Steve Hayes wrote:

Next year the theme [at the AABT convention] will be on processes ("mechanisms") of change ... we will need to be there with boots on.

... In addition to the emphasis Steve is placing upon process studies of mindfulness as a mediator of treatment response, we have another major mission in the development of ACT. Specifically, ACT needs to become designated as an "empirically supported treatment" and, as we know, the powers that be are still enamored of creating this appellation on a disorder-by-disorder basis. I still believe there are not enough randomized clinical trials being conducted looking at ACT with various behavioral disorders....

It's one thing to understand the process of acceptance/ willingness and how that is promoted by mindfulness-type interventions. It is quite another to have ACT universally accepted as an effective treatment for the various disorders that have become the stomping ground of the AABT and world behavior therapy gurus. Let me be clear about this. I don't actually believe that these are really separate disorders at |

all. I think they all originate with some very common themes that ACT universally addresses. However, the academic and mental health establishment wants to talk about what treatments work for what conditions. In that sense, ACT is off to a very promising start but is also very exposed to being criticized for overstepping the available data (as has actually occurred in an article in the Behavior Therapist).

I was always taught that process studies are important only to the extent that an intervention has established its effectiveness with the target problem of interest. Then, the examination of what the process mediators are. So, my hope is that we keep the "boots on" in both sectors....

EVIDENCE-BASED PRACTICE EST status; disorder/ syndrome vs. functional process [cont'd] Steve Hayes	... I agree we need to bang away at syndromes, but the real game seems to be functional processes. We will get there - but we are not there yet. We do not yet have a functional nosology ... so we play the syndromal RCT game but in the long run that is not where we will end up, (methinks / mehopes). Right now, RCTs on syndromes are necessary.
EVIDENCE-BASED PRACTICE EST status; disorder/ syndrome vs. functional process [cont'd] **PSYCHIATRY** **Psychopathology - failings of/ potential of ACT/RFT [11-26-02]** Rainer Sonntag	... I think we should be clear about the sad role of the current psychopathology in psychiatry and perhaps the mental health community at all. The phenomenological psychopathology of Kraepelin, Jaspers, and Schneider - which was, after all, a clinical approach - is gone. One must not overlook the fact (as it seems to me) that psychiatry and the whole mental health field devastatingly lack a scientifically-based clinical approach, i.e., an approach that links whatever laboratory research (may it be neuroscience, behavioral or whatever) to what happens in session and is directly observable by the clinician (this has been called a "clinical taxonomy" by Alvan R. Feinstein in his still-readable book "Clinical judgement," 1967). This lack of a scientifically-established psychopathology has lead some psychiatrists to abandon the psychological domain altogether, calling themselves "clinical neuroscientists." Others - even well known researchers working in a natural science paradigm like Eric Kandel - look to psychoanalysis as an adjunct to neuroscience. DON'T BE TOO MODEST! RFT/ACT has more to offer than a treatment package that, of course, should be empirically validated. It is a new and comprehensive approach to psychopathology, diagnosis, treatment, and clinical thinking. What is most fascinating for me is not that mindfulness stuff which should not be overemphasized. What is really thrilling (at least for me) is that RFT/ACT for the first time in the history of psychiatry and clinical psychology provides a grounding for clinical principles and management that is based on experimental research and not only personal clinical wisdom and experience and consensus. Think, for example, of a RFT/ACT-transformed mental (behavioral) status examination. What this might look like you may see at the RFT website where most of you presumably have found the very helpful ACT case formulation approach. Traditional signs and symptoms of psychopathology await a recasting in terms of RFT/ACT. For example, formal thought disorder may be functionally conceptualized as resurgence of early verbal repertoires in the service of emotional avoidance, escape from task demands, or social attention rather than be seen as elements of vague clinical syndromes in a formistic way. In addition, we may look for reason giving, issues of "right and wrong" (e.g., in paranoid delusions), or excesses of a desire for "understanding" as new and functional items of such an exam. For me as a physician, the lack of a scientifically-based psychopathology most clearly shows up with respect to psychopharmacology. In fact, there is no scientifically serious clinical "psycho"pharmacology. There still is a huge gap (which has been called a "hermeneutical hiatus" by a German author) between pharmacological neuroscience and the domain of clinical phenomena. At the pharmacological level biochemical mechanisms are described in all technical (e.g., molecular) detail. At the psychological level, however, lay language still dominates. I think there is a great need to join in with behavioral pharmacology in order to describe mechanisms of change in a scientific way also at the behavioral or psychological, i.e., clinical, level. How do psychotropic agents work at the process level? How do they influence derived relational responding? What happens when a deeply depressed human again is affected by positively reinforcing consequences after several days on antidepressant medication? How do verbal behavior and drugs interact? E.g., I explain the function of antidepressant agents to my patients as a kind of establishing operation that does not elevate mood by itself but enhances or reestablishes the effects of positive events (i.e., goals linked to chosen values); thus it is not enough to take the pill; in order to move forward he/she has also to change behavior. Perhaps it would be interesting to test this instruction + drug combination in a placebo controlled trial. I have a dream that RFT/ACT will close this gap of a clinical science. So that, for example, a pragmatic use of drugs may be based on an analysis of behavioral processes linked to observable behaviors rather than on syndromes. Furthermore, such a clinical science would reach far beyond psychiatry and clinical psychology into medicine in general. This is because all medical treatments - in the end - are about behavior: e.g.,

	GOING to surgery, TAKING pills, EATING healthy food, DOING exercise etc. etc. Kelly Wilson's and Miguel Roberts' application of an ACT perspective on anorexia (see *Cognitive and Behavioral Practice, vol. 9*, 2002, pp. 237-243) may give us a first idea of how general practitioners may confront medical problems from a behavioral viewpoint: "as examples of the unworkability of control" or with respect to "their interference with the client's ability to pursue her (or his) values."
	I am neither a researcher nor a prolific writer. What I would like to see from the experts is standard textbooks written from a RFT/ACT perspective that may really turn around the field.
EVIDENCE-BASED PRACTICE EST status; disorder/ syndrome vs. functional process [cont'd] **PSYCHIATRY** Psychopathology - failings of/ potential of ACT/RFT [cont'd] Kirk Strosahl	... The idea that the RFT/ACT theoretical framework provides perhaps the first empirical supported basis for a testable theory of human dysfunction is something I've long believed, even though I cure any topical insomnia by wading through some of this stuff. To have people get interested in this model in terms of the clinical science of psychopathology/human suffering, we have to figure out how to make it more "consumer friendly." Is there a way we could do a book called, "Relational Frame Theory For Dummies"?
	Tuna mentioned the idea that we could do a "manipulated training" RCT looking across a spectrum of different clinical complaints in what I presume would be applied delivery system settings. I think this is a huge idea that directly tests the clinical effectiveness (as opposed to efficacy) of ACT. All we would have to do is have a system with a willing group of soon-to-be-trained ACT therapists, sufficient patient volumes and methods for establishing the (I ache as I say this) diagnostic reliability of how patients are categorized.
	Georg Eifert mentioned ongoing elaborations of the ACT model with anxiety disorders, combined with RCTs. I agree that each manifestation of suffering will need some particular detailing, because there are many different forms of experiential/emotional avoidance that our patients learn. If we don't get precise about these conceptualizations and the theoretical basis in RFT, we could end up just being another dog in this fight.
	The Stonybrook study of ACT vs. CBT with social anxiety is a very good example of the potential for core ACT concepts to be blended with other mindfulness interventions and thereby misconstrued. Early on, I talked with Jennifer at an AABT about 2 years ago and they were having a lot of problems "measuring" acceptance. Taking the intervention largely from the book, they had put together an "ACT" treatment protocol. Since ACT is more of a "space" than a set of techniques, it is anybody's guess what this treatment actually was. This is not meant to be critical of Jennifer whatsoever, but more or less indicative of the problem we face. On the one hand, if you can't disseminate a treatment because it is idiosyncratic to the "master," it is worthless as a point of attack. On the other hand, you can't have a free-for-all environment in interpreting what the treatment is at the point of clinical implementation. I guess this argues for some type of treatment fidelity check for such studies, provided by "experts" in ACT. In this case, I provided whatever assistance I could but have no idea whether the eventual clinical protocol, process or outcome measures were worth a rat's ass. So, now we are back to Steve's original comment; we have to get the boots on and develop solid methods for measuring acceptance (the behavior and the mental stance) and committed, valued action (a la Kelly's work).
EVIDENCE-BASED PRACTICE **Ethics of using ACT where no good data [7-21-03]** Trent Codd	Mike Twohig wrote: It seems to me that in clinical work we have an obligation to use the most supported treatment that we know how to do.... So, is it ethical to use ACT with populations where there is not good data? Is it ethical to do ACT if the supported treatment does not work out?
	My opinion would be that it's ethical to use ACT if:
	1. There is no empirically supported tx available for the type of problem you are treating.
	2. The client has failed with empirically supported treatments.
	3. There are empirically supported treatments for the problem, but you are not trained in the tx and/or no one in your locale is trained, or those who are trained are not accepting patients. In other words, the patient won't have access to the EST.
	4. You get informed consent in which you explain the empirical limitations of ACT, and/or explain that other empirically supported treatments are available to them and they don't have to choose ACT (this assumes they are competent to give informed consent). You might also explain that at any time they can decide to discontinue ACT at which time you would then deliver the EST, or complete a course of tx with ACT and if it "fails" deliver the EST to them (you, of course, would need to discuss the risks and benefits of each tx).
EVIDENCE-BASED PRACTICE	Personally, I don't think it's unethical for a clinician to use ACT in lieu of an empirically supported intervention, but a couple of conditions would have to be met. First, my assessment would have to clearly point to experiential avoidance and language-based processes being at the root of the problem. Second, INFORMED consent is a big issue. I would want the client to know that other treatments exist, and that some have much more extensive research support for the client's particular problem than ACT may have.

Ethics of using ACT where no good data [cont'd] Doug Woods	That said, if I thought ACT was more pertinent to their situation, and had a greater chance of success, I would not hesitate to tell this to the client. This is a good issue though, because on this listserv, I read a lot from people who want to try ACT for this or that, but I never read mention of the functional analysis that would lead the clinician to try such an endeavor, and I never hear about how or whether the clinician discusses alternative treatments with the client. Perhaps these clinical explorations are based on a well-thought out RFT-based functional analysis and perhaps the clinicians did inform their clients that alternative empirically supported treatment existed. I guess we just don't know.
EVIDENCE-BASED PRACTICE Ethics of using ACT where no good data [cont'd] John Blackledge	... Even if the literature says CBT has been indicated to be relatively effective with a particular population, I often suspect (with many problems) I'd have a better chance of making a difference by doing ACT or a more traditionally behavioral treatment involving exposure or skills training. This strikes me as a bare-bones practical issue that simply has not been subjected to enough research-- If a therapist is not competent in treating a particular problem with an approach that the empirical literature prefers, is it best for that therapist to attempt to use that approach, or to do what he/she knows how to do best if there's a reasonable rationale for doing so? Clearly, the standard 'best choice' in such cases would be to refer the client to a therapist who is competent in the 'preferred' approach, but how often is that actually feasible? ...
EVIDENCE-BASED PRACTICE Ethics of using ACT where no good data [cont'd] Matthew Smout	Here's a can of worms: what empirical literature exists tends to overstate the difference between "therapies" for client outcomes. Even when you can demonstrate the integrity of different treatment approaches and show that therapists aren't all doing basically the same thing, the results for client outcomes may be equivalent (as in Project MATCH). Or worse, in the NIDA collaborative cocaine treatment study, although training in CBT helped the therapists do CBT "better," the relatively unskilled drug counselling approach produced greater reductions in cocaine use. There's only a limited amount of variance in client behaviour that can be accounted for by the therapist and within that amount, less still will be due directly to the clinician's theoretical orientation. In my opinion, the diversity of theoretical approaches available is for the clinician's benefit - so that the clinician can find a "map" that suits them as they negotiate the tricky business of listening to a client empathically while trying to take the conversation in some consistent direction. I'm sure therapists who trust their "map" will end up devoting more attention to their clients, and will behave confidently in a way that inspires confidence in their clients. If you truly believe ACT offers the best hypotheses for how human behaviour functions, I'm sure the quality of your interactions with your clients will be better if you deliver ACT. ACT-minded therapists would acknowledge the successful empirical track record of CT in clinical outcome studies, but presumably being ACT-minded would be looking at factors other than the "restructuring" of automatic thoughts as the process of change. Surely ACT therapists can operate as effectively through these non-cognitive-restructuring aspects of CBT as CBT-trained cognitive therapists.
EVIDENCE-BASED PRACTICE Ethics of using ACT where no good data [cont'd] **Process vs. package** **ACT/ RFT** **Development philosophy** **ACT cf.** **CBT/ CT - process-outcome link**	I think we need to think of empirically supported processes, not packages, and interventions need to modify processes that are functionally present. Syndromes help very little in organizing this. The empirically supported treatment (EST) list is too linked to packages and manuals and syndromes and too little to processes. Is positive reinforcement a "package"? That's why the ACT / RFT issue is so critical. ACT never was / will be a "package" -- it is an orientation to psychotherapy linked to a philosophy and theory. It includes techniques that alter processes, but these techniques evolve everyday and creative ACT clinicians invent new ones everyday (if an old line behavior analyst came up with cute new something that reinforced behavior in an individual case, no one would call it a "new treatment." It is still contingency management. If an ACT therapist develops a new defusion technique it is still defusion). The reason we do ACT in the ACT group at UNR is that the supervision group is part of a clinical program and ours is for training ACT. We filter clients on the way in; we modify what we do inside the team with every case; we sometimes refer out. If there are no data supportive of ACT-focused processes in problems that are functionally of the kind we are treating, I'm nervous about why our team has the case and I'm looking either for a referral or a way to alter what we do to fit the case. Furthermore, the content of a specific case -- though ACT is the treatment structure -- is modified by the literature. If we have a panic-disordered client, we will include methods of dealing with the five component processes in effective manuals for panic: interoceptive exposure; situational exposure; dealing with negative cognitions; psychoeducation; and breathing. I do all 5 in my own ACT work with panic. I deal with negative cognitions with defusion and exposure/acceptance (which is probably much of why CT works anyway ... see

ANXIETY **Panic - intervention processes, ACT treatment of [7-23-03]** Steve Hayes	Teasdale's review and which itself has a decent and growing research base ... heck the process-outcome link in ACT is much better than it is in CT in my view, just data-wise); I do exposure (of both kinds and more) but in the contexts of defusion and acceptance and focused on response flexibility -- and there are data available for all of that, including some now coming from Barlow's shop; I always do some simple psychoeducation and normalization about what panic attacks are. I watch for hyperventilation and sometimes train breathing if necessary. Am I doing Barlow's manual? No. But, heck, that is changing in an ACT direction anyway, and I think just on *empirical* grounds ACTified exposure (etc.) is more likely to work. What is hard about this approach is that much of the EST literature does not give a darn for processes and principles ... in part because the theories are poor and often don't work very well; in part because we've bought into syndromes and manuals instead. The theory that underlies CT has been stumbling through relative failure for 25 years and people sort of act as if it doesn't matter and they should do the whole package anyway. Is THAT empirically supported treatment?! Then you (finally) do a component analysis and voila the whole package adds nothing to the treatment of *depression*, which is where the whole CT thing started. Heck, Rob Zettle and I did a CT component analysis (and a comparison to ACT) 20 years ago ... that bubble was popped in my own mind and shifted in an ACT direction in the early-1980s. Yet people act as if EST reasoning means you *have* to do Beck's package with depression. Nonsense. We need ESTs, in the sense of Ts linked to empirically supported principles. ACT structures that very process of linkage based on a modern theory of language and cognition. I know of nothing that is empirically supported that conflicts with ACT at the level of process, so if you are willing to incorporate processes and procedures in a case by case fashion you can do a heck of a lot of EST, within an ACT framework.

EVIDENCE-BASED PRACTICE
 	
   Ethics of using ACT where no good data [cont'd]
 	
   Process vs. package [cont'd]
 	
ACT/ RFT
 	
   Development philosophy [cont'd]
 	
ACT cf.
 	
   CBT/ CT - process-outcome link [cont'd]
 	
      Steve Hayes
	Doug Woods wrote:
	
	    Steve makes great points about process over package. A couple things to think about though, and I believe they are integral to the discussion...
	
	    1. Understanding the processes of the various behavioral presentations is still in its infancy, I think. For any one person, do we have the assessment technology to say that we know what is and is not linked to cognitive fusion, experiential avoidance, directly encountered contingencies? It seems we have to know this, and have this technology down before we can even begin to make use of an empirically supported process paradigm.
	
	There is a difficulty, but it is no better going in the technology direction. It just appears to be, because the area of ignorance is hidden.
	
	In a technological approach the manual is the variable; adherence shows you've implemented the variable. Voila! Psychotherapy fits within an FDA approach. You "know" what you did and you can assess whether "it" worked. But in almost every EST, there is minimal evidence that adherence predicts outcome. Translation: what is in our manuals is not what is literally producing the change. What is? Usually we do not know. "Competence" is a fudge in fact (not in principle), is related to the independent variable in unknown ways (thus, the "don't know" phrase in the previous sentence), and is contaminated by outcome, among other problems.
	
	Knowing what is effective in Rx is in its infancy but (as I just mentioned) that is the way it is no matter what we do. No one in the EST literature has yet solved it. Even the pharmacotherapy types haven't, because their controls are usually inadequate (witness the SSRI v. placebo debacle). And pharmacotherapy is a 100 times easier in this area than psychotherapy in principle.
	
	Process is used in two different ways. The implications for ESTs are different. Reinforcement is a process. It is a basic principle about a sequence of events. The therapeutic relationship is a process. It is not a principle -- it is a global aspect of therapy that is inferred from therapy. This makes a difference analytically.
	
	Understanding processes in the sense that we measure what is going on in Rx and try to infer what is producing change is barely off the ground. Process in the sense of functional relationships of known importance is not in its infancy. "Reinforcement" is like that. RFT concepts are like that. I was noting today (to Mike Twohig, by coincidence), that our data right now for RFT concepts is probably greater than the data for direct contingency concepts when they were applied.
	
	    [DW] 2. Do we know well enough yet, that ACT components have a specific effect on the different processes that we believe may be related to various behavioral presentations? Do we have an adequate measurement strategy for these processes?
	
	Component data are important, but you are mixing two issues here. You don't need ACT component data to look at processes [though we do have fledgling component data (due to the huge variation in manuals and due to a few component studies such as the pain study in *Psychological Record*)].

I think we DO know about the domination of verbal rules and the repertoire narrowing effect of verbal stimuli; we do know that experiential avoidance is bad beans; we do now have some evidence that ACT alters these processes (and others); we do have some data that these alterations predict outcome. Are they limited data? Yeah. But sheesh, after 25 years of trying CBTers can hardly get their mediational analyses to work. In ACT they seem to hit regularly. I don't want to overstate the case, but RFT evidence is growing very nicely and the link to ACT is growing. This is very new literature. Many of these pieces are not yet in print. Few in the field, other than the direct contingency folks, have done the bottom up -- processes to procedures approach. Others often only have "therapy process" variables to fall back on. ACT has processes in the sense of basic principles and sequences of change linked to them. That makes the theory / therapy link a heck of a lot more powerful.

> [DW] 3. This whole debate seems to me a catch-22 in terms of widespread scientific acceptance. To be accepted in the current scientific culture, we need to do well-controlled studies with well-formed manuals. However, it almost seems that by manualizing the process, you get away from the process, and as soon as you get away from that, in some circles, your science may be viewed as suspect. It's a tough situation.

Scientific acceptance should be based on a philosophy of development, not approval alone. Approval will come (or not) but what is important is that there be something worthwhile to approve of. If the existing strategies of treatment development were so grand, why is the result a growing applied/basic gap; why isn't our science obviously and powerfully progressive? The FDA approach is not working. It had value but the value has largely been extracted. We need something different.

The ACT / RFT philosophy of development is unusual, but it is actually well tested -- I think it is essentially the same as early behavior analysis. The ACT book walked through that philosophy and we've kept true to it in the world ACT community (look at the Sweden conference and you'll see it in action).

In a local sense, no one need agree with the development philosophy. In concrete terms it just meant that we spent years on basic data and philosophy, delaying the day for what empirical clinical types would understand to be the "real" science. We now are manualizing the treatment. We do it in as flexible and as functional a way as you can ... but so does Marsha Linehan and lots of fellow travelers and no one complains. And we measure defusion / acceptance / values / etc. as best we can, knowing full well what we have now is inadequate. But we also know that the RFT / ACT link has a chance to solve this over time. And so you get the grant. You do the study. You get the data. You publish it. And you post the manual on the ACT website.... If adherence doesn't predict outcome you work harder to link the manual to possible functional processes, and you find ways (experimentally / well defined ways) to produce competence. And you look at the impact of that training (ACT has some data of that kind at least ... 95% of the ESTs have none). The science looks the same as what is out there. We aren't asking for something goofy, like qualitative research is to be viewed with as much credibility as quantitative data or some such.

But when you have done your RCT, this is *an* ACT manual, not *the* ACT manual. And you don't take the literal procedures to be the functional treatment. And you watch the RFT (etc.) literature and change as you go. And you feel free to modify treatments for functional reasons as long as the processes you are targeting make sense ... no centralization / no permission from Rome. And the theory and the process-outcome link is as important as the outcome data per se (have you noticed that most ACT studies have looked at that ... while many, many ESTs have still not looked at it with any care).

To me, this is more of an empirically-supported Rx development program than the simple, brute force FDA style program most ESTs seem to be following. Yet it comports with the EST movement (which I've been part of for 15 years, from behind the scenes work to get the Division 12 thing to happen, to AAAPP, to the Practice Guideline Coalition, etc.). Much of the "big picture" background for the EST movement is in Hayes, S. C., Follette, V. M., Dawes, R. M., & Grady, K. E. (Eds.). (1995). *Scientific standards of psychological practice: Issues and recommendations*. Reno, NV: Context Press. From that context at least there is no basic conflict between the EST idea and the ACT implementation of it.

POLITICS

Application of RFT principles [3-2-05]

Steve Hayes

Tony Biglan wrote:

> What does this discussion [re values/ choice] imply for one who wants to build a community of people with like-minded values?

I think this discussion does not say much about Tony's question.., but if you take an RFT angle on how to work to create certain desired ends and not others, there are many things to say. This is not "values" in the ACT personal choice sense so much as it is in the social/cultural sense (the two are related of course). I think we need to work this out empirically inside the RFT community and thus I will cross post to that list. Off the top of my head here are some ideas [warning: they may sound manipulative -- I'm talking about this the way a political advisor might if RFT implications are correct. And I'm a progressive so my apologies to right wingers on the list ... my point in putting up this post is to look at the process, not the content per se but I will engage the content Tony asks about from the point of view of someone who is progressive. The same points could be made by taking the opposite political stance]. If folks see other RFT implications for Tony's question let's get them out there.

RFT implications for building political/social values:

1. Ride the horse in the direction it is going. It is easier to amplify an existing relational network than to modify it. Find a way to cast the future in a way that does not challenge the existing network. For example: if the electorate is religious, link religion to your desired ends. I think the Democrats foolishly criticize the "religious right." Bad idea. 85% of the electorate is religious; 95% value spirituality. Criticize the "right." Drop the word "religious." Instead link a progressive agenda to spiritual, moral, and religious values. Same with freedom; democracy; etc. etc.

2. Take a long view. Relational networks evolve over time. You cannot create them all at once. Take what you can get if it builds a better consensus and moves the normative network in your direction and leave the rest for later.

3. Turn wedge issues in your direction verbally or through compromise linked to your key concepts, and if you can't, don't engage them. The key issue is to build the relational network and protect organizing principles and terms from harm. As things come up you need to keep wedge issues from harming your central concepts and ideally you want to use them to pull down your opponents. This is hard. The right has learned how to beat up progressives with sexual concerns, for example. Progressives are so afraid of back sliding on overarching concerns that they sometimes cannot make compromises, so they get drawn into wedge issue fights that hurt them hugely. The goal is not just to win. It is to win and build your key concepts. If you can't do that, compromise and link the compromise to a verbally central concept. This is especially good if the verbally central concept can then be used as a wedge issue in favor of your views in other areas. Grudging compromises do no long term good because the relational network is not being built in your direction. A fight that leads to a nominal win but weakens your key concepts is actually a long term loss (this is how progressives have lost control of Congress and are about to become a permanent minority). A fight that leads to a loss but strengthens key concepts is a long term win. The worst is to fight, lose, and weaken your key concepts. Progressives have been on that end of the stick regularly since Reagan. For example, suppose you have an agenda to create "strong, responsible families." You link it to progressive issues such as minimum wages increases; better schools; etc. Now along comes a wedge issue: say, parental notification in abortion. I would rather have strong advocacy for parental notification (with good quality judicial outs for kids with abusive families) and link it to the program "to build and support strong, responsible families" than to fight parental notification and win on the basis of fears about undermining "freedom of choice." Using "freedom of choice" in this context moves this key concept in the direction of "sexual anarchy" and then you've lost ground across the board because the culture will not support sexual anarchy as a value. Next thing you know you have right wing ads of pictures of gays kissing with the term "freedom of choice" and a picture of John Kerry next to the picture. The right wing has such pictures up right now in key states to attack the AARP. And it will work. Even if they lose they will have gained in the long run. That is because the right understands that this IS a cultural war, and a cultural war is about values.

4. Coherence is critical. The more coherent the relational network, the more resistant to change. For that reason this strategy cannot work if you don't actually have values that are important. You have to be building toward something. When I look at the political landscape I despair because I see that the right has a coherent set of values they are building toward and progressive forces by and large do not. People desire coherence -- it is built into human language to do so. Why did the right attack Kerry on flip-flopping? Because they know this. The right gets it -- they know it is a values fight. When Clinton was elected before he even got into office he had to deal with gays in the military because the right forced the issue. They wanted to try to show that anyone who wanted both fiscal responsibility and social progressivity was immoral. Bill compromised (he knows these principles intuitively) and slipped the punch but he was a bit more vulnerable on the issue. Whitewater then hurt more because it had the same focus and he was weaker. Then Bill unzips, lies about it, and gives the right everything needed to avoid a historical realignment under DLC values: Gore loses as a direct result. Progressives will suffer for a generation and we are at great risk of seeing a historical realignment under right wing values that bring together the monetary goals of the rich and the social/cultural fears of the middle and lower classes. That combo is a 51-55% win as far as the eye can see.

5. Long term vision helps provide motivation and coherence, especially if they are concrete and almost sensory. Futures that can be imagined in almost sensory terms but not fully tested are a motivative augmental that can help organize the network long term. Bush managed to link his policies to both the horror of world wide terrorism and death; and to world wide democracy. These are powerful long term visions, both positive and negative. I thought the progressives could have played the long term vision of peace through strength, democracy, compassion, and religious tolerance. The fight against terrorism is actually a fight against religious intolerance and cast that way it helps restrain the violent, jingoistic, "feed the military and to hell with the bill our grandkids will pay" policies of the right that bring together their "rich + social fears" strategy. But without a real long term vision we had a Bush-light vision with a little

"multinational cooperation" thrown in. "Multinational cooperation" can easily be rolled into "bureaucrats in some foreign land will control us." Hell the Brits won't even buy that and they don't have the oceans and frontier tradition that the US has that makes it a *horrible* sell here. I'd use "multinational cooperation" only in its inverse form: the US is increasingly hated around the world. Kerry did that and then backed down at the first sign of resistance because he'd hid it behind the skirts of "foreign leaders have told me" and then because he could not say which ones had, he looked like a liar or (shall I say it) flip flopper. Brilliant move on the right wing's part. Anyway, he could have said "the US is increasingly hated around the world because people do not see that we stand for strength, democracy, compassion, and religious tolerance." That gives you multinational cooperation without the cost of that term. Bush did a much more effective positive/negative combo. Those are some of the things that come to mind....

POLITICS

Communicating with mental health establishment

PSYCHIATRY

Medical model, alternative interpretation of [10-20-02]

Rainer Sonntag

[Re: a call for comments on the (US) Commission on Mental Health in the context of perceived influence of pharmaceutical companies]

As a psychiatrist I am a physician; and as a physician I notice an interesting paradox. I would call it the "medical self-misunderstanding of psychiatry." When, in these times, psychiatrists try to get closer to medicine by biologicalization they in fact get more distant. Often they violate basic principles of medicine. I think there are more commonalities between medicine and behavior analysis than between medicine and biological psychiatry: the experimental method, direct assessment, reluctance to accept hypothetical constructs (who has ever seen a behavior gene; not to speak of the long and complex ways from genes to behavior: DNA makes RNA makes PROTEIN makes … makes … etc.), and a premium on the establishment of unambiguous and clear functional relations - between manipulable environmental events and physiological processes. Most of these principles of science - for me - seem to be absent from modern (biological) psychiatry.

With respect to the so-called Medical Model, this most often seems to imply the model of a genetically transmitted metabolic disease. However, there is another Medical Model that may even be more important and that has been highly successful in the past: the model of infectious diseases. This latter model may be a highly productive metaphor to communicate with the medical field. They (we) know it all and it is close to more traditional as well as RFT behavioral thinking. Think of antecedents, consequences, rules, instructions, evaluation, reason-giving, or contextual cues as non-verbal and verbal "infectious" agents that influence us and others. (Think of an epidemiology of verbal events; e.g., what was the impact of that famous song "Don't worry, be happy"?)

As ACT therapists we try something that may be similar to an immunization of our clients so that they can live their lives without continuously struggling with "verbal infections" (I hope I'm not too far off the mark with this interpretation). On the other hand, politically, this (infectious disease) Medical Model means - I think - that every voice spoken out loud counts. Therefore, let's stand up and say what we have to say. If we find the right way to talk and they hear us it will influence them and, hopefully, transform e.g., the multiple stimulus functions of drugs. (By the way, it is this transformation of stimulus functions that all totalitarian regimes like the Nazis in Germany fear and why they always try to control the free public opinion. Let us not be controlled by our feelings of hopelessness and then not be heard.)

PSYCHIATRY

Diagnosis - DSM categorization, limitations of [8-10-05]

Kelly Wilson

Todd Kashdan wrote:

A few of my colleagues and I have been discussing the latest study by Kessler and his colleagues (Kessler et al., 2005 in NEJM): How can 25% of our population have a mental disorder? Even Kessler stated that at least 10 of this 25% is so mild and transient as to represent an emotional "hangnail." If this is the case, then why are they comfortably classifying these individuals as having mental "disorders"?

We have persistently been in the camp critical of the diseasifying of every aspect of human suffering. I have frequently cited Kessler. To me the take-away message is not that something like a third of the population has a mental disease during a given year, but that suffering is ubiquitous. If one equates suffering (with enough boxes in the checklist checked a la DSM) with mental diseases, this is what you find. I personally think what these numbers suggest is a crappy diagnostic system. When you look at the notion of comorbidity, the picture gets even worse. If I am recalling correctly off the top of my head, something like 70% with one "disorder" will meet criteria for another. This means that co-morbidity so-called is more common than simple morbidity. Again, if we (1) buy the diagnostic system, and (2) folks endorse the right number of symptoms, then it follows that there are this number of cases. Myself, I find very little merit in the whole DSM system. For example, I think co-morbidity is an artifact of the category-splitters mentality that has run amok in DSM land over the last several iterations. Art Houts has written with great intelligence on the proliferation of DSM categories.

So, my take is that Kessler's data are interesting, not because they tell us about the prevalence of mental diseases--though I am certain that the APA lobbyists will use them in this way. I just think they reflect what the Buddha said in the first of the four noble truths or from someone a little closer to my own cultural tradition: The mass of men lead lives of quiet desperation.

WORK **Misuse of ACT, potential, concerns re [4-29-05]** Steve Hayes	Monica Pignotti wrote: I have a number of concerns about using ACT or any other therapy or personal growth method in a business setting. My concerns fall into two categories: possible inappropriate violation of personal boundaries in a business setting and the danger of manipulation and undue influence. These are good points. If you aren't mindful of them it can indeed be a big problem. I think you are making some assumptions about how you would do this kind of thing in a work setting, though. You don't do ACT workshops at work the way you do them at, say, the Summer Institute. Frank Bond may want to weigh in on this (and some of these issues are addressed in the "ACT at Work" chapter in his book). You can handle 90% of your worries by cutting sharing way down -- virtually to zero. Do a lot of private work. Have them "share" with themselves, with workbook exercises and things of that kind. Don't ever allow that stuff to be seen in the workshop -- have them take it home. Keeping it very low key and voluntary, and give folks ways to set the exercises to fit their own purposes -- including in essence not doing anything at all if they want (and without detection). It still works that way, surprisingly. And people -- when you take away all the pressure -- still work on things. They see the personal relevance. That handles 90% of your worries but not this one: why are they there in the first place? For that I prefer an agreement on the way in: you cannot require that people attend and you have to give extensive informed consent. But if folks know you won't make them do anything and you will protect their privacy 100% ... they will most often take advantage of it. It is still dicey at times with co-workers but this handles the vast majority of problems.
WORK Misuse of ACT, potential, concerns re [cont'd] Kelly Wilson	Following up on Steve's post. I don't think you can emphasize enough--in any setting --the voluntary nature of the work. I flat out beg people. Do not do this for me. Do not do this because people around you expect or want it. Haven't you had enough of that? I take it as one of my central responsibilities to communicate the fact that I am really really asking without prejudice. Amy Murrell and I talk in the Guilford values chapter on this issue of choice and its centrality. I am not referring here to the choice/ decision distinction. I mean the experience of choice under appetitive control - choice *for* something--as opposed to choice under aversive control.
WORK Misuse of ACT, potential, concerns re [cont'd] Steve Hayes	Mike Kirkeberg wrote: I hope I don't get splattered all over the wall for having this thought (consider it coming out of my limited understanding), but in a way it sounds like what is being said is that ACT is true in a clinical one-on-one setting, but not necessarily true in the real world? Naw, it is amazingly transportable to non-clinical settings. We already have more going in that area than almost any empirically supported "clinical" approach I can think of. You'll notice in the stigma study we did in *Behavior Therapy* we called ACT "Acceptance and Commitment Training" to recognize its non-clinical use ... but it is still just ACT. I think what's being said is that you have to adjust the approach to respect the situation. You can't just go in there guns blazing without really thinking through what you are doing from the point of view of the persons you are working with. The privacy issues are different. The context is different. etc. If you are doing, say, a prevention group in a school you'd better be mindful that you may have someone in there who is not really willing to be there and won't say so; so a gentler approach is needed. Fewer assumptions can be made. Even in clinical workshops (etc.) this can happen but the danger grows as you move into new settings. Some of the methods inside ACT can be extremely evocative. In the right moment that is great, but there is a time and a place. ACT is essentially about creating an analysis of these processes that will bring them into our science and make them safe and available for the culture. Many of these methods have been rumbling around for a long time and the psychological / functional space has been known for thousands of years. We are bringing science to it; we are bringing it into the healthcare system; the schools; even the work place. But Monica is right -- there have been cultish forces that have tried to do that. Without the protection of science and an open, self-critical culture they've sometimes created harm as well as good. We have to be more wise; more cautious; less arrogant; more mindful; and more open to learning how really to serve others in these settings.
WORK Misuse of ACT, potential, concerns re [cont'd] Frank Bond	Over the past 9 years, I have conducted a very large number of ACT workshops in organisations of all kinds: UK government departments, ad agencies, lots of banks. In addition, I use ACT with clients in a traditional clinical setting. The feel of the two are almost entirely different; to be sure, there are common threads, but the vibe is not the same. I think the reason is that the goals are slightly (but importantly) different and so we tailor ACT techniques accordingly. In an organisation, we don't even mention the term ACT (sorry Steve); instead, we offer 'work and life effectiveness training.' This term is not a ruse to snare

and cuckold the naive, rather, it truly reflects what we are trying to do with core ACT techniques in that setting: give people skills that they can apply to all facets of their life. Yes, we and trainees mention the word 'stress' now-and-again, but we mention far more often how we can all use 'mindfulness' (that's the term we use, as it is in the common parlance) to make our lives work better for us - be it in our work, with our work colleagues, friends, partner, family...

We also tell them that we have data showing that these techniques can allow people to work more effectively and that these skills predict job performance (see the ACT website for details on this published research). Thus, we show people that they can use these techniques, this approach to living, to help them in all aspects of their life. We're very open about the fact that these can help people perform better; and, they usually love hearing that. My experience has been that we get very few people attending our workshops who don't want to do their job well, even if it is just to get a pay rise. My feel is that most people would love to have tools available to them, in order to live a more effective life. I fully acknowledge that most every organisation that brings me in is doing so in order to increase productivity, and that is fine with me: I believe our ACT training stands a good chance to do so AND I believe that we can also help people live a more valued life. The two are not mutually exclusive; indeed, I think that they are very much intertwined, and our data suggest this, too. If, through such training, a person decides that they are in the wrong job and want to leave (I've seen this twice), then the organisation is actually better off for it, and most know this very keenly.

To me, the likeliest ethical trap in my work is that the Organisation may tell me what to do, force people to attend, or have a stooge in the group who reports back to Big Brother. I have never encountered any of these situations, to my knowledge. In fact, the biggest complaint is that the organisation makes it difficult for people to attend, owing to workload. I am also very much concerned about participants gossiping about other participants, and this is why we've designed our protocol so that it ensures that no one is even encouraged to share (except for stating a value at the end, but we typically get something high in social desirability, such as, 'I want to be a better worker, father, etc.'). We spend 1/3 of the time on values, and all of this is done with either me prattling on or them working on their own (with paper and pencil). We show how we do this in Steve and Kirk's Practical Guide.

The core of my view is that ACT identifies principles that are common to every aspect of our life, and we can tailor any ACT-based intervention to be applicable to any setting: we do not have to use it from the perspective of a clinician. Psychodynamic clinicians saw this in the 1940s, and they developed organisational change interventions, based upon their theories, which still dominate the I/O field to this day. ACT is offering the same types of interventions, but ones that are based upon a (granted, small but growing) evidence base. To me, this is far more ethical, as we can offer people and their organisations something that stands a better chance of creating a whole and meaningful life.

WORK

Stress - ACT interventions

EXERCISE

Evaluation - Cross cutting categories [8-16-04]

Steve Hayes

Joseph Ciarrochi wrote:

Can anybody come up with a nice way to induce [work] status evaluations?

One we have taken to using in ACT workshops is designed to get beyond evaluative categorical talk applied to others ... it's not quite on point but it might be tweaked for your purpose:

We call it "cross cutting categories" [originally tested out in a study of Barbara Kohlenberg's on ACT and self stigma in substance abusers in recovery]. The idea is to overload our verbal evaluative tendencies by bringing in unusual and emotive dimensions.

A while after the introductions we ask someone to volunteer to answer some intimate questions. I used to do it randomly but now I pick out someone who did a slightly odd introduction and I ask them privately at a break if they are willing. So I then have that person remind the group of what he or she said during the introductions and I ask the group to notice what their minds were doing when they heard this the first time. If the person said strange stuff of course what was happening (I don't tell people this or have them say it aloud ... I just assume it) is they were chattering evaluative stuff.

Then I ask the volunteer questions like "when was the last time you cried?" and I let the person answer. Then come several other such cycles (e.g., "what do you care most about in your work? What do you worry about most in your immediate family?"). These are unusual questions and they are hard to sort people on them into easy categories. It in essence blows up the evaluative cartoons we functionally let substitute for "other people."

As these questions are asked and answered I ask the group to notice what is happening again.

What happens is that a human being shows up. The simple evaluative cartoon slips away.

Sometimes I then ask them to look around the room and notice as each person is seen what their minds start to do. Sometimes I coach this a little, but again what is happening is categories and characteristics and evaluations (old/ beautiful/ Asian/ dressed weirdly/ fat/ etc. etc.).

I think you could push this by taking the middle part and deliberately asking for comparatives (e.g., find

	something that you don't like for each person in this room; find something you like better in you than in them for each; find something about them that your mind evaluates as better than you; etc.). You could push people in a social fear direction ("what is the secret about you that if you said aloud you would most fear the reactions of others?"). You could set up a competitive exercise (and then not do it) and ask people to watch what their minds started to do (I will … or I won't … do better than others). [E.g., "as an exercise I am going to have each of you give a 2 minute talk on a police topic I will give to you after you stand up. We will start in about 30 seconds, so get mentally prepared" … then ask what their minds started to do.]
	The badge on the chest exercise might work well as a defusion exercise rolling out of this if you asked people to out at least one thought their minds started putting out as this competitive situation was considered that they are willing to let go of.
WORK Stress - ACT interventions [cont'd] Jonathan Weinstein	I don't know how much of the values piece you've done, but here's how I might approach it. 1. Mindfulness exercise of your worst day at work (see below only substitute worst for best). 2. Mindfulness exercise of your best day at work-- See if you can think back to your best day on the job. Try to imagine what you were wearing, where you were, and who was with you. How did people interact with you on that day? How did you interact with others that day? See if you can notice your thoughts and feelings from that time. If there's an evaluation in there, just notice it don't try to make it go away. See if you can picture hour by hour where you were, who you were with and what you were doing. Notice thoughts, feelings, memories, sensations, evaluations etc. Go through their entire day. At the end, ask participants what made that day so special. Ask them if there are any barriers standing between them and having another day like that. 3. Make values present-- in those last two exercises at what moments were you the least and most proud to be a cop? What stands in the way between you and having days in the future like your best one? 4. If participants say other people are in the way--clarify whether it's their avoidance of thoughts, feelings (antecedent control) that prevents them from attempting to improve those relationships. Ask them if they would be willing to have all of these aversive thoughts if they could have days like their very best one in their future. If they say no-- have them imagine the shape of their career 5-10-15 yrs from now. If they say yes, it's time to design and assign exposure homework. That is going back and cleaning up messes they've left behind. You can do this too in the context of 5-10-15 years exercise only now they have the chance to change the future by acting today.
WORK Stress - ACT interventions [cont'd] **EXERCISE** **Journaling [8-17-04]** Joseph Ciarrochi	Following on Jonathan's point 4, I thought I'd use the journaling exercise to do the exposure in session. Here are the journaling instructions from Pennybaker's research.... *Instructions for journaling* What I would like to have you write about for the next … (insert time) is the situation you are struggling with (insert topic here). The only rule we have about your writing is that you write continuously for the entire time. If you run out of things to say, just repeat what you have already written. In your writing, don't worry about grammar, spelling, or sentence structure. Just write. Whatever you choose to write, however, it is critical that you really delve into your deepest emotions and thoughts. You might tie your personal experiences to other parts of your life. How is it related to your childhood, your parents, people you love, who you are, or who you want to be? Again, in your writing, examine your deepest emotions and thoughts.
WORK **Stress management, RCT re** **EVIDENCE** **Process of change (acceptance) - workplace stress RCT [11-25-02]** Frank Bond	My colleague, David Bunce, and I conducted a RCT that looked at the effectiveness of ACT, applied in a group format, at work. (A media organisation based here in London.) As it was a worksite stress management intervention (SMI), we did not attempt to target a specific DSM disorder. We did, though, examine the process by which ACT had its effects. Using the Acceptance and Action Questionnaire (16 item version), we found that acceptance was the mechanism, or mediator, by which our ACT intervention (see Bond & Hayes, 2002) improved general mental health (General Health Questionnaire), depression (BDI), and a performance-related variable (Propensity to Innovate). The Dysfunctional Attitude Survey did not serve as a mediator for any of these changes. We compared the ACT SMI to a stressor-reduction intervention, which was not quite as successful as the ACT one, and it had its effects through a different mechanism of change, or mediator. Quite apart from anything else, I think that this study shows that it is not too difficult to examine both process and outcomes in the same study. Details of the experiment are in: Bond, F. W., & Bunce, D. (2000). Mediators of change in emotion-focused and problem-focused worksite stress management interventions. *Journal of Occupational Health Psychology, 5*(1), 156-163. The ACT protocol that we used can be found in: Bond, F. W., & Hayes, S. C. (2002). Acceptance and Commitment Therapy at work. In F. W. Bond & W. Dryden (Eds.), *Handbook of brief cognitive behaviour therapy*. Chichester: John Wiley & Sons. We are currently comparing the outcomes, and mediators of change, of both ACT and a traditional CBT amongst UK local government workers.

Chapter 2
<u>Comparing ACT with other Therapies and Traditions</u>

Questions as to how ACT compares and contrasts with other therapeutic approaches have represented a recurring theme on the listserv. This chapter contains a selection of posts on this theme, many of which discuss ACT in relation to its antecedents in the behavior therapy tradition - notably cognitive-behavior therapy - as well as its companion "third wave" therapies, such as Dialectical Behavior Therapy. Also included are discussions concerning therapeutic strategies and techniques not necessarily confined to one particular form of therapy, such as exposure, cognitive restructuring, and the seeking of insight.

Many writers to the listserv have drawn parallels between ACT and the religious tradition of Buddhism, and the chapter includes posts dealing with this comparison. For example, there is discussion of the Buddhist practice of meditation, as compared with ACT's use of mindfulness practice. Other posts contain material from Buddhist sources reflecting and illuminating ACT-consistent perspectives.

ACT cf. **Behavior Therapy - 1st, 2nd and 3rd waves defined [7-18-03]** Steve Hayes	John Bush wrote: What is meant by "2nd wave CBT" and how does it differ from 1st wave CBT? Traditional behavior therapy: first wave; Traditional CT / CBT: second wave; The currently ill-defined collection of more contextualistic changes occurring in the behavioral and cognitive tradition [bringing in aspects of eastern and less-empirical clinical traditions; retaining the science commitment; and trying to do a better theoretical analysis ... such as DBT, ACT, FAP, MBCT, MBRP, IBCT, etc.]: third wave.
ACT cf. **Behavior Therapy - compatibility with ACT** **COPING STRATEGIES** **Relaxation - ACT rationale [5-9-05]** Lizabeth Roemer	Sue Orsillo and I have developed a treatment that integrates ACT and mindfulness strategies with existing behavioral treatments for GAD. Within this context, we use applied relaxation and diaphragmatic breathing, but are clear that their intent is to increase awareness of internal sensations, thoughts and feelings. We say that relaxation may follow, and it may not, and either is ok. Of course, often clients do find these techniques relaxing. However, we do not feel that these techniques actually reduce negative emotions. They do help the person be more in the present moment, and be more aware of the thoughts and reactions they are having. And this can reduce the secondary distress that is often associated with trying to push feelings and thoughts away. We find it important to make sure that clients don't begin using these strategies to avoid however....
ACT cf. Behavior Therapy - compatibility with ACT [cont'd] COPING STRATEGIES Relaxation - ACT rationale [cont'd] Steve Hayes	Relaxation training is not incompatible with ACT if you cast it correctly. Contact with the present moment is a great example. The original rationale for Jacobsonian relaxation training was pretty good too. I originally learned progressive muscle relaxation training as means for learning how to let go. You can hardly get more ACT than that. "Relaxation as a opponent of anxiety" may have conflicts but this rationale is not the method itself and I know of no evidence that this rationale adds to its effectiveness. In fact, I don't know of *any* behavioral methods that are incompatible with ACT ... it is only the rationales that sometimes get sideways....
ACT cf. Behavior Therapy - compatibility with ACT [cont'd] COPING STRATEGIES Relaxation - ACT rationale [cont'd] James Herbert	The key is the function relaxation is designed to serve: increased awareness and ultimately acceptance of distressing private experiences vs. a change in the content and/or intensity of such experiences. In my experience, this distinction, while technically simple, does not come easily experientially. In fact, one of the biggest problems is the tendency to become focused on the content/intensity changes that frequently do occur, which puts you right back in the trap. As someone far wiser than me noted, "if you're not willing to have it, you've got it."
ACT cf. Behavior Therapy - compatibility with ACT [cont'd] COPING STRATEGIES Relaxation - ACT rationale [cont'd] Dermot Barnes-Holmes	If I recall correctly, Wegner found a paradoxical effect in one of his studies on relaxation (i.e., folks showed higher levels of arousal when told to relax). This contrasted with "just notice what shows up" condition. Seems to fit exactly with a critical role for the rationale underpinning the relaxation exercise itself.
ACT cf. Behavior Therapy - compatibility with ACT [cont'd]	It seems that the same could be true for "distraction"; that the rationale is about control of unwanted private events while the effectiveness, when it works, might hinge on increased contact with the present moment.

COPING STRATEGIES Relaxation - ACT rationale [cont'd] Patty Bach	
ACT cf. Behavior Therapy - compatibility with ACT [cont'd] COPING STRATEGIES Relaxation - ACT rationale [cont'd] **FUSION/ DEFUSION** **Meaning of [5-10-05]** Steve Hayes	Shoshana Isenberg wrote: But the Jacobsonian relaxation training (and many others) is still about control, rather than just awareness. It doesn't have to be about control. I would agree that it is not just about awareness ... but remember all of those raps about how relaxation was learning to do nothing and to let go of all muscular activity? It was said you could not "do" relaxation by muscular activity because any muscular action shortened muscles. Rather relaxation was the action of non-action -- of letting go -- but you were to focus on the sensation very closely so you could learn the difference between how your muscles felt when tense and relaxed. This is such a close parallel to an ACT rap I hardly need to point it out. For example, defusion is not the deliberate (i.e., rule based) action of stepping back from thoughts, because even that thought you need to step back from. Rather defusion is letting go of the domination of literal meaning and focusing on the process of thinking itself so you can learn the difference between how it works when you are fused or defused. Same with acceptance. Same with the present moment. So, yes, the rationale is usually off. And then you are setting people up (needlessly) for things like relaxation induced panic. But the point was that it is easy to change that. An empirical prediction: Relaxation plus an ACT rationale and a few acceptance/ mindfulness/ defusion/ contact with the present moment examples will be more powerful and less dangerous than relaxation plus a heavy control rationale and a few distraction / think of nice things not bad ones / don't let the bad feeling and thoughts dominate examples. There's a nice dissertation. Probably a small effect size so you'd need a big N but doable. ACT is a model for how to do behavior therapy (or if you think of the word "behavioral" in a narrow way, for how to do behavioral and cognitive therapy). There is room for just about every empirically validated technique -- and every behavioral technique of that kind I know of. But yes, it is also different. That is why it is a new model. So you have to fit the technique to the model. James [Herbert] mentioned thought stopping but I'm not sure that is an exception ... the data on it are minuscule and I'm not sure it makes behavioral sense. Some cognitive techniques conflict (e.g., thought disputation) but there too the data are minuscule that this element really helps. The overall traditional CBT packages include many techniques that can be brought into an ACT consistent stance. Sometimes people get so caught up in the power of what is relatively novel about ACT -- at least novel in empirically-supported treatment land -- that they forget the hard won knowledge from our empirically-supported traditions. That does not make sense (except in research studies designed to focus on components). As we say in the 1999 ACT book, in the final analysis "ACT takes on the character of traditional behavior therapy, and virtually any behavior change technique is acceptable. The difference is that behavior change goals, guided exposure, social skills training, modeling, role playing, couples work, and so on are integrated with an ACT perspective."
ACT cf. Behavior Therapy - compatibility with ACT [cont'd] COPING STRATEGIES Relaxation - ACT rationale [cont'd] Brian Glaister	I now view deep relaxation training as a method of developing the observational (or transcendental) self and awareness of the present moment, in which the focus used for training is the muscles. This is analogous to using breathing, or any other perceptual focus, for the purpose.

ACT cf. **Behavioral Activation - re depression** **DEPRESSION** **ACT cf. Behavioral Activation [3-14-04]** Nico van der Meijden	... In the Dutch journal of behavioral therapy of this month there is a review of a book of Jacobson: *Depression in Context: Strategies of guided action.* C.R. Martell, M.E. Addis & N.S. Jacobson. (2001) New York: Norton. ISBN 0-471-18970-7. Price: ¢43,00. It's a book about the treatment of depressions (unfortunately the review is not available on the internet). In the manner the reviewers describe the content of the book I recognized a lot of the way of thinking that characterizes ACT. The two approaches seem to fit seamlessly. The reviewers are enthusiastic: they characterize the book as a masterpiece. They describe the behavioristic background of Jacobson; it's not the form or content of a thought or act that's important, but the function. No mentalism, but functionalism. Depressive behavior is based on a learning history and is maintained by certain schedules of reinforcement (a vision already expressed by Skinner 40 years ago). According to the reviewers the translation to practice of this model has been obliterated by the rise of the cognitive model. They think a valuable approach was 'nipped in the bud.' Martell, Addis and Jacobson pay in their book a lot of attention to the context of behavior. Summarizing the review: depressive behavior can only be understood against the background of events and experiences from past and present. A decrease of positive reinforcement by certain events or an increase in negative consequences lead to certain reactions or symptoms (cognitive, behavioral, biological), which the subject experiences aversively and tries to control or escape from. These 'digging' behaviors (to use the ACT term) which give short term relief, worsen the aversive symptoms in the long run (it felt like reading a part of the ACT book). Relying on this review, this book seems to be a good supplement to the ACT book, especially with regard to the treatment of depressions. It also seems to give a good impression of contextualistic behavioral thinking....
ACT cf. Behavioral Activation - re depression [cont'd] DEPRESSION ACT cf. Behavioral Activation [cont'd] Jonathan Kanter	I know the Martell, Addis and Jacobson book quite well so I thought I'd use this as an opportunity to make a quick comparison with ACT, for those who don't know it as well. First, glad that you have found the behavioral activation manual; it is a nice treatment with important similarities to ACT. Both share a contextualistic, anti-mentalist framework and suggest it is futile to directly change thoughts and feelings. Contextualism as described by Martell et al. is not as clear as ACT's, but that is a minor point and they should be credited for trying. But there is an important difference. ACT goes a step further and says, not only is it futile to directly change thoughts and feelings, but it is a flawed agenda and not what life should be about. You do not need to be less depressed in order to lead a valued life and ACT helps you get moving toward those values. In contrast, Behavioral Activation does not attack the agenda; it WANTS you to be less depressed - it just suggests that the best way to do it is by getting active and moving toward values, instead of directly targeting thoughts and feelings. It goes outside - in. So while ACT is purely and totally contextualistic, you could argue that Behavioral Activation is not. Also behavioral activation does not stress the values piece very much and I have known several behavioral activation therapists who add the ACT values component into their Behavioral Activation treatment in order to dignify the hard work of activation. To be fair, I also know therapists interested in ACT who have chosen Behavioral Activation instead because it is simpler, and if you have an inactive depressed client and assess that cognitive fusion is not a major problem it seems like an o.k. choice. As an aside, my own read of the "Scientific foundations..." book by Clark, Beck, and Alford is that it is quite biased and NOT an accurate review of the cognitive literature, which is considerably more mixed than the authors make it sound. But I of course am also biased.
ACT cf. Behavioral Activation - re depression [cont'd] **ACT cf.** **Other contextualistic approaches [3-15-04]** James Herbert	Jonathan, I think you captured very nicely some important distinctions not only between Jacobson et al.'s stuff and ACT, but between several of the other newer contextualistic approaches and ACT, including mindfulness-based CT for depression, MBSD, and DBT. It's always struck me that the latter are often inconsistent in the message about changing unwanted private experiences. That is, the control agenda is left mostly intact, while acceptance moves are considered useful tools for achieving changes in private events. In addition, mindfulness/defusion exercises are not as explicitly linked to behavior change, thereby missing ACT's pragmatic stance on these exercises. Finally, as you note, the values piece is not emphasized as much, and it is simply assumed that therapist and client share similar values and goals (e.g., reducing depression, forming more stable relationships).
ACT cf. **CBT - cognitive restructuring**	I'm wondering, can cognitive restructuring ever be in the service of determining whether something is workable? I understand that in ACT we try to break the link between unworkable agendas like requiring that our clients have a certain type of thought or feeling in order to act in a desired way. However, sometimes perspective taking seems essential to see whether something is workable. Take for example, a

COGNITIVE RESTRUCTURING **Use in ACT [5-24-05]** Lawrence Needleman	context in which a client with paranoid behavior has the thought called "she's trying to get me fired." The client may learn to see these types of thoughts as thoughts and realize that they are part of her mind's old and unhelpful pattern. However, at least early in therapy, it often seems necessary to evaluate the evidence and explore alternative explanations. Moreover, the client's interpretation may be correct and it's important that s/he determine as well as possible if this is the case. I guess my hope is to convince them that their paranoid thoughts are simply thoughts (don't map with reality, aren't workable) and once they see it that way work with them on defusion. Do you ever find yourself using old-style cognitive restructuring? If so, in what kinds of contexts and how?

ACT cf.
 	
   CBT - cognitive restructuring [cont'd]
 	
COGNITIVE RESTRUCTURING
 	
   Use in ACT [cont'd]
 	
PSYCHOSIS
 	
   ACT cf. CBT [5-24-05]
 	
Scott Temple
	I don't think that a 'formal' Acceptance and Commitment Therapy stance would incorporate the same cognitive restructuring approaches that are customarily associated with cognitive therapy. On the other hand, I have found that guided discovery (gentle curiosity and Socratic questioning) allows me to flexibly assess evidence without ever asking 'what's the evidence for that belief?' At least as important, particularly in my work with psychosis, is the use of guided discovery to get at the workability issues you raise. This leads to issues pertaining to the patient's values, and to the cost paid because of their living as though certain propositions are true. For example, if having loving relationships is important, then staying home to avoid the prospect that family members can hear one's persecutorial voices gets in the way of loving relationships. People are often willing to tolerate painful inner content in the service of getting at something of deep value to them, as is well articulated in ACT. In fact, Steve Hayes has spoken about the courage that psychotic patients show every time they take their voices with them into public venues ... very humbling. In a recent CBT trial I did for psychosis, I found the ACT focus on values, willingness, and commitment to be incredibly helpful, even if I did not use the same kinds of defusion interventions that are specified in ACT. But, like a lot of folks who do CBT for psychosis, the two clinical trials of ACT with psychosis have caught my attention. I did 20 sessions, and got good results. ACT trials employ what, 3 - 5 sessions, and get impressive results? Something's going on here. I've had some difficulty using defusion exercises, etc., with psychotic patients. But I'm willing to look into this further.

ACT cf.
 	
   CBT - cognitive restructuring [cont'd]
 	
COGNITIVE RESTRUCTURING
 	
   Use in ACT [cont'd]
 	
PSYCHOSIS
 	
   ACT cf. CBT [cont'd]
 	
Patty Bach
	As Scott mentioned, a focus on values can lead to being willing to take action towards valued outcomes in the presence of negatively evaluated content - even delusional beliefs.
	
	Someone else on this list (I can't recall who) shared his experience of doing groups with clients with psychosis and noting that when the clients started doing values work they were much less focused on symptom content.
	
	In ACT the thought itself is not viewed as workable or unworkable - it's just a thought. Action in context - e.g., in your example of the client who thinks someone wants him fired from his job - get rid of this thought; stop going to work; work harder; talk to supervisor about my work performance; yell at co-workers/supervisor; get a new job; etc. is what is workable or not workable.
	
	A focus on employment or values related to employment leads to many possible actions he might take no matter what the thought content and no matter whether he gets fired or maintains his job.
	
	Suppose a client believes that he is NOT going to get fired. He probably wouldn't be upset by this belief, in fact, he would be unlikely to ever mention this belief in treatment since it is not distressing - and he might suddenly find that he is fired.
	
	And then would it be more useful to examine his belief that he wasn't going to be fired, or to examine his behavior on the job?
	
	I might even make this move with a client who believes he is going to be fired - e.g., ask what changing the belief to "I am not going to be fired" will accomplish - will changing the thought have an impact on whether or not he is fired? And if it will, how? E.g., if he said, "if I believed I wasn't going to be fired then I would go to work instead of calling in sick" I might explore what that's in the service of (usually making the thought stop) and then what happens the next time he goes to work (which might be an increase in the thought since he has called in sick). Does whatever he has been doing ultimately work to stop the thought? What's the cost? What is in the way of going to work in the presence of the belief "she wants to fire me"?
	
	Is the client who thinks he is going to be fired more interested in changing the thought or in staying employed? If he quits his job the thought might stop; is that a good outcome?
	
	Is it the belief that one is (or is not) going to be fired that leads to being fired, or is it behavior that leads to being fired or keeping one's job no matter what one's belief?

ACT cf. CBT - cognitive restructuring [cont'd]	... To probably oversimplify, ACT puts behavior over thought. CBT (Beckian) considers thought 'primary,' if you will. Both models, in practice, treat thought contextually, in the sense that thought arises in a broader context of body sensations, emotions, behaviors, and environmental contingencies (internal and external). Treatment in both models is about increasing the person's capacity to flexibly respond to daily life, although ACT does so in a less "DSM focused" manner. In terms of treatment strategies, guided by theory,

COGNITIVE RESTRUCTURING Use in ACT [cont'd] PSYCHOSIS ACT cf. CBT [cont'd] Scott Temple	ACT bypasses engagement in examination of content; CBT deals with content directly. I have a question, and let me ask by using an example that actually arose in a group that I run in our partial hospital program. I'm making it more detailed than the group did: Let's say you are on the 'savannah' (15,000 years ago). There's a fire lit, but ready to go out if you don't toss on another log. You notice that the gourd holding water is nearly empty. There is a stream beyond the circle of light. Between you and the stream is a brush patch. You hear a rustling sound in the brush. You are startled. Your children are asleep by the fire and you know that you will need water during the night. You value having water for your children, and you get up to walk to the stream. You wonder: "Is that a sabre tooth tiger in the brush, or is that the sound of the wind, causing the brush to clatter?" That is a thought, an appraisal. Do you pursue your valued goal, at the risk of being eaten, or stay in the light till morning, later feeling foolish if there are no tiger tracks to be found? Can you collect evidence to inform you whether there is a tiger in the brush? How? A patient in the group, who has an anxiety disorder (also BPD), said, essentially, "It matters to me whether the threat is 'real' or not." Plug in Larry's example, if you want: paranoia shares properties with anxiety disorders in the sense that threat estimates are involved. It seems to me that it is a strength of Beck's model that it can aid in making more flexible, adaptive estimates of threat, which can then guide one's behavioral response. The purpose is not to get rid of the 'sabre-tooth tiger thought.' How does ACT help people with psychosis make these threat estimates, especially when they believe they'll be eaten by a tiger if they go for the water?
ACT cf. CBT - cognitive restructuring [cont'd] COGNITIVE RESTRUCTURING Use in ACT [cont'd] PSYCHOSIS ACT cf. CBT [cont'd] Patty Bach	While the Saber-tooth tiger example describes threat appraisal it does not seem to describe an anxiety disorder. How much thirst would it take for the cave man to venture to the water? The anxiety-disordered client might die of thirst in the service of avoiding the tiger. Threat appraisal has its uses and most people in therapy for anxiety disorders are seeking treatment in relation to threats they already know are very low probability (e.g., plane crashing); threats that are vague as in GAD; fears that will more than likely come true, e.g., having a panic attack in the panic disordered client or a flashback in PTSD; and fears that are unrelated to the valued action in question as in many social phobias. Threat appraisal might have some bearing on paranoid delusions and other delusions are not based on the appraisal of the probability of some future event, and instead on the 'truth' or 'reality' of some condition, e.g., "I am Napoleon." Also, by definition, delusions are beliefs that persist in spite of overwhelming evidence to the contrary. In the case of paranoid delusions, I like Bentall's theory of delusional beliefs functioning as a defense against low self-esteem. Instead of seeing one's self as a failure, one can blame the state of one's life on the actions and evil intentions of vague others. Target reality of the delusional belief, and then what? Same with other kinds of delusions. "I'm not a failure, I'm a rock star"; "I'm not a loser; she's in love with me." Target the reality of the belief, then what? Target values first - get the client moving in a valued direction, and there is less investment in the delusional belief since there are more sources of positive reinforcement and less to defend against. Also, risk appraisal suggests that we can know the outcome, and we often can't. I'm seeing a rape survivor in treatment who is angry because she took great care to protect herself against the possibility of sexual assault. Her accurate risk appraisal didn't protect her because we can't take every possibility into account. Some flying phobics have certainly boarded planes that crashed, and they didn't die in a plane crash because of poor threat appraisal and died in spite of the accurate appraisal that the odds of a plane crashing are very remote. ACT data suggests that threat appraisal can increase the function of threat-related verbal content - that is, it becomes even more important to think about possible threats.
ACT cf. CBT - cognitive restructuring [cont'd] COGNITIVE RESTRUCTURING Use in ACT [cont'd] Lawrence Needleman	I recall (cognitive process) in the 1999 ACT book, the authors suggest that cognition is designed for survival not for happiness. However, it seems to me that all the ways that cognitive processes and content are necessary for survival - a value, they are necessary in the achievement of all of our values. Specifically, cognition helps in predicting, organizing, strategizing, communicating, goal setting, etc. Sometimes "a thought is just a thought," or "worse," a lure away from valued action. Other times, a thought can be useful information, informing choice. To broaden the discussion beyond threat appraisal, prediction more broadly can be in the service of valued action (or take us down the wrong path). If I value being a good friend and can accurately predict based on my learning history with a person how s/he is likely to behave in response to my behaviors, I can use that prediction to improve/value the relationship. Often, cognitive content spontaneously arises that predicts someone's behavior and that content may be on target or not. Moreover, I believe that reflection on the

content can often improve prediction -- e.g., exploring the evidence, thinking of alternative explanations (decreasing confirmatory bias), etc. If upon reflection, the content (prediction) was on target and suggested a valued direction, great -- act on it. On the other hand, if the content was not supported by evidence, don't act on it and realize it was off base, to (hopefully) improve future predictions [i.e., cognitive restructuring].

Patty, in the case of the employee who predicted he would get fired, as you suggested, the thought could be the context for valued behavior -- including talking to his supervisor about his performance. In this case, the content of the thought may have been signaling that if he values his job, he needs to improve his performance and perhaps that would mean choosing to sacrifice other valued behaviors of lower priority than keeping his job. Or, not; he might be a stellar performer who has content that does not map with his job situation. If this is the case, it also could be helpful for him to know, because he can then choose to allocate time and energy to other important areas of his life. [Similarly, other behaviors, besides thoughts, can provide us with useful information. If a young child feels uncomfortable with an adult neighbor and doesn't know why, it might be a signal to get away from him (or it might just be noise; neighbor may be safe).]

It occurs to me that when I act in a valued way - it is often not just "with cognitions" coming along for the ride but rather the cognitions help plan, organize and execute it - both with what we often call effortful or intentional thinking as well as intrusive thoughts. Intrusive thoughts also just don't go along for the ride but can serve as a brain-storming generator (Salkovskis suggested this when theorizing about OCD processes). When the mind goes "blah blah blah," there are often gems imbedded, and we often incorporate them when deciding if and when and how to act.

I guess the bottom line for me is that the cognition is important. After all, if it weren't would we be spending so much time on listservs? Isn't it true that we believe that shaping up our cognitions in this process will help us with valued behavior? I guess the trick is to know what it's in the service of, when it's workable and when it's just noise.

ACT cf.

   CBT - cognitive restructuring [cont'd]

COGNITIVE RESTRUCTURING

   Use in ACT [cont'd]

RFT

   Should clinicians learn?

THERAPIST

   "Don't believe a word I'm saying" [6-1-05]

   Steve Hayes

Cross References:

See 4-185 to 4-188 for later posts in the thread:

RFT

Should clinicians learn?

See 7-324 for a later post in the thread:

THERAPIST

"Don't believe a word I'm saying"

It seems a bit weird to have to respond to the idea that cognition is important.

Is there another approach in applied psychology that built its own comprehensive basic research program in cognition? What about all those RFT language training studies; studies on motivation; studies on values; studies on deictic frames and sense of self? They are all about building and using relational repertoires.

We don't tell clinicians "learn RFT or you can't be an ACT therapist" because that would be like saying "run a marathon and we will let you train to be an ACT therapist." The barrier is too high. But people on the list should have no doubt. In the long run you cannot FULLY understand ACT without understanding its theory and philosophy. That is why Chapter 2 and 3 is in the ACT book even when there was a big push to kill them. Sooner or later -- if you get into ACT enough -- learning all of this is work (hard work!) that needs to be done....

If you get on top of RFT you will see this issue differently and it will be easier to detect the clinical uses of language and the actual technical analysis. The clinical use is more in the direction of restriction of Crel methods because they are so dominant and if you don't do that you are lost.

We way over use Crel interventions including with ourselves and (in mainstream CBT) with our clients. We should use them when they work and not when they don't but when you are using them all the time you can't even see the issue. For example, the ever troublesome "don't believe a word I say" is done in the section of ACT when you are breaking through excessive Crel control. It does not mean "belief is never useful" or "cognition is unimportant" or "what you think does not matter." It is clinical language designed to implode the excessive Crel control through an inherent paradox. Paradox is one of the few methods around to do that. It is not hidden or manipulative paradox we are talking about: it is evident, open, and inherent paradox. e.g., "Be spontaneous." And in that sense it is 100% so: literal belief cannot by itself detect the limits of literal belief.

Technically / scientifically / clinically -- you need Crel methods. There are many sections of the ACT book that use them. For example, when we say "the problem is deliberate, purposeful control," we are following up a Cfunc method (creative hopelessness) with just a little bit of Crel intervention to throw the mind a bone. etc. etc. The issue is establishing contextual control so that you can use Cfunc methods that permit more direct shaping as well as Crel methods. The technical analysis of values work very much involves Crel issues as you note ... that is said in the ACT book too but it is not said very loudly. You will see a lot more in the RFT book. Clinically it does not need huge encouragement: when folks begin to do new things they naturally contact new contingencies and guess what: they formulate new cognitions.

Metaphorically, this issue is like this situation:

You have developed a whole theory and research program that explains how to get objects rolling and how to slow things down. But there is this huge problem with heavy runaway trucks on mountain roads. So you apply this work to that problem and you make a lot of progress. So you write a book about how to deal with heavy runaway trucks on mountain roads and guess what: it has a huge emphasis on brakes, and using your engine to avoid getting going too fast, and steering in ways that don't increase speed, and the like. When

	someone says "hey, but it is also important to be rolling!" one part of the answer is "yeah. True." And we have a whole research program on how to get things rolling. And there are even many things in the book on trucks that are about that -- they are just buried because anything that gets things rolling also presents the problem of learning how to slow down and until drivers learn that part it is not that helpful to do much about how to get rolling. If you read the science book on runaway trucks it would include major sections on getting and keeping things rolling ... but the scientist is not the truck driver. That book has a different purpose given that 95% of the problem with heavy runaway trucks on mountain roads is slowing things down………….. It is like that.

ACT cf.
 	
   CBT - cognitive restructuring [cont'd]
 	
COGNITIVE RESTRUCTURING
 	
   Use in ACT [cont'd]
 	
CAUSE
 	
   Thought - role in causal chain
 	
THOUGHT
 	
   Causal chain, role in [6-1-05]
 	
     Kevin Vowles
	Just a few things to add to the discussion.
	
	First, it's probably safe to say that most behaviorists hold that thoughts are important. As others have pointed out, there are lots of good things (and bad things) that cognition allows us to do. I think the 1999 ACT book suggests that cognition is one of the primary reasons that humans have been able to do so much with our world. Along these same lines, many of the "old guard" of behaviorism (Skinner among them - particularly in Walden II I believe) have discussed the relevance of thoughts.
	
	I think some of the confusion lies in whether thoughts are root causes of behavior. Common sense dictates that if I think something (e.g., "I am thirsty.") and then do something (e.g., take a drink of water), then the thought caused the behavior. Within traditional behavioral theory (and ACT/RFT), however, thoughts are not viewed as causes of behavior. Rather, it is the current environment (including the actual setting and things that are happening in the setting), as well as past experiences that determine behavior. These three variables comprise at least some of the "context" in contextual approaches.
	
	Therefore, a contextual definition looks a bit further back in the "chain" of thoughts/behaviors to identify the cause. So, instead of:
	
	Thought > Current Behavior
	
	It is:
	
	Context (past behavior, current environment, current contingencies of environment) > Thought > Current Behavior
	
	Or, others have suggested that current thoughts and current behavior co-occur with neither being the "cause."
	
	If taken back to the "beginning" of a certain behavior (imagining that was possible), the assumption is that the identified root cause is something in the context, rather than the occurrence of a spontaneous thought. With regard to the water example, I know that water gets rid of my thirst because it has in the past and presumably someone made me drink it as a kid when I was thirsty, therefore, I make an assumption that it will do so again. This approach suggests that treatment would best be focused on the context, rather than the thought.
	
	Among other things, what RFT adds is a theoretical model concerning inter-relations among language, cognitions, and actions. Also, ACT adds a method of disconnecting the common sense approach that thoughts MUST be causes of behavior with the defusion exercises. The "thought is just a thought" statement is one of these exercises and (my understanding of it) is to allow some of the gravity and importance often ascribed to thoughts to be weakened. The exercise is not, "thoughts are not important." So, even if I think I am thirsty, I don't have to take a drink. More clinically relevant examples include if I am feeling depressed, I can still go out to dinner with friends/family or if I am in pain, I can still go to my kid's baseball game. From an ACT perspective, I would choose to do these activities if they were personally-relevant, related to values, etc. I could just as easily choose not to do them if they were not worth it to me, related to goals/values, etc.
	
	With regard to cognitive restructuring exercises, I suppose it depends on your definition or practice of "cognitive restructuring." If the practice is entirely a cognitive enterprise that depends on replacing a maladaptive thought with an adaptive thought, then the above contextual approach would suggest if the context is not changed, then the thought will not change either. Further, some relevant data suggest that the more one attempts to control or change a thought (or sensation such as pain), then the more it will occur or the longer it will last. So, replacing a thought with a thought may not work very well.
	
	On the other hand, if one approaches cognitive restructuring in a manner which includes some of those contextual variables, the approach may lead to cognitive change or, perhaps more importantly (?), behavioral change. It sounds like Dr. Needleman was including some of this contextual stuff in his post when discussing cognitive restructuring, but I don't want to assume. Finally, I think the ACT perspective suggests that values-directed behavioral change can occur in the absence of that cognitive change as well. That addition is particularly important when treating the many chronic conditions that are out there, where unpleasant thoughts, feelings, and sensations are ongoing. The whole discussion of form vs. function of thoughts is important here as well.

ACT cf. CBT - cognitive restructuring [cont'd] **COGNITIVE RESTRUCTURING** Use in ACT [cont'd] **CAUSE** Thought - role in causal chain [cont'd] **THOUGHT** Causal chain, role in [cont'd] Patty Bach	To extend the example to prediction of future events, does the prediction "it's going to rain" lead to taking an umbrella, or does the observation of dark clouds occasion both the cognition/prediction and the behavior of taking the umbrella? I might predict how a stranger will respond to my behavior if I am given a lot of information about that person; and if that person is a friend, my predictions AND behavior are based on shared history with the friend - the history doesn't cause the prediction which then causes the behavior - the history 'causes' both. Cognition is certainly useful, and in clinical contexts, I doubt we'd see someone present for treatment regarding the accuracy of a prediction such as "I think I am going to get fired" - in most instances such a thought would lead to behavior change and not getting fired (unless it's too late), or to ignoring the thought and not changing behavior and getting fired (or not getting fired, if the prediction was not accurate). The person coming for treatment in relation to the thought "I am going to be fired" usually presents for treatment when s/he recognizes that the thought is accurate and wants to learn how to improve his/her behavior on the job; when s/he recognizes that the thought is 'irrational' and is distressed by the thought itself and wants it to go away; when the thought was accurate and s/he has been fired and is distressed about the job loss; when s/he acts inappropriately - e.g., confronting the boss, and presents for treatment because of the inappropriate behavior; and other matters related to the thought - behavior relation rather than to the accuracy of the thought content per se. There are many histories that might lead someone to have the thought "I am going to be fired" and many of the contextual cues occasioning such a thought may have little to do with the work environment per se or the probability of actually being fired, and problems with respect to the thought that lead people to seek psychotherapy are usually related to how one responds to one's thoughts rather than to how accurate the predictions/evaluations are. And if someone comes in for treatment complaining about uncertainty regarding the accuracy of a prediction, then we might look at prediction skills, and/or at the person's relationship to certainty/ uncertainty.
ACT cf. **CBT - cognitive skills training [3-31-05]** John Blackledge	I've been wading through CBT for kids literature to prepare lectures for a Child & Adolescent Therapy class I'm teaching (Joseph Ciarrochi finds it a source of gleefully sadistic amusement that I was tagged to teach CBT), and I've had a few thoughts I didn't expect to have. One, some of the components used in cognitive therapy can neatly fall under the umbrella of stimulus discrimination. For example, some of the components involve increasing awareness of the child's surroundings and interpreting social cues in conventionally sensible ways (including sharpening appraisals of others' motivations and intentions). Clearly, from an RFT perspective, sharpening such stimulus discrimination skills would involve teaching the child to reframe aspects of her experience, in addition to shaping her to attend to important stimuli in various contexts. Two, hardcore cognitive techniques that involve teaching clients to think logically and to recognize and weigh evidence have some appeal, and I can see that some (particularly children) might have deficits in these areas. The RFT supposition is that language is useful when it allows us to effectively solve problems, and such techniques, taken at face value, could be helpful in appraising situations and making sensible choices--which, when yoked to values, could help enable a child to move toward them more effectively. My clear line of departure with the cognitive model lies in using such strategies in the service of emotional and cognitive control (as well as in imparting the belief to clients that thoughts cause emotions and other behavior). Additionally, it seems a given that the ACT-consistent way of teaching these skills would be done in a way that imparts lesser degrees of fusion with their products. But the web is starting to feel a little bit sticky, and I'm curious to see if others have grappled with this issue. One of the things I've noticed since my career path has switched from adults to children is that skills deficits in kids tend to be more frequent and more pronounced (or at least more obvious) than those seen in many adult clients. I was always taught by Steve that skills training and ACT can go hand in hand, though I've rarely explicitly focused on formal skills training (traditionally defined) with adults. With any population (perhaps particularly with kids), the sensible ACT-consistent thing to do seems to involve finding out what the client really values, assessing barriers to movement toward those values, then giving them the strategies they need to get through those 'real' or entirely verbally constructed barriers. If experiential avoidance and excessive fusion are in the way, then we work with them to break down those walls. If true skills deficits are in the way, then we rectify them. What I'm wondering is, what are people's thoughts on how and when to combine defusion strategies and cognitive skills training that focuses on a child essentially reframing her experience, in a way that is theoretically coherent and consistent?
ACT cf. CBT - cognitive skills training [cont'd] John Blackledge	You know, the more I think about this, the less sticky it becomes for me. I was coming from a coherence perspective--i.e., if you've chosen to adopt an ACT-based treatment model with a child, how do you (can you?) integrate components that have commonly fallen under the cognitive skills training umbrella with ACT in a way that doesn't confuse the client and therapist, and that globally doesn't muddy the conceptual

	model. The solution, to me, appears to be to focus on cognitive skills training components like problem solving and evidence-based appraisals of others' intentions, motivations, and how they 'stand' with respect to you. In other words, those skills that deal with getting a conventionally reasonable survey of the land and that provide the tools to successfully notice, conceptualize, and solve problems occurring outside the skin-- with the ultimate goal of moving more effectively toward what is valued. Logic, attention to detail, and an ability to frame interpersonal and other situational cues in a roughly conventionally standard way (such that you are playing roughly by the same rules as others when this is required for effective action), all appear to be helpful in being effective in the world. Working to enhance these skills in a child (or an adult, for that matter), while addressing the world inside the skin with defusion and acceptance strategies, seems entirely consistent with an ACT model to me.
ACT cf. CBT - cognitive skills training [cont'd] Patty Bach	Why not skills training? It seems to me that the answer to what interventions to use when and with which clients is within ACT itself - simply ask yourself, "what's that in the service of?"
ACT cf. CBT - cognitive skills training [cont'd] **Behavior Therapy - compatibility with ACT** **COGNITIVE RESTRUCTURING** **Defusing effect of** **[4-1-05]** Matthew Smout	Perhaps the time has come for a book which combines the ACT procedures outlined in the 1999 book with behavior therapy 101 guided by a theoretical framework which integrates the ACT hexaflex, basic operant and RFT principles. I think Joe (and others previously) rightly points to the "B" in CBT as being quite effective and compatible with ACT. The fundamental difference between ACT and other topographically similar approaches lies in the treatment of "inside the skin" - the "C." At present, the 1999 text seems to prime the reader to "look out for" chronic unworkability - immediately unsettling the therapist about to treat a relatively un-therapied client. In practice, experienced ACT clinicians seem to have no problem in switching to concentrate on one of the other core processes - valued action; defusion; acceptance (something the hexaflex model encourages). However, clients also present with problems that basic behaviour therapy would be great for, and it seems weird that clinicians might feel like they need to choose between ACT and CBT to do BT. This may be an artefact of ACT being developed amongst people who live and breathe behaviour therapy so everyone can assume that knowledge. As ACT goes global it seems to encounter less people who think BT first, CT next. Steve's case conceptualisation outline includes a lot of basic behavioural assessment with ACT interventions in the context of BT. I guess because it's not ACT-unique, the BT gets lost in communicating the model sometimes. Based on studies comparing BT and CT, it is fair enough to ask when and why would you add the "CT" - and then why not the "ACT." In my experience cognitive restructuring very often appears to have a defusing effect. It's just that it has the potential to amplify the problem, so hopefully our ACT defusion exercises don't carry this risk. As ACT practitioners we could still do cognitive restructuring - and if I do cognitive restructuring now it would be to get defusion - but this is very different to what I was shooting for with a distress reduction, thought-elimination goal of earlier days. Steve has outlined clearly the difference between ACT and CT as philosophical (pragmatism is part of ACT's philosophy), far more so than technological. It is the philosophy and theoretical framework that guides our timing, sequencing and selection of interventions. I'm not sure what CT could offer that ACT couldn't in addition to BT. I might predict the risk of further struggle and confusion by switching philosophical horses mid-therapy stream. Of course this is an empirical matter, but for now, maybe we should be mindful to package BT with ACT.
ACT cf. **CBT - comparisons; transitions; integration** **[10-24-02]** Steve Hayes	ACT Listserv Member wrote: ... any ideas out there re: linking ACT with CBT in psychological services? ... how are people seeing the two approaches co-existing? I'm personally a bit of a primary behaviourist and have never been whizzbanged by CBT, considering it to be a bit too medical and blaming in its approach, but it clearly works for a lot of people. ACT seems to me to be worlds away from CBT in terms of its conceptualisation of mental events and I suppose my worry would be patients getting angry (justifiably) if they've had a trial of ACT and not done well with it only to be sent to a CBT therapist who tells them the exact opposite re: how to manage their experience! .. my guess is that CBT largely works because of the defusion that results from distancing (in Beck's sense of that term) and because CBT folks ask people to do different things in the presence of noticed thoughts (e.g., to "test" them; to do homework). Those two moves are central in ACT. In CBT they are means to an end, but the impact is immediate. This was why we originally called ACT "Comprehensive Distancing." We thought we could just take these earliest moves and build them out to the extreme. That overlap, plus the movement of CBT into acceptance and mindfulness, plus the fact that ACT reduces believability of thoughts as a central process of change, makes it fairly easy to build a transition for CBT - ACT or ACT - CBT in agencies that can work together as a team. I think I would say something like this for CBT - ACT: "There are a variety of ideas about how people work, but one thing we know for sure -- if you get all entangled in negative thoughts and feelings, and put

your life on hold in the meanwhile, life tends not to move forward. The therapist you worked with before tried to help you get disentangled by looking at the content of these thoughts and feelings and by putting aside thoughts that were not rationally based. Those approaches have been helpful for some people, but for you it apparently was not fully satisfactory. I would suggest that we do something else entirely. Instead of trying to win that war so that you can move ahead in life, we will work on how to step out of it altogether."

I have used that rationale with former CBTers and it has always worked. If I was a CBTer who knew ACT and got an ACT failure to work with I might say: "There are a variety of ideas about how people work, but one thing we know for sure -- if you get all entangled in negative thoughts and feelings, and put your life on hold in the meanwhile, life tends not to move forward. The therapist you worked with before tried to help you get disentangled by letting go of these thoughts and feelings. That works for some people but for some others we simply have to try to work on their content as well. You can continue to use what you've learned if it works, but in here I want us to take the additional step to look at the actual basis of these thoughts." etc.

We've actually dabbled in integrated programs that contain all of this in one package. I don't think it is impossible. ACT will change thinking -- and quite rapidly. If you hold thoughts lightly you can mix the message. Something like this:

"The biggest harm from negative thoughts comes when we buy into them. It doesn't hurt to notice that some of the thoughts we buy into have little empirical support, are much too black and white [add your favorite cognitive distortion]. And we will do some of that work here -- so when we catch thinking of that kind, we will gently note that in addition to thinking that way we can also think another way. But we are historical creatures so even as we change what we think, old forms of thinking will hang around for a long time, and it's not always the best thing to be correcting every error as if that will stop the force of history. Maybe even more than catching all of our cognitive errors, it helps to notice that thoughts are thoughts. They are what they are, not what they say they are. So we will do some of that work in here too, because it will help us to move ahead -- even when thoughts and emotions occur that encourage us to do what does not work."

That mixed message can fit into either transition (ACT-CBT / CBT-ACT). By the way, all of these rationales are a bit more cognitive than I would normally do them, and they talk about things in a more specific way than I might early on. I'm not meaning for these to be said word for word but to point to a path ahead given the question asked (and given the desire to be brief in this context). I would put in more stuff about emotions / actions / values etc. in a normal context for example, and I ask more and listen more etc.

There is a larger message in here worth noting. While it is true that ACT has very different assumptions than some forms of CBT -- and apparently works by a different process -- I see little to be gained by trying to start wars within the behavioral camp broadly speaking. We are all empirical clinicians and wars are not good things.

That does not mean, however, that we should fail to see the differences -- especially when our science hats are on our heads. I think we should all keep our eyes open and try to work out what processes and methods are most helpful. As I look at CBT I see fairly little evidence that the "disputation" part makes much difference. The behavioral tests; distancing; and homework parts seem much more important -- and those I can explain from an ACT / RFT perspective. I think looking at CBT that way explains why Behavioral Activation is turning out to be as effective as CBT, and why there is such an early response to CBT.

Variants are emerging within CT itself (esp. MBCT, Borkovec, etc.) that also challenge the normal CBT model. The transition problems you speak of will eventually happen within shops dedicated entirely to CT.

ACT cf. **CBT - effect on content of thought/ feeling** **ACCEPTANCE** **No change in content of thought/ feeling, does not mean** **ANXIETY** **Panic - flying phobia**	Hank Robb wrote: If you think of flight phobics ... there are two issues: (1) not getting on airplanes; and (2) having stuff inside your skin that you would rather not have there when flying. The order of treatment operations has to be FIRST get on airplanes (move in the direction that you determine is important for you to move). Second, go on your travels more comfortably. ACT works great for number one but has nothing to offer for number two because, as far as I can see, ACT thinks of things inside your skin as just "how things are." I don't think it is correct to say that ACT has nothing to offer in this second area ... "acceptance" does not mean "things will not change" simply because it literally involves abandoning a change agenda. Getting present with what is going on is an active process. Functionally speaking, acceptance is the most radical form of change I know. A lot of the ACT book is focused on this very point (for example, how dramatic changes in content can come from acceptance and re-establish the original problematic context). In the specific area of plane travel: I used to have a neurotic fear of throwing up on planes (complete with panic, anticipation, avoidance etc.) which I dealt with by applying ACT principles. What ACT offers in the area of private events is exposure, extinction, response variability, values, and effective action, among others ... these are quite active processes. For example, ACT-based exposure may

EVIDENCE

Panic - emotion suppression/ acceptance [9-2-03]

Steve Hayes

Cross Reference:
See 1-38 for a later post in the thread:
EVIDENCE
Panic - emotion suppression/ acceptance

do a better job than some existing "exposure" programs because it helps remove obstacles (esp. fusion and avoidance) to effective exposure that pure exposure-based interventions do not. A recent study on exposure to bodily sensations in panic fits in with that idea. ("The Effects of Acceptance versus Suppression of Emotion on Subjective and Psychophysiological Response to Carbon Dioxide Challenge in Patients with Panic Disorder." The authors are Jill Levitt, Tim Brown, Sue Orsillo, & Dave Barlow.) ... 60 patients with panic disorder underwent a carbon dioxide challenge. 20 got a brief ACT-based acceptance orientation; 20 got a match suppression orientation; 20 read a story. The acceptance group was significantly less anxious and less avoidant than the suppression or control groups in terms of subjective anxiety and willingness to participate in a second gas challenge.

The idea that you have to consciously work to change things inside the skin or they will not change confuses form with function. In controlled studies ACT appears to move these internal measures as well or better than treatments that target them directly for change.

To go back to 1980. I'm afraid I will throw up on a plane. I'm focused on my internal sensations. They are linked verbally to an effort not to get sick, because it would be repulsive to spew chunks while stuck in the middle seat etc. I try not to think about spewing. But trying not to think that a) elicits spew-related thoughts and b) increases the importance of spew-related thoughts. Thus, trying not to think about spewing has both Crel and Cfunc effects. A question about traditional CBT: does a focus on the form or occurrence of thoughts increase the importance or decrease the importance of these thoughts? I have to think it increases the importance. This is the weak link in CBT, it seems to me. In the effort to make a Crel intervention work (think this, not that) they must simultaneously provide Cfuncs for these very thoughts (it is important what you think). ACT works directly on the Cfuncs, which it turns out, alters the network anyway but without that inconsistency. That doesn't mean that you can't do ACT-based work on the network itself, but RFT suggests it should be easier to do that in ways that do not increase the Cfunc impact of existing negative thoughts.

In my case, I started with accepting any and all emotions that might be associated with throwing up ... and committed to remaining present with them fully and without defense, whether I threw up or not. Thus, neither throwing up, nor the emotions I experienced about throwing up were held as consequences or matters of importance beyond noting their presence. When thoughts about throwing up came up, I watched them dispassionately for a moment and let whatever thought came next come next. I didn't argue back, believe them, deliberately distract myself, and so on. When bodily sensations emerged, I noted them and did whatever else was there to do (reading; resting; talking; watching movies), not to distract myself from the sensations, but merely to ride the plane. I avoided no flights. While I asked for an aisle seat (still do ... I just prefer it) if it got mixed up I welcomed being placed in the middle or at the window as an opportunity to feel what comes up when placed there. I did not take drugs. I did not avoid any trips. I noticed lots and lots of anticipatory fear and anxiety.

I had in fact actually thrown up on planes and the new forms of conditioning took some months to take hold. In the meantime I was flying and mostly it was not all that painful. Sometimes it was unpleasant or even extremely so (if you haven't felt the draining of your blood when a nausea/anxiety rush hits, you do not quite know what such a thing feels like ... it is not what you would call pleasant). Still, if you stay present, it is as alive a moment as any other.

Full extinction took years as new situations were encountered (e.g., extremely rough rides; riding while having the flu; riding while packed in like a sausage). I still occasionally (once a year?) have a throw up related thought, but it is empty and devoid of any punch. Usually it evokes only a smile.

ACT is a context for behavior therapy. If I was devising an ACT intervention for flying I would include lots of deliberate exposure, but I would make clear that the purpose is not to remove these feelings, bodily sensations, or thoughts, but to practice seeing them as they are and to practice letting go of their "importance" or the need to avoid them. Ironically (and I would not say this initially) this is exactly the place from which change in content is particularly likely.

To my mind, this *is* a form of ACT.

This will all be worked out empirically. ACT-based exposure treatments are coming. I don't know if ACT will move people more or less than other treatments in the "number two" areas, but so far it looks good and it does seem incorrect to say that ACT offers nothing in this area, as if the ACT message is "content will not change, so just slog ahead." Content is actually very likely to change, particularly when we remove the self-amplifying effects that rule-governed change efforts can provide. The paradox is clear, but it is one that comes from the old form / function issue when human language is involved.

ACT cf.

CBT - effect on content of thought/ feeling [cont'd]

Hank Robb wrote:

Steve makes some points I would greatly agree with but I think in doing so sneaks CBT (or to my mind REBT in particular) back in, which is GREAT with me. Here's how. Yes things will change. But to do something FOR THE PURPOSE OF ACHIEVING CHANGE is not to abandon the change agenda. So

ACCEPTANCE No change in content of thought/ feeling, does not mean [cont'd] **DEFINITION/ INTERPRETATION** **Belief [9-3-03]** Patty Bach	ACT can't go straight up on the problem. ... in fact, to get the changes Steve experienced, he states he intentionally stopped BELIEVING certain things. Before change is possible one usually must abandon the change agenda - put down the shovel. It seems to me that there is a change agenda in successful ACT; however I doubt it is ever the same change agenda that the client walked in the door with - "I need more confidence"; "I have to make the anxiety go away"; etc. These are the unworkable agendas that are abandoned. It is interesting to consider the etymology of "believe"; it is from the Germanic 'belieben' which means 'to hold dear' and the Latin 'libido' - love, desire. Thus, belief was originally not so much about objective truth or fact as about holding dear, loving (attachment?). This reminds me somewhat of the ACT discussion about confidence as a feeling versus as a quality of action. It seems that belief may be regarded somewhat similarly. Choosing not to believe a thought is then not to question its objective truth so much as to stop holding it as dear to let go of attachment to it. It seems to me that not believing a thought is not the same as changing the thought. Not believing a thought means ceasing to hold onto it as dear (function); changing a belief means replacing one belief with another (content). You might say that one "changes belief (verb)" as changed action in relation to content, rather than that one "changes beliefs (noun)" as changed content. Effective action does not require that a belief such as "That would be awful" is replaced with "That would not be awful," instead one moves forward with the thought "that would be awful" and doesn't hold onto the thought so dearly; it is acknowledged and let go of. One must let go of belief before beliefs can change just as one must act with confidence before one feels confidence or must put down the shovel before a new tool can be picked up.
ACT cf. CBT - effect on content of thought/ feeling [cont'd] Tuna Townsend	... As I see it, CBT/REBT is distinguished from ACT by the fundamental difference in focus on content or context, respectively. I believe (using the word advisedly) that the effectiveness of REBT/CBT derives from the client's ability to defuse from their maladaptive beliefs/cognitions; and that this is accomplished, in effect, by multiple-exemplar training, piecemeal, by addressing the content of specific beliefs/cognitions. Although the client may believe that they are extirpating problematic thoughts/beliefs (or even problematic cognitive styles/habits generally), the result is to instill a healthy 'distrust' of the automaticity of one's own 'mind'... I have no doubt that it is effective, but I'm unconvinced that it is as efficient as it might be. By contrast, ACT (and mindfulness-type training in general) seeks to undermine the process by which maladaptive beliefs/cognitions take hold in the first place, and the process by which they influence our behavior generally. The subtle-but-important difference is that content is addressed in a fundamentally different way. I really don't mean any of this as an "ACT is better than CBT" argument - but by way of pointing out that it appears to me that they are doing very much the same thing; and that the functional/contextual focus in ACT may be doing it more efficiently. So I guess I _am_ saying that ACT is better than CBT....
ACT cf. **CBT - personal impact on therapist [7-16-03]** Matthew Smout	Joseph Ciarrochi wrote: 　We train therapists in 2nd wave CBT at our university. I have always been struck by two observations: 1) many graduating therapists don't seem very inspired by the approach; and 2) they don't seem to apply much of the CT part to their own lives. ... I found learning CT quite difficult initially, which struck fear into my heart at the start because I wondered "If it's cumbersome for me, what's it going to be like for a client whose head is already full?" I was impressed by the apparent boom of outcome studies - particularly the panic control studies and was excited by the prospect that this technology could make a difference. Once I stepped out of univ. into practice - it became apparent that clients rarely if ever were inspired to do DTRs for homework, rarely "restructured" their automatic thoughts the way CT would have them, and particularly in the midst of distress, were rarely inclined to analyse their thoughts. This led me to become pessimistic that cognitive therapy worked by the mechanisms it was theorized. Behavioural activation and the therapeutic relationship stuff seemed far more potent. ACT initially inspired me mostly because I think it's true. ACT doesn't make promises that you're scared the clients' experiences won't match like CT. After seeing Kelly's workshop, I saw an even bigger picture - and experienced the value of valuing in a richer way than intellectual understanding.
ACT cf. CBT - personal impact on therapist [cont'd] ACT Listserv Member	... I agree with you Joseph, after graduating from the clinical masters, I didn't feel inspired by the CBT approach that we were taught to use with clients. I did use it in my own life to a limited extent, but this didn't affect my life in any major way. In fact I wonder if this is one of the appeals of the CBT approach (as it was taught to me in my masters program) that it is not something that you need apply to your life as a

	therapist. It is much less confronting that way, and you get to pretend to be an expert into the bargain!
	I came away from Kelly's workshop with the feeling that ACT makes a whole lot of sense to me. I now have a taste of how wonderful it would be to be delivering a therapy that I could believe in whole-heartedly (rather than mouthing some rationale which I don't really believe but which I hope will convince my clients to do what I ask). To be honest, I feel I'm on the cusp of something that could change my life, and the lives of my clients....
ACT cf. CBT - personal impact on therapist [cont'd] Eric Morris	I trained in Australia but now work in the UK. My observation is that over here CBT is synonymous with clinical psychology, so much so that a trainee I have jokes that on her doctoral course they get exposed to "both kinds of therapy, cognitive AND behavioural" (much like hearing both kinds of music played in Texas, country AND western).
	Maybe as a result of its dominance, or perhaps because of contact with the contingencies of doing therapy(!), amongst trainees I have talked to the CBT focus does not seem to inspire great enthusiasm, even if it seems like it is a technology that is popular and valued by consumers and managers.
	I think that ACT dramatically changes your perspective (hmm, self-evident perhaps) as a therapist, especially if you have been trained as a CBT therapist. It is hard to go back to cognitive restructuring and 2nd wave CBT when experientially you have discovered that thoughts work in a different way to what is predicted from the cognitive model(s). Another colleague of mine described reading the ACT book as like getting some form of mind virus that alters the functions of talking about thinking - because "life works by addition" she can't go back to 2nd wave CBT; her experience of it has been fundamentally changed (perhaps Kelly and Steve like the sound of that?!).
	ACT does inspire enthusiasm and I think a sense of freedom as a therapist because the perspective is radical/ fundamental in a way that 2nd wave CBT isn't. I don't think that this is just due to therapists looking for a "new thing" for the sake of it, but because CBT therapists already have experienced the limitations of content-level intervention and ACT provides a way out of that quagmire.
ACT cf. **CBT - transition from/ use alongside ACT** **THERAPIST** **CBT, transition from/ use of ACT alongside** **METAPHOR** **Fusion/ defusion - mind's sales pitch [8-28-03]** ACT Listserv Member	Leslie Telfer wrote: The obstacle [to my practicing ACT] is my fear of not doing it right. When I've tried to do it, I've gotten tangled up in the client's content and fallen back on safe and familiar strategies, which gets us way off course. I'm also ambivalent about the ethics of doing a therapy that I don't feel well-grounded in yet ... How have other people gotten started doing the actual therapy?
	... At the time I got involved with ACT I was a committed CBTer. I was committed not only because of the results with my clients, but also the results of utilizing it with my own tricky, and frequently unkind, mind. Two things happened, though. The first, is that I noticed in myself, after a year or two, that my own cognitive challenging was much less effective than it had initially been. To be blunt, it just didn't <u>work</u> that well for me anymore. And I also noticed this with some of my clients. It seems like initially, the mind welcomes this new challenging and for a time it brings relief. However, as ACT so poignantly stresses, the mind works additively, and it seems like the mind simply habituates to your cognitive challenging and you are back at square one. The second facet of my switch to ACT revolved around my own powerful interest in Eastern thought/Castaneda and wanting to live my life to the fullest, and in freedom. In other words, having the fewest points to defend. To discover a rigorously tested and incredibly thought out theory/therapy that paralleled this was really exciting.
	The change wasn't immediate, though. What I began doing was using CBT as a first-line therapy and, if it didn't work, to then try ACT. Eventually, I reversed this order, until finally I couldn't bring myself to utilize cognitive restructuring, as it felt like I was colluding with the verbal community at large, which is antithetical to the way I want to live my life. I remember listening to a CBT therapist, who was transitioning to ACT but was still holding on, as he argued with Steve about CBT. REM's "Losing my Religion" popped into my head and I knew just how he felt.
	As to feeling relatively competent with doing ACT, Steve's suggestion of reading transcripts makes a lot of sense. At the time I started, that option wasn't available and I found that reading the book was the key. Several times. Each time I understood it at a deeper level and I just learned to think more from that perspective. The techniques, exercises, and metaphors, also begin to become more and more second nature.
	Despite all this, I still struggle with my mind's fears about driving away clients. To be honest, I have never really taken the plunge with regards to implementing Creative Hopelessness with clients. Also, I haven't screwed up the courage to do the Milk, Milk, Milk exercise, in my thin-walled office, next to my ten other colleagues' offices. My own passengers are certainly alive and well...
	With regards to defusion, one technique that I use is to help the client look at thoughts, feelings, etc... in terms of sales pitches. Then I can say, "your mind's really selling that thought well, huh?", or "that one's pretty easy to buy, isn't it." Or you can throw in some witty repartee about getting your shirts whiter, or changing phone companies. I find this a useful adjunct to the core chessboard and bus passenger metaphors.

ACT cf. CBT - transition from/ use alongside ACT [cont'd] Jonathan Kandell	At the risk of going against "the religion" :-), I think CBT and ACT can work together. CBT works for those aspects of internal experiences which are able to be controlled, ACT for those aspects which can't. (Why make room for something painful if you don't have to?) In looking at internal and external barriers, some can be lessened, others gone around; still others can't. The former can be controlled, the latter need to be accepted. I guess I'm more of a "serenity prayer" ACTer than a more radical devotee. And don't forget the choice of willingness is itself a cognitive step-- sometimes you have to remind yourself to be willing again and again, e.g., remembering the right metaphor. (Marsha Linehan emphasizes this in DBT.) ACT has influenced my CBT though: I now emphasize with clients that CBT is not designed to eliminate unpleasant automatic thoughts or emotions as they emerge-- they will happen as they will. But wise thought at that point can lower the amplification of unpleasant emotions (i.e., "dirty discomfort"). So CBT can involve a lot of acceptance.
ACT cf. **CBT/ MBCT; ACT approach to CBT** **[9-30-04]** Scott Gaynor	Mary Politi wrote: Does anyone have any suggestions for ways to incorporate ACT without deviating from the [CBT] manual too much? At the last AABT Zindel Segal (Mindfulness-based CT) did a presentation where he suggested that teaching clients to evaluate the evidence for negative thoughts and coming up with more rational thoughts based on the evidence (e.g., by using the Thought Record -- the main disputational device in cognitive therapy) may help, at least in part, because it allows clients to experience negative thoughts as simply mental events, rather than as the self. They (e.g., Teasdale, Segal) call this metacognitive awareness. So even if the classical CT perspective is on changing content, an important side effect of the process (underappreciated in the classical, second-generation approach) may be changing the relationship to the negative thoughts (i.e., their function) rather than changing their content per se. In my lab a grad student and I have been treating college students with significantly elevated depressive symptoms and low self-esteem using only the thought record (in one of the study conditions). We are doing it as close as possible to how it is presented by Persons et al. in their book and videos. We are finding that not only do we get significant improvement on measures like the ATQ and DAS, but also the AAQ, consistent with Segal's suggestion. What this suggests to me for your situation is that in the context of the disputational approach make sure to also play up the parts that promote self as perspective (the observer self), help clients discriminate thoughts as thoughts (and not facts) and distinguish evaluations from descriptions (standard ACT moves). So it may be that even within the disputational approach, important defusion work can be done in the sense of clients seeing thoughts as ideas and opinions colored by their history rather than objective facts. It is not full blown ACT, but you can try to highlight the areas where some overlap exists. This it seems to me is the way third generation CT is going anyway. Indeed, in an in press article in BRAT on metacognitive awareness in CBT, Fennell describes moving clients from their "old perspective" of "I am bad/ useless/ inadequate" etc. to a "new perspective" of "I am a normal human being but I believe that I am bad." This involves components of self as perspective work (ACT), a replacement thought (classical CT) and an accompanying recognition of "I am bad" as an evaluation not a description (ACT). ACT is much further along the path (so it feels to you like doing standard CBT moves is a step back) and ACT is grounded in a much better underlying theory, but at the technical level there is clearly some convergence that you might build on to function in your current context.
ACT cf. CBT/ MBCT; ACT approach to CBT [cont'd] Steve Hayes	Not sure I have a solution, but if you can forgive me Mary for noting the conflict for another purpose: I can't count how many times CBT folks have challenged ACT on the grounds that it is nothing new. (These are always folks who have not been to an ACT workshop ... somehow people can read a little ACT stuff and come to that conclusion, which has ever been a puzzle for me.) Earth to traditional cognitive behavior therapy: It is not the same, in fact, in some areas it gets close to a direct conflict. Your very difficulty shows the problem.
ACT cf. CBT/ MBCT; ACT approach to CBT [cont'd] Mary Englert	When I've woven ACT in with traditional CBT manualized approaches, I use the "Fight the Thoughts" step to simply help the client gain greater perspective that these intrusive and ever present thoughts have no evidence behind them. The thoughts can then more easily be viewed as used car salesmen desperate to make a sale. Even with kids, I use Rapee's "Detective Thinking" to expose the frauds. This step segues nicely into ACT stances of noticing these thoughts, seeing them as uninvited guests; who are trustworthy anyway - these thoughts or your experience and evidence?
ACT cf. CBT/ MBCT; ACT approach to CBT [cont'd] Jonathan Kanter	There are ways you can do CBT and be ACT-consistent up to a point. This requires, first and foremost, abandoning the change-private-events agenda that lies at the heart of CBT. Then, you selectively pick certain interventions, such as behavioral activation and cognitive defusion (e.g., asking your client, "How much do you believe that thought?", treating thoughts as hypotheses rather than facts) which are

	components of CT that are fairly easy to work into an ACT conceptualization (although not perfectly).
	However I have found this approach to be more work than it is worth. And, at the point you are at with your group, when you are about to starting disputing, challenging, and changing thoughts, there is really no way to be ACT consistent. Like Steve says, it is simply a conflict. So I think you are in a real bind.
	I personally really appreciate that bind. I have been teaching both CBT for depression and ACT to my students (my research focuses on how to improve CBT for depression with a behavior analytic/ functional contextualistic model) and we all feel the bind. I personally like inhabiting the space of that contradiction - really challenging the students to try the CBT change agenda full throttle and the ACT acceptance agenda full throttle (with different clients) because it is the best way for them to really grow as therapists. I don't want them to simply believe me when I say "ACT is right and CBT is wrong" - I want them to struggle with it, experience it in their own lives, work it out, be confused again, and so on. Then they really get that CBT and ACT are different in a very fundamental way, even if there are aspects of CBT that may be consistent with ACT at certain times.
	I emphasize "world views" to them and state my own preference, which is that it is better to pick a world view and try it on completely and fully, then pick another and try that one on, than it is to be eclectic, where you just throw interventions together even if the interventions are theoretically incompatible.
	When I do CBT-change agenda with my clients I am similar. I don't say what the Beck book tells me to ("If you just keep at it, you will learn to change your thoughts and you will feel better"). Instead, when a client is really committed to the change agenda I say, "O.K. let's try this out, and as we do so we need to really stay in contact with our experience of if it is working for you in both the short run and the long run." Then I really try to commit to the change agenda full throttle, become as much of a true believer while I'm doing it as I can (value with my feet, I guess, but that needs more explanation I think), and trust the experience. If I do the CBT-change agenda only half-heartedly than I'm wasting everyone's time, because neither I nor my client is going to learn much from an experience that was set up to fail. My stance is something like, "Well, if, for whatever reason, I find myself in the position where I'm going to do this intervention which doesn't really fit my world view, what can I do to really make the most of this experience for my client?" This of course is easier said than done.
	These experiences almost always have the effect of reinforcing my belief in the ACT model. But not always; and that's when things get really interesting. That's what I like about this work: no easy answers.
ACT cf. CBT/ MBCT; ACT approach to CBT [cont'd] Patty Bach	One of the many things that has stuck with me from a class in my first year of grad school was some of Steve's comments about "eclecticism." To loosely paraphrase, 'technical eclecticism' is fine while 'theoretical eclecticism' is problematic, and one is most effective clinically when interventions - no matter how eclectic - are based on a single, coherent theory of behavior/ behavior change.
	E.g., Physicalizing, "Milk, milk, milk," the Observer exercise and many others used in ACT originated within different traditions. And an ACT therapist might use the Two Chair technique, Free-association or any number of interventions and still be doing ACT. These interventions are 'technically eclectic' and they are unified functionally/theoretically in the context of ACT therapy with a given client.
ACT cf. **DBT - Borderline Personality Disorder clients** **PERSONALITY DISORDER** **Borderline - ACT/DBT; use of ACT interventions [1-29-04]** Ann Bailey	My colleague and I run a Borderline Personality Disorders Clinic. We worked purely from a DBT perspective until we discovered ACT. We now weave ACT expressive techniques around the containing, more supportive DBT components.
	Our question relates to the issue of the extreme identity disturbance found in the Borderline client and the use of the observer exercise. We were nervous about trying it out, but did on our clients who have almost finished the 12 month program. We decided to use the exercise as we feel DBT does not address the central issue of identity disturbance and self-fragmentation in the Borderline Population.
	Our observations were that the exercise was very powerful. The clients understood the concept, achieved great insight, however, in some cases felt extremely threatened by it. Their insight did not serve to change much. In fact their new awareness seemed to highlight their level of fragmentation, rather than highlighting the constancy of the 'observer self.'
	We have trialed this exercise with anxiety-disordered clients and had very different responses. Obviously, BPD is far more complex and we would not expect similar results but our questions are as follows:
	1. Is the observer exercise too 'hot' a technique to be used with clients with such extreme identity disturbance?
	2. Do you feel ACT alone is too expressive a technique to use without the containing element of DBT with Borderline clients?

ACT cf. DBT - Borderline Personality Disorder clients [cont'd] PERSONALITY DISORDER Borderline - ACT/DBT; use of ACT interventions [cont'd] Jacqueline Pistorello	I have been applying ACT and DBT independently as well as in conjunction. The archives contain a prior message I posted on this issue, where I elaborated in more detail.... [see below] My basic stance of when to use full-blown ACT with someone diagnosed with Borderline PD is that: - the client is no longer in stage 1 (severe safety issues); or - there have been multiple treatment failures, including DBT, applied competently. I find it hard to justify using full-blown ACT with this population as a first resort when DBT has been empirically validated already. Although it is obviously an empirical question. I have successfully transitioned clients from DBT into ACT when they stabilize some and have come to see the two not only as compatible but also as complementary. In terms of bringing elements of ACT into DBT treatment: I do that regularly in my practice, particularly in terms of metaphors, defusion, values, and explanation of concepts. I typically stay away from "heavy" experiential exercises (e.g., child within) and any paradoxical components (e.g., "What you hear me saying is not what I am saying"). I have successfully utilized some mindfulness exercises that require an observer perspective (e.g., giving shape and size to a feeling or a thought) for the sake of defusion and emotional regulation. Depending on people's reactions to this type of exercise, I proceed further. I do not start out with the observer exercise, for reasons you have alluded to. I rely on the bus or the chessboard metaphor instead to instill that sense of "observer self." It is more concrete and visually accessible. Eyes closed exercises can be dysregulating with this population, particularly for those with a trauma history. Interestingly, just last night I was at a meditation group where the issue of "no self" in Buddhism came up. The speaker pointed out that you must have some sense of self to be able to "transcend" it. It might be a developmental issue, where only after achieving some sense of ground can one experience groundlessness as it is. In that sense, the observer exercise might be "too much" for someone in Stage 1 of DBT. I believe (although others disagree) that this is one of the conceptual differences between ACT and DBT: ACT assumes that the person "has everything she needs" to move forward whereas DBT relies heavily on the idea of skills deficits that need to be addressed....
ACT cf. **DBT - coping skills/ control vs. acceptance (BPD)** **PERSONALITY DISORDER** **Borderline - ACT/DBT; coping skills vs. acceptance [9-4-03]** Victoria Follette	Scott Temple wrote: Lots of [my group] patients are not only affect-phobic, but they rather quickly and impulsively employ maladaptive coping responses, or safety behaviors.... I find that I begin working first to shore up alternative coping skills, such as early identification of affects, and employing coping skills before escalation into maladaptive safety behaviors. I know that might only bolster the sense that feelings are 'dangerous.' However, my sense is that some of these patients are so phobic and so impulsive, that perhaps they need coping skills first. Several of us … have worked on this clinically and are trying to measure it in the lab to clarify the issues. This is why we have used DBT skills as an adjunct to our ACT work. Because of dialectics we are able to work within the acceptance and change framework. I find that some of our people come with such a weak repertoire of coping skills that they are not ready for the full ACT work; this is controversial I know, but it has been our clinical experience with trauma survivors who have some BPD issues, or complex PTSD depending on your thoughts on those issues. We have worked hard not to invalidate basic ACT concepts but doing the skills and it seems to work - a number of cases have gone very well this way. On another note, I have used ACT to get myself in airplanes and it has worked but that is a really long story.
ACT cf. DBT - coping skills/ control vs. acceptance (BPD) [cont'd] PERSONALITY DISORDER Borderline - ACT/DBT; coping skills vs. acceptance [cont'd] Jacqueline Pistorello	I have been using both ACT and DBT in my practice at a counseling center, and have been experimenting with combining (or not) these two treatments for the last five years. Having been ACT-trained first and DBT-trained later, I was originally very uncomfortable with the idea of relying on any control-based strategy (e.g., distraction, self-soothing) directed at private events when using DBT. I had lots of ambivalence about suggesting things like watching a comedy when one is feeling depressed in order to "change the emotional state." Since working with folks presenting with BPD features on a regular basis, I've found some ways of dealing with this clinically (more later). I've been writing and revising a paper comparing ACT and DBT for a few years now, in conjunction with Alan Fruzzetti and in consultation with Steve H., as it seems to have become an area of immediate interest/need to folks. One of my conclusions is that, along with ACT's emphasis on defusion, the handling of private events (e.g., acceptance versus control), at least in terms of what is "said/done in session," is the main difference between ACT and DBT. ACT, in session, is often all about bringing an accepting posture towards private events (more on that below). DBT advocates a dialectical perspective, with both control and

acceptance strategies being encouraged, with effectiveness being the ultimate gauge.

I have a few thoughts about why there is this difference between the two: one has to do with differences in population and the other with differences in theory.

There is the obvious fact that DBT was particularly designed for individuals (women) diagnosed with BPD. And, as you and Victoria have stated, the issue of dealing with private events may be different when people get so close to the "edge."

I have some data that pertains to this. In collaboration with other colleagues, I have administered the Thought Control Questionnaire (TCQ, by Davies and Wells) to two different samples: a college student sample and a sample of women presenting to a DBT partial hospital. The TCQ has a subscale called Distraction. When I looked at the relationship of distraction to measures of psychological distress (SCL-90) among these two samples, I found that distraction was significantly and negatively correlated with psychological distress in the BPD sample ($r = -.32$) but not in the college sample ($r = .00$). However, when I looked at means, the college sample scored significantly higher on distraction than the BPD sample. My interpretation of these findings is that distraction, within a sample that is significantly less likely to be able to distract, may have a salutary impact. However, as distraction increases (perhaps as it becomes more pervasive and generalized), it loses its utility. [These are correlational data, however, so all the usual limitations of this type of data apply here.]

Considering that both ACT and DBT are based on a functionalist philosophical stance, talked in terms of "workability" in ACT and "effectiveness" in DBT, the issue of addressing control vs. acceptance of private events, in both treatments, is based on what works. I believe that, it is not that in ACT, control in any private events area is always problematic. In theory, we target areas in which control has not been working and it is possible that in some areas more "control-based" strategies may be working just fine for the individual. However, what I find is that NOT to confront (directly or indirectly) in session any and all attempts to control private events in ACT has the potential impact of inadvertently reinforcing fusion and perpetuating non-acceptance in areas where acceptance is called for. Because the control agenda is so pervasive in society and difficult to budge clinically, intervention needs to be relentless in this area. Basically, I think that the ACT approach of challenging IN SESSION any and all control attempts directed at private events, is based on workability in moving the client, not on an all-or-nothing "rule" that "control is 'bad.'" It has to do with the theory behind ACT of how to bring about meaningful change.

In ACT we talk about applying control in areas where it works (outside) and not in areas where it doesn't work (inside the skin). However, I've come to think that some contextual control could be applied to the world inside the skin, given a high level of mindfulness of one's private events and workability of one's "moves." I guess it all boils down to the function of the behavior. Topographically, even following one's breath could be a "control-based" approach, whereas going for a run when one is distraught could also function as either a control or an acceptance-based move.

The data I presented above would suggest that some control-based strategies such as distraction (assuming that people are not distracting by cutting or drinking, for example) might be "effective" with folks who are severely distraught. However, even when coaching clients on using skills such as distraction in DBT, I emphasize the need to do so mindfully and keeping effectiveness in mind. Also, when clients come up with a crisis plan that involves control-based approaches in DBT, I say something like: "For now, this is OK, but eventually, we will need to look at that and see if there is a more effective approach to take to this in the long term." In my experience so far, for individuals with BPD features, I start out with a DBT approach and switch to an ACT approach later. Recently, I've interviewed a client who followed this order of treatments, and she noted that she does not think she would have been able to do the "other" group (an ACT group) before she had done the skills group. She said something like: "I don't think I could have even asked myself about values when I didn't even know when/if I was sad." To come back to Scott's question, could severely distraught folks "tolerate" an acceptance-only approach in terms of private events? I think it is an empirical question. However, when it comes to treating chronically suicidal, BPD folks, I find it hard to justify not starting out with an approach that has been empirically validated for that population (DBT in this situation).

I agree with Scott that BPD folks are almost like "expert suppressors" (a term I first heard from Elizabeth Simpson--Liz, are you there?) and I have some data to suggest that might indeed be the case. My dissertation involved instructing 51 women diagnosed with BPD to suppress, accept, or monitor a personally-relevant unwanted thought (following the typical thought suppression methodology: Participants are told "do X for 5 minutes," then everyone is "released" from instructions and can do whatever). There were two interesting findings. First, even when instructed to accept the unwanted thought, these folks found themselves trying to suppress it some of the time (according to self-report: "how much did you try to suppress the thought?"). During debriefing at the end of the study, those in the suppression group would often say "I found it very easy to do it. I do this all the time." Basically, acceptance of unwanted private events is VERY difficult to do for folks in this much suffering. Second, although individuals reported significantly less subjective distress on the suppression condition (relative to both acceptance and

	monitoring), they talked more during the second 5 minutes (relative to acceptance condition), when they were no longer asked to suppress, accept, or monitor. Basically, this points to the "cost" of suppression, I believe. Yep, one may be able to suppress and it may even feel "better," but one needs to talk non-stop to keep the thought away! AND, later, at the end of the study, the women instructed to suppress who were LOW on a measure of experiential acceptance (AAQ), actually found a coloring task LESS pleasant. Again, suppression may "work" in the short term, but it has a cost, even for folks who are highly distressed.
	I keep these findings in mind when instructing control-based strategies for BPD folks, and sometimes share these findings with them.
	Despite the length of this message, I still feel that I've only touched the surface on this issue...
ACT cf. **DBT - types of mind (DBT) cf. senses of self (ACT) [cont'd]** **Mark Webster** *Cross Reference:* *See 4-165 for an earlier post in this thread*	The DBT mindfulness skills are split into the 'how' skills - observe, describe, participate - and the 'what' skills - non-judgemental, one-minded, effective. Being effective is about pursuing valued goals, as in ACT. Wise mind, emotion mind and reasonable mind tend to be used as tools or even a metaphor to quickly orient the patient to think about the state of their mind. It is a simple form of distancing, perhaps, as a first incremental step to an observer position. This more atomistic approach of DBT is useful with difficult patients, such as the Personality Disorders.
ACT cf. DBT - types of mind (DBT) cf. senses of self (ACT) [cont'd] John Blackledge	... At a technique level, I wonder if the "wise mind" concept might confuse things a bit if used in ACT. It carries (at least for me) the connotation of rationality, logic, etc.--all things typically associated with the word machine we're trying to unhook ACT clients from. I'm sure my caricature of wise mind here differs from the proper way DBT therapists use it, but I'm simply concerned that to use the phrase in a therapy where "mind" is something to step back and unhook from in problematic situations might breed confusion rather than clarity--regardless of how carefully the distinction between "mind" as generally discussed in ACT and "wise mind" is presented to the client.
ACT cf. DBT - types of mind (DBT) cf. senses of self (ACT) [cont'd] Jonathan Kanter	Some more thoughts on mindfulness and "wise mind" in DBT vs. acceptance and distancing in ACT: As Pat said, it is mostly a mistake to equate the three senses of self in ACT with the three types of mind in DBT. They don't map too well, although there is some overlap. "Reasonable mind" and "emotion mind" are basically examples of cognitive fusion so they map onto self-as-content. DBT is much more judgemental about this stuff than is ACT: reasonable mind is generally seen as good; however it is hard to act from reasonable mind when one is emotional. A certain amount of emotion mind is also ok; however BPD clients are in it much too often. Basically, reasonable mind is when self-as-content works and emotion mind is when it doesn't. "Wise mind" maps onto self-as-context and in fact many of the DBT mindfulness techniques are similar to ACT techniques and metaphors in this stage. When I was learning DBT I often came in to group therapist meetings with ACT exercises and they were always well received. As Mark said, the "how" and "what" DBT skills are easily incorporated into ACT, and have a similar feel. I'm sure Steve and Marsha cite at least some common sources to these aspects of treatment. That is, DBT skills are easily incorporated into ACT at least at the level of technique, with some minor changes in language to fit the rest of the treatment. For example, I agree with J.T. that the use of the term "wise mind" can be problematic in ACT if there is a history of using "mind" to represent cognitive fusion, as in "thank your mind for that." The term "mind" is so loaded with meaning in our culture; the ACT usage undermines and exploits this while DBT does not challenge the common usage. Of course, we don't want to define our treatments by our terminology; ACT can be done without using the term "mind" and still be ACT. At a theoretical level, however, I think there are some problems with the integration. The ACT approach is so completely theoretically and philosophically consistent that, when DBT is viewed through an ACT lens, it falls apart a bit. The DBT emphasis on dialectics, for example, I think unnecessarily complicates things; ACT simplifies. For example, "wise mind" is described as a dialectical integration of "emotion" and "reasonable" mind, as wise mind "depends upon the integration of all ways of knowing something." The term "integration" is strange and doesn't quite work in this context but is in keeping with the idea of the dialectic, which of course is important to DBT. The ACT distinction between selves, to me, and the emphasis on self-as-context is much more straightforward and leads more directly to clinical techniques.

ACT cf. DBT - types of mind (DBT) cf. senses of self (ACT) [cont'd] Patty Bach	"Translating" terms from one therapy approach to another is as challenging as translating idioms from one language to another! It does seem that in practice and at the technique level, 'wise mind' shares features with self-as-context. And at the level of description, the way 'wise mind' is described, as an integration of emotion and reasonable mind, it can then only be more content. Metaphorically, if context is the 'board' and content 'the pieces,' say 'emotion mind' the black pieces, and 'reasonable mind' the white pieces, then 'wise mind' is described as sort of "the best of the black and white pieces." It seems that ACT would both 'integrate' the different 'minds' in the sense of accepting not trying to avoid them - "I accept them as content," and diffuse and deliteralize - "I am not my thoughts or emotions (or 'minds')."
ACT cf. DBT - types of mind (DBT) cf. senses of self (ACT) [cont'd] **FUSION/ DEFUSION** **Meaning of [4-30-03]** ACT Listserv Member	I see a problem with the mapping of "emotion mind" onto cognitive fusion, although it makes sense to do so with "reasonable mind." In ACT, while we talk about private events in a broad sense to include more than cognitions, when we talk about fusion or defusion it invariably becomes "cognitive." Is the implication that underlying all emotion is a conscious appraisal process at work? Emotion theorists such as Zajonc and others have made a persuasive case for pre-cognitive judgments in emotions and situations where emotion has "primacy." Findings from neural science from LeDoux among others also point to dual pathways into the limbic system, ergo supporting the phenomenon of primacy of emotion. If this were so, wouldn't we need to consider "emotional fusion" and apply defusion interventions as appropriate? Isn't DBT about defusion from emotion? If I feel it must be true... Separately, if sensations can be viewed as a separate system from subjective experience, perhaps we could consider "interoceptive fusion"!
ACT cf. DBT - types of mind (DBT) cf. senses of self (ACT) [cont'd] FUSION/ DEFUSION Meaning of [cont'd] Jonathan Kanter *Cross Reference:* *See 3-107 to 3-110 for later posts in the thread:* *FUSION/ DEFUSION* *Meaning of*	When I said emotion mind and reasonable mind are cognitive fusion and thus map on to self-as-content, it perhaps would have been more straightforward to not equate them both with cognitive fusion but instead simply state that they exemplify self-as-content. As you suggest, equating emotion mind with cognitive fusion requires some explanation. As you suggest, I actually do think more in terms of fusion with private events as a general category than cognitive vs. emotional fusion. We don't really want to do a microscopic analysis of "was that a thought?" or "was that a feeling?" Without agreeing with cognitive primacy people like Kihlstrom, I think we can say that any experience of emotion will have a verbal component, at least historically, as in learning to label the emotion, etc. The bidirectional nature of verbal stimuli, and transformation of function, suggests that any given "thought" may have respondent (emotional) qualities, and any given "emotion" may have verbal qualities. It is this constantly active, thinking, feeling, whirling (monkey) "mind" we try to defuse from/accept. It is a bit of a jumble. That said, if we are doing ACT traditionally from start to finish, the cognitive defusion/deliteralization exercises are distinct from and come before the emotional acceptance exercises, and that is because this distinction and the staging are often useful. We deliteralize/defuse from thoughts in order to facilitate the non-evaluative experience of emotion from a self-as-context perspective. In DBT, this experience of emotion from a self-as-context perspective is "wise mind," not "emotion mind," while when you are fused and not accepting and your emotions are in control, you are in "emotion" mind.
ACT cf. **DBT; ACT/DBT synthesis [2-23-05]** Ann Bailey	Jason Gosnell wrote: Has anybody worked up a synthesis of ACT and DBT for PTSD-Borderline work? I wonder if they would complement each other or if DBT is sufficient and there is no need to integrate. Within our clinic we work with Borderline Personality Disorder which is a 12 month program comprising group and individual therapy, and have created a synthesised ACT/DBT group program which we have been using for some time. In answer to your questions: Is DBT alone sufficient? From our experience the answer is no, we feel there is the need to integrate DBT/ACT for a number of reasons (this is not based on anything empirical as yet). Because you are working with people who engage in experiential avoidance through very harmful means, cutting, burning etc., our experience has shown us that using ACT alone is too 'expressive' or 'hot' a technique for such clients in the initial phase of therapy. Exposing to intense affect early on runs the risk of self harm increasing due to the Borderlines' tendency to experientially avoid this way. Thus, basic distress tolerance skills need to be acquired so that harmful avoidance can be replaced with less harmful avoidance. However, once this has been achieved, the second phase of our program focuses on ACT experiential techniques of contacting internal experiences so that the clients can change their relationship to their feelings, rather than just 'tolerate' them. We feel that this is not emphasised enough in DBT and is crucial for clients with this

diagnosis (or any other). We think of the synthesis of these approaches in line with supportive / expressive continuum, DBT providing the supportive, containing aspect of therapy, while ACT providing the expressive. We alternate the delivery of the ACT / DBT modules during the 12 months, starting with a greater emphasis on DBT distress tolerance as discussed earlier to keep things balanced.

The other nice crossover between the two approaches is the DBT core mindfulness skills and the self-as-context ACT interventions. Ultimately, we are trying to help the Borderline client develop their reflective functioning, their observer self so that they are more able to be less reactive to affect when it arises.

In saying all of this, our experience has taught us that caution is important in the use of some of the more expressive techniques. We recently asked our group of clients to make commitments after 12 months in the program and they all decompensated, requiring us to take them through distress tolerance skills for some time before they settled. As distressing as this was for the clients, and as anxiety provoking as this was for us as therapists (which is another issue entirely), there were some incredible moments during those commitments, which long term we hope were very valuable. Nevertheless, we are questioning our decision to use this task with them in future and I would appreciate any thoughts people have on this issue out there.

ACT cf.
 	
  DBT; ACT/DBT
  synthesis [cont'd]
 	
EXPOSURE
 	
  General inc. consent
  seeking, "distraction"/
  defusion
 	
CONSENT
 	
  Exposure work
  [2-23-05]
 	
  Kelly Wilson
 	
  Cross Reference:
  See 6-260 and 5-213
  for later posts in the
  thread:
 	
  EXPOSURE
 	
  General inc. consent
  seeking,
  "distraction"/
  defusion
	I don't know enough about DBT to speak with any authority. But a note on something like a commitment exercise: I think it is best to think of these things as *in vivo* exposure on steroids. Really it is defusion, since the things the client is being exposed to are heavily verbal. Standing up and publicly pronouncing a genuine intention is one of the most profoundly meaningful, terrifying, and human moments I have ever seen--given any history. Given the right history, you will get lock up - total fusion.
	
	When I say to think about it like an exposure session, what I mean is that I try to read the person's moment to moment reactivity and titrate the exercise. The problem here is, as you point out, these folks have access to an operant behavior that is highly effective and at very high strength: para-suicide. With any exposure session though, if the session is too intense the client leaves (physically or psychologically). When I say too intense here I do not mean too intense in any absolute sense. I mean too intense in the sense that it exceeds your permission to take the client to painful and frightening places. Intensity, as I think of it, is not relative to "the human capacity for tolerance" rather it is relative to the extent to which we are willing. After all, the monks during the Vietnam war poured gas over themselves and sat passively burning to death. This suggests that "capacity" may be nearly unlimited--at least very very high. But, and I think this is key, they were choosing this. Doing exposure with clients this translates to permission. It is so very very easy to slip from doing hard work with permission to doing hard work in as coercion. It can shift in an instant and we need to watch for the signs of it. And, this is an especially slippery slope with this population, because the interpersonal slope is often so slippery. The problem with these folks is that when we go too far, too fast, without enough permission, the backlash is brutal.
	
	How to read and titrate? Well, my take is (and this is a general take applicable to any sort of exposure) watch for dysfluency and physical inflexibility. Walk folks up to the edge of that inflexibility and then work right in that middle zone until you start to see flexibility emerge. All who have been at my workshops over the past couple years know how I love that middle zone--that place right between doing and not doing, saying and not saying. (What we in my lab fondly think of as the "Camus Zone." Get ready Wales--I will introduce you to this densely ambiguous and interesting place next week.) I think we often move too quickly to doing (or not doing) without lingering at the edge until choice emerges as a possibility. The second piece that I believe is critical to weave in is the permission piece. Exposure chosen is different than exposure that is not chosen. And here, I don't mean nominally chosen. I mean really chosen. No coercion. We have a responsibility to make "no" a real choice and offer it without prejudice. Practically, it means moment by moment checking on the state of the therapeutic contract (again, not nominal checking, *real* checking). We have to work very hard as therapists in this situation to keep control in the hands of the client. We need to work hard to keep ourselves mindful that it is their therapy, not ours. That it is their burden to lift and on their schedule. What comes with this persistent attention to the tx contract is that clients can get the respect that is inherent in the posture.
	
	Other technical matters to attend to--I think that recognizing the life cycle of an exposure session is worthwhile. Doing exposure we crank up and then ride the wave. There is a place when we slide down the other side of the wave when we can tell that the work is done--at least that bit. Premature termination of an exposure session is problematic. Maybe this is why I have such a hard time staying inside prescribed session lengths--I think of it all as exposure and I am watching for a naturally occurring break in the work. Or, maybe I am just undisciplined?
	
	I hope this helps some. Words fail. This is my best shot though at describing the sort of things that are organizing my behavior in treatment.
	
	Here is a haiku--as a contribution to the poetic offerings posted on the list lately:
	
	   I have known darkness; known the deepest blue, my friend; Have you traveled there?

ACT cf. DBT; ACT/DBT synthesis [cont'd] Carla Walton	Like Ann, I work in a clinic that provides treatment for persons with Borderline Personality Disorder. Our program runs along fairly classic DBT model lines. I work as both a skills trainer in the program and an individual therapist (not the same clients). As most of you would have experienced, ACT has a funny way of getting under your fingernails AND it also seems to make so much sense for this population. As such, having been exposed to ACT, I found it hard to not start integrating it and have interwoven ACT in my work using DBT as a skills trainer and as an individual therapist. I was aware that Ann had been integrating DBT and ACT in the clinic where she works and have (gratefully) been able to learn from some of her experiences in integrating them. In skills training (group therapy component) I have weaved some of the ACT concepts / metaphors / experiential exercises throughout the DBT material and have found that this has worked really well. It seems to really enhance the DBT material and clients seem to really connect with it when I bring ACT into the sessions. One of the things that people are often surprised about when they have contact with DBT groups is how supportive the clients are of each other. I have noticed that the clients now use some of the ideas from the ACT metaphors in the way they support each other. For example, the clients will often say to each other (when they notice someone is avoiding painful emotions) "Is that Joe the bum at the door? Are you going to let him in?" I have also incorporated it into my individual work with clients and have found that getting people in touch with their values can be very motivating to do the work required in the DBT program. I also have a case example where I believe the introduction of ACT in addition to DBT was instrumental in helping someone to shift. I was handed over a client in the DBT program who had been chronically suicidal for a number of months. I was told to not be too hopeful as she had a fairly poor prognosis. The client was a 24 year old deferred student with BPD and Anorexia. She had pervasive thoughts that she didn't deserve to eat and deserved to die. The turning point in therapy was when she expressed to me that she felt she had been too passive in therapy. When I asked her what she wanted to do differently, she said that she had 2 options and needed to make a decision: firstly, to go back to Uni, get her own place and build up relationships again and secondly, to kill herself. We discussed how she was (and had been for a long time) stuck between trying to make a decision between those 2 and agreed that the only way to get unstuck from the decision was to move towards building the life she wanted whilst defusing the thoughts of suicide. Within a month, she had started eating, applied to return to Uni (she commenced her final year of her studies 2 weeks ago and is doing well). When we reflected on what had been helpful, she said that that discussion had really stuck in her mind as she had always thought that she wouldn't be better until she stopped thinking about suicide, but now accepts that suicidal thoughts are just thoughts and that suicide is an option (and will always be), but is less appealing the more she gets back to enjoying life. If you told me 2 years ago that I'd be working on defusing thoughts of suicide, I would have laughed at you (well, once I'd figured out what defusing meant). Linehan talks about a number of stages in DBT (Stage I - decreasing suicidal behaviours, therapy interfering behaviours, quality of life interfering behaviours and increasing behavioural skills; Stage II - decreasing post-traumatic stress; and Stage III - increasing respect for self and achieving individual goals). Beyond Stage I (which involves skills training), I have used ACT as the Stage III intervention. Because some of the theoretical principles of ACT and DBT are shared, this seems to complement the earlier work done in DBT very well.
ACT cf. DBT; ACT/DBT synthesis [cont'd] **COPING STRATEGIES** **Distraction, function of** **[2-24-05]** Sonja Batten *Cross Reference:* *See 6-260 and 5-213 for later posts in the thread:* *COPING STRATEGIES Distraction, function of*	I think that this is an important topic, as there are a lot of things in common between the two therapies, and obviously PTSD and emotion regulation disorders (like BPD) go hand in hand. I routinely use the DBT skills with patients with PTSD, even when there's no BPD present. I do think there's a subtle distinction to be made, however, because the theory/ rationale underlying the two treatments is slightly different and if you're not careful, can cause problems with your ACT rationale. Sue Orsillo, Robyn Walser and I have a book chapter coming out where we deal, in part, with this issue, and Victoria Follette and colleagues have written about it as well. The core mindfulness skills are obviously important for reducing experiential avoidance and for helping to develop the perspective of self-as-context for experiencing private events that we talk about in ACT. I also love using distress tolerance handout 1, which gives the client several strategies that can be used to get through a crisis without acting impulsively or self-destructively, such as mindful breathing exercises, techniques for self-soothing using the five senses, and a variety of modes of distraction. But wait!! Isn't distraction .... avoidance?!? And aren't we working on reducing avoidance in ACT, not teaching folks new ways to avoid??? Well, yes, and yes. But as a pragmatist, I had to notice that teaching these skills to trauma survivors in the beginning stages of therapy was really helpful. So, I now routinely still teach some of the DBT skills, but I clarify that the distraction and avoidance techniques that I'm teaching them are not a long-term solution. In the long-term, we're still working toward

	willingness and acceptance without having to use distraction. But it may take us a while to get there and be able to use acceptance in a consistent way. So in the meantime, these skills may be helpful to at least get the client through a difficult moment without doing something that she'll regret later. As therapy goes on, we work together on using the distress tolerance skills less and placing more emphasis on willingness to experience whatever private events show up.
	It's just important to think about your theory and rationale if you're thinking about combining treatments - otherwise you've got a good chance of getting yourself in a bind when your client points out that you were saying one thing last week, and another thing this week!
ACT cf. **Focusing therapy [2-26-04]** John Blackledge	Matthew Smout wrote: Anyone out there familiar with focusing therapy (Eugene Gendlin's work)? From what I gather, this approach teaches people to use their "bodily wisdom" to guide them in decision-making and in particular, in therapy, the aspects of personal history and experience to attend to and possibly re-think. I wonder where the "felt sense" (as this bodily wisdom is referred to) fits with ACT. Is this more private content which is observed dispassionately or is this a possible link to the "vitality" aspects of valuing? I think there are some similarities in focus and process between Gendlin's focusing work and ACT. As I recall, he advocates focusing client attention for extended periods on a "felt sense," which is essentially the physical aspects of aversive emotions attached to problematic aspects of the client's life. I also recall that during such exercises, he repeatedly asks his clients not to focus on verbal explanations of what this felt sense means or is, but rather let the felt sense 'define itself' after consistently focusing on it. So, there seems to be extended exposure, implicit (perhaps even explicit) acceptance of the aversive stimulation, and some defusion facilitated by therapist directives to focus on physical sensations rather than language and to not rush to verbal judgment on what a set of aversive physical sensations "are" and what they mean. All points in common with ACT. There are also some substantial differences. Focusing doesn't explicitly try to defuse language--if memory serves me, the techniques mentioned in the last paragraph are the only ones there that seem likely to serve a defusing function. In fact, Gendlin's directives to let the felt sense eventually "define itself" seems to explicitly call for more languaging. Also, no work in Focusing on values (not that I recall).
ACT cf. Focusing therapy [cont'd] **ACT cf.** **Other traditions generally [3-1-04]** Steve Hayes	Focusing is linked to the experiential psychotherapies more generally. Check out the "Focusing Institute" and you will see Les Greenberg and folks like that all over it. Not surprising. The front of the ACT book has the word "experiential" on it for a reason. And Les has a (nice) review of the book on the back cover for that same reason. The Gestalt - behavior analysis link goes way back. The first Gestalt book, Perls, Hefferline, & Goodman had a behavior analyst / rat runner (Ralph Hefferline) as a co-author. A lot of the cool techniques in Gestalt Therapy come right out of contextual behavioral thinking. I have a file that gets increasingly thick called "just like ACT." There are innumerable connections, overlaps, and similarities between ACT and other traditions, especially non-empirical experiential and spiritual traditions. That (to my mind) makes it more likely that there is value in the work. So what is different? Personally, I believe it is this: so far as I know the ACT / RFT / contextualism package is one of the first and today the most comprehensive attempt to link a scientific approach to these issues (from scientific philosophy, through basic theory, applied theory, component analyses, process analyses and outcome analyses) that is simultaneously true to these core issues as they are experienced (not necessarily as they are interpreted) outside of the scientific community. As a purely applied matter, what that *might* mean is that ACT can be simpler, more focused, and yet broader when it needs to be -- because it has a validated theory, linked to validated basic processes. For example, I've seen a lot of acceptance work in other traditions that is not linked to values and behavior change. I think ACT / RFT can explain why that might not be a good idea; etc. Techniques, charismatic leaders, interesting raps, assumptions, and cool new things come and go -- but in the history of human kind, only science has proven its ability to progress. Art today is not "better" than art a thousand years ago. The science of today is infinitely "better." The functional contextual ("behavior analytic") wing of psychology did fantastically well until it hit the barrier of human language and cognition. RFT seems to have found a way through that barrier. If that is so, we are in for a multi-decade ride ... who knows what folks can do with a workable theory. My advice: we should feel free to borrow the techniques wherever we find them. In the long run what will matter though is how well we develop the theory, basic processes, measures, data, and ways to train all this.

ACT cf. **Functional Analytic Psychotherapy [7-31-05]** Kelly Wilson	Gareth Holman wrote: Weeks ago, Kelly wrote: 'As to FAP being more a part of the "whole banana" (strange image Steve) I think that Carmen Luciano put it in a way that I think is right. I have heard her say something to the effect of "If you aren't doing FAP, you aren't doing ACT." Seems right to me.'... Kelly or others, can you be more specific about how 'if you aren't doing FAP you aren't doing ACT'? In the briefest way--I see as the central tenets of FAP (and I am no FAP expert): 1. a genuine concern for the persons with whom we work. 2. a functional rather then formal understanding of client behavior. (The example here would be the client who struggles with issues of whether they can trust their own judgement who comes in a critical juncture in therapy and says that they want to take a couple months off from therapy. This may appear formally inconsistent with moving ahead in therapy but might be just what the doctor ordered in terms of the client making a beginning of making and exercising their own judgement (the good kind of crb).) 3. reinforcing, not by some contrived response, but rather by one's genuine response to a client we care about who is doing something progressive in their life. 4. considering your reactions in therapy as data. They are not the enemy. They may be telling you something about your own idiosyncratic history, but also may be telling you about the reactions the person is experiencing in their day-to-day life. 5. re the data considered in #4, if judged to be like the reactions the client's modus operandi is generating in the world outside of therapy, are grist for the mill in therapy. There is an article of faith here that interpersonal interactions in therapy will mirror important aspects of interpersonal interactions outside therapy. (How could it be otherwise--they are one person.) Of course, this is not all of FAP--just my own idiosyncratic read on some important pieces. However, if the above are not part of your doing of ACT--in my opinion, you are missing some important aspects of ACT. What did Carmen mean? Can't say for sure, but I suspect it is at least related to some of what I describe above. As I mentioned in my advanced workshop at ACT SI II in response to a question about reactions to a client: Bob Kohlenberg is my guiding star on this issue. Bob is the one who really sensitized me to pay attention to my own reactions and to what extraordinary assets they are in working with clients....
ACT cf. **Integrative Behavioral Couples Therapy [3-14-04]** Steve Hayes	I do think the IBCT conception of acceptance is different [to that of ACT]... However, unquestionably IBCT is contextualistic and a fellow traveler. Neil [Jacobson] was very clear about its philosophical roots ... he wrote about it in several places ... and you don't have to look very far to see functional contextualism and indeed ACT sensibilities inside both IBCT and his version of Behavioral Activation. That connection goes way back ... to 1986 at least. I've thought that the differences are probably pragmatic. Neil and Andy [Christensen]'s approach has a certain directness to it that fits the couple's situation. ACT, in a way, is more deeply psychological. Putting aside for the moment the fact that IBCT is empirically supported in this arena and ACT isn't, if I had a time to do an intensive ACT couple's workshop with say 20 hours of contact (like we do intensives normally), followed by individual couple's sessions, I'd do it ... I'd love to see that model tested. But if all I had was several hours to do normal couple's therapy I'd be worried. It will take some real creativity on someone's part to learn how to put ACT comfortably inside that structure in a way that can be replicated by others. I've seen good ACT therapists pull it off (Liz G for example) so I'd guess it can be done. IBCT fits nicely, but perhaps that is why it simplifies some of the acceptance message: it is easier to do it that way. We won't know until folks try seriously to develop and test ACT protocols with couples. Personally I've avoided it, but perhaps part of that comes from 2 divorces and the fact that I seem to drive women crazy (not in a good way, sigh) -- my mind beats me up enough without having to face the "fraud" nagging it would throw at me. Avoid, avoid.
ACT cf. Integrative Behavioral Couples Therapy [cont'd] Steve Hayes	One of the differences is that ACT is always talking about accepting experiences (which, by the way, does not mean they cannot / do not / or should not be changed -- Hank regularly reminds us of that and that's right. Sometimes they do/can/should -- or any combination of those -- and sometimes not, it is just that on workability grounds it is "not" more often than folks had realized ... the bigger point is to experience them and do what works), while IBCT sometimes is talking about accepting behaviors, and usually the behaviors of others. I don't think ACT has spent much time on that ... though if you really accept your own experiences, very often the behaviors of others become less of an issue because you actually were trying to change them in order (unnecessarily) to change your experiences. Sorry for the convoluted sentences....

ACT cf. **Morita therapy** **[1-30-05]** Jonathan Kandell	Morita therapy appears, from cursory glance, to bear a striking similarity to ACT…. Was ACT influenced by Morita or are they accidental cousins? Here are some quick excerpts from a Morita article and a Morita web page: "One of the main tenets of Morita Therapy is that our internal experience (feelings and thoughts) is basically uncontrollable by our will. If we feel anxious about going for a job interview we can't necessarily make ourselves feel relaxed and confident. If we experience doing our income taxes as frustrating and tedious, we can't just snap our fingers and suddenly find the task satisfying and exciting. Most of the reasons for procrastination have to do with 'internal barriers' like fear, anxiety, indecision, perfectionism, etc…. I call these barriers the *Demons of Inaction*. Traditional therapies generally suggest that you must conquer such demons through various strategies such as insight, self-talk, motivation, or increased self-esteem. But Morita Therapy offers a set of tools that is less about *conquering* and more about *co-existing with*. Rather than vanquishing your anxiety about the job interview, you simply take your anxiety along for the ride." (reprinted with permission from "Morita Therapy: the Japanese Psychology of Action," by Gregg Krech in *Thirty thousand Days*, Vol. 12, No. 4: ToDo Institute, www.todoinstitute.org) Morita's basic premises: Know Your Purpose; Accept Your Feelings; Do What Must Be Done … From a Morita site … **The Naturalness of Feelings** (Arugamama) If we find out that we have just won the lottery, we may be excited and happy. But if we find out about the death of a loved one, we may feel sadness and grief. Such feelings are natural responses to our life circumstances and we need not try to "fix" or "change" them. Arugamama (acceptance of reality as it is) involves accepting our feelings and thoughts without trying to change them or "work through" them. This means that if we feel depressed, we accept our feelings of depression. If we feel anxious, we accept our feelings of anxiety. Rather than direct our attention and energy to our feeling state, we instead direct our efforts toward living our life well. We set goals and take steps to accomplish what is important even as we co-exist with unpleasant feelings from time to time. Feelings are Uncontrollable There is an assumption behind many Western therapeutic methods that it is necessary to change or modify our feeling state before we can take action. We assume that we must "overcome" fear to dive into a pool, or develop confidence so we can make a public presentation. But in actuality, it is not necessary to change our feelings in order to take action. In fact, it is our efforts to change our feelings that often makes us feel even worse. "Trying to control the emotional self willfully by manipulative attempts is like trying to choose a number on a thrown die or to push back the water of the Kamo River upstream. Certainly, they end up aggravating their agony and feeling unbearable pain because of their failure in manipulating the emotions." -- Shoma Morita, M.D. (from www.todoinstitute.org See this website for further information on Morita Therapy) Once we learn to accept our feelings we find that we can take action without changing our feeling state. Often, the action-taking leads to a change in feelings. For example, it is common to develop confidence after one has repeatedly done something with some success.
ACT cf. Morita therapy [cont'd] Jason Gosnell	For people on this listserv interested in the narrowing and broadening attention issue, he [Morita] discusses this in that book [*Morita Therapy and the True Nature of Anxiety-Based Disorders* edited by Peg Levine]. The basis for the first phase of his treatment was in fact to allow the narrow, fixated aspect of attention that neurotics tend to have to open up. He called it the "opening of the peripheral aspect of attention" (a rough translation of *mushoju-shin*). This is a change that softens the neurotic fixated quality of attending to things or "staring" at things as I put it--staring at emotions, sensations, etc. Locking onto them then obsessing about them, doing battle with them, etc. In the first phase of treatment, the background field of awareness opens and a person can easily shift between objects of focus--allowing foreground to become background, and new objects of attention to emerge from the background and be foregrounded. This is actually a state of mind, probably the same as FLOW. I suspect that meditation accomplishes the same thing if it is practiced regularly. I also suspect that living an ACT or Constructive Living lifestyle may--in the process of working in this way--accomplish the same thing. I don't know….

ACT cf. **Motivational Interviewing [5-24-05]** Matthew Smout	Lawrence Needleman wrote: Motivational Interviewing seems to be helpful. It seems to me that many of the evocative questions that are at the heart of MI elicit people's values. Does the MI approach have anything to offer ACT? Absolutely. The general MI approach emphasises being cautious about giving information - asking permission before offering information or advice. This style fosters the kind of respectful, listening, egalitarian relationship essential for doing ACT work. The second edition of MI book [Miller, W.R., & Rollnick, S. (Eds.). (2002). *Motivational Interviewing: Preparing people for change* (2nd Ed.). New York: Guilford Press.] actually includes a chapter on values - making the connection even tighter. I recommend any psychotherapist familiarise themselves with the MI approach as it teaches the counselling microskills in a way that is very conducive to doing ACT effectively.
ACT cf. Motivational Interviewing [cont'd] Steve Hayes	We have an RCT coming showing that participation in an ACT workshop before training in MI makes it more likely that you can learn MI, including even as reflected in behavioral measures of MI interviewing; it does so generally as well or better than participation in a personally focused MI workshop as a front end; and it does not contaminate MI (that is, people do MI without insisting on inserting ACT into the interviews even if that was not part of the MI training).
ACT cf. Motivational Interviewing [cont'd] Matthew Smout	This is important because Miller has written himself on the difficulty of training people to do MI - generally many staff are over-confident that they do MI, yet observation of video-taped sessions show they are not doing it. That ACT could alter this is a big deal. In my experience, familiarity with MI and ACT enhance the practice of each another. There are parallels in their purpose. We started with technology to "change people" - e.g., exposure for anxiety and skills training for drinking - but surprisingly a large number of people didn't want change imposed on them. Both MI and ACT serve a purpose of guiding people through deciding to commit to new behaviour (from contemplation to action, in the 'Stages of Change' model). IMHO, ACT orients clinicians to the magnitude/gravity of change more impactfully than training in MI generally would. MI training is a little less conceptual and "big picture" than ACT training and includes a lot of practical phrasing for clinicians and examples of client dialogue indicating resistance and change talk, which is very helpful for the behaviour analytically-oriented psychotherapist (such as the ACT therapist). There are some differences. MI orients the clinician to shaping statements of confidence from clients - MI adopts a conventional understanding of self-efficacy-behaviour relationships. I've been pondering how ACT deals with this issue. Still pondering. Kelly's chapter on substance abuse in the new Practical Guide to ACT book addresses the issue of resistance. MI goes into even greater detail. ACT goes into more depth about exploring client values. Of course there are also the defusion and acceptance exercises but this territory is not really the focus of MI so it's a little unfair to compare them at this point. Both ACT and MI help the client find "the will"; ACT would keep going at a point where MI would leave the client to find "the way."
ACT cf. Motivational Interviewing [cont'd] **CLIENT** **Involuntary/ semi-voluntary - integrating ACT/ MI [5-24-05]** Patty Bach	In work with clients with serious mental illness I often integrate some MI into ACT at the front end - as a way of addressing resistance/increasing willingness in involuntary and semi-voluntary clients. I think this could be helpful in working with clients in any less than completely voluntary setting (e.g., inpatient, parole and probation, substance abuse, anger management, behavior medicine, half of a couple). Rusch and Corrigan (2002) found that MI increased treatment adherence and insight in persons with schizophrenia, and I see MI as useful in any setting where treatment adherence is low. The completely voluntary client who seeks out a therapist may not benefit from the addition of MI and the less-than-voluntary client may become a little more voluntary after MI. I agree that there are a few conflicts between MI and ACT around self-efficacy/ behavior relations, and I like that both have the respectful stance of starting where the client is and having the client look to his/her own experience for guidance rather than having shoulds and values imposed by the therapist.
ACT cf. Motivational Interviewing [cont'd] CLIENT Involuntary/ semi-voluntary - integrating ACT/ MI [cont'd] Patty Bach	... Miller makes it clear that resistance is a therapist problem - that resistance doesn't mean that the client is 'doing something wrong' or 'isn't motivated enough'; instead he suggests that resistance is present when the therapist/treatment provider is ahead of the client.

ACT cf. Motivational Interviewing [cont'd] **CHOICE** **Reasons, with cf. for** **CAUSE** **Reasons are not causes [5-24-05]** Kirk Strosahl	In my work training behavioral health clinicians to provide rapid, effective interventions in primary care settings, the issue of motivation to change is omnipresent. It isn't restricted to alcoholics or drug abusers, but to virtually every kind of behavioral health issue people face in their lives. Controlling one's diabetes, stopping smoking, making lifestyle changes that reduce health risk, taking a medicine as prescribed--these and many more. So, inevitably, the whole issue of how to use ACT in a way that promotes a readiness to change is central. Comparing ACT and MI is a little like comparing apples and oranges. I think the traditional MI model is, at heart, a second generation cognitive behavioral model. It effectively reframes the issue of choice as a matter of weighing the pros and cons of staying the same versus the pros and cons of making a change. In this sense, I think MI really is a "decision" model, even though it is very respectful of the client's right to make this decision without being cajoled, pressured, etc. In that sense, MI draws a clear line of delineation for "who is responsible for what problem and who is going to do what about it." I find this part of MI very consistent with the ACT approach. The original version of MI didn't specifically draw a connection between the "decision" and the client's values. I don't think it's an accident that the 2002 edition of MI includes a chapter on values because by then, ACT had been on the scene for 3 years in terms of the first published volume. The transformation of MI to a more values-oriented exercise is reflective of the influence the "C" part of ACT has had on the behavior therapy community. I still think there is a core difference between ACT and MI and that is in the conscious distinction between choice and decision that is so central to the ACT space. People don't make decisions to enter treatment or change behaviors because the "pros" outweigh the "cons." They choose to change their course of action because of a desire to behave in a way that is consistent with valued directions in life. They MUST understand that a choice is always made WITH reasons, but not FOR reasons. This is because the relative weighting of the pros and cons for deciding to do something can shift from day to day. A choice is made not with reference to pros and cons, but with respect to one's own values. Values are more immutable than pros and cons and they don't have a "true-false" value to them. So, my "moves" with primary care patients focus on the behavior organizing and activating properties of value-based choices. I share the MI perspective that this is essentially the patient's problem and the patient will be the one choosing or not choosing a new course of action. I also emphasize that not choosing is a choice. In fact, it is impossible not to choose and this is where I think ACT shows another distinction with MI. I would consciously try to rephrase client language that "implied" that the client was "forced" to engage a behavior, rather than chose that behavior. I think MI tends to let patients roll reasons that attempt to masquerade as causes into the decision matrix. The ACT approach would be to specifically reconstruct the grammatical properties of pluses and minuses to separate reason giving from true causal relations. Although Steve may have his own sense of why ACT adds to the ability of counselors to apply MI more properly, my guess is that ACT very heavily cements the distinction between deciding and choosing and creates a space in which the therapist can sort out reasons and true causes. Choosing a behavior is a true cause of that behavior. Posing private events (urges to drink, urges to inject) as causes creates much less behavior change leverage and makes maintenance of change very difficult. At the same time, ACT is inclusive of the fact that these private events will constantly be circulating in the client's life space, even as the ongoing choosing is occurring....
ACT cf. Motivational Interviewing [cont'd] **THERAPIST** **Being "in the moment" - cf. Motivational Interviewing [5-25-05]** Matthew Smout	... A thing that struck me reading the MI (2nd ed.) book which I invite ACT trainers to consider: The MI book now spends quite a lot of space orienting the clinician to what the client says in session - this strategy really orients the clinician to being with the client. My feeling is that there is less for the clinician to keep in their head and more of a focus on what's happening for the client. A lot of ACT writing is very philosophical/ theoretical/ conceptual/ big picture stuff - all good and important - but sometimes the clinician is left wanting for a broader range of client speech samples, or cues that can be used to keep them "in the moment" and less off in their heads wondering about "the ACT model." ACT advocates being in the moment with clients, but a lot of my colleagues who have received ACT training struggle to DO "in the moment" because of being overly conscious of the ACT verbal stuff. MI doesn't TALK ABOUT "in the moment" but I think has moved toward fostering DOING "in the moment" quite effectively. This is the value I see for ACT clinicians.
ACT cf. Motivational Interviewing [cont'd] ACT Listserv Member	Something that is missing... is the concept of response-ability and responsibility (blame/ownership). To encourage and motivate a client by demonstrating the ability to respond is great; placing the onus of what choice is made back on the client can be tricky and may have some unintended side effects. Here at the institute I work for, we train our direct line and nursing staff in MI techniques to help them in motivating the client to participate in programming. What I have seen even when following the training well, is the patient still seeing their choice as right or wrong, and evaluating their choice one way or the other, even if

	the alternatives are all "acceptable." That is why I prefer using workability to motivate change, spending time returning to the concept of workable choices, evaluating choices based on their functionality.
	Lastly … as someone that was trained in radical behaviorism, I still view choices as being shaped by reinforcement history and free-will as being a meaningless construct. We have choices, but the choice of what choice we make is learned and determined by contextual/ environmental variables. This leads me to steer clear of any implication of responsibility. Altering the context of and the function of choice seems a better way to motivate participation in therapy.
ACT cf. Motivational Interviewing [cont'd] **CHOICE** **ACT concept of** **[5-29-05]** Niklas Törneke *Cross Reference:* *See 4-160 for later posts in the thread:* *CHOICE* *ACT concept of*	This might be to say something that is obvious to all on this list but as talking about choice in an ACT context sometimes is misunderstood, I'll risk that. When we talk about choice in ACT this is not a philosophical or scientific statement, made as an argument for "free will." In ACT choice is a kind of common sense term or, even better, an experiential term. Human beings constantly act without being able to know (verbally) the actual causes of that behavior. We play games that we have learned, and in these games it is as if we really know why we did this and that. This is helpful, especially in social action. But it can also constitute a trap; that's why we target this in ACT, of course. As we act the actual causes of that behavior are forever hidden in history, so to speak. So what term are we to use for this "action without knowing the causes"? Choice. There is no better word for this actual experience.
ACT cf. Motivational Interviewing [cont'd] Jonathan Kandell	Maybe I'm missing the nuances, but I don't see conceptual conflicts between MI and ACT. Doesn't MI fit right into the "creative hopelessness" stage of ACT? I don't take the heart of MI to be weighing the "pros" and "cons" … (though that is part of it); but rather *developing discrepancy* between the client's actions and values, and *validating ambivalence*. Use the conflicts between the client's values and actions to deconstruct their "resistance." There is a playful rolling with resistance which parallels ACT. Remember, Miller thinks of MI as a strategic therapy. Like ACT it is strategic and directive at the same time. You first deconstruct the client's unworkable system (which MI thinks of as resistance and ACT thinks of as a language game), and then you assist the client in bringing his or her actions and values into consistency. ACT and MI both contain the paradox (or hypocrisy?) that while they don't tell the client what to believe, they think there is a "right" telos we are helping the client move toward. We just have to nudge them toward seeing it. Since MI is only intended as a way to raise motivation, not as an entire model of human suffering, I don't think it's fair to compare MI to the parts of ACT beyond creative hopelessness, or to ACT's deeper metaphysical and epistemological assumptions.
ACT cf. Motivational Interviewing [cont'd] Patricia Juarez	I am an MI trainer and I am also on the MI trainers' listserv. So I can also say one of the main goals in MI sessions is to develop discrepancy between the problem behavior and what the person really wants for his/her life. This is done under the assumption that every person, to one degree or another desires a better life, and that our job as "change facilitators" is to promote reflections that would lead the person to make better decisions for his/her life (i.e., intrinsic motivation), and at all times, the person gets the message that she/he is responsible for their decisions, even if it is to stay the same. Also, agreeing with what Jonathan says of MI as being a counseling style designed primarily to increase motivation, a recent meta-analysis suggests that MI has a greater impact when applied as a prelude to more formal kinds of treatments, because it seems to increase commitment to more specific change strategies. (If interested in this meta-analysis, see the article "Motivational Interviewing" by Jennifer Hettema, Julie Steele, and William R. Miller at: http://arjournals.annualreviews.org/toc/clinpsy/1/1;jsessionid=nrCDHHAknew4 This article also includes a section on the theory of Motivational Interviewing, that may be of interest to those curious about this therapeutic intervention.)
ACT cf. **Rational-Emotive Behavior Therapy**	… REBT is not just about taking an irrational belief and disputing it. The point of REBT is to get to what is referred to as the Elegant Solution. The elegant solution, as I am viewing it today, doesn't include the person constantly assailing and disputing every irrational belief that comes up, but to get to a spot where the irrational thoughts are likely to occur less often because of a context of acceptance. "Acceptance" is a word

[9-7-03] Daniel Moran	used quite often throughout the decades of REBT literature. The Elegant Solution, once fluently enacted, leads to a philosophical life stance where evaluations of one's personhood have less sting, perhaps no influence at all at times, and may then be less likely to lead to discomfort. It is a level of acceptance that is arrived at through a different means than the way ACT approaches it. Does REBT try to change content (Crels)? Yes. Does living life according to the Elegant Solution influence context (Cfuncs) in a clinically helpful way? I think it'd be interesting to find out. My guess is that the answer is Yes. I'll hit the books to develop this idea. And then perhaps on to the lab. Indeed some of the content orientation of REBT is well criticized by relational frame theorizing, but there is a context orientation to REBT (as I understand it) that is rarely mentioned on this listserv (or in many places, unfortunately), and may be comparable to the mission of the members of this listserv. A few months ago, I recall Steve suggesting two types of informed consents: one for ACT if CBT failed for the client in the past and one for CBT if acceptance failed in the past. I think there is room for both in one's therapeutic repertoire. Using the techniques judiciously is the challenge for an artful/ scientific, effective therapist....
ACT cf. Rational-Emotive Behavior Therapy [cont'd] Tuna Townsend	... In my very first encounter with Steve Hayes some eight years ago, I indicated my great admiration of Albert Ellis' "Reason and Emotion in Psychotherapy," with particular reference to the passage in which he (Ellis) describes the epiphany he'd had when a client (upon whom Dr. Ellis was performing psychodynamic therapy) suggested with words to the effect that "... it's not what happened to me back then that's messing me up; it's what I'm telling myself NOW about what happened back then that's messing me up..." In that moment, Dr. Ellis writes, he was converted to RE(B)T, although it took him some time to develop it. REBT in particular has gone a long, long way (in my opinion) to remedy what was/is wrong with so much of what passes for 'psychotherapy' - chiefly, a reliance upon the spurious and putatively curative powers of 'insight.' I'm not saying that insight is wholly irrelevant, but that as someone else recently quoted (I thought the late Richard Alpert/Ram Dass was the original source), "'Understanding' is a consolation prize...." Considering the historical/cultural context in which RE(B)T evolved, it was a pretty amazing and powerful shift away from the prevailing model. I think that ACT represents a similar advance, and this time it is the vantage point provided by the shoulders of Dr. Ellis and his cohort that allows us to see a little bit farther....
ACT cf. Rational-Emotive Behavior Therapy [cont'd] ACT Listserv Member	To me REBT and its "elegant solution" is very much about acceptance and is something I thought to be compatible with the Buddhist ideas of letting go or non-grasping. Letting go of rigid demands, de-awfulising, greater tolerance of discomfort, letting go of global ratings of self and the world … this philosophical shift caused disturbing thoughts to fall much more lightly on my shoulders (and to slide off) … increased acceptance and patience … less judging of self and others … a Teflon coating for all irrational/non-helpful beliefs. I very much respect the teachings of Uncle Albert.
ACT cf. Rational-Emotive Behavior Therapy [cont'd] Hank Robb	... I think there are, perhaps, two fundamental differences between ACT and REBT. I say, perhaps, because I don't think they have to be there but they are at the moment. One is the basis for organizing one's life. REBT, I think, stands in contrast to ACT in making the fulfilment of one's deepest DESIRES the organizing point of one's life. This opens the whole issue of what does "moving in a valued direction" mean. If it means going in a socially-desirable direction but one that doesn't touch your "soul," then REBT says "go for what fills your soul." If you really more deeply desire to work on your novel, your fishing, your flute playing, or shooting up drugs than your marriage, food for the hungry, or money for your children's education, then go do that. From an REBT perspective, the problem is not failing to forgo desire in order to move in a valued direction. The problem is being sure you are not sacrificing long term fulfilments for short term fulfilments and not sacrificing what you care most deeply about for something you care less deeply about because pursuing the former is harder than pursuing the latter. Thus, the REBT admonition, "The aim is not to feel better but to get better," meaning not to be deterred from pursuing your deepest desires because the road is difficult. Second, and I think DJ has this, REBT thinks that putting things like "I can't stand it," or other "irrational beliefs" such as "it's awful" in a frame of coordination with just about anything is unhelpful, and it is more helpful to put those contents into a frame of opposition instead. By itself REBT did not, and I don't think would have ever come up with, changing the Cfunc in the technical way put forward by RFT. But since it also would work, REBT is happy to be adding it because it does work. (For example, as far back as 1957 Ellis wrote about the difference between how you are affected by what someone says to you and how you would be affected by the same words from the same person if that person were saying them with their head sticking out the window of a mental hospital. Same words, same person, different context, and, thus, different effect. But this is not the technical and forward-moving analysis offered by RFT.) That is also why I say, REBT can go "straight up" on primary problems. The REBT position is that things like anger,

	anxiety, depression, and guilt are not "natural." They are the result of putting responses such as "it's awful" in a frame of coordination with whatever did, does, or could, happen to you. Yes, you wouldn't have to take it seriously, i.e., you could change the Cfunc, but you could also change the Crel, the "usual" REBT move. Maybe it is "natural" in the sense that frames of coordination are the first frames used. But there is nothing "natural" about remaining stuck there when doing so doesn't work. Applying more "advanced" frames when doing so works....
ACT cf. Rational-Emotive Behavior Therapy [cont'd] **ACCEPTANCE** **Not effortful cf. process of learning acceptance [9-9-03]** Steve Hayes	Joseph Ciarrochi wrote: REBT: The vital path involves a "forceful struggle." One learns to vigorously dispute irrational beliefs, in order to weaken their power. ACT: the vital path involves an effortless shifting of context. The shift is not hard, it is tricky. And it is easy to forget to do. "Vigorous disputing" is seen as another potential control move. It is also seen as further entanglement in the language machine. Hank Robb replied: "Effortless shifting of context" only comes after a great deal of effort for most people. If it were so "effortless," therapy would end in about a session and "no talking retreats" in about 3 hours. "Tricky" things are "hard" if you're not well practiced at the trickiness. ...just one little tweak about this dialogue between Joe and Hank. The focus of the word "effort" is shifting meaning here. The action is effortless -- the process of learning that action generally is not. Acceptance and defusion are not effortful in the sense of forceful expenditure of energy. Much as muscles relax by non-stimulation, not by stimulating counter contractions, the context of acceptance/defusion is simply different and that can happen in an instant. Yet the process of learning NOT to struggle is a struggle for virtually all of us because the language-based stimuli that occasion struggle are both ubiquitous and subtle. It is tricky. Generally we have to extinguish the struggle process through huge amounts of struggle and failure before any alternatives present themselves (that's exactly why "creative hopelessness" is important in ACT -- it's one giant extinction process for the struggle). In principle, however, this could all be easy -- and wouldn't THAT piss us all off (the story of the monks trying to kill the new 6th patriarch of Zen is relevant here ... monks didn't like that a new cook in the kitchen could just walk in and do it so well he'd be named patriarch without decades of study and toil).
ACT cf. **Self-help books, Claire Weeks' [10-24-02]** Steve Hayes	ACT Listserv Member wrote: I've been a fan of the self-help books written in the late 70s/early 80s by Claire Weeks, an Australian psychiatrist, for some time, and now that ACT is on the scene have realised that there are similarities to Weeks' work - it's based around 'acceptance' and 'floating' through (perceived) negative experience. Has anyone else noticed this? ACT is clearly not derivative of her stuff and is obviously backed up by the RFT empirical base, but I think there are some interesting comparisons. I always liked the Weeks books. I don't think any of the ACT book authors consciously borrowed from her but she is working in the same space. [By the way another one is Gary Emery who moved in that direction post Beck (His book *Rapid relief from emotional distress* is still useful for clients.). I actually did borrow from him. "Accept, Choose, Take action" is his phrase ... I knew it was not original but I could not find who I'd borrowed it from until after the ACT book came out, so it has that cheesy footnote saying in essence "we know this is not our phrase. Sorry to whomever wrote it."] Unfortunately, the clients who've come in to see me having read Weeks have tried to turn the thing into a new control move. I know that is not her fault but it does point to the difficulty of writing lay books. As an adjunct to ACT, though, I think some parts of them could be helpful.
BUDDHISM **ACT/ RFT cf. Buddhist ideas [5-25-04]** Steve Hayes	Some general comments on Buddhist ideas and ACT / RFT. Niklas commented a while back that ACT / RFT notions differ from Buddhist notions and that is right. Fusion is not quite the same thing as attachment to permanence. The arising of the self is not the same as deictic frames. These things are related, but quite different. I see Buddhist ideas as insightful but also pre-scientific, and in their details they seem unlikely. Self simply does not arise in the fashion supposed; attachment is not really the core issue and impermanence is not really central to suffering. I don't think permanence is the issue until you have temporal and evaluative frames ... then it becomes an issue. My dog has time alright; and he has comparison in the sense of preference; but he is not "attached." No one has ever been able to construct an adequate scientific system out of Buddhism, and why would they? It is like trying to construct a scientific system out of the Bible. You can construct a psychology, but it is not based on basic principles that you can show in the animal lab (or the human infant lab). It starts 20,000 feet up with a fully verbalizing creature and when you do that you miss the key issues that put you in the position you start with ... for example, bi-directionality, arbitrary applicability, etc. A few students of mine (Chad Shenk, Aki Masuda, Kara Bunting) and I have been writing a chapter for a book on Buddhism and keep running into issues between Buddhist scholars. Level after level of tiny (but

very, very important!) battles over wording, concepts, and theories. I've secretly sworn never to write formally about Buddhism again ... I'm sure I will break the vow but really I think we have to follow our own path and see where it leads. That is exactly what has been happening ... and ironically that is *why* folks want us to write about Buddhism -- it led to a similar place. But not the same place. And I sure don't want to end up inside a tradition with level after level of tiny (but very, very important) and totally irresolvable battles over wording, concepts, and theories. The great advantage we have is we have a way to resolve our little battles. If RFT serves as a base for a relatively adequate functional analysis of language and cognition, it will be barely recognizable 50 years from now. Buddhism will be Buddhism 50 years from now, as it was 50 years ago and 50 years before that and 50 years before that and so on and so on.

Scientifically speaking:

It is fun, interesting, and worth noting the relationships, esp. it is worth seeing if basic behavioral concepts (e.g., inside RFT / ACT) can illuminate complex concepts inside various traditions inc. Buddhism. For example, this thread on suffering is great;

maybe (but I'm skeptical about this one) held very lightly it could occasionally be worth seeing if Buddhist ideas suggest things we are missing;

but mostly it is worth following the inductive behavior analytic path and seeing where it leads.

I'm skeptical about the middle part because it is always harder to go from complexity to simplicity than it is from simplicity to complexity. There have been many psychologies that have tried the former path and have progressed for a while only to be swamped in complexity. BA is one of the few that seriously followed the latter path and refused to move off it, even when psychology tried to bury us or simply walked away in disgust. It is not time to abandon the inductive path simply because we are now better able to address complexity empirically. The exact opposite ... it is esp. now that we need it because we will be swimming in complexity with regularity.

This is part of why I think in the long run RFT is more important than ACT, though in the shorter run ACT holds more interest.

BUDDHISM **Meditation, ACT/ RFT view of** **CONTROL** **Strategies - variability of destructive effects [6-4-03]** Kelly Wilson	Joseph Ciarrochi wrote: Can meditation become just another control strategy (e.g., an attempt to reduce stress, as presented in the book the "calming method")? Is there a type of meditation that is ideally suited to ACT? Isn't there an old story about the fellow who goes to a monastery and asks-- Master, if I meditate eight hours a day, how long will it take for me to reach enlightenment? The master replies-- 10 years 2nd question-- What if I meditate 12 hours per day? The master replies-- In that case, 20 years. I suspect that there are more and less destructive control strategies. For example, I have seen self strangulation (twist a belt around your neck until you black out), cutting, burning, drinking to blackout, combining massive doses of dangerous drugs, having sex with 8 or 10 people within a single evening, getting A's on every report card and every assignment, always being very, very nice to everyone, avoiding conflict at all costs, running ten miles per day, and on, and on. On the scale of things, I suspect that strategies have multiple effects and work how they work in different areas. Some strategies are more pervasively destructive than others. Functional identity (all experiential avoidance) doesn't equal identical effects in all domains. Form is important too. Now, take something like exercising, or meditating or systematically doing deep muscle relaxation (DMR)--these things have effects over and above whatever agenda drives them. For example, if I shoot myself in the head to stop a disturbing thought, the thought will stop, but so will my heart. Another example, Tom Borkovec has shown that if you get GAD folks to do DMR prior to exposure, you get better effects from the exposure. So, some of these practices (even as control strategies) should alter sensitivity to contingencies, general health, relationships, etc. I would expect real net benefits on multiple levels from some. In the case of DMR, there is probably not much in there that can hurt you, and plenty that can help. Same for any sort of mindfulness meditation practice or probably exercise (which can have a decidedly meditative quality depending on the exercise and how it is done). The question is, both theoretical and empirical, what are the relevant change processes? Are the effects of these practices altered by the agenda of the practicer? I would guess yes. The Zen story suggests yes. Wholly altered? I would guess not. Lots of work to do here.

BUDDHISM Meditation, ACT/RFT view of [cont'd] **CONTROL** Strategies - variability of destructive effects [cont'd] Mary Politi	This message is in response to Kelly's assertion that some control strategies are less destructive than others, and that mindfulness/control techniques are not wholly altered when the practicer has some agenda on his/her mind. I'm not sure I agree. The exercise/running 10 miles per day example in an anorexic would not reap many positive benefits in his/her life--the agenda is control, and the exercise probably leads to more destructive physical and psychological health. On a personal level, I have tried meditating to help fall asleep on nights when I struggle with insomnia, and it has the opposite effect--the meditation only frustrates me when I still can't fall asleep (whereas I can meditate fairly well when I have no "agenda"). I think the form and the agenda of the practicer are central in the effectiveness of the technique, and they can be wholly altered. Any other thoughts?
BUDDHISM Meditation, ACT/RFT view of [cont'd] **CONTROL** Strategies - variability of destructive effects [cont'd] Kelly Wilson	Sure Mary - I wouldn't disagree that these things can be very destructive and work in the complete opposite direction to that intended. What I meant to express was a matter of degree. It is the "wholly altered" part that may need consideration. I agree that agenda is an important aspect, but not the only aspect--maybe even entirely so in some circumstances. On the other hand, we cannot ignore the positive effects of some interventions--e.g., exposure, relaxation-- even when they are delivered with an explicit control strategy. Ultimately these things work how they work and for what they work for. Which leaves us lots of work to do.
BUDDHISM Meditation, ACT/RFT view of [cont'd] Niklas Törneke	Comparing ACT and Buddhism is a huge project. Looking closer at meditation experiences from an RFT perspective seems to me to be helpful and to give at least a hint to answering questions like the ones you put Joseph. Maybe it can also give a hint to why RFT is so crucial to ACT work, especially in the long run. ... I'll take one of the basic Buddhist techniques as an example, what is usually called "mindfulness of breathing." The initial instruction is to focus on something in the perceptual field, like the sensing of the air as it passes your nostrils. This is not "thinking about the breath" but attending to the direct contingency of the sensation. As you do this other things will "ask for your attention" but gently you stick to your focus, or return to it if you lose it. As you continue doing this there will be a lessening of thoughts, usually described as "muddy water settling down." You will still have thoughts coming up, but to a lesser degree. From an RFT perspective this can be described as discriminating actual non-verbal contingencies and as you keep doing it there will be less derived relational responding taking place, probably as a result (at least partly) of less contextual cues for such behavior being present. In lists of ACT techniques this is sometimes called "focused mindfulness." At this point you can change your discrimination somewhat. You make your focus a bit wider, noticing thoughts coming up. But you notice them "as thoughts"; that is, you discriminate the relational responding as such. Doing this you can also discriminate the functions of this responding (what happens as these thoughts come up), differentiating these from more direct functions ("what is really there," as sensations, thoughts as thoughts etc.). The way of widening your focus to "whatever turns up" is called "open mindfulness" in lists of ACT techniques. The discrimination of relational responding as such (when it is taking place) is the key process of what is called defusion in ACT. But the two discriminations aid each other. In a way I guess you can say that it is much easier to discriminate derived relational responding as such as there is less going on per time unit. The effect of the above is that verbal control over behavior weakens, which has a point from an ACT perspective, as excessive verbal control is considered a problem in many contexts. I guess you can do meditation exercises with other purposes in mind, both within the context of Buddhism and other traditions. These could be more or less ACT consistent.
BUDDHISM Meditation, ACT/RFT view of [cont'd] John Blackledge	I think meditation can be neatly conceptualized as a defusion/acceptance technique similar in function to standard ACT techniques (with an added component of more expansive present-centered awareness). Of course, to think that this conceptualization captures the effects of meditation greatly cheapens the experience (it's much bigger than words, of course), but that holds for everything from an ACT and a Buddhist (and a Sufi, and a Hindu, and a Sikh, and a Taoist, and a Native American...............[insert mystical wing of any religion here] perspective). In many of the Buddhist books I've read, the authors consistently refer (sometimes obliquely, sometimes

	directly) to the problems people face when they attempt to use meditation to gain something, whether the gaining involves more positive thoughts and feelings and less negative ones, enlightenment, etc. Michael Palin (one of my favorite Monty Python guys) illustrated this common gaining perspective people approach Buddhism/meditation with on one of the travel shows he did (Around the World in 80 Days). Before spending a week with Buddhist monks at a monastery, he asked one, "What will I gain from this?" The monk looked perplexed, and simply answered, "Nothing." You gain nothing if a part of you is banking on relief or ecstasy--only by surrendering to what's really there on its own, nonverbal terms do you gain anything. Paradox in a nutshell.
	One of the differences between ACT and Buddhism is that ACT yokes acceptance and defusion to the pursuit of values. There is no intention in ACT to get people to defuse all the time (otherwise they would defuse from values as well), and there is no necessity to consistently get people to become expansively aware in the present moment. Present centered awareness and prolonged defusion/acceptance are great (I personally value them very highly, and consider meditation a very valuable tool that I try to sell to my ACT clients), but perhaps not necessary to live a more meaningful life.
	As far as whether specific meditations tend to elicit more of a control agenda: I've seen a few in books that specifically mention the technique as a way to feel better or get rid of unwanted thoughts. This is an empirical matter, but I suspect this might backfire. I think it's almost inevitable that people will at least initially use meditation as a way to try to avoid, but we can twist anything to that purpose.
BUDDHISM Meditation, ACT/RFT view of [cont'd] Madelon Bolling	To say that Buddhism promotes acceptance and present-centered awareness without the pursuit of values is somewhat mistaken. That is the purpose of the Four Great Vows (to save all beings from suffering, to abandon greed, hatred and ignorance, to be awake to ubiquitous opportunities for realization [a poor translation, sorry], and to embody the Buddha's way fully) that all Buddhists take and are reminded of constantly. The extent to which individual Buddhists actually succeed in pursuing these values of course varies widely.
BUDDHISM Meditation, ACT/RFT view of [cont'd] John Bush	Indeed, the moral-philosophy aspect of Buddhism is saturated with values. Perhaps the main difference with ACT practice is that Buddhist values are universal for all persons and broadly defined, whereas in ACT we're concerned more with personal values, some of which can be relatively specific. Buddhism says (much like the Hippocratic oath) "Do no harm to sentient beings, even your enemies."...
BUDDHISM Meditation, ACT/RFT view of [cont'd] Madelon Bolling	John Blackledge wrote: Those who have practiced Buddhism formally would know better than I, but isn't one of the ultimate goals of Buddhism to defuse even from a literal understanding of the Four Great Vows (as well as from the Eightfold Path, etc.)? That is, to get to a point where you aren't purposely trying to attain anything, but rather completely defusing and becoming completely aware (as often as possible), and in the process paradoxically attaining enlightenment and embodying the Four Great Vows? This is a good approximation of the Zen view.... -- I say approximation since we tend to be allergic to buying language, period. I hesitate to say that this is "defusing" since I'm not an ACT adept, but that might be the right word here. From the beginning it's an error to try to attain anything. "Attain," if you look at it, is an agenda, a rule that points away from the immediacy of experience, from the contingency-shaped realm. The whole problem seems to be--how to be a languaging creature in a way that doesn't upset the balance of the whole system, where most of the other elements (sentient and non-sentient) are contingency-shaped or balanced by equally regular laws (gravity, weather, succession of bloom). Our languaging allows us to overrule :) these checks and balances. The question is how to language (in the broadest sense) without killing off the world.
BUDDHISM Meditation, ACT/RFT view of [cont'd] **RFT** **Relational framing - effects of meditation/ ACT [6-6-03]** Patty Bach	Joseph Ciarrochi wrote: I wonder if any of these meditation/defusion practices actually reduce the general tendency to engage in relational framing. My personal experience with meditation has been that, while meditating, I have the subjective experience that there is reduced languaging/relational framing. I find that when I am meditating regularly the way this seems to carry over into the bulk of my time when I am not meditating is that, while I do not seem to experience any less languaging/relational framing activity, I am more mindful/aware of when I am languaging, and therefore more easily able to defuse from thoughts/feelings that show up. Do ACT interventions attempt to reduce relational framing activity, or responding to verbal stimuli? I have understood ACT to do more of the latter than the former. It seems that reducing relational framing would not be very different from "don't think about X," and that the stimulus functions of language/private events are the targets of change rather than the content/frequency of relational framing/languaging activity.

	On another note, another interesting Buddhist perspective - Pema Chodron, in her writing on a Tibetan Buddhist approach to meditation, says much that sounds consistent with ACT. She points out that one may use meditation or any practice in the service of avoidance. In Tibetan meditation sometimes meditation proceeds similar to other meditation practices described in this 'Meditation and ACT thread,' then there is an approach (I think maybe called 'insight meditation') where one deliberately focuses and meditates on distressing private events to increase understanding of how one operates. There is a slogan encouraging this practice that she roughly translates as "meditate on that which provokes resentment."
BUDDHISM Meditation, ACT/RFT view of [cont'd] RFT Relational framing activity - effects of meditation/ACT [cont'd] Steve Hayes	I think you are right about primacy of processes Pat, but empirically speaking when believability of clinically important negative thoughts goes down, generally frequency gradually follows. If we can take these clinical data to reflect the two RFT processes (Cfunc / Crel) it makes sense. Take away the functions of framing and framing itself should weaken somewhat. Of course if you did that deliberately, the "deliberation" would itself provide both Cfunc and Crel contexts, so we would be back to the "don't think about X" paradox.
BUDDHISM Meditation, ACT/RFT view of [cont'd] RFT Relational framing activity - effects of meditation/ACT [cont'd] Niklas Törneke	From a practical point of view I think the question Joseph raised points to something which is clear in all Buddhist (at least) meditation and which maybe is a bit different than most defusion techniques in ACT. Focusing is always stressed as a starting point. From my own experience, as Pat writes, that reduces framing. This could be used as avoidance, and from my experience of working in therapy with people who have meditated regularly (or are doing it) I would say it is used this way by many. Nevertheless, if focusing is combined with "opened mindfulness" (as is encouraged by most traditional Buddhist instructions) I would say it aids the real goal of discriminating AARRs, that is, attending to verbal stimuli as to "what they are and not what they say they are." Is it not reasonable to think that focusing on sensations, for example, would by itself reduce the amount of Crel and Cfunc present? The classical ACT intervention that would work this way, of course, is "milk, milk, milk..." A mantra technique? It is clear that this would not work "deliberately" (Steve's point), that is, if the instruction was "do this so that you will not think of what milk really is." The aid of focusing is a "side effect." It is like counting sheep to go to sleep. As long as you do it "just for counting sheep" it may actually help putting you to sleep. Sleep will be given to you as you count.... If you do it to go to sleep ... there you are getting frustrated!
BUDDHISM Meditation, ACT/RFT view of [cont'd] RFT Relational framing activity - effects of meditation/ACT [cont'd] Niklas Törneke	What do you think of these speculations? Too far off, maybe, but it gets me going.... Focusing on actual contingencies (the sound of "milk, milk...", the sensations from your nostrils as you breathe) lessens the presence of stimuli functioning as Crel (and, of course, Cfunc also). (Actually, according to Buddhist instructions, if you continue "just focusing" you will reach levels of experience where there is no thought at all, they call it different levels of jhanas.) Choosing to widen your focus there will be more stimuli functioning as Crel but as you are in a better position to discriminate your responding as it happens in the moment that will affect Cfunc, the consequences of your behavior (as you sit doing this very thing) will change, you discriminate that etc. ..... Defusion?
BUDDHISM Meditation, ACT/RFT view of [cont'd] RFT Relational framing activity - effects of meditation/ACT [cont'd] Dermot Barnes-Holmes	Sounds good to me. Also, seems like the importance of deictic frames should be emphasized here. For example, when you talk about "choosing to widen your focus" this is done from a perspective, right? Seems like this is most likely done from I, Here, Now (self-as-context), and although relational framing may increase, that activity itself is responded to as I, There, and Then, rather than I, Here, Now (i.e., you don't "buy" the thoughts and feelings, good or bad, that show up). In short, defusion seems to involve a transformation of functions of relational framing activity itself, in that the activity acquires the relational functions of I, There, and Then, rather than I, Here, Now. One method that seems to facilitate this transformation of functions is mantra-type exercises, because they provide an exemplar of the relevant transformation of functions for a single word or set of words (e.g., saying the Rosery in the Catholic tradition). Of course, the trick is to get this transformation of functions to generalize, under appropriate forms of contextual control, to the individual's ongoing and dynamic relational framing activity.
BUDDHISM Meditation, ACT/RFT view of [cont'd]	Yes, good! This also gives an example of how complex this kind of behavior is, I think, even in this (from the perspective of languaging in general) "simple" form. Not so strange that we need these kinds of "unnatural" exercises to discriminate what we are doing, and still a lot of it escapes us!

RFT	
Relational framing activity - effects of meditation/ACT [cont'd]	
Niklas Törneke	

BUDDHISM Meditation, ACT/RFT view of [cont'd] **RESOURCES** **Meditation, nature/ benefits of - client handout** **EXERCISE** **Milk, milk, milk [6-19-03]** John Blackledge *Cross Reference:* *See 3-124 for a further post in the thread:* *BUDDHISM* *Meditation, ACT/RFT view of*	I've given out the following description of the nature and benefits of meditation in ACT workshops I'm conducting for my dissertation. It was an attempt to inoculate clients from using meditation as a control agenda, and in a way consistent with ACT. Not sure if it serves that purpose or not--I'd love to hear feedback. How is Meditation Beneficial? It teaches you how to directly experience the present moment. We spend virtually all of our time caught up in our heads, often upset about the past or worrying about the future. When we're this caught up in our heads, it's as if the bad things that have happened or that might happen are happening right now. Mindfulness exercises like meditation remind us that what's really happening right now and what our minds say is happening are two very different things. It gives you a chance to experience unpleasant emotions and thoughts in a safe setting. We are all brought up to believe that unpleasant thoughts and feelings are things that need to be gotten rid of, things that indicate there is something wrong with us that needs to be fixed. Activities like meditation give us a chance to see what happens when we don't struggle to get rid of these unpleasant thoughts and feelings. While our minds usually tell us that this is a bad or a dangerous idea, the experiences of those who try it wholeheartedly say that it's not as bad as you'd expect, and that it takes less effort and comes at a much lower cost than struggling. It teaches you when and how you avoid. We've become such experts at pushing away unpleasant experiences that we often take steps to avoid them even before we are consciously aware they are there! Avoidance is fine when it doesn't cause problems for you, but when it keeps you from moving in a valued direction it is counterproductive. Mindfulness activities like meditation give you much better insights into what kinds of feelings you try to avoid, how you try to avoid them, and even some of the costs of these avoidance attempts. As mentioned above, it also teaches you that you don't have to avoid in the first place! It teaches you that no thought or feeling is permanent. When we feel bad, we often automatically assume that we're going to feel that way forever (or at least for longer than we can bear). Actually, all thoughts and feelings (whether pleasant or unpleasant) ebb and flow like waves on the ocean. Ironically, when we struggle against unpleasant feelings or otherwise try to avoid them, they usually stick around even longer and become even stronger! It gives you an opportunity to commit to a course of action and stick to it, regardless of how you think or feel. Once we decide what we value in life and what work we need to do in order to work toward those values, we very quickly find that we don't always feel like doing that work, or that we think we're not capable of doing the work. Meditation can give you a very solid example of how you can do such work even when you don't feel like it or don't think you can. Simply commit to meditating for a set period of time, every day. Do it even when you don't feel like it, don't think you are doing it right, or don't think you are getting anything out of it. Treat these thoughts and feelings like you would any others while meditating-accept them, don't fight them, and focus back on your breath. In return for a few minutes of your time, you get a daily lesson that you can do something even if your mind says no. It can provide an experience of calm and peacefulness. It doesn't always (especially if that's what you're trying to make happen!), but hey, it's nice when it does. It can make you feel more connected to the world and people around you. Much of the unpleasantness we experience comes from feeling separate from the experiences that surround us. Meditation shows you, bit by bit, how connected we actually are. You can think of feeling connected to the people and things around you in the moment as being a lamp connected to an electrical outlet. Vitality, like electricity, flows from connectedness. The lamp still exists when it's not plugged in, but it doesn't have the life that was intended for it. Such connectedness is also at the core of spirituality and religion. It can teach you to be less judgmental of yourself and others. Bit by bit, meditation teaches you that all the negative evaluations and judgments we make about ourselves and others have little, if any, basis in fact. Since efforts to "earn" evaluations such as "better than," "good enough," "loveable," "happy enough," etc. are very often at the core of our suffering (especially when we believe we've fallen short of these evaluative states), learning to believe them less and less is a very productive process. Those who frequently make negative evaluations of others (especially when they believe these evaluations) also tend to make more negative evaluations of themselves. Making and believing negative evaluations also disconnects us more and more from our surroundings and from the present moment, destroying the vitality that comes from such experiences. It teaches you that your mind isn't very good at describing your experience. Direct experiences are much

more complex than words can convey. Try to describe a time where you were almost ecstatically aware of your surroundings (for example, walking in the woods, in a flower garden, or at the beach and noticing how brilliantly colorful, beautiful, and peaceful your surroundings are), or simply try to describe to someone a trip you took to a place he or she has never been (that is, what it was like to actually be there). How close does you verbal description come to the actual experience? It seems pretty safe to say, "Not very close at all." Direct experience is simply a lot bigger, and a lot different, than words. More to the point, unpleasant experiences (even the really, really, really unpleasant ones) are often very different from what our minds tell us they are. In short, they are typically (and, in the minds of many who have experience with such a perspective, always) more bearable, less destructive, and more vitalizing than the "struggle against unpleasant experiences" option that our minds insistently offer us instead.

It teaches you that words are just words, and that reality is something quite different. Try saying the word "milk" over and over again, out loud, for a minute or two. When you first start saying it, you can almost actually see and feel the physical qualities of milk. You can taste it, feel it going down your throat, feel how cold and creamy it is, etc. After you've repeated the word for a minute or so, you only hear the actual sound that speaking the word makes. Where'd the milk go? It's just a word, but words have the ability to carry the features of the things they designate unless you take special steps to experience the words as they actually are. Milk is a benign example, but what if the words were "I'm bad" or "I can't take this," and these words occurred along with intense feelings of self-loathing and desperation? Your mind may be very convincing about the truth of these statements, but does your direct experience communicate the same message? Like the milk, the brute force of these words tends to fade when you focus in on the experience that actually lies under the words and allow it to be there as it is, not as your mind says it is. The feelings don't disappear, and often neither do the words, but the experience is always different from what your mind says it is. If it isn't, it's usually a good sign that you're still struggling and not fully settling into the experience.

Meditation gives you a continuing lesson in the difference between direct experience and talk, and an eventually convincing lesson that direct experience simply feels much more real than words.

BUDDHISM

Mind - Room of a Thousand Demons
[5-24-04]

Graham Taylor

... This story is one I have used for many years in preparing clients to do defusion / exposure to painful and unwelcome memories of trauma. The source is given at the end. I'm not sure how much I have changed the story from O'Hanlon's tape - I know the last paragraph is me. In ACT terms the notion of self as observer is obvious, as is exposure in the service of valued ends.

The Room of a Thousand Demons

Once in the life of every Buddhist monk in Tibet, a ceremony called the Room of a Thousand Demons is performed. This ceremony gives the participants the opportunity to obtain rapid Enlightenment. Participation is optional, but the chance comes only once in a lifetime. If the opportunity is not taken, the faithful must make the longer path towards enlightenment, going through perhaps several reincarnations along the way. But there is a price to be paid for rapid enlightenment, and the ceremony is not named the Room of a Thousand Demons for nothing. This is what the faithful are told.

The Room of a Thousand Demons is well named. The demons which inhabit this room have the ability to enter every corner of your mind, and take on your deepest fears and traumas in the most vivid form.

The Room of a Thousand Demons has two doors. You enter the room at one side, and that door cannot be re-opened from the inside. The only exit is a door on the other side of the room. Many people have made it through the door on the other side, to enlightenment, but some people have never made it out. They remain tortured by the Demons. In order to help you choose whether you will enter the Room of a Thousand Demons, here are two pieces of advice.

Whatever you experience in the Room of a Thousand Demons, *always remember* that your experience is *only* a projection of what is stored in your own mind. If you have a fear of heights, you will not *really* be standing on a narrow ledge above a 1000 foot drop, it will only *seem* that you are. If you have a fear of spiders, it will only seem to you that the room is filled with spiders. The experience however, seems so real that most people forget this advice.

So remember this. The second piece of advice is simply: *keep your feet moving*. For whatever you experience in the Room of a Thousand Demons, if you keep your feet moving, you will get to the other side of the room, open the door, exit, and experience enlightenment. During our work I will be with you, as you walk your Room. I cannot see your Demons for they are yours, not mine. I do have my own Demons, but they are in my Room. But I can see your struggle, and I can be with you, and remind you to keep your feet moving, and help you through.

Acknowledgement. This version is adapted from a story from Bill O'Hanlon's audio tape, "Keep Your Feet Moving: Favourite Teaching Stories from Bill O'Hanlon," available from Possibilities, 7914 West Dodge #387 Omaha NE 68114, USA.

BUDDHISM **Mind vs. experience -** **Parable of the Arrow** **[4-21-04]** Andy Santanello	I hope that this isn't too Buddhist for the list, but I have always found this passage extremely profound. It's called "The Parable of the Arrow." A man approached the Buddha and wanted to have all his philosophical questions answered before he would practice. In response, the Buddha said, "It is as if a man had been wounded by a poisoned arrow and when attended to by a physician were to say, 'I will not allow you to remove this arrow until I have learned the caste, the age, the occupation, the birthplace, and the motivation of the person who wounded me.' That man would die before having learned all this. In exactly the same way, anyone who should say, 'I will not follow the teaching of the Buddha until the Buddha has explained all the multiform truths of the world' - that person would die before the Buddha had explained all this." I think this passage cuts right to the heart of ACT. Often we take our mind's advice when we should listen to the wisdom of our experience (the physician). All of us have poisoned arrows sticking out of our rumps at one point or another. If we don't take the steps to "pull them out," the poison of experiential avoidance eventually will cripple us by gradually whittling away adaptive behaviors.
BUDDHISM **Suffering, notion of** **[5-25-04]** Jim Bastien	Just a quick comment on the Buddhist notion of suffering. Buddhists discuss various forms of suffering including the more common sense of physical and emotional pain. However, the more primary notion of suffering in Buddhism stems from the experience that nothing is permanent. However wonderful our current situation, it will eventually change. If we are attached to it, we will suffer when it transforms into something else. Over time, one comes to see that everything is constantly changing and nothing remains the same. This is the notion of impermanence. Reinforcers are like this. Their efficacy fluctuates with relative states of deprivation. It is the constant cycling of gain and loss that in time fosters an underlying sense that permanence is unattainable. This underlying dis-ease with one's ability to achieve a lasting sense of satisfaction through the pursuit of what we want vs. what we don't want Buddhism calls *dukkha* or suffering. So even when things are going well there is already suffering inherent in this situation if one clings to the futile hope that it will last or consistently recur. Liberation from suffering comes when one no longer chases one's desires in an attempt to "get it all." If things are going well that's ok because it is part of the way life works. When things are not going well that is ok because that is the way life works. The middle path is not to cling to any form of reinforcement.
BUDDHISM **Words, discourse on -** **Chuang Tzu** **WORDS** **Discourse on - Chuang** **Tzu [6-1-04]** Andy Santanello	This is a little discourse on words by Chuang Tzu, the Taoism sage. "The purpose of a fish trap is to catch fish, and when the fish are caught, the trap is forgotten. The purpose of a rabbit snare is to catch rabbits. When the rabbits are caught, the snare is forgotten. The purpose of words is to convey ideas. When the ideas are grasped, the words are forgotten. Where can I find a man who has forgotten words? He is the one I would like to talk to." Chuang Tzu I got this from Schiller, D. (1994). *The Little Zen Companion*. New York: Workman Publishing. I think that this little quote is interesting from an ACT perspective on a few levels. First, this quote alludes to the fact that words are empty vessels that carry meaning. There is no wisdom or meaning in the vessels. In other words, words are just messengers. I think people get caught up with "killing the messengers" when they are just innocent bystanders. Second, there is a function/content theme in this quote. Chuang Tzu seems to be suggesting that words are useful for what they are useful for (i.e., conveying an idea), but that ultimately they fall short. Ultimately, I think that the experience of living cannot be fully captured in words because this experience is not an idea, it is reality.
COGNITIVE **RESTRUCTURING** **Does ACT result in?** **[1-11-05]** John Blackledge	From an RFT perspective, we have to acknowledge that changing the way you think changes the stimulus functions that are present (i.e., changing the way you frame your experience changes how the stimulus functions that comprise that experience are transformed). The issue is, I think, changing the way you think about your experience only works when you can change the way you think about your experience. When you can't, you're stuck, and you have to learn how to defuse that way of thinking and accept what remains (if you can't accept it already). I suspect this isn't a small caveat, as existing ways of thinking can be pretty resistant to change.
COGNITIVE RESTRUCTURING Does ACT result in? [cont'd] Patty Bach	I think ACT certainly leads to a change in one's thinking - and that as compared to cognitive reappraisal a major difference would be in considering how thinking is changed. Cognitive reappraisal seems more focused on changing content while ACT is more focused on changing process and how one responds to whatever content shows up-and in order to reappraise a cognition in the moment one must first be mindful of one's cognitions in the moment - perhaps this is where there is some similarity to ACT or other

	mindfulness approaches, and a difference in ACT is that one does not necessarily change the appraisal, instead one notes that it is merely an appraisal/evaluation and hopefully chooses an action with or without a change in any particular cognitive appraisal.
COGNITIVE RESTRUCTURING Does ACT result in? [cont'd] Kelly Wilson	Also worth noting that changing the way you think, reframing, reappraisal, are not analyses, they are all behaviors requiring analyses (for behavior analysts anyway). Creating a context in which people actively engage in thinking about an event in different ways ought to increase flexibility with respect to that which is thought about. Look at Ellen Langer's wonderful book *Mindfulness*--not behavior analytic at all, but demonstrates the point well. What we need to understand is what are the contexts that foster this sort of psychological flexibility. This points to the central difference between behavior analysis and most of the rest of psychology. We don't count behaviors as independent variables. For us, they are always the dependent variable. Likewise, framing relationally does not constitute a behavior analytic explanation. The explanation is the context (IV) that generates and maintains framing relationally (DV). This is by the way, a key distinction between RFT and network theories of meaning. If you want to get this issue, the best read (I think) is the Hayes & Brownstein, 1986, behavior-behavior relations paper. It is said elsewhere--it is in Skinner, of course. But this is a very clear explication of the issue. If you get this, you have gotten something central about behavior analysis.... Hayes, S. C., & Brownstein, A. J. (1986). Mentalism, behavior-behavior relations and a behavior analytic view of the purposes of science. *The Behavior Analyst, 9*, 175-190.
COGNITIVE RESTRUCTURING Does ACT result in? [cont'd] **ACT cf.** **CBT - cognitive flexibility/ cognitive restructuring [1-11-05]** Steve Hayes	Cognitive flexibility (think about it many ways and do what works) is probably more important than cognitive reappraisal in the sense of "thinking about it (always) in the right way." Cognitive flexibility implies cognitive change - but not directed change into a specified and narrow form (including "rational" thought).... Let's remember that the mediational analyses in traditional CBT rarely work. So if reappraisal defined as "thinking in the right way" is so good, why don't these mediational models work and work really well? They don't. And Ruth's point about mindfulness is a good one [Ruth Baer wrote: "I've read some ... papers on reappraisal and suppression, and their evidence looks pretty good that suppression is not very healthy and reappraisal is better. But they don't tell us anything about how mindful observation/ acceptance/ allowing would compare."]: in basically all of the studies I'm aware of when you allow a test of changing the function ... via acceptance/defusion/mindfulness vs. changing the form, the former wins out. In ACT there is lots of work that does in fact change the form of cognitions. We are cognizing organisms. But it is always held lightly and is always subordinate to workability: don't BELIEVE even this; how does that work for you?; can you integrate those same facts into another story - and another? Defusion and flexibility is key. If some of the variants of thought include forms that support effective action you can have your cake and eat it too: you get the benefit of cognitive change in the sense of having verbalizations comport with effective action and you get the benefits of cognitive flexibility. If none of the variants of thought include forms that support effective action and you can get effective action anyway, then the cognitive forms will over time come into line with action. This is a double headed arrow. If the cognitive forms are narrow and fused and don't support effective action, you are in trouble. But ACT targets that situation in an easier and more generally effective way than directed cognitive change strategies do -- or so would be the claim. Ways to test this: head to head comparisons; mediational analyses; correlational analyses. A few of these have been done, but a lot more is needed. So far, the ACT / RFT model has won out in every case I know of. Comparing cognitive reappraisal to suppression is not relevant to any of these tests. Joe [Ciarrochi who wrote "I think traditional CBT folks already are saying that ACT is nothing more than repackaged CBT."] is exactly right: the traditional CBT crowd is now fully off of "this will not work" or just "huh?" and fully into "this is what we do anyway." If ACT / RFT is more in the ballpark of what the universe shows, eventually "we knew it all along" will settle in and these sensibilities will be the new normality -- we are not there because what "is the same" is not yet understood. Those of us who were doing this work 15 years ago remember what it was like. It is hard to let bygones be bygones - but we don't need to hang on to the history. We have no need to make others wrong. If "this is the same" was really true I would not care, and CBT is indeed changing. But real differences should not be papered over in the interests of harmony. The same folks saying "this is what we do anyway" a) have never been in an ACT workshop, and if they had they would not be saying they do the same thing b) do treatments that show empirical differences in processes of change with ACT, and c) still do cognitive restructuring, exposure to change emotions, etc. etc. even though these have demonstrable dangers.

	I think we need to draw this into high relief - not everywhere and not always, but strategically, compassionately and carefully. Thesis / antithesis / synthesis. You don't get change unless there is a difference.
	There is a difference.
EXPOSURE **Acceptance and** **[1-28-05]** Steve Hayes	Patty Bach wrote: Acceptance is staying present with whatever shows up. We don't bring aversive private events into focus in order to accept them; when we make an acceptance move the event/experience accepted is already there; it's shown up without a deliberate effort to bring it about or attend to it. If something is present we accept its presence. We would no more try to focus on anger or anxiety etc. than try not to. Yes, except in deliberate exposure work. That catholic posture toward such events may be part of why ACT produces pretty cool natural exposure in some studies -- do the defusion / acceptance / self / values work etc. and people start naturally doing things that are hard (that OCD study Mike Twohig just did is a nice example). Deliberate exposure work is fine but can easily have a tiny seed of "I need to make this feel different." In ACT workshops there is a lot of guided exposure work, but by really emphasizing the acceptance side it reduces that danger. What is being learned is the move you can make when things show up outside of ACT workshops - it's not a content move.
HYPNOSIS **Altered states,** **literature re** **EXPOSURE** **Stimulation during** **(EMDR etc.) [1-6-05]** Steve Hayes	Russ Harris wrote: The problem both with tapping therapies and EMDR is working out which bits of the protocol are helpful. Tapping on parts of your body, following a finger from side to side with your eyes, listening to alternating auditory clicks - all of these create a trance state. Is that state 'mindfulness'? I'm not convinced it is. It seems more akin to a hypnotic trance - a dissociated state. But maybe I'm wrong about that.... It seems that at least some of the reasons for the rapid effectiveness of these methods when compared to CBT.... Are there good, controlled studies that show rapid effectiveness for these methods relative to traditional CBT? I need a few references. No need to explain differences until we have differences. Are there differences? As far as trance states and such I used to follow the hypnosis literature (years ago) until I was convinced (by Ted Barber and others) that there was literally nothing that you could do through hypnosis that you could not do with high social demand. The language of "trances" and "altered states" and such isn't relevant until you have a discrete phenomenon to chase. I haven't rechecked in - not for years ... so maybe the literature has moved. But this got a good careful over decades look by some really good psychologists and they were never able to document that the "altered state" idea had merit (and some really wanted it to be true). Regarding tapping, clicks etc. This is not a literature I know, but again first we need evidence that they make a difference (is even that firm yet? I doubt it). Then we need a model. My suspicion is that they will *sometimes* help but that almost any stimulus would do the same (e.g., not just taps, or eye movement, or clicks, but also repeated novel smells; turning the person upside down; moving the chair in random patterns; etc. etc.). My suspicion of mechanism when they help at all: response flexibility / varied contact with the environment while in simultaneous contact with the feared event. In animal models forced contact with the environment during unreinforced exposure to a CS increases operant and respondent extinction. Freezing / narrowing / etc. can be forms of avoidance and requiring contact with the environment undermines that function. Same with humans but not all humans avoid in that way. If they do, some stimulation might be helpful - but that is usually in exposure protocols anyway so it might not add much beyond what folks already do. If that is the mechanism, virtually any seemingly credible method to ensure response variability should also be helpful. Dance the rumba while bringing to mind traumatic memories. Remember Wolpe's cats? Eating during exposure helped. His model was later shown to be wrong but the procedure might be helpful for other reasons. It makes sense of some anomalies. Remember the goofy data on relaxation and SD? (i.e., muscle tensing works as well as relaxation in aiding exposure). It would make sense of that. Just guesses though. But in the meantime, we need real differences before we get too interested.
INSIGHT **Function - leads to** **more effective action?** **[5-20-04]** Niklas Törneke	Regarding "insight into the past" I would say it very well can function as a starting point for more effective action, but it need not. Experiencing anxiety (say) now as "a result of this and this that happened there and then" (programming I now discriminate) can change the context of that experience now and thus start new behavior. That does not contradict, of course, that "trying to get insight about the past" can be a verbal trap.

INSIGHT
 	
  Therapies; insight in therapy
 	
THOUGHT
 	
  Suppression, effectiveness of [3-28-04]
 	
    ACT Listserv Member
	Steve Mahorney wrote:
	
	    [The ACT book] states, "This is why insight-oriented psychotherapy may make sense at times." What do we mean by insight and what are its categories? At what other times would it "make sense"?
	
	Insight is self-awareness of previously 'unconscious' material, either emotional or intellectual, that is assumed to be at the root of psychological dysfunction. Two traditionally accepted forms of insight therapy are psychoanalysis (Freud, Jung, Adler, etc.) and Gestalt (Perls, etc.). Insight oriented therapies make sense to most because they recapitulate Western cultural belief that 1) there is an underlying cause and 2) that knowing the cause alone will create change. To me the quote is hinting to this, that insight driven therapies seem to make sense, because they are so close to our culturally acceptable practices of seeking reasons/causes, in this case in our unconscious mind or childhood or both (or in the case of Freud in biological recapitulation of evolution of our species, also). Insight is fine if it happens, but it should not be the goal of therapy, as it doesn't usually bring about change....
	
	As for the insight experience in therapy, ACT might look at it this way: when we talk of creating a safe space for the client to talk about their problems, we are really talking about altering context through bringing about different contingencies for discussing private and often painful material; due to the shift in context some thoughts that the client was suppressing may be verbalized. Think of it this way, if you felt that you could say anything and not be evaluated negatively by your peers/ therapist/ priest, etc. and you felt that you wouldn't be abandoned with the thought (in other words you were supported) what would you say? Therapy does this, it provides a safe place to say anything, so the need to suppress a thought is gone....
	
	Are there things that are not verbally governed? Sure they can be governed by external contingencies that naturally occur, such as touching a hot stove leads to a burn. The unconscious question is tricky - I do believe (and RFTers help me out here) that some cognitive material can be out of our direct awareness at least temporarily and partially. Through languaging we can temporarily suppress thoughts; if it didn't work sometimes we wouldn't do it. And although we are not directly thinking of something (say Elvis), through the bidirectional nature of language and transformation of stimulus functions, whatever we are thinking of instead of Elvis is still "attached" to the stimulus Elvis. What I mean here is that although I am not thinking about Elvis, 1) I have to check that I am not thinking about Elvis, which is thinking about Elvis and 2) because some of the stimulus functions associated with Elvis will transfer to whatever I utilize to not think of Elvis, I will in essence still be thinking of Elvis (this is what I meant by partially). The Chocolate Cake exercise illustrates this point much better than I just did.

INSIGHT
 	
  Therapies; insight in therapy [cont'd]
 	
    Francis De Groot
	I think insight-oriented (IO) therapy indeed can make sense sometimes. The example given in the book can be generalized. IO therapy can help you see things from a different perspective, put things in a different context. If you can discover the frames of coordination you are putting events in, and the consequences thereof (my father abused me - my father is a man - I hated the abuse; so I hate men; or RFT book p. 208: being a man means having control - women have no control - women are victims; I can rape women), you might be able to change (just by the different context, by making them more rule-governed and making place for values, ...). But it won't be easy, and most of the time it will not be enough just to have the insight.

INSIGHT
 	
  Therapies; insight in therapy [cont'd]
 	
    Kelly Wilson
	I think this is essentially right Francis - in as much as the behavior is under operant control--that is sensitive to consequences. However, we shouldn't underestimate the possibility that lots of "problem" behavior is under strong antecedent control (i.e., respondent). If the latter is the case (and both almost certainly are always so) the solution will come from procedures that look like defusion/exposure (here exposure meant the way I speak of it in my values chap for Guilford). IO therapy may well also have some effects as result of exposure/defusion.
	
	There is a twisty dark side possible too, however, with IO. It can be like "if I understand - then problem over" - strong antecedent stimulus control is typically not like that though. For example, all of the insight in the world will not change a snake phobic's response to a snake--you gotta get in there and be with the snake for that to change.

INSIGHT
 	
  Therapies; insight in therapy [cont'd]
 	
AVOIDANCE
 	
  Effectiveness of [4-1-04]
 	
    ACT Listserv Member
	Steve Mahorney wrote:
	
	    We talk about clients avoiding unpleasant thoughts or feelings. Is it possible that their avoidance efforts have been successful enough that they are unaware of them (unpleasant thoughts or feelings) and that "insight" into when they are influencing behavior may play a role in facilitating ACT steps?
	
	There are two questions here:
	
	1) Is it possible that their avoidance efforts have been successful enough that they are unaware of them (unpleasant thoughts or feelings)?
	
	Yes and no. Yes avoidance can be successful - if it were not we would not use it and I suspect that with very unpleasant memories we can bury them under a lot of language and behavioral restriction so as to not

be immediately aware of their influence. They become like hearing; we always hear, even in our sleep we are receiving audio input, but we don't listen to everything in our environment. Some of the noises fade into the background; think about sitting at a coffee shop talking to a friend, there are lots of noises (other conversations, music, etc.) - most of us can focus our hearing on the person in front of us and the rest is there, it is heard but not listened to...similarly, some thoughts and memories become like background noise. Thing is we still hear the music at the café, and we still feel the effects of the unpleasant thoughts and feelings and like the music sometimes they take the foreground even when we don't want them to, so no too.

2) Can "insight" into when they are influencing behavior play a role in facilitating ACT steps?

I think Kelly answered this earlier and I would only add that we must take care that the "insight" doesn't become an explanation for behavior, and the focus on it is minimal so it too can be treated like what it is, a thought/memory/evaluation/etc. When it becomes the "cause" of behavior it leads to more verbal traps, like justification for the behavior or insight can become the focus of therapy for the client and block progress because they "cannot" move past it. Also, is it possible to address the problem behavior without "insight" and still show improvement in functioning? What are the current consequences that are maintaining the problem behavior?

Just my thoughts, I don't believe them.

UNCONSCIOUS

ACT/ RFT view of

Memory, repressed - ACT/ RFT view/ treatment approach [4-5-05]

John Blackledge

Mark Taylor wrote:

> Per a discussion with my wife, she questioned what ACT would say about the unconscious. I stated it probably doesn't recognize it, or at least doesn't call it by the same label. She asked about repressed memories then.

Not sure if this was where your wife was coming from (or if it was just sheer curiosity), but some psychological concepts (like the unconscious) have been around so long that people assume they are real entities that MUST be explained by a theory in order for that theory to be valid. I think it's important to remember that the "unconscious" is just one psychological construct among many (and one that can only be inferred and can never be directly measured, at that). From an RFT/ACT perspective, I think the kinds of things referred to by the unconscious fall into two categories:

(1) Verbally derived relations that we are not explicitly aware of at a given moment in time (for those not fluent in RFT, think of verbally derived relations loosely as implicit assumptions that have been indirectly deduced from your experiences);

(2) Aspects of our behavior (broadly defined to mean thoughts, feelings, and overt behavior) controlled by contingencies we are not verbally aware of.

Regarding how repressed memories might be conceptualized from an ACT/RFT perspective, I think there might be at least 4 categories:

(1) The experience or thought being "repressed" is aversive, and thus the target of experiential avoidance. Sometimes the avoidance of the thought would be successful enough to largely keep it from arising. Sometimes avoidance of it might simply consist of refusals to admit its presence..

(2) The memory isn't really "repressed," but rather consists of a specific thought or thoughts (referring to a past experience) that 'hasn't been had' before. The thought could involve, for example, an evaluation of a specific historical experience, an assignment of motive or intent to someone else's behavior, etc. From a behavioral perspective, memories essentially consist of verbal re-creations of events from our history, so there is always room to re-create aspects of the experience in a novel way.

(3) The memory isn't accurate, but rather reported because the current context is 'pulling for it'--i.e., the person is being reinforced for endorsing the memory, or the person is elaborating a relational network and the memory coheres (in plain English, the person is thinking about an event or experience in greater detail than in the past, and the "repressed" thought comes up because it seems to fit well with other aspects of what is remembered--and thinking about things coherently is typically reinforcing).

(4) Someone else is aware of a seemingly significant negative life event you've been through (from your youth, for example), you don't remember it, and the assumption is made that you must therefore be repressing the memory.

UNCONSCIOUS

ACT/ RFT view of [cont'd]

Steve Hayes

JT's answer is very thorough. Just a small addition.

Phil Hineline once pointed out that non-behaviorists believe that conscious processes are relatively easy to understand but that unconscious processes are strange, hard to understand, and a bit frightening. Conversely, behaviorists believe that unconscious processes are relatively easy to understand but that conscious processes are strange, hard to understand, and a bit frightening.

RFT is all about what is strange and a bit frightening to behavioral folks -- the unconscious is just old home

	week. Non-verbal organisms are not "conscious" in a verbal sense of what they do / feel / sense -- nor are we much of the time. But causality is not put into "the unconscious" as an entity. Unconscious learning is due to contact with events -- it is that history and that context that is the "cause" of what is attributed to "the unconscious."
UNCONSCIOUS Memory, repressed - ACT/ RFT view/ treatment approach [cont'd] Jason Luoma	Monica Pignotti wrote: How would an ACT therapist intervene with a client that presents with ... beliefs and issues about having to "recover ... memories" to get better? ... Those sorts of beliefs enforced by years of therapy, can really keep these people stuck in their lives because they are indoctrinated to believe that they have to "resolve" these before they can begin to live their lives. This sounds like several clients I've had in the past.... This is just a more extreme version of the context of experiential control, basically the client has some content (thoughts, feelings, etc.) that is not acceptable and it needs to be eliminated before they move on in their lives. Or in this case, they don't have the right content and if they could just get the right content, then everything would be OK. The place I would start if this theme was prominent is with creative hopelessness. How has doing this been working for them? Has trying to recover repressed memories or understand how their history has gotten them to where they are fundamentally improved their life, allowed them to do the things they want to in their life, to be the person they want to be? I'd focus on workability. What does their experience say vs. what their mind says? They are still in therapy after all.
UNCONSCIOUS Memory, repressed - ACT/ RFT view/ treatment approach [cont'd] **INSIGHT** **Therapeutic goal?** **CAUSE** **Etiology, utility of exploring [4-7-05]** Sven Rydberg	Yes, I have also had a good number of such (and similar) requests from clients. My solution so far has been to ask the client: "What do you want: to get better first, or first to know why you got worse?" If a client wants to know "Why" first, I say that it will take time and does not guarantee that she/he will get better. If a client wants to get better first, I can say that if they then are interested in the "Why worse" answer, it often can become more clear later. For instance, they probably have changed their behavior. At least 9 out of 10 of my clients have wanted to get better first.
INSIGHT Therapeutic goal? [cont'd] CAUSE Etiology, utility of exploring [cont'd] James Herbert	Most patients come into psychotherapy with an implicit (or often even explicit) notion that the purpose is to understand the etiology of their problem in order to change it. This is the result of at least two factors: the powerful legacy of psychoanalytic theory, and the impact of our collective histories with regard to verbal problem-solving. Psychoanalysis is based on the idea that insight into the (historical) origins of current problems is necessary (and in some cases even sufficient) for change. And our verbal repertoires are built around problem solving, which of course generally works well in the world outside the skin, but often runs into problems when applied inwardly. But let's step back and be honest for a moment. Consider any client (or any person for that matter). Do we really understand what makes him/her tick? Do all the assessment -- whether traditional, behavioral, or otherwise - that you'd like, and generate an etiologic story. How certain are you that this is really the cause of the behavioral target in question? We don't even understand the etiology of something as common as depression. Sure, as scientists we have discovered pieces of the puzzle (e.g., both genetic and psychosocial vulnerabilities). But the picture is far from complete. And that's just for the condition in a general sense. When trying to piece together the cause of any individual's behavior the task becomes far more daunting. Of course, this doesn't stop clients from wanting to know the cause, nor the vast majority of clinicians from happily offering them one. Someone experiences a loss, then becomes depressed. Bingo. But what about all those folks who experienced equally powerful losses but who didn't become depressed (the base rate problem)? What about the possibility of illusory correlation (*post hoc ergo propter hoc*)? Etc. etc. The point is that the stories we tell about the causes of our clients' behavior (or our own behavior) are just that - stories. They may or may not be accurate etiological accounts in a scientific sense. An alternative approach is to examine the function these stories serve. Sometimes they can provide a helpful context within which to make changes. But more often than not they only serve to keep one stuck in the past, trying to sort through an ever-increasingly intricate web of historical events rather than moving forward with life.

	Fortunately, for most of the problems we deal with in psychotherapy, we don't need to understand the etiology of the problem to intervene effectively.

So, when clients start the search for an explanation, I discuss these things with them openly and directly. I note that we could spend lots and lots of time piecing together a story, but there would be no guarantee that it would be accurate. And in fact, I could pretty much guarantee that the story would be highly incomplete at best, and grossly inaccurate at worst. Alternatively, we can focus on what the client wants to change (e.g., values clarification and appropriate goal setting), and how to achieve that change.

Finally, I'm anything but nihilistic about the search for etiology. When wearing my scientist hat, I very much want to understand the causes of behavior, both "normal" and pathological. Over the past couple of decades, the scientific community has made impressive progress in some areas, perhaps most importantly by ruling out once cherished explanations (e.g., the schizophrenogenic mother). But it's naïve to believe that we understand any disorder very well, especially in any individual case. And this applies not only to traditional case formulations, but the cognitive case conceptualizations of the cognitive therapists and even many of the functional analyses that the behavioral types are so fond of.

In the psychotherapy context, the search for causes is almost always an unnecessary and even harmful detour. |
| INSIGHT

Therapeutic goal? [cont'd]

CAUSE

Etiology, utility of exploring [cont'd]

James Herbert | Sven Rydberg wrote:

I think "maintenance of the problem" may slow down and even prevent "recovery."

Causes can be broken down in many ways (recall Aristotle's four causes, for example). Causal accounts that focus on proximal, maintaining factors are probably more likely to be both accurate, and to provide direction for intervention. But it still does not follow that interventions *must* target these maintaining factors in order to be effective. Consider the old aspirin analogue: aspirin may be effective for headaches from multiple etiologies, and such effectiveness may tell us little about the etiology of any particular headache - it may not be due to a lack of aspirin in the CNS, for example.

The degree to which accounts of maintaining factors lead to better treatment is an empirical question. From a strictly functionalist perspective, the accuracy of the accounts isn't even the issue. Such accounts, whether accurate or not, have "treatment utility" to the extent that they facilitate treatment, relative to treatment uninspired by such accounts.

My thesis is simply that most etiological accounts are not only highly incomplete, often grossly inaccurate, and misleading, but that they probably have "negative treatment utility," i.e., they interfere with rather than facilitate treatment. But again, this is a testable proposition, so maybe I'm wrong. |
| INSIGHT

Therapeutic goal? [cont'd]

CAUSE

Etiology, utility of exploring [cont'd]

James Herbert | Just to clarify, I did not mean to suggest that etiological questions are unimportant, nor that good etiological accounts of psychopathology might inform interventions. Let's certainly hope that this is the case! As science progresses and causal accounts become more complete, hopefully developments in intervention and especially prevention technologies will follow.

Rather, my points were: (a) in spite of our rhetoric, we currently know very little about the etiology of any particular patient's problems; (b) despite this, patients typically seek causal answers, and therapists are generally happy to comply; (c) such incomplete (or even inaccurate) causal accounts often constrain rather than promote positive behavior change (e.g., by fostering a victim mentality); and (d) causal analysis does not *necessarily* dictate the most effective intervention strategy.

.. Putative causal accounts can sometimes serve a useful function, as descriptive narratives that provide a context for subsequent behavior change efforts. Such narratives may sometimes be helpful, but are risky if taken too literally as historical fact or if they constrain rather than promote positive changes. And ... such narratives can sometimes have powerful placebo effects. But IMHO they remain risky, and should therefore be used with caution. |
| INSIGHT

Therapeutic goal? [cont'd]

CAUSE

Etiology, utility of exploring [cont'd] | The behavioral model is a medical model if by that we mean understanding the history, etiology, course, and response to treatment of well specified functional processes.

The "medical model" behavioral folks despise is the "label the person and be content" model -- but that is not the medical model anyway.

It isn't in physical medicine. Labeling syndromes in physical medicine is just a way station to understanding the etiology, course, and response to treatment of well specified functional processes and where that does not work (e.g., in cancer) they tool another course to get there (e.g., the basic process work on oncogenes).

In general the syndromal strategy is low pay-off when multiple causes lead to common outcomes or single causes lead to multiple outcomes. The syndromal does not work very well in behavioral disorders - multiple causes lead to common outcomes or single causes lead to multiple outcomes. In the mental health fields folks hung on (too long) to basic accounts that were not sufficiently helpful (psychoanalytic models that |

PSYCHIATRY **Medical model; syndromes, utility of** [4-13-05] Steve Hayes	were too vague as a scientific guide; brain-behavior accounts that are often too global as well). So we need to do what the cancer researchers did: go basic. RFT is that move and it is part of the etiological / causal / medical model work of the ACT / RFT community. I heard a good paper by Brian Iwata who argued that experimental functional analysis in behavior analysis is a very high form of the medical model since you show you can both produce and eliminate the problem. He cited several old Claude Bernard quotes that looked like they were written by behavior analysts. Eventually, if successful, we will work out etiology but we have to do it from the ground up. James is quite right that patients (or therapists) telling stories is not real etiological analysis - it's story telling.
INSIGHT Therapeutic goal? [cont'd] **CAUSE** Etiology, utility of exploring [cont'd] John Bush	Years ago, when I was first practicing CBT, a client said: "Oh, I see. Insight [in the psychoanalytic sense] is the booby prize."
INSIGHT Therapeutic goal? [cont'd] **CAUSE** Etiology, utility of exploring [cont'd] **PHYSICAL ILLNESS** **Cancer - acceptance of unknown etiology** [4-14-04] Jeffrey Porter	I am a psychologist in a cancer treatment center and I have been utilizing an ACT approach for the past couple of years. This issue that you speak of is especially pertinent with the majority of cancer patients. It shows up in many forms (i.e., why me? how did this happen? what did I do to cause my cancer?). The drive to understand why the cancer is in them is incredibly strong for most patients and I find your [Monica Pignotti's] observation that any explanation is preferable to no explanation to be very accurate. My experiences have been that one of two outcomes usually occurs when a patient is struggling with this issue. Either they latch onto an explanation that explains the cancer and puts them at fault in a tangible way (e.g., "It was all the diet Coke I drank in college" or "It's because I try too hard to please others and I disregard myself") or they get stuck asking the question and looking for the answer and stay in this state for a long time. Both situations are problematic inasmuch as they usurp attention and energy for a purpose that distracts the person from engaging in more meaningful activity. With respect to the second scenario of getting stuck in a pattern of searching for the answer, I often see patients soon after they have been diagnosed with cancer and consequently I usually do not call attention to the fruitlessness of this struggle right away. I sincerely doubt that many people would be willing to let go of this (very important) question prior to investing significant time and energy into trying to answer it. So initially, when it comes up in therapy I use more of a CT approach to the issue, something like, "I can see that this question is really important and it's difficult to live with it in an unanswered state. What answers has your mind come up with?" Then I participate in evaluating the likelihood of each answer being accurate/right. At some point down the road, maybe weeks or months, when it is clear to both of us that the patient has struggled and suffered with this question, I shift to an ACT position on the issue. When the context is appropriate, I'll say something like, "You know, you've been working on trying to find the answer to this question of why you have the cancer for a while now. We've put our minds together and haven't solved it. You've done reading on your own/ searched the internet/ talked to your oncologist (whatever fits) and still you don't have the answer. I know you don't want to hear this, but is it possible that the answer, you know the real answer, is not available? That maybe another challenge of this cancer is that you have to live with not knowing why it happened and only knowing that it did happen? I'm not telling you that this is the thing to do--I don't know what it's like to be you. I just know that you and lots of people like you struggle and suffer with this question and never find the answer. And I wonder if this is really how you want to spend your time." My experience is that in the majority of cases, this leads to a letting go or at least a loosening of the grip on this question. When that happens, the relief that comes from giving up the struggle is quite reinforcing and the issue rarely shows up again. In the first situation, where a person has adopted an explanation/story to explain his/her cancer and that explanation blames the individual and this blame leads to additional self-punishing behavior, defusion is obviously what would be helpful but my experience has been that it is very difficult. I have used the metaphor of clinging to a life buoy only to find out that it is more of an anchor than a buoy. I describe how being diagnosed with cancer can be like being thrown off of a ship. It's instinct to grab onto anything within reach. Sometimes that is an explanation for why you have the cancer. However, if the thing you have grabbed onto isn't what your mind told you it was (a solution) and is pulling you down more than it is helping you stay afloat, maybe it's time to ask yourself if you'd be better off holding onto nothing. This is a difficult behavior pattern for a person to change because life is on the line and the mind says, "I have to know why this happened to be able to deal/live with it."

INSIGHT	Jeff, Interesting observations. I do have one question though. You wrote: "I sincerely doubt that many people would be willing to let go of this (very important) question prior to investing significant time and energy into trying to answer it."
Therapeutic goal? [cont'd]	
	I'm just wondering out loud if this is one of those pieces of accepted clinical wisdom that may not in fact always hold true. That is, is it really necessary for patients to struggle with self blame for a period of weeks or months in order to appreciate the futility of the quest? Or might it be possible to reach that point sooner with a little nudging? I've found myself moving more quickly in this regard lately, with what seem like good results.
CAUSE	
Etiology, utility of exploring [cont'd]	
PHYSICAL ILLNESS	
Cancer - acceptance of unknown etiology [cont'd]	
James Herbert	
INSIGHT	My experience is similar to James's. In general, here's what I do:
Therapeutic goal? [cont'd]	- Ask how long they've been trying to explain their predicament (let's call this "Activity X"), and with what result.
	- Ask what they might do to make their lives as good as possible now and in the future (we'll call that "Activity Y").
CAUSE	- Suggest they experiment with pursuing goals they have a fighting chance of attaining (Y), while spending less time on X (digging for explanations of things that have already happened regardless of how they came about).
Etiology, utility of exploring [cont'd]	
PHYSICAL ILLNESS	Rationale: It can be very hard to stop doing X, even when you're being punished for it, unless you see Y as an alternative. (Example of the "don't think of a white elephant" paradox.)
Cancer - acceptance of unknown etiology [cont'd]	
John Bush	

Chapter 3
<u>Core Processes in ACT</u>

A post in Chapter 1 (1-18) introduced the "Hexaflex model" – so called because it arranges the six main components of ACT into a hexagon with psychological flexibility at the center. These components - acceptance; defusion; self-as-context; contact with the present moment; values; and committed action - are explored in the posts presented in this chapter. In the case of defusion, many of the discussions deal also with its potentially problematic counterpart (fusion), which, had it been easily separable, might have been included in Chapter 6. Two additional topics in this chapter are: mindfulness, the practice of which may be seen as closely related to several of the Hexaflex components; and vitality, a quality often associated, in the listserv community, with a life lived in a values-consistent manner.

ACCEPTANCE **Connotations of, unhelpful [3-26-04]** James Herbert	Joseph Ciarrochi wrote: ... people often do some unhelpful relational framing when they hear the word "acceptance." They think acceptance = "passive" or "giving in" or "letting people walk all over me" or "being weak." Good point about the connotations of "acceptance." I've struggled for a word that conveys the idea better, and the best I've come up with is "embrace."
ACCEPTANCE **Fate, of [11-18-03]** Steve Hayes	A student of mine (Dosheen Cook) recently completed a study that compared a Buddhist with a Confucian sense of acceptance (the latter being heavily linked to acceptance of one's fate) ... the former predicted health outcomes, the latter did not, both in Asians and Anglos. Acceptance of the moment -- moment by moment -- includes acceptance of the presence of events that we do not and cannot control. That is a kind of acceptance of "fate." But the concept has a history and it is not a psychologically helpful one. In Greek mythology "the Fates" were three goddesses who controlled the lives of human beings and beyond that even the Gods (Zeus himself was controlled by them on occasion). Fates and destiny thought of as causal entities that we do not control but that somehow control us are just control and fusion at a higher level (I don't control events but SOMEONE does; I don't understand why, but SOMEONE does; I can't figure it out or make it go away but that's because someone else is operating on me and I guess I just have to give up since I have no other choice; etc.). Resignation is like that. The control/fusion agenda is not being abandoned ... Psychologically, the important thing is acceptance in the moment of a lack of control in many areas and yet the continuing attempt to show up, care, love, and make a difference in the face of uncertainty, randomness, death and disease, loss, pain, and the other ailments flesh is heir to.
ACCEPTANCE **Mindfulness, and - core components/ self-report of** **MINDFULNESS** **Acceptance, and - core components/ self-report of [8-8-03]** Steve Hayes	... Mindfulness / acceptance has three components I think. The ability to defuse from thoughts. The ability to stay in full contact with what you are already in contact with. Finally, the ability to contact what is there to be contacted but is not now being contacted. Self-report of the first is hard (because the self-report itself tends to be taken literally) but not impossible. Self-report of the second is also hard but not impossible. ACT studies have crude measures of both of these. It is that last one that is most difficult, because of the "feature negative" problem -- it is hard to see what one does not see.... This three way division brought together for me why mindfulness and acceptance are at their core much the same phenomenon.
ACCEPTANCE **Self/ others - Whole, complete, perfect exercise** **EXERCISE** **Whole, complete, perfect [5-26-03]** Steve Myles	Joseph Ciarrochi wrote: I am trying to understand this idea that we can accept ourselves on faith as 'whole, complete, and perfect."... Is a pedophiliac perfect? The words "whole, complete, and perfect" are great at setting off minds doing what they do best (i.e., deriving lots of relations). In particular, for most people, these words set their minds off deriving lots of self-relations, many of which are negatively evaluated. One way in which this is useful in therapy is that it provides a great opportunity for the client to practice choice making in the presence of negatively-evaluated content; in this case, the choice to (or not) accept oneself (hold oneself lovingly, to use a metaphor) with all these negatively-evaluated self-relations in play. Someone who is deriving lots of negatively-evaluated self-relations after being asked to say the words "I'm whole, complete, and perfect" is very unlikely to be able to make a decision to accept herself, because she has abundant reasons not to. She can, however, make a choice to do so, in the presence of all these reasons not to, because choices are not made for reasons, but may be made with them. Another way in which it can be useful is as an opportunity to practice defusion. Once the client starts deriving negative self-relations, she can be guided to take "a step to the side" and observe the process. A question that can be asked at this point is "Can you accept yourself as a human being who has a mind that does what minds do (i.e., derives negative self-relations)?" An image that springs to mind is that of a man standing in front of a bathroom mirror, noticing his body. He notices many things that he doesn't like, and labels himself unattractive, ugly, repulsive. He is unacceptable to himself. He then has an out-of-body experience and sees himself from a couple of steps to the side. He observes himself looking in the mirror, finding things he doesn't like, labeling himself negatively, and not accepting himself. From this out-of-body perspective, he finds himself more acceptable, as a human being with a mind that does what minds do (i.e., derives self-relations, many of which are negatively evaluated).... The "out of the body" move in this metaphor is about shifting from the conceptualized self (where the guy is all caught up in responding literally to his self-relations) to the observer self (where he's noticing the process of deriving self-relations)....

ACCEPTANCE Self/ others - Whole, complete, perfect exercise [cont'd] EXERCISE Whole, complete, perfect [cont'd] Patty Bach	I like to think of 'perfect' in terms of being, and that one gets there by acceptance; that is, seeing one's self or others as perfect is an acceptance move. Kind of like the idea of 'love the sinner hate the sin,' does e.g., 'pedophilia' describe a person or a behavior/characteristic of a person? One may evaluate oneself as 'perfect' while also negatively evaluating one's behaviors or characteristics just as one may accept things and events without liking them. If 'perfect' means 'complete,' then it seems that the move to 'perfect' is a move outside of 'good/bad.' I think that evaluations come into play when we think of 'perfect' with respect to *doing* rather than *being*. In any given moment, from the perspective of me/here/now one is always perfect or complete, in the sense that one could not be anything other than what one is right now; and if perfect/complete one may move in a valued direction from where one is right now without anything needing to be different.
ACCEPTANCE Self/ others - Whole, complete, perfect exercise [cont'd] EXERCISE Whole, complete, perfect [cont'd] Steve Hayes	Etymologically perfect means "thoroughly made" (the "fect" part is the same root as in the word "factory"). I usually use the "whole, complete, perfect" exercise early in treatment (or workshops) to show that held as a belief, it is IMPOSSIBLE to do. Since most of us are playing for self-esteem at some level, this impossibility is disconcerting but informative. It is a game you cannot win (first you lose, then you play) because the very conditionality of this comparative frame ... esp. when linked to time or causality ("if I do this, then I will be whole") contradicts the desired outcome ("... so right now I'm NOT"). Even if you have it, if you can lose it, you just did; and if you don't have it, you can't get it. Later on we return to it, after defusion and choice work has been done. That's how I do it anyway. By then, it is easier to see that you can only hold it as an assumption. But held as an assumption it is NOT an evaluation or conclusion and it is not conditional. Are you willing to start from the assumption that you are whole, complete, and thoroughly made? Yes or no. If yes, will you still stay yes when your mind is screaming at you that it cannot be done and should not in your case? Yes or no. If yes, cool. Start there and all the things that you definitely need to change in your life (the pedophile example is just an extreme one, but if you want more, just look in the mirror) can be worked on with your feet on a strong foundation of deliberate, supportive, non-evaluative, recognition of your presence here as a living being. Yes, it is a faith-move -- but not faith as a belief or a conclusion. Faith as an act of self-fidelity (same Latin root, BTW).
FUSION/ DEFUSION **Attention, and** **MINDFULNESS** **Attention, and** **[11-23-02]** Rainer Sonntag	ACT Listserv Member wrote: It seems that defusion may be, at least in part, a manipulation of cognitive processes, such as the focus of attention. When I defuse, I shift my attention to observation by invoking the executive control of attention. I don't think that the language of attention is the best level to describe fusion-defusion. As I understand RFT, the processes at issue are more basic. Actually, "attention" may be part of fusion, at least when it includes "verbal attention" or "conscious attention." What we see, feel or think as named things or objects (trees, cars, feelings, thoughts), i.e., what is in the focus of attention at a given moment, is already direct experience + verbal activity, that is direct experience and verbal activity fused. And, of course, they constantly fuse, so we cannot escape the process or context of fusion. In fact, it would be rather bad to abandon the general process or context of fusion; in such a state of "general defusion" anything would lose its meaning, even values. What is trained in ACT may be seen as a kind of differential discrimination, i.e., to develop a habit of constantly defusing the derived relation between private events and verbal activity. And the first step of defusion is to note the process or context of fusion - that there are thoughts and feelings that (as part of their verbal content) say things about themselves proposing to be something that contradicts direct experience (e.g., anxiety saying about itself that it is dangerous which in fact, as a feeling, it is not - anxiety is not dangerous). Shifting the focus of attention seems more to be like looking from one (fused) content to another (fused) content. It is never, however, according to my understanding of RFT, shifting from fusion to defusion. With respect to mindfulness (and defusion), there seems to be an inherent paradox involved. That is, "an attentional focus of mindfulness" - so to say - always means that there is no focus of attention. Mindfulness involves letting go of any control over the content (i.e., focus) of attention, thus the mind can wander freely and there are no deliberate efforts to avoid or keep hold of any content of "consciousness." (By the way, in the cognitive literature focusing attention is often conceived of as "effortful," involving "controlled processing," and "allocation of resources.") To come back to the clinical domain, what most clients have actually done in their struggle with their thoughts, feelings, bodily sensations and so on, is to shift the focus of attention by distraction, by deliberate attempts not to think bad thoughts and shift to nice thoughts etc. Thus, shifting the focus of attention is a common part of experiential avoidance, which is based on fusion. This leads me to one final thought. Shifting the focus of attention has to do with motivation. It is a

	motivated act that has been brought about by rules (over expansive tracks, augmentals) specifying that some kinds of experiential content should be avoided while others may be sought. Thus, the motivational power behind shifting attention, this is a result of rule governance.
FUSION/ DEFUSION Attention, and [cont'd] **MINDFULNESS** Attention, and [cont'd] **Use in ACT** **METAPHOR** **Fusion/ defusion - language bicycle [11-27-02]** Steve Hayes	On defusion and attention: "Attention" has always been a difficult topic, especially for behavioral folk. The traditional behavioral view is that attention is a matter of stimulus control. When stimuli are functional you are, by definition, "attending." "Attend" comes from Latin roots - the "tend" part is the same root as "tension" - it means "stretch." The metaphor of "attention" is that the observational faculties of the mind are being stretched to cover something. Attention goes beyond pure stimulus control because of the verbal component that is added. It seems to me that attentional manipulations are usually verbal orientations toward stimulus domains and dimensions that are contacted "from I, here, now" in the RFT sense. This is itself a kind of stimulus control but it is over a response that in turn produces stimulus control of the more traditional sort. Defusion is the weakening of the domination of stimulus functions that are due almost entirely to relational frames (let's just call them "literal functions"). Mindfulness contains defusion elements because the practices orient the thinker toward the process and not merely the products of relating events verbally, which weakens literal functions. They also orient people toward direct perceptual functions that are "here; now" (e.g., what breathing feels like) precisely because it is these functions that are dominated over by literal functions. However, note that mindfulness practices virtually never direct attention toward literal functions ("and now I want you to become aware of the truth of these thoughts. Are they accurate or inaccurate? How true are they? What evidence contradicts them? What great thinkers would agree with this position? Is the position logical? What would happen in the future if this position is true" etc. etc.). That is why I think it is a mistake to think of mindfulness purely as a matter of attentional control. The whole reason we have a problem with attentional control in the first place is because literal functions dominate over other functions and the range of behaviors and relevant stimuli narrow greatly as a result to literal matters of right/wrong; logical/illogical; good/bad; if/then; and so on. The pivot point is not attentional control, because a) it matters very much what else you attend to, and b) the need for it comes from another core problem. The pivot point is the narrowing of behavior that comes from literal functions. Defusion is focused precisely on that. Attentional control can be (and almost always is) in part of defusion technique. There are other defusion techniques, however, and these are key to ACT. Mindfulness practices can help build these out, but I think mindfulness is safest if done dominantly as a defusion technique. I heard a person say at an AABT presentation that when we begin to be overwhelmed by anxiety, we can always follow the breath. That was worrisome, because we are now very close to using verbal orientations toward stimulus domains and dimensions that are contacted "from I, here, now" in the service of functions that are evaluative, literal, and future oriented ("if I follow the breath, I won't be overwhelmed"). I think we need tight analyses of all of this precisely so that we can throw what is not needed overboard. Avoiding being overwhelmed is not needed - it is an illusion of literal language in the first place. We also need them to develop new methods. If defusion is key, perhaps we can develop new methods that go beyond those that have been shaped by thousands of years of spiritual traditions. In other areas of science, such things have happened. And, by the way, of course fusion and defusion will cycle. Sometimes fusion is useful (or at least not costly). Other times it is lethal. The point is to ride the language bicycle, always falling out of balance, yet always correcting in time to avoid a face plant - and meanwhile moving forward.
FUSION/ DEFUSION **Control agenda, use in service of [1-16-05]** Steve Hayes	ACT Listserv Member wrote: > My client, who is quite smart, noticed that her emotional reactivity decreases shortly after various defusion practices. Recently she has been eagerly engaging in defusion and reports feeling "better." It seems to me that the old control agenda is back and the decrease in emotional reactivity is starting to be reinforcing. The model of extinction in your dissertation emphasized initial arousal followed by reduction of arousal so I'm guessing this impact worries you - and it could indeed lead to problems but usually it does not. Defusion quickly reduces arousal in many patients. There is a little danger inside that odd fact, but only if the client then fuses with yet another control-based rule. If action and flexibility is there I wouldn't be too concerned yet and would simply gently apply defusion to the new rules that pop up as well. There is also a nice benefit - even if they later start to struggle - they have seen something counterintuitive and odd -- I like to use it as evidence that our minds are often very poor in predicting the future. And their experience directly approaching content differently changes its function ... so other odd ACT techniques can be more likely to be tried. Finally, big responses predict an unstable existing pathological system - and that predicts

less resistance to change and better outcomes. ANYTHING really new is good news and signs you are moving.

BTW Acceptance techniques can have the same quick impact, and the same risks and benefits. Self as context and present moment stuff too. Depends on the client.

As you say: "In CT, the basic assumption is that a (content) change in thought leads to a change in congruent emotion."

But defusion is not a content change. It is a context / function change. Whether that immediately changes arousal varies (in general it does but not this dramatically) but that is not the most important thing - it is flexibility and ability to act that is most important because that then feeds a true change in the patient's style of living.

[AS] Is cognitive defusion relying on a similar assumption, although it works with a contextual change?

No, because neither content nor arousal is argued to be key.

So, I'd be playful with her. If she says she is feeling "better" do some work with her to see if she is also willing to FEELING better. Just because defusion reduces arousal does not by itself mean that the old control agenda is back. The fact that a decrease in emotional reactivity is starting to be reinforcing is not a big problem in itself unless it leads to a new set of avoidance rules - and if it does you (and she) will know it very quickly because those new rules won't work long at all. So a gentle warning (a wink; a wiggle of the eyebrows) is all that is needed - so that if it does blow up you aren't blamed.

It is not negative reinforcement that is our clinical enemy: it is rule-based rigidity. It is not emotional change per se that is a problem ... though it is a temptation to do unhelpful things it is also just more content (albeit "positive" content).

I'd react in a light way unless you sense cognitive entanglement in a control agenda (sensing too big of a concern from you when arousal is down per se could overemphasize the content issue just as she used to - but just inversely) and shift the focus to the real core of the work: the ACT question. That question contains nothing one way or the other about emotional content.

If you sense entanglement, then confront that (e.g., "You are feeling better. Is that what we've been doing in here?! I didn't think it was" etc.) but not decreases in arousal per se.

FUSION/ DEFUSION Control agenda, use in service of [cont'd] Steve Hayes	John McNeill's question reworded by Steve Hayes: "Would it be accurate to say that defusing content may or may not result in a content change, in the sense of a change in the trained and derived relations in which the word participates, But what is important is that there is a change in context as a result of the defusion technique, thus altering the previous functions evoked by the words [the transformation of stimulus functions] without necessarily altering the relational network in which the word participates [the network of trained and entailed relations]?" To which I'd say: exactly!
FUSION/ DEFUSION **General - inc. in relation to values** **METAPHOR** **Fusion - chocolate cake mix/ stir fry [7-6-04]** **CLIENT** **Inarticulate - fusion with verbal events [cont'd]** ACT Listserv Member *Cross Reference:* *See 5-209 for an earlier post in the thread:* *CLIENT* *Inarticulate - fusion with verbal events*	I like visuals so here is a way to "look" at fusion: imagine baking a chocolate cake (from scratch not a mix). When you start you have separate ingredients: eggs, flour, chocolate, etc. You take the ingredients and put them into a bowl - when you start you can still discern each ingredient. But with a little mixing it becomes harder, you may still see the egg a little, but some ingredients aren't separable; if you mix a little more you can't tell what you started with at all. If you are the bowl, and the ingredients are your words, feelings, evaluations, etc...fusion is like the cake batter at the end. There are various levels of fusion, like when you first start mixing the cake batter you are still able to see some ingredients (cognitions etc.) as separate, and in the extreme there are those cases where you can't. What starts as separate events, emotions, experiences, etc., becomes something that as time goes by (as we mix our cake ingredients), our mind, through languaging and transformation of stimulus functions, can no longer discern between the thought and the thinker or between the thought and the real events. There are several possible "reasons" that the client with PTSD was unable to identify that they were feeling anxious. First, when someone lives with a higher level of anxiety as a more or less constant state, they become desensitized to the symptoms as anxiety. This could be due to fusion with the symptoms, "it's just the way I am" or it could be the "watch effect" (when you wear a watch for a long time you "stop" feeling it on your wrist). Doing PMR (progressive muscle relaxation) or some other relaxation exercise, often helps the client realize how tense they are keeping their body. If you did PMR and the client still could not ID their emotional state, then it could be that they lived in an environment where their emotions were devalued by others (it literally never mattered to anyone what the client was feeling); or they were punished for talking about emotions (we all see a form of this in the grocery store with the "I'll give you something to cry about..." parent); or the client's identification of emotions could have "caused" the parent to start reacting in an aversive manner (such as when the child is feeling sad, instead of comforting the parent starts talking depressed and threatens to kill themselves). Most likely it is the first "reason," the desensitization -

	it is common in PTSD or hypervigilant clients not to be able to identify that they are showing the signs of anxiety simply because they no longer notice them.
FUSION/ DEFUSION General - inc. in relation to values [cont'd] **METAPHOR** Fusion - Chocolate cake mix/ stir fry [cont'd] John Forsyth	…I think you make some interesting points here and I like the cake metaphor. Yet, we need to be careful not to confuse (or imply) that fusion is bad or that it naturally leads humans down the road to psychopathology and suffering. Personally, I can't imagine any 'functional' aspect of human experience where fusion does not play some part. Fusion, in my humble opinion, gives life a quality and richness that would be hard to contact without it. Fusion can become a problem though when it gets in the way of workability. So, here are a few thought questions I have been mulling over more recently. Are there limits to defusion? Can it be taken too far? Here I am thinking of Spock from Star Trek as an example of defusion to the extreme but I am sure there are others that are more true to life. Some of us may even know people like this, and perhaps some of the personality disorders and other clinical conditions may be characterized by extreme forms of defusion?
FUSION/ DEFUSION General - inc. in relation to values [cont'd] **METAPHOR** Fusion - Chocolate cake mix/ stir fry [cont'd] ACT Listserv Member	Can defusion be taken too far? Most certainly...without some amount of fusion with our thoughts, our thoughts would be "meaningless." Our thoughts would become akin to an English language speaker that has no contact with any other language, hearing a speech in say Japanese on the radio. It is in fact the bidirectionality and the ability to transfer (and transform) various stimuli, that gives language its power. Words and thoughts without some amount of fusion, would be funny or nice sounding noises made by vocal chords. Everyday life is a bit of both mental and physical - we may experience things in the physical, but almost instantly we assign meaning through language (think of seeing an opera - you may not know exactly what is said, but still get the "meaning" through the visual stimuli). This becomes problematic when the mental and the physical become divergent or out of balance and the mental "becomes the physical" or has more importance in how an individual interacts with their environment. What defusion in ACT means to me is simply taking a step back, to retain some of the individual flavors of the ingredients while still appreciating the taste of the mixture. To return to a food metaphor, optimally defusion would be like Japanese stir fry, let's use chicken teriyaki. Very good teriyaki sauce will interact (fuses) with the meat and vegetables to create new flavor but also let the eater still taste the broccoli, meat, etc. Also, with teriyaki, you can still see the ingredients which also lends itself to that balanced state of fusion and defusion if you will. The chocolate cake on the other hand, becomes an altogether new flavor so that most people cannot taste (nor would they want to) the flour, eggs, etc. (this is fusion taken too far).
FUSION/ DEFUSION General - inc. in relation to values [cont'd] **METAPHOR** **Defusion (is not distancing) - what are hands like? [6-8-04]** Kelly Wilson	A physical metaphor I sometimes use--from way way back when we had to explain how "Comprehensive Distancing" was not distancing "to get away from." I hold my hand up tight covering my eyes. And then I pose the question to myself (out loud) "What are hands like?" Then I answer, "Hands are mostly black and dark, with little lightening sparks in them, and they stretch out in all directions as far as you can see, and they press against you. And, that is what hands are like." (Basically, just describing what I can observe.) Then I hold my hand about a foot and a half in front of my face. And do the same thing: "What are hands like?"--"Hands are pink and white and have little lines all over and they have these wiggly things on one end and the wiggly things have little hard parts, and at the other end, they are attached to this long thing (my arm), and that to my body, etc." Then I ask--"In which situation was I in contact with more aspects of my hand?" In this physical metaphor the distance is not "to get away from my hand" rather it is to appreciate my hand in a richer and more articulated way. I use this in training, and also at times with clients to describe what we are up to.
FUSION/ DEFUSION General - inc. in relation to values [cont'd] Kelly Wilson	Chad wrote: I'm inclined to think that defusing values is a bad idea, perhaps a very bad idea. I don't think it is a bad idea. What defusion produces is not meaninglessness, at least that only momentarily, but instead flexibility. The problem we encounter with fusion is lack of flexibility--it is the "must," the narrowness that is the problem. When I defuse reactions with a snake phobic, I don't make the snake phobic incapable of avoiding, it is just that avoidance becomes a more flexible piece of a broader repertoire. Avoidance can now be engaged in with sensitivity to context. Like stay when it is with your kids at the zoo. Jump away when it is on a trail near a pond in Mississippi. And even the latter, draw back closer and look if it has a long uniformly narrow head (non-venomous), but stay back a ways if it has a diamond shaped head (likely venomous). Here is why even values are sometimes needful of defusion--even a value can become an event that turns on you and becomes a source of aversive control. Like "I have to do this for my kids." (quit drinking, climb out from under the bed, or whatever). Here the value has turned on you: the client is not working to be a

	sensitive, engaged parent (appetitive control), they are working to avoid being a bad disengaged parent (aversive control). Whatever they do runs the risk of being tainted by the aversive control that is organizing the behavior.
	When I do defusion, it is to confer flexibility and thereby to introduce the possibility of choice. Sometimes you have to act against a value momentarily in order to serve it over the longer time scale (move your family to rural Mississippi, leaving their dear friends behind). Sometimes you have to act against one value to serve another (lie to prevent a death). If we are jerked around by our values reflexively--well, it ends up not being a very effective way to live one's values.
FUSION/ DEFUSION General - inc. in relation to values [cont'd] Steve Hayes	If you are talking about chosen values, you already have a bit of defusion in there, because humans can't do "choice" (as compared to reasoned judgments and decisions) without it. In ACT we do go after "IT IS important" (the fused version) to "I hold it as important," or more technically correct but too odd to say in normal discourse, "I am importanting about it." The old "nothing matters" stuff in workshops is right on point about that and is in fact a defusion exercise situated inside values work. However, once we are dealing with chosen values, further defusion work of a traditional sort is not normally helpful ... because if you "take it too far" you lose contact with the quality that is inside the verbalization of values that is shared with acting in a valued direction. What is helpful, however, and is a kind of defusion, is using the distinction between what is and what is described to keep values linked to that ongoing quality. We sometimes say that values are verbal ... and that is right. But values are more than that: they are a quality of what we do. A declaration of values can have inside it a quality, and if all is going well it is the same quality as actions taken that accord with that declaration. If you get to that, we now are doing values-in-action, and that is a powerful place from which to work. But to get there you can't have the declaration of values BE the values, alone and cut off -- and that cut off sense is exactly what fusion produces (the finger pointing at the moon IS the moon). Suppose there was an arrow pointing in a direction and you oriented in that direction and began to walk. The arrow contains a direction, and it is the same direction as the walk. Suppose, however, you took the arrow to BE the direction. That would be like taking the arrow off its stand, sticking it in your pocket, and then walking around aimlessly -- confident that you now HAD the direction since you have the arrow. Fusion can do that inside values work. So, traditional defusion work inside values work (e.g., say "love" 100 times) -- I've never seen it be useful because it can indeed go too far and cause us to lose contact with the quality that is at issue. Other, more subtle defusion aspects as part of values work -- I think so, because they help us make contact with that quality.
FUSION/ DEFUSION **Image, defusion of** **IMAGE** **Defusion of [10-9-04]** Jonathan Kandell	Russ Harris wrote: > Sometimes distressing cognitions are predominantly images rather than verbalisations - especially in the flashbacks characteristic of PTSD. I'd like to know how other ACT therapists are defusing these distressing images. The main technique I've been using is borrowed from NLP. Imagine the disturbing image on a TV screen, then 'play with it' - e.g., alter the volume, contrast, colour, brightness; flip the image upside down or sideways; speed it up, slow it down, change it to black and white, add music etc. This seems to work well, and I'd be keen to know of any other methods that people find useful. Horror movie analogies ... e.g., "The Ring"... Suppose you're stuck in a house watching the movie, rotting away, transfixed on the screen ... as long as you think it's real you're fused with it... but once you realize it's just a movie you're free.... Painting analogies ... Look at this painting on my wall ... Look at it from the point of view of its 'meaning'... now look at its shape and colors ... aesthetic balance ... now look at it from the point of view of an engineer…. The same 'thing,' the same 'image,' can be seen in any number of ways…. The images that flash through your mind are just like that....
FUSION/ DEFUSION Image, defusion of [cont'd] IMAGE Defusion of [10-9-04] Audrey Lowrie	I use ACT along with other approaches. I have found that when dealing with images, morphing them into more positive images can work well. I use sand-tray work to do this because it is the most dynamic of the creative therapies, in that the person can elaborate, move, subtract from, add to, etc., in the one sitting. I have found that a person creating a sand-tray after we have been speaking about a traumatic episode in their life will represent both who they see themselves to be in reaction to the situation, and what the current reinforces for that aspect of identity are. However, they will also represent other aspects of themselves, aspects that they like about themselves and that currently have positive consequences for them. There will be some form of relationship between these two aspects of their identity. Through dialogue and elaborating the preferred mode, the preferred images can be made richer, more compelling and more motivating.

FUSION/ DEFUSION **Literature re** **EXERCISE** **Milk, milk, milk, study re** **EVIDENCE** **Defusion, helpfulness of - Milk, milk, milk exercise [1-23-04]** Steve Hayes	David Fresco wrote:
	I am working on a writing assignment where I wish to make the point that what has been christened "defusion" in Hayes et al. (1999) has been studied much longer (e.g., deliteralization, etc.). ...I was wondering if someone can point me in the direction of the work within the ACT tradition that preceded defusion.
	Defusion within the ACT tradition:
	The usual published starting point that I cite for ACT and (to a lesser degree) RFT is this piece:
	Hayes, S. C. (1984). Making sense of spirituality. *Behaviorism, 12*, 99-110. It was written while I was still at Greensboro.... By this metric ACT / RFT is 20 years old this year (!?).
	The article has about a page or two on this issue, saying things like "What is common to all these traditions is the selection of procedures that might weaken the literal quality and thus the rule-control exerted by self-talk while enhancing the salience of you-as-context." It also notes how old the issue is.
	There may have been a little on the defusion issue in this earlier chapter, however:
	Zettle, R. D., & Hayes, S. C. (1982). Rule governed behavior: A potential theoretical framework for cognitive behavior therapy. In P. C. Kendall (Ed.), *Advances in cognitive behavioral research and therapy* (pp. 73-118). New York: Academic.
	I don't have it at hand to check.
	The first place that ACT is talked about extensively is in this publication: Hayes, S. C. (1987). A contextual approach to therapeutic change. In Jacobson, N. (Ed.), *Psychotherapists in clinical practice: Cognitive and behavioral perspectives* (pp. 327-387). New York: Guilford.
	... and the next big one is: Hayes, S. C., Kohlenberg, B. S., & Melancon, S. M. (1989). Avoiding and altering rule-control as a strategy of clinical intervention. In Hayes, S. C. (Ed.), *Rule governed behavior: Cognition, contingencies, and instructional control* (pp. 359-385). New York: Plenum. (now available through Context Press)
	Both of those have obvious sections on defusion (but the ways it was talked about wander quite a bit ... distancing, recontextualization, loosening equivalence classes, undermining rule control, deliteralization)... You will see that undermining literality is a major issue in this stuff.
	I think the first empirical piece that bears on all of this from an ACT perspective is Zettle, R. D., & Hayes, S. C. (1986). Dysfunctional control by client verbal behavior: The context of reason giving. *The Analysis of Verbal Behavior, 4*, 30-38.
	By the way, Aki Masuda, Mike Twohig, Casey Sackett and I have a little test of the "milk, milk" exercise coming out in BRAT showing that defusion alone is helpful:
	Masuda, A., Hayes, S. C., Sackett, C. F., & Twohig, M. P. (in press). Cognitive defusion and self-relevant negative thoughts: Examining the impact of a ninety year old technique. *Behaviour Research and Therapy*. It will be out in the next issue. That "milk, milk" exercise goes back to 1907, and was studied in the 40's and 50's by Osgood and others.
	The connections on defusion (however you describe it) go back for many years ... the issue is as old as psychology and beyond. But as far as ACT and RFT: that issue has been central from day one.
FUSION/ DEFUSION **Meaning of [cont'd]** Patty Bach *Cross Reference: See 2-73 for earlier posts in this thread*	I don't see how sensations (or emotions and thoughts) could be viewed as separate from subjective experience - they ARE subjective experience. While 'cognitive fusion' is described in ACT, I think there would be nothing inconsistent with saying "emotional fusion" or "sensory fusion," etc. Emotions or cognitions are not merely 'fused,' they are 'fused with....' Languaging/the client's language system is the 'glue' that 'fuses' one with their thoughts, emotions, sensations, etc. in a way that makes them indistinguishable from "me" - and thus aversive if negatively evaluated, instead of being experienced as the content "my experience." Deliteralization techniques are used to defuse language, not cognition, emotion, sensation (though they might also eventually be experienced as being 'defused').
	I find it interesting, and maybe confusing too, that we speak of 'cognitive fusion' and of 'defusing language.' 'Diffusion' means to break up or separate, while 'defuse' means to make less harmful or potent (literally, to remove the fuse from). In other words, could one say that in ACT we 'defuse language' in order to 'diffuse' private events? Or is it to defuse and diffuse private events? Or to defuse private events, and diffuse private events from self?
	Fusion/Diffusion AND Confusion ... I seem to remember a therapist pitfall about taking deliteralization too literally, and right now fusion/defusion/diffusion is starting to look like milk, milk, milk, milk.... :)

| FUSION/ DEFUSION Meaning of [cont'd] Steve Hayes | Actually, "defusion" was not used in the sense of "defuse: to remove the fuse from" (as in "defusing a tense situation"). It is a neologism that came from the use of the term "fusion" to talk about excess literality. We used "fusion" instead of "excess literality" and "de-fusion" (and thus "defusion") instead of "deliteralization" for a simple reason: after years of trying few could say "deliteralization" without stumbling. I'm serious.
| | Oddly, though I did not know it when I used the term at first, "defusion" already had a history in Freudian thinking and a somewhat similar use. The OED said it thusly:
| | [tr. G. entmischung (Freud Das Ich und das Es (1923) iv. 50), f. de- II. 1 + fusion.] A reversal of the normal fusion of the instincts
| | So if editors tell you that defusion is not a word, refer them to the OED.
| | "Diffuse" -- although ultimately tied to the same root (fuse ... which means to pour together) has connotations and denotations of dissipation, having a wide range, vague, or even confusing [the last is especially unhelpful since it is the same root but the opposite meaning to de-fuse]. As Pat noted, it can mean "to break up" but all of these other meanings also apply and many are unhelpful. I've always corrected others when they use "diffusion" to mean "defusion." Too dangerous.
| | Bottom line: one can certainly fuse with emotions, thoughts, bodily sensations, and so on, but for a common reason: language functions (arbitrarily applicable relational responding) enter into all of these.
| | In the line of "does a dog have Buddha nature?" here is a question: "can a dog fuse with its emotions or bodily sensations?" Defined in terms of relational framing, the answer seems pretty clear: nope. It is precisely because that it so, that the first query is meaningful. Fusion is the source of attachment in a Buddhist sense. Deliteralization (defusion) is a key component of mindfulness /detachment. That is one reason I think RFT may add something to the Eastern thinking that is already so well developed ... but that is another story for another day.
| FUSION/ DEFUSION Meaning of [cont'd] **RFT** **Verbal, relational meaning of [5-1-03]** Kelly Wilson | Mind and defusion:
| | In an *attempt* to clarify ... "fusion" and "mind" are ways we talk about verbal processes. This is really RFT stuff as Jonathan suggests. When we say verbal in ACT (really RFT) we mean relational stimulus control. That is, a *stimulating event* is said to be verbal if the event has at least some of its psychological functions as result of derived relational learning processes. When we say *a behavior* is verbal, we simply mean that the behavior is at least partially under the contextual control of events that have their psychological functions as result of derived relational learning processes.
| | This is a very special meaning of verbal--it is our own. It is not what Skinner meant by verbal. It is way far from what the lay public means by verbal. Why? We think that there is something special about verbal behavior. Following Skinner's analysis, verbal ends up resolving to discriminated operants where the contingencies are arbitrarily organized by another organism. The rat pressing the lever ends up being verbal. In a sense, this is absolutely right. The piece that was not available to Skinner--having worked the theory out by 1945--was the rising tide of phenomena that started out under the umbrella of stimulus equivalence and now has expanded far beyond (thankfully). What Skinner intuitively understood, but had no technical analysis of, was the ways that arbitrarily applicable, arbitrarily applied relational responding might generalize, massively propagate, and become more complex, among humans, given a history of multiple exemplar training.
| | So, something that looks like a conditioned response like fear (i.e., respondent) could be verbal in the sense that it is under antecedent control of an event that acquired the eliciting functions through relational learning processes.
| | So, to come back around to the discussion a little anyway--comparison and evaluation are some of mind's primary occupations, but since comparison and evaluation are dominantly verbal activities for human subjects, they do not in any way exhaust verbal. Verbal = derived relational responding--this essentially means that *any* psychological function an event could have could be established through relational means and be verbal (using our definition), and as a corollary, *any* response could be verbal in the sense that it is under this sort of stimulus control.
| | Defusion means the lessening of the domination of specific verbal functions. We know that under certain conditions, verbal functions will dominate over directly and immediately experienced contingencies--when the dentist says sit still, we respond to "sit still" even though the directly experienced contingencies "say" get the hell away.
| | So, from my talk in Reno last summer:
| | Fusion: certain verbal functions of an event dominate over other directly and indirectly available functions;
| | Defusion: is the process whereby these verbal functions become less dominant, and others become

	available.
	Well, at least that is my current best thinking on this matter.
	It is not that verbal is the enemy. Verbal also gives us valued action extended over long time frames and under the control of "defective" contingencies. This is why I highlight the fact that *certain* verbal functions dominate over *both* directly *and* indirectly available functions....
	ACT seeks to undermine the domination of certain verbal functions, when the domination of those functions restricts the client's (or my) ability to participate fully in a valued life.
	Hmmmm … somehow I doubt if that clarified anything at all … so it goes … fun anyway.
FUSION/ DEFUSION Meaning of [cont'd] RFT Verbal, relational meaning of [cont'd] Steve Hayes	Two small tweaks of Kelly's response. Re: When we say *a behavior* is verbal, we simply mean that the behavior is at least partially under the contextual control of events that have their psychological functions as result of derived relational learning processes. That's mostly so, but we have to add that arbitrarily applicable relational responding (AARR) is itself verbal behavior (said in another way, verbal behavior framing events relationally) and AARR is not at its base regulated by contextual cues that result from AARR (i.e., it has to start somewhere else, logically). Which takes me to the second tweak. I've been cautious about the language of "relational stimulus control" because it encourages the idea that the relations are in the stimuli. A key to Relational Frame Theory is that AARR is arbitrarily applicable -- thus the relatedness of stimuli are not solely in the stimuli per se but in additional sources of contextual control (even in the case of pragmatic verbal analysis ... a technical point that is too difficult to cover in a short email). From fairly early days we toyed with the idea of calling all of this "relational" instead of "verbal" (e.g., Hayes & Hayes, 1992, -- the *American Psychologist* piece). I'm OK with ambiguity on this point since it is mere terminology. Either side has problems. "Verbal" confuses RFT with Skinner and with lay use. "Relational" confuses RFT with traditional relational learning. (To see the latter read the commentaries on the book by McIlvane/ Salzinger/ Malott/ Osbourne/ Spradlin and our response that is coming out in *Analysis of Verbal Behavior*. Should be out by ABA.) I suspect both terms will be used indefinitely, and my pragmatic heart says that is OK -- just fit the use to the audience....
FUSION/ DEFUSION Meaning of [cont'd] **RFT** **Emotion, meaning of** **EMOTION** **Meaning of [5-1-03]** John Blackledge	In the interest of providing multiple exemplars with Kelly and Pat's posts, here's another possible way of saying it: I think it would be consistent with RFT to view "emotion" as (in part) the entanglement of interoceptive stimuli (e.g., physical sensations, urges, cravings) and relational responding that frames the 'meaning' and 'implications' of such stimuli. From this perspective, fusion with an 'emotion' would be the same thing as fusion with the relational responses tied to these formal stimulus properties--literally the same thing as cognitive fusion. Take anxiety as an example. At a purely formal level, anxiety could be described as rapid heart rate, tension in the chest and shoulders, sweating, shaking, dizziness, and so on. Nothing to defuse from there--these are formal stimulus properties. Anxiety-the-emotion (as we often think of emotions) would include a variety of relational responses (direct and derived) that transform the functions of those formal stimulus properties. In a context of cognitive fusion, those formal stimulus properties may be transformed by negatively self-evaluative relational responses that greatly enhance their aversive functions, by causal relational responses that prescribe avoidant behaviors and proscribe more adaptive responses, etc. From an RFT perspective, emotions are not something separate from derived relational responding--relational responding is a defining component. Thus, to defuse cognitively is to disrupt the verbal component of emotion and expose oneself to the formal stimulation that remains.
FUSION/ DEFUSION Meaning of [cont'd] RFT Emotion, meaning of [cont'd] EMOTION Meaning of [cont'd] Niklas Törneke	ACT Listserv Member wrote: When emotion (intense emotion vs. a milder mood state) is a limbic event, the chain might look like: perception > "limbic storm" = emotion > action disposition > behavior (impulsive, nearly automatic responding, possibly/likely outside of awareness). In this case language functions (read, neocortical activity) may not be present in the sense that Steve mentions... Kelly writes: "There is little of your experience that is not touched by relational conditioning processes." How do relational conditioning processes relate to experiencing intense emotions? It seems that language functions are not present, but I have to admit that I don't know RFT. Instead, we promote a new and more adaptive chain: perception > emotion > action disposition > observation > valued action/behavior activation. I think the key is in what Kelly writes; relational framing "touches" everything. It is not (metaphorically speaking) "at the root of" everything. (It is at the root of human language, though.) As for emotion the term is a bit tricky, of course, but from what you write I assume that what you mean is some form of basic emotion or affect. For the sake of argument, at least, let's buy the sequence 'perception > "limbic storm" = emotion > action disposition > behavior' without language. Arbitrary applicable relational responding could enter at any point in this "chain" as anything is discriminated, emotion for example. I am a bit unsure here,

if you mean that this "emotion" would not be discriminated? But if so, in what way is it meaningful to speak of "intense emotion" that is not discriminated? For a language-able human being everything that is discriminated can be framed relationally. That means that even if a kind of basic emotional state "arrives" without relational framing, in that very moment it will be framed. There is no way for a human being to experience anything (including basic affect) as it is "in itself" for anything but extremely short periods of time. Once language able-caught in language! In clinical work, for example, "intense emotion" is at the table because it means something to the individual (that is, it is framed relationally). Even if "the meaning" of a particular intense emotion is just "I can't take this" or "empty" or "the thing I can't describe," this would still be relational framing (in common sense terms, this would have "meaning") and that framing will transform the functions of that emotional state (and, I think, will be experienced as an integrated part of it, which is what we call fusion). Naturally, relational framing can also precede your "chain of events." Whatever is "perceived" can have its function due to its partaking in a relational frame.

FUSION/ DEFUSION **Meaning of** **EXERCISE** **Timeline - detecting fusion [11-29-04]** Steve Hayes	Fusion is a dimensional process that involves the domination of verbally derived functions inside unawareness of the process of relating itself. Some of the time it is harmless - though dangerous. Some of the time it is quite harmful. Until you work on it, it is as invisible as air. Here is an exercise: -- Long ago recent past now soon to be distant future Put your finger where your mind is in time. If you are thinking about or talking about the past or future, move your finger to point to where it is. Move it continuously as the temporal focus shifts. Do this for about 5-10 minutes continuously (you can talk to others etc. as you do it). Points about fusion: a) "Now" is not necessarily common. b) If your finger is anywhere other than now, you *know* that the verbal functions are dominating. That can be so even if it is pointing to now, but it is necessarily so if it isn't. c) You will find it hard to track - you "disappear" periodically into the past or future. b and c are the sure "tracks in the sand" of fusion, and this is just with one verbal relation: time. Add evaluation, hierarchy, (etc. etc.) and it is amazing how entangling it all is.
FUSION/ DEFUSION **Meaning, debate re [cont'd]** **MINDFULNESS** **General [9-28-04]** John Blackledge *Cross Reference:* *See 6-279 for an earlier post in the thread:* *FUSION/ DEFUSION* *Meaning, debate re*	Joseph Ciarrochi wrote: If I might summarize then, just to make sure I am getting it? ... [Mindfulness]... disrupts the context of literality, by ... response prevention. People notice thoughts and feelings, in a "being mode," and don't "do" anything about them, or behave according to what they say. Thus the thought does not lead to its normal consequences. E.g., if I merely notice my thought "I must not feel anxiety" and don't do anything in response to it (e.g., avoidance moves), then the thought will lose its power eventually (whereas before it was reinforced by the immediate benefits of avoidance). Am I getting this right? I really like this notion of mindfulness (or defusion) as response prevention. More technically, the defusive component of mindfulness would work as verbal response prevention because it would establish a context that, by definition, does not support verbal responses. When you consider how each new evaluation (or any response--verbal or otherwise) can serve as a contextual cue for subsequent (and related) thoughts/evaluations, even a very brief moment of defusion might have some very meaningful results, as it introduces something new to the context in which the negative evaluations and verbal rules are occurring. Once mindfulness results in defusion, it might set the stage for responses other than the negative evaluations and problematic rules that were previously being emitted--responses involving awareness, acceptance, or even more adaptive verbal responses occurring with respect to the products of the defusive episode (e.g., "Wow--it's not really true. It's just a bunch of words!").... [JC] ... mindfulness may help us to see that the emotional pain and valued action are part of the same thing, and thereby help us stay committed to values ... I think mindfulness would reveal immediate, direct contingencies/stimulation that was both relevant and irrelevant to values. Defusion (as facilitated by any defusion techniques, mindfulness included) works to make formal stimulation and direct (non-verbal) contingencies more salient, and verbal (abstract) stimulation and verbal contingencies less salient. [JC] ... So some mindfulness practices might target all of the ACT-relevant processes? I think mindfulness (as I understand it to be practiced by Buddhists) would definitely involve defusion and acceptance, though it wouldn't necessarily involve a values component beyond that of valuing mindfulness ... From an ACT perspective, mindfulness can be yoked to specific goals in the same sense that acceptance and defusion can be practiced in order to facilitate movement toward a personally held value.

	[JC] Perhaps interventions that focus almost exclusively on mindfulness (e.g., MBCTD) are still indirectly targeting valued action? It depends on what the mindfulness is used for. If its function is to avoid aversive thoughts and emotions, then from an ACT perspective you would say it doesn't target valued action. If its function is to pass through apparent cognitive and emotional barriers to values-consistent action, then I think it could be said to target valued action.
FUSION/ DEFUSION Meaning, debate re [cont'd] Kelly Wilson	I would not say defusion/fusion is the same as direct/verbal. I have been defining it, over the past couple years like this: Fusion is the domination of *particular* verbal functions over other potentially available direct and *verbal* functions. Fusion describes a narrowing of available functions--both verbal and nonverbal. Defused = flexible, context sensitive, etc. Fused = inflexible and relatively insensitive (except with respect to the particular dominant function)....
FUSION/ DEFUSION Meaning, debate re [cont'd] John Blackledge	... One reason I like thinking of complete defusion vs. fusion as equivalent to no relational responding vs. relational responding is that there appears to a clear-cut, precise delineation between the two--and because it points directly and practically to contextual manipulations that can be made to instantiate defusion (i.e., find out the critical contextual features that control relational responding and remove them to create defusion)....
FUSION/ DEFUSION Meaning, debate re [cont'd] **EXERCISE** **Saliva [9-28-04]** Kelly Wilson	... Fusion: the domination of a particular derived psychological function of a stimulating event over other potentially available psychological functions of that event and of other events in the organism's environment. Where the former "derived psychological functions" means: those established through a history of derived relational responding and where the latter "potentially available functions" includes both directly available functions and/or those established through derived relational conditioning processes for the stimulating event and for other events in the organism's environment. This should be marked by decreases in response flexibility, variability, and context sensitivity. Defusion as a process: The lessening of domination by a particular psychological function, increases in response flexibility, variability, and context sensitivity. Where the increases in flexibility and variability are in part related to the potentially available functions mentioned in the definition of fusion. I can think of a variety of means to assess this empirically (this one is in planning--just got my shock generator), although I do not think it is an entirely empirical question. For example, what if I constructed a simple 3-three member equivalence class and gave one of the members strong shock functions through classical conditioning. Now I have the person sit in an experimental space, hooked to the shock generator. I expose them to members of the shock class on the computer screen. I then take them out of the experimental chamber and ask them to name as many objects in the room as possible, the color of those objects, the number, etc. This should be entirely different for the subject if shock versus non-shock class members were presented. You could also use visual figures in the equivalence classes and let the orientation, color, etc. of the figures vary. My suspicion is fused subjects would be able to answer fewer questions about these directly available functions. Why? The derived shock functions dominate over all other potentially available functions. If they were doing a talk aloud, I would anticipate the fused subjects would show variability in talking about the meaning of the experiment, what to do next, how long it would take, etc. if they were encountering non-shock stimuli (these are all verbal functions of the experimental context). Whereas if the shock stimuli showed up--all narrow, inflexible, avoidant all the time. This is just an example. And, I don't think the verbal versus non-verbal distinction is any simple measurement problem either. Do you have some measure of that? And, I can give you an example of fused/not fused in your experience that will show you the distinction as I slice it. As you sit there read the following one line at a time without scanning ahead: Notice the saliva in your mouth, close your eyes for a few moments and let yourself notice all of the details of the sensory experience of the moisture in your mouth. Notice how slippery your tongue is made by it as your tongue moves across your teeth. Notice also where the moistest and least moist spots in your mouth are. Take a couple minutes, eyes closed and then come back. OK now close your eyes again and think of all of the facts you know about saliva and what it does for you--digestion, mastication, Ph, where it comes from, what produces it. Close your eyes and let yourself. Imagine a list of facts and check them off slowly, mindfully, one at a time. OK now imagine that you gather that moisture up in your mouth and imagine that you spit it out into a

	clean glass.
	Now imagine that you drink it back down.
	Done in a room full of people, slowly and deliberately, with their eyes closed, I guarantee that you will see all of the functions, and flexibility disappear. You will see big time domination by disgust functions and avoidance responses and all of that tactile stuff *and* verbal stuff is gone. It is a neat trick and readily demonstrates what I am talking about.
	The other thing--one can have available verbal functions without being fused (at least by my definition). See the first part of the exercise--aids in digestion, antacid properties are all verbal, but no fusion. They were present, but did not block other available psychological functions....
FUSION/ DEFUSION Meaning, debate re [cont'd] John Blackledge	... It still strikes me that the essence of defusion involves temporary removal (synonymous with weakening) of stimulus functions arising through verbal processes--with the target(s) of this process ranging from a single problematic frame to an entire network. This seems to clearly distinguish between strategies that attempt to alter one's relationship to language (and indeed undermine language's ability to "influence" behavior in problematic ways--and I use the term "influence" as a proxy, of course) vs. strategies that attempt to work within a context of literality to make changes. I would assume that this process would lead to the same kind of behavioral flexibility, variability, and context sensitivity you have discussed as an outcome....
FUSION/ DEFUSION Meaning, debate re [cont'd] John Blackledge	Joseph Ciarrochi wrote: I thought that defusion had more to do with undermining unhelpful stimulus functions than reducing the rate of relational responding? ... Doesn't defusion involve setting a context where these thoughts no longer act as barriers? ... I would say that defusion "undermines unhelpful stimulus functions" by disrupting the relational responding that gives rise to those functions. Once the person has experienced these transformed stimulus functions being torn away from the words he is struggling with at least once, a couple of things could potentially happen: (1) the defusion episode, having changed the person's learning history with respect to the problematic thought(s), results in different stimulus transformations arising when the thought next arises; or (2) the person learns to create a context of defusion the next time the problematic thought arises and works as a barrier, through the channel described in this paragraph's first sentence. So, from this perspective, defusion would "involve setting a context where these thoughts no longer act as barriers" (as you said), as the thought would still occur, but would not function in the same debilitating way that it used to.
FUSION/ DEFUSION Meaning, debate re [cont'd] Kelly Wilson	... consider this example of why I don't think verbal/nonverbal fused/defused doesn't work. While it is certainly the case that if we do a 'milk, milk, milk' type exercise with a devilish thought, we will eventually get to a place where all that is left (mostly) are the non-verbal auditory functions. Verbal functions go poof and we see emergent flexibility. But eliminating verbal is not necessary for defusion. Consider this clinical example: client comes in and says: "My wife criticised me this morning and it was the strangest experience. First I noticed that I was having feelings of anger, I noticed I was feeling like retaliating against her. Criticism is always such a hook for me. I just sat quietly a minute and noticed that there was a hint of sadness present. The moment sort of unfolded for me in its complexity. I had memories of criticism from school, from my parents. Then I had thoughts about my relationship and how important it is to me. The anger was not gone, but it was a fragment of this very complex moment. I looked over towards my wife, who was busily getting ready for work, saw that her brow was knit. I had thoughts about how stressed out she had been lately at work, how I could see that written on her face. I went on with what I was doing. Didn't slam things around, which would be my usual response. Didn't get all sullen. Later that evening we met up after work and went to dinner. It was the strangest thing." Would you say that client was fused? Tons of verbal stuff going on there. What is not there is domination by that initial anger, or anything else. I mean would you do a defusion exercise with this client. Not me. I would just say. Cool man. Life is a trip isn't it. Though I did not explicitly define it in this way in the Values chapter with Amy Murrell in the new *Mindfulness and Acceptance* book, the spirit of this definition in elaborated form is definitely in that chapter. And, yes, I do think this is the best way to slice it, at least for now. I think this way of thinking about it links up nicely to the non-verbal complements in basic operant and respondent conditioning (see the Wilson and Murrell chapter on this)....

FUSION/ DEFUSION Meaning, debate re [cont'd] Kelly Wilson	... I am interested in all instances of fusion where immediate life-threatening circumstances are not at stake. My interest in instances of fusion is because of its life constricting qualities. So, if you are standing on a street corner, about to step into the street, and I yell WATCH OUT FOR THAT CAR! Fusion in this instance is a good thing--you need immediate life constricting stimulus control in order to stay alive. If, on the other hand, you are about to go for a walk in Sydney (where the cars drive very fast through the city), I might say "watch out for the cars" - no need for life constricting fusion here. Dangerous cars are part of a complex array of available functions as you walk out to the street. I actually do not want people fused with valued ends. I seek flexibility and a context where choice is an appropriate way to speak....
FUSION/ DEFUSION Meaning, debate re [cont'd] John Billig	... Kelly's comments about not fusing with valued ends really struck me as being very important in working with patients in therapy. Not fusing with valued ends is often what is most freeing for patients I see in therapy. In fact, many patients come into therapy and are hurting because the valued ends that they set for themselves have been blocked in one way or another, by internal and external barriers. Helping a patient identify and feel their important values while expanding the repertoire of available means to live those values is what ACT (and a life lived fully) seem to be about.
FUSION/ DEFUSION **Skill - reversal of automatic process [5-31-04]** Everdien Tromp	[Re: Deliteralizing language - pp.154-158 of the 1999 ACT book] Several exercises are described to help people improve their skill of looking *at* the process of language instead of looking *from* language. Thoughts are used to structure our perception of the world. We don't even notice that we look at the world *from* our thoughts, because we believe them in literal way. To look *at* the process of language involves focusing attention on language as language, cryptic as this may sound. A bit of defusion from literal 'understanding' can be achieved by watching the direct stimulus functions of language like sound, the feeling of your muscles, the sight, etc. An elegant way to watch your attention switch from the symbolic function of a word to some of its direct stimulus functions is by repeating a word over and over again for one or two minutes. This is the classical *milk, milk, milk exercise* (Titchener, 1916). Present it as an experiment or experiential exercise and help the client notice how the literal meaning of the word disappears and one can see the word as an instant of the language process. I like the notion of skill learning here. Deliteralization is a skill you can practice, it's not another rule to follow. One can play with direct stimulus properties and thereby loosen the 'grand illusion of language' by realizing that the symbolized *thing* is not there at all. The only thing that's there is sound, movement, breathing and so on. And this is not a fact, but a skill, something you do....
FUSION/ DEFUSION **Taboo language, defusion exercises re [11-26-04]** Steve Myles	Joseph Ciarrochi wrote: It is one thing to repeat "milk, milk, milk" and another thing to repeat the "c" word. How many ACT practitioners would be willing to participate in this defusion exercise? I think that it is a great idea to use these more difficult words in defusion exercises. As therapists, we need to be willing to work with these words when clinically necessary, and to get to that point we need practice in being defused from them. The way of the world is that clients/patients don't only get fused with easier words to work with like "worthless" and "loser." They get fused with very nasty things like (from my work) "fucking ugly spastic" and "mongol."
FUSION/ DEFUSION **Terminology - distancing, deliteralization, defusion** **Clinical dialogue/ illustration of concepts** **ACT** **Original name (Comprehensive Distancing) [2-26-04]** John Blackledge	Joseph Ciarrochi wrote: Can any of you old-time ACT folks comment on why the term "defusion" came to be preferred over "distancing"? ACT was originally called comprehensive distancing, but was changed because comprehensive distancing was a term used in cognitive therapy that had some purposes/connotations that were inconsistent with the goals of ACT. Then the term deliteralization was coined to more specifically describe the language-disrupting techniques and processes used in ACT. But that term is, quite simply, too difficult to say without stuttering. So it was changed to defusion (as in cognitive defusion), which implies the opposite of fusing or binding with the content of language. I actually never use the word "defusion" with adult or child clients. I always refer to it as "not believing your mind," "unhooking from your thoughts," or "not buying into your thoughts"--things like that. Phrases like this strike me as more directly specifying the behavior being prompted than a phrase like "distancing."

FUSION/ DEFUSION	Well … back in the day, ACT was called "Comprehensive Distancing" or, by an affectionate few "Big D.," Beck had distancing and we had Big D. Anyhow, distancing was pretty much uniformly misunderstood. People got that if negative cognitions and emotions were bad that a little distance helped--which is true enough, but really only alters the effects of these by attenuating them. For us, distancing is more akin to what happens when you look at a Monet from 2 inches away as opposed to 20 feet. Actually, both are great, and doing both will get you in contact with more of the stimulus functions of the Monet. From an ACT perspective (at least mine), distancing is done to increase contact--especially the richness of contact.
Terminology - distancing, deliteralization, defusion [cont'd]	
Clinical dialogue/ illustration of concepts [cont'd]	As to use with clients, I have *never* used the term defusion with a client. I don't even use it with other therapists unless they ask for it (like by coming to a workshop or a talk). Why? It's just a technical term that means something to a very tiny group of people. There are much more accessible and common sense ways to talk about the same thing. Or better still, experiences that can illustrate it.
ACT	
Original name (Comprehensive Distancing) [cont'd] Kelly Wilson	I also don't use the term distance, since it is so easily confused with an avoidant strategy by the same name.
FUSION/ DEFUSION Clinical dialogue/ illustration of concepts [cont'd] Kelly Wilson	I think my use of the [emphasised] "never" was probably a bit pontifical. Sheesh. Some days it is so embarrassing to be me. But anyhow. "Unhooked from" is good. I tell clients, especially those who don't like being bossed around, like kids, like me, that the issue here is not whether thoughts come or go, but whether they get to boss us around or not. Like a bully at school, do they get to run your life? Also, exercises like the Passengers on the bus both individually, or acted out in a group, help to bring home the idea. And, the mindfulness-type exercises can also provide a direct experience of what it is like to not be dominated by thoughts, emotions, etc.
FUSION/ DEFUSION Clinical dialogue/ illustration of concepts [cont'd] Hank Robb	I keep a pair of yellow "clip on" sunglasses on the table next to where I work. I pick them up and hold them close to my eyes and note "now everything looks yellow." Then I pull them away noticing, "It's the sun glasses." I ask clients to do the same and then ask if this isn't the same sort of thing that happens when you notice you are seeing from a thought rather than seeing the thought. As Kelly notes about the additional "stimulus functions" ... one thing you notice when you move the sunglasses away is that they have edges which you find it difficult to notice when they are up close to your eyes. So you see more, and different, not less.
FUSION/ DEFUSION Clinical dialogue/ illustration of concepts [cont'd] Graham Taylor	My client (and I) can 'have' a thought that 'I haven't done a good enough job' when faced with negative feedback - and hey, given the learning history *and* the present context, that thought has *got* to show up, but do we have to 'buy' it - like I used to? Just like at Christmas time I get reminders of Father Christmas and his band of elves busy making toys in a factory near the North Pole, but I don't buy it that that exists like I used to. I can draw a picture of a thought inside a head vs. a 'thought' in a thought bubble, or as in the cartoon pictures which were discussed on the list a year or so ago, I can take my thought balloons along for the walk....
FUSION/ DEFUSION	In part it was because distancing had dissociative connotations ... as if you had to "get away from" something. That is why ACT was created as a name (thankfully ... it would be lousy to be living under the Comprehensive Distancing label now ... we'd have to be waiving off the dissociative connotations in every talk). Also distancing was used in Beck's approach not to undermine the functions of thoughts but catch thoughts in flight so as to establish a target for change. It was a limited part of his protocol. Staying with the term would suggest that this move in ACT was the same thing as in CT, and it is not ... it is much more elaborated, more central, and has a different purpose. I still occasionally find myself using the term though.
Terminology - distancing, deliteralization, defusion [cont'd]	
Clinical dialogue/ illustration of concepts [cont'd]	In the hiatus between the early days of ACT in the mid 1980s and its full emergence in the late 90's, we spent most of our time refining the theory and philosophy, as well as developing the technology based on clinical experience. As RFT began to emerge we had a more technical account of where we had taken the "distancing" process (which is pretty far now from distancing in CT). A number of ways of talking about it emerged (recontextualization; deliteralization) that were linked to RFT. "Defusion" is a neologism (automatic spell checkers still regularly change the word to diffusion, and sometimes new ACT folks think that is the actual term) that we finally settled on merely because "deliteralization" is too darn hard to say (even though it needs less explanation than defusion).
ACT Original name (Comprehensive Distancing) [cont'd] Steve Hayes	I think there is a need for much more focused research, both RFT work and ACT work, on defusion. We need to learn more in the lab about how to weaken Crel and Cfunc control. And we need studies like the one coming out in BRAT on the impact of the "milk, milk, milk" exercise. Our measures of defusion are also inadequate. The AAQ style measure is not enough ... we will need more subtle or behavioral methods

	to really get at this adequately. We also need defusion measures that apply to specific problems.
	It is very easy to come up with new defusion techniques. I've borrowed something from Graham Taylor (thanks for the tip Graham) and commonly now in ACT workshops have the audience practice defusion methods on each other (using the working list which is downloadable on the website), and then have them make up their own. Recently, for example, someone had their "client" repeat their difficult thoughts with an imaginary hand puppet. Seemed to work. "You're a bad person" has different functions when "Mr. Hands" is saying it to you, and it set up some nice ACT questions: e.g., is it OK to have your puppet saying that? Thank the puppet for his contribution. etc.
	You do have to be careful with some of the more creative defusion moves to make sure the client is collaborating and in the right spirit ... defusion is not dismissing or judging the mind, or a way to criticize its products. It is there to catch the relational process itself -- to peek through the illusion of language in flight....
FUSION/ DEFUSION **Verbal functions, defusion particularly relevant to [7-6-05]** Steve Hayes	Russ Harris wrote: Steve, you wrote .. "I think of defusion as more related to thoughts than emotions per se." This brings up an interesting issue about the dividing line between emotions and cognitions. So far as we know, relational frames can interweave with just about everything ... ... and as soon as you ask if they do in a specific instance the answer will likely be "yes" (if not always before the question then almost certainly after you ask it). ... it's [verbal functions] that make defusion particularly relevant. Pull them out and it sounds odd (e.g., "I defused from sweating" is a weird sentence. "I accepted that I was sweating" is not). In the real world though, these verbal functions are usually there. I suppose that is why in the AAQ acceptance and defusion items load on a common factor.
MINDFULNESS **Definition of [1-27-04]** Steve Hayes	Luke Moynahan wrote: I have been attempting to provide a generic descriptor of "mindfulness exercises" and have not been able to find a definition of the type of behaviour (or rather response relations) that is attempted when carrying out such exercises. There is a definition (fairly cognitive) coming out in Clinical Psychology: Science and Practice. I have written a response to that paper that broadly outlines a more behavioral definition. [Hayes, S. C. and Shenk, C. (2004). Operationalizing mindfulness without unnecessary attachments. *Clinical Psychology: Science and Practice, 11*, 3 (pp.249-254).] Might be helpful. In "hexaflex" terms ... most forms of mindfulness seem to involve acceptance, defusion, contact with the present moment (both non-verbally and verbally in the sense of self-as-process -- the ongoing observation and description of experience), and self-as-context. The response takes a stab at why this is so.
MINDFULNESS Definition of [cont'd] John Blackledge	... I view mindfulness as defusion + awareness + acceptance. It seems to me that directly experiencing the sensory aspects of each moment--especially while noticing the occurrence of thoughts as thoughts-- creates a context incompatible with the context of literality required for the entailments and transformations inherent to language. It seems some core elements of defusion are there--direct experiencing of formal stimulus properties, and viewing the process of thinking rather than fusing with the content. Since any of us except (possibly) for the proverbial monk on the mountain will fade in and out of mindfulness countless times when we practice it, the context of literality will correspondingly fade in and out, and this experience may likely shape some helpful (or perhaps even harmful) verbal behavior that could take the form of formative augmentals (among other forms). But it seems to me that mindfulness, pure and simple, is about defusion from language, not about the production of one type of languaging over another. It also seems to be about a fairly expanded awareness of physical sensations (sights, sounds, movements), of the process of thinking, and complete acceptance of all this stimulation....
MINDFULNESS **Meditation - acceptance vs. control [7-29-03]** ACT Listserv Member	... I believe that meditation can be utilised in the control of something else: the amelioration of suffering, unsatisfactoriness, dukkha or whatever Sid Gautama meant 2500 years ago (the 4 noble truths). I for one am very willing to accommodate the innate paradox of acceptance versus control that (I think) is involved here. Before I had even heard of ACT I was intentionally utilising mindfulness to reduce (control) the emotional pain that resulted from my thinking and I believe this practice facilitated much defusion (though I did not call it this) and produced many ACT like metacognitive insights (e.g., self as context). While mindfulness involves a non-judging acceptance of *whatever* presents in one's field of awareness, my experience is that this acceptance ameliorates negative emotional consequences, and due to negative reinforcement I have been conditioned to repeat the process. My agenda is the production of the respite and refuge that mindfulness delivers: the ability to disengage from my thoughts into the present moments of my breathing or whatever I might be doing. It's control but it seems to work for me.

MINDFULNESS Meditation - acceptance vs. control [cont'd] Ruth Baer	It doesn't work very well to use individual meditation sessions as control strategies. That is, if I sit down to meditate thinking, "I'm going to meditate now so that I can slow my racing thoughts, relax my body, and feel better," I may be disappointed because there's no guarantee that a meditation session will do that, though sometimes it does. Also, the experts all seem to agree that this is not the purpose of sitting down to meditate. Rather, the purpose is to practice being present with and accepting of whatever's there, which might be racing thoughts, tense body, feeling bad, etc. However, over time, if I consistently practice being present with and accepting of whatever's there, then I find a trend toward greater equanimity and reduced suffering.
MINDFULNESS Meditation - acceptance vs. control [cont'd] **CONTROL** **ACT anti-control stance - pragmatic not scientific** **LANGUAGE** **Contextual approach [7-30-03]** Steve Hayes	The anti-control stance of ACT should not itself be taken too seriously. It is more like a pragmatic clinical warning than a scientific principle. In its clinical use in ACT, not everything is anti-control anyway. You can control your life, and you can control trauma, for example. But you need to be wary about controlling pain in an immediate or local sense. Standing way back, we can derive scientific rules about predicting and "controlling" behavior that literally contradict the ACT warnings about control. The ACT literature itself shows that letting go tends to reduce negative private experiences (thus, in one sense of the term, you can surely "control" them). But you need to hold that knowledge lightly. My guess, Ruth, is that even when you notice that practice being present with and accepting of whatever's there reduces suffering, you have to let go of the verbal tendency to turn that into a simple formula or the very practices that create that effect are functionally no longer the same practices. Language constantly creates such paradoxical effects. A contextual approach to language frees us up to have our cake and eat it too if we focus on function and don't insist on "consistency" if that isn't helpful. We have no control. We have total control. It depends on domain and purpose of the talking as to whether that talk is useful.
MINDFULNESS **Meditation, ACT and; formal & informal practice [1-13-05]** Hank Robb	Archana Jajodia wrote: What is the place of a daily practice of meditation in ACT - i.e., do ACT therapists encourage their clients to take up such a practice? Is it recommended for the therapists themselves? I introduce just about every client to first identifying their spontaneous (unbidden) thoughts, images, and sensations (TIS) and then to how they could relate to them from at least three different perspectives, such as the "Observer" perspective, e.g., "Whether a thought is true or untrue it is still nothing more or less than a thought," or "True thoughts are nothing more or less than true thoughts," i.e., the "true thought" of "I am sitting in a chair" when I am sitting in a chair, is not the experience of actually sitting in a chair, same with images, same with sensations. I then encourage them to practice about 10 minutes a day, preferably early in the day. Most don't do it consistently even though I regularly encourage it and try to troubleshoot problems such as doing it in the car after they park at work but before they go in the building instead of at home because of hectic schedules getting children to school. I analogize that a singer or musician would do a tone up or tune up before they started their performance and we are going to be performing with TIS all day long and might as well get ready to do so. Those who do the practice seem to "get" that they don't have to "believe" their thoughts or respond to their images or sensations as anything other than images or sensations a little sooner than those who don't, but no smashing differences that I note. …
MINDFULNESS Meditation, ACT and; formal & informal practice [cont'd] Kelly Wilson	I am pretty much of a know-nothing on this topic--but given that, it looks to me that the practice of meditation is so extremely varied that one would have to ask what precisely would count. For example, I haven't done it much lately, and I know it is weird, but I like to iron clothes. I once had someone I was rooming with at a conference comment after watching me iron that it looked like a meditation. I had not really thought of it that way, but I had noticed the singleness of the act, the focus. When I was doing that, I was not doing anything else; all focused attention on sights, sounds, smells, and a precisely repeating order to it. Was I meditating? Now, my favorite somewhat similar activity is to turn my old tube guitar amplifier up to 10. At that level, the strings become incredibly sensitive to the slightest touch, and if you move the knobs to *just* the right place, the tones, ahhhh. Each tiny movement and touch to the strings speaks. It is wholly sensory focus. Am I meditating? I realize that these don't look like what most folks are talking about when they say "meditation practice" but I am curious what the meditators think.
MINDFULNESS Meditation, ACT and; formal & informal practice [cont'd] Russ Harris	Hi Kelly. Your experience of ironing could be considered classic 'mindfulness meditation.' Jon Kabat-Zinn is one of the experts on this, and the mindfulness-based CBT approach is based on his approach. He defines mindfulness meditation as 'paying attention in a particular way: on purpose, in the present moment, non-judgementally.' Domestic chores are often used as a practice for mindfulness meditation, e.g., washing the dishes, with your full attention on the sight, smell, sound, movement of the washing.

MINDFULNESS Meditation, ACT and; formal & informal practice [cont'd] John Forsyth	Mindfulness meditation is about being fully present with experience as it is. This is an action, not a state, and requires practice. Mindfulness is not the same as concentrative meditation practices where the goal is often peace and tranquility so long as the meditator is meditating. Rather, the goal of mindfulness is to use the posture day in and day out -- to wake up to experience as it is, not what the mind says it is.
MINDFULNESS Meditation, ACT and; formal & informal practice [cont'd] Archana Jajodia	I too find that a 'formal' practice of meditation (whenever I can manage to sustain it) helps me greatly to be more 'mindful' the rest of the day, or in ACT terms, helps me defuse from my thoughts and mind and experience the moments as they occur. I am one of those who get very caught up in their thoughts and I found that I did not really 'get' defusion until I began a daily mindfulness/ meditation practice.... With my clients I have found that getting them somehow to commit to a homework regimen (or 'therapy exercise' as I call it in session) of 'formal' meditation helps them greatly identify the observer part of themselves and realize that someone exists that is not their thoughts.
MINDFULNESS Meditation, ACT and; formal & informal practice [cont'd] John McNeill	Mediation as life-project: I, too, encourage a variety of daily life meditation practices in my work with clients. A range of approaches are emphasized such as shamatha concentration; vipashyana insight; tonglen and other compassion practices; *liang xing* and other dialectic practices; death meditation, present-centeredness in ordinary daily activity; use of allegories, metaphors, slogans, and so on; retreat work, Sangha refuge, and devotional practice; *tai chi* and yoga; bibliodharma; etc. While strongly encouraged, one's immersion into a life-project is ultimately a choice left for each to decide. As for forced practice: A horse drinks on its own accord, not when coerced. The most important point I think, is to emphasize that the practice is intended to cultivate a skillful means for *relating to/staying with* rather than *moving away from* one's ongoing experience of others, the world, or oneself. The practice should not teach one to become a more skillful 'avoidant responder' in life. All too often, Western application of the practice is [mis]applied in service of experiential control, which is contrary to traditional Eastern practice. Properly employed, the practice helps us move toward rather than away from our history and experience. But this is an old idea - at least for many in the East. Also stressed is the slogan: 'We are transformed not by what we think, but rather by what we do.' While words do something, we must be careful that we do not allow them to fix truth in what they say. Words serve a navigation function for life [*dao*-ing functions]. In terms of practice, sitting in forgetfulness [Ch., *zuo wang, wang xin*] or mind-fasting [Ch., *xinzhai*] means to be so empty of thoughts that the ego-self loses its distinctiveness and separateness in the world. By such practices a cognitive to somatic shift in knowing unfolds, an "epistemological reorientation" that both neutralizes the dualist cognitive roots of knowing and exposes the somatically-induced nonthinking mode of awareness [Nagatomo, 1992]. This quality of lived experience is characterized by a nondual, nonexclusive, noncontentious engagement with the world, or what Nagatomo calls a non-tensional mode of existence [somatic attunement], which facilitates the coming-together of self and world as indistinguishable features of each other. The transition from *I* to *Who* occurs as the self becomes appropriated by or assimilated into the field of lived experience. Realizing our emptiness frees us from the illusion of self to become one with our surroundings. In the spirit of 'sharing about our practice,' I have included a doc. attachment [below]. Mindfulness-Awareness[1] *Guidelines for Meditative Practice* Most people approach meditative practice with an idea of personal gain. But impositional desiring is compromised by wants, hopes, and preconceived ideas that can in a rigid sense objectify the world and thus upset the self-creative possibilities and rhythms of otherwise noncoerced experience [Ch., *wu wei*]. Meditative practice is yielding, choiceless, expansive, accommodating, nonjudgmental, and not shaped by one's desire to define, possess, or control the occasions or outcomes of practice. Thus, the practice reflects the achievement of what could be called *deferential desire* [Ch., *wuyu*], which is characterized as the ability to abandon ego-self in the manner of casting oneself as fully as possible into the matrix of ongoing experience, unmediated by verbal construal. C. Joko Beck [1989] notes that mindfulness practice is not performed for idealized purposes of: 1- Inducing psychological change. 2- Gaining enlightened self-understanding. 3- Attaining power and mastery over others, the world, or oneself. 4- Achieving a blissful, transcendental, or detached state of experience. 5- Cultivating a set of special powers. 6- Attempting to induce positive experience. 7- Avoiding negative experience.

8- Establishing a curative state of physical health.
9- Making one an authority on anything.
10- Instilling virtuosity or spirituality into one's life.
11- Gaining compassion about others, the world, or oneself.
12- Creating insight about the Cosmos.

The How-ness of Now-ness

Accordingly, proper meditative practice encourages a move from an achievement to non-achievement orientation, which is not infested with discriminated objects of desire. Just as a mirror reflects its manifold situation without opinions about it, meditation is the practice of observing one's mind, a choiceless pursuit, responding without storing. We are reminded that meditative process is at base 'nothing special' (Ch., *wu shi*).

Considered pragmatically, to quiet one's mind does not mean to cease the activities of mind. The very effort to control the movement of thoughts only keeps the thinker stirred up in the thoughts. Thus, in trying to accord, one naturally deviates and in the act of emphasizing change, deference is stifled. Instead, we are advised to abandon any effort to cease the process of thinking! What this amounts to is recovering spontaneous vital process without deliberate action [Ch., *wu wei*]. The power of attunement can be seen in the harmonizing of psychological struggle, which eases when we are able to join with the environing world, unmediated by biased construal.

So what is it that one does?

Meditative practice emphasizes the importance of self-cultivation through a life-time of committed application to everyday affairs of living, particularly the development of behavior and activities intended to optimize personal experience, vital process, spontaneity, and creativity in life. Self-cultivation notes a particular kind of skillful means through which the practitioner knowing how, whence, and where generates effective action. A distinctive form of skillful action is the kind of mental-attending that is responsive to change and the relational context of momentary experience.

As a particular kind of Shamatha-Vipashyana practice:

- Sit in stillness.
- Breathe naturally without attempting to control it.
- Remain awake, present, and with eyes open – observing, participating spontaneously, detaching from evaluation, focusing on the rising and falling details of experience.
- Simply label thoughts as 'thinking' whenever they surface then nonjudgmentally return back to breathing.

Note that if you lose interest in or become discouraged with meditation, it may be because your practice has become idealized or romanticized in some way.

[1]Some portions directly pirated from source texts. Sources include: Acharyas Pema Chödrön and Dale Asrael. Learning to Stay, Buddhist Workshop sponsored by The Rocky Mountain Shambhala Center, August 2003; Charlotte Joko Beck (1989). *Everyday Zen: Love and Work*. San Francisco: HarperCollins; Nagatomo, S. (1992). *Attunement through the body*. Albany, N.Y.: State University of New York Press; Suzuki, S. (2001). *Zen Mind, Beginner's Mind: Informal talks on Zen meditation and practice*. New York: Weatherhill; and Thich Nhat Hanh (1987). *The miracle of mindfulness: An introduction to the practice of meditation*. Boston: Beacon Press.

MINDFULNESS Meditation, ACT and; formal & informal practice [cont'd] Francis De Groot	I want to put a more skeptic point of view toward some of the practices praised in these discussions. Shouldn't we be very careful and more hesitating before fully embracing practices like meditation, yoga, tantra-I-don't-know-what, Buddhism, and perhaps even mindfulness? Not that these things are wrong, on the contrary: they can be very useful, just like Gestalt-exercises can. But, before embracing them too enthusiastically, shouldn't we keep aware we're using them in *a different context*? I want to use Gestalt exercises, though without the Gestalt philosophy. So I don't tell patients they are Gestalt-exercises. The practices referred to are linked with eastern thinking, new age.... Regular practice is very important, we know that from fluency training etc. But some things are very much related to eastern thinking, and less to ACT. ACT, as I see it, has many ways that lead to cognitive defusion. Defusion is the thing we're working to, and self-as-context. Mindfulness exercises can be very useful, but maybe the name "mindfulness" itself is even dangerous, because it's linked to philosophies other than functional contextualism. It might be framed relationally to very different things ... you also have to defuse from.

MINDFULNESS Meditation, ACT and; formal & informal practice [cont'd] Patty Bach	I tend to agree with Francis' point about caution. While mindfulness and meditation seem to be useful, the original question was about the place of daily meditation in ACT and the "ACT position" on daily homework. In some sense I suppose that we (the list) as ACT practitioners reflect "the ACT position," AND ultimately we must ask "show me the data." While there are a couple of studies using ACT + mindfulness, I know of no studies comparing ACT + meditation/mindfulness versus ACT alone. I don't think any client (or therapist) practicing meditation is necessarily being "ACT inconsistent," and a therapist assigning daily meditation might be ACT inconsistent, a la "what's that in the service of?" BTW - Steve Hayes sent a brief paper [Operationalizing mindfulness without unnecessary attachments] to the list a few months ago ... about the place of the term mindfulness in the science of psychology.
MINDFULNESS Meditation, ACT and; formal & informal practice [cont'd] Steve Hayes	Defined in certain ways, ACT is a mindfulness-based technology, but meditation per se is a technique. It can fit or not, work or not.
MINDFULNESS Meditation, ACT and; formal & informal practice [cont'd] Jonathan Kandell	I also think complete absorption is distinct from mindfulness. Complete absorption, what Kelly describes with his guitar, is Csikszentmihalyi's "flow" experience, isn't it? (Flow involving a sense of playfulness, a feeling of being in control, concentration, mental enjoyment of the activity for its own sake, a distorted sense of time, and a match between the challenge at hand and one's skills.) I think of flow as the good form of tuning out (i.e., tuning out without avoiding). "Mindfulness" is in many ways the opposite--the detailed and non-judgemental observation and cataloging of experience. Not exactly flowing! In the former you're less aware of details, in the latter more. I think a lot of people confuse these two: the DBT literature for instance incorporates both into its definitions of mindfulness.
MINDFULNESS Meditation, ACT and; formal & informal practice [cont'd] Patty Bach	I think 'complete absorption' may be construed as a form of mindfulness and that one is attending to detail though not necessarily 'noticing that one is noticing' even while evidence of awareness of detail is evident in observation of the process of and/or products that arise out of periods of complete absorption.
PRESENT MOMENT **Not living in [5-30-03]** John Forsyth	ACT Listserv Member wrote: ... how sad it is that so many people try to live in the past or the future, neither of which do we have...so I ask, are those people 'living in the past/future' really living? I think the issue of living in the past or the future is one of degree. We all have a history, and this history may be wonderful and worth reflecting on in the present. Considering the future -- where we would like to be -- also can be exciting and an opportunity for goal setting, changing one's life track, hope, etc. The problem I think comes when one chronically lives in the past or the future, and particularly when the past is the centerpiece for justifying problems in the present (e.g., if only I had a different childhood, set of parents, went to a different school).
PRESENT MOMENT Not living in [cont'd] Ruth Baer	I was just thinking similar things. I believe my quality of life would be reduced if I never got absorbed in thoughts/memories/fantasies/images/etc. about the past or the future. Sometimes, as you say, this can be enjoyable and/or useful. But not always, which is why it's valuable to be mindful of these things when they happen.
SELF-AS-CONTEXT **Discrimination of - cf. defusion generally [5-27-04]** Steve Hayes	Niklas Törneke wrote: As Kelly noted, self-discrimination will be different for a human being (compared to pigeons for example) due to derived relational responding. There is still a twist to this, it seems to me, a twist that is central to what we try to do in ACT. Not only is the behavior of (self-)discrimination different but what can be discriminated is also different. That is, a pigeon can not self-discriminate the behavior we call arbitrary applicable relational responding (AARR) for the simple reason that there is no such behavior with the pigeon (as far as we know) to discriminate. Helping people to do exactly this (to self-discriminate AARR as it occurs) is central to ACT. The concept of cognitive fusion is a way of describing the fact that we as humans very often do not do this,

we respond to the result of this special kind of response (AARR) rather than to (self-)discriminate the response as such. This, it seems to me, is the point of defusion or deliteralization.

The behavior recently discussed on the list, "self-as-contexting," is a particular form of AARR (a kind done framing "I-here-now") and for the client to self-discriminate this as it occurs is the point of the typical ACT interventions. This, of course, in the service of psychological flexibility.

This seems right on. The only twisty thing is discriminating "self-as-contexting."...

Discrimination -- like everything else! -- seems to have both a verbal and a non-verbal sense. When we verbally discriminate, features of comparisons enter into relational frames. This is greener than that. A bird may discriminate the two colors, in the sense of having these two events control differential responding on the basis of differential reinforcement, but the colors are not in verbal categories, hierarchically related to a verbally abstracted and named dimension, and entered into a frame of comparison or distinction. In a sense, the bird is not discriminating "C-o-l-o-r" at all ... "color" is what the *scientist* is discriminating verbally, not what the bird is doing.

Non-verbal discrimination can exist in humans without any verbal discrimination. Fine motor activity is like that. Verbal discrimination supports and over time may produce relatively non-verbal discrimination ... like how learning to drive eventually leads to automatic driving skills with minimal verbal involvement (until the flow is disrupted and the verbal aspect leaps to the fore). But the two processes are still distinguishable ... at least conceptually and sometimes empirically.

When we discriminate AARR in flight, it seems to me we are engaging in a kind of verbal discrimination, so arranged in ACT (etc.) as to make it easy for non-verbal discrimination to be or become part of the behavioral episode over time. We "so arrange" it by doing even this in a defused way.

When we are dealing with perspective taking this process becomes even more slippery since "I here now" is an aspect of virtually all verbal discriminations, once perspective taking is established in the verbal repertoire. I say "virtually all" because children make verbal discriminations before this repertoire is established (so it must still be possible later) but they have a hard time remembering that they did so after self as perspective taking emerges.

So, when you verbally discriminate self-as-contexting (if we need a verb the older version used originally in this line of thinking -- self as perspective taking -- seems easier ... it must be why I'm using it in this post when I rarely do anymore ... contexting sounds inherently implausible as an act) this very discriminated verbal repertoire is part of that act of verbal discrimination. So much so that as you focus ON this component of AARR, the very action you are noting disappears into the background as an implicit part of the verbal discrimination process itself.

That is not the case with other forms of AARR. I can watch and notice my thoughts until time ends ... as I do so I will generate more but then I verbally discriminate those. Catching "I here now" as an object of verbal consciousness is not like that ... it is more like non-verbal discrimination. You "show up" and "stay in the here and now" through practice. Verbal discrimination starts that process but it can't fully carry it.

I think this means that defusion is somewhat more relevant to noticing thoughts as thoughts. Consciously showing up in the here and now is not just a matter of reducing literality (though that is an important part of it) -- it is a both verbal and *non-verbal* process of discriminating an ongoing aspect of all AARR (at least in fully verbal humans).

I'm not sure of all this by the way … but it seems right.

SELF-AS-CONTEXT Discrimination of - cf. defusion generally [cont'd] Niklas Törneke	Thanks, you really have the gift of pointing to the central issue. In therapy this is so clear. In my experience it is much easier to help clients watch their thoughts and benefit from that than to help them use perspective-taking as an ally. And of course, it is easier to watch content than to watch the one watching. Or, as we say in therapy, "if you could watch the one watching, who was watching that?" You can not really step out of it, at least not verbally. It is interesting that the words we can use for that behavior is "staying on, being present" etc. It is more like "sitting down" than discriminating. Weird, but experientially "true." Maybe you are right that it could be described as non-verbal discrimination. Other views on that? This also brings in the discussion on Buddhism, I think. This experience (in doing mindfulness of breathing for example) must be at the base of what Buddhists call the experience of "no self." There is nobody there. There is just "being." Watching yourself watching, you see you are not there. Or, you don't even see that (etc. etc.). By this I don't mean we should buy all the Buddhist interpretation of this. I think you put this well, Steve, in your earlier note on this. One reason I believe this kind of discussion is important is that it could bring us closer to what is really the core of the now so popular "mindfulness." Would it be too provocative to suggest that that concept has some of the same weaknesses as Buddhist terminology? That is that "It starts 20,000 feet up with a fully verbalizing creature" (quoting Steve on Buddhism). As for "self -as contexting" I agree it is not so helpful as a term. But I think we need to return to a verb from

	time to time. It is so easy to slip into objectifying "self as context" and treat it as if it is "something." Self as perspective taking is quite good, though.
SELF-AS-CONTEXT **Dissociation/ depersonalization, cf. [4-5-04]** Niklas Grebäck	Rhiannon Patterson wrote: I think I've read that depersonalization can be induced by meditation for some people. I think of it as the pathological version of "observer mind." This is something which concerns me a little about the recommendation to develop observer mind ... for some people that stance can lead to dissociative states that probably aren't healthy or useful. I had a client who responded to the observer exercise in just that way. S/he felt uncomfortable with "dissociating" and wondered how this went with the rest of the work. As I see it, the crucial point is the function of it (observing/depersonalizing). Depersonalizing is in the service of ridding one self from unwanted psychological content/processes, but observing is in the service of getting in contact with it, wanted or unwanted. Looks the same, works the opposite.
SELF-AS-CONTEXT Dissociation/ depersonalization, cf. [cont'd] Patty Bach	Nik, I like the distinction you make between depersonalization and observing. I wonder if the distinction might be in differentiating content and process To extend Gareth [Furber]'s mirror metaphor ... to notice a reflection of a reflection of a reflection of a reflection etc. we increasingly narrow our focus to a very tiny part of the one whole mirror ... there's only one reflection, and the description of it rather than the reflection itself is recursive. I see two ways this might occur in observing-self exercises. Mindfulness is not rule-governed and mindfulness can have that same recursive quality of the reflection of a reflection if one tries to be mindful of being mindful. Perhaps the only thing one cannot do mindfully is to be mindful - it's like trying to follow the rule, "be spontaneous." In many mindfulness exercises/practices one is mindful of one's breathing or of noticing thoughts without 'buying' them, or of bodily sensations, etc. If one tries to notice mindfulness itself, then mindfulness becomes content and the recursion of 'being mindful of being mindful of being mindful ...' might lead to increasing distance from self as context and self-awareness as one gets stuck in the recursive loop of being mindful of mindfulness. When one 'succeeds' in doing something mindfully, one is not mindful of being mindful until after the fact and reflecting back on the experience. Perhaps in depersonalization the observing-self itself is avoided. The ACT book (p. 200) describes how some clients are fearful of the experience of self-as-context fearing a sense of nothingness or annihilation. Self-as-context is experiential. If one is noticing self-as-context it is no longer self-as-context, it is self-as-context-as-content. If one is noticing depersonalization then one is not 'depersonalized,' perhaps it is experiencing the observing self as negatively evaluated content and 'buying' it as the observing self rather than as content about the observing self? In my experience, the physicalizing exercise can sometimes be useful for getting at depersonalization, e.g., after several cycles of going through physicalizing various thoughts/feelings/sensations one might 'get to' the observing self which might be positively experienced or negatively evaluated and avoided....
SELF-AS-CONTEXT Dissociation/ depersonalization, cf. [cont'd] Matthew Smout	I think it is possible to get a sense of "observer you" without engaging in a trance-like meditative process that might be more likely to lead to the unsettling feeling of dissociation. I currently see a client who is the most experientially phobic person I have ever seen - he could not tolerate sitting still for more than 60 seconds in his first session. He was willing however to persevere over sessions, and now he can engage in mindfulness exercises for about 5 minutes. We used the observer you exercise in a very rapid way to fit within his 5-minute tolerance period (he is an ex-drug user with a very "fast" mind). We concentrated mainly on memories from different ages in his life, and concentrated on the continuity of perspective despite the changes in his physical appearance, surroundings, thoughts and feelings at those times. We went fast enough so that his mind didn't get a chance to wander off too much and he could stay with each memory. Although I'm sure this is not how the exercise is usually done, I think it achieved the desired effect as giving him somewhere to stand while we continue defusion - as evidenced by his asking less questions along the lines of "who am I?" "what am I if I'm not my thoughts and feelings?" "how do I decide if I don't do what my mind says?" Even if he couldn't articulate who he was, I trust he has a sense of who he can be besides his mind/feelings.
SELF-AS-CONTEXT Dissociation/ depersonalization, cf. [cont'd] Jonathan Kandell	I agree this is a crucial difference that has not been explored enough in the literature. The "observer" metaphor hedges the fence between an unemotional relation on the one hand (almost information gathering), and an active experience on the other. Some ACT exercises--especially those aimed at defusion--promote the former (e.g., word-repetition; labeling thoughts as "thought," feelings as "feeling," since in both cases one is moved away from *experiencing* when one is labeling); but other ACT exercises promote

the latter (viz., the Gestalt exercises like Looking for Mr Discomfort aimed at "contact" and "showing up").

In short, there is a fundamental ambiguity within ACT between defusion and mindfulness-- "just noticing" versus "showing up." (Why would willingness be so difficult if one could "de-fuse" away all of the discomfort?) My feeling is that in the end this is a strength of the theory, not a contradiction. Each component has its own therapeutic purpose: defusion creates distance, crucial for those overwhelmed by their emotions ("you are not your thoughts," "the room can revolve and it's fine if you have a steady chair to sit on"). However, "contact" has its purpose for those who go too far toward avoidance. Most of us do both.

This is one reason I prefer the "Bare Attention Self" (a term which comes from some forms of Buddhism) instead of the "Observer self." (I raised this topic in an earlier listserv thread.) Bare-attention, by definition, is not depersonalized, since it involves an experience of the emotion at hand. However, the caveat "bare" indicates that one is not to wallow in the emotion or thought. A common Buddhist metaphor is to be like a person greeting guests at a party-- you want to welcome each one but not spend too much time with each person. Notice you do not just want to observe the people coming in (that's poor hosting!), but to actually experience them in their pleasant and unpleasant natures. (This metaphor can easily be incorporated into the ACT "Bum at the party" metaphor.)

I suppose this suggestion moves ACT closer to DBT, since it views either contact or distance from experience as valuable depending on the context at hand. You can think of contact-distance as a dialectical continuum. All the better in my book! If you take a quick look at Steve's PowerPoint summary of ACT, it really does fit right in.

SELF-AS-CONTEXT Dissociation/ depersonalization, cf. [cont'd] ACT Listserv Member	All this talk about dissociation vs. depersonalization, made me want to clarify and differentiate the two phenomena from one another. Dissociation is the separation of thoughts, feelings, activities into a separate part of consciousness; mild forms of it are seen in compartmentalization of tasks. More severe cases of dissociation result in distinct personalities that function independently of the "core personality." I treated a young man, who came in to therapy because his internship brought him in contact with abused children which had triggered a breakdown in his ability to avoid his memories of his sexual abuses in childhood. At the beginning of therapy he was utilizing visualization techniques for relaxation, and spoke of a little boy there that he talked to, that was flag number 1. Then he had me paged - when he had been out with his roommate and a couple of female friends, he started to get anxious and left; the next thing he knew he was home, in a scalding shower, scrubbing himself and screaming. This is dissociation, what may start off as attempts to distance oneself from a feeling, event, memory, may, due to incredible bad circumstances (such as multiple rapes in childhood), develop into an uncontrollable problem. Coincidentally, the client above, never experienced the same feelings he had with the dissociative events during the observer exercise. Depersonalization is the sensation of not being a real person or that some part of you isn't really a part of you; usually a body part becomes not you. Depersonalizing can also be of other people as in the Japanese medical experiments in WWII in which they called their human subjects "wood." My own experience with the observer exercise, is similar to the feeling I get when I lay out at night looking up at the stars. I feel small, and lose that "self centered" perspective for a while, and the memories become a little like watching home movies (from the observer self perspective), still me just me at a different time and a different place. Maybe that is a little dissociative, but I don't think it is, because I never lose my "self," I don't experience a loss of memory, nor do I feel it is not me.
SELF-AS-CONTEXT Dissociation/ depersonalization, cf. [cont'd] ACT Listserv Member	Several of the clients with whom I worked reported the fear of being "nothing" when practicing self-as-context. To me this is an example of fusion with self-as-content, and/or self-concept. The mystical traditions have long encouraged people to realize that they are "nothing" first and "everything" thereafter. With sufficient practice opportunities, the self-as-context feels solid and not dissociative. I often make this distinction by relying on the chessboard metaphor: the pieces remain connected to the board, they are not floating in a dissociative way.
SELF-AS-CONTEXT Dissociation/ depersonalization, cf. [cont'd] Steve Hayes	I recall that the original use of the term "Observer self" in ACT came as a take off of the term used by Deikman in his book on the Observing Self. It has always felt like a slightly dangerous term, because of its dissociative connotations, but from the beginning (Comprehensive Distancing?) ACT has faced that problem. It has stepped around the problem primarily by acknowledging it and coming up with metaphors and definitions (e.g., backing up from a painting so that you can see it) that make sense of the steps proposed. Defusion is a matter of reducing the stimulus functions that occur only in the context of literality / reason-giving / etc. Often discomfort will go down, but that is not what defusion is for. It is about experiencing

	events more directly ... including experiencing *that* you are thinking instead of just experiencing the world as thought about.

SELF-AS-CONTEXT
 	
Explanation vs. experience
 	
ACT
 	
Strategic importance of [10-14-02]
 	
Steve Hayes
	ACT Listserv Member wrote:
	
	    Are there any suggestions about how a simple-to-understand treatment rationale about [discovering and defusing self] could be provided to clients?
	
	My usual rationale is that it is simply not possible to accept and defuse from difficult content until you have a solid place to stand. I use the metaphor of the board and pieces etc. and talk about how you HAVE to fight at the piece level because other pieces seem life threatening so you simply CANNOT expect yourself to do anything like acceptance or defusion until your feet are on solid ground. If you ARE the pieces, you really are screwed, because at that level the war will go on.
	
	That rationale lets us go exploring. Then the exercises open up a domain and the actual wordless experience of "known from here now" shows up and people know they are solid. But even then -- during, say, the observer exercise we periodically warn "do not believe this -- belief will be of no help." Attachment comes largely from belief and the last thing we need is another "self" to believe in.
	
	Re:
	
	    [ALM] I would assume that ACT intends to undermine attachment to all "selves" on the basis of content vs. context. Isn't this simply "metacognitive awareness," "decentering," or "disidentification" a la Teasdale, or is there more to this concept?
	
	The only place attachment is usually an issue is with the conceptualized self. Self-as-process is fluid and self-as-context is quite literally no-thing at all, so there is no-thing to be attached to -- thus the warnings above. Self-as-context is based on the "I-here-now" established by deictic frames, that in turn contextualizes consciousness itself. The material in the RFT book is more theoretically advanced than the ACT book on these issues, but a lot more remains to be done and the experimental work going on with deictic frames, perspective taking, empathy, etc. will hopefully flesh this out.
	
	I think this IS the same thing as Teasdale or any of the mindfulness folks are talking about at the level of experience. At the level of concepts about the experience, well, there are differences. I think RFT is tighter and more focused technically, but then I would. But all that is for the clinician or researcher, not the client.
	
	Re:
	
	    [ALM] Second, is any focus brought onto the self-evaluative processes and their negative consequences in the sense that the self, defined as the observer consciousness, is above evaluation? This would not be unlike the self-acceptance vs. self-esteem concept of Albert Ellis.
	
	Yes there is (and yes, it is very like Ellis's idea) but the cool thing about this is that the experience itself does the work. You can say it if you want, but you hardly need to. The part of us that is unchanging (I-here-now as a context for what is known), is not thing like and only some-thing can be evaluated. You cannot evaluate no-thing (every-thing). Sometimes I actually say that to clients, but even if I don't, people absolutely KNOW that -- if it is the EXPERIENCE of I-here-now is what is at issue. In all my years of doing this, I have NEVER had a client who connected with the experience try to turn it into a thing to be evaluated -- other than wishing to "be there" because that feels so calm and solid (but often then quickly realizing that this very wish is just more content to be noticed from here now).
	
	[To make this simple: Stay with the experience and the cognitive worries reflected in your post will not be a big issue.] That means you have to trust a bit too -- and not rush to try to "explain" all of this to your clients etc. When you say "I have found that some faculty and graduate students have a hard time grasping these concepts" I of course understand what you mean, but start with the experience (and not the concepts we grasp and handle) and then the concepts will not be hard because you can hold them lightly to point to a domain, not BE the domain. The concepts are not the experience and held tightly they actually interfere with finding the contextual pony in that pile of evaluative / temporal / causal / referential self pooh ["I am like such and so and that is (pick one) good / bad etc."]....
	
	Anyway, this issue is the huge burden ACT carries. It has to be said but what is being said goes after the impact of saying itself.
	
	On a related but distinct matter, while I have folks' attention.
	
	It keeps becoming clearer to me why ACT may be important. It is not the technology. All of that is either stolen or ultimately obvious. It is that ACT has formulated the issues and linked them to basic processes in such a way that we can use the best of the more experiential/ humanistic (etc.) traditions (and what we make up on our own, etc.) and even play a little with language itself, and yet have a fairly tight analysis that guides us clinically and allows all of this to be researched. That is why ACT may be part of something truly new, because it shifts us away from the old divisions (empirically clinical folks can now play with the most loosey-goosey stuff) yet it takes the whole field in a more empirical and basic process direction. That is a

weird combination.

For example, the concept of defusion allows us to play with psychobabblish methods of mind-blowing ... and not have to then hang on to these ideas as if they are true, or as if they are technical accounts. For example, when I said earlier "self-as-context is quite literally no-thing at all, so there is no-thing to be attached to," we do not then have to do what eastern psychologists do -- come up with a term for no-thing-ness. No-thing is not a technical term in ACT or RFT. That sentence of mine was not a scientific statement -- it was a clinical one. We were just talking. But the technical account provides guidance and gives us a secure place to play. The technical account would explain why this kind of talk might be useful. An account might look something like this: "no-thing" looks superficially like a name that is in a frame of coordination with an object, but when you use it that way and then try to apply the normal temporal/ causal/ comparative frames to it, the network brought to bear by the term itself cancels out those very temporal/ causal/ comparative frames, which in turn attacks the context of literality that is necessary for terms to have verbal meaning at all. Said another way, some of those sentences above are defusion techniques, but since the actual experience of "I-here-now" -- self-as-context -- is facilitated by defusion (part of what we meant by "discovering self, defusing self"), these statements work functionally, and the account explains why.

If I am right about this and ACT gets sufficiently known, the field of empirical clinical psychology will go in two directions at once, tighter and looser, but without incoherence.

That is what seems important about ACT.

If I am right, though, it means something truly terrible to folks on the listserv. Ultimately, all of that stuff on contextualism and RFT etc. will actually be relevant (and if the ACT book is difficult at times, try those suckers).

Then again I may be dreaming.

SELF-AS-CONTEXT

Purpose of [6-18-03]

BUDDHISM

Meditation, ACT/RFT view of [cont'd]

THERAPY

Instruction, use of [cont'd]

Steve Hayes

Cross References:

See 2-84 to 2-89 for further posts in the thread:

BUDDHISM

Meditation, ACT/RFT view of

See 7-326 for an earlier post in the thread:

THERAPY

Instruction, use of

In the original ACT manuals self as context work shows up after confront the agenda; control as the problem; a bit of defusion; and willingness. Why there? It is often cast in terms of safety. Now that we are shifting to an agenda of FEELING good, rather than feeling GOOD, we need a place from which that is possible -- since once you are attached to a piece (shifting to the chessboard metaphor) experiencing events as they are seems to be life threatening. Self as context work reminds that person that he or she is not really at risk (though the conceptualized self certainly is -- kill yourself everyday).

Self as context, in other words, is cast as a means to experiencing events as they are, not as what they say they are, and doing what moves in the direction of chosen values in this moment and situation. Said in another way, it is in the service of participation / exposure / expansion of repertoires / effective action. ACT is not about navel watching. As one of the posts in this string said, ACT is a behavior therapy.

One worry I have about meditation practice is that it sometimes seems to be in the service of something else (e.g., how you feel when you meditate -- or even what you don't feel as much when you meditate). The practices are not at fault. It is the agenda that people bring to them. ACT is rather direct about the agenda, but even then based in the client's own experience (to jump to another string about how direct one can be -- Kel's answer seems right on -- as direct as one needs to be to get the job done ... being mindful that language is a two-edged sword).

SELF-AS-CONTEXT

Unchangeability of [5-11-04]

Steve Hayes

Joseph Ciarrochi wrote:

The observer self is described as being "critical to acceptance work because it means that there is at least one stable, unchangeable, immutable fact about oneself that has been experienced directly." Sometimes I wonder if this description of the observer self is not one more attempt to have something permanent and unchanging. Is this the one control strategy we unconsciously allow ourselves?

I wouldn't think of "it" as unchanging.

However, the experience of being here now is not an "it" and that experience is what it is, not whatever we think OF "it."

When you are absorbed you are also aware or you would not be able to say anything later about what absorbed you; when you are asleep and aware of your dreams YOU are aware or you would be unable to say anything about them. If you are asleep and unconscious and unaware of anything ... well in that case you believe that you were asleep or unconscious but you did not consciously experience being asleep or unconscious. That contradiction is an issue, but it is not same as "you" coming and going so far as "you" are aware. By definition.

I can't recall talking to clients about "one stable, unchangeable, immutable fact about oneself." I suppose it could have happened but it would not be common. I would instead go for the experience, which is rather like hitting ground. Of course we BELIEVE that "here now" comes and goes. I talked about that in the 1984 paper and claimed, rather boldly, that God is helpful in part because there is no such contradiction between the experience of "no-thing / everything" and the belief that we come and go.

I think we can be more or less aware of awareness ... that comes and goes. I suspect that is what you mean.

But even when "it" goes ask yourself this question: who noticed that "it" went?

There you are again. As always.

So exactly why is the content of your experience a threat? Who or what is threatened? Apparently not you.

That's the point.

SELF-AS-CONTEXT Unchangeability of [cont'd] **EXERCISE** **Find a free thought [5-11-04]** Steve Hayes	Joseph Ciarrochi wrote: Ah, I think I'm gradually getting there ... I mean I get it at an experiential level, but my analytic mind can't quite make sense of things (because the observer self is not a thing).... So the observer self is a perspective that is always there, even if we are not aware of the perspective.... Using the chess board metaphor, one can be at the piece level (the level of content) or the board level (self-as-context). The board is always there, holding all the pieces, even if we are not at the board level (e.g., aware of the self-as-context).... The metaphor of the board is "from here / now." Said another way it is pure consciousness, not what we are conscious of. Anything we are aware of we are there to be aware of. When a person gets entangled with the piece level of mental activity they've gone from who they are to who they aren't. There is an exercise we sometimes do in workshops called "find a free thought." We ask people to watch their thoughts and find one that is free and unprogrammed; unconditioned; linked to nothing else. Of course this is very frustrating ... every thought seems to be historical, linked to other things. Even attempts to be random have the same quality. Then we ask the attendees to do it again and while they are in search mode we add a simple question as they watch their minds: "who is watching?" Sometimes I add "and is that part of you machine like?" It sometimes is quite jarring to catch yourself right inside a moment of cognitive entanglement and to realize you've been there all along. And it is instructive that this part of us does not seem to be machine like or programmed (hard to do so ... there is no-thing to it!). It is like the "person in the hole" metaphor. How does one get out of the hole? At one level: notice who's noticing you are in. [JC] Yet ... The ACT book (page 184-185) suggests that the observer perspective develops via reinforcement from a social community. E.g., "... In order to have the ability to report events verbally in a sophisticated manner, however, it is necessary to develop a sense of perspective or point of view and to distinguish it from that of others."... Does this imply that there was a time when an observing self was not developed? From an RFT point of view, yes. Before deictic frames established a sense of "I-here-now" and "you-there-then" then there is no observing self. The analysis claims that perspective taking is a side effect of language training ... particularly what we now called deictic frames. Infantile amnesia seems related to this same issue actually ... when "you" show up, "you" can remember. Sense of self is why the deictic frames training (e.g., with developmentally disabled kids who do not have a sense of self ...) is so important. There was a recent RFT publication (Louise McHugh is the senior author) showing the developmental trends with these frames, and there are some data showing that they can be trained and that they can effects on "theory of mind" tasks. The grand prize would be to show that they impact empathy ... the theory says "you" show up at the same time that "I" show up ... and empathy seemingly requires that you being able to see the world as another might and relate that to your own processes of experiencing events ("do unto others as you would have them do unto you" etc.). In that ACT workshop "eyes on" exercise this "board to board" quality is quite powerful. [JC] If there was only one human and no language, would that one human still have an observing self?

From an RFT point of view, no. In that 1984 *Behaviorism* piece on spirituality I noted that with your science hat on from this analysis the soul was a side effect of language. This is the quote:

> Spirit is defined as an "immaterial" being; and matter is the stuff of things. Spirit is thus a being non-experienceable as a thing. You-as-perspective seems to fit this definition rather well. As was argued earlier, the essence of a thing or object is "this-not that." To see a thing we must also see "not-thing." Thus, all things must be finite-they must have edges or limits. It is the edges or limits that allow us to see a thing. If a thing was absolutely everywhere, we could not see it as a thing. For the person experiencing it, you-as-perspective has no stable edges or limits-it is not fully experienceable as a thing. Perspective is precisely the aspect in which things are held. As soon as perspective is viewed as content from what perspective is it viewed? Perspective must move one step back. It seems plausible, then, that the matter/spirit distinction has as its source the content / perspective distinction established as a necessary side effect of language. Quite literally, it may be that verbal behavior gave humankind a soul.

Of course I also apologized for the heresy ... and acknowledged that from a faith point of view quite a different answer would be given. This was the footnote on that point:

> 1. This statement, and to some degree this entire paper, might be thought by some to be sacrilegious. It is not my interest, however, to say literally that God or spirit in a religious sense does not exist independent of humankind. To the contrary, God could have created the very mechanisms I am describing that makes spirituality knowable. The paper is only meant to talk about spirituality within the game we call science.

SELF-AS-CONTEXT Unchangeability of [cont'd] Kelly Wilson	The stability of observer self is a shaped property of the response. Awkward as it might be, "selfing" is probably more accurate. Seeing and speaking from a consistent perspective is shaped operant behavior. Shaped by the social verbal community, who generally dole out reinforcement and punishment for consistency. As such, self is not an object (no thing as Steve says in Making Sense). We need to be careful about objectifying behavior (heck, behavior analysts--at least the contextualist folks-- don't even treat stimuli as objects).
SELF-AS-CONTEXT Unchangeability of [cont'd] John Forsyth	Kel is right on. This may be off track, but I tend to think of the observer self -- self-as-context -- as being the most pure form of experiential knowing. You might think of it as responding to direct and derived contingencies as they are. Nothing more, nothing less. Young children are masterful at this. As a dad of three little ones, I am continually awe struck by the subtle changes that are emerging as my kids grow and as their language abilities develop. There is a beauty and peace in how children respond to the world that is hard for we adults to do once evaluative and other relational verbal processes get more entrenched via socialization. Young children are masters at being present with the world and responding to that world as it is (self-as-context), not how they say it is (self-as-content).

VALUES
 	
  ACT concept of; goals, vs.
 	
  Happiness, pursuit of - a valued direction?
 	
ACCEPTANCE
 	
  Situations, no ACT call for acceptance of
 	
EMOTION
 	
  Happiness, pursuit of - a valued direction? [3-12-03]
 	
  Steve Hayes
	Joseph Ciarrochi wrote:
	
	> It seems like you are saying that a client can choose any valued direction except "the pursuit of happiness." This is a strong restraint, given most people rank the pursuit of happiness as one of their most cherished values.
	
	ACT takes a particular stance on values and goals. Values are qualities of an unfolding sequence of action. They exist in the very moment you orient in a direction and they continue to exist so long as a particular unfolding sequence is headed in that same direction. They can never be obtained ... only instantiated. Goals are things that can be obtained as one moves in a valued direction.
	
	Ask two questions "does it exist in the moment you orient in a direction?" and "can you obtain it as an object?" If the answer is "yes" and then "no" -- it perhaps can be treated as a value. Another way to say this: values are issues of being as you are doing.
	
	Example: caring for others. The moment you choose to matter about that, you are headed in that direction. To care about caring is a kind of caring. Before you begin you have arrived -- you are being caring. However, no matter how much caring you do there is more to do ... you can never obtain it as an object.
	
	Pursuit of happiness might be like that ... or not. Mostly it seems not. Mostly people want to FEEL happy ... it is a result, not a quality of action. They are not BEING happy, DOING happy, they instead are pursuing happy. That's a goal, not a value, and it doesn't work very well methinks. If they don't have it they mourn. If they do they worry about losing it.
	
	It would be like trying to create a loving feeling not by BEING loving and DOING loving, but by doing something else so as to FEEL loving (or loved). But those other things are themselves almost always not a loving thing to do -- you are treating yourself and others as an object and you know it.
	
	Happiness is like that too. You can only pursue what you do not have. How can the affirmation of NOT produce IS?

Whenever I do the "little kid" exercise in workshops what shows up as what we wanted is self-acceptance, love, caring, participation, being seen, safety, respect, and things like that. I can't think of once that "happiness" showed up as what we as children wanted ... if we have these other things, sometimes we are happy, sometimes sad, but always alive.

By the way, it is the present focus that allows values not to be just another way to beat ourselves up. Values in a true ACT sense of the term are not REALLY about the future anymore than me being oriented west is about San Francisco. ("Outcome is the process through which process becomes the outcome.") That is why values can work anywhere in ACT work ... still human minds turn them into things that are achieved somewhere else than now ... that is where the difficulty can come in.

[JC] I have been extremely poor...to the point of living out of my car. I stood still, and much of my potential was being wasted. I could radically accept my situation, but this acceptance would not have been sufficient to get me moving. I needed to get my arse out of poverty. I needed to get myself educated.

... acceptance is not a matter of accepting situations. ACT is also a radical change strategy, and usually situations call for change. What we are called upon to accept is our history, our continuity of consciousness, and what emerges in situations as a result. All else is on the table.

Sorry for the guruish quality to this post ...

VALUES **Anti-social/ harmful** **Goals, cf. [8-1-05]** Casey Capps	Audrey Lowrie wrote: Most of us have seen clients referred for counselling who think that they have a right to hit women, enjoy images of child sex abuse, hurt animals... I think if you ask the human being that is hitting women (or men), abusing animals, or abusing children if this is really what he/she wants his/her life to be about, if this is what he/she wants to be remembered for, with kindness and compassion, withholding judgment, the answer will almost always be no. There is no way to know for sure, but this is my sense. My sense is that this is usually some avoidance move or lack of skillfulness. The other piece I think is that values can be just another place to get stuck if they are understood as an outcome, somewhere to get to (I have to get married, have kids, have a house; happiness). If one is always looking toward the future and evaluating where he/she is in relation to the value, he/she is missing this present moment completely and most likely not living each moment fully. I understand valuing to be about living what you want to be about in each moment. One's non-verbal experience will let one know if valuing is occurring; the mind need not be involved any more than necessary. I think of that Rilke quote, something like loving the questions themselves and living your way into the answer. (Rilke, 1903)
VALUES Anti-social/ harmful [cont'd] ACT Listserv Member	I think people do what brings them reinforcers - the method is really dependant upon learning history. The majority of people find that treating others with kindness provides them more opportunities for reinforcement, due to more possible deliverers of reinforcers staying in their social environment. If you spend a lot of time attacking others, only a few will remain; if you treat others in a manner they find reinforcing (kindly) they will stay, and behave in ways that will lead you to reinforce them. Raise a child in an impoverished environment, with a struggle to obtain food, little or no positive attention for doing "nice" things, and where aggressive behavior is attended to and positively reinforced by peers, and you end up with someone more likely to behave aggressively; same goes for those raised in homes where violence is modeled. Certainly not everyone raised in these types of environments will be "bad" people, but it is more likely....
VALUES **Anti-social/ harmful; conflict with therapist's values [6-4-03]** Sonja Batten	John Bush wrote: If an ACT client's values assessment included "Torment as many people and small dogs as I can," would we want to help him carry out his program? Moving from the theoretical to the practical level, when I do values work with clients, I will often say to them something to the effect of that they can choose their own values, and I'll support them in anything they choose, as long as it doesn't involve hurting self or others [including dogs ;)]. They can choose to value those things - they're free to do so - but as a human being and a therapist with my own values, I have my limits as to what I can support.
VALUES Anti-social/ harmful; conflict with therapist's values [cont'd]	Tony Biglan wrote: Would a person who was experiencing their thoughts and feelings with openness and no efforts to control adopt a goal such as tormenting dogs? Many ACT clients, when they contact this issue, react almost with a panic. "If values are a choice, what if I choose badly?" There are two parts to this concern: that maybe one has the "wrong values" and the

Violation of; "wrong" choice of [6-4-03] Steve Hayes	possibility of violating their own values. The former is an illusion, because by definition to have "the wrong values" one would have to have the right ones that when applied to the wrong ones determined that they were wrong. This is the sense in which values is one of a very few things (self as context being another) that are always perfect (not in an evaluative sense, but in the "whole and beyond evaluation" sense). I do believe in the possibility of evil (if values are a choice, you almost have to believe that) but at this level I have just not yet seen it. If I did, I would get away. The latter issue is not an illusion. We all do it everyday. It is the basis of "sin." It is apparently bad etymology, but I have an old unpublished paper on "faith, sin, and grace" that argued that we can make good sense of "sin" by linking it back to the similar Latin word (and the Spanish one) meaning "without." In a religious sense sin is without God -- to turn away from God's love. In a psychological sense it is also to turn away from love but that includes especially the foundation of love, which is acceptance. Acceptance applies not just to self but also to values. We have the values we have. When we turn away from ourselves and our values and enter into a world of conditionality in these areas we pay an immediate price. "The wages of sin is death" seems right on -- we immediately lose vitality and we pay for it with our lives. That is one reason the Genesis story is in the ACT book. When we apply literal, evaluative language to the foundation on which we stand, we immediately are hobbled and disempowered. Tony's post thus turns into this question: Are there folks whose basic psychological posture is loving who -- as an expression of that -- value torture of others? I can barely conceive of it; I've certainly never seen it. Underneath rapists and murderers I've worked with I've found Betty Crocker [mythical housewife-spokeswoman for General Mills baking products in the US]. A Zen teacher of some note who is interested in ACT ... told me that what ACT seems to add is a technical account (e.g., defusion) and a sensitivity to "self as context." What it is missing is a set of values and a set of practices. That seems right to me. But if we add a set of values and practices, we slip away from the behavioral health and scientific psychology niche into something else. That's fine, but I'd rather have ACT support people in doing such things if it is there for them to do that, rather than having ACT itself be about that. I hope that out of the ACT work more people will act to save the world in concrete ways (e.g., feeding the hungry). But ACT is not about feeding the hungry ... or any particular value. The closest to a values conflict I've yet seen in the ACT work is the use of ACT to help Mormon gay folk adjust to a life without gay sex. Personally -- though I would definitely not do it myself -- I'm OK with it (with some discomfort, I admit). Compared especially to the alternatives, ACT is a gentle and loving approach to this issue, emphasizing self-acceptance, acceptance of sexual feelings, validation of values, and choices about sexual behavior. If you are cool with vows of celibacy or poverty (as an ex-Catholic, that was big in my training) then I think we have to allow for folks to make values choices of this kind too. That's the closest I've seen but I'm sure there are other values conflicts out there.
VALUES Anti-social/ harmful; conflict with therapist's values [cont'd] **CHILD & ADOLESCENT** Values, anti-social; accessing values [6-4-03] Laurie Greco	In my work with children and teens this happens quite a bit -- mean lady therapist undermines [seemingly?] values-driven agenda once again. Seriously though, I have found that sometimes a client's stated values and supporting actions are functionally equivalent to, "I wanna be a more effective [you fill it in ... neurotic person, drug user, anorexic, dog killer, school refuser, delinquent...]. This is my choice and value, so can you help me, please?"... I had a teen client who was rather attached to and swore by his "value" of being someone that other people feared (essentially, he wanted to continue moving towards and achieving some sort of high-level bully status). Did I support my client's stated program for the sake of helping him travel in a chosen direction? Hell no. I also did not tell him it was wrong, stupid, immature, or the like. Instead we explored this value - mindfully and openly (without judgment/defense) rolling around in what it means to be feared, to be a bully, always coming back to "and then what?" So then what happens when you're King of Bullies and everyone and their Mom is terrified of crossing your path to the point that they wouldn't dare challenge you?" And on and on we go, looking closely (mindfulness exercises great here), pealing away layer by layer...and I think Steve is right. At the core of this bad-ass adolescent I catch a glimpse of Betty Crocker. And this stated value of "bullying/being feared" might be nothing more than a dressed-up version of, "I want to be respected by my family and peer group. I want to be someone that other people listen to and respect." Or maybe ... "I want control in areas of my life where it simply is not possible." Now we've got somewhere to go. Okay, so he holds some personal values within peer and family domains ... I can support this program. What has he tried, and how has this worked? (... perhaps creative hopelessness re-enters the scene at this point...). I love these kinds of cases because the values work is so intense - such a taxing process for all involved and certainly challenges my acceptance as a therapist (which is great incentive for me to continue with my own acceptance work!).

VALUES Anti-social/ harmful; conflict with therapist's values [cont'd] **CHILD & ADOLESCENT** Values, anti-social; accessing values [cont'd] John Blackledge	It does seem like values clarification with kids isn't qualitatively different than with adults--pro-social, workable, and envitalizing outcomes are there, but the means to the end can get convoluted. One difference with kids (and with Charles Manson), I guess, is that kids can tend to be more shocking about their unclarified "values," which can catch us off guard and make us start demanding pliance.
VALUES Anti-social/ harmful; conflict with therapist's values [cont'd] **CHILD & ADOLESCENT** Values, anti-social; accessing values [cont'd] ACT Listserv Member	I agree with Laurie's comments in the case of the kid who values intimidation. I incorporate ACT and DBT in my work with incarcerated adolescents. I encounter these sorts of stated values with great frequency. When these issues come up I attempt a reframe, and validate what is valid about the stated value, withholding judgment about the harmful means, and often incorporating a discussion of the pros and cons of continuing to live the value as they have in the past, versus alternative means. Hopefully the reframing and validating process will open the door to a brainstorming discussion about alternative ways to live the value.
VALUES Anti-social/ harmful; conflict with therapist's values [cont'd] **CHILD & ADOLESCENT** Values, anti-social; accessing values [cont'd] Laurie Greco	I'm not sure that values work with children or Charles Manson (!) is much different than values work with non-serial killer grownups. Perhaps it looks different topographically - at the level of technique - and might require a little creativity to enhance the workability of it all. But when used functionally, I think we're doing and uncovering much of the same. Re: technique - with children and teens, I often try to incorporate fun, "artsy" activities into values work, such as by creating personal Values and Struggle Collages in session, using pictures and symbols from teen magazines. It often comes as both surprise and relief when the grown-up therapist presents a very similar-looking collage depicting a very similar-looking struggle. I might not create collages with Charlie. Who knows, though -- maybe he'd dig this sort of thing, giving us a place to connect. I wouldn't be surprised, though, to uncover (perhaps striking?) similarities between some of Charlie's deeply-held values and my own. Maybe through values work, some seemingly clear-cut distinctions (e.g., grown up-child, animal lover-dog tormenter, healer-murderer) become a bit blurred such that the initial and often safer notion of separateness begins to dissolve. I got no data, but I'm wagering that beyond all of Charlie's stinky layers, we could catch at least a momentary glimpse of one suffering Betty. Like any challenging client population, the route to Betty might be a bit more indirect and 'convoluted,' requiring a number of back-door approaches and lots of patience. Which is linked to John's comment about demanding pliance. I have found a layer-peeling, backdoor approach useful in undermining pliance-counterpliance that often shows up with teens (e.g., "I chose this because my friends did, and it really feels crappy to be on the outside"; "I chose 'left' because my parents are pushing 'right,' and I resent being treated like a little kid.")....
VALUES Anti-social/ harmful; conflict with therapist's values [cont'd] **CHILD & ADOLESCENT** Values, anti-social; accessing values [cont'd] David Lee	These posts on children/adolescents and values have been very interesting and useful. The examples of stated values have been extreme; more often, I find, even the less extreme examples of stated values require some exploration. For example, the 12 yr old who doesn't care about school because her stated value is to be a "rapper"--never mind that there is no apparent talent being displayed by the child. The other examples, i.e., dog killer, Charles Manson, are similar in that they are "names" or embodiments (concrete statements) of stated values. I would wager that even a putatively reasonable stated value still needs a bit of exploration. For example, it would surprise me if a child said her value is "world domination through peace love and understanding." I'd still want to know what's up with that. I certainly agree that the more fun that is brought into session, the better the connection and discovery of values that takes place. I tend to do less art but more gross motor examples--get up, move about, and exaggeration of the values, etc. Also, I am informed by the child's history about where to look and promote a more "abstract" version of the stated value; e.g., the "rapper" has a long history of being moved from home to home, has an indifferent parent, etc., so the relations between the stated value and being accepted, loved, cared for are fairly obvious. The "fun" during session really has to do with bringing those relations into the present (though not stated explicitly, as I am doing here). Another stated value that I find particularly interesting is the "anarchist." These adolescents are often a bit brainy and have a logical structure, based on an extant literature, built up to support their values. I find it

	challenging to be accepting and supportive when "reasonable" values are presented. In these cases, I find that deliteralization exercises lead to values work in a sly fashion. I would like some feedback on what I find are the most typical cases involving children. It is usually the case that someone else, a parent or caseworker refers a case for a problem, but from the child's perspective, there is no problem. The statement, "If they would just leave me alone," shows up frequently, for example. Sometimes the statement is indicative of the "problem," but sometimes it doesn't seem so. And I often wonder if I should "raise awareness" or come at it a different way, or just leave it alone.
VALUES Anti-social/ harmful; conflict with therapist's values [cont'd] **CHILD & ADOLESCENT** Values, anti-social; accessing values [cont'd] Laurie Greco	Our examples have been leaning towards more extreme cases - perhaps to drive home some point. I would say that most of the kiddos and teens I work with aren't dog killers OR budding sociopaths. But in some sense, those extreme and not-so-extreme adolescent cases are alike. They're me (and you?) ten years ago - or today - searching fruitlessly for some solid ground to stand on, defining and redefining valued directions while wandering in a world of desire, attaching to internal chatter (and the like), often reacting more to the past and anticipating the future than relating directly with the unfolding present. At a practical level, I agree that there's always room for some rich values work and ongoing clarification (whether the stated value is to become a dope rapper or to achieve world domination through peace/love or collecting human heads). Re: values that sound too "reasonable" -- I know whatcha mean and seem to get this with shy/anxious little ones (smells like pliance?). I'm not sure, but to me it's very similar to supporting and accepting client values that appear shocking or abhorrent at first glance. Out of curiosity, what kinds of deliteralization exercises have you found most helpful when this comes up in therapy?
VALUES Anti-social/ harmful; conflict with therapist's values [cont'd] **CHILD & ADOLESCENT** Values, anti-social; accessing values [cont'd] David Lee	What is entirely fascinating is this transition from a world of possibilities that all seem entirely plausible, e.g., the existence of Santa, to an ever-narrowing world of also-rans (e.g., "I coulda been a contender"). The shift from that anything's possible world children see to fairly realistic and possible choices, e.g., famous rapper, in adolescence and slightly beyond to mundane occupations that lead people to comment, if only to feel better, "I don't work to live, I live to work," contains the elements for values work with children/teens. I think it is a very important work to strip away the notion that a thing to do is the same as a thing to be. At some level, a simple message--I care, and I care very deeply about you--seems to make the difference; it seems to put before the child/teen something new that is not quite the same. Sometimes a kid will ask me *why* I care, and I won't answer that question, except to say, that's the bottom--there is no other reason; it is simply the fact of the matter. [Re: deliteralization exercises] Of course, "it depends." One really quick thing I do nearly every time almost as a test for curiosity is to briefly build up the power of language with examples of reason giving the teen uses; then I put a pen in my hand and invite the person to tell the pen to rise to the ceiling. And then I try to share some puzzlement about how words seem so powerful, and yet... The milk, milk, milk exercise is fun and produces the intended effect almost always. The hoods on the bus is fun too, involving lots of movement. I find that the bad cup metaphor is very useful for "young philosophers"--they ask lots of questions as they chew on this one. Also, I like to "be their mind" and walk them through various events they report have happened in the prior week to physically show distinctions between their words and them; this is especially useful when the walk down memory lane (noting that the same "you" was there during various events in their lives) has been successful. BTW, I stopped saying "in the service of" because I got too many strange looks. Now, I say either "does that work to" or "does that help you to" in relation to values.
VALUES **Choice (with reasons, not for reasons) [2-25-05]** Joseph Ciarrochi	Russ Harris wrote: In conceptualising ACT, I like to come back to this quote by Kelly: "The core ACT goal, in the most abstract sense, is to help the client live a rich and meaningful life while accepting the suffering that surely comes to all of us." Why is this our goal? Presumably because living life in such a manner gives a deep sense of satisfaction, or vitality.... So when my doubt starts nagging away, it says to me that statements such as "It's not about feeling GOOD, it's about FEELING good" are not quite accurate - because living a rich and meaningful life does feel 'good,' in the long term, even though it may feel 'bad' in the moment. I think it is another trick of the mind to never stop asking why do I want to do this? What is my "real" motive? But not everything can be justified. You must start out with life premises (values) before you can do anything. It's like taking a journey. You have to choose a direction to go before you can go. You don't have to justify that direction. I mean, I guess you can say, I want to go towards X because it gives me pleasure. I'm not sure the "because it gives me pleasure" part adds anything. You could ask, "why does it give you pleasure? is this a good enough reason?" and the mind will keep going and going, trying to find the "true reason."

	A cat does not need to justify its preference for chasing mice. In a way, a tree values sunlight. It is always trying to get to the sun. And the tree grows just fine without all these human reasons. One of the most difficult parts of ACT for me is getting that you can just choose values, with reasons (they show up), but not for reasons.
VALUES Choice (with reasons, not for reasons) [cont'd] John Forsyth	In my book values are on the table because they are what most of us want out of life -- living well, fully, richly, meaningfully ... doing what matters. We judge values by what people do, not in terms of how they feel about what they do. Being a parent, a loving spouse, a neighbor, colleague, friend to someone often comes with its share of pains and hardships. If feeling good was the only guide and the expected outcome, then many of us would simply stop engaging these and other life domains. A related issue you raise is about pain and feeling good. I honestly don't think that most people live out their lives guided by the goal and value of feeling good. This seems like a dead end -- chasing the feeling. There are countless examples of people who have lived out their lives with every possible disadvantage, every reason to give up, who experience enormous pain and hardship, and yet continue to go after what they care about and do what matters to them (Mother Theresa). Values are what we do with our hands, feet, mouth, eyes -- they are actions. Unnecessary actions that get in the way of this doing, in turn, are (or can be) problems.
VALUES Choice (with reasons, not for reasons) [cont'd] Steve Hayes	The ultimate basis of all symbolic systems is an assumption outside the system. Providing a mathematical proof of that was considered to be one of the greatest scientific advances of the last century. The "why" questions you are asking can only be fully "answered" by staying inside the system, but then they are not fully answers. If you say "vitality" is your answer your mind (which IS that very symbolic repertoire and thus CANNOT go outside the system) will eventually say "why vitality?" The assumption that is outside the system in ACT is non-verbal knowledge. It is the so-called "two by four" solution. I walk through it in: Hayes, S. C. (1997). Behavioral epistemology includes nonverbal knowing. In L. J. Hayes & P. M. Ghezzi (Eds.), *Investigations in behavioral epistemology* (pp. 35-43). Reno, NV: Context Press. That is why values are a choice. You cannot answer "why" because, by definition, a choice in ACT is undefended and unjustified verbally. It is based on non-verbal knowledge - about which one cannot adequately language. Of course, you can choose vitality as a value, but don't tell me I have to -- if I have to it's not a value. Is there a feeling that comes with living according to your values? I think so. Let's see. If you say it is vitality, I'd say "fine. Seems that way to me too." If you say "I live that way *in order to* produce vitality" I'll say "why vitality?"
VALUES Choice (with reasons, not for reasons) [cont'd] Nico van der Meijden	Take e.g., the social practice of psychotherapy: if you're a psychotherapist and value being a good one, you probably have some image of what constitutes a good psychotherapist (based on role models, studying, seeing colleagues at work, supervision, tradition etcetera). However, becoming a good psychotherapist requires a lot of effort and practice and alongside successes you'll have setbacks and failures and all the negative evaluations and feelings that come along. If you're not willing to have those, it'll be difficult to become a good psychotherapist, because avoidance will diminish the behavioral flexibility a good therapist needs. So I would say FEELING good in this case is a process goal in the service of becoming a good psychotherapist. But being a good psychotherapist shows itself ultimately in behavior and outcomes, in the quality of our daily practice and what we achieve by it, it doesn't show in the positive private experiences that are merely a side-effect. The quality of our behavior is not something completely subjective as it can be judged by others that participate in the same social practice, like our clients or colleagues. So I would say a sense of meaning, satisfaction and vitality is a side-effect of the quality of our behavior on a day-to-day basis.
VALUES Choice (with reasons, not for reasons) [cont'd] Steve Hayes	Russ Harris wrote: If a client asked you, "Why should I bother to live according to my values?" or "Why should I just choose?" how would you answer them? You seem to be asking "how do you convince the patient that they should care." You don't. If you try to answer the questions you ask you are doomed. But, to be frank, questions like this are more often asked by ACT therapists than real human beings [note the frame of distinction :)]. We get to values by asking what a person wants to have their life be about. We call that "values." If a person asks your question: "Why should I bother to live according to my values?" in the sense of "Why

should I have my life be about what I want it to be about?" there is not much you can say other than "God bless you" and "come back when you've suffered some more."

I go through this in the "2 by 4" chapter. It is like the person stuck under a refrigerator calling out for help but when you go to move the refrigerator they say "But wait! Why should I care if it is removed?" or "How will I even know if it is working to have it removed?" or "How will I know that I know if it is removed?." The proper response to all of this is to smile. Then leave.

Verbal knowledge is ultimately based on non-verbal knowledge. If you ask "why" you are demanding that non-verbal knowledge ultimately be based on verbal knowledge. That is a no-win game - it is time to leave saying "call me back when you are ready."

You know it works to get a refrigerator off you the same way you know it is on you. If your suffering is not enough, my pitiful answer to your why question will add nothing.

I would not dream of telling clients they should care. I'm about empowering people to move toward what they care about.

As for choice: we get to choice by pointing out that you cannot get to values without choice.

VALUES	Values provide the metric for evaluation. Rational judgments and decisions involve applying these metrics to behavioral alternatives. If you try to do values via rational judgments and decisions you enter into an infinite regress: I picked *this* metric because doing so passed the test of *that* metric. The obvious question is: how did you pick *that* metric? If you try to answer on the basis of rational judgments and decisions you have to say I picked *that* metric because doing so passed the test of *yet another* metric. It can never stop until you say "I picked this metric because that's where I stand and that's where I start." That is a choice.
Choice (with reasons, not for reasons) [cont'd]	No choice: no values.
Steve Hayes	Means-end values (process values) you can do as rational judgments: I value the rule of law because it fosters non-violence and I value non-violence. The first "value" can be a rational judgment, but it has to be based on one that is a choice (i.e., not verbally defended and justified by an appeal to still some other metric), or you enter into the infinite regress problem.

VALUES	Aaron Meyer wrote:
Choice (with reasons, not for reasons) [cont'd]	> Would you explain this statement a bit more: "Verbal knowledge is ultimately based on non-verbal knowledge."
Steve Hayes	[The *Behavioral epistemology includes nonverbal knowing* chapter] actually does attempt a technical account, and I could repeat it but it is late. If I were a better business person I would provide a link to Context Press to buy the book. Instead, the chapter is attached.

It is late - and it somehow seems OK to be a little more poetic. Would it be OK if I did that?

You cannot have symbolic systems without assumptions that are outside of that system. If you demand that they be fully inside the systems they enable, you have to create a self-delusion - but like an itch we need to scratch we are only a "why" away from collapse. The only thing that can stop it is to stop it. Naked. Out of nothing. Or so it seems from the point of view of the systems that this "choice" enables. We have to plant our feet firmly in thin air and break all of the rules by acknowledging what it is that we actually assume; or choose; or want to be about. Just because. (With reasons / not for reasons)

Truth criteria are assumptions. They enable symbolic systems but they are not and cannot be fully inside them. You cannot have a pragmatic truth without a goal. But this means that goals too are not fully inside the system. Choice is outside the system. By definition. (Not for others: for the scientist *your* assumptions, truth criteria, goals, choices and so on are fair game inside *their* systems - but to put them there they needed their *own* assumptions, truth criteria, goals, and choices that are outside of theirs.) "Why" can only be answered inside the system. "Why" is a demand for a coherent relational network -- as if that is *all* there is (or *all* we are). But what of the life that enables and supports relational networks themselves? What was there before there was a symbolic system? What is outside of it? Right now. Can you really be so sure that everything is inside simply because your word machine says so and thus (seemingly) makes it so. What was and is there that is beyond all of that? RFT will indeed shed light on that, as will behavior analysis generally. BA was the very science focused on that question (which cost it its dominance in psychological science and darn near killed it).

Before we learned the invention of language we still had purpose. We had workability. My dog Biji would definitely know if he had a refrigerator on him; and he would know when he was set free. And he would not need someone else to tell him which to prefer. He didn't have verbal truth, poor thing. We do. It can take us to the stars or to the brink of destruction. Minds demand we know what we cannot "know." Minds are only about one kind of knowing. But there is more to us than that - and this other part was there first. Do you suppose that my dog Biji demands that life be meaningful? Does he fear his own death? Does he realize that the Universe itself will die? Does he face finitude, emptiness, and meaninglessness? As humans if we do face these things - or even embrace them - what comes next? Do we stop functioning? Do we stop caring? Why not? My dog Biji would definitely know if he had a refrigerator on him; and he would know when he was set free. And he would not need someone else to tell him which to prefer. And are we really so different? If I give this process a form my mind will claim it, and squeeze it nearly to death to make it give up its secret. Here is about as much form as seems safe for me to hear myself say (for tonight at least):

I care about my children. I need to pee. I love my wife to be. I weep for those who suffer. I'm hungry. I want to survive. I want to make a difference. Now I take a breath. They are all equally so.

If I start from what is so, living with a mind is possible. If I do not, only minding is possible.

Values are a humble acknowledgement of what is *so. That is why when we touch them - really touch them - we cry. I don't think we do that because we are not living up to them - though that is a source of sadness. I think we cry because in that moment there is a suchness* that is overwhelming and just for a moment pops the illusion that we are our minds. We truly do care. We faith in ourselves. It is as real as a breath. Not because I (or anyone) says so -- because you know so. Only a human, strange little creatures that we are, could have that sense of what is so ever at their fingertips and seriously ask "why."

Here is a way to get in touch with the sadness of that "why" question: if you have children picture them and connect with your love for them (if you don't have kids, do this with anyone you love absolutely and always have). Now ask yourself as if you really want an answer: "why do I love them?" Immediately, in the very hearing of the question, see if there isn't a sense of betrayal - as if we know that our minds have friggin just gone one step too far even to ask such a shameful question. "Senator McCarthy, have you no dignity? Have you lost your last shred of common decency?" We, we who know we will die and that the Universe itself will either go dark and expand forever or collapse back into an infinitely dense pea, we also yearn. We care.

Deny it if you will (and minds will!) but first try to see what is under that denial. Like that song: what if God was one of us? Why does that song bring a tear? What if we really could be about having love in our life? And what if that leap of faith was itself a tremendously loving thing to do? What if that very leap was the substance of things not seen? Sorry. Thank you for indulging me. The chapter will do better. To bed. Peace, love, and life.

VALUES Choice (with reasons, not for reasons) [cont'd] Steve Hayes	Nico van der Meijden wrote: What you say can only be valid if we don't have absolute or ultimate criteria by which to judge our values. If we say values are personal choices based on what 'we feel is so,' there are no absolute criteria. There are only personal choices and preferences. But when there are only personal choices, with no absolute criteria to refer to, the choice of values is arbitrary. What "absolute or ultimate criteria" do you have in mind? One of usual sources for such things is religion but it requires an act of faith to become so. That act of faith is a choice the way I am using the term -- in every theology of which I am aware anyway. I deliberately referred to that connection in my "substance of things not seen" comment in that last message (the Christian definition of faith). I'm definitely not arguing against faith -- I'm arguing for choice. Without choice you can't do faith, so far as I understand it. If you are referring to evolution the counterargument is more complex. I'll hold off on that for now. Those two are the usual suspects. Did you have something else in mind? It is not correct to say that choices are arbitrary. The animal operant lab studies choices -- in what sense are they "arbitrary"? Selecting among alternatives not based on verbal formulations of pros and cons or cause and effect, does not mean selecting among alternatives from outside the natural universe. It means selecting them not entirely inside the verbally constructed universe. Your line of thinking is why people recoiled from pragmatism: they want a way to be a good boy and to know that they are being so. "If values are choices then how can I say Hitler was wrong?" or to use the example Marxists used in their rejections of Jamesian pragmatism: how can I disagree that "what's good for General Motors is good for the country?" I think these ideas are confused. You can resolve values conflicts. It is just that YOU have to do it. Here's how: choose. What's good for GM is NOT necessarily good for the country once you say what you are seeking. Same goes for Hitler. It is anything but arbitrary.

VALUES
   Choice (with reasons, not for reasons) [cont'd]
     Steve Hayes
	... I would agree that values can't be separated from language ... I'm pretty sure I haven't said otherwise in that chapter or elsewhere.
	
	I just argued that all verbal knowing stands on a base of non-verbal knowing....

VALUES
   Choice (with reasons, not for reasons) [cont'd]
     Steve Hayes
	A couple of points. You [Nico van der Meijden] wrote this:
	
	    But suppose I say: 'I'm a sea-captain and I ought to do what a sea captain ought to do,' I would say I have a valid metric for evaluation.
	
	But how did it happen that the person chose being a sea captain in the first place? You say many things in your post but let me just pull out two sentences:
	
	    "A value is a principle that has authority over us independently of our feelings, attitudes or preferences. How I feel at a given moment is irrelevant to the question of how I must live" and later "The other option is using non-verbal passions, desires or processes like classical and operant conditioning as the base for values."
	
	I think language games are being confused in this entire thread (I'm not focusing exclusively on you here Nico) and we need to pull them out and consider them separately. The language of choice used in ACT is in the service of empowerment. It is a clinical language. Said a bit loosely, it is about how to create sea-captains. The thread we have had on the non-verbal basis of knowing is philosophy of science talk. Philosophy is a process of articulating, and taking responsibility for assumptions. Since assumptions are required in analysis (back to Godel's theorem) having them is part of the scientific process; owning them is part of a responsible approach to science. When we are doing philosophy of science we are speaking for a slightly different purpose than when we are speaking clinically. Some of the philosophical things we've been writing here in this thread would rarely be said clinically. Some of the thread has been still another kind of talk: scientific analysis itself. When we have intimated that the basis of non-verbal knowing is contact with contingencies, that is an example. Much of the language you are using is a language of justification, linked to processes of social and personal regulation: what would normally be spoken of as moral philosophy. You spoke in an earlier message of "ultimate" and "absolute" values; you speak in this post of "authority" and what one "must" do and you pit that way of speaking against various terms including passions, desires, feelings, attitudes, preferences, or conditioning. And social authority is indeed how verbal processes initially produce persistence in the face of immediate contingencies, and these terms are referring to that set of more immediate processes. I think they emerge in this conversation because this is how the clinical talk presents itself when viewed through the filter of a language of justification and moral training. It is telling that most of the terms you are pitting "authority" against are not terms that have been explicitly introduced into the conversation (e.g., passions, feelings, attitudes).
	
	Any talk that is useful clinically has a behavior regulatory role: that is the sense in which it is "useful." So the clinical use of "values" and the social / personal regulatory use of "values" overlap. And I do think our social history is very much involved in the values we have. But when we are working as clinicians we do not have the authority to use values talk in a moral sense except in a very limited way that enables that role (e.g., rules about therapy -- such as you cannot physically hurt yourself or others while in therapy or I will intervene). As I recall, the very word "moral" comes from a root that means "manners" and "customs" -- but we are not in a clinical role as a representative of society, attempting to teach proper manners. We cannot say what the right values are; or why our clients should have one set of values or another. This is not because we are behaviorists: it is because we are there in a role as a psychologist (etc.) and not there as religious or moral leaders.
	
	That does NOT mean that we will not invoke values in that way in other contexts and other roles: political, moral, religious and so on. Said in technical terms focusing on a speaker: a scientific analysis of values is a tact. The moral and political use of values is a mand. You can do a scientific analysis OF a mand, but that does not mean that this analysis now serves the functions of a mand. For statements to serve the functions of a mand on others (in RFT terms, focusing on the listener, for it to function as a ply) you must embed words in a context of explicit social control. Scientists and clinicians do that, but primarily in other roles -- except in ancillary ways not in their roles as scientists and clinicians. Just because you are tacting in your role as a scientist, it does not mean that you foreswear manding in other roles. Ask my children: we have "musts" in my home. You must not hit others, for example. You must be considerate of others, for another. But that is in my role as a parent. I would never say to a client "you must be considerate of others." I would definitely look at the effects of the client's behavior on others, and I would set up conditions for the person to discover if being considerate is one thing they value. If they discover that, ACT will help establish conditions under which the personal regulatory effects will follow. It is not by accident that "Acceptance and Commitment Therapy" has that word COMMITMENT in it. You speak of the importance of such things as being able to enter into marriage vows. I agree. And look at the actual data on ACT and you will

	see that it empowers persistence: ACT is not about teaching clients how to be regulated by passions, feelings, and attitudes in the sense in which you use those terms (which seems to be to pit short term contingencies over and against the persistence that can be produced by the "authority" of moral rules).
	But if you try to do ACT from the perspective of DOING moral rules, you are no longer doing ACT. They are just different language games. I can tell my daughter about how marriage vows are forever: I would never say such a thing to a client. Rather, in ACT, I would talk in such a way that the person can discover their own values. I would look at the pain that comes from not living in accord with them. I would help teach ways of persisting and changing in the service of chosen values. This opens up a space in which it is possible to "vow" something (whether that be to a marriage or to a changed social condition or to raising a healthy child). With those skills in hand values can take on a different quality. They are not just moral rules: they are chosen life paths.
	ACT opens up a possibility of commitment. Clients can choose their *own* vows and know what they are doing, mean it, and live it.
VALUES Choice (with reasons, not for reasons) [cont'd] Niklas Törneke	I think one problem with this thread is that the word values, as a common sense term, of course can be used to mean different things, all legitimate from different perspectives. I'll try to sort out how I understand this, from a clinical ACT perspective.
	First, from this perspective (as I understand it) there is only organisms (humans) who act, behave. There are no "things" like values, that is only a way to speak about a particular behavior. So from this perspective there is really no useful way to differ between valuing and values. What we are talking to clients about is their behavior.
	To clarify what we want to talk about it is convenient to talk about two kinds of behavior, choosing and valuing (or, in more common language; choice and values). It is important to stress, though, that talk about the nouns rather than the verbs has a danger in it, which I think is relevant also for the discussion on this list. The use of choice and values (rather than choosing and valuing) easily tricks us into objectifying these "things," making it seem like if we need to specify what these things "are" and there we go off ... (at least off from what we want to do in ACT...).
	One more introductory; these ways of behaving is not something we need to teach people to do. All humans choose and value, in the ACT sense of these words. What we do is that we help people self-discriminate these behaviors as we assume that will increase behavioral flexibility.
	What is the point we want to make in ACT, talking this way?
	1. Choosing. This comes close to what most people would call "just acting." There is no escape; we do it all the time. We act, as a result of all the different contingencies up to the point of that particular action. Language easily tricks us into acting as if other actions (verbal) "forces" specific actions. "I can't...," "because... ." In ACT we talk about choosing to put people in the experiential position of (self discriminating) the possibility of "just acting" regardless of what verbal behavior goes on at the same time. You just put your foot where you put it. No verbal action forces you to put it in a particular place. This is what is meant by arbitrary. Of course choosing is not arbitrary from a scientific point of view. Whatever act is done is a result of the whole chain of contingencies up to the point of that particular action. But as those contingencies are not possible to discriminate verbally for the organism, the experience is "radical choice." This is the experience, the position, we want the client to discriminate. This is the possibility we want to point to. For a purpose ... that is;
	2. Valuing. With the experience of verbal barriers broken down (the possibility of choosing, of "just acting") where will you put your feet? How do you like the place where you put your feet just now? This is the central "values-question." A human being is not "free" in a scientific meaning. But experientially we are, as we cannot verbally discriminate the whole chain of contingencies leading to our actions.
	So, in this position, what about putting your feet in the direction of what you want (verbally constructed, globally desirable consequences)? What people actually want is a result of both verbal and non-verbal contingencies in their history (and the history of the species). As verbal is late (both for the individual and for the species) verbal always rests on non-verbal, as the chapter which started this thread points out.
	Trying (in therapy) to figure out "true valuing" by finding out "the non-verbal base" will just be a way of returning to the trap the client (and therapist?) was stuck in from the start as that would be an effort to solve verbally what verbal behavior cannot solve. Back to choice, "just acting..."
	But valuing in the ACT sense is verbal behavior. It is constructing globally desirable consequences and putting your feet in that direction. This is verbal behavior that is useful as it increases the probability for appetitive consequences in the long run.

VALUES **Choice (with reasons, not for reasons)** **EVIDENCE** **Mediators of outcome - epilepsy study [7-7-05]** Steve Hayes	Shoshana Isenberg wrote: How is the same "mind" that one is learning to trust less for most evaluation, thoughts, etc. suddenly a reliable source for what one values, or if they are getting closer or further from them, or feeling more "vital," or whatever. Isn't this the same cognitive process of evaluating? Your worry could come true if values work is not done properly. Good values work has to be defused and accepting. That does not necessarily mean it needs to be last. Values are more than evaluations. See the stuff in the book on choice vs. judgments. They are more contingency shaped and beyond mere words ... even though they lead to verbal forms. The book goes into this re the need to avoid pliance; the need to avoid justification, etc. One way you might assess this empirically is to ask about reasons for values. In an ACT perspective, the cleanest reasons are non-reasons. They are close to "just because" or "because this is what I want to be about." If you have the same form with funky things like "because then Mom will like me" you know you're in trouble. Check out ... work by Sheldon on "personal strivings" for empirical evidence on that point and possibly also a way to assess for this. Joe C & JT put us on to this originally. Good stuff. The model is different but the bottom line is relatively consistent with an ACT approach. ... [Sheldon] shows that if you are motivated to attain goals for less pliance-based (my term, not his) or avoidant reasons and more personal "just because" reasons you have more sustained effort, more goal attainment, and better impact on well-being. ... you can search for publications by Kennon M. Sheldon in PsychLit or elsewhere. He had an article in JPSP in 1999 on it (he calls it a "self-concordance" model ... if you enter that search term it will pull the articles as well). By the way, Tobias and JoAnne have some neat things coming on their Bull's-eye values measure as well. The mediational analyses in their wonderful epilepsy study support acceptance, defusion, AND values as mediators even in a fully predictive way (e.g., changes in the mediators occur before changes in outcomes but then account for a major portion of the outcomes seen even a year later -- the range was 42-53% of the variance accounted for, depending on the process measure). In support of what I'm saying [above], I just took a peek at Tobias's data and if you factor out acceptance and defusion changes, the values stuff doesn't work and vice versa. This is pretty supportive of the ACT model, and it provides empirical support for the idea that values work is NOT just evaluation ... and indeed if it is done solely that way, it doesn't work ...
VALUES Choice (with reasons, not for reasons) [cont'd] Steve Hayes	Monica Pignotti wrote: ... the ACT position is that the choice of values does not involve the reasoning of the mind. However, it is also not based on emotions, according to what I have read on ACT; it is not about what one feels like choosing to do. What then, is the basis for choice of values? What does it mean to "just choose"? We are mixing clinical and scientific language. The idea that "the ACT position is that the choice of values does not involve the reasoning of the mind" makes no sense if it is taken literally and scientifically. We are talking about defusion, not mindlessness. We are not becoming dogs and cats. Values work in ACT reduces the participation of reasoning as such but it still involves "the mind" and thus cannot eliminate all aspects of your verbal history being involved. The language of choice helps us get closer to contingency-shaped behavior, but values are in large part verbal. These are quotes from the ACT book (chapters on values and committed action): Language is very useful in judging and evaluating actions relative to given standards. Logically, however, we must reach these standards in some other way than by judging and evaluating. If we evaluate values, by what values do we evaluate them? *In this sense,* valuing transcends logical analysis and rational decision making. Selecting values is *more like* postulating, assuming, or operating on the basis of an axiom than it is like figuring out, planning, deciding, or reasoning. Valuing is a choice, not a judgment. (italics added) While ACT focuses on undermining self-defeating forms of verbal control, it also tries to build verbal control where such control works. Valuing is one of those areas. Values are *verbally construed global desired life consequences.* (italics in original) So, yes, values involve "the mind" which we define as our total verbal / cognitive repertoire. All normal verbal humans have the capacity for values, for this simple reason: constructing futures is a basic language function that emerges very early in development, certainly by the pre-school years.

Valuing requires only this ability, combined with a degree of disentanglement from the more elaborate verbal functions of reason giving and justifications. Thus, developing values in adults is more a matter of removing verbal barriers than it is establishing the construction of verbal futures. Oddly, when values--a verbal event--are treated too verbally and intellectually, they cannot function properly.

So we are talking about a verbal process plus defusion from a common aspect of verbal processes.

Next chapter:

Not all verbal behavior is problematic. *Formulating valued ends and intermediate goals is necessarily a verbal activity.* At the same time, behavioral activity that moves a client toward a valued end *has an important nonverbal quality.* For example, looking at a compass and figuring out which way is north could be considered a verbal event; however, once oriented, stepping north has an important nonverbal quality. It is only through committed action, and its associated intended and unintended effects, that the client can move from knowing what it is he or she wants from life, to finding out what actually works to achieve those ends.

Put more technically, committed action is the mechanism through which unworkable plies and inaccurate tracks will be undermined and socially valued but individually meaningless augmentals will be abandoned or significantly reformulated. If the values work described in the previous chapter has been successful, the client has developed or reestablished augmentals that provide overall verbal purposes where those are most helpful.

So, back to the question:

[MP] The bottom line is how does one choose values if not by emotion or rational thought? Is it done intuitively by whatever happens to strike a person and if so, wouldn't that ultimately mean that they were at the mercy of their history or whatever other forces were acting upon them, rather than actually choosing?

Well this avoids the issue of how one *would* choose values through emotion or rational thought. Try to answer THAT scientifically and you will see myriad problems. What looks simple is nothing of the kind.

Putting that aside this question is close to the same as "where does behavior come from." The answer: from the totality of our history, our biology, and the current context. In the case of values does that include emotion and judgment? Yes, but it is not justified and explained by them, so this clinical move reduces their role (but does not eliminate it ... defusion is not the same as "nonverbal" ... it is a matter of degree).

So scientifically, yes, of course, we are "at the mercy" of our history, form, and the current context. We are part of the natural world. But defusion loosens the grip of one particularly pernicious aspect of that history. But then, remember, defusion work in ACT is now also part of that very history. So we are constructing special social verbal contexts to create broader and more flexible repertoires, but we are not leaving the natural stream of events. ACT is firmly situated in a natural science perspective ... but as viewed from a contextualistic vantage point.

The closest we can come to speaking about what we are seeking experientially is the language of freedom and choice. But are we LITERALLY and SCIENTIFICALLY dealing with "free choice"? No, of course not and I know of no progressive science that has ever been constructed that takes that view literally. Science is all about constructing and using regularities. ACT is based on a philosophy that allows multiple language systems for different purposes, however, so we can embrace both the language of freedom and the language of determination where each is most workable.

So, how do we value? Answer: with our whole selves.

(The "2 X 4" chapter helps here: Hayes, S. C. (1997). Behavioral epistemology includes nonverbal knowing. In L. J. Hayes & P. M. Ghezzi (Eds.), *Investigations in behavioral epistemology* (pp. 35-43). Reno, NV: Context Press.)

As for intrinsic values:

The only intrinsic value I see in ACT per se is love. Why that is so requires more time than I can give it so close to ACT SI. In thumbnail form the reasoning is this: acceptance is inherently "loving"; acceptance is not possible without a self-as-context; a transcendent sense of self is established by deictic frames; you cannot have deictic frames without both "you" and "I" -- according to RFT "I" does not exist except in relation to "you"; thus acceptance of one's own experiences requires acceptance of others experiencing their experiences; that too is "loving"; thus you cannot do ACT without loving yourself and loving others.

It is intrinsic not as an a priori but as an empirical result of the ACT model.

The other values in the ACT / RFT work are the values linked to science itself.

An article I wrote on that in 1998 explains my position. [Hayes, S. C. (1998). Fighting for science values. *The Behavior Therapist, 21*, 205-206.]

VALUES

Choice (with reasons, not for reasons) - not arbitrary

FUNCTIONAL CONTEXTUALISM

Concepts - choice; truth; non-verbal knowing [2-9-04]

Steve Hayes

Joseph Ciarrochi wrote:

ACT suggests that values are chosen *with* reasons, but not *for* reasons. Reasons, presumably, are just more private experiences (like thoughts, sensations) that show up when one is valuing, but these reasons don't have to affect the valuing. Taken to its extreme, it almost sounds like the choice of values is arbitrary.

Some philosophical stuff on truth and the concept of choice might help here. [See a relatively obscure 1997 chapter (on what my lab called the "2 x 4" argument) that was basically my attempt to answer this question from a contextualistic framework. [Hayes, S. C. (1997). Behavioral epistemology includes nonverbal knowing. In L. J. Hayes & P. M. Ghezzi (Eds.), *Investigations in behavioral epistemology* (pp. 35-43). Reno, NV: Context Press.] It should help. Before I finally found the file for this chapter on another computer I'd attempted the outline of a response re: the arbitrariness of values. I've included it below, though now that I've re-read the chapter, I rather prefer it....

The truth criterion of contextualism is successful working.

In order to mount that truth criterion you need a specified goal against which you can evaluate whether or not something works.

However, you cannot justify the goal because selecting the goal is what allows "justification" within that philosophical system.

Choice is a selection among alternatives that is not done for reasons.

Reasons are verbal formulations of cause and effect: they are verbal justifications.

So selecting a goal must be a choice for a contextualist, i.e., it can be done with reasons but not for reasons.

Choice does not mean literal freedom -- it means "from the inside" freedom.

It does not mean literal freedom because:

a) functional contextualism as a scientific philosophy seeks order (while allowing for randomness) -- order in the sense of "prediction and influence with precision, scope, and depth."

b) Analyses are true within this philosophy of science to the extent that this goal is achieved.

c) Thus, about absolute randomness nothing true can be said, because it means in that specific area the goal has not or even cannot be achieved.

"From the inside" freedom can, however, be analyzed from the outside.

Humans are not just verbal organisms; they are also influenced by non-verbal processes.

Reasons are forms of verbal knowing.

Selecting among alternatives not for reasons (from the inside), may be based on processes not verbally known (e.g., contact with contingencies).

If so, these acts are not random and they are not "arbitrary" even though they "feel free."

When non-verbal processes are analyzed successfully there are "reasons" *for the scientist* but the behavior is not thereby governed by the verbal formulation ... even if the scientist is evaluating his or her own behavior.

Valuing is that kind of behavior.

A shorter version of the argument:

Godel's theorem has by now been proven scores of different ways within mathematics. It presents all human knowledge with this sobering conclusion: we can never justify and know everything within any analytic system. We have to start with things that are outside of the analytic system.

From a behavior analytic viewpoint it is non-verbal knowing that stands outside of verbal systems, enables them, and can never be fully brought into them.

Or, in other words, verbal knowing is based on non-verbal knowing.

Thus there will always be limits to verbal knowledge.

Values are like that.

An even shorter version of the argument:

You do what you do; you get what you get.

Values are like that.

VALUES

    Choice (with reasons, not for reasons) - not arbitrary [cont'd]

FUNCTIONAL CONTEXTUALISM

    Concepts - choice; truth; non-verbal knowing [cont'd]

FLEXIBILITY, PSYCHOLOGICAL

    Need for [2-10-04]

      Steve Hayes

Joseph Ciarrochi wrote:

The [*Behavioral epistemology includes nonverbal knowing*] article still raises some questions for me, which I wish to describe here. I would appreciate any thoughts and criticisms.... Assume someone says, "I choose X. I do not have to provide any reasons to choose X. I choose X because I choose X." Now, from a scientific perspective, there are at least two things that this "unreasoned" choice can be based upon.

1) Nonverbal knowing, as described in the Hayes article. This knowing is based on direct processes (operant, classical conditioning), and is anything but arbitrary;

2) "Languaging (arbitrary applicable relational responding)" that the person is unaware of and that the person cannot state explicitly.

I think both of these bases for valuing, can, in certain contexts, be problematic.

You betcha.

[JC:] Here's why ...

1) Nonverbal knowing may not work if the learning history is "out of tune" with the present moment. People who have been abused in the past may "know" at a nonverbal level that other people are likely to hurt them. This "knowing" may then drive their choices (e.g., they may choose to work 80 hours a week, and therefore not have "time" for relationships). So ... there is nothing in the learning history that would lead the person to choose relationships. However, let's assume that the person does not realize that (s)he would, in fact, really enjoy being in a relationship.

The ACT solution to this, I think, is to encourage people to develop new experiences and make contact with what is in the "now." When they do this, they will presumably become more in tune with the present moment and make better choices (i.e., choices that are sensitive to present environmental contingencies).

or at least better situated choices

[JC:] 2) Basing choices on "unconscious languaging" is probably not particularly vital. For example, terror management research suggests that if people are reminded of their own mortality, they come to identify with their ingroup more strongly (a relational framing process) and they become more prejudiced.

Note that this is a fusion / avoidance process.

[JC:] The explanation is that people are defending against the terror of death by seeking to live past death via their group (e.g., "I will live on through my family"). People don't seem to be realizing that they are basing their "choices" on a fear of death and an increased identification with a group (relational framing).

right

[JC:] I think the ACT solution to this is to help people to become mindful of their defensive processes and their languaging.

Yes ... and build acceptance / defusion skills.

[JC:] Hopefully, they will learn that they do not have to run from thoughts of death. Once they stop running away, they may be in a position to make better choices.

So ... this is a rather round-about way to getting to the applied problem. It seems like there is good choosing and bad choosing.

Yes, but be careful. Measured by what metric?

[JC:] Only the person choosing can know the difference. The difficulty of ACT practitioners is that 1) we want to accept and validate an individual's choice, and 2) we might want to encourage people to explore other choices, especially when we suspect that the first choice is non-vital and out of tune with the moment.

right

Kel was the first to bang the drum of psychological flexibility and these questions show why we need it: it is what ties all of this together. Values/committed action can help produce greater response flexibility, but they are much more likely to do so in the context of defusion and acceptance, self-as-process (contact with the present moment), and self-as-context. Values alone are helpful because a) choice itself does this by loosening the automatic linkage between your verbal history and action, and b) you learn greater persistence and change linked to values -- undermining two key forms of response inflexibility (inability to change; inability to persist). But all of the other processes are needed to balance this out properly.

Acceptance and defusion undermine the most pernicious effects of

"'Languaging (arbitrary applicable relational responding)" that the person is unaware of and that the person cannot state explicitly…'

Self-as-context and contact with the present moment helps people show up and make contact with the ongoing flow of situated experience.

Personally, I don't do values without at least some of these other things for exactly the reasons you point to. Sometimes "values" carries along too much of the Trojan Horse of the dark aspects of implicit verbal conditioning (e.g., hidden avoidance; disguised self-righteousness). And values should be allowed to change, also for the reasons you mention. That's one reason I like to revisit values near the end of therapy if it was done at the beginning.

If we can establish greater psychological flexibility, life itself will be the teacher. It often hurts to learn this way -- yet at least we do learn.

So far as I know, that is the best we can do. At least then when you DO see a way forward, you have a great chance of following that way.

As Willard Day, one of the fathers of behavioral contextualism, once exclaimed with incredulity and just a touch of crossness when he saw us struggling with this general issue (basically, how to know what is right): "… but … you're trying to be a good boy!" Then his face softened and he had a good laugh.

VALUES Choice (with reasons, not for reasons) - not arbitrary [cont'd] **Vitality - metric for evaluating values?** FUNCTIONAL CONTEXTUALISM Concepts - choice; truth; non-verbal knowing [cont'd] **VITALITY** **Values, metric for evaluating? [2-11-04]** Patty Bach	Joseph Ciarrochi wrote: It would seem useful to evaluate valued directions in terms of their vitality. E.g., "I feel vital when I do x, and dead when I do y. I choose to do x." However, this sounds like one is providing a reason for doing y…. An important part of values is that they cannot be evaluated unless from another set of values, this is at the heart of functional contextualism. If I ask "does it or does it not leave you feeling vital?" then I am coming from the position that vitality is something that one should value, which may or may not be something the client values … this is the 'radical' part of 'radical acceptance.' I personally value vitality, and does this mean that others 'should' also value vitality? "I need more vitality" does not seem especially different from, "I need more confidence," "I need higher self-esteem," "I need less anxiety," "I need to get rid of my depression" … and then everything, including me, will be okay…. And what of all the things I value, or activities that are consistent with some value, that do not leave me feeling especially 'vital,' and may even leave me feeling rather low? Giving a student a failing grade, paying bills and taxes, standing in line to do paperwork or deal with bureaucracies, doing the dishes, etc. … We do things 'with' reasons because when someone asks 'why?' verbal relations are bound to show up. I think that *with* reasons suggests the relevant response has been more contingency shaped, while *for* reasons suggests that it is more rule governed…'With reasons' are reasons that contact the response and me directly, while 'for reasons' are often about others and participate only in verbal rule governed networks … e.g., I value being physically active and I especially love the game of flag football, running, and weight lifting…vitality is certainly a part of it, the strategy and physicality, being outdoors, the social aspect of being on a team - and just as much the mindfulness/flow that can occur whether running alone or during a team sport, the competition, I have more energy when I am more active…I am physically active 'with' all of these reasons… If I were active in sports 'for' reasons, those might be reasons such as, "My Dad told me being in sports is good," "it looks good on my resume," "My boss gives more promotions to people on the team," "I might meet a significant other on the team." … None of those 'reasons' are 'wrong' or 'bad,' they merely suggest that the relevant value for sports/exercise is not, "being physically active," and instead that the relevant value is "being social," "pleasing others," "getting ahead," "meeting others," etc., because none of those 'reasons' contact the direct contingencies of activity/sports per se, only the verbal contingencies of them. I think this is why the question, "what is that in the service of?" is so important in identifying values. The person who realizes they value sports only as a means of pleasing others or meeting others may be relieved to be able to give up doing the sports they hate and to do something they enjoy more because of the direct contingencies in the service of meeting others, etc.. ACT is not value free … the paradox of functional contextualism is that you value the right to reject any value because values are only valuable in context.

VALUES
 	
    Choice (with reasons, not for reasons) - not arbitrary [cont'd]
 	
    Vitality - metric for evaluating values? [cont'd]
 	
FUNCTIONAL CONTEXTUALISM
 	
    Concepts - choice; truth; non-verbal knowing [cont'd]
 	
VITALITY
 	
    Values, metric for evaluating? [cont'd]
 	
      Steve Hayes
	Joseph Ciarrochi wrote:
	
	    Ok, I absolutely won't believe my mind when it says there is any way to evaluate values. If I do believe this, I will hit myself with a "2 x 4," as Steve has instructed in his 1997 article. Let me take one more crack at getting at the essential point.... People's verbal statements of what they value are often out of tune with what their behavior "says" they value. I might say that I really value family, but in fact what I really do is work 100 hours a week and ignore my family. Or, as Patty suggests, we may say we engage in football because we value health and fitness, but we might really be engaging in it because we value approval from our father. We are so often unaware of what we are valuing (behaviorally).... ACT seems to be about increasing awareness of valuing rather than targeting the content of values.

The fact that you cannot *justify* values, does not mean that you cannot distinguish between what works and what does not. You can. You know it like you know you are breathing. Here, however, is the problem: if you fail to hold that knowledge lightly it will either slip into self-contradiction or ossify in self-righteousness.

It is a conundrum -- and from that same old story: a) the limits of language itself, b) the contextual nature of language itself. Are we speaking as scientists? Clinicians? Individuals? What works in each of these domains varies in the area of how we speak about this issue. And what of processes that are at the edge of or beyond language itself. Can we speak of these as well? *Must* we speak of these as well? In all roles?

It don't think we are trying to help people become "aware" of values primarily. I think we are in the business of empowerment and liberation. In that context, what we are trying to do is helping people *do* valuing ... especially with their feet.

Go back to the refrigerator. Can you know when a 1,000 pound refrigerator is on you? If so, can you know when it is off?

When I have a client who says "but how do I know what works?" I never provide a direct answer, because that answer will be verbal, literal, evaluative, reasoned, and all of the other things that tend to get in the way of the processes we are trying to establish.

I might reply with "minds are amazing things, are they not. Here all the rest of creation is somehow managing without being able to ask that question." I might hold up a couple of fingers and ask "tell me, how do you know what you see?" Or even just "what does your experience tell you?" If the person is a Christian I might quote the New Testament "lilies of the field" saying (a faith/fidelity quote -- and this values move is in essence a leap of faith/fidelity).

It is true that ACT says nothing about the content of values per se, but it says a lot about how to avoid dead ends and to empower the function of values. We need to weaken pliance, literality, reason-giving, evaluation, avoidance, etc. because these interfere with the kind of valuing that makes the kind of difference we are seeking clinically.

A local clinician here, Sandy Evarts, used to say something like this "imagine there is no 'right' and 'wrong.' Imagine no one need ever know except you. Imagine it could be anything. Imagine you are free. If it were like that what would you choose to be about here?" I confess I always had a slight fear reaction when I heard him say "imagine there is no 'right' and 'wrong'" (my Catholic upbringing?) and you will occasionally have clients who deep down fear that if they are free they will be monsters. In fact, however, I have never dug down (beneath pliance, literality, reason-giving, evaluation, avoidance, etc.) and found bed rock values that seemed perverse. I can imagine it; and I believe that evil is possible. I just haven't seen it.

Sometimes folks, seeing that, say there are universal values. I see why that happens, and I've even heard it within the ACT community, but it would be dangerous for ACT folk to go there. The next step would be to make the universal list and "voila" you have a religion. That is not our role as clinicians.

You know when this process is working in the room (or in your life). Just between you, me, and the fence post, if I were to put words to it "vitality" would be pretty darn good. "Freedom," wouldn't be bad. But as soon as we say this, if we turn it into a justification or a formula or something to "understand" we will slip off the point.

Clients know when the refrigerator is off them. Clinicians know that too. And if the process itself is interfered with by literality, evaluation, etc. then we have to hold this all very lightly because our own "understanding" can disempower us clinically.

With my science hat on, it is a different matter. There I can do an analysis of valuing (what this odd bit of behavior comes from, what controls it, etc.). In this analysis there is no "free choice." And you can see if work of this kind leads to behavior change; and you can look at how to do it so that change happens. But if anyone asks "who says behavior change is important?" you've just moved back OUT of science, and the scientist won't have anything coherent to say about it.

It's the usual conundrum.

VALUES **Desires, deepest, cf.** **CHOICE** **Freedom, experiential position of [1-7-04]** Niklas Törneke *Cross Reference:* *See 6-257 for an earlier post in a related thread*	Hank Robb wrote: Niklas' response points out what, again, seems to me to be a problem with ACT's current conception of "values." His question, "... what do you REALLY WANT (caps. mine) your actions to work for?" is indicative of "deep desires" not arbitrarily chosen ends-in-view. To my thinking there are two things here. 1. Choice. This is an experiential position of "freedom," that can be discriminated by the person being there. This is arbitrary in the sense that whatever is there on the inside (reasons, feelings, deepest desires, deepest fears etc.) you can choose to put your next step…. (This, of course, is not a statement on scientific truth of "freedom" but a description of an experiential position.) To help clients discriminate this experience or position is crucial to ACT, as this experience has the potential of freeing someone entangled in verbal constructions from those very constructions. 2. Values. These are verbally constructed consequences and are not arbitrary. Technically they are constructions, like the entangling ones. It is more like once you are in the position described above, where will you put your foot? In a way it would be correct to say "anywhere (except the usual place, given that that is not working) could be helpful" as that will increase the behavioral repertoire. But a human being, experiencing the above, will not in fact put his foot "anywhere." If I can choose, why not something I care about, something I value? This is always a possibility at hand. The point of "grace" so to speak. This, by the way, is the point with the ACT exercise "Argyle socks." Asking the question "what do you really want?" is to facilitate the above. In ACT, as I get it, there is less stress on "finding the true need" or even "finding my true values." This I see as a danger with the way you put it. Maybe this is not true to your position but if you stress "deepest desire" as something "that must be found" you put something verbal between yourself and action. That can be useful (it often is in life), but can easily be a trap. In therapy you usually work with people where this is the problem, this is the trap at hand. To my experience even work with values can fall into this. By objectifying values as something "that must be found," you easily just repeat the old agenda. It is as if you have to wait until "you find it." But there is no "waiting" from taking steps. Waiting is just another step. So you are back on 1. above.
VALUES **Difficulty accessing - "don't know" clients** **Valued Living Questionnaire [7-22-02]** Kelly Wilson	… Do not expect people to immediately be articulate in talking about or thinking about these valued domains. People get very crosswise with their values and being psychologically present to an unfulfilled value is painful and often avoided. Also, understand that I do not think that values are "there to be discovered." I would say that they are constructed in a lifelong social interaction (including the therapeutic interaction). They seem to already "be there" because the social interaction was already there. What we are searching for in the interaction [the Valued Living Questionnaire] leverages is something that the client and the therapist can commit to, something that dignifies and directs the hard work of therapy (exposure, defusion, behavioral activation, committing and recommitting).
VALUES Valued Living Questionnaire [cont'd] Kelly Wilson	John Bush wrote: Is the questionnaire used in conjunction with the Values Assessment Homework you did with Steve and Kirk? I use the VLQ in place of the ratings in the book - but still use the writing sometimes. Both the writing and the VLQ are intended to leverage a strong conversation about where the client would like to aim their life. We build the therapeutic contract around that emerging sense of direction.
VALUES Difficulty accessing - "don't know" clients [cont'd] Niklas Törneke	In working to help patients choose what they value, with their feet, my main problem is in process…. What to do when people say "I don't know"? That, of course, could mean "help me clarify!" That is one kind of work. I find it more difficult when it really is a way of not going there at all, when the "I don't know" functions as avoidance in the interaction in therapy. Theoretically the answer is clear, I guess, "make it not function!" But I quickly run out of tools in this. I remember listening to Kelly giving helpful "checklists" in other areas (as "detecting mindiness"). I need a checklist on making the "I don't know" not functioning…
VALUES Difficulty accessing - "don't know" clients [cont'd] Tuna Townsend	I wonder about a process of 'choosing values' - seems pretty arbitrary… and the fact that cultures usually provide vague and high-minded models for what one *ought* to value; one needn't look far for an answer to the question, 'what *should* I value?' And, there appear to be any number of 'therapies' which would happily join that question, at least implicitly. One of the things that drew me to ACT, and commands my respect, is the unwillingness for the ACT provider to do so, at least at the level of content. The fact that one might be stumped for an answer itself prompts a critical question. I might suggest that if I couldn't tell you what I valued (with my feet, mouth, or any other organ or appendage), I might really value keeping myself in the dark, perhaps so that I wouldn't have to confront some of the really bad choices I've

	been making... or even acknowledge that they *are* choices, and not simply forced upon me by circumstances.
	For myself, I start out with 'what do I actually value now, as seen by my actions?' An accurate answer to this question can be pretty embarrassing, and a place where most folks might be tempted to stop and scratch their heads rather than confront how petty and constricted and not particularly 'honorable' one's actual values actually are. Some folks might well answer something like, 'I value getting high, staying high, blaming others for my circumstances, and generally avoiding feeling badly at pretty much any cost.' Also, when viewed this way, one can see what commitment really is - the extent to which we will act (or not act), the lengths to which we will go, the sacrifices we will make, in order to live in accordance with those values.
	As you've suggested, "I don't know" can sometimes mean "I don't want to know" or "I know, but I don't want to say it out loud."... The 'reasons' we have for why our lives aren't working too well often sound pathetic and weak and stupid when we speak them aloud. All the more reason to do so, I would think.
	The fact is that we all have 'values' to which we are 'committed' - that's what we have to work with. The 'Headstone' process gets to the point pretty quickly. Once I can tell you what I think would be inscribed there today, I can begin to think about what I might rather have written on my tombstone at some later date, and perhaps begin living *that* life now.
VALUES Difficulty accessing - "don't know" clients [cont'd] Robyn Walser	One consideration - perhaps the "I don't know" is how the client spends his/her life. It functions to distance and keep things unclear. I recently had a client who wanted things made clear as he "didn't know" what his values were and how to do things differently. I leaned in a bit and asked where else "don't know" shows up in his life. Turns out - all over the place. He uses it as a means to remain a victim of circumstance or history, or he can blame failing relationships on not knowing. Every time he said he didn't know, we cleared it out of the way and I asked, "now what is left to be done." Of course, he said don't know again and we did this for 15 or so minutes in the session. He was able to connect with the fact that "don't know" was preventing him from taking valued steps - generally those steps had something to do with being loving and committed (looked like quitting laying on the couch and complaining to his partner how he doesn't know what to do or how to solve his dilemma and getting up and taking action).
VALUES Difficulty accessing - "don't know" clients [cont'd] **EXERCISE** **Walk, taking an existential [8-22-02]** Steve Hayes	I see two major, related barriers here. One is the illusion that a choice not to choose is not itself a choice. The other is the attempt to be right about choices -- turning them into big, heavy, rational judgments.
	Values are an aspect of ongoing actions. They are an organizational principle of patterns of behavior -- namely, "what is this behavior in the service of?" They are not "in the future" and they are not things you can be right about. What we do in ACT is we help people take responsibility for the patterns of behavior they are establishing moment by moment and instead of simply being regulated by reinforcers (the organizational principle for all other creatures), or by implicit verbal (in an RFT sense) purpose (the organizational principle for mindless human action), we add in the possibility of taking responsibility for verbal purpose by making it explicit and by seeing purposing itself as an act.
	When a person says "I don't know" they are DOING something but the illusion is created that they are doing NOTHING, and they are waiting for something (the right decision?) to occur so that they will be able to begin to do something. If "I don't know" is "a way of not going there at all" the therapeutic job is to help the client take responsibility for that act. All of the old ACT technology about avoidance functions applies ("is that old?"; and "and what is THAT in the service of?"; and "what would you have to give up to let go of an attachment to 'I don't know'"; and "has 'I don't know' been a problem for you in the past? Is this one way you dig?" etc. etc. etc.).
	It is not a problem that the person says "I don't know." This is exactly what they need to say, because this is one of their problems and by saying it they helpfully bring it into treatment right here right now. So it is not a barrier to doing something in treatment -- as if filling in a values sheet is the real goal ... it is treatment. The goal is taking responsibility for a human life. I would rejoice in "I don't know." Respond with "that's great! Super! ... And how has that worked for you in your life?" or something like that.
	I sometimes take clients like this on a walk. I just suggest that it is a nice day and that we can talk as we walk. For a while all seems normal as I lead the way out of the building. Then when choice points in the path come up I step back and act as if I have no preference or idea about where to go. The client will eventually pause uncomfortably and say "where should we go?" I act stupid. I might say something like "where do you choose to go?" They are often confused but almost always quickly realize that this is a physical metaphor. If I know some of why the person has been choosing not to choose I sometimes will add a few things in. Suppose the person is afraid of being hurt. I might say "but, you know, there could be dangers down that path ... or that other one. There may be someone there ... or there ... who will hurt you." (etc.) If the client hesitates I add "but if we stay there may be dangers here too. So, you could choose to stay here, or go there, or go there ... but all of these will be choices." And I smile and wait.

Anything the client does is fine ... the goal is to see that each moment is in fact a kind of choice. The future cannot be known ... that is not what taking a walk **is.** But you can **intend** to go somewhere -- to take a direction -- and then a walk becomes a journey. "Outcome can be a process through which process is the outcome." What should that direction be? Well, that is the very question of values. Getting there is not the issue. Going is the issue. That is where the vitality is. Often the client will finally say something like "let's go to the cafeteria" and then the walk is very smooth. Each turn makes sense. Or sometimes the client says "let's just meander and look around." Once again the walk is very smooth. Each turn makes sense. Once there is a flow I sometimes raise issues that bump the client off course. I might write down a thought on a piece of paper and give it to the client. I might say something like "here, read this and then stick it in your pocket" and give them a note card saying "I can't choose to go anywhere unless I know it is the right place to go." Later, back in the office, the whole walk can be used as a metaphor ("so, was it possible to walk to the cafeteria carrying a card that said 'I can't choose to go anywhere unless I know it is the right place to go?' Is that any different than this values sheet issue?"). Etc.

The other problem with "I don't know" is that the person is trying to make it into some big deal to be right about, as if there is a "right" set of values. Occasionally people will secretly fear the flip side -- that their true values are disgusting and not in accord with what they would want to be ("Deep down I'm a psychopath and that is horrible"). Values are always perfect from the inside out because they enable evaluation -- they are not the result of evaluation ... If you fear that you have bad values then you have the good values that enable you to fear the bad ones. You can't be wrong about them ... though they do evolve (sometimes rapidly). You also can't be right about them. They are just what you are playing for. And they are not external to you -- values are not "out there." You don't HAVE to value anything. It is just what humans do as they live. If people put values in things they end up with so many out there oppressing them that they cannot actually do anything.

Sometimes I use the language of games to help lighten it up. In a game there are rules and purposes. The key underlying principle is "you are not there yet." If that is not true, the game is over. In football, you have 60 minutes to score more points than the other team but you are not there yet. In baseball, you have 9 innings, 3 outs each, to score more runs ... but you are not there yet. So, which do you choose to play right now -- football or baseball? It is not a big choice really but it will make a big difference in what you do over the next little while. Let's add in a few more: which do you choose to play -- football or baseball or reducing world hunger or raising a family or being a great friend?

Sometimes I use small children as an example. It is so obvious that games are fun and that children love them. They really show that "Outcome can be a process through which process is the outcome." The pretense that (say) one base is "safe" and touching you with the ball makes you "out" enables such joyful play in, say, 6 year olds. It is obvious it is not REALLY about the base. It is about play. It is about LIVING.

If life was a game, and no one would giggle, and you could be about anything, in the area of (choose a domain) what would you want to be about? If you know some of the options the client is looking at, give them game names (do you want to play intimacy tag? Loving baseball? Family football?). If you still get "I don't know" and you think it is the heavy "I have to be right" dimension that is suppressing creativity here, make it more immediate. "So, let's talk about therapy itself, right now. In this very session. In this very moment. If you could play for anything ... what would it be? What kind of relationship are we building here?" If you still get "I don't know" raise the stakes just to see how far the "no choice choice" is going to be taken.

You could do something like "I'd like to be more close to you as a human being and to support you in getting out of therapy what you truly want. So I want to play here for honesty, and closeness. If you could play for anything in this interaction between us ... what would it be?" You could do the same move in even more direct aspects of human relationships ... all the way down to life and death. Let me give an example. "So, suppose I suddenly fall to the floor choking on my pencil. {I might even fall to the floor here and stick my pencil down my throat} In this very moment. If you could play for anything ... what would it be?" [I'm wondering will they even play for saving a human life? How frigging far will they take "I dunno" for god's sake.] If the person still says "I don't know" maybe I'd start to choke to death... are they willing to let someone die just to show that they can "do nothing" and pretend that they really did nothing. I might even start hollering "Someone is dying here! [choke; choke]. What do you choose to be about in this moment! Are you just going to let me die!? What is this goddamn inability to move in the service of?! Do you need an engraved invitation from God to start living?" Hopefully something that dramatic won't be needed ... I'm just exploring a principle in this fantasy session -- namely, helping the client to take responsibility for the action of inaction.

99.9% of clients will step up to the challenge when it is playful and immediate but as soon as they [choose?] ANYTHING at all, you now have a new route to build on, because if THIS moment can be about something (anything) then the NEXT moment can be and in fact the moment when the client says "I don't know" can be and so on. If the client does anything you can be amazed ("so, you CAN make choices!") and

	build from there.
	Here is a fantasy bit of a session: Sometimes we talk about values this way -- it is like a pencil stuck down through the chessboard. The track left behind shows where you've been going. When you sit and say "I don't know" that is one more little pencil blip along a very old track. Now sight along that track. Look at where it has been taking you. Imagine that direction will continue your whole life. Is that what you want to be about? Is that what you want on your tombstone? Here lies Sally. She didn't know. If that is not what you want, what will you DO? What direction will you take your life in? If you again say "I don't know" then right here, right now, you lengthened that pencil line. Look at where it has been taking you. Imagine that direction will continue your whole life. Is that what you want to be about?
	This reminds me of a famous Koan: "If nothing you can do, will do, what will you do?" I sometimes give that Koan to over-intellectual folks trying to be right about values and realizing the internal problem in that. Values are not enough. Not nearly enough. Nothing you can do, will do. I agree. OK. Now. What will you do? OK. Now. What do you want your life to be about?
	At the deepest level, your client is asking this fundamental question: can I live? My answer? You already are. So let's DO IT.
VALUES Difficulty accessing - "don't know" clients [cont'd] Steve Hayes	Hank Robb wrote: Consider this story sometimes used as an ACT training aid. Person A is walking on the beach after a great storm which has tossed hundreds, if not thousands, of starfish up on the beach. Person A encounters Person B who is throwing starfish, one at a time, back into the ocean. Person A says to Person B, "Given all these starfish that will not be saved how does what you are doing matter?" Person B picks up another starfish, throws it back into the ocean, and says, "..." There are actually two ways this story can end that are of interest to me. The first is the one I have typically heard in ACT trainings. Person B says, "It matters to that one." The second is for Person B to answer, "It matters to me." I've not used the starfish story in an ACT training but both answers you have listed are not ACT consistent in my view. The problem with both "It matters to that one" and "It matters to me" is that caring is placed outside the person and their relationship to events. Nothing matters TO you (or to anyone else, starfish or human) and IT doesn't matter. YOU matter about things, and since you -- in some important sense of the word -- are not a thing, one good way to say it is "No thing matters." I sometimes ask clients to imagine whether anything would matter if all living creatures in the Universe were dead. All (so far) have quickly said "no." The mountains will tumble but no one will care ... including the mountain. But put in caring creatures and all is different. Humans will go to war over mountains (look at the middle east). We still occasionally do the "prove to me that anything matters" exercise in ACT trainings to drive this point home (no one can ever do it ...). The whole point of the values part of ACT is that **people** care about what they care about. In trainings I usually use the example of late night tear-jerker commercials for starving children funds. People initially say that they care but with a little bit of probing you find that very few write a check. The inevitable result of this kind of "caring" is numbness as the number of things that "matter" multiply beyond comprehension or the capacity to action. In the end, it screws up the ability to care at all to equate this kind of externalizing guilt version of caring with actual caring. True caring is vitalizing and empowering -- not oppressive and numbing. When you matter about something, you act in regard to it. Values are a quality of action: without action, they do not exist in the sense that ACT is focused on. They are not statements on a piece of paper. The honest truth is that the vast majority of people do not care about starving children because they do not take care with regard to them. If these folks have the capacity to care -- fully, vitally -- I am not worried at all. They have nothing to be ashamed of. We have plenty enough caring to go around. If trying to squeeze a few bucks out of them is at the cost of crushing the capacity to care in a vitalizing way ... it is just too high a price. So here is the starfish question with my answer: "Given all these starfish that will not be saved, how does what you are doing matter?" Person B picks up another starfish and says, "It doesn't. I do. Wanna see?" [throw] If the actual starfish situation happened I would probably not throw them back in, so my point is not that you should. My point is that in either case, it is YOUR mattering, not IT's mattering (TO you or not) that is at issue. I think "having a ball" and "follow your bliss" are unsafe ways to speak about this ... though in the hands of an Ellis or Campbell I'm not really worried. Still, they sound as if we are here to have some particular kind of emotional reaction.

	ACT is about empowering human beings to live. HOW depends on what they choose to have their life be about. That choice includes socialization, but it is not synonymous with it -- which is why there are long sections on pliance and going beyond it in the ACT book, and so too in moral development and rule following sections of the RFT book (among other places). I think we went pretty far down that road, but if you say that values are ONLY about the individual and "fulfillment" I say "sez who."
	Hank -- you say:
	"One can, I think accurately, say that, as long as you are passing along your genes and personally surviving, LIFE doesn't care if you are miserable. On the other end, as long as you are doing your social duty, SOCIETY doesn't care if you are miserable. Thus, in my view, the individual had better busy him or herself finding and achieving his or her own INDIVIDUAL, PERSONAL fulfillment"
	The gene and meme point is true and we've pointed that out in the ACT book. But be careful when you talk about misery and INDIVIDUAL, PERSONAL fulfillment. It is not by accident that misery and miser have the same root. The miser is trying to hoard everything to himself for his or her INDIVIDUAL, PERSONAL gain. Yes, it is the individual who acts. Yes, values are personal. If you value the peace and fulfillment of fishing, well god bless you. I'll support you in that. If you try to justify those values on the basis of fun or avoidance of misery ... then you lose me. There is no such rule book. If people value Mom, the church, and apple pie, then none of us should say "gee, that is not INDIVIDUAL and PERSONAL." There is no such rule book.
	There is an easy metric to distinguish empty pliance from chosen social values. One is oppressive. One is vitalizing. Look and you can see it.
VALUES Difficulty accessing - "don't know" clients [cont'd] Kelly Wilson	Guilty - I have used it and have spoken too loosely about mattering. Of course Steve is absolutely right that *no thing* matters. I think I try to make that clear to folks, but should be more careful about a topic that has clear hooks for people. *Things* mattering is a critical element in a formula for a life in which one is oppressed by one's values. Not the kind of life I want for myself or my clients.
VALUES Difficulty accessing - "don't know" clients [cont'd] Steve Hayes	A connection to values helps distinguish vitalizing acts of caring, compassion, and action from automatic emotional and cognitive reactions that are often called "caring" but are destructive, defended, guilt ridden or even shame ridden, and rarely linked to "taking care." "Caring" usually does involve emotional sharing (whence the word "compassion"), but I don't think emotion is the end of the story. We behave in many ways. Do I think that it is good that people hurt when they see others hurt? Sure, but I want to know what comes next. If it is defense, I'm not impressed. If it is vitality, I'm all for it.
	... I want to make it acceptable NOT to expect caring in all circumstances, precisely so that human beings can pick and choose where to focus their time and energy: fully, joyfully, and without (bought) guilt and shame. In the place in which it really, truly is OK not to send any money to the starving children of country x, it is also OK to call up your best friend and ask for substantial money for a cause you DO care about, despite the sense that you are breaking a big time social rule.
	Caring is not just emotional conditioning. Caring is not just social rules. Caring is touching and being touched ... on purpose. It is that last values piece that lifts caring from conditioning and rule-governance to something more profound.
VALUES **Difficulty accessing - esp. involuntary/ youth clients [6-10-05]** Julian McNally	... In previous work I've done with prisoners and substance abuse clients (some voluntary, some semi-, some in-) I found motivational interviewing ... and narrative approaches useful. E.g.:
	MI - "What does behaviour/ thought/ mood X buy you?" [Whatever they say:] "And what does that buy you?" [Keep digging for what really matters.] "What do you 'sell' to get it?" or ask, "What do you enjoy about X? And what's good about that?" But you have to really BE curious about their responses not just ask to get an answer. You'll see a shift when they get that you're interested in their experience of valuing without having an "adult-world" judgement attached ("oh, that's a good value to have - that's the right one.").
	Narrative approaches - Two that I've used here:
	1. Restraint theory as outlined by Alan Jenkins in *Invitations to Responsibility*, Dulwich Centre Press, 1990. "What has stopped the problem from getting worse" or (more agency implied) "How have you stopped the problem from getting bigger? How come you're not violent/ stoned/ truanting all the time? What has held you back?" The answer often is or points to a deeply-held value - self-respect, respect for others, acceptance of own responsibility, desire to work and earn money, get along with others - also sometimes to plys like parental, social or peer approval that MAY be able to be authentically transformed to a deeply-held value: "You say you don't want to let your parents down again. Does that say about you that you love them and want to give something back to them? Maybe in appreciation for what they've done for you?" The "what do

	your highly-valued actions say about you?" question often gets to core values.
	2. I think with some clients, especially young ones, the unwillingness to commit to or speak values is driven by a belief, sometimes unconscious, that 'I don't matter' [Aside: our culture drives this belief home in young people - you'll really have a place in society when you have a job, because money/status is what counts not who you are. This is what drives a lot of youth suicidality IMHO.] So I get at that by some variation of the miracle question. "Just suppose anything was possible and you knew your life could make a difference to somebody... who would it be? And what difference would you want it to make?" Then sit back and listen, but listen by way of more of that authentically curious questioning - "It sounds like this is really important to you. Does anybody know this about you?" The answer is often 'no' which just means you've been granted a huge privilege.
VALUES Difficulty accessing - esp. involuntary/ youth clients [cont'd] Jeremy Gauntlett-Gilbert	Some extra thoughts: 1. Make explicit the distinction between values-driven action and doing it because you're 'meant' to. Do this early. I give an example of two adolescents doing exercise (on a pain management programme). One is doing it because the physio is scary and their mum said they had to. The other is doing it because they really want to get back to skateboarding, or travel the world, or whatever. Who will still be doing their exercises 6 months after the programme? Who will keep going in tough times? This explains why it's important to really understand what's important to you ... if you do this early, it undermines the 'because I should' or 'because you said so' responses from the start. 2. We've had some success with using 'heroes and heroines,'... usually do up to three stages here - we use this in a group setting - a.) identify the hero (can be living, dead, comic book, whatever - preferably not friends or family as the issue is clouded by 'because they're always good to me'). People can get stuck at this point and need help. b.) explain why this person is a hero (there are a whole bunch of different reasons to admire Nelson Mandela) - usually do this with the adolescents in pairs. c.) ok - now imagine I've got a syringe here. I'm injecting your arm with 'essence of Nelson Mandela.' what will the next couple of months be like? What might you do a bit different? Of course, the 'danger' is that someone will come up with a thug as a hero. I think that this is one of those ACT moments where one has to take a deep breath and go with it. Is a thug really a problem? If they're a well-known thug, then they must be doing something effective :). And one can always deal smartly with answers like "because he's tough" - "well, sure, but lots of people are tough - what's so special about him?"; "how did he deal with difficulties and discouragements in his life?" ... I think that we all still need to do some thinking about the developmental context of values around this age.
VALUES Difficulty accessing - esp. involuntary/ youth clients [cont'd] Leslie Rogers	With my early on exposure to adolescents and even some adults in therapy - I too would have difficulty getting clients (especially adolescents) to explicitly state what they value. Oftentimes my reaction to clients with difficulties stating values would be this strong desire to scramble (use metaphors, ask 50 questions about values) and help the client figure out how to say what it is they care about or figure it out. What I have been doing instead of explicitly going after values is several things: 1) focus on a Choice angle with my adolescent clients; 2) the content that shows up after a couple creative hopelessness exercises (value/vulnerability); or 3) as what we talk about in Oxford is to –WAIT-build rapport-build more rapport- and the values will come. Other things we talk about with the client to maybe get at values is what is the presenting problem getting in the way of. With regards to choice, more times than not adolescents are forced to come to therapy and they aren't happy that they are there or think they live in a world where there aren't many choices. Asking if coming to therapy is difficult? Is having choices something you are interested in? Is having choices something you value? Most of the time the answer is yes. If none of these tactics work - then we WAIT. To make whatever is happening in the therapy room their choice.
VALUES Difficulty accessing - esp. involuntary/ youth clients [cont'd] Julian McNally	... all these moves go better with Rapport - The Essential Ingredient! I like your juxtaposition of choice with values - something that may give these clients a stronger sense of personal power and agency. I haven't tried it but something like "What would you rather be doing if you didn't have to come here? And what would that be in service of [asked in culturally-appropriate language of course]?" might work too.
VALUES Difficulty accessing - esp. involuntary/ youth clients [cont'd] Kelly Wilson	Although it isn't identical, substance abusers are often in treatment because someone else thinks it is a good idea. In [my chapter in the *ACT Practical Guide* on treating substance abuse] I talk about a couple different presentations that we see in substance abuse that you may also see among adolescents. For example, apparent (but not real) compliance, sullen withdrawal, active hostility. In the chapter, I describe working on the value of being able to choose one's own way.

VALUES **Difficulty accessing - esp. psychotic/ elderly clients [7-6-04]** Leslie Telfer	I have run into some problems working in this area [values], in particular with two of my client groups: psychotic patients and some very elderly, debilitated patients. Perhaps the problem is my discomfort with the clients' emotional pain. In both cases the issue is one of values as well as goals; the one seems to entail the other. For example, the value might be to have a loving, intimate relationship, and the goal to be married. I have a number of psychotic patients who are constantly symptomatic and live in a nearby care facility. I am in some cases the only person that they have any kind of one-on-one relationship with. To come into contact with the loneliness and isolation in their lives is painful for both of us, and unlikely to change in any substantial way. In the case of very elderly, debilitated (but not demented) clients, the ship has sailed on many of the things they might have wanted to do in their lives. To get in touch with what they might have wanted for themselves as children and young adults, then survey the path they actually took in life, brings them into contact with intense regret, which is okay when someone can reset their course, but here the other people are dead and the careers are over. While I might be able to see the possibility of living in accordance with their values NOW, I have not been successful at getting them to see this, and I have backed off, feeling that I was doing more harm than good. With less extreme cases (not so old, not so psychotic), I have felt that I was imposing the idea of living a value-driven life on retired people who just want to play golf. Okay, I am exposing my bias. Clients come in who feel depressed, and can't figure out what's wrong, when they "have everything": financial security, a 50-year marriage, grown children, a comfortable retirement, a decent golf handicap. But they are bored and their relationships aren't very intimate and I end up feeling like I'm torturing them. The values work has gone best for me with younger clients (say, 25 to 65; I rarely see anyone younger because I work exclusively with military veterans) who are not psychotic.
VALUES Difficulty accessing - esp. psychotic/ elderly clients [cont'd] Theresa Glaser	Keep in mind I'm VERY new to this (ACT) and this is just anecdotal, but here goes ... I actually tried to do a values exercise in a group once and had that same experience where people got depressed when they realized their functional roles were fairly limited. I think there may be difficulties using pre-determined values domains for this reason. I am interested in how people define themselves, especially after trauma (i.e., it is what my dissertation is about) and try to distinguish between functional roles and the structure of the self (in other words, can you have a differentiated self while not having many functional roles--e.g., worker, friend, partner, golfer ...) I think it's hard to do this as this society is pretty focused on defining people in terms of their social roles. Anyway, I think the same goes for values--how to help individuals see themselves broadly/flexibly enough to be able to connect with values work. How are they able to see how this may apply to them? I personally love card sorts. I have tried Miller's values card sort [see the motivational interviewing website: http://motivationalinterview.org/library/valuescardsort.pdf] with a couple of patients so far and I think it helped broaden the spectrum of what they might want their life "to be about." There are something like 100 of them, so usually people can find something they value in the mix (actually, they are forced by the exercise to sort them into "not important to me," "important to me," and "very important to me"). I'd be interested to know if other people have used this and what they think. Of course, this values work imposes structure (contrary to what I said earlier). I also struggle with the notion that people "should" have values--I think the word itself is very "value laden" (ha ha, I know). The long and short of it is that I think everyone can benefit from elaborating values in the "here and now." I think it takes some work to help people think flexibly enough to see what kinds of values they might have if their life scope is fairly limited. It is the "chicken or the egg," because what we are trying to do is increase cognitive flexibility, relying on methods that require cognitive flexibility.
VALUES Difficulty accessing - esp. psychotic/ elderly clients [cont'd] Matthew Smout	I think Theresa raises an excellent point about adopting a very broad and open approach to values (the Miller card sort exercise sounds pretty cool - never heard of it before, I'd like to hear more!). The life domains are just a convenient marker to get the ball rolling in a discussion, but with the client populations you've been talking about it makes sense to approach valuing with different conversation pieces. Some past listserv discussions opened up the concept of values for me. In a sense most behaviour can be thought to be value-driven, but language can frequently obscure this. Taken literally, the statement "I choose not to value anything" implies people can be without values, but functionally, the choice not to value is also a value-based choice. So while it might not be functional to talk to people with psychosis living in boarding houses about how they want to enact their career goals, or talk to a dying cancer patient about how they want to enact their value of a close relationship with a father that already died...these people continue to live out values everyday...in how they interact with their care-givers, in how they spend their time alone...in their ruminations. From a behaviour analytic view - their thinking is a kind of purposeful behaviour. Their fantasies/musings may be in the service of suppressing pain or in creativity, learning

	(summarising what they've learnt from life), humour, whatever. Do I spend my time alone engaged in self-punitive rumination, unproductive "figuring out," bitter evaluations of others, or do I spend my time alone recalling life highlights, composing a letter/poem/artwork, thinking about interests…. The workability dimension comes in to what's possible to enact, not what's possible to value, and thinking can be a valued behaviour (or not!).
VALUES Difficulty accessing - esp. psychotic/ elderly clients [cont'd] Jonathan Kandell	Leslie, from my own experience in a community mental health clinic, the ACT values categories and worksheets and vocabulary are somewhat counterproductive for severely limited clients, e.g., very uneducated and poor, or severe psychotics. The point of those worksheets is to open up all the possibilities; but that mission is somewhat over-the-top for these folks. Even at best, numerous boxes full of text is not always helpful. However, let's not miss the point: whether they can or do verbalize it, everyone non-comatose has values and it only takes one to do ACT--so there's no need to let the cart lead the horse. What I've ended up doing in situations like you describe is to find *some* activity the client is/was *genuinely* interested in (i.e., the miracle question), and then carefully draw out value(s) from that. This then creates the necessary context and motivation for extensive exposure. (Don't forget: there's no need to get all the values on the table ahead of time; if successful you can always generalize later.) No need to use the term "values" or to specify with exactness the "values narrative" (the point is: "this matters to you, this is who you want to be"). Without using fancy words, you can also use as a teaching model situations where the patient is already consistent with his values, e.g., "Just like you didn't cheat on her because of who you are - though that didn't feel very good at the time - might you try to get through this feeling so you'll like yourself tomorrow?" Even limited folks understand the expression "get a life." With this population especially, you need to be careful the values are truly genuine and not just programmed ("pliance"), especially by mental health professionals. (Describing their values with jargon is a dead give-away.) I find this step alone is crucially liberating and validating to folks who have been radically invalidated most of their lives. You'll know you're on-track if you sense the person's motivation when you start exposure. If not it's time to go back and reexamine if the person really values this activity after all. In fact, I'd go so far as to say that with this population, drawing out valued-action is even more important than people who are less limited. These people make a career out of managing symptoms, and forget to actually live a life while doing so.
VALUES **Employment, domain of [8-14-02]** Kelly Wilson	Vijay Shankar wrote: > A client of mine is struggling with formulating her value in the domain of employment. She asked me if I had any examples that she could use that would point her in a direction and I found myself struggling too. Would appreciate people sending me examples from their practice/experience. Here is a taste of the issues that will be raised in the [Valued Living Questionnaire] users' manual ... with respect to employment. When I think about the area of employment, I think about who I want to be as an employee. There are several relationships that are important to me in this domain. Who do I want to be with respect to my fellow employees (or more broadly to others in my discipline)-- what sort of force am I among my fellow employees? Am I a gossip? Do I spread stories (true or not) and how does that work? Do I work to bring people together? to make the place I work a little more pleasing? Do I ask people how they are (and mean it)? Am I genuine and constructive in those relationships? A second relationship of relevance is my relation to my employer. Here I am particularly sniffing out cynicism. I have entered into an agreement with my employer. Did I say yes and mean it? Or did I say yes, then spend my time dissing the company, sitting and complaining among my fellow workers, creating a culture of "ain't it awful." This is very, very seductive. I am compelled by my own history here--growing up working class, and in the sixties to boot, dissing the fat cats, owners, bosses, employers is right! Why as a teen growing up in the late sixties and very early seventies it was practically a virtue to steal, obstruct, and lie to "the man." I am suspicious though. While activism in the area of workplace safety, fair wages, and the like can be a great value to pursue, very often, our complaints about our employers are just something we use to license behavior that would otherwise be unacceptable to us. If they are *bad* then it becomes ok to steal their time, their pencils, to create an atmosphere of discontent with regard to them. The trap here is the same one of playing the right/wrong game anywhere: I have to keep them wrong or else I have to live up to my own values in my behavior--or that I haven't been living up to them. Such negativity is also a way to protect ourselves from our feelings of hopelessness and powerlessness to take responsibility and to create a life worth living in this domain. If our problem is *them*, then we cannot rightfully be expected to *do* anything. *They* would have to change. Do understand here that my concern is not for the employer. They are not my client. My concern is for the corrosive effect of living a life in which I am actively valuing (with my feet --and mouth) values that would embarrass me if I were to say them out loud and explicitly. Like on your tombstone "He made sure

everyone knew how unfair the boss was!" Now there's one I'd want to be remembered for.

ACT is really about unilateral, authentic living. The values questionnaire is about leveraging a conversation that explores who and what you want to be in this domain (and others) that occupies a major portion of each day. How long can we stay well while living inauthentically for half of our waking life? Or if not in ways that betray our values--walking around unconscious about our values there and at least not actively pursuing them.

If this seems moralistic--rest assured that I am looking for the client's morals here-- not mine. What difference to them if they violate mine--but if they violate their own, my fear for them is that it is toxic. Now employment can also be more broadly connected to career and discipline, so someone like me might be asked about my relation to the discipline--who am I in behavior therapy, in psychology? what am I creating there?

I hope this gives a taste of the conversation that I want to have with the client on this topic.

(PS if anyone finds themselves reading this and thinking that it is puerile, or naive, or maybe even moralistic --I would ask that you check yourself out with respect to your own employer--if I am puerile, naive or moralizing, do you get to ignore my questions? What do you get to keep doing? What do you win by labeling me--even if it is true that I am puerile, naive, and moralizing--which I am fully capable of on any given day? And what do my personal flaws have to do with you and your relation to your work? As with most of ACT, a good place to start looking at interventions is in one's own world. Hmmm this has me thinking about the coming academic year and what I will play for in my own department. hmmmm.)

VALUES Employment, domain of [cont'd] Frank Bond	I agree with Kelly that a clinical psychologist would do well to have one's client look at his/her 'own world' when banging on about dreadful work conditions (e.g., lousy hours, a tyrannical boss, etc.); but, I firmly believe that, for work (or I/O) psychologists who consult with organisations, merely intervening on the level of individual employees' psychological processes should not be the primary focus of an intervention. (Indeed, for those of us in the European Union, EU directives mean that an organisation that does this is legally liable.) Instead, primary focus needs to be on changing unhelpful work and organisational characteristics that exist in a company, and the work design literature has done a pretty good job, over the past 25 years, in identifying those characteristics that are helpful and harmful to employees. For example, there is a good deal of evidence that a lack of control over aspects of one's job (e.g., in terms of task variety, sequencing, and pacing; and procedures and policies in the workplace) is a great predictor of everything from mental ill-health, poor performance, and lower back problems to death by cardiovascular disease. Primary focus on changing such work characteristics does not mean, of course, that one cannot help individuals to become more psychologically accepting and more committed to their values/goals. Indeed, our research has found that work organisation characteristics, such as job, control interact with acceptance to longitudinally predict outcomes such as mental health and objective measures of job performance; such that those people who have high levels of job control have better mental health if they are also more, as opposed to less, 'psychologically accepting.' I think that this is a good example of how a focus on both the organisational and individual level is helpful; and that work psychologists, in particular, cannot afford to ignore the former. Indeed, I believe that to do so is colluding with the 'fix my workers' attitude that, sadly, many of us see in organisations. I am not having a go at Kelly, here. I am sure that he would agree with this 'level of analysis' perspective. I just think that it is important, for those of us who work in organisations to keep in mind the context in which employees work; and to try to make it less toxic to these people.
VALUES Employment, domain of [cont'd] Kelly Wilson	Sure Frank - I agree completely. Because I know Vijay works with individuals (at least assumed that) I answered as if the client is the individual and that I have little or no ability to intervene on the worksite. For such a client, I want to either find a way for them to say yes to what they are doing (and mean it), or to say no (and move on). Or to say no and be about actively working to change the place. What I wanted to get out of though was a lifestyle that is invested in how crappy life is. One ends up having to keep life crappy in order to stay right and justify values-aberrant behavior. Now if the workplace is the client, I would work on values issues with the workplace, management -- getting explicit about what they are up to and how that is working. From their perspective they need to look at what their practices do with respect to workers. If they crap on the workers, they will be writing licenses to steal, cheat, stay home sick, do shoddy work, etc. Having worked in a number of factory jobs prior to psychology, I saw a lot of pennywise pound foolish organizational practice. Good way to create an adversarial culture. Hated every company I worked for. My ideal would be to work both ends. In fact, we are playing in my lab group with what a utopian research group would be like (a workplace of sorts)--like what would full on integrity mean practiced by the entire group towards one another? How would the group organize itself? What practices would be fostered?

	Which banned? Don't know where we will find ourselves, but it is shaping up to be a very fun and rewarding group in which to work--probably not for everyone, but it suits my tastes. To get a flavor of the culture we are building in this workgroup, check out the lab manifesto link off my home page....

VALUES
 	
    Present moment, being in - a valid value?
 	
PRESENT MOMENT
 	
    Being in - a valid value?
 	
METAPHOR
 	
    Self-as-context - sky [10-20-03]
 	
    Joseph Ciarrochi
	I just found an excellent metaphor for context in the Segal, Teasdale, and Williams book [*Mindfulness-based Cognitive Therapy for Depression*]. The mind is "... like a vast, clear sky. All our feelings, thoughts, and sensations are like the weather that passes through, without affecting the nature of the sky itself. The clouds, winds, snow, and rainbows come and go, but the sky is always simply itself, as it were, a 'container' for these passing phenomena."
	
	... On another, related point. Would an ACT practitioner consider this to be a valid value: "Being in the present moment"?

VALUES
 	
    Present moment, being in - a valid value? [cont'd]
 	
PRESENT MOMENT
 	
    Being in - a valid value? [cont'd]
 	
    John Blackledge
	"Being present" could definitely be a value. I'd likely be suspicious, though, if a client presented with it. This bit of verbal behavior could be participating in a control agenda; i.e., the client may think something like, "If I'm present, then I won't feel as bad as I do right now." (of course, all of us on this list know the spiels on why control agendas can cause problems). Or, saying one values being present could be demonstrating pliance, in at least a couple of ways. A client might suspect you value being present (based on the kind of exercises and metaphors used in ACT) and endorse this as a value to please you. "Being present" is also kind of 'hip' right now, and someone could endorse it as a value because they're 'supposed to' value it, according to the sub-culture they reside in.

VALUES
 	
    Sources of [3-4-04]
 	
    Steve Hayes
	Matthew Smout wrote:
	
	    Just wondering whether physical experiences, from an ACT/BA point of view, are seen as a legitimate source from which to inform values (nonverbal knowing?), or are generally regarded as "private content," held lightly and to be defused from if individuals allow it to obstruct committed action?
	
	Isn't everything a legitimate source from which to inform values? Thoughts, feelings, bodily sensations, etc.... And isn't *everything* to be held lightly? "Held lightly" doesn't mean "don't let it participate in behavioral regulation." I think it means "don't take your verbal formulation of it to be it." That includes body sense. You notice what you notice. Sure, let it be part of the total picture (it already is). See how it works from there.
	
	I do worry when some body folks seem to say that "true" knowledge can be found there in a way that goes beyond other sources of knowing. Makes me suspect that folks want to learn the right answer, or learn how to be good boys and girls. All forms and targets of knowing have a role. Beyond that it is an empirical question. I know of no evidence that body work is more true or effective than, say, mindfully noticing thoughts.
	
	Is there any such data?

VALUES
 	
    Sources of [cont'd]
 	
    Steve Hayes
	Hank Robb wrote:
	
	    I want to agree that thoughts, feelings, bodily sensations, etc. are LEGITIMATE sources from which to inform values but it seems pretty hard to do from Self-as-Context where "all they are" is a bunch of thoughts, feelings, etc. It seems to me they can only do their work from Self-as-Process.
	
	If values cannot and need not be justified, "legitimate" is not really the issue. Etymologically "legitimate" means "according to the law." Can't get more rule-governed than that.
	
	From a scientific point of view, choices are "informed" by many things: some verbal and some non-verbal. Self-as-process is important because it is a repertoire of noting the flow of events verbally in a descriptive sense. That helps link experience to what we know verbally. But thoughts, feelings, and bodily sensations have effects that go beyond that.
	
	From the inside out, I'm guessing that self-as-process seems like the only place they "can do their work" because this is the only place (other than the conceptualized self) where they can do their work that you can talk about and thus make the influence "legit."
	
	There is another alternative. Let go of trying to make them legit.

VALUES "Straightforward" problems, application to; power of [4-6-05] Mary Politi	I just want to comment on how powerful values work can be for clients-- you all may know this, but as a "newbie" I am surprised every time. I am working with a fear of flying case, and last week, I couldn't quite figure out where his anxiety about flying was coming from and why it was so intense this last time compared to every other time he has flown in the past. It turns out that this client is less anxious than he is ashamed about something he has done recently that is antithetical to how he wants to be living. Just asking him about his values led to a radically different session--panic right in session about how he might be remembered if the plane were to crash while he was on it. It just got "real" very quickly.
	I wonder how often people are asked "what is it that you really want?" in a meaningful way.
VITALITY Quality of action [5-8-05] JoAnne Dahl	In the self-help book for ACT and chronic pain that we are working on I have found one issue difficult to write about in a comprehensible way. I also find this same issue difficult for students to learn and subsequently difficult for them to do in therapy. It is the issue of vitality. I think this particular issue of "quality" of action to be an essential point that ACT adds to traditional CBT programs but it isn't easy to teach. This is how I try. I say that the process of taking steps in therapy is two-fold, a kind of check and balance system. Before you make your choice as to what step to take you need to reconnect to your valued intention. You might use questions like: "In which of my valued directions would this step be in the service of?" "What is most important here?" "What is my most important intention here?" And after connecting to your valued intentions, you would choose an appropriate step that you can only judge would be in alignment with that direction. And because this step was based on your "judgement" you need to evaluate that step you have just taken by gauging its "vitality." This means that you need to stop and reflect on how this step "feels." Alive or dead, vital or non-vital. It isn't easy to know why you choose to take steps, it is easy to fool yourself (your mind fooling you), but the feeling of vitality is reliable. If you take a step for the wrong reasons (someone else wants you to) you will notice that in your evaluation that the quality of vitality is lacking....

Chapter 4
ACT Foundations:
RFT, Contextualism, and Behavior Analysis

This chapter contains dialogues on the concepts, theories and traditions with which ACT is associated, including in particular Relational Frame Theory (RFT). RFT has its own separate listserv, and although some e-mails were cross-posted to both the ACT and RFT listservs, the RFT-related material presented here does not purport to reflect the more detailed examination of RFT topics found on that listserv. Nevertheless, these posts provide introductions to RFT and suggestions for further reading, as well as addressing important questions such as whether clinicians need to learn RFT in order to practice ACT.

Reference is made to ACT's roots in behavior analysis, and to the functional contextualist philosophy that underlies ACT. The chapter also includes expositions, from a contextualist viewpoint, of some key concepts, such as cause, choice and context. In addition, a number of other definitions and interpretations from an ACT perspective are provided (for example, of the word "confidence"), often by reference to the etymology of the word in question.

BEHAVIOR ANALYSIS

ACT as applied behavior analysis; RFT [6-22-05]

Kelly Wilson

Doug Woods wrote:

> What if we just stopped calling this ACT/RFT and started calling it "comprehensive behavior analysis"? Isn't that what we're really talking about?

Yes that is exactly what we are after. I have always said that I am a behavior analyst and what I do in the applied realm is applied behavior analysis. It is mystifying to me when people talk about ACT as if it can sensibly be set in contrast to applied behavior analysis, except insofar as it is applied to some domains where traditional applied behavior analysis has not been applied. Likewise "blends" of behavior therapy and ACT seems an odd concept to me. I use anything and everything that makes sense from a behavior analytic perspective--including management of direct contingencies, homework (gasp!), psycho-education, and even highly directive advice (gasp! gasp!). People have heard my caution about these matters as prohibitions. It would be nonsensical to prohibit them. What I prohibit is the therapist *using* them to manage their own anxieties in therapy. I think that will have a downside and it is very easy to start sliding down that slippery slope. When I prohibit them in a new therapist, it is so that I can bring them into contact with what would happen if they let go of those strategies for a moment--what else is there and available? I want the use of these strategies to be under the control of client needs, not therapist anxieties. Of course, this comes from an analysis of the contingencies driving therapist behavior--which is not an area that has been addressed by many applied behavior analysts--with a few exceptions (Bob Kohlenberg comes to mind).

So, if it is just applied behavior analysis, why not call it that?

Names are strategic. I hate the name ACT as much as I love it. Brand names have an up and a downside. If we had gone to AABT a decade or two ago and said - we are doing applied behavior analysis (or comprehensive behavior analysis) people would have immediately stopped listening.

Some, because they already do applied behavior analysis, hence nothing new to learn. Some, because applied behavior analysis is old stuff and we have moved way beyond that now. The problem is that applied behavior analysis as a brand name did not say functionally what needed saying. One has to speak to an audience in a way that moves the conversation ahead.

Things have changed a bit. Over the past couple years, I have been in front of pretty large audiences at AABT talking in terms of stimulus control and they are not running screaming from the room. The brand name ACT got us in front of that audience talking about behavior analysis--partly because it distanced us just enough from "behavior analysis" that people could hear over the roar of what they already knew about "behavior analysis." We have to speak in different ways to different audiences in order to be heard. I give a different talk in a department of psychiatry, an EST-oriented CBT program, and a different one still at SEABA. Different audiences, different language systems, histories, etc.

The downside of brand names is that you get statements like "I don't do behavior therapy, I do ACT." Yipes! ACT is behavior therapy. It is an unfortunate side-effect of the language game we played to get heard. So, we need to dance back and forth. What is different, what is the same? If you say things that sound like "it is the same" there are folks who will get offended. If you say things that sound like "it's different" some folks will get offended. Sometimes you offend both with the same words, but for opposite reasons.

I have said on several occasions (and I am pretty sure I have heard Steve say pretty much the same thing) that eventually, ACT just disappears as a brand name because the strategic utility will have disappeared. Behavior analysts will be applying behavior analysis to a broader set of issues--the ones we brought to the fore and others we haven't thought of--and "behavior analysis" will have stopped being a dirty word outside ABA.

BEHAVIOR ANALYSIS

ACT as applied behavior analysis; RFT [cont'd]

Kelly Wilson

Monica Pignotti wrote:

> ... what I have observed is that because ACT draws on many different sources (ABA being only one of them) people with a variety of different backgrounds are attracted to study it.... ABA is only one part of the picture.

One may or may not be a behavior analyst and one may suggest that ACT can be understood best as an existential or gestalt therapy. However, it would be a mistake to characterize the origins of the treatment as having behavior analysis as one among many theoretical sources. ACT was explicitly developed from a behavior analytic perspective. Behavior analysis, including what we know about operant and respondent conditioning processes, are altogether central to the development of ACT and to ACT as it currently exists-- at least from the perspective of its developers. Where we have borrowed from others, for example, from gestalt approaches, it has involved a behavioral analysis of those techniques. Our borrowing from existential psychology was an attempt to make a behavioral analysis of the phenomena of interest to existential folks. Behavior analysis is the thread that holds it all together. Without it, ACT is a mish mash of techniques. In fact it would be incoherent to suggest the importance of RFT absent behavior analysis. RFT is a behavior analytic theory.

	One can understand ACT in all kinds of ways, but to understand it from a theoretical perspective other than behavior analysis, would, in my estimation be making a reinterpretation of ACT. One could do it, but one could not do that and rightly characterize it as consistent with the theoretical origins of the treatment.
BEHAVIOR ANALYSIS **Extinction - not eliminative [8-10-04]** Steve Hayes	William Kordonski wrote: The brain works by addition and not subtraction…. However, how do we explain to colleagues extinction? For example, a man who can't go over a bridge is successfully treated and feels nothing as he crosses bridges on a regular basis. Or the drug addict who after many years of sobriety states he no longer feels urges to drug? These instances appear to be examples of getting a "behavior out of the brain." Thoughts, please. Extinction is not eliminative. In response reacquisition procedures that is readily shown. "Extinguish" a response and later retrain it and it will retrain more easily. Resurgence also shows it. "Extinguish" a response and later "extinguish" another response and subjects will revert to the earlier extinguished response ... more or less in order. [For an example from derived stimulus relations work see Wilson, K. G., & Hayes, S. C. (1996). Resurgence of derived stimulus relations. *Journal of the Experimental Analysis of Behavior, 66*, 267-281.] Kel first put me on to this view, but in hindsight it is startling to me that we haven't all been talking this way in behavioral psychology all along (at least the more contextualistic wing). It's one of those profound but "of course" insights. What extinction is, is the establishment of alternative response functions in the presence of a given situation. Say I'm afraid of bridges. I avoid them. Escape and avoidance becomes the dominant response function for bridges: given a bridge, nearly 100% of my behavior is escape and avoidance. So I expose myself. During exposure I initially do escape and avoidance behaviors (what else?), including its physiological associates. But extinction kicks off greater variability (why? Evolutionary reasons. When the food goes away, for gosh sakes do something else or you might die) and behavior is inherently variable if you stop narrowing the repertoire, e.g., thru language (why? Evolutionary reasons. Without variability nothing new can be selected and we wouldn't be here because we could not adjust to ecological changes). So eventually I start to do other things. I look around. I talk. I notice my breath. If I'm lucky [e.g., if I have an ACT therapist ... :)] my therapist *ensures* that responses other than escape and avoidance occur, and *ensures* that functionally it is not present even when other response forms occur. Joke. Eat. Find the worst hairdo in the crowd. etc. And yes, do your defusion work; acceptance work; mindfulness; etc. etc. As these responses occur my response repertoire is flattening and is becoming more widely distributed. It looks like the earlier response is being eliminated, but not so. It is just *relatively* less dominant because other responses are now occurring in that situation. Some of these are reinforcing ...and so they build. The old responses are then even less dominant ... relatively. So it is that the drug user ultimately "no longer has urges" … but what a dangerous way to say it! Talk to any addict in recovery and he will tell you that even after a decade urges will sneak up when situations show up (e.g., after a major loss; a major win; at an old stomping ground not revisited before; etc. etc.) that still have the narrow behavioral functions. The "it's behind me" syndrome has ensnared many an unwary person in recovery. That is why it is always "one day at a time" precisely for the reason you started your comment with: because the brain [or, shall we just say, the human being] works by addition, not subtraction. Once in, always available. The goal is broad, flexible, and effective repertoires (a nod to Kel and Liz who first started talking that way in my lab anyway). That is what protects us from being consumed by dark spaces and the narrowing of behavior they produce. Nothing is ever eliminated.
BEHAVIOR ANALYSIS Extinction - not eliminative [cont'd] Kelly Wilson	Just to add a note - some of the psychological functions that will start to show up as the repertoire fattens will be respondent in nature. Amy Murrell and I discuss this in our values chapter in the new Guilford book. SO, for example, aesthetic appreciation may start to show up. This latter is behavior under strong antecedent control. I had this experience with snakes and talk about it at workshops a lot. Not only did my operant behavior broaden--I could *do* more stuff with snakes--hold, feed, look, but also behavior that is under respondent stimulus control--like a sense of wonder, appreciation, interest, an almost visceral appreciation of the beauty of snakes. That was really the aspect of the change in experience that caught my attention. Nowhere in the "extinction" literature had I ever seen anything about this additive quality to extinction--especially on the respondent side. But when you think about it--theoretically--it's a big Duh! of course. Incidentally, I also talk a lot about self-as-laboratory. This is a case study in that. My thinking about this issue changed in part as result of dense theoretical training in behavior analysis--but it was really that analytic sense brought to bear on my own personal experience. (It's an ACT thang.) Carl Rogers said "That which is most personal is most general." There is something to that I think.

BEHAVIOR ANALYSIS Extinction - not eliminative [cont'd] John Forsyth	To add one piece. There is a growing literature on contextual control over previously extinguished respondents. Mark Bouton has written extensively on this. Mark's arguments are very much in line with Steve's -- extinction is not elimination, it is new learning. Acquire a fear (say of a snake) in Context A, run extinction procedures in Context A, and later test for fear of snakes in Context A, and you won't get much of a blip ala fearful responding to the snake. Yet, acquire the fear in Context A, extinguish in Context B, and test again in Context A and you get a big blip or what some folks call "renewal" or "return of fear." Renewal also occurs with the following arrangement -- Context A, extinguish Context A, and then test Context B, and with an A - B - C arrangement. The largest renewal effects occur with the A - B - A arrangement. Most of this has been shown with rats, with contexts being experimental apparatus or drug states. Some studies are starting to come on line with humans though. We have some preliminary data showing similar effects in humans following a fear conditioning preparation and another one due to start soon. I believe folks in Leuven have a study or two due out shortly. This work has been extended to issues related to relapse following successful exposure therapy, leading to recommendations that one ought to make the extinction context as a therapy context as similar as possible to the contexts found in the client's natural environment. Would be cool to show how verbal processes function as context here, particularly with renewal.
BEHAVIOR ANALYSIS Extinction - not eliminative [cont'd] John Blackledge	(Just a point intended to highlight the apparent potential for defusion to facilitate more flexible verbal responding as well as direct contingency-based responses like respondents....) Additionally, some or many of the psychological functions that show up when one's repertoire "fattens" will be verbal. Defusing from a debilitating thought may help a variety of verbal responses that are not debilitating emerge. The sense of wonder (for example) that Kel mentions strikes me as one example--I would guess that non-verbal animals do not experience wonder as we do, but rather that wonder requires relational responding. We don't target such thoughts directly as ACT therapists given the assumption that they do not impede movement toward values.
BEHAVIOR ANALYSIS **Scope of [6-5-04]** Jonathan Kanter	I am first and foremost a clinical behavior analyst, and to me this means ACT, in one way or another, infuses almost everything I do clinically. However, being a clinical behavior analyst means more than ACT to me. It also means that I continue to learn about idiographic functional assessment and shaping of behavior through environmental control, continue to struggle with how to reformulate traditional non-behavioral phenomena like depression, love, and the self into behavior-analytic terms that include RFT as well as traditional processes, continue to develop behavioral models of the therapeutic relationship and other non-specific treatment factors, continue to learn basic behavior analytic research on establishing operations, stimulus control, rule-governance, reinforcement as well as RFT and how to apply this research in clinical settings, continue to develop my skills in single-subject research methods and how best to investigate clinical phenomena, and continue to learn and perfect other behavioral techniques such as behavioral activation and exposure protocols that - although similar topographically and perhaps identical functionally to ACT - nonetheless are still seen by many as different at this stage in the development of behavior therapy.
CAUSE **Private events, role of, in "causing" behavior** **FUNCTIONAL CONTEXTUALISM** **Context, role of, in causality** **ACT cf.** **CBT - role of private events in "causing" behavior [9-16-03]** Steve Hayes	Joseph Ciarrochi wrote: I am trying to understand how one would describe the causal role of F.E.A.R. in promoting human suffering. ...I understand the behaviourist principle that private behaviour (e.g., emotion) does not cause public behaviour (external act). Rather, the cause must be something that is external to the behaviour and that can be manipulated. Yes, but actually, the public / private part has little to do with the point. You could say the same for public behavior and public behavior, it's just that we rarely make the mistake there. If we ever said "he's a good quarterback and throws a great spiral because he's a great ditch digger and really can shovel better than almost anyone" we'd immediately realize that we need to account both for how one act related to another (what about ditch digging leads to good spirals? Is that always true? Why is it in this case?), AND how the excellent ditch digging was established in the first place. If you say the same thing but put some other *form* of behavior in the second place (thoughts, feelings, and so on) we now dumb down because we think we have two domains, not one, and so it sounds like we are going outside of the first domain. For example, listen to how these next sentences sound and note how much more complete they seem to be than the first one: "he's a good quarterback and throws a great spiral because he's more confident than almost anyone" "he's a good quarterback and throws a great spiral because he can visualize himself doing it" "he's a good quarterback and throws a great spiral because he can sense the ball in his fingers" "he's a good quarterback and throws a great spiral because he has no fear" The first one, the ditch digger example, is obviously the same domain and we see the problem. The last four

appear to involve different domains so it is plausible that the second domain may provide a causal explanation for the first. But the last four are all psychological events -- behavioral folks call these "behaviours" but regardless of the language these are all dependent variables for psychology. So really they are the same as the first example. It is just a trick of language that this is missed.

[JC] So, F.E.A.R. is caused by the historical contingencies of reinforcement and punishment (presumably under different contingencies, F.E.A.R. would not exist, but neither would language).

Right.

[JC] Let's say someone experiences an activating event (traumatic life event) that leads to an aversive memory. The person evaluates the memory as bad and seeks to avoid it. Then, via fusion/relational framing, there is a gradual expansion of what is aversive and what is avoided. The more the person avoids, the more restricted his life becomes, and the more intense the suffering. What would the behaviourist say is the cause of the suffering? Is it the activating event plus the historical context that led to F.E.A.R.?

Yes. And the current context. And the context that led to the behavior-behavior relation.

[JC] can we also say that F.E.A.R. is actually part of the causal sequence (although it is behaviour)?

Sure.

[JC] Can a private experience (e.g., avoiding)...

Be a little careful here. Avoiding is a function ... there may be private events that go with that function, but we need to be precise about what we are talking about.

[JC] ... be a necessary, though not sufficient, condition for another private experience (e.g., suffering)?

Sure, but this is a tricky point. The ACT / RFT folks have written a fair amount about it because it is absolutely essential to ACT and RFT. Indeed, this general issue it brings up (the role of context; views of causality; what is considered to be an adequate analysis) is THE most important difference between ACT and CBT etc., it is the most important difference between behavior analysis and other perspectives, and it is the most important difference between RFT and other theories of cognition.

Given the goals of prediction AND influence, no psychological dependent variable CAUSES another. Many psychological dependent variables (call them behavior / feelings / thoughts / or what have you) relate to other such dependent variables and they can participate in overall "causal" relations but the only variables that can meet the goals of prediction AND influence, are contextual events in the "manipulable in principle" environment.

Some pieces that will help see why: the '88 review of Pepper's book in JEAB... The 1986 paper on behavior-behavior relations. It is in *The Behavior Analyst*. Hayes and Brownstein. I like this article more than any other philosophy of science piece I've written and I think it really is essential as a basis for ACT / RFT in the philosophy area)... The Context Press books on contextualism and behavioral epistemology will help too.

As an outline of the argument:

As a contextualist / behaviorist there is no "cause" in a mechanistic sense. Events are understood by appealing to context, but that is understood by appealing to context, and so on ad infinitum. Eventually reach the totality, and the one is not caused by anything. My usual example, stolen from Kantor via Linda: sufficient heat + oxygen + combustibles = explosion. When welding combustible metal in a vacuum, if we ask "why did it explode?" we are likely to answer "because we lost the vacuum." We will not say "because there was a spark or flame" because welding always involves that. In a mine, grain elevator we say "because there was a spark" because oxygen and grain dust is assumed. And so on. But if we have all the elements, there is an explosion not because any one thing caused it but because all these things working together IS an explosion. The causal talk differs in different settings because what is assumed changes with the context.

What saves contextualists from an infinite regress is that analysis has a purpose. Causal talk is used to help our purposes be accomplished and to indicate when they have been achieved.

The environmentalism of behavioral folks comes from their interest in prediction and influence, and to influence any system you have to get to what you can manipulate ... and no one can directly manipulate "dependent" variables (that's why we call them that).

[JC] A 2nd wave CBT'er might claim that the cause is the activating event combined with the unhelpful belief (e.g., "I can't stand the memory"). Is there something inadequate with this claim from a behaviorist's perspective?

Yes. In different contexts, the "belief" will NOT have this effect, and thus you have to specify how the current context established a relation between the event and the belief. That same model "the cause is the activating event combined with the unhelpful belief" is exactly why CBT is CBT and ACT is different.

What you just said is the same normal cognitive model as in "I lost something dear to me; I believe it's awful; I'm depressed" or "I had something painful happen; I think in black and white terms; I'm depressed." But exactly what ACT does it says: that behavior-behavior relation depends on a context. Mess with the context, and you change the function of the belief. ACT spends a lot of time on these contexts and how to alter them by establishing a new social / verbal community. That is why ACT has defusion (etc.) front and center while few other treatments even see the issue: you can't see it unless you focus on the contextual features that establish behavior-behavior relations (contexts of literality, reason-giving, control, etc.). If there is nothing inadequate with this claim, there is no need for ACT: we already had REBT; CT; CBT; etc.

Now, your example sounds just a bit tricky because the specific belief you are talking about is close to a statement about the need for control of private events. People have such things, but the social / verbal community establishes that context of control *whether or not* you can state it verbally ... so, as above, be careful about turning contexts into beliefs. The metacognitive folks do this all the time when they come right up to the core issue and then slip in a cognition to make it seem as though it is just a formal cognition at another level that we are speaking of. The context of emotional control is not the same as a simple belief "I can't stand the memory." Not to say people don't have such beliefs. Often they do. But part of what is powerful about ACT is that defusion/ acceptance / etc. is NOT just another belief, so you don't have to deal with the issue logically -- you can deal with it experientially -- whether or not there is a belief there.

Anyway. Back on point.

In addition, you have to account for the belief itself: what is it, where did it come from, why does it function in that way, what brought it into the current behavioral stream. RFT does that and as it does it keeps coming back to history and context. Everything is manipulable in principle. RFT goes farther than any theory of cognition I know of to avoid the "structuralistic error" that comes by turning dependent variables into independent ones.

That is why ACT has to have RFT: without it ACT will not be able to answer fully the great question you ask. And without an answer, ACT adds nothing to what CBT already did.

Bottom line suggestion: I like questions like this or the values one earlier etc. because it shows there is some coherence to the whole rap. The things we worked on in the hiatus between early and late ACT RCTs are often precisely the things folks ask about now ... and there is a kind of developmental progression (does this sound arrogant? Sorry if it does). So a brand new ACT person would not ask this question, Joe; it takes some sophistication even to see it clearly. I was talking to some of my former students in Sweden and we were reminding ourselves that things we worked on years ago ... and maybe don't talk about that much anymore ... are often important for folks coming into contact with ACT. Not that there aren't new issues ... but often the issues have been worked through to a degree by others.

Sometimes it is hard for folks to remember to work through the issues with newer folks -- once one works though it, it begins to lose interest. For example, these old contextualism issues captivated ACT folks in the late 1980's and then interest waned a bit as we worked it out.

Fortunately, a lot of this is in writing. It's not real satisfying just to say "slog though some of this stuff a bit more. Here's the reference" but sometimes that's what needs to happen (so much has been written that it is silly to try to put the whole rap into a quick email)....

CAUSE **Thoughts don't cause behavior [3-29-04]** ACT Listserv Member	... As far as thinking causing behavior, well not directly, though our fusion with our thoughts may give the appearance of cause - when we become fused with cognitions, we can react to them as if the actual contingencies were relevant, and therefore react to our thoughts as if something real happened...or will happen...so indirectly thoughts can act as occasions for behaving. Isn't that the purpose of utilizing metaphor and experiential exercises early in ACT? To defuse us from our thoughts/ feelings/ evaluations, so we can see them not as impetus for behavior, but as thoughts/ feelings/ evaluations....
CAUSE **Thoughts/ rules cf. context [3-26-04]** Steve Hayes	On the causality front and the difference between thoughts and rules: The point is to keep dependent variables as dependent variables while acknowledging that actions do relate to actions. The "why" is pragmatic: only things you can directly manipulate can be directly linked to the goals of prediction-and-influence. When actions relate to actions, you look to the context of each, and to the context of their relation, because you can alter these contexts. Rules can be expressed by others. They can be built into the social/verbal culture in which we behavior. External rules are easily manipulated, and can in some cases usefully be treated as "causes" (though in contextualism remember there are no ontological causes at all ... in fact there's no ontology at all other than the assumption of the one or "real" world). Thoughts you cannot manipulate directly. Self-rules are the same as thoughts. You need to keep track of them, and you acknowledge their controlling role as part of an overall causal relation, but you look to the contexts (literality/ control/ reason-giving/ etc.) that created that causal relation as the focus of

	interventions.
	What we target overtly in ACT on the rule front are the rules in the social / verbal community that we may be able to change in the therapeutic relationship; and the contexts that support unhealthy behavior-behavior relations when we are dealing with self-rules (e.g., unhealthy thought-overt action relations; or thought-emotion; or emotion-overt action; etc.).
CHOICE **ACT concept of [cont'd]** ACT Listserv Member *Cross Reference:* *See 2-81 for an earlier post in this thread*	Although it may not be helpful to our clients for them to look for the reason for action or causes of their behavior, we as the clinician may want to keep looking for the contextual variables and some of the possible reinforcers (negative or positive) that may influence and predict the choices made by the client. Finding relationships between certain variables that occur together with the choices that have led to behavioral restriction, or suffering, may help us in helping the clients. When I do functional behavioral assessments, I am not looking for reasons for a behavior occurring, I am looking for function of behavior to help treatment planning. In therapy, looking for themes in the client's languaging allows me to find function of their language and their non-verbal behavior, which helps in recognition of when the therapy should progress to the next stage.
CHOICE ACT concept of [cont'd] Niklas Törneke	Yes, I think you put in well as an ACT position, looking for contextual change in relation to the choices clients make. I think it is an interesting point, though, that that is the exact strategy we use, talking about choice the way we do in ACT. Talking about "taking a step" regardless of whatever reasons, thoughts, feelings etc. are present (that is talking about choice), is *changing the context of those very reasons, thoughts, feelings etc.* For clients (as for the rest of us) these reasons, thoughts, feelings etc. have the function they have from the context of literality. This is the context we change by pointing to choice, in the experiential meaning of the word. Together with other ACT interventions, of course. This is why choice is an important concept in ACT, even though it is not an argument against the behavioral position that there are historical contingencies controlling whatever behavior there is....
CHOICE **Free or determined; subjective sense of [3-4-03]** John Forsyth	Hank Robb wrote: ... how one relates to the presence of thoughts, images and sensations is always a choice. Similarly, how one relates with their hands, feet, etc. to events outside their skin is also always a choice (except possibly for things like air puffs to an open eye). Interesting point about choice. My lab group and I have been struggling with this issue and related concerns such as free will. I agree that choice is important, but I think we need to be careful about how that term is used. Choosing is an act, meaning to select freely and after consideration, to decide on, or to have a preference for. Our struggle concerns whether one can be free to make choices in the absence of a history (direct or derived) for choosing. So, is it possible for a client to make a choice not to respond to their own responses if that is all they know? Probably not. Are clients free to make choices among alternatives in the absence of an experiential history for doing so? Again, probably not. Being response able -- that is, able to choose -- in this context would seem to require new relational training, shaping, and contact with direct contingencies (i.e., alternatives). I believe this kind of work goes on within ACT, and clients learn that there are alternatives, that life is not unidimensional, and that choices can be made that were not previously known or clear. When a client walks in the door we try not to assume that they can choose freely, or even know what that would look like. Rather, we assume that they are more or less stuck, or trapped within their limited histories and are behaving within the constraints of such histories. A good part of ACT seems to involve helping clients get unstuck by expanding their limited repertoires with respect to a world of possibilities (i.e., valued choices that are available and can be responded to or not) via direct experiential exercises.
CHOICE Free or determined; subjective sense of [cont'd] Patty Bach	I agree that we have to be careful about using terms like "choice." Choice cannot be primarily about generating alternatives from which to choose, as there are plenty of people who generate all kinds of alternatives and who then feel paralyzed about which alternative to choose. It seems that whatever I am doing is what I choose to do. Under what conditions would I do something I am not choosing to do? I often do not have the subjective experience that I am 'choosing,' yet how could I ever do anything that I am not choosing? I like the exercise of walking with a client and then debriefing about his choices. 'Choosing' seems to be nothing more than behaving; if 'choosing' is behaving, then 'conscious choice' might be behaving overtly while simultaneously verbally tacting my own behavior, or "being aware that I am behaving," or perhaps behavior partially under the control of the thought "I have a choice." 'Making a choice' or deciding among alternatives, is a different behavior (that is itself chosen).

Feeling or sensing that behavior is not chosen occurs only after the behavior of interest - noticing that one just did something that one did not notice one was doing while in the midst of doing it.

"Free choice" is maybe behaving without first generating verbal 'reasons' for behaving.

I recently did a little experiment with myself around choice. Of course the N = 1, so this has little validity!

I quit smoking about two weeks ago (it's become increasingly difficult to maintain both behavior analysis and smoking - too much cognitive dissonance!). In the weeks prior to quitting I 'chose' to begin tacting my own smoking behavior - when I both had an urge to smoke and noticed that I had an urge to smoke I would tell myself either "I choose to smoke" and smoke or "I choose not to smoke" and do something else until the next urge. I cut down my smoking about 40% this way.

Could I say that I did not 'choose' to smoke on those occasions when I forgot to notice and verbally comment on and 'make' a choice? Am I choosing not to smoke? Right now I am not smoking. Is that a 'choice'? "Not smoking" is not even a behavior! I am thinking, typing, listening to the radio, chewing gum, sitting, fidgeting and swivelling in the chair. I 'chose' those behaviors (the fidgeting and swivelling do not 'feel' chosen, and I occasionally notice them); "not smoking" is not a part of what I am 'doing' right now.

We also have to be careful about saying things like clients choose not to respond to their own behavior - 'not responding' is NOT behavior! 'Not responding' is responding with a different behavior.

It seems we cannot 'choose among alternatives in the absence of a history of choosing among alternatives' (Hmmm. In other words, I cannot choose to choose!). However, the behavior of choosing among alternatives can be shaped by a therapist or learned given a history of rule-following behavior. There is something tricky here about what we are talking about. I am having the thought "That's not it!" And that is precisely the point about the matter of choice.... Creating alternatives seems to 'shake up' some of the verbal stimulus functions of 'reason giving' to maybe increase contact with consequences.

Kind of like 'choosing,' I have observed that I have tended to say "I am 'trying' to quit smoking." What in the world is 'trying'? I am smoking or I am doing something other than smoking. Where is the 'trying'? It seems that 'trying' is only doing something while simultaneously having the thought that one wants to or should be doing something else! Choosing is perhaps only doing something while tacting or noticing that I am doing it, as opposed to 'just doing it,' and 'making a choice' is the behavior of generating verbal 'reasons' for behavior that then have various stimulus functions with respect to the behavior of interest....

I am thinking that some of ACT with respect to matters like 'choice' is extinction procedures with respect to verbal behavior that has been negatively reinforced. I am not exactly sure what I am talking about (yet), and I suspect that something like that is involved.

I want to smoke right now, so I am choosing to log off and go for a walk....

CHOICE	
Free or determined; subjective sense of [cont'd]	As a theoretical matter, I always assume that the subject could only have done what they did, given their history. This is determinism as a working assumption. As Burrhus says in Walden II, "behave as you ought damn you" is always wrongheaded. The subject always behaves as they ought. If they don't we have merely failed to appreciate the contingencies.
Kelly Wilson	The piece that interests me, in the realm of choice, is the analysis of the subject experiencing themselves as choosing freely. I am interested in people experiencing their lives as chosen, not coerced. This is a different piece to analyze than choice itself. I assume choice to always be determined, but we sometimes experience it as coerced and sometimes as free. What are the conditions under which our clients, students, experience themselves as choosing freely (me too)? Skinner was all about this. Walden II was a thought experiment-- How do we organize an environment where we make maximal efforts to reduce aversive control? It is the presence of aversive control that generates a sense that one is coerced rather than free to choose.
	The piece that was unanalyzed in Walden II or in Beyond Freedom and Dignity, in my estimation, was the contingencies that could allow people to experience themselves as freely choosing in an environment that is *apparently* filled with aversive contingencies. The world is not Walden II. My question is, how do we generate Walden II in an individual's experience, even in the face of coercive circumstances? Or, to cite a specific case, how was it that Victor Frankl was able to experience his life as chosen, even in a concentration camp?
	I really think that the heart of this matter is to be found in the fact that human beings are the only creatures that know about their own death. We are the only creatures for whom living is a choice. Once you get that you are alive by choice, you can no longer be coerced. It is knowledge of death that frees us to live by choice under any and all circumstances.
	Bottom line, it is language processes. This is all fruit of the tree from which we ate in Eden. The dark side of eating the fruit was the ability to know shame and suffering in the midst of plenty. Remember, suffering was there before Adam and Eve were cast from the garden. Truly it was the bite itself that cast them from the garden. The light side of eating the fruit is the fact that we can also experience our lives as chosen, as

free, as glorious, in the midst of horrors.

ACT is about creating Walden II in our client's experience (our student's, our family's, our own). In training, it is about creating our work-space as a place where it is made clear moment-by-moment that we are there by choice-- regardless of circumstances.

One of the most liberating experiences I have had in my life, an experience that made possible extraordinary, life-transforming change, occurred in 1985. I stood right out at the edge. It was dead calm. I could taste my life welling up around me. No thing mattered. I leaned just a bit forward. The rope strained. I realized that one step would bring it all to an end, and that I could do that regardless of anything or anyone. I was possessed of an awareness that the ability to end my own life could not be taken away from me. In my best moments, I hold that space close. There is no coercion possible in that space. All is experienced as choice.

| CHOICE

Free or determined; subjective sense of [cont'd]

Patty Bach | To understand technically the contingencies influencing behavior "X", 'not X' is not a behavior. If I am a smoker and want to quit, 'not smoking' is not a behavior. Presumably, if I have been doing 'X' it has been reinforced. If I am doing 'X' and report that I do not want to do 'X' or wish that I could stop doing 'X' and I continue to do it anyway, then I cannot be having the experience that I am 'choosing X.' I must feel compelled/ coerced into doing 'X' or unable to choose some other behavior - choose 'not X.' In other words, if I am a smoker and have the subjective experience that I want to quit, and I continue to smoke (and have probably 'tried to quit' in the past) I am likely to have the subjective experience that I 'can't' quit.

Doing "X" for the sake of "Not Y" is negative reinforcement; a rat that has been shocked (Y) will press a lever (X) to avoid or escape a shock (not Y).

If 'X' for the sake of 'Y' is positive reinforcement.

'X' for the sake of 'not Y' is negative reinforcement.

'not X' for the sake of 'Y' is positive punishment.

'not X' for the sake of 'not Y' is negative punishment.

I think we subjectively experience less 'choice' under conditions of negative punishment and negative reinforcement; that is, I experience less sense of choice when I am doing a behavior I 'do not want to do' to avoid losing a positive consequence, or not doing a behavior I 'want to do' to avoid a negative consequence. For example, "I am smoking because I can't tolerate withdrawal symptoms when I stop," or "I like to smoke and I am quitting so my wife will stop nagging me." Under conditions of positive reinforcement and punishment, choosing 'X' for the sake of 'Y' or 'not X' for the sake of 'not Y' I may experience more of a sense of choice. For example, "smoking relaxes me" or "I am not smoking so I won't get cancer" experience more choice when I am behaving for positive reinforcement or decreasing a behavior to avoid negative punishment.

If we assume that 'choosing' is reinforcing, to go even one step further in the language of operant conditioning, I wonder if one might say that, if I am interested in doing 'not X' in order to decrease behavior "X", through a DRO intervention (differential reinforcement of other behavior) "I am choosing not X" is a discriminative stimulus for positive reinforcement of any behavior other than X. "I am choosing Z and not X" would be DRA (differential reinforcement of alternative behavior) (Z in this case). |
| CHOICE

Free or determined; subjective sense of [cont'd]

Patty Bach | Choosing is behavior with respect to consequences. When more than one possible thing to interact with is present, saying that "I choose it," this is a shorthand for 'I move towards X instead of towards Y.'

"Choosing" is about consequences. It is a *general* description of any kind of action of moving towards a thing that has a desired consequence, as in 'the chimpanzee chose the banana instead of the orange,' or 'the chimpanzee chose to play with the ball instead of to eat the banana.'

We feel that we do not have a choice when we get the behavior and consequence link wrong; we sort of 'don't know what we are really choosing.' It will be especially difficult to sort this out when the consequences are negatively reinforcing or punishing, because those consequences are determined by what does NOT happen.

Humans can choose among things that are not present and can choose among consequences that are very delayed. If I asked a pig "do you want chocolate or vanilla" it would not choose. If I presented it with chocolate and vanilla and it ate chocolate the choice would 'mean' something like "I prefer chocolate to vanilla." Such a choice is not so simple for humans. If I chose chocolate that might mean "I like chocolate better," but it also might mean, "Aunt Emma's feelings would be hurt if I chose vanilla," "Bob told me the chocolate is better and he's usually right," "I really don't like either one, but they will think I'm rude if I decline both," "I have been dieting all week and I deserve this" or "everyone else is choosing chocolate, so I'd better have it" or "last time I had vanilla it was awful" or "the chocolate has fewer calories than the vanilla" or "the chocolate costs less than the vanilla." |

With respect to chocolate and vanilla, I am 'choosing' chocolate.

However, I will experience myself as not having a choice with respect to chocolate and vanilla if my behavior of 'choosing' is done with respect to some other consequence. In the 'above' examples, I am not really choosing between chocolate and vanilla. I am choosing not to hurt someone's feelings, not to be seen as rude, to listen to Bob, to cut calories, to save money, etc.

Essentially, feeling that I have a choice is being a good behavior analyst with respect to my own choices. When choices have multiple consequences we feel that we have 'no choice' when we 'want to' choose one behavior and find ourselves doing another. I think one could argue that either we actually absolutely always or never choose to do what we do, and that we experience a sense of choice when we can correctly identify the contingencies. I will feel choice if I can say "I chose chocolate so as not to hurt Aunt Emma's feelings"; if I can only say "I really wanted vanilla but Bob would have been annoyed" I will feel no choice, because I was 'choosing' behavior with respect to Bob, and feeling 'no choice' with respect to chocolate and vanilla. I will 'feel' I wanted vanilla and did not choose it, but with respect to Bob, I did 'choose' to be negatively reinforced by choosing chocolate to avoid Bob's annoyance.

Kind of like choosing to drink to avoid anxiety and saying "why do I do this when it gets me in trouble?" Because I am not 'choosing' it in relation to 'getting in trouble' I am 'choosing' it in relation to the consequence of anxiety.

CHOICE

Free or determined; subjective sense of [cont'd]

CULTURAL DIFFERENCES

Linguistic practices [3-11-03]

Tuna Townsend

Dermot Barnes-Holmes wrote:

> This thread got me thinking about some of the cultural differences I have seen in reactions to ACT, and in particular its emphasis on choice and response-ability.

I think the within- and across-cultural differences with respect to ACT are differences which are familiar to linguists and cultural anthropologists, although they may not see them in quite the same way. The (Benjamin) Whorfian hypothesis is very RFT-like in that it suggests language-based contextual control of an individual's 'perceived experience' of the world. A given language, or even regional dialect, may contain features or implicit assumptions and biases which differentially shape an individual's experience and 'stance' toward all kinds of experience, including that of the things we've been discussing on this list lately ... choice, responsibility, pain, suffering....

For example, in the Hawaiian culture (in which the extended family is FAR more important and enduring than the individual), the dominant 'language' is a Creole known as Hawaiian 'pidgin'; in pidgin, the first-person-singular is rare - practically non-existent ... one almost never hears a 'local' person refer to themselves as the cause or initiator of action. On the other hand, the self-as-object ('such-and-such always happens to me') is completely ordinary.

As you might imagine, the concept of personal responsibility is quite different than one would find in the wider English-speaking culture, and especially in the mainland-American, where the individual is regarded as supra-ordinate. This absence of the "I" in local culture seems to facilitate practices of consensus-building, 'agreeance' (I love 'new' words) and unanimity... it's a lot harder to have a 'personal point of view' if there's no place to keep it.

In the population with which I was working ('local' guys, 18 years old and up), the concept of 'self' - and even 'thinking' - was much different than any I'd ever considered. Virtually all of these guys were unaware of their own 'self-talk' until we performed some simple experiential exercises. I was minded of Julian Jayne's 'bicameral mind,' in which one's thinking ('private languaging'), when tacted, was thought to be the 'voices' of the gods, or one's ancestors, or king ... but not one's 'self.'

I think it's a useful exercise to try to imagine how one's experience might be very, very different by merely 'tweaking' some of our most transparent assumptions ("I exist apart from everything else in the universe"). These assumptions and biases are the inevitable products of the arbitrarily-applicable nature of language. Our language - as the voice of our culture - 'forces' some discriminations upon us, and utterly ignores others. More insidiously, though, it merely 'favors' some, and subtly discourages others.

One of the defining characteristics of American culture - a truly bizarre (if you stop to think about it) experiment in 18th-century Western European notions of free-will and determinism - is our fierce determination to preserve at least the illusion and rhetoric of individual freedom, even as we throw it away. BFS's point (as I interpreted it, anyway) was that human beings are extraordinarily susceptible to manipulation and control *precisely* in the name of freedom and dignity ... viz., the steady assault upon Americans' civil-liberties in the name of 'homeland security' under the ever-present (thanks to periodic 'alert-level' adjustments) 'threat' of sudden and unpredictable attack.

With respect to choice, it might be useful to reflect on the accuracy of our own assessments regarding our own 'choosings.' How much of it is what we say it is, and how much of it is post-hoc confabulation, to preserve a (n incomplete) sense of autonomy? See "Telling More Than We Can Know" (Nisbett, Wilson;

1977). We are demonstrably incapable of accurately identifying/ reporting the factors which actually determine our 'choices.'

Even within and among English-like language speakers, the functional properties of responsibility and blame are conflated, to varying degrees... as are the functions of 'acceptance' and 'surrender' or 'resignation'; or 'commitment' and 'being stuck with'.... And, the language-trap is so imbedded with action that one is inclined to engage the relevant discriminations on the level of semantics, ultimately leaving function practically untouched. ACT is clearly committed to engaging at the level of function and context, and dealing only very lightly with 'content' - and always 'as content'- and is therefore fundamentally distinguishable from almost all other psycho-social approaches to behavior change. There is a very important difference between changing the function of the *content* of one's thoughts, and changing the function of 'thinking' itself. There may be an argument to be made for top-down or bottom-up approaches, but not for me.

Wittgenstein's suggestion that we 'pass over, in silence' those things for which we have no language is easy to accept as a suggestion that we ignore experience for which we have no words. ACT (I think) calls upon us to learn to experience what we do without the compulsion to label, judge, evaluate, compare, or 'understand' (someone once told me that "'understanding' is the universe's 'consolation prize'..."), but rather continue moving in 'flow' with what it feels like to be living a valued and 'fulfilling' existence.

Some cultures seem to embody a kind of 'pride' in their ability to 'suffer,' and cling to histories which emphasize it ... by contrast, we (U.S.A.) Americans seem to take similar pride in our ingenuity in avoiding and escaping suffering ... go figure.

The Dalai Lama once suggested that the purpose of life is to be happy; taken with the 'four noble truths' - all of which are concerned with the existence and universality of suffering - this clearly does *not* require the elimination of suffering, but learning to practice compassion, equanimity, creativity, generosity, and, yes, 'happiness,' in the presence of suffering.

CHOICE **Reasons, with cf. for [7-3-04]** John Blackledge	Marcelo Mombelli wrote: I still don't get the distinction between choice for reasons and choice with reasons. Try thinking of it this way: Making a choice for reasons is the same as making a choice because of reasons, while making a choice with reasons is the same as choosing to act in a given way regardless of what reasons may be present. For example, let's say you chose to write a letter to your grandfather. If you were writing the letter for reasons, the reasons would have to be conducive to you writing the letter--e.g., you'd have to "feel like" writing it, you'd have to have enough important things to say, you'd have to be in the "right frame of mind," etc. If you chose to write the letter with reasons, you would write it regardless of how you felt, what frame of mind you were in, and what you feel like doing--in short, you could choose to write the letter regardless of any reasons for or against writing that you may think of. The distinction is made, in part, to break through the belief that we need good verbal reasons to act in any way. In fact, we are free to act in any way that doesn't defy the laws of physics at any time, regardless of what verbal reasons may or may not be present.
CHOICE Reasons, with cf. for [cont'd] John Blackledge	Ata Ghaderi wrote: Choice with reason (i.e., the act of making a choice) is most probably a contingency-based behavior while choice for reasons is a rule-governed behavior (i.e., a verbal behavior). The problem here is that almost everything we do is verbal, or at least it becomes verbal as soon as we try to understand it. Just a thought... Choice with reason is when we do the way of "Just do it"? Yes, I think you've got it-- choice with reasons is a direct-contingency based behavior, and choice for reasons is rule-governed behavior. And I like the way you phrased the last part— "choice with reasons is when we do the way of 'Just do it,'" as it implies that you are 'just doing it' rather than doing it because of the verbal rule/reason, "Just do it."
CHOICE **Term, use of [9-14-04]** Kelly Wilson	Hank Robb wrote: ... we often, don't "choose" we just "act." ... I actually once was in the presence of a child, potentially, drowning in a river. My first response was the generation of alternatives, "Is there a rope, a log, shall I swim?" However, the father, who had been sitting beside me, was already in the water. As far as I could tell, he did not "choose." He just acted. Choice is not a technical term, and I think we should remain sensitive to the context in which it is being used. So, for example, I might be inclined to speak of every instance of action (and inaction) as a choice were I attempting to disrupt an avoidant strategy in which a person either behaved as if they had no choice, or behaved as if they could avoid choosing. As we have spoken of--maybe in the book, who can remember-- not choosing is a choice too.

	We use the language of choice when we wish to richen the client's experience of possible alternative acts.
	I doubt if I would have been moved to use the language of choice in the near drowning incident.
CHOICE **Who chooses (if not mind/ observer-self)?** **METAPHOR** **Chessboard/ Bus - choice of direction [4-11-03]** Steve Hayes	Joseph Ciarrochi wrote: I understand how the mind is not your friend and how one can choose to drive in the valued direction (bus metaphor) or move the "chessboard" despite all the mind's blabbing. But ... who chooses what direction to move the chessboard? Who chooses what direction to drive? The observer self (e.g., chessboard) has no content and cannot choose. It merely observes. I usually say "your mind is not your friend ... and it is not your enemy either." I think I stole that from Kirk. Lots of things are best done by decisions. I think ACT merely tries to open behavioral regulation to more control by sources (e.g., contingency shaping) that are not literal and evaluative ... but even then only when literal and evaluative sources have not proven to be useful. That doesn't eliminate these other sources, by the way. From Mt. Olympus, everything participates in choices (as to *who* makes choices: people do) but seen from the inside choices are not explained or justified by reasons (verbal formulations of cause and effect). In essence that weeds out (or at least weakens) time and comparison treated literally. [JC] Is there some intuitive system ---beyond mind, beyond reason and logic--that is presumed to be the most valid director of our lives? The word "valid" is a give away. It suggests you mean "is there some other system that knows how to do it right?" I think the answer is "no" because "right" (or "valid") is itself a verbal comparative and we are talking about finding ways to interact with the world precisely when verbal comparatives fail us. Contingency shaping is all the rest of creation has and as the bible says, the lilies of the field do quite well, thank you. But the lilies (and the doggies etc.) never ask about whether their choices are valid. I think this question contains a trap. "Who does it and how do we know it is valid?" cannot be answered literally and still be on point. The question looks like (dare I say it given our previous discussions) a strange loop, because it purports to be about an answer, but taking the question too seriously prevents one. Suppose I reach for an orange juice and suddenly I find myself thinking "I don't think it is proper to reach for the juice until I am clear who just made that choice -- if it even was a choice -- and until I know if it is a good one." The best answer for such a question is not a verbal explanation. A bout of reassurance will only further confuse. The best answer would be to drink the juice. Or not. I'm not being cute here (really I'm not).
CHOICE Who chooses (if not mind/ observer-self)? [cont'd] **ACT cf.** **DBT - types of mind (DBT) cf. senses of self (ACT) [4-29-03]** Patty Bach *Cross Reference:* *See 2-72 to 2-73 for later posts in the thread:* *ACT cf.* *DBT - types of mind (DBT) cf. senses of self (ACT)*	Joseph Ciarrochi wrote: Linehan describes reasonable mind, emotion mind, and wise mind. "Wise" mind is kind of emphasized in DBT as being "the good" (though Linehan is careful not to denigrate the other modes). Here is a quote from Linehan: "Wise mind is that part of each person that can know and experience truth. It is where the person knows something to be true or valid...." Is this view inconsistent with ACT? Would I be acting inconsistently with ACT if I were to discuss the three types of mind? The three senses of self - as opposed to mind - distinguished in ACT do not seem to me to parallel Linehan's 'reasonable mind,' 'emotion mind,' and 'wise mind.' To the degree that I am familiar with DBT, I have viewed 'wise mind' as a process, a way of minding - not as 'some-thing.' One context where Linehan's 'minds' seem similar to, though not exactly parallel to, ideas in ACT is around choosing and making choices 'with reasons' (wise mind?) instead of 'for reasons,' instead of seeing reasons, thoughts, and emotions as 'causes' of behavior (emotion and reasonable mind?). It is useful at times to speak of 'mind' as a thing, and I like the ACT use of 'minding' as a verb that is something I, as a whole organism, do, as opposed to conceptualizing 'mind' as if it is somehow independent of the whole person. I would not say that 'my legs walk'; I walk, and my legs are necessary for me to do so, and would not do so independent of me as a whole person. My mind does not think, evaluate, compare, etc.; *I* think, evaluate and compare; my 'mind' is necessary for thinking, and it is "I" who thinks. My personal view is that, rather than needing to figure out which 'part of me' is the most valid or effective director, I, as a complete person, need to become a more effective director, including figuring out what I can and cannot 'direct' (hmm... 'and the wisdom to know the difference...'), and 'using'/ 'making the most of' my conceptualized, ongoing self-awareness, and observing senses of self in order to do so. No one sense of self exists, functions, or directs independent of I as a whole person. I am the self that can experience myself in all these different ways. Each experience of self may play a useful role in how I direct my life. They are not 'selves' but 'senses of self.' They are not independent parts of me, they are processes, ways in which I, as a whole person, may experience myself at any moment. They are all 'my self' and none is myself.

CHOICE Who chooses (if not mind/ observer-self)? [cont'd] METAPHOR Chessboard/ Bus - choice of direction [cont'd] **Values - beacons in stormy sea [4-29-03]** ACT Listserv Member	... Clients will sometimes ask me if values are "mindstuff." For example, are they a part of the "board" (when we are using the chessboard metaphor)? I have found myself answering this using (and sometimes mixing) several metaphors. Using the chessboard metaphor (where the chessboard can move in any valued direction), I tend to conceptualize values as being almost innate predilections from outside of ourselves, which are like beacons that help us guide the "board." A second metaphor I have kind of created is that of a stormy sea where we are often battered about this way and that by the mind. Values are like a shining lighthouse in the distance which keeps us on track, and helps us reorient, when we so often lose our direction...
CHOICE Who chooses (if not mind/ observer-self)? [cont'd] METAPHOR Chessboard/ Bus - choice of direction [cont'd] Values - beacons in stormy sea [cont'd] **VALUES** **Directions, as [4-29-03]** Steve Hayes	Of course, in a clinical context all of this is "coach talk" not "reporter talk" (or for that matter "scientist talk") but sometimes consistency is helpful even in that context. I like ALM's metaphors [above]. Values are like beacons ... it is just that we choose the beacons. If the chessboard can move in any direction, we are speaking of the direction itself. One very cool thing about direction is that it is obviously and undeniably true that once you are headed in a direction, you are headed in that direction. Direction enables the unfolding of a coherent process of events, and there will even be outcomes in that direction ... but no matter how far you go in a direction, there is still more direction to go. The end result (being headed in a direction) was there from the very first moment to the very last. The happy news in that is that you don't have to wait for life to start. "First you win, then you play." Hard to accept that, of course, since we constantly use conditionality to beat ourselves into shape ("you'll be OK when ..."). Someone (Pat Bach?) mentioned in an earlier post that in one sense "I" am everything and that is surely the case. "I am the board" is helpful not because it is literally true, but because it avoids attachment (literal fusion) with anything (since the board level is not definable as a thing ...). It is a pragmatic, not a literal, move. In line with Pat's point, however, it is worth noting that it is the board *and* all the pieces that move in a direction.

CONTEXT
 	
Control of behavior - antecedent vs. consequence [4-1-04]
Kelly Wilson
	Matthew Smout wrote:
	
	    I've noticed that you often give very clear responses to peoples' questions by distinguishing between behaviour controlled by antecedents vs. consequences. This makes good sense to me. If I've understood you correctly, identifying behaviour as antecedent-controlled suggests exposure-like interventions will more than likely be helpful, whereas consequence-controlled behaviour suggests presumably interventions where the therapist might "shape" the person's behaviour through words and actions might be better.
	
	    However, ACT articles have tended not to use the A & C terms (although I assume they contribute to the "context" of the behaviour). I feel like maybe there's a black hole here in my education, or maybe it's an obvious point that only I have failed to appreciate the significance of, but I don't really recall anyone else placing much emphasis on drawing the distinction between whether the main influence over behaviour (in a given case) is antecedent or consequential. What kinds of work are you drawing on when you talk about this - basic lab (rat/other animal) research, or particular clinical writers that might have escaped my attention?
	
	Hmmmm. Well, the work is behavior analytic. And, you are absolutely correct, antecedents and consequences and a history thereof, are ways of speaking about context. I can think of a couple reasons that it isn't spoken of a lot in terms of antecedents and consequences. First, I suppose, is that the underlying basic behavior analysis is assumed. The second reason, speaking at depth in technical behavior analytic terms leaves a lot of clinically trained folks out of conversation because they do not have much background in BA. Also, we fought so hard to raise the RFT type issues above the fray among behavior analysts--we focused on what RFT added, and perhaps we stopped talking as much about the basic BA process issues--though never let them go. If you look at the things that are written specifically for behavior analytic audiences, you will see more of it.
	
	I have had a ton of training in BA and just plain think in those terms--a sort of nuanced contextual behavioral perspective--I guess. In terms of antecedent and consequential stimulus control--what I mean by that is that it is useful to think about behavior in terms of the relative contribution made by antecedent and

consequential control. We can think of this in terms of the operant and respondent distinction.

Operants, of course, require careful attention to *both* antecedent and consequential stimulus control. When consequential control is an issue, we will have to think about two kinds of antecedent control: both operations that establish discriminative control (events that "signal" the availability of a consequence) and also operations that will make a consequence effective (establishing operations).

Respondents, by contrast, are relatively insensitive to consequential stimulus control. These are typically categories of responding built upon evolutionary imperatives--orienting to a novel sound in the environment, salivating in the presence of food, cringing when struck, etc. Classical conditioning processes are of primary interest. However, respondent functions may be acquired through relational conditioning processes also.

Now some folks teach the operant/respondent distinction as if respondents and operants are really two distinct kinds of behavior, but the distinction I am making is not ontological it is pragmatic. In fact, there is only one organism. It does not have a little kit bag of this and that kind of responses. Many respondents can be brought under operant control--skin temperature for example, crying *very* quickly. And you can't find an operant where there aren't aspects of the behavior that have respondent qualities. For example, look at my chapter with J.T. Blackledge in Mike Dougher's edited Context Press book (download chap from my web page--better still, buy the book). It refers to a pigeon example. Pigeons that are pecking a key in an operant chamber for food reinforcers peck a little differently than they peck for water. When they peck for food, their pecks look more like eating movements; for water, like drinking movements. In the grossest sense, both pecks are under consequential control, but the minutia of the form of those pecks is under strong antecedent control. The key has become classically conditioned to either the food or water (because interaction with it immediately precedes the consequence). Having those psychological functions, the bird responds to the key in some respects as it would respond to the food/water. You could attempt to shape the eating peck for water reinforcers, but my suspicion is that (1) it would be tough, and (2) you would see persistent drift back to the drinking pecks. (see early work on the misbehavior of organisms--Breland and Breland, 1961). If you want to manage pecking, pay attention to the operant contingency. If you are concerned with the precise form of the pecks, you need to pay attention to the respondent contingency.

As you suggest in your email--when consequential control is central, attention to the operant contingencies is best--establishing operations, discriminative control, and operant procedures, like shaping and fading. (Of course, all of these can be made psychologically present through direct acting or verbally established psychological functions.) For the therapist, shape behavior and fade stimulus control to the naturally occurring stimuli in the person's environment.

When strong antecedent control is at stake, we need to attend to the respondent contingencies. Here exposure and defusion strategies will be important.

Note however, that pretty much any exposure/defusion procedure will contain operant components (shaping mindful attending to disturbing bodily sensations or thoughts, for example). The reverse is also true. Any behavior that is shaped by the therapist will also have important respondent components. So, for example, if you are shaping social skills though social interactions with an underskilled client, they will feel anxious during the exercise. We are likely to see some conditioned suppression (see Wilson and Murrell, in press). This anxiety and conditioned suppression are under antecedent control--hence, defusion/exposure should be part of the intervention too.

As to things to read. Gosh, I would say that Charlie Catania's *Learning*, 4th edition (Prentice Hall) had a big influence on my thinking. I read a million things though--so who knows, talk about complexly determined behavior. Not to say I agree with everything in the book at all. For example, I don't use it beyond chapter 12. But still, I learned from it and continue to use it in my teaching. Likewise Skinner. Lots to disagree with, but that is the most central historical antecedent of the intellectual line. I imagine also that I was very, very influenced by Linda Hayes (see also Linda Parrot). I took more classes from Linda in grad school than anyone else. She put me in front of J. R. Kantor. Linda is hard, but perhaps the most brilliant and intellectually honest person I ever met. Read Linda and be edified. I suppose I am a sort of Skinner/Kantor hybrid, polished by the Hayes' in Reno, and by my own oddly converging history.

Lord, that was long, and complicated I suppose. I tell the undergrads here at the University of Mississippi that if they want a simple learning course, they should take it from someone else. These processes mix together for me, and I teach them that way. It's harder, more complex, but seems more sensitive to the subject matter. I think of behavior as an ongoing, evolving stream in dynamic interaction with the environment. This operant/respondent piece is a critical part of that perspective.

CONTEXT **Meaning of [2-21-04]** Nico van der Meijden	I've read the ACT book thoroughly and although I believe I understand the theory fairly well, I still find it difficult to get a grip on the concept of 'context' as used in the book. It has some kind of elusive quality to it. I'll just write down how I understand it, perhaps someone is willing to comment... Probably it is not as complicated as I think....

I understand that for a behaviourist the context of behaviour of a person is the combination of his/her learning history and the current situation - the past made present by the current situation (and of course language enables us also to construct a future in the present, based on our past experiences). In operant conditioning a reinforcer strengthens the link between a context (Sd) and an operant, so the chance a person emits the reinforced behavior in the future, given the context, increases. In evolutionary theory a (changing) environment selects those animals of a certain species which have characteristics (genes) that favour survival and reproduction in that specific environment. The pragmatic goal of a behaviour analyst is the prediction and influence of behavior. For influence to be possible, the context has to be functionally linked to, but outside behavior itself. Context is the independent variable. Dependent on the behavior you want to influence (your goals) an infinite amount of possible contexts is conceivable, with all kinds of abstraction levels. A Marxist may, e.g., talk of 'a context of unequal distribution of wealth and means of production'; a fashion designer may have to deal with 'a context in which men wear trousers but no dresses,' a priest with 'a context of increasing secularisation,' et cetera. A context can be in the outer environment, but also inside the skin (e.g., 'the context of the observing you,' 'the context of acceptance').

Suppose I'm reminiscing about an old high school love (to use an ACT metaphor) and I compare this old love with my current relationship, which changes the stimulus functions of both. When I fuse with this relational frame of comparison ('it's how reality is') is this relational frame a context, is it behaviour or is it a behaviour in a context of literality?

In the 'Acceptance Process Measure' (downloadable from the ACT web site, I can recommend it...), Khorakiwala, Hayes & Wilson write (page 4): "... one might notice a feeling of anger simply as a feeling one is having. This is taking the observer perspective. Conversely, one might be dealing with the stupid things that people do (and that "makes you angry"). In this case anger is a context for looking at the world and interpreting it -- a kind of filter through which the person is looking."

Is anger in this example a context or a behaviour or again a behaviour in a context of literality?

As I understand it from the book, thoughts, emotions et cetera are behaviours and the context (that which is linked to, but is outside behavior itself) is the context of fusion or literality versus the "context of the observer you" (these contexts are of a very abstract nature). Therapy is about changing context in order to make fusion with language less dominant and the contingencies of current situations more dominant.

When, in the above example, fusion with the relational frame of comparison damages my relationship, I can become aware as an observer of the thought and enjoy my relationship more....

CONTEXT Meaning of [cont'd] Steve Hayes	"Context" is a broad philosophical term. Technical behavioral analyses (or the technical analyses from any true contextualistic theory, from Marxism to feminist psychology) will have specific terms for various contextual events (e.g., "discriminative stimuli," "conditioned reinforcers," ... if you are an RFTer things like "verbal discriminative stimuli"). I think the question can be addressed in a more philosophical way and it actually begins to disappear as an issue once you get technical and specific so philosophy first. Part of the problem is that context is not a thing … it is a function … so what is context in one moment is not context in the next. Pepper's writing about contextualism is very helpful on this point. As an example: "the analysis of an event consists in the exhibition of its texture, and the exhibition of its texture is the discrimination of its strands, and the full discrimination of its strands is the exhibition of other textures . . . and so on from event to event as long as we wish to go, which would be forever or until we got tired" (Pepper, 1942, p. 249). The other part comes not from contextualism per se but from functional contextualism ... if you put the "prediction and influence as a goal implies manipulability" filter on analysis, only certain contextual events are relevant to behavior change. Where this comes together is in the role of behavioral events as context. Behavioral events are part of the current historical and situational context (e.g., they are part of our learning history, etc.) but as soon as you look at a contextual behavioral event, it has functions that are dependent upon other contextual events. Consider a response chain: a rat picks up a ball, carries it up a ramp, puts it down, presses a bar to open a hole, and drops the ball in the hole. Question: is carrying the ball up the ramp context for later dropping the ball in the hole? In one sense, sure. It is part of that behavioral stream. But if I am interested in getting a rat to pick up a ball, carry it up a ramp, put it down, press a bar to open a hole, and drop the ball in the hole, that answer will be of little use -- I will need to understand the contingencies used to get the rat to pick up a ball, and the contingencies involved in getting a rat to carry a picked-up ball up a ramp, and the contingencies involved in getting a rat to put down a ball once at the top of a ramp, and the contingencies involved in getting a rat to press a bar to open a hole, and the contingencies involved in getting a rat to drop a ball in the hole that opens up. Skinner struggled with this too. In his response to the reviews of his canonical papers in that special issue of

Behavioral and Brain Sciences, he says something like "it is true that in one sense behaviors are controlling variables over other behaviors, but they are not originating causes." Something like that. [I still don't have a clear electronic copy of the 1986 "mentalism, behavior-behavior relations" paper (Hayes & Brownstein). I'll get one done and get it posted ... because even though it is an old dog I think it is the most elaborated version of this argument.] I personally avoid all behavioral "causes" whether the behavior involved is public or private (so, for example, thoughts do not cause overt behavior; and throwing a football well does not cause good baseball pitching) because while ontologically there *are* no "causes," there is a utility to causal talk ... and I'd rather reserve the term for variables that have the utility (prediction and influence) I'm looking for. If forced into a corner, I might say something like "a controlling behavioral event that is part of an overall causal relation."

So, let's bring that to

> "... one might notice a feeling of anger simply as a feeling one is having. This is taking the observer perspective. Conversely, one might be dealing with the stupid things that people do (and that "makes you angry"). In this case anger is a context for looking at the world and interpreting it -- a kind of filter through which the person is looking." Is anger in this example a context or a behaviour or again a behaviour in a context of literality?

The entire behavioral stream is part of one's history and therefore part of context, but if you take that to be the whole story, you quickly remember that we could go "from event to event as long as we wish to go, which would be forever or until we got tired" (Pepper, 1942, p. 249). In essence, if we keep pushing the entire universe is context for everything: "The quality of blowing your nose is just as cosmic and ultimate as Newton's writing down his gravitational formula." (Pepper, 1942, p. 251). Skinner saw this too, and had the pragmatic solution to it: "It is true that we could trace human behavior not only to the physical conditions which shape and maintain it but also to the causes of those conditions and the causes of those causes, almost ad infinitum" but we need take analysis only to the point at which "effective action can be taken" (Skinner, 1974, p. 210).

In the context of literality, emotional control, and reason-giving, anger has a function. In the context of defusion and acceptance, anger has a different function. This is one of the key differences between ACT and the CBT mainstream. The message of ACT is that, yes, thoughts and feelings are critically important, but no, they are not causal. At most, they are "a controlling behavioral event that is part of an overall causal relation." It is up to us as therapists to change the contexts that support unhelpful causal relations. In the verbal side of things, we do that by manipulating Crel and Cfunc events.

I think you are sensitive to this issue when you say:

> Suppose I'm reminiscing about an old high school love (to use an ACT metaphor) and I compare this old love with my current relationship, which changes the stimulus functions of both. When I fuse with this relational frame of comparison ('it's how reality is') is this relational frame a context, is it behaviour or is it a behaviour in a context of literality?

Framing events relationally has huge impacts. Your example is a good one ... just a comparative thought like that can turn a current lover into an ogre or a queen. The relational act is part of the context in which that effect occurs, but as soon as we start to analyse this effect, the relational act will itself be a historically and currently situated act. If we stop with the act itself we are back to the old dead end of "thoughts cause overt behaviour." It is a "dead end" in the sense that there now is a gap between so-called causes and actions the therapist needs to take. The ACT style of analysis is "in a context thoughts occur and in a context thoughts relate to overt behavior" ... and that whole stream is causal if it can be shown to be so with experimental analysis (i.e., through direct alteration of manipulable events)."

So I would look for the events that gave rise to a comparative frame, for contexts of literality (etc.) that gave rise to a function for that action.

If you do all that, the answer to the question:

> When I fuse with this relational frame of comparison ('it's how reality is') is this relational frame a context, is it behaviour or is it a behaviour in a context of literality?

will be "yes" -- it is all of those but then as you begin to do more with that answer, certain aspects of that answer will be more useful than others.

As mentioned earlier, this whole issue "actually begins to disappear as an issue once you get technical and specific." In order to see the larger set of issues it helped not to go there first for that exact reason. But let's do that now. A relational frame of comparison, by definition, is regulated by Crel events. Those events are not the framing itself. So

> When I fuse with this relational frame of comparison ('it's how reality is') is this relational frame a context,

The answer is "sure" but it occurred within a context. What were the Crel events? Speaking loosely why did the old flame "come to mind" and why was a comparison made? And you speak of "fusion" with this action of relating ... "fusion" is a Cfunc issue. What were the Cfunc events? Speaking loosely, why were the results of the comparison taken to "be how reality is"?

"Context" is not a technical term in behavior analysis, RFT, or ACT. It is a broad, philosophical, orienting term that encompasses many specific technical terms. The confusion won't show up at that level because technical contextual terms are manipulable events in behavior analysis, RFT, or ACT. But when you apply these concepts clinically, you have to take note of the other side of the behavioral coin because the stimulus side of things only exists functionally when there is a responding side of things and vice versa ... and what we tend to see clinically first is streams of action.

That's how it seems from here anyway.

CONTEXT **Meaning of [3-19-04]** ACT Listserv Member	Everdien Tromp wrote: It seems to be that the term context is essential for understanding ACT, but I miss a clear description of what context means in an ACT context. Is context everything around us? Or even everything around us, including our inner milieu? Or is it everything around us that is relevant and/or known to us? Or is it everything around us that influences our behavior, like for instance retrieval cues? Is context as broad as our 'knowing what others know' or Theory of Mind? Are pliance, rules, or tracks context? Context is very important in ACT, and depending on with whom you are speaking, it can be all of the things you mentioned. For me context is our social/reinforcement history paired with current stimuli (both environmental and internal) that influence how we behave and how we interpret events/behavior/cognitions. Context is like parameters of a computer program - if certain conditions are met by the presence of or absence of certain variables/stimuli, then action X is done. Context defines the significance of actions/events/stimuli, etc. Topographically similar behavior (commonly called the same, though they are not), can have multiple 'meanings' or hold more or less significance not only to different people, but also to the same person depending on the context in which it occurs. Movies, books, TV, etc. are all good examples of how behavior takes on different meaning in different contexts. Writers develop characters and put them in different contexts and have actions take place. Take for example a man kissing another man - if you were watching "La Cage aux Folles" it would mean something different than if you were watching say "The Godfather." The latter would mean death, the former love. Context is more complex than that; it is also important to remember the function of the behavior in the context (hence functional contextualism). For now it is fine to just keep in mind that no behavior happens independently of setting and history....
CONTEXT **Social/ verbal [3-5-04]** Steve Hayes	Francis De Groot wrote: ... when defining the social/verbal context of behavior, you [Leslie Telfer] include "everything we tell ourselves, as well, about how things are and how they work." This means our own thinking. So our own thinking is the context of our own thinking? Next you write that this social/verbal context can influence overt behavior. This means our own thinking can influence our overt behavior, and thus can be used to change our behavior, which is denied further on in the book (p.22-23). I think my reasoning might be wrong, but I don't know what I'm missing. I think of the social / verbal context as the contingencies maintained by a language community that gives language events functions. Things like contexts of literality, emotional control, reason-giving, say-do correspondence and the like. Think not so much of *what* people think as of what you have to do to, say, children to get them to respond in particular ways based on what they think. You do things. Things like: "why did you do that Johnny?" "There's your Daddy" "Tell me where it hurts" "Stop crying or I will give you something to cry about" etc. etc. In ACT we establish a therapeutic relationship: which is a mini social / verbal community. But the rules of the language game (the social / verbal context) have changed. Client: "I'm mad" Therapist: "Is that OK?" Client: "I'm bad" Therapist: "Cool. Let's say that over and over again fast" Client: "This is why I can't" Therapist: "Very good. Thank your mind for that thought" etc. etc.

DEFINITION/ INTERPRETATION **Acceptance; cognitive defusion (RFT) [10-8-02]** Dermot Barnes-Holmes	Yvonne and I were just thinking about RFT-type definitions of acceptance and cognitive defusion. We figured the following. Acceptance occurs when direct and derived aversive eliciting functions produce direct and derived operant approach responses rather than avoidance responses. In this sense, Crel control remains unchanged but Cfunc control does not. For example, a client who finds young attractive women "dangerous" or "threatening," because he was previously rejected by such a woman, may still find attractive women aversive but deliberately NOT avoid contact with them or behave in a hostile way towards them. Of course, such acceptance moves may eventually lead to a transformation of the eliciting functions, but then this would not involve acceptance because the eliciting functions are no longer aversive. Cognitive defusion involves changing entailment functions. In the Milk, milk, milk exercise, for example, the entailed relations between the word milk and those events typically associated with the word are attenuated (e.g., the word starts to sound like a duck quacking). Having attenuated "harmless" eliciting functions, attenuating entailment functions (as a response class) may transfer via an analogical network to more threatening eliciting functions. In the example above, for instance, the young man might see the thought "Any girl that is attractive must be dangerous" as just more words that show up for him in a possibly intimate situation. In this sense, cognitive defusion provides a set of often neutral exemplars that facilitate acceptance of threatening psychological events. The above is just our first stab at these issues. Any comments etc. welcome.
DEFINITION/ INTERPRETATION **Confidence [7-30-03]** Steve Hayes	Joseph Ciarrochi wrote: Check out these ACT-inconsistent inspirational quotes. It seems like the popular culture works directly against ACT-type principles (e.g., unhooking thoughts/feelings from behavior): "Self-confidence is the first requisite to great undertakings." -- Samuel Johnson "With confidence, you can reach truly amazing heights; without confidence, even the simplest accomplishments are beyond your grasp." -- Jim Loehr "Experience tells you what to do; confidence allows you to do it." -- Stan Smith There is an easy way to make all of these ACT consistent: treat them as descriptions of actions rather than descriptions primarily of feelings. Confidence means, etymologically, "with fidelity" or "with faith." Confidence the action is to be true to yourself. Feeling what you feel and doing what needs to be done (e.g., acceptance and valued action) etc. is an extremely confident action. If you are willing to feel a lack of confidence and behave effectively anyway, you are DOING confidence. That action sometimes produces confident feelings. But non-confident action (e.g., denying or covering up non-confident feelings) never does because it is a non-confident action. Replace the word "confidence" in the quotes [above] with "being true to yourself" (which is what confidence *is*) and they are great ACT quotes.
DEFINITION/ INTERPRETATION **Confidence; comfort [12-11-03]** Steve Hayes	Ed Zahra wrote: [I am a little confused as] to the derivation of the word CONFIDENCE in terms of CON (meaning "with") and FI (meaning "fidelity"). My understanding of CON, however, is that it means "against" rather than "with" (as in pro vs. con). The prefix "con" doesn't mean against. It is a form of the Latin "com" (in classic Latin, the word "cum" I believe). It means "together or together with" (from which English later generated the prefix "co") and also "altogether" thus "completely" or "intensive." In the words confidence and comfort, two versions of the same prefix are used. They mean "with faith" (combined with the Latin fides) and "with strength" (combined with the Latin fortis). Good ACT messages in there. Act with self-fidelity or faith; and get with your strength. That's what ACT is all about. Confidence and comfort (properly understood as actions, not emotional results ... though these actions often *eventually* produce emotional results of that kind ... but as usual if that is the goal then you aren't doing the actions).
DEFINITION/ INTERPRETATION **Self, ACT concepts of [3-8-04]** Steve Hayes	Self as Context: The No-thing self. Self as "here now." Self as perspective. Transcendent self. The context of consciousness per se. Side effect of deictic frames according to RFT. Self as process: The continuous processes of descriptive awareness of each moment. Now I feel this; now I see that. Referential, but continuously in the present. Conceptualized self:

	The verbally constructed self. Self as object. Self as content. Evaluative. Temporal. Reasoned. Literal. "I am a person who ..."
DEFINITION/ INTERPRETATION **Self, ACT concepts of [12-3-04]** Steve Hayes	Russ Harris wrote: Could someone please clarify this for me. As I understand it, self-as-process is the ongoing self-awareness of what we are experiencing in the present moment. Yet when I've seen or heard written statements representing self-as-process, they all revolve around feeling and sensing in the present moment (e.g., I am feeling sad; I am cold), and they don't seem to include awareness of doing (e.g., I am breathing, I am typing). Does self-as-process include awareness of what we are doing in the present moment (e.g., I am sitting; I am looking at the computer screen)? Or is it more like "I am feeling myself sitting; I am sensing myself looking"? (Or is there no distinction, given that we only know what we are doing through feeling or sensing it?) The distinctions do not seem to be important to the concept. Self as process involves observing and describing what is present as a continuous process of verbal knowing. That includes everything. It could include feeling, thinking, other forms of action, and even "external events" since, by definition, if they are known they are also psychological events (e.g., the known chair is not merely the chair as an object - we are speaking of the chair as a locus of behavioral functions). Ontologically we are not making "feeling - thinking - doing" distinctions but then ACT is part of a philosophical system that is aontological to begin with. The "known / not known" distinction within psychology is worth making but it can be confusing. To know something verbally versus knowing it purely non-verbally involves different functional variables and sometimes folks are speaking of that. Truly unknown events (i.e., neither know how nor know that; neither *scire* nor *gnoscere* to back up to the Latin roots) are not psychological events at all and sometimes folks are speaking of that when they use the broader concept of "contact with the present moment" - meaning both verbal and non-verbal contact [but that more general term sometimes seems to be used to mean the same thing as "self-as-process" or "ongoing self-awareness"]. A bit confusing, that.
DEFINITION/ INTERPRETATION Self, ACT concepts of [cont'd] John McNeill	I would consider sensing, perceiving, feeling, thinking, motor responding, and so on as discriminated features of one whole psychological event - that is, as co-dependent and co-arising features of one continuous act of 'doing.' Usually we are only aware of a truncated portion of the field of psychological experience and likely only that limited portion is discriminated and available for verbal articulation. As further elaboration: In each of your examples, your language indicates an 'I' doing something 'other' designation, and in doing so the logocentric dualist trap is sprung. The act of speaking from a Indo-European language context with its emphasis on noun-verb distinctions makes it difficult to transcend the I/Other distinction. Moreover, logocentrism [and its realist ontology] dupes us into believing that the words used for describing our experience are literally one and the same. Ultimately, human beings are incapable of producing a pure sense datum sentence, thus the language about experience always falls short of the real thing. That's one reason why structuralist introspectism failed. So, while words can be put to discriminated features of our ongoing experience [self-discriminated process: languaging about one's ongoing sensing, feeling, thinking, etc.], they are not on literally equal footing, and thus we should not confuse one for the other [e.g., taking consensus reality for experiential reality] - a kind of confusing the 'map' for the 'territory' metaphor. A quote by D. T. Suzuki is instructive in this regard: "The contradiction so puzzling to the ordinary way of thinking comes from the fact that we have to use language to communicate our inner experience, which in its very nature transcends linguistics."
DEFINITION/ INTERPRETATION Self, ACT concepts of [cont'd] ACT Listserv Member	Self as process seems to be a further discrimination of perspective taking as a frame of coordination. We learn through multiple exemplar training from our verbal community to discriminate behavior that is performed by the body we occupy, and to label that as me or self. This self is verbal and arbitrary - for evidence of that work with autism diagnosed children who do not have a verbal concept of me, self, you, etc. This ability to discriminate between me and not me, functions primarily as a method of communication - it helps us answer questions such as "Who did this?", and "Did you do that?"; ultimately this self comes to act in equivalence relations with not only what happens externally, but as tact for covert operants like thinking, feeling, sensing, etc. Self as context focuses on seeing the "me" as an behaving entity, and elevating the awareness of those behavior both overt and covert. It is analogous to seeing a car as not only an object/machine that we can operate on in complex behavioral patterns to move our bodies, objects and others from one location to another, but also focussing on the electrical, chemical, mechanical, etc. processes that are occurring in a coordinated manner to allow this to happen on a moment to moment basis. In human terms, if you are having a conversation with another person, that is the overt behavior of self; the thoughts that occur prior to or simultaneously with the verbal behavior of speaking and listening are covert;

	then there is the self as process. The self that would involve recognizing on a moment to moment basis, that you are constantly thinking, feeling, evaluating and how that affects your conversation (verbal and nonverbal content, etc.). In other words, recognizing there is a self and its behavior as it happens.
DEFINITION/ INTERPRETATION Self, ACT concepts of [cont'd] Steve Hayes	ACT Listserv Member wrote: ... I ask, "Can you ever be not me/I/Self?" We are always self, so ultimately self as context and/or process are perspectives/frames of reference. They are ways to help someone see thoughts as events/behavior that only have power due to the function and nature of language; cognitions are behavior, but often are treated as extant entities that can, and for some, do act in ways that interfere with living a full valuable life. ACT has come across some techniques borrowed from the eastern religions/philosophies that help people by helping them look at their feelings/thoughts and evaluations from this other perspective. Religious references aside, they don't ever remove self/I/me from the picture; they aren't transcendentalist, more like looking at all of behavior from the perspective of the observer, like watching the cognitions and overt behavior on TV. They aren't literally transcendentalist. The argument would be that the perspective of "I / here / now" established by deictic frames, when developed and amplified and noted, is limitless from the point of view of the person engaging in these actions. "Transcendent" or "spiritual" (if not reified) is a reasonable way to speak of the "no - thing" (or every - thing) quality of such an "event" (that is not experienced as an "event" ... that is what we mean by boundless). Engaging in other actions in the context of this seemingly boundless action alters the quality of those actions in useful ways. Self as context is another one of those concepts in ACT / RFT that seems to work scientifically; and seems to work clinically; and trying to make them both at the same time seems not to work. It's like talking ABOUT the now, while being IN the now. Both work on their own turf, yet taking one to *be* the other doesn't work. In the note [above] the voice / context / language game shifts subtly sentence to sentence ... which is fine. It's just worth noting what game is being played in a given moment.
DEFINITION/ INTERPRETATION Self, ACT concepts of [cont'd] Steve Hayes **WORDS** **"Get in the way"** [12-6-04] Steve Hayes	... Note that the "me/I/Self perspective" being talked about in [the Zen] tradition is NOT the "I / here / now" perspective taking being talked about in ACT/ RFT under the rubric "self-as-context." The "me/I/Self perspective" being talked about is more like the conceptualized self. Self-as-context is more like "no thing self," or "big mind," or "one mind" you hear being talked about in other ways. … These language similarities cause confusion and I just wanted to acknowledge that since the words are so similar but their meanings are so different. The way ACT folks talk about "self" sometimes creates a barrier for trained Buddhists - but I've never yet had anyone trained in that tradition look at it really closely who had an issue with it (even Zen masters have done so, so I'm beginning to think there is no issue). Usually the issue if there is one is more in the area of community; practice; and things like that -- frankly some of the things are just things spiritual and religious traditions can do more so than therapy traditions. Sigh. Sometimes these words seem to just get in the way. When I was a sophomore in college at Loyola-Marymount (did I ever tell this story?) I wrote an anguished message to my therapist at the time (Dr. Carlo Weber - good guy) which consisted of a page, single spaced that said "Words, words, words, words, words, words, words, words, words, words, words, words, words, words, words, words, words, words, words" and so on for the entire page. This was before computers - it took a bit to produce such a document. I think the last line was "line after line of mother f------g words." Like I said, I was really in anguish about the issue so perhaps my rude language can be seen in that light. The next page just had one sentence on it. It said something like this: "between the fourth and the fifth word on the fifth line two days passed."
DEFINITION/ INTERPRETATION **Strange loop** [4-7-03] Steve Hayes	Dermot Barnes-Holmes wrote: I think the concept of "strange loop," as used in the ACT book, is metaphorical, not technical (e.g., when first used, it appears in inverted commas). In fact, a technical analysis of strange loops and the like is required. I use the term "strange loops" clinically in ACT ... I say it directly to clients. It's not a technical term in those circumstances. I use it to refer to inherently paradoxical (Dan Wegner calls them "ironic") rule-based processes (times when following a rule produces less of what the literal content of the rule specifies as the outcome of the rule). Clients don't identify them from the rule-based process, however. What they notice is

that they are deliberately trying to produce an outcome and the more they try the less that outcome manifests itself.

The term "strange loop" is used just to remind clients to look for fusion with a rule in these circumstances, and to consider using other skills (usually defusion, acceptance, valued action, etc.) instead of more effort spent following the rule, different and more creative means of following the rule, better ways of following the rule, etc. Start from the end and work backwards. If you are ending up where you specifically intended not to be, suspect a strange loop and look for fusion with an unhelpful / unworkable assumption, agenda, plan, means, strategy etc. (often implicit).

In terms of a technical account, strange loops contain a process (when treated literally) that functionally contradicts the literal outcome. "Relax or else awful things will happen" contains an eliciting function that transfers through a relational network (the reaction to imminent awful things) that is not relaxing. "Be spontaneous!" places a rule in a regulatory position over a behavioral property that cannot be rule-governed. "Stop being so afraid -- You need to try to be more confident" links a non-confident action to a fused negative self-judgment ... nominally in order to produce positive feeling states, whereas both of these processes (non-confident actions; fused negative self-judgments) directly produce negative feeling states. Etc. etc. In general, strange loops are cases in which the behavioral process at issue is not readily or helpfully rule-governed in the first place.

FUNCTIONAL CONTEXTUALISM

Application to personal goals [3-16-04]

Patty Bach

I might agree that

"aiming to change private events such as thoughts, images, and sensations does not, necessarily, mean one is something other than a functional contextualist." [Hank Robb]

However, the unit of analysis in functional contextualism is the act in context, and "aiming to change private events" is not an act in context. A functional contextualist might ask, "in what contexts is changing private events useful?", and "does changing private events work?"

Also, the goals of functional contextualism are the prediction and influence of events. In a functional contextual account one cannot directly manipulate behavior, one can only manipulate context. To use the example of a flying phobia, if the goal is to reduce anxiety, then phobic avoidance is successful working.

If the goal is to feel less anxiety in the context of flying then taking Xanax, or drinking three martinis before flying might also be considered successful working.

When the context is widened from the narrow context of flying, phobic avoidance, taking Xanax, and drinking martinis may not be so successful.

The values work in ACT and the question "what's that in the service of?" link it to functional contextualism. And where ACT differs from many other treatment approaches is that it targets the context. Q - "What do you want your life to be about?" A - "less anxiety." If less anxiety is the goal - and the goal need not be justified in functional contextualism - then the client's phobic avoidance is an ideal solution.

"I have to feel comfortable when I fly" suggests an agenda where discomfort is bad and should be avoided. As a goal, does that agenda work? Does it operate only with respect to flying, or is it present in other contexts as well? And is there evidence that techniques to change private events work?

In what contexts is changing private events a 'valued outcome'? One might want to feel less anxious, and one might dislike feeling anxious. One might use relaxation or other strategies to reduce situational or baseline anxiety in some specific contexts, and as a valued outcome or goal does anxiety reduction as an end in itself increase or decrease behavioral flexibility overall or in other or larger contexts? (Of course, this presumes that 'increased behavioral flexibility' is associated with successful working, and since decreased behavioral flexibility is a defining characteristic or outcome of anxiety disorders, addictions and other compulsive behaviors, and perhaps eating, sexual and other clinical disorders, I'm comfortable suggesting that decreased behavioral flexibility is not likely to be associated with successful working for most persons.)

ACT is not sadistic; the goal is not to feel uncomfortable. One doesn't usually get on an airplane in the service of feeling anxious. One gets on a plane in the service of travel, recreation, work, education, etc. If the goal of flying were 'comfort,' no one would fly, not necessarily to avoid anxiety, but also to avoid standing in long lines, hanging out in airports, sitting for hours in a cramped seat, etc. Sure, maximize comfort - and flying isn't primarily about comfort, it's about getting somewhere. And possibly, though not guaranteed, the most effective way to reduce discomfort while flying over the long term is repeated exposure to flying, not in the service of decreasing discomfort, and in the service of attaining other valued outcomes.

"Successful working" is always defined in context. ACT, in a sense, facilitates the client becoming a functional contextualist.

(And while I would doubt that many persons do much of anything 'in the service of feeling anxious,' I would wager that "having the experience of being alive" is often experienced in contexts where anxiety

	might also show up, and that contexts where anxiety is not likely to ever be present, such as watching television alone or doing laundry, are not strongly associated with 'feeling alive.' Maybe this is a, 'can you have your cake and eat it too?' question ... are negatively evaluated private events less 'vital' than positively evaluated private events? [And if so, in what contexts?])
FUNCTIONAL CONTEXTUALISM Cause - pragmatic cf. literal meaning **CAUSE** Contextualistic view - pragmatic cf. literal meaning **THERAPIST** "Don't believe a word I'm saying" [12-5-02] Steve Hayes	... Pragmatism is integrated into the ACT / RFT work and I frequently realize that the sticking points people encounter have philosophical roots having to do with the odd qualities of pragmatism. At the AABT ACT workshop a number of folks were stumbling over "don't believe a word I'm saying" for example, but the underlying issue appeared to have much to do with the idea that the truth of a statement is to be found in the functions it serves.... [Ata Ghaderi (personal communication) wrote:] It feels quite strange and interesting when you know things experientially (or you think you know, because the report is verbal), and cannot clearly express them in language. It's a hell to use language to present a clear description of something that is beyond language.... Given my background in mechanistic behaviorism, I am having serious problems in defining CAUSE of behavior in relation to verbal rules. Could we say that behaviors are caused by their consequences given the context in which they occur (i.e., the learning history, the specific antecedents and establishing operations connected to that specific behavior in that context, and expected consequences)? Some additional reading will help. The Context Press books on *Varieties of Scientific Contextualism* and *Investigations in Behavioral Epistemology* will be useful. Then mentally put the word "cause" in quotes every time you use it. That will help too. More substantively - in a contextualistic view nothing literally causes anything, because if there is literal cause then there truly are parts, not just constructed parts. WE divide up the world - it is not already divided. For example, you might say "this ball sits apart from that one." Really? The heat in ball one is part of the other. The gravity in one envelopes the other. Where does the "ball" precisely begin and end? Contextualism assumes a real, one world. But the divisions are ones we impose. That does not mean divisions are arbitrary, because some divisions work better than others - not for reality (it was doing quite well before we started to divide it) but for us in interacting in and with the one world. The language of CAUSE is pragmatic. Skinner says it this way: the law of gravity is not why objects fall. The law of gravity allows scientists to interact successfully with the world. As far as my own writings on the issue, the following chapter is useful: Hayes, S. C. (1997). Behavioral epistemology includes nonverbal knowing. In L. J. Hayes & P. M. Ghezzi (Eds.). *Investigations in behavioral epistemology* (pp. 35-43). Reno, NV: Context Press. [AG] If we can agree on the above and take the specific properties of the verbal behavior into account (i.e., bidirectionality, stimulus equivalence, etc.), then it should be okay to put verbal behaviors (verbal rules, as stimulus or consequence, etc.) in different parts of operant/ instrumental chains of behaviors, where they can have antecedental, consequential or motivational properties, and thus contribute to the contingencies of the behavior we are studying. In lay terms they can contribute to CAUSE behaviors. Is it right? Yep. Just remember that this is only a useful way of speaking. [AG] Defusion and acceptance strategies in ACT are aimed at changing the context of literality, emotional control etc. We want to make our clients understand (experientially, not verbally: don't believe a word of what I'm saying) that they are having different thoughts and emotions, and that they are not their thoughts or emotions. We want to help them (and ourselves) create some distance/ space and we use self as context in this endeavor. We deal with reason giving so we stop presenting our thoughts and emotions as causes of our behavior. Does this mean that we, in our analysis, are giving verbal rules causal properties? The rules about how to do therapy might be said to have causal properties for us as therapists, but that is within a scientific context that establishes these functions. Within a functional contextual system verbal rules about causes are those that directly lead to the prediction and influence of behavior with precision, scope, and depth. Individuals are influenced by the literal content of rules and we might say that this is a "cause" but until we include the in-principle manipulable context, that statement must be incomplete since no behavior-behavior relation can directly lead to the prediction and influence of behavior with precision, scope, and depth. (I go through that in this paper: Hayes, S. C. & Brownstein, A. J. (1986). Mentalism, behavior-behavior relations and a behavior analytic view of the purposes of science. *The Behavior Analyst, 9*, 175-190.) When we include context, technically we could say "within a social verbal community that establishes and maintains the functional control of literal rules, client rules are controlling behaviors within an overall causal relation established by that social / verbal community." ACT directly alters that context somewhat in the social/ verbal community within an ACT therapeutic relationship, which is why the "same thoughts" are no longer the "same" functionally. It is also why we caution "don't believe a word of this" - because if ALL

we do is to establish new rules, we limit the degree to which a non-literal context can now be part of the situation.

[AG] If we agree that behaviors are caused by their consequences given the context, then are we somehow saying that verbal rules can also cause behavior (given the context), but instead of changing these rules (i.e., content) we change the context (because strategies used to change contingency-based behaviors are ineffective when applied to verbal behaviors)?

This is not bad. Even if we DID change the rules, however, we would do so only by changing the context (such as that experienced in the therapeutic relationship). Cause is a particularly limited way to speak when we forget it is a way of speaking. It can still be useful even then, but it is limited. If I say "why did it explode?" and someone answers "because of the spark" then combustible material, oxygen, and heat is assumed. If I am welding combustible metal in a vacuum and I say "why did it explode?" and someone answers "because of the break in the vacuum" then combustible material, a spark, and heat is assumed. If I keep track of everything that goes together to make up an explosion when I say "why did it explode?" then the only technically correct answer is "there is no why ... it is an explosion when all of these features occur." The whole event has features, but none cause the whole event. Combustible material, oxygen, a spark, and adequate heat IS an explosion. None are causes ... or perhaps all are "causes." If ALL are "causes" then "cause" loses some of its pragmatic quality and only the full description is left. This is why contextualism cannot have literal causes - they collapse into all or none as more and more of the context is considered. Contextualism does have figurative causes, however, that are found in descriptive functional relations and are used pragmatically: to avoid explosions, avoid vacuum loss when welding metal, don't avoid sparks. In a grain elevator, avoid sparks, not vacuum loss.

FUNCTIONAL CONTEXTUALISM **Function vs. object [5-2-04]** Steve Hayes	Nico van der Meijden wrote: I've noticed that an important distinction often made between contextual theories and mechanistic theories is that in contextual theories something 'has a function,' while in mechanistic theories something often is considered as an object…. As I understand it, a function is something that somebody acquires or learns during his/her history and that can change, while an object is an existing, given fact that doesn't change. But I wondered if this is perhaps too simple and there is more to it…. Objects are things: formally characterized events with spatiotemporal boundaries. They are usually given ontological status. How they are known or used; or your history with regard to them is irrelevant to what they supposedly ARE. In mechanism parts are fundamental. The whole is derived from the parts. Basically you begin with objects in mechanism ... functions are built up from relations between objects. When Skinner defined verbal stimuli as he did he was using the term "stimulus" without it necessarily having to "stimulate" anything. That's a behavioral no-no: "stimulus" w/o "stimulation" is behavioral nonsense. A function is a dynamic relation. Contextualism is holistic, so whenever you divide up events you are aware that the very "events" you are speaking of are only "events" as aspects of the whole. Thus, everything is dynamic. Context is a function -- is implies responding. Responding is a function -- of history and current context. etc. Basically there *are* no objects in contextualism. "It is not behavior alone and cut off that we mean. It is behaving in and with a context." (paraphrase of Pepper). Especially since contextualism is aontological - even claims of the existence of external objects are only parts of an act in context (by the knower claiming ontological status for an object).
FUNCTIONAL CONTEXTUALISM **Utility not ontology, appeal to** **RFT** **Falsifiability of [10-11-03]** Steve Hayes	Joseph Ciarrochi wrote (referring to an unfavorable review of the RFT book by José Burgos): Burgos seems to make the following argument (and I hear this argument a lot): Functional contextualists are inconsistent, because they make ontological statements such as "essence," etc. (page 30). They claim to have theories that are falsifiable (page 33). Other statements that seem ontological are: "There are four scientific world views (from what world view does one make this statement?)"; "you always have to be standing somewhere" etc. People argue that FC's secretly assume the above statements are claims about reality. Essence can mean "the foundation of being" -- and to use a foundational claim to justify a concept would indeed be inconsistent with all forms of contextualism. But "essence" can also just mean what you consider to be the functional core ("the essence of the problem is x") -- and that use can be justified by the utility of considering it that way, relative to your goals.

There is nothing in the RFT or ACT books like the former use ... so far as I know.

This is a kind of gotcha game ... much like the days when folks would jump with glee when Skinner said he didn't mind doing something and folks would say "See! See! He said Mind!" Ooooohh. Woooow. Skinner was eventually driven to disclaimers before he talked, poor guy ("yeah, I know I will talk mentalistically at times ... you can't speak friggin' English otherwise."). It's a silly game really.

[re: "They claim to have theories that are falsifiable"]

Sure. RFT can be falsified in one of two ways, and both are contextualistically sensible. We pointed to both in the 2001 RFT book:

1. It is shown not to be useful:

"As a pragmatic theory, if Relational Frame Theory cannot lead to interesting and useful outcomes in important domains of human concern obviously relevant to human language and cognition, then it is functionally false." (intro to Part II)

2. It is not coherent because the functional features of the claimed processes do not comport with the data.

"Part I of this book was theoretical but in many areas it was supported by data specifically generated to test the analysis. Most major points were buttressed by at least some experimental research directly focused on them. If these points are wrong, the theory is falsified in a traditional sense of the word." (intro to Part II)

An example would be the claim that relating is an operant. If relating is shown to have nothing to do with one's history with contingencies (for example), the claim is false. While this is a kind of falsification that lines up with the traditional sense of the word, I did not mean in terms of ontology. I meant you throw the theory out because it does not work empirically.

What is tested empirically in contextualistic science is not the world but the utility of our analyses. Testing the claim that relating is an operant is not testing a reality claim, because in the hands of a contextualist it is not that operants exist as units independent of our analysis -- it is that they allow us to interact successfully with the world. As Skinner says it: bodies don't fall because of the law of gravity: humans are able to interact successfully with the world in certain circumstances if they bring their behavior under the control of this verbal formulation. But if one makes such a claim you have to show that the formulation actually works. Skinner said it this way: "[Scientific knowledge] is a corpus of rules for effective action, and there is a special sense in which it could be 'true' if it yields the most effective action possible. . . . (A) proposition is 'true' to the extent that with its help the listener responds effectively to the situation it describes" (Skinner, 1974, p. 235).

That is why behavior analysis is the *experimental* analysis of behavior. Manipulation of contextual events is how we show that prediction-and-control (as one unified goal) with precision, scope, and depth is accomplished. This is not correspondence. It's function. I wrote a chapter on this point some time ago that might be useful if the point is of interest: Hayes, S. C. (1997). Behavioral epistemology includes nonverbal knowing. In L. J. Hayes & P. M. Ghezzi (Eds.). *Investigations in behavioral epistemology* (pp. 35-43). Reno, NV: Context Press.

[re: 'Other statements that seem ontological are: "There are four scientific world views (from what world view does one make this statement?)"']

This was dealt with by Pepper and we addressed it in the Pepper review years ago. The four world view division seems useful. In the Pepper review in JEAB we said that "hazards may be minimized, if not altogether avoided, if behavior analysts clarify their philosophical assumptions. Pepper's analysis may be helpful for this purpose." It helps explain why some conflicts are not empirical (there is nothing in the world of research that RFT could do to solve Burgos' problems with the theory. They aren't empirical problems) and why some are. We linked the whole thing to goals:

"Behavior analysis is a position with a history of success in achieving its goals, but a position that fails to develop is a position that fades away (Reese, 1986b). How can behavior analysis find its way, while retaining the useful qualities that made it what it is? Pepper shows behavior analysts what is truly unusual and important about their position. His book helps put behavior analysts' hands on the tiller of their philosophical vessel. It may steer better from there."

I think it is pretty clear that we were not turning the concept of world views into some ontological thing. But like Skinner's "mind" comments you basically can't speak English if you get too neurotic about this.

I think Pepper's theory is itself a contextual theory. So what? It doesn't pretend to be otherwise. Conducting an analysis does not mean you are an essentialist. It depends on what you are doing.

[re: '"you always have to be standing somewhere" etc. People argue that FC's secretly assume the above statements are claims about reality.']

Pepper says it this way: whenever you corner a contextualist on such things, they will slip away saying "try and catch me." Contextualists can look like mechanists, but the core of their game is different. Contextualists get to play at the other world view if it serves their purposes without being tied to them, but they can do so without ontological baggage. Those outside of the contextual perspective are frustrated by what they see as loose thinking. But meanwhile functional contextualists are busy creating useful data, and useful interventions, without getting lost in the dead ends of what is "really" there. In some areas of science it may not work to play the game contextualistically. But within psychology the history of behavior analysis suggests that it is a powerful game.

But you can't say a sentence without realizing that ontology is a hair's width away -- because the illusion of ontology is in language itself. (RFT explains why actually.) But commonsense ontology in language itself is not the same as ontological claims.

... As a contextualist, you could have prediction as a goal ... or *any* goal. Why not? Goals are a priori events in contextualism. You could even choose predictive verification as a goal (or "I'll be a good mechanist") as a goal and *still not be a mechanist*.

In the review we said it this way:

> "A powerful implication of this truth criterion is that on contextualistic grounds one can adopt the analytic strategy of an alternative world view in a given situation if doing so is useful toward some end. For example, a philosophical contextualist might adopt a mechanistic theory because it is useful in identifying ways of "controlling" behavior. Strategic integration of this sort does not violate Pepper's warning against the destructive effects of eclecticism, because no integration of the underlying root metaphors is implied. The machine metaphor is merely used in the service of a contextualistic agenda; and the truth of the analysis based on that usage is evaluated against a successful working criterion."

Mechanists use predictive verification to confirm the ontological truth of the model. It is not an arbitrary goal. It is the very purpose of science. You don't get to pick it or not. It is the avenue to the truth and the truth is in a pre-organized world that is discovered, not constructed.

LANGUAGE

Etymology - relevance of [11-30-04]

Steve Hayes

Daniel wrote:

> Scholars often use the etymological legacy of a word to give extra umph to the meaning. It is fascinating. I am intrigued by the historical meanings of words, and the many new meanings that a word picks up through the centuries. But does this exploration of the history of the word help us know more about the "meaning" today? I thought, as behavior analysts, we actually "define" a word by what stimuli occasion it. I want to know what occasions the utterance of "pain" vs. "suffering" from a person. Knowing the etymology adds to my scholarship in general, and may turn around to be a useful therapy tool with my client ... but is there something that it adds to the behavioral analysis?

Meaning is use, but etymology is the study of the history of use ... and cultural practices are historical across many lifetimes.

RFT seemingly refines the "meaning is use" stance of behavioral folk on language. We need to think this through in more detail. From an RFT point of view direct stimulus relations are not the primary focus -- Relational frames are the focus. Thus a word does not just "mean" the stimuli that occasion it. To take a bit of a cartoon example (I know this one is slightly unfair but unpacking all of that leads to a paper, not an email): If I say "hot" in a rising voice and the person replies "cold" this does not signify that cold means hot. The meaning of words involves the relata, derived relations among them, the derived functions that are transformed by them, and contextual cues that occasion all of this. On the listener's side it involves all of these processes as well. Direct stimulus functions are part of the whole as well, but they are not the defining features. (Actually the very first comprehensive presentation of RFT was a paper the late Aaron Brownstein and I gave at ABA in 1985 on speaking with meaning and listening with understanding ... and we essentially defined "meaning" and "understanding" in RFT terms). ..

Anyway, back to etymology. Modern day language is filled with frozen metaphors, reified into causal entities. Those metaphors constitute the original relational networks the term participated in, and almost always the metaphor is more closely linked to the issues of blood and bone that surrounded language as a basic regulatory system. Skinner often used etymology to make that point (e.g., his paper on cognitive language). This is important clinically as well ... RFT explains how language gets us farther and farther away from direct contingencies. ACT ties to break down the excesses of that process and to bring it under contextual control. I find that the world as viewed by languaging creatures who had a few thousand words (before we created and then elaborated the concepts of emotion, mind, etc. etc.) is a bit more ACT sensible.

I would not want to go back to that world ... science and technology depends on much of what we've done with language just in the span of written language ... but I do want to edge in that direction when it helps to do so. Etymology is useful in that regard.

Clinically it also helps us detect the connotations that occasion current use whether we are verbally aware of it or not. For every word there are many synonyms and connotations echo down through the ages in

	subtle ways in the practices of verbal communities. When I know that "but" originally meant "be-out" I begin to see that in fact I now use it as a fighting term. I begin to wonder if a sense of not being able to breathe is really worth the struggle with "anxiety." I begin to hesitate when I hear a client cast acceptance as persisting "despite" emotion because I detect the fight in "spite" and I wonder if the client is unknowingly leaking a misunderstanding of what we are working on.
	Those are the two big reasons etymology is so frequent in behavior analysis that I am aware of: it undermines the reification that is built into language & it orients us toward subtle aspects of current use.
LANGUAGE **Words as tools; "subliteral" communication** [4-23-03] John Blackledge	... one reason I think the ACT technology (and its ancestors) is so valuable--it helps us use words (and pictures of these words) helpful in communicating a point in a 'subliteral' fashion. To paraphrase a long-gone Buddhist master, it can be easier to find the moon if there's a finger pointing at it--and critical to remember the finger is not the moon itself. The thin line we walk as scientists, contextualists, and ACT therapists involves how to use words as tools without them using us.
RFT **Assessment, RFT-based, utility of** [4-22-03] John Blackledge	[Re] the issue of how much utility explicit RFT-based assessment might have in treatment. There are, of course, RFT-based assumptions that form cornerstones of ACT treatment. These include the assumptions that much of the suffering observed in clients comes from the fact that they frame private events in a causal relation to overt behavior, that they derive that private events can and must be controlled and that they remain confined to the mandates of a variety of other rigidly-held but counter-productive rules (perhaps causal and evaluative relations play a role here), and that they negatively self-evaluate (e.g., via comparative and hierarchical relations). I imagine that good ACT therapy involves good ideographic assessment of how a given client specifically frames these aspects of his experience, in a way that allows defusion techniques (etc.) to be directly tailored to the SPECIFIC ways that the client frames his experience, rather than being applied in a more general and didactic fashion.
	My subjective feeling is the more I "know" about how a client is framing problematic aspects of his experience, the more able I am to directly target specific problematic relational responses with defusion techniques, and the more able I am to predict the kinds of experiences that cause trouble for a client. When I can do this, it really helps me sink relevant ACT interventions into the areas where an individual client most needs them. If this process could be facilitated by more explicit RFT-based assessment (whether filtered through some as-yet-fictional self-report instruments, visual depictions of relational framing, etc.), I'd be all for it....
RFT **Attitude change - smoking prevention strategy** [5-16-05] Steve Hayes	Tony Biglan wrote: Ok, gang, if you could put one thing from ACT into a mailing to 9th and 10th graders that was designed to prevent smoking among those who don't smoke and to encourage quitting among those who do, what would you put in? I'd embrace what they believe, then find an attribute of what they believe that moves the network toward what you want so that it is functionally different though formally the same. Suppose kids think smoking is "masculine" and masculine is a positive attribute. Sexist, true. But can we use this to help kids not smoking in the first place or even to put it down? What are the attributes of "masculine" that can help you? Suppose you find that folks believe that men don't take advice even when they should (e.g., they don't ask for directions; and they reject good directions given by others as if that means they are weak). If I had a TV commercial (I will put my answer in this format trusting you can convert it to other formats) I might build this out by showing men getting into trouble (a couple of times -- to set the theme) by trying to pretend that they don't need to ask for directions or follow them even when given good directions. Then I'd say something like: "It probably is true. Smoking is 'masculine.'" Then I'd pause for a split second and have a couple of sentences, probably shown in a way that deliberately parallels an earlier part of the commercial - the person being given good directions and ignoring them (e.g., the same person in the same scene, but now the message is about smoking), that include whatever anti-smoking info you want to have listened to less defensively. Ideally this info would even link over to another aspect of "masculine." For example, you might find that folks believe that it is a masculine trait to weigh evidence. Then in addition to your informational appeal you might include "weigh the evidence" once or twice in your message (no need to specifically link that to "masculine" -- it will probably be more effective if used but not really described self-consciously). If this works it will begin to transform the functional meaning of the attribute: instead of smoking being masculine in the sense of you get to do strong things as an adult and smoking shows that -- it is masculine in the sense of stubborn; prideful; stupidly self-directed and *not* smoking is masculine in the sense of weighing evidence, taking tough stands and so on. One cool thing about that is if advertisers later try to play up the smoking is "masculine" theme, they could actually be supporting your campaign since you are

relating the negative aspects of that category to smoking and the positive aspects to not smoking. Repeat this same move with a series of commercials targeting critical aspects of the network. You might echo the line in each "It probably is true. Smoking is 'X'." and systematically dismantle things like strong, independent, cool, sexy etc. Sorry for the sexist qualities of this example ... one of the creepy things about using media to move people is having to start where folks are and if they believe that "smoking is masculine" we may need to deal with that. Of course there has to be limits on that move since there is more at stake than smoking here. Gender bias for example. To do this approach well you need data on the network as it is normatively but you can probably guesstimate based on focus groups and available data.

This is all RFT consistent but I'm pretty far ahead of the actual available data. I'm not sure this will work. It should though if the theory is powerful. This basic research on attitude change from an RFT perspective needs to be done. Anyone looking for a thesis or dissertation?

RFT **Beginner's summary [4-1-04]** Rhiannon Patterson	I have been resistant to trying to understand RFT for some time, mainly because it looked like I'd have to learn a large and frustrating new vocabulary before I could even begin to understand the content. However, having read John Blackledge's introductory article in BAT (2003, vol. 3, issue 4), along with Chapter 2 in the ACT book, I finally feel like I might get it. Even better, what I get seems to make complete sense! I would like to put forward my preliminary understanding of what RFT is about, along with a comment and a question, and see if people think I'm on the right track. It seems like there are three basic points: 1. People learn relations among "things" (stimuli). The learnable relations available to us are parallel to logical or mathematical relations: equivalence and transitivity. Equivalence includes: * A = B implies B = A (mutual entailment) * A = B and B = C implies A = C (combinatorial entailment) Transitivity includes: * A > B and B > C implies A > C (also combinatorial entailment) These learned relations are called derived relations because they do not result from direct learning experiences / direct training. The learned relations are said to be "arbitrarily applicable" because they don't just apply to inherent, formal properties. I.e., you could learn "Coke tastes better than 7-UP," "7-UP tastes better than gin," and you might then prefer Coke to gin without ever tasting any of the three, or knowing the formal properties associated with tasting better. 2. These learned relationships (which in themselves could result in rigid thinking) also have big implications for mental health, in large part, because they result in a corresponding transformation of stimulus functions. That is, if A is scary and needs avoiding and A = B, then B is scary and needs avoiding too. 3. All these relations (as well as the transformation of stimulus functions associated with them) are learned, through operant learning / reinforcement. One thought I have about these derived relations: as I was initially thinking about all this, I kept thinking, "But humans must surely have an INNATE capacity to construct certain relations. It can't all be learned." Specifically I was thinking about logical / mathematical relations. Understanding transitivity is learned, true, but the learning feels more like it is about discovering underlying (and undying) truths, rather than learning something about the way the world happens to be now (a contingent truth?) On further thought it occurred to me that maybe this is why derived relations feel so much like truth, when usually they are not. We believe them as if they were formal truths, because our minds are applying logical reasoning to the categories in question. Our minds are forgetting, however, that the objects of our reasoning often are not objects that genuinely (inherently) possess the properties we've associated with them….
RFT Beginner's summary [cont'd] Patty Bach	Rhiannon, you are right on track - RFT is not nearly as scary as it looks at a glance. I'd add to #1: Transitivity includes: * A > B and B > C implies A > C (also combinatorial entailment) and also implies that C < B, C < A, and B < A One of the trickier parts to grasp (at least for me) is that = means 'coordination,' not = in the same way it is used in mathematics where = is always =. What I mean is, if A = B entails B = A, we could substitute for (=), A > B entails B < A; A is the opposite of B entails B is the opposite of A; A is a member of class B entails class B includes member A (hierarchical); A is different from B entails B is different from A; A is better than B entails that B is worse than A, etc.

	[Referring to RP's final paragraph] Exactly! We probably have the innate capacity to construct relations generally, and as for certain relations, 'logic' is itself relational. It seems absolutely logical to say that "I am not moving," and from the perspective of outer space I am traveling at 100,000 km per hour through space along with planet earth, and spinning around at 4,500 km per hour. And that 'hour,' or time, is a 'measure' of the 'rotation of the moon' as it moves '15 degrees' in its 'orbit' 'around' the 'earth.' And the 'kilometer' is '1/10,000' (now known to be inaccurate) of the 'distance' around the 'equator.' It is all relational. Depending on the frame of reference it would be just as 'logical' to say that "gravity made the cup fall to the floor after I dropped it," as to say "the cup didn't move and gravity made the earth slam into the cup after I let go of it." AARR is pervasive and 'logical' in context - and this logic allows us to 'name' the relations and 'talk about them' with others - and it is the way we talk about the world that determines the way we perceive the world to be, not the way the world is that determines the way we talk about it. Arbitrarily applicable and not arbitrarily applied.
RFT Beginner's summary [cont'd] Patty Bach	My point about 'abstractions' was perhaps more about the 'arbitrary' than the 'abstract' - where this most links to the clinical, for me, is in the area of choice and values and it can play a part in cognitive defusion too. And that's just me, so not arbitrarily applied! Many ideas/things that we take as 'given'/ 'objective' are highly abstract, relational, and arbitrarily applicable. Much of physics, which seems very 'logical' can be reduced to abstract relations among very few phenomena. The 'meter,' which seems fairly objective, in the sense that we can agree that an object is one meter in length, is the length of the 'official meter' stored in France - that's pretty arbitrary - and it is not 'arbitrarily applied.' I would not have success as a physicist if I suggested that a 'meter' is some other length than that object in France. The advances in the physical sciences and engineering demonstrate the utility of making 'the meter' non-arbitrarily applied through truth by agreement. But what of, "a good person" - is there a place in France or elsewhere where I can find the "official good person" or "The official good life" - The official good relationships; ideal moral stances; good/bad behaviors; irrational beliefs; good parent/child/friend/significant other; worthwhile hobbies; correct income; right religion, political party, etc.? Do I get to or have to choose? In existentialist terms, is 'arbitrarily applicable but not arbitrarily applied' 'freedom' or 'responsibility'? If I get to choose … my response is "yikes!!!" … is that a 'good' or 'bad' response? Is choice a freedom or a responsibility - or is that too a choice? I wrote and deleted "don't believe a word I am saying" ... instead, I'll write, "you are free to choose to believe or not believe a word I am saying."
RFT Beginner's summary [cont'd] ACT Listserv Member	[Referring to PB's comment: "Exactly! We probably have the innate capacity to construct relations generally, and as for certain relations, 'logic' is itself relational."] Or relational framing is the by-product of multiple exemplar training that occurs during language acquisition early in childhood and continues throughout our life becoming more complex as we build our repertoire. This position would seem to be supported by the fact that organisms (humans included) with language deficits or no language do not adeptly (or at all) construct relations as well as verbally competent adults. Also, it is possible to train clients with cognitive delays to discriminate based on relational properties of stimuli and bring it under contextual control (see studies on say-do correspondence by Yvonne Barnes-Holmes for good examples of this). Relational framing seems to be a by-product of differential reinforcement for matching to sample training across multiple settings, within a wide variety of contexts (at home, school, work, etc. and with mommy, daddy, teacher, etc.), with a variety of tangible and verbal reinforcers, with progressively more difficult discriminations being shaped by the demands of our culture. In fact, education (and possibly that fuzzy concept of intelligence) is really a measure of our acquisition of, use, and the latency of forming relations among stimuli and verbally reporting it in a contextually determined fashion.
RFT **Intellectual performance [5-4-05]** Steve Hayes	Is anyone yet doing RFT work with actually improving IQ? Sooner or later that will come. A good software programmer could do a lot based on RFT right now (who knows if it would work but some of the things to try are fairly clear). I would think that defusion / willingness etc. would create more psychological flexibility in the area of intellectually challenging tasks just as it does with emotionally challenging ones (lots of studies on that) and physically challenging ones (the emerging sports psychology work). The dividing lines between these are probably more arbitrary than functional.

RFT	Bryan Roche wrote:
Intellectual performance [cont'd]	Great idea re the relationship between emotional and intellectual flexibility.... Steve can you point us in the direction of any studies in particular you are thinking of that are relevant to this?
Steve Hayes	Solving problems and being creative requires that you be able to sit with "not knowing" ... sometimes for long periods of time. This seems psychologically challenging in much the same way as sitting with anxiety is for the panic disordered person. I didn't actually claim a research base for the connection in my note but in fact there are research strands that make sense seen in that way.
	For example, the literature on learned industriousness has data on the correlation with problem solving tasks and even creativity. Folks who can persist in the face of unpleasant feelings did better. We are seeing similar things in the AAQ world in the I/O applications. Those in the Langer tradition have similar mindfulness data.
	I can dig up the refs but they are not hard to find. There was a review of the learned industriousness literature a few years ago. Interesting area, relevant to the cluster of related processes we are talking about here (e.g., distress tolerance, experiential avoidance, fusion, mindfulness etc.).
RFT **Introduction to [3-2-04]** Joseph Ciarrochi	There ARE readable descriptions of RFT (see Blackledge, J. T. (2003). An introduction to relational frame theory: Basics and applications. *The Behavior Analyst Today, 3*(4), 421-433.).
RFT Introduction to [cont'd] Graham Taylor	Bryan Roche has a very simple introduction to RFT which you can get to off the ACT website, but it's a bit tricky to find - there is also a link to it from my website [www.therapist-training.com.au] go to Workshops, then ACT, and it's there.
RFT Introduction to [cont'd] Serafin Gomez Martin	... it could be of help to read pieces in which there is RFT stuff but with special emphasis on applied clinical issues. Some examples of this that I recall now may be:
	Kelly et al.'s chapter in Dougher, M. (Ed.). (2000). *Clinical behavior analysis*. Reno, NV: Context Press. book and the chapter in the RFT book (Psychopathology).
	Dermot et al., Chapter in Mike Dougher (2000) book (Problems of Self).
	J. Blackledge article ...
	Hayes, S. C., & Wilson, K. G. (1993). Some applied implications of a contemporary behavior-analytic account of verbal events...
RFT **Online tutorial** **[8-18-04]** Eric Fox	I am pleased to announce the release of "An Introduction to Relational Frame Theory," an interactive, web-based tutorial designed to introduce the basic concepts and approach of Relational Frame Theory (RFT). RFT is an innovative new approach to studying language, cognition, and other complex human behavior, and serves as the theoretical basis of Acceptance and Commitment Therapy. RFT is based on the principles of behavior analysis and several decades of research on derived stimulus relations.
	You can learn more on the tutorial's home page at: http://www.contextualpsychology.org/rft_tutorial
	The tutorial was written and designed for a very broad audience. It is hoped that everyone from undergraduate psychology students to doctoral-level psychologists to any educated person on the street (or on the web!) will find the material accessible, engaging, and relevant.
	"An Introduction to Relational Frame Theory" is freely available to everyone, and is also a great way to incorporate cutting-edge educational technology into your course or training program! It's easy for instructors to make the tutorial an assignment or extra-credit project for their students: simply register an instructor account, create a course, provide your students with the Course Access Code, and that's it. You will then be able to log in to see which of your students have completed the tutorial, along with their performance on the tutorial quiz.
	Here are some unedited, anonymous comments provided by individuals who completed an early version of the tutorial:
	-- "This is by far the best and most efficient presentation of RFT I have ever encountered. It presents very complex concepts in a shockingly easy to understand and approachable manner."
	-- "Very visually appealing and easy on the eyes. Graphics lent themselves to the teaching--they were not gratuitous and unnecessary."
	-- "Fantastic. Interactive. Concrete examples."
	-- "It provided a relatively painless way to master some unusual and complex ideas."

	-- "Very easy to use and very much enjoyed the playful style." -- "The language is clear, the humor is nice, and the movement through the concepts is logical." -- "Good examples that are easy to understand and relate to, and good questions starting at a basic level. Clearly structured and just the right amount of humor :)" -- "Vivid depiction of complex--abstract concepts--accompanied by clear examples - I finally seem to understand RFT!!!!"...
RFT Online tutorial [cont'd] John Blackledge	I just wanted to put out another plug for Eric's excellent RFT tutorial, which you can find a link for on the ACT webpage. If you're an ACT fan afraid of approaching RFT or even disinterested in it, I can't recommend this tutorial more. There is ACT-specific material in it as well, so if you always wondered how RFT is relevant to ACT, now you can find out.
RFT **Relational framing - does ACT decrease?** **[1-7-04]** Steve Hayes	Joseph Ciarrochi wrote: Much of ACT is seen to undermine contexts that involve the unhelpful transfer of stimulus function (Cfunc). Yet the deeper I get into RFT, the more I am convinced that ACT also directly targets Crel. Do not many of the ACT technologies set a context where relating of stimuli is discouraged? (I am not sure if this is a controversial statement. I guess I'll find out.) For example, ACT practitioners often create contexts where unhelpful reasoning and sense making is actively discouraged, or at least not rewarded (e.g., via confusion, paradox, exercises such as choose being right versus being alive, etc.). Does this not mean that they are using contingencies of reinforcement to reduce relational framing (reasoning)? Nice question. There is a fine point in here and I think it can be argued multiple ways.... Consider the "milk, milk, milk" exercise or the "leaves on the stream" exercise. Both seem to alter Cfunc, and they provide few specific Crel cues of the sort so common in CBT ("don't relate x to y -- relate x to z"), but would it be wrong to say that they weaken Crel control more generally? I used to argue ACT that way, but I'm unaware of much RFT writing on general and specific forms of Crel control. Rainer Sonntag sent me an interesting statement on stimuli controlling "generalized relational operants" as an entire class that is in line with the idea that there are general forms of Crel control as well as the more specific kinds (specific: A is the opposite of B; general: relate A to B).
RFT Relational framing - does ACT decrease? [cont'd] Niklas Törneke	I think it is correct to say that certain things you do in ACT decrease relational framing as such. Milk, milk, milk, is a good example. In that exercise both Cfunc and Crel decreases. Whether the decrease of relational framing in the exercise generalizes to life in general is not so clear, though, to my thinking. The transformation of function definitely should generalize, if ACT is helpful. This connects to the discussion Rainer and I had on the RFT list just before Christmas regarding mindfulness. As far as I understand the reason traditional mindfulness meditation would use focusing techniques, especially initially in the exercises, is that they reduce relational framing as such. Focusing on your breath, for example, contextual cues for relational framing (Crel) would decrease. In meditation manuals this is described as "clearing the mind" etc. Relational framing (thoughts occurring) is still there, but less so. This (according to meditation teachers) helps meditation, as there is less to pay attention to. "Monkey mind calms down" which is the starting point of Vipasana meditation and helps the development of what they call mindfulness. I would guess the same process takes place in certain ACT exercises. But I still think this is more like "help on the way," the change in Cfunc being the critical thing.
RFT Relational framing - does ACT decrease? [cont'd] John Blackledge	The issue strikes me the same as the point that while mutual/combinatorial entailment and verbal transformation of function are technically two separate things, you can't have one without the other. It seems to me that any defusion technique that successfully and completely disrupts verbal transformations of function does so by disrupting the full set of relational responses giving rise to all verbal transformations. I guess you could technically say that defusion techniques target Crel (read as the contextual variables supporting all types of relational responding) in order to effect change in Cfunc. But Crel and Cfunc seem as interdependent to me as entailments and transformations, so is it pragmatically useful to make this fine-grained distinction? Cognitive therapists could, of course, arrive at changes in Cfunc as well, but would do this by creating a new Crel rather than disrupting Crel.
RFT **Should clinicians learn?** **[3-6-04]** Kate Partridge	I'm just a front-line practitioner, not an academic or a researcher. I'm an experiential, non-intellectual person - that doesn't mean I'm not intelligent. I don't have the time or the type of mind to be able even to read all the RFT-related emails, not to mention the theory itself. Having started out as an enthusiastic study-grouper, I've been numbed and paralysed by the theoretical discussion so far. This sort of discussion just feels like obsessional thinking to me - how many angels on the head of a pin. I'm sure Rainer is right when he says: *I have the impression (and believe me I know it from my own*

experience with my own rational mind) that those folks that are most interested in RFT need the most exposure to the experiential aspects of ACT.

I'm feeling so frustrated about this - I hope I'm not being offensive - I'm just trying to articulate how impossible it is for me, and I'm sure for a number of others, to be able to connect in any deep way with the theory, <u>when it is presented as verbal theory</u>. Steve's experiential exercise of the woven 'Chinese' finger trap (what ARE they called?) gave me an immediate and direct understanding of the trap of the verbal net. I'm also a mindfulness meditator, and that helps a lot.

I hope to heaven that there IS some way for this stuff to be accessible to "right brain" practitioners like me. I just want to know how to do the work!

Having got that off my chest, I feel much better. Best wishes to all.

| RFT

Should clinicians learn? [cont'd]

Patty Bach | Joseph suggested that learning RFT is itself a sort of defusion exercise, and Rainer and others that learning about RFT increases 'ACT flexibility.'

This discussion might itself be a defusion exercise...what shows up for someone who identifies with or values ACT when reading "learning about RFT is important"? Or "learning about RFT is for intellectuals who probably don't have an experiential life"?...

Niklas said:

    My guess is that the process of becoming a great therapist involves an understanding of theory and that the outcome of understanding is flexibility in practice (Rainer's point as I got it). You and I determine what is enough for you and me to be as great as we choose to be and we will act accordingly, no matter what others say.

Behavior analysis is always about the behavior of the individual and that applies to therapists too - I will always practice "therapy according to Patty" and there's "therapy according to Niklas; Joseph; Steve; Rainer; Hank; Kelly; Dermot ... etc."

We all find our greatness in doing what works.

I don't see this discussion as a question of "what makes a great therapist?" so much as a question of "is there some amount of training and experience and/or knowledge of theory one must have to say 'I am doing ACT'?" As Rainer said, that is an empirical question...

Paraprofessionals (and that probably includes all human beings) with little formal training can help others solve many problems and persons with a great deal of training often have little impact...

I often train front line staff such as nursing assistants and mental health technicians in basic behavioral principles and techniques such as positive reinforcement and extinction. And I usually begin the training by saying something like, "if you are a human being you already know something about behavior interventions...all of us are interested in and know something about describing, understanding, predicting, and influencing the behavior of ourselves and others..."

At the same time, I am not so sure there are any "minor problems" - if a problem brings a person to a therapist then that problem is anything but minor to that individual.

If behavior change were simple we'd all be out of a job - no one would need to consult a professional and there would be no need for complicated theories of something so self evident.

How can something so obvious (e.g., quit smoking) be so challenging and difficult? How can anything be so simple and complicated at the same time as behavior (or ACT)? We are all walking, talking paradoxes. We are astonishing. Holding that thought seriously yet lightly is at the heart of ACT, and holding it lightly gives ACT (and maybe even RFT) a playful quality.

This listserv probably has as many purposes as participants - it is interesting, challenging, useful, and educational - and a never ending opportunity to practice defusion and to laugh at myself - and it is also a playground.

Being on this listserv has enhanced my ACT flexibility both verbally and experientially and the listserv is itself a great experiential exercise…. Do I choose to reply or not reply? And if I do or don't what's that in the service of? Am I participating at the piece level or the board level? Is everyone welcome including the bums who say "I matter about RFT" or "I don't know or care about the difference between Cfunc and Crel"? Can I accept whatever shows up as it is and not as it says (or I say) it is? Can I defuse from that content? Is that a 'bad comment' or is the 'bad' in my interaction with the comment? Can I look at that passenger? "Cfunc, Cfunc, Cfunc, Cfunc, Cfunc, Cfunc." I shouldn't have said that; there's a whole bunch of observing selves reading this from numerous loci...no wait, that's just more digging ... I'm having the thought that I shouldn't have said that … BUT, no AND, most important of all, how can I get more listserv members to wear argyle socks? |

RFT Should clinicians learn? [cont'd] Steve Hayes	I felt a great deal of sympathy for Kate's post. See if this is so: Most people come to the ACT work through experiences of personal or professional relevance at workshops; or they have a similar experience reading something. Then as they try to expand their connection with the work, they enter not into more experiences of that kind but into this bizarre language community. Some of what is there is bizarre because it is behavior analytic, contextual, and so on. Zen behaviorism, I heard someone call it. Hard to make sense of it at first. Some of what is bizarre is that the language being used changes voice ... now literal, now figurative, and always to make a difference. That quality comes from ACT and its underpinnings (back to contextualism, radical pragmatism etc.) but it is maddening until you click into the game ... esp. on email where you can't determine the voice by the tone, manner, etc. Minds exposed to it just want to reject it as so much bullshit (which it is in a sense, but it is BS designed to make a difference). My advice to beginners who are going nuts with all of this: Get to another workshop ... you'll remember why you are here in the first place. Hold this listserv lingo lightly. Focus more on the protocols, the practical guides, etc. ... and less on the discussion about ACT ... (but do hang in on this other stuff). Let your clients teach you. And eventually, who knows, this BS may also make a difference with you. Till then, keep the faith.
RFT Should clinicians learn? [cont'd] **METAPHOR** **RFT, should clinicians learn? - car driving cf. fixing [3-7-04]** ACT Listserv Member	Reading the last few posts in this stream, this analogy came to mind - tell me if it captures the situation... Most of us on this list can drive a car, only some of us can fix a car (i.e., be mechanics), and even fewer of us can explain the engineering (chemical, electrical, physical, etc.) processes that actually make the entity called a car possible. Doing ACT is like driving a car; most of us, with some driver education and practice, can learn to drive competently. With workshops, and the book, and practice we can learn to do ACT competently, and make a difference in our clients' lives. Some on this list want to know some more on the parts and read the RFT books, and even some of us want to know the underpinnings of that and read about contextualism, radical pragmatism, etc. Do we all need to know how to fix a car to drive the car? Do we all need to know the physical, electrical, etc. properties and the interactions between them that produce the thing called car and its functioning? Probably not. It doesn't hurt for us to know a little basic roadside maintenance (in ACT to know about the root metaphor, understand the theory, etc.) - this makes us better drivers.
RFT Should clinicians learn? [cont'd] METAPHOR RFT, should clinicians learn? - Car driving cf. fixing [cont'd] John Blackledge	I really like this metaphor. To extend it a little more--If you have an intimate understanding of how a car is designed and the principles that make it run, you may be in a better position to get peak performance out of it while driving. And when unanticipated things go wrong and the car breaks down in the middle of nowhere, knowing how to fix it is a very good thing. There are definitely multiple ways to get to ACT fluency/expertise (reminds me of the Buddhist saying, "There are 84,000 doors to enlightenment"). But Kate's focus on the primacy of direct experience over any possible verbal explanation is key. I think RFT fluency allows a better ability to improvise and focus clinical work (to 'push it to the limit,' so to speak) and still keep it ACT-consistent. That, of course, is ultimately an empirical question, though.
RFT **Should clinicians learn? [cont'd]** Rhiannon Patterson *Cross Reference:* *See 2-60 for an earlier post in this thread*	I am interested in hearing from clinicians about whether you feel that learning RFT has helped you in being a good ACT therapist. I find RFT rather tedious and time-consuming to study (although the tutorial was somewhat helpful), and since I don't have a purely intellectual interest in learning the details of a new theory of language and cognition, I'm trying to figure out whether the investment of time would pay off in terms of clinical understanding and skills in any way. If people have illustrative examples of instances where a deeper knowledge of RFT has given them added clinical insight or skills I'd be especially interested in those. My guess is that learning RFT thoroughly could be useful for conducting basic research on underlying psychological processes, but may be irrelevant for clinical skills and even for treatment development ... do people agree?

RFT Should clinicians learn? [cont'd] Jeremy Gauntlett-Gilbert	Here's a concrete example of how I benefited (or how I think I've benefited). After a bit of reading, I think that I genuinely appreciate the difference between Crel and Cfunc (took me a while). It made me think about my clinical practice. I think that I have been tending to teach patients a new rule - "you don't need to have the right thoughts to move forward." Which of course is another example of literal sense-making and my attempt to get the correct 'content' into my patients' heads to help them move. Not a terrible clinical move, of course - quite a good rule, really, if you're going to be interested in rules. Appreciating the difference between Crel and Cfunc from an eye-strainingly difficult behavioural point of view helped me to appreciate what exactly I was doing there. Old CBT habits die hard! I had read the ACT book repeatedly before this point; I appreciated the material about making sense, paradox, metaphor and verbal inexpressibility. However, getting to grips with the RFT material (from the ground up, with all of its technical difficulty) allowed me to see what I was doing with fresher eyes.
RFT Should clinicians learn? [cont'd] **METAPHOR** **RFT, should clinicians learn? - museum traffic light [6-3-05]** Jeremy Gauntlett-Gilbert	Tony Balazs wrote: What would be the Cfunc alternative to teaching a new rule? I am still struggling with the difference between Cfunc and Crel. I think it would be to step back and look at the whole issue of rules. A Crel move would be to alter relationships between things "on the same level." That is, to rearrange thoughts or rules into other thoughts or rules - to change "I need to think more positively to move forward" into "I don't need to have the right thoughts to move forward." This probably is progress, and is classical CBT-style progress. Nothing necessarily wrong with that; I've replaced a rigid and less workable rule with a better one. I think that Cfunc would be to shift the whole context. Why would I need to have the right thoughts, any more than I would need to be wearing the right shoes? How did I get to the point where I thought that fleeting mental events might have any necessary impact on my behaviour? "I don't need to have the right thoughts..." - whoops, there goes another fleeting mental event... Imagine a person stopped at a red traffic light. So far so good - but they are standing in front of an antique light in a museum. I can see this. I say to them "you don't need to stop there, you're on foot in a museum!" "Oh!" he says, and whips out a copy of the highway code. "Hang on - yes, I've got the page and it says that stop lights don't apply in museums." I groan quietly. I say "no, you don't need your highway code here!" He says "oh!" - and rummages in the back of the book, then says "ah yes, I've found the section on 'when you don't need your highway code'." ... I groan again. This guy doesn't need to shuffle around pages in his highway code, or make little notes in the back (dealing with the problem within the same system). He needs to clock that the whole Context (there's the big word) has changed. It's completely different. He's not in a context where highway codes are even vaguely relevant. Telling people that they don't need to have the right thoughts is like going back to the highway code. I'm giving them a new, logical, plausible-sounding change-the-content solution. Not a bad one, but it remains a logical, plausible sounding, change-the-content solution. It's trying to solve the problem at the same level, within the same rules, by changing the relationships. Museum guy's solution lies not in changing the stop light to green, or finding new rules that allow him to ignore the stop light; instead he needs to realise that stop lights don't have to function like that here. And thoughts don't have to function as behaviour influencers.
RFT Should clinicians learn? [cont'd] Rhiannon Patterson	What I'm picking up from people's responses is that the key addition which RFT makes to clinical interventions is the following. It helps the clinician remain aware of the importance of the function of thoughts / behaviors (functional analysis), rather than focusing just on whether the client's rationale for their thoughts / behaviors is accurate or not (CBT) and where those thoughts / behaviors come from (psychodynamic). The clinical implication of a CBT approach is: change incorrect thoughts (and thereby change maladaptive behavior, when a behavior is viewed as the problem); the clinical implication of a psychodynamic approach is: discover the origins of thoughts and thereby change thoughts (and again, thereby also change behavior, when a behavior is viewed as the problem); the clinical implication of a FA approach is: identify the function/ effect of the behavior at issue, and if that function/ effect is not consistent with the client's goals or values, point that out, and explore other behaviors that would have a more effective function. An FA approach need not ignore working on the content of thoughts (CREL issues?), nor the etiology of thoughts and behaviors. But the important addition of the FA approach is that, when addressing the content or etiology of thoughts does not suffice for behavior change, the clinician has another, often more powerful tool - focus on the function of the behavior (e.g., avoiding doing X lets me avoid feeling Y) and asking explicitly whether that function (avoiding feeling Y) is really so important to the client, that the client wants to sacrifice the function they would gain from changing the behavior (do X lets me get Z, though I will also feel Y). (In this example, X could be "going to after-school tutoring," Y

	could be "feeling inferior," Z could be "learning math") Is this about right? If so, then could we say: What is useful about RFT / FA is that it brings to light the functions that are actually in play for the client, and the functions that are being avoided/ refused, which perhaps the client couldn't see clearly before ... And once the real choices being made are clearly identified, it becomes somewhat easier for the client to make choices in line with their values - or at least, they are aware of why they struggle to do so, and they can use ACT defusion strategies to help them move in the direction they value.
	Does this seem like an accurate synopsis to people? I feel like I'm probably missing something about the arbitrarily-applicable relational responding (AARR) piece, but maybe the important clinical point about AARR is simply to note that the content of thoughts can derive from all sorts of histories / contingencies (via AARR) and to realize, therefore, that defusion/ reducing believability can be a useful clinical intervention, when particular thoughts are so seductive / powerful to a client, that they feel unable to engage in effective behaviors in the presence of those thoughts.
RFT Should clinicians learn? [cont'd] Steve Hayes	Great summary, but the clinical impact goes a bit deeper ... For example, you can easily use RFT to create powerful new clinical metaphors in flight / in session that are uniquely suited to the specific client and the client's specific issues.... It explains why avoidance and fusion emerge naturally, why they are harmful, and what to do about it. It informs how to do values; and how to increase and decrease motivation verbally. It tells you how to establish a sense of self etc. etc. (I could easily add 20 such items to a list). But the biggie for adult outpatient work you've described very well.
	BTW I am very grateful that the RFT researchers see the importance of ACT and the issues it raises for RFT; and I am gratified that many clinicians see the importance of RFT and the issues it raises for ACT ... but ACT folks need also to retain the big picture especially when dealing directly with the wonderful RFT researchers around us (like the whole Irish mafia). I've once or twice witnessed interactions that had the feel of "justify yourself by proving that I need to know about you to do my work" (I'm not talking about this thread ... but things I've seen directly at conventions etc.). It made me cringe a bit because it felt so parochial. RFT is much bigger in scope than ACT and it is not here to serve ACT any more than physics is here to serve engineering. We have to let RFT be RFT. But is there applied value in visiting the strange land of RFT? You betcha. Not absolutely necessary; but it will eventually help your engineering. My usual advice though is to go slowly and let experience be your guide.
RFT Should clinicians learn? [cont'd] Kelly Wilson	On the issue of what, or how much RFT is necessary: For me, the issue is densely pragmatic, but there are multiple levels of workability that need to be watched.
	1. At the level of clinicians doing ACT, I think that some of the clinical trials suggest that we can train folks in a protocol and have them execute it and produce reasonable effects without training in RFT or even much about behavioral principles. However, what happens when things go sideways? Or if the population, setting, structure, etc. are altered? Flexibility is needed and a rule-based approach is more likely to fail because of its insensitivity to change. Sometimes the sensitivities that might moderate problems are already shaped, but not articulated in behavioral terms, among good clinicians. Even here though, the organizing value of a broadly applicable theory (I mean behavior theory generally, including RFT) can keep one on track. I have done some recent consulting where I have, for example, talked a lot about basic behavioral issues such as the effects of aversive and appetitive control. I think that understanding these at a pretty basic level can provide good orientation in moment-to-moment therapeutic interactions, and can enhance even well-developed, but not theoretically-organized, clinical behaviors.
	2. At the level of treatment development: here I think that broad dissemination, treatment innovation and variation delinked from basic theoretical and empirical science runs the risk of extraordinary wrong turns. Right turns are possible without empirical science, but empirical science has a way of reeling us in when we get off track and does a better job of doing so than theory alone. In my Wilson, 2001 theoretical constructs paper I suggested that an elegant theory is always more cooperative than data. So, I think that in this realm (treatment development) we need our connection to basic bench science--both theoretical and empirical. There is a burden here: our basic and applied sciences need to be talking to one another--and I mean a lot.
	3. At the level of the community we are developing: I think that if we are hitching our wagon to science as a means to drive improvement in treatment, the link to basic science is absolutely critical. There have been plenty of groups centered on practice that have come and gone or become marginalized for lack of a good connection to basic behavioral science. Sometimes the communities are very tightly knit (like our own); however, that alone does not look like it is enough to keep the work progressive, growing, and evolving.
	If in order to do limited interventions knowledge of RFT and other behavioral principles is mandatory, we are toast. For a progressive science though, it looks like a must to me.
	I think that our community is working very very hard to keep this connection alive and vital. Everyone does not have to do the basic to applied stretch (although this is what I most like to train). However, I do think that if we all value it as a community, we are less likely to fall prey to long and costly wrong turns and also

less likely to fall into the basic/applied split that we currently see within organizations like the APA.

We all have to work at this. So, my unsolicited advice to the applied folks is stretch a bit (and a bit more) to see what the basic science is telling us. And my advice to the most basic lab folks is stretch a bit (and a bit more) to make clear the relevance of basic work to human problems. If we all work at this we can make something extraordinary happen--something on the order of the birth of behavior therapy. The birth of behavior therapy was the last *big* basic to applied stretch, but it lost steam. We have a chance here to mid-wife the next wave. There is a role for all. For the basic folks, keep it relevant. For the applied folks, value it, nurture it and stretch a bit to consume a little more of it. Together, we can make something happen.

RFT **Summary of [1-8-04]** Rainer Sonntag	Over the holidays I took some time to review my understanding of RFT. The result is the summary below. Steve read part of it and encouraged me to post it....

A short summary of RFT (with some extensions)

Relational frame theory describes (and "explains") human behavior on the basis of several interlocking contingencies. These contingencies are: mutual entailment, combinatorial entailment, generalized derived relational responding, transformation of stimulus functions, and rule-following.

1. Relational Responding

1.1. Mutual entailment is shaped through an operant training process with multiple exemplars by which humans abstract relations between two stimuli which do not share topographic similarities.

A common example is naming. Through multiple examples of name-object and object-name presentations together with a contextual cue (which specifies the particular relational response and can be viewed as a name for it) humans abstract a relation of coordination. In colloquial terms, for example, a real car in the street IS "a car." Or, to give another example, by training with multiple examples of "X is bigger than Y" and "Y is smaller than X" a relation of comparison is abstracted.

Basically, these training processes are similar to concept training with interlocking contingencies of generalization and discrimination training. The difference is that in ordinary concept training the concept is abstracted from formal properties of the stimuli presented.

1.2. Combinatorial entailment is shaped through an operant training process with multiple exemplars by which humans abstract relations between at least three stimuli that do not share topographic similarities.

Again naming may be a convenient example. When at least two name-object relations (e.g., "dog"-dog, "Hund"-dog [Hund is the German word for dog]) together with a contextual cue are trained a third relation is derived ("dog"-"Hund"). This third relation has never been directly trained. All three stimuli are related coordinately and it is said that they participate in a relational frame of coordination. If a derived relational response (hear "dog" - say "Hund") is reinforced the whole "system" of related stimuli and responses may be indirectly reinforced.

1.3. Stimuli are related not only coordinately. There are a lot of other relations that may be abstracted through the aforementioned operant processes: opposition, comparison, distinction, hierarchy etc.

This multitude of different specific relational processes (A is the opposite of B; A is bigger than B; A is different from B; etc.) is a context where through an operant training process with multiple exemplars of different specific relational responses, derived relational responding is shaped as an unspecified generalized operant (relate A to B).

This process again is similar to a concept training with interlocking contingencies of different relational frames. The result, however, is both a generalized response class and a generalized stimulus class.

As a response unspecified derived relational responding is just the tendency to frame any stimulus contacted relationally (This may include selecting relational frames by chance and, thus, a kind of "relational drift" - analogous to genetic drift in population genetics which leads to a sampling error of genes so that a small population can literally drift in a random, unpredictable direction during evolution).

1.4. The behavioral significance of these processes lies in the transformation of stimulus functions. Responding relationally to stimuli allows for changes in the stimulus functions of each stimulus in a set of related stimuli.

For example, if a certain amount of bread is coordinately related to a piece of paper with the words "one dollar" on it and if this piece of paper is also coordinately related to a piece of metal worth "one Euro" then the stimulus functions of one Euro will be the same as those of one dollar, i.e., both will prompt a baker to give me the same amount of bread.

The signs of language (whether spoken or written words or other signs as well) like money are a universal tool to exchange stimulus functions.

1.5. Self-observation (or experiential awareness) of derived relational responding over many instances with a specific relational frame, results in an abstracted experience of specified derived relational responding (e.g., opposition, comparison/hierarchy) that is without content but has the experiential quality of a concept, i.e., of a generalized stimulus class. This may lead to self concepts like "I always do the opposite," "I always take the position of an underdog."

Once these more abstracted self concepts have been verbalized, they (and the whole response class they "contain") can be related to experiential measures of workability (i.e., delayed consequences) which may transform the stimulus functions of the (e.g., oppositional) behaviors and, finally, lead to behavioral change (e.g., oppositional behaviors are dropped because they have been related to their destructive consequences).

One way to do this in therapy may be through "Socratic cubby holing," i.e., asking the client whether a specific relational frame was implemented (e.g., "Did you say this in opposition to what I said before?", "What are you doing this moment; are you comparing yourself to your brother?", "As you give me that answer do you take a submissive position in relation to me?").

1.6. Self-observation (or experiential awareness) of derived relational responding over many instances with many different relational frames results in an abstracted experience of unspecified derived relational responding that is without content and also has the experiential quality of a concept, i.e., of a generalized stimulus class. However, this "self concept" is even more abstracted and may be formulated as "I relate." It may be a technical formulation for the self-as-context because derived relational responding as a generalized stimulus class is without content. [As I write this it tastes a little bit funny and, yes, uncomfortable because it reminds me of Descartes' "Cogito ergo sum" - or is there more in this "cogito" than has been realized so far by philosophers!?] The experience of unspecified derived relational responding as a generalized stimulus class (an abstracted concept), however, cannot be an object of derived relational responding, i.e., there is no verbal response to this generalized stimulus class or concept because any verbal response would be a turn away from this kind of self-observation. To the most general forms of Crel we can only respond nonverbally so that we may have a link, here, between verbal and nonverbal knowing/behavior.

With respect to therapy, then, this kind of looking at the verbal from the nonverbal may be at the heart of mindfulness which, as I discussed before on the RFT list, may not be a weakening or subtracting of Crel but an abstracting of specific instances of Crel to the effect that general forms of Crel (being without content) lose their "power" to transform stimulus functions. Without this power (of specific and content-laden forms of Crel) the natural functions of stimuli may become better available.

2. Rule-following

2.1. Rules. Finally, the socioecological or evolutionary significance of these four processes (mutual entailment, combinatorial entailment, derived relational responding, transformation of stimulus functions) is that they are the basis for verbal communication, i.e., instructional influence, between different human beings.

However, it is obviously not enough for one person to say "Killing a human being is bad and should not be done" that all people listening to this sentence will do what it says. Even when they understand it, i.e., perform the appropriate transformation of stimulus functions and, for example, feel bad if they think of killing another person, some people may kill other persons.

What has to be added to listening with understanding is another operant training process that shapes the fifth component of effective verbal behavior, i.e., rule-following. According to RFT the rule, however, is not in the head of the listener or the speaker.

The rule is either an explicit instruction or it is an abstracted description for a complex set of derived relational responses during an observed or reconstructed behavioral history.

For example, the training history described in the paragraph on combinatorial entailment may be abstracted by the rule "'Dog' in English means the same as 'Hund' in German." Both an appropriate training history as well as the seemingly simple instruction do not put a rule into the head of a person. Rather the stimuli "contain" the rule once it is given; their functions are changed either by the training or by the instruction/rule.

RFT distinguishes between four kinds of rule-following.

2.2. In pliance, a rule/instruction that has been understood is followed because of a history of contacting socially-mediated reinforcement for the correspondence between the rule and behavior. Here, doing what the rule says is socially reinforced not because the rule describes behavior that naturally results in social reinforcement, but because following the rule (whatever its content) is socially reinforced per se.

For example, if an important person (e.g., father, mother) says to a child "I want you to become a rich man" then working hard may not be reinforced by the pecuniary value of the money gained, but because money is framed coordinately with father's or mother's approval.

In pliance, contingencies of derived relational responding and nonverbal rank order behavior may interlock.

2.3. In tracking, a rule/instruction that has been understood is followed because doing what the rule says has been reinforced in the past by consequences that result from rule-following, but has not been based on social reinforcement for the correspondence between the rule and behavior.

The consequences may be environmental or result automatically from the rule-follower's behavior.

For example, effective use of a road map (a track) may result in arriving at the expected destination; thus, following the road map is reinforced.

Following a track like "I have to stop thinking this bad thought" may be automatically reinforced by any activities to achieve this because the track transforms the stimulus functions of those activities (what may be formulated as the rule "It is good to do this because it will help me to get rid of my bad thoughts"). At the same time, however, the term "bad thought" (or whatever substitute) is coordinately related to the bad thought and therefore elicits the same emotional responses as the bad thought itself. Finally, any avoidance activity may be coordinately related to the bad thought, thus paradoxically eliciting the same responses as the bad thought itself.

2.4. In augmenting, understanding a rule/instruction alters the capacity of events to function as consequences. There are two types of augmenting that can be distinguished.

2.5. In motivative augmenting, a rule/instruction that is understood alters the capacity of such events to function as consequences that have been established as functional consequences already before the rule/instruction was given. After the rule was given that capacity may be greater or smaller.

The relevant consequences may be environmental or may automatically result from the rule-follower's behavior.

For example, following the motivative augmental "Try this vanilla flavoured, chocolate coated ice cream" may be reinforced by buying the ice cream because the verbal description of sensory or perceptual functions of consequences works in a way that enhances the reinforcer value of a consequence and evokes operant behavior that results in contact with that consequence.

In the same way, following the motivative augmental "If you try harder you will soon feel as good as in better times" may be automatically reinforced by increasing the frequency and/or intensity of activities performed to achieve the specified goal. "Feel as good as in better times" may function as a short hand verbal description of sensory or perceptual functions which are related to "better feelings." The latter are at least temporarily contacted as part of their verbal description and they are related coordinately to the performed activities (trying harder = feeling better).

2.6. In formative augmenting, a rule/instruction that is understood alters the capacity of events to function as consequences that have NOT been established as functional consequences before the rule/instruction was given. I.e., such rules establish new reinforcers or punishers.

Again the consequences may be environmental or result automatically from the rule-follower's behavior. With respect to automatic reinforcers, formative augmentals may - like pliance - lead to behaviors that have lost any connection to environmental events.

For example, imagine a person who has neither been reinforced with pills for some behavior nor has been told before that pills are good things. For this person, following the formative augmental "Take this pill and your depression will fade away" may be reinforced by taking the prescribed pill because the rule has established the pill as a reinforcer even if the promised consequence is never contacted. So the person takes her pill year after year in spite of ongoing depression.

3. Selection

3.1. One of the biggest challenges for any evolving line of organisms are changing environments. Many organisms have solved this problem by adding more and more structure in a rather unsystematic manner (as Nobel prize winner Francois Jacob wrote in 1966: evolution works like a tinkerer). The downside of this growing complexity is an also growing burden of constraints and loss of flexibility or adaptability. (There is an inherent paradox in here: more complexity for more flexibility resulting in more constraints and ultimately loss of flexibility.) Therefore, complex organisms have "invented" processes (like learning) to enhance plasticity (see West-Eberhard: Development and plasticity, 2003, for a book length treatment).

3.2. Most learning processes are situationally quite specific. Generalized imitation is one big achievement to provide for a process that is able to generate a principally unlimited number of novel behaviors environmental contingencies may operate on in order to select the most useful.

Derived relational responding is another "big bang" and it may be as important for the development of individual behavior as sexuality is for the evolution of populations. Both enormously enhance variability and thus adaptability through recombinatorial processes. And like sexuality, derived relational responding has its dark side (with respect to sexuality I think of the burden that sexual selection may pose; e.g., the huge antlers of some deer species that lead to their extinction).

3.3. The dark side of derived relational responding, in my opinion, is most intriguing in formative augmenting. In formative augmenting, it appears that tracking and transformation of stimulus functions

	interlock. It seems to be that process by which we learn from others by language, for example, when one hunter-gatherer said to another "Don't go to that wood; there is a dangerous wolf pack" or "You must go to that big tree over there and you will find some delicious fruit." Through these sentences the stimulus functions of the wood and the tree are changed; the first now functions as an aversive consequence (approaching the wood will be avoided), the second as a reinforcing one (the tree will be approached). In the second example, formative augmenting may still be limited by natural contingencies because when the tree no longer has fruit, following the rule may no longer be reinforced and hence selected as a response option. However, in the first example, the wood may never be approached again because it is impossible to "test" the rule when it is followed.
RULE-GOVERNED BEHAVIOR **ACT algorithms; pliance & untestable tracks [8-11-04]** Steve Hayes	Francis De Groot wrote: The FEAR and ACT algorithms are instigating rule governed behavior; it seems to me; and there's nothing wrong with rule governed behavior, as long as they result in a better life. Sure. All verbally regulated behavior is rule-governed. Mostly in the rationale underlying ACT we have worried about pliance and untestable tracks. Why? Same answer in both cases: relative rigidity of responding.
RULE-GOVERNED BEHAVIOR **Non-verbal (rule consistent); ACT consistent rules [12-11-04]** Steve Hayes	Joseph Ciarrochi wrote: Does ACT/RFT distinguish between verbal and non-verbal rule-governed behavior? (or must rules be verbal?). People may behave "as if" they have a verbal rule, even though they deny believing the rule when they hear it. There is a difference between rule-governed and rule-consistent behavior. Non-verbal classes of responding can be rule consistent (scientists can formulate rules that describe the pattern). They are not rule governed, in a behavioral sense of that term. That 1989 book on rule-governed behavior that Context Press just reissued goes into all of this ... The first chapter is by Hayne Reese and he does a good job disentangling all the different senses of the term "rule" [it has a great etymological history that makes perfect sense of the confusion ... Latin for "a straight line" eventually came to mean "one who lays down the line" like a ruler of a Kingdom. The cognitive sense of the term is actually an older sense / the behavioral sense is a newer one]. [JC] We often help the client to connect their control rules ("I must avoid my traumatic memory") with unpleasant contingencies ("my life has become small and without value"). In a sense, are we using experiential methods to help people cognitively restructure how they think about the control rules? We are changing the way their control rules are framed. In some ways, are we not doing something similar to that found in second wave CBT (cognitive restructuring)? Client rules change with experience. We are verbal/ cognitive creatures and we will talk about everything. But there is the usual paradox here. Experiential control comes from fusion. When ACT uses experience to contact the workability of old patterns and actual verbally formulated rules, even the new rules that spontaneously form are to be held lightly. If a client came into an ACT session moaning "I just haven't learned to accept my own emotions" I might say "so just notice your mind is saying that" or "and what do you do with that thought?" or "and how does that thought work for you?." It would not matter that the target thought was supposedly ACT consistent ... if it had a fused flavor it is an issue. So, sure, third wave treatments are doing things that are like second wave treatments (and first wave too). Still they are different, even in the areas where they overlap, because the whole is different. The purpose is different. The sensitivities are different.
RULE-GOVERNED BEHAVIOR **Therapy, induced by [3-11-04]** Gareth Furber	The movement from rule-governed to experiential based behaviour has always been the selling point and the stuck point for me. I have yet to be convinced that a therapist can do much more than introduce a more workable rule system. That rule system may encourage a client to take a different philosophy with regards to their thoughts, feelings and experiences, but ultimately will the mind not "store" this in some form of rule? In my life I have always attempted (in some way) to work with what I have learned from my training as a therapist. I have used CBT successfully in my life and more recently used ACT strategies, particularly the acceptance and exploration of difficult emotions. I still feel though that I have merely added a new "rule" to the system, albeit one that is highly adaptable.
RULE-GOVERNED BEHAVIOR Therapy, induced by [cont'd] Steve Hayes	[responding to GF's first paragraph] Yes, but that is itself something to be wary of (even though it will always occur). That second order wariness is unusual in most empirically supported approaches and very characteristic of ACT. If you hold the rule tightly "don't follow rules" aren't you merely changing the form and not the function of rules? And isn't changing the function of rules part of the whole point -- part of the process that creates more psychological flexibility? (Don't believe this.)

RULE-GOVERNED BEHAVIOR Therapy, induced by [cont'd] Matthew Smout	Gareth, I suspect what you're struggling with is that although theoretically, verbal behaviour and nonverbal behaviour are separable, in practice they almost always co-occur together. Once you have language you can get at just about any nonverbal experience verbally. Also you derive rules from interactions with others, which have a non-verbal aspect to them. ACT as therapy tries to add interactions that disrupt adopting new literal rule-following (e.g., "thank your mind for that thought," "let's say that over and over again," "never mind your mind"; "don't believe a word I say"), but it can't prevent clients abstracting verbal rules from the therapy and attempting to follow them (not that it would necessarily want to).

RULE-GOVERNED BEHAVIOR
 	
Therapy, induced by [cont'd]
 	
Matthew Smout
	Gareth Furber wrote:
	
	    That raises further questions:
	
	    1) what verbal rules do the clients abstract from what we are doing?
	
	    2) should we monitor these rules?
	
	    3) how can a ACT therapist successfully engage in ACT therapy without understanding the RFT principles?
	
	    If I were to spend a number of sessions asking questions like you just indicated in an attempt to disrupt adopting new literal rule following, at some point I will slip and introduce a rule especially if asked "why you talking like this?" Surely I need to understand what relations I am weakening to have the courage to keep going? I realise these are questions that require more experience on my part but they are like a brick wall to me at times.
	
	IMHO...
	
	1) Clients could potentially abstract any number of rules - some might be helpful some might not
	
	2) Yes - just as we routinely attend to the rules the client brings to our first session with them, we remain attentive to the influence of unhelpful rule-following and that extends to the rules they pick up from their work with us.
	
	3) I think the main principles an ACT therapist needs to be aware of are:
	
	a) the client's values direct therapy (we aim foremost to help clients pursue their values);
	
	b) workability dictates whether any given client or therapist practice is advocated - if it gets clients closer to their values - great; if further away or not closer - scrutinize;
	
	c) we can only add to minds we can't erase from them;
	
	d) words don't cause behaviour.
	
	This is pretty rough and I may later reflect I've neglected something important - but I would guess that these principles get me by at least 80% of the time.

RULE-GOVERNED BEHAVIOR **Workability of** **[3-10-04]** ACT Listserv Member	Francis De Groot wrote: The things I most keep in mind from this part of the ACT book [pp. 26-36] are what the rigidity rules can induce and the warning to be cautious about using the therapeutic relationship to induce specific rule following. I can see this, and I agree with it, but (in ACT terms I should say "and") I find this very difficult. Certainly in a psychiatric hospital inducing rule following is a most common thing: don't smoke in your room, it's time to go to occupational therapy, don't forget your homework .... Patients do a lot to please their therapist, nurse, … you often can get things done because of your good relationship. Are there rules about when to use pliance (rules) and when not to? You have a good question, and have picked up on one of the key concepts for an ACT therapist (at least I think it is). Most therapies really are efforts to change the "rules" that the client lives by, usually the ones pertaining to what they think about themselves and how that affects their behavior. Some rules are good to follow - most of the ones pertaining to the external world fall into this category. Imagine if we did not have rule governance, people would drive however they wanted, whatever speed, ignore traffic signals; they would have sex with whomever, whenever; they would steal ... on and on, you get the point. Rigidity of rules, especially rules that are concerned with our feelings/thoughts/memories and the like, is, I think, what is being cautioned against in the book (rigidity even in external rules can run awry; what is the Buddhist saying - which is it better to be a blade of grass or tree??). Rule following serves a purpose, workability should be the test for when it is or isn't good. Most avoidance of cognitive material starts with a simple self rule, "Don't think/feel X." It works in the short term, for most, but the truth is that long term it makes us think about it more. I think the book references some of the thought suppression research to get more on this. It is this kind of rule following that usually is at the root of creating more behavioral restriction, and increasing suffering. In order not to think/feel X one needs to not do Y because Y brings you in contact with verbal and environmental stimuli that are in relational frames with X. When we as therapists, simply try to

	supplant our rules about thinking and behaving, it may work for some and it may work for a short period of time - what we need to keep in mind is long term workability of following rules. Rules are neither good or bad in themselves; it is the context, and workability that establishes that. For example, two people (person A and person B): A and B both wash their hands a lot, it takes up a good portion of their day, it is done in a very ritualistic manner, with a specific type of soap, with a specific water temperature. Both A and B are washing their hands because they are worried about contamination, their own and others'. Both A and B are rigidly following rules about hand washing, and on the surface, if this was all the info you had, you may think both have OCD, but...what if one of them was a surgeon, then would the rigid rules about avoiding contamination be bad?
RULE-GOVERNED BEHAVIOR Workability of [cont'd] Andy Santanello	I think that the comment about workability is right on, and I think one little piece needs to be added. ACT encourages a move from rule-governed to contingency shaped behavior. In other words, clients are encouraged to check the workability of their mind's "strategery" (to borrow a term from Will Ferrel doing his impersonation of G. W. Bush) against the yardstick of their experience. Our clients have been taking their mind's "word for it" when it tells them "avoidance works, keep doing that." If the therapist starts saying "don't try to stop thinking, accept your thoughts instead," he or she is reinforcing the client's habit of buying into the mind's insistence that controlling internal events is necessary and that this strategy will work. ACT tries to help clients experience for themselves the unworkability of the change agenda. This is why ACT is unique, and why it is so powerful. ACT helps clients see for themselves what works for them in their lives, regardless of what their mind, or the therapist's mind for that matter, tells them. Lastly, it encourages clients to be honest with themselves. If someone wants to learn how to play guitar, he or she must be willing to get blisters, miss strings with the pick, and play the wrong notes from time to time because these are all things that will happen during the learning process. To be a good musician, you have to practice everyday, no matter how many mistakes you make. I think ACT is about practicing everyday, and making room for playing some wrong notes from time to time.
SCIENCE **Philosophy of - alternative views; recommended readings [9-17-03]** Kelly Wilson	I teach a course in learning in which I pack a month-long lesson in philosophy of science into the front end of the course. Why? Because we can't even talk about behavior analysis--and be talking about the same thing without it. If I don't do this, I describe a contextualist account and they hear mechanism. Even if they hear something else, it quickly slides over into mechanism.
	An even deeper problem for folks is breaking loose of what I call in class "the received view of science." When I unpack the received view of science folks cannot even get that it is A view of science--IT IS SCIENCE. I make folks read Larry Loudans' delightful article "A Confutation of Convergent Realism." This very tasty little paper unpacks the problem with convergent epistemological realism and its handmaiden referential theories.
	In brief the received view of science is:
	- Theories represent the world/domain (re present)
	- Terms in a theory refer or correspond to aspects of the "real world"
	- If the model is correct, it will allow for remote (and non-intuitive) prediction
	- This ability to make remote prediction tells us about the accuracy of the model
	- Current theories are not wholly true (i.e., accurate re-presentations), but they are truer than old theories and the scientific method ensures (at least over time) the development of increasingly accurate representations of the world over time.
	This view is described by Loudans as Convergent Epistemological Realism (CER)--that's a mouthful. I believe that conventional science is realist in its ontology, CER in its epistemology, and contains a completely subterranean theory of language--that is, a referential theory of language.
	It is almost impossible for folks to get, without experiencing extraordinary distress, what is meant by a nonreferential theory. You can literally watch them twist in their chairs in class as they try to get their heads around the idea of a nonreferential theory-- "Well if it doesn't refer to the "real" world, what does it refer to? AHHHHH!!!"
	A physical metaphor I have used to make this point is as follows. I stand at one end of the room and make exaggerated steps across the room. I say: "My goal is to get across the room. Walking got me from one end of the room to the other. What do my steps refer to?" and then, "I want to predict and influence behavior. I talk, and talking like this allows me to predict and influence behavior. What does my talking refer to?" The first question seems goofy to people. The second does not seem goofy at all.
	Why is it so difficult to get the concept of a nonreferential theory? Because understanding a nonreferential theory of language is excruciating. This is why, I think, Skinner was almost universally misunderstood. Without imposing extraordinary distress on folks they cannot hear it as anything but an incoherent (incorrect) version of what they already think. A referential theory of language is built into lay

	understandings of language and virtually all of philosophizing. Certainly all of the logical positivist, operationist, logical empiricist folks are way far gone on this. It is likewise there in the sophisticated thinking of folks like Maccorquodale and Meehl in their classic 1948 paper on hypothetical constructs and intervening variables. The thing is though that the referential theory of language is COMPLETELY invisible, unstated, assumed. A few folks have gotten this--Wittgenstein got it. The pragmatists like Dewey got it--though I don't think the pragmatists unpacked this idea sufficiently. It is in their talk, sometimes explicitly, but mostly intuitively--language as use. I think that this core piece--a nonreferential theory of language-- may have been what marginalized American Pragmatism as a truly dominant school of philosophy.
	Bottom line, letting go of ontology is distressing. Letting go of reference is distressing. Very hard stuff to hang onto. But, it may just turn out to be worth it.
SCIENCE Philosophy of - alternative views; recommended readings [cont'd] Kelly Wilson	Graham Taylor wrote: I sense the vital nature of this, and need some help here - can you post or suggest some BASIC readings to have a go at. Or class handouts you use, or anything. Dermot and Steve have both published on this issue. Also, consider my little pub "Some Notes on Theoretical Constructs" which you can download from my homepage. My students say that it is pretty clear (but they may just be sweet talking me). Niklas also thought it was useful, so maybe it is. The paper deals with a slice of these issues--namely implications for types of theoretical constructs and for different types of theorizing. Anything Steve or Dermot have written on contextualism is worthwhile. Dermot's paper on reality and truth is very tasty (warning: will mess with your head).... To get how some of this fits with mainstream psychological theorizing it doesn't hurt to have a sense of the opposing view, so things like Smitty Stevens' classic work on operationism provides a killer counterpoint to this perspective. Stevens lays out his position on operationism nearly 70 years ago, and I don't think that psychology has moved a hell of a lot beyond it. Really, I think that the whole set of papers in the 1945 September issue of Psych Review are worth looking at. The issue contains a symposium of then current thinking on operationism--with all the biggies weighing in. Skinner's paper on the "Operational Analysis of Psychological Terms" is a stunning counterpoint to every other article in this issue. (Skinnerphiles know this paper affectionately as "The '45 Paper.") I tell students that if they want to get what Skinner was up to, they need to understand the '45 paper. This paper represents Skinner's mature thinking. In the paper, Skinner provides a psychological answer to the problem of operationism. He makes it clear in this paper that he applies the same functional pragmatic approach to the use of psychological terms by psychology theorists as he does to any other behavior performed by anyone else. If you get this paper, you get what was truly radical about radical behaviorism--behavioral to the root. Another very worthwhile read is Larry Smith's excellent book "Behaviorism and Logical Positivism." Smith does a very nice job of unpacking the distinction between Skinner's behaviorism and the other behavioral positions that emerged alongside it. I think that you can extrapolate from the analysis of early learning theorists to modern cognitive psychology because they are the same type of theories. The constructs change name, but not type. Yesterday's "habit strength" is today's "memory trace."...
SCIENCE Philosophy of - alternative views; recommended readings [cont'd] Dermot Barnes-Holmes	For short and really basic, try Barnes & Holmes (1991). *The Psych Record*. This has a mix of philosophy, history, and very simple RFT. I use it with my own undergrads and no one's head has exploded (yet!).

Chapter 5
<u>ACT with Particular Client Groups and Clinical Problems</u>

Posts in this chapter concern the application of ACT in a variety of clinical contexts, organized by reference to presenting problem or client characteristics, and the delivery of ACT in group format. Dialogues regarding the sequencing of ACT components are also included here for the reason that debate on this topic often focuses on the varying therapeutic needs of different client groups. A further selection of posts discusses ACT-relevant considerations in relation to cultural differences in client populations.

ALEXITHYMIA **ACT conceptualization (link with EA) [4-1-04]** Steve Hayes	Mary Politi wrote: I was wondering if people have used ACT to treat patients diagnosed with alexithymia. Measures of alexithymia correlate very highly with the AAQ. One of the authors on the AAQ study found this but it came in too late to include in the validation article. Chronic and early experiential avoidance, esp. due to the deep structure of family traditions / early trauma / etc. = alexithymia. That would be my guess anyway. And, sure, ACT should help. Remove the props for avoidance, and then do emotional exposure and training of emotional discrimination. Psychotherapy usually does some of the latter but not systematically and usually without the former (except the presence of a supportive relationship). An ACT approach should be a better combo.
ANXIETY **Anxiety Sensitivity Index - link with EA** **BOOK** **ACT for Anxiety Disorders [4-30-05]** John Forsyth	Mary Politi wrote: Has anyone looked at the Anxiety Sensitivity Index (ASI) and how it relates/does not relate to experiential avoidance measures? It seems to me that they overlap, in that the ASI measures a person's willingness (or unwillingness) to feel anxiety... We have a few studies out showing exactly what you suggest, and there are more from other groups too. I think you are right on re: the connection between AS and EA. AS denotes fear of anxiety sensations, or fear of fear. Within the context of EA, AS makes complete sense. AS does not make a whole lot of sense in the context of experiential acceptance. Honestly, I think EA drives AS and other related constructs, not AS to EA. Georg and I talk about this connection a bit in the *ACT for Anxiety Disorders* Book...
ANXIETY **Panic - flying phobia** **COPING STRATEGIES** **Enjoyable activities, attention to function of [3-17-04]** Steve Hayes	Gareth Furber wrote: Once you have got on the plane, I would assume that you are then free to explore any variety of methods to make the trip more enjoyable with workability as your guide.... As a therapist, is the exploration of these methods (to make the flight more enjoyable) reinforcing of the belief that the flight must be enjoyable? "Enjoy" comes from a word that originally meant both "taking pleasure in" and "welcome." If you are afraid of flying -- while you may not be able to take pleasure in it right now, you can certainly welcome and celebrate the moment ... which is (in a sense) "making the flight more enjoyable." There are lots of things to do while flying: sleep, read, watch movies, consider your mortality, play games, talk to others, look around, look out the window, breathe, feel your butt get numb, imagine, write, work on your computer, listen to music, feel afraid, let go of control, eat great food ... well, maybe not that last one. I think helping people connect with all the things there are to do while flying only makes sense. If the purpose is to *subtract* some experiences (as opposed to putting them in a larger context) it probably feeds a destructive agenda, however. There is the same amount of life in *every* moment -- no more, no less. What differs is our psychological presence, not what a moment of life affords ... if the purpose is to show up to your experiences with flying, and to expand the number of things you can do while flying, it probably feeds a healthy agenda. I used to be terrified of throwing up on planes. For years flying was only about that: nausea and keeping the little bag close. I could come close to throwing up just by walking through the door of a plane. So first I had to make room for the thoughts and feelings and fears, as they are and not as what they say they are. No BS. I give up. If I throw up I throw up. Nausea is nausea, etc. Then I could begin to figure out what I like to do on planes. If I tried to do step two before step one, I would be less likely to do step one because step two would now be (in its function) the step of "not one." Playing solitaire would now be NOT being nauseous. But that is not playing solitaire, really. Sleeping would now be NOT fearing throwing up (but as soon as I wake it is now more of an issue). Almost anything we do will alter internal events. And I don't think there is a hard and fast rule "don't alter them." But if altering internal events were the golden path folks think it is, why would we need things like ACT anyway? We need it because it is not so easy, and some of our most powerful methods (e.g., drugs, alcohol) bring along a whole set of problems as well. With fear of flying I'd do psychoeducation about what these feelings are physiologically, and I'd look for hyperventilation, and I might even do relaxation training (as training in letting go), and I'd do exposure in imagination and in vivo, but I'd put all of that at least in the context of acceptance, and defusion since I think the data are pretty good already that these processes help with response flexibility and exposure; and

	if I had the time and permission I would probably add self-as-process work (learning to contact the present moment), self-as-context work (in part of make acceptance truly possible), and values work, and committed action linked to the exposure work...
	These last ones are not as well established data wise in this area....
ANXIETY Panic - flying phobia [cont'd] **COPING STRATEGIES** Enjoyable activities, attention to function of [cont'd] **ACT cf.** **CBT - re phobias [3-18-04]** Gareth Furber	I think I am beginning to understand a key distinction between the fundamental aspects of my training and the processes of ACT. In my training, the treatment of fear of flying would involve 1) exposure 2) some form of cognitive restructuring regarding the interpretation of physical symptoms, 3) some relaxation training (to counteract physiological response). This does not differ much at all from what an ACT therapist might do. The context in which this work is done though differs considerably.
	In my training I would have conceptualized the fear of flying as a physiological/cognitive and behavioural response to a set of core beliefs/assumptions/rules (whatever you want to call them). This implies that the therapeutic goal is the modification of these rules etc.
	In ACT I see the therapeutic goal as the achievement of being psychologically present, accepting of whatever experiences come your way and finally (having had some success with the first 2) pursue freely other experiences that may be available at that time.
	While the techniques in CBT aim to weaken pre-existing rules (e.g., chances are I won't throw up on this plane), techniques in ACT promote the willingness to experience what comes ("I'm willing to throw up and then more")....
ANXIETY **Panic - interoceptive exposure** **EXPOSURE** **Interoceptive - acceptance cf. control agenda [10-1-03]** Steve Hayes	Archana Jajodia wrote: Does anybody have an ACT protocol targeted specifically to panic disorder? Has anyone tried interoceptive exposure from an ACT perspective?
	Exposure of that kind has always been a key feature of ACT. That exact package for panic disorder is actually where ACT started 24 years ago, in part because that combo is what I was doing with myself when panic was a major deal in my life. The result basically formed the core of ACT, and all other ACT manuals....
	It is very easy to do interoceptive exposure from an ACT perspective. That has been a study worth doing for 20 years (PCT/MAP stripped of all the inconsistent control junk and thoroughly ACTified). In fact I tried to talk the developer of interoceptive exposure into doing a grant with me on that exact combo sometime in the early 1990's or earlier....
	The only tricky business is keeping the ACT message in the work, especially as they start feeling less anxious. As a means to THAT end, ACT will be no more successful than anything else.
	I don't mean by that that ACT won't reduce anxiety or that it won't reduce it more than other things. Possible it will. What I mean is as folks start to experience reductions they link the ACT techniques to an anti-ACT agenda. You can do lots of cool things in ACT for anxiety, including exposure or even relaxation, but you have to be very clear with what you are doing or the dominant agenda in the culture will overwhelm your message. Exposure is a willingness exercise in ACT. Its purpose is to increase the flexibility of behavior in the presence of feared events. I.e., its purpose is empowerment / freedom / choice / valued action. But anything ... even ACT ... can be linked to the poisonous message of "out with the bad stuff first." And as a vehicle for THAT, ACT will be no more successful than anything else.
ANXIETY **Stress - values-based intervention [8-19-02]** JoAnne Dahl	Kirrilie Smout wrote: I am wondering what an ACT approach to stress management might be like?
	I work with stress and adults who have so-called burn out and ACT. My working hypothesis is that a negative stress reaction is due to "ill values" or that one's feet are not going in the same way as one's values or intentions. Our results show that on the values instruments people who are stressed have disregarded important dimensions in their lives and are, for example, spending more time on certain things like in my clients' cases, taking care of others but almost no time in taking care of their own needs. The treatment of stress in our case would be to find out using the values instrument what values have low activity or big discrepancies between intention and own activity and support the client in building repertoires there. This instrument is very revealing and explicit.
BIPOLAR DISORDER **Manic phase - use of ACT**	William Kordonski wrote: I've been using Kelly's form and Steve's with a man who is in the manic stage. He is constantly having new love affairs. He has lost his home recently too. But when we look at his values and how he is living them there are few discrepancies. Has anyone had experience using ACT with Bipolar folks in the manic phase?

VALUES	I would suspect that avoidance may be preventing him from filling out the forms accurately (unless, of course, changing love affairs and a lost house aren't inconsistent with his values). Maybe he's afraid how you will perceive him if significant discrepancies show up on his paperwork. Or maybe it's too aversive for him to take an honest look at how well or poorly he's living a valued life. Maybe a bit of both. It's not uncommon for defusion work to be required to get an accurate assessment of values and movement/lack of movement toward them.
Discrepant behavior, unacknowledged - bipolar client	
FUSION/ DEFUSION	Another possibility would be that he doesn't have a complete picture of how some of his behavior impedes movement toward his values. If so, this would place an extra burden on you as the therapist to mark behaviors he reports that you feel may impede progress toward one or more of his values, then bring them up in a collaborative fashion (e.g., "I wonder if doing X might be moving you farther away from value y"). This may be a particular concern when he's manic--short term consequences are Emperor (rather than just King) at times like that, and he may need some extra help connecting the dots.
Values, re - bipolar client [5-12-04]	
John Blackledge	
BIPOLAR DISORDER	William Kordonski wrote:
Manic phase - use of ACT [cont'd]	> Could you please elaborate on the term "defusion work" especially in relation to this man. Also, I've met with him 4 times thus far and he continues to act the "naughty little boy." So I think your thoughts are on the right track, i.e., a combination of avoidance and not connecting the dots. I continue to be okay with his reports and assure him that his life is not mine to live. I think I'm seeing a slight shift toward honest reporting in the light of my non-punishing stance.
VALUES	Assuming you've done much of the standard defusion work with him (e.g., distinguishing between descriptions and evaluations, using standard ACT exercises/metaphors like the "milk" exercise and those experientially showing the distinction between direct experience and talk about those experiences) and assuming that this is an avoidance issue, I'd consider doing something like this:
Discrepant behavior, unacknowledged - bipolar client [cont'd]	
FUSION/ DEFUSION	Find a values domain you feel is a particular hot spot for him (one that is very important to him and that he has likely fallen short on a lot). Ask him to elaborate on that value and what about it is important to him. For example, have him discuss in detail a couple of times that he really lived that value--what happened, what it felt like, etc. Then have him picture (perhaps in an eyes-closed exercise, with you providing prompts to picture various details) what his life might be like if he lived that value often. Be alert for any negative evaluations (particularly self-evaluations) he verbalizes during all this. If they come up, give prompts that point out the evaluative (vs. descriptive) nature of those thoughts--e.g., "That's an interesting thought your mind is giving you. Is that a solid fact, as real as this table--or is that one of those airy evaluations?", and "Can you sit with the pain that's underneath that evaluation for a few moments with me?" Sometimes, things like condensing a particularly potent negative self-evaluation to a short phrase (e.g., "I don't deserve it") and repeating it over and over as in the milk exercise can cut through an evaluation that is tightly fused with. If no evaluative barriers come up in the course of his elaborating on his value, ask him what gets in the way of living that value. Then jump in with techniques like those just described. I'd be interested to hear how others cut through avoidance during values assessment, as well.
Values, re - bipolar client [cont'd]	
John Blackledge	
	Avoidance could be tightly intertwined with a potential failure for him to 'connect the dots,' as well. Part of the purpose of values work in ACT is to use language to maximize a client's ability to move toward their values. In order to do this, the client must be able to verbally specify what behaviors get them in trouble, and what behaviors move them toward what they value. Avoidance can play a role in this because it can be very painful to show up to all the things we are doing that move us away from what's important to us. So, even if an intervention somewhat along the lines of the one described above isn't completely called for, the extra practice defusing from evaluations may not be wasted as it can apply to avoidance of 'connecting the dots' as well. Regardless, it might be a good idea with a client like this to 'guide his pencil' by providing him with prompts that help him more thoroughly consider the values-affecting consequences of his actions. Particularly when he is manic and only thinking one step ahead.
BIPOLAR DISORDER	I advise against using ACT with persons with bipolar disorder in the manic phase until symptoms remit - however, most of my experience is with individuals meeting criteria for manic episode with psychotic features, so I'm not sure if the same caution applies to individuals with less severe symptoms.
Manic phase - use of ACT [cont'd]	
VALUES	I do not find the lack of discrepancy between the values and how he is living them surprising. While I have not used the forms with anyone meeting criteria for a manic episode, I have observed a striking lack of awareness of or insight into negative consequences of behaviors often seen in mania, such as substance abuse, indiscriminate sexual behavior, impulsive major decisions about career/finances/relationships, illegal activities etc.
Discrepant behavior, unacknowledged - bipolar client [cont'd]	
Patty Bach	However, once manic symptoms remit the client may see the relationship between his or her behavior and values quite differently.

BODY DYSMORPHIC DISORDER **Functional analysis, need for [7-6-04]** Nico van der Meijden	Sven Rydberg wrote: Any ACT ideas on BDD (Body Dysmorphic Disorder, imagined ugliness)? A client of mine ... is obsessive about loss of his hair.... I think it's important to look at the function the obsession with hair loss has for this client and to make some functional analyses. Perhaps you have already made some assessments, but from what you write it's difficult to get a clear diagnostic picture of this client, e.g., is it social anxiety or fear of social judgement he's avoiding? How is the relationship with his parents? Are there separation problems/ dependency conflicts: is he afraid of the problems and responsibilities of mature life facing him when he would leave home? Are there sexual problems or anxieties? You don't write anything about his history or background (or his 'context' as they would say in this group). To get a clearer picture of the function of this behavior I think it would indeed be wise to have a meeting with his entire family.
CHILD & ADOLESCENT **ACT metaphors/ exercises [7-18-02]** Chris McCurry	Kelly Wilson wrote: We just hit a small grant ... to do a pilot treating kids at our local high school using ACT. The target population will be kids 14-18 who are at risk for academic failure/drop out.... Any thoughts on ... ACT interventions you like with this age group? In terms of ACT moves - I've found the bus metaphor to be appealing and useful. I have VERY carefully used Steve's "you have to kill yourself everyday" move with some success (nobody's died yet). The corpus delecti issue is often big with adolescents, as well as mattering. I don't know how well this would work with your group but I had some success with an anxious adolescent undermining literality by going on the net to dictionary.com and translating her stock anxious thoughts (regarding an upcoming oral surgery) into Portuguese. "I can't stand this" became "Eu nao posso estar este" and when she had this thought instead it lost a lot of its bite.... Here in the Pacific Northwest we have a lot of snowboarders. Probably not big in Mississippi. I will talk with them about control- in snowboarding you increase control by leaning back (to a point). In skiing, and other tasks, you increase control and effective working by leaning in.
CHILD & ADOLESCENT **Autism - group intervention for parents** **GROUP** **Parents of autistic children [12-10-03]** John Blackledge	... I ran weekend ACT workshops for parents of autistic children (2-day workshops, about 7 hours each day)--small n (20). Post data indicated modest but significant reductions in general distress as measured by the General Health Questionnaire-12 and the Brief Symptom Inventory, and a slight but significant reduction in depression, with one measure of general distress maintained at 3-month follow-up.... ... the "group workshops" were not group workshops in the strictest sense, since so few people attended them (the n for each respective workshop started at 7, then dwindled to 6, 4 and 3 for the last three workshops--prompting me to ask that age-old question, "What if you gave free therapy and nobody came?"). Perhaps this, coupled with the abbreviated workshop format, helps explain why there wasn't that revolutionary, post-ACT workshop glow that many of us have experienced after attending a marathon ACT workshop. My subjective sense after running these workshops and looking at the data is that the problems potentially shared by families/parents may be conducive to a workshop format. But a one-shot, weekend format with no follow-up sessions may not be the best way to go if you want robust, maintained change. If I do more workshops like this for an outcome study, I'll make sure there are more people in each group, and schedule a couple of follow-up sessions (perhaps individual follow-up sessions) to drive the points home.
CHILD & ADOLESCENT **Group intervention with adolescents [10-29-04]** Joseph Ciarrochi	J.T. Blackledge and I have recently created a brief workbook for adolescents, based on some of the visual metaphors and exercises used with adults. I have just completed a pilot with 8th graders, and they seemed to respond well to the materials. ... I sent two emails to J.T. describing my experience with this intervention and what seemed to work. I insert these emails below. The pilot consisted of 2 x 3.5 hour sessions with a group of 15 8th graders (8 girls; 7 boys). Comments after the first 3.5 hour session: I had to go away from my best laid plans, once I got into the moment, but it all worked in the end. Dealing with 8th graders is like dealing with a tree full of chattering monkeys (who have just snorted cocaine). You won't keep them quiet for long. ***Values The values bit took a lot longer than planned, nearly 1 1/2 hours. Kids offered an awful lot of compliance-type things ("I want to be good" type of stuff), so I had to work a bit at getting at the core values. Kids put "establishing" and "building" strong friendships as their top value, above values related to family and other domains. I am planning to do a lot of experiential role play next week, to help them

interact more effectively with their classmates, teachers, and parents (it allows them to experience all the ACT-relevant processes in vivo).

This first 1.5 hours was also spent getting kids to distinguish between value consistent and inconsistent behaviors and to notice the sorts of emotions and thoughts that come up when engaging in values (e.g., anxiety, self doubt).

***Creative hopelessness/ Acceptance

During the second 1.5 hours, I spent about 40 minutes on creative hopelessness/acceptance. I did the "don't think about a chocolate cake," "lie detector," and "don't get eaten machine" exercises. They seemed to get things experientially. I also did a bunch of experiential exercises to illustrate how spontaneously negative self-evaluations occur and how futile it is to hope to eliminate them (e.g., whole, complete, and perfect; have the thought "I am perfect in every way"; the prevalence of self-doubt even in the most talented athletes, etc.). I also helped them to identify how their own valued action often involves risk and can elicit self-evaluation, anxiety, and frustration. The one control move I focused on was "avoiding a valued direction" in order to not have the anxiety or self-doubt.

My intuition was that I did not have time to get them to identify other control moves (e.g., distraction, changing one's attitude). I think this would have been very difficult for them to understand...with more time maybe.

***Defusion/ Self-concept defusion

We explored the distinction between descriptions, evaluations, and rules. Kids worked on an individual problem on the worksheets, and I worked on a common problem on the board (the problem was "getting picked on by a teacher"). The worksheets worked well. And helped structure the whole experience. The kids definitely got the description and evaluation distinction, but I did not have enough time to give them the rule distinction in much detail (more next week). I think they won't have trouble getting the rule distinction....

The Milk, milk, milk exercise worked real well. I also got 4 kids to say one word each from "I'm not good enough." They were to say it in a funny voice. Kids really got the idea (had the experience) that whilst these evaluations felt powerful, they were just words, and words are not substantial and don't need to push them off their valued path. The "Bad cup" metaphor was particularly powerful, especially for the kids who, I could tell, got picked on regularly. (I was actually surprised at how easily kids got this stuff.)

***Willingness/ Commitment

I did a bit of work here, especially with the notion of carrying their feelings and evaluations with them. I'll do more next week.

Overall, I really enjoyed working with the kids. They are so much more expressive than adults, and their defenses are far easier to recognize....

I definitely see that working with kids will improve one's work with adults. You have to stay close to experience and values, or you lose them to horseplay....

Exhausting!

Comments after the second 3.5 hour session:

Man, the intervention went fantastically today. The kids came in and seemed really keen to start (unlike the first session, when they were like a tree full of chattering monkeys). Everybody was into it, and I think they got the distinction between descriptions, evaluations, and rules.

The experiential role play stuff was a huge hit (e.g., two people interact, with one role playing a bully and the other role playing the bullied). When adults do this exercise, they can usually fake good, and you have to dig a bit to get to what they really do. With kids, they just put all the ineffective stuff right out in front of you. You can then put what they do next to what they state they value and proceed from there. I think the ACT-ified assertiveness stuff was amongst the most useful material....

The whole time they did the experiential role play stuff, I was helping the kids to identify feelings (or descriptions), evaluations, and rules as they showed up. I also had them identify the values they wanted to put into play. Then I had them role play various responses they might try in real life. After each response was played out, the group rated the response on a scale of 1 to 10 (10 most effective response). So "spreading nasty rumours" was rated a 3 response, whereas "asserting" was rated an 8. This task went off!!!

We did another exercise that I think really worked well (it was created in the room in the moment). Basically, we wanted to role play what kids might try when they are getting picked on. So one kid volunteered to play the role of the person that gets picked on, and the group agreed to pick on him (hot stuff, I know). Rather then have the group come up with insults that the kid might take seriously, I had

	them generate insults they commonly hear and had them write these insults on pieces of paper. We then randomly gave each person in the group the piece of paper, and each person read their insult to the kid. It was a great defusion move, because one could hear and feel that the insults were just words (they were just stuff someone was reading). I then asked them to contrast how they reacted to these read words compared to how they normally react when someone says the insulting words to them.
CHILD & ADOLESCENT Measures - WAM, AFQ & CAMM **MEASURE** Child & adolescent measures [3-26-05] Laurie Greco	The child and adolescent measures are now on the ACT website (Yay!). For those of you who have been using the initial 50-item version of the WAM, here's the run down: We split the 50-item scale into two separate measures based on results of factor analysis. Also, it made sense to do this based on how factors correlated with each other and with other variables. **One measure clearly taps into willingness and action -- 14 items, Willingness & Action Measure (WAM) **A second seems to get at experiential avoidance and fusion -- 25 items, Avoidance & Fusion Questionnaire (AFQ) Our initial findings suggest that the WAM may be a stronger predictor of good stuff (e.g., quality of life, success in relationships), and the AFQ may be a stronger predictor of bad stuff (e.g., physical and emotional pain). Interestingly, the two measures don't correlate with each other. Kids seem to be responding differently to negatively worded items. We're back in the schools now getting retest and follow up data and are conducting structured interviews with around 30 children and adolescents. We're trying as best we can to crawl into their minds to see if and how they understand these funny questions. We're playing around with wording on the WAM and are testing an 18-item version. We should have recommendations for which scale(s) to use by this summer. For now, I'd say go ahead and use the 14-item WAM as a measure of willingness and action and the 25-item AFQ as a measure of experiential avoidance and cognitive fusion. Compute total scores by simply adding up responses. No need to reverse score. High scores on the WAM = high willingness. High scores on the AFQ = high avoidance/fusion. Ruth Baer, students Sarah Dew & Trish Lipani, and I are working on the manuscript(s) now and will post something soon! (Uh oh, said it out loud) Ruth, Sarah, and I are also piloting the Child Acceptance and Mindfulness Measure (CAMM) in the schools. Writing child-friendly mindfulness items sure is tricky!!
CHILD & ADOLESCENT Metaphors - stingerless bees, nocturnal monsters etc. [5-20-03] **IMAGE** Ideas for ACT pictures [cont'd] Mary Englert *Cross Reference:* *See 7-307 for an earlier post in the thread:* *IMAGE* *Ideas for ACT pictures*	I use a metaphor with worried kids that we often end up drawing, so a ready-made picture would be ideal. I have them imagine they are hiking in a beautiful new park and as they go along the trail they get swarmed by bees. When I ask them how they'd feel, they always answer "scared." Then I go on to say that just as the bees begin to swarm, the park ranger comes over some loud speaker system welcoming park visitors and saying "BTW, all of the bees in this park lack stingers." When I then ask them how they'd feel, the answer is always some form of "relieved." We go on to compare their OCD, health anxiety, separation anxiety or whatever thoughts to the stingerless bees - sure they are yellow/black striped, buzz, swarm etc., but they are harmless. Calling the intrusive thoughts "the bees" keeps us away from calling them "bad" thoughts. So being swarmed by stingerless bees may make a mighty fine drawing.
CHILD & ADOLESCENT Metaphors - stingerless bees, nocturnal monsters etc. [cont'd] Ragnar Storaasli	This metaphor reminds me of a time my daughter, about 5 years ago, was stung several times by bees and subsequently began having "bee nightmares" and was afraid to go to sleep at night. Not surprisingly, comfort and reassurance that no bees would sting her while she slept didn't work so well. The conversation we then had was on the difference between real bees and "thought" bees. Only real bees can sting. I told her if the thought bees showed up that she should invite them in for some lunch and honey. She embraced the buzzing thoughts and their stingers disappeared.

CHILD & ADOLESCENT Metaphors - stingerless bees, nocturnal monsters etc. [cont'd] Steve Hayes	This reminds me of a time when my daughter became very afraid of the "little blue monsters with big teeth" (think the movie "Gremlins") that she feared would bite her in her sleep. I think she was 9 or 10. She delayed going to bed for fear they would appear in her dreams, which they did. After some days of this she asked me what to do. I said with some passion that the poor blue monsters lived in her dreams and they had nowhere else to go. We needed to be kind to them since it wasn't their fault that they were scary. We made a bed for them in a cardboard box and put it by her bed. That way, if they came to her, they'd have a nice place to stay with her. Oddly, they never came.
CHILD & ADOLESCENT **Parenting - ACT interventions; barriers [5-15-03]** John Blackledge	David Heyne wrote: Is anyone able to provide any leads regarding currently available ACT-based parenting materials...? I've run a couple of dissertation ACT workshops with parents of autistic children, as well as a few dozen parenting classes using Glenn Latham's book (The Power of Positive Parenting--an excellent, user-friendly behavioral parenting book). My experience has been that ACT works seamlessly into the skills-training approach inherent to parent training, as I believe it does to any skills training approach. Once the skills are in a parent's repertoire, other factors (e.g., avoidance) can tend strongly to block their emission. If you're considering an intervention with the primary purpose of improving parenting skills, the logical sequence seems to be what Kristoffer suggested--teach the parenting skills, let the parents have a little practice implementing them, then do an ad-hoc functional analysis to see what's keeping them from creating workable behavioral plans and applying consistent consequences. Chances are, avoidance is a chief culprit (whether avoidance of the discomfort of a tantrum, a child's disapproval, the discomfort involved with designing a plausible behavioral plan, feeling like a villain, etc.), which points the way to some focused defusion and acceptance work, along with a heartfelt focus on what their values are as parents. I'd like to be able to say that I've come up with some strikingly original departures from typical ACT work to address these issues, but the fact is the targets of avoidance so resemble the kind of things people struggle with in areas having nothing to do with parenting that I've found typical ACT exercises appear to work fairly well. Once a parent has made contact with a heartfelt value that resembles wanting to raise a child who is relatively well-adjusted and capable, a few specific prompts regarding sticking points with their children during standard experiential exercises seem to facilitate some useful defusion and acceptance. Worrying about what others think about your abilities, being able to accept high levels of anxiety, frustration, and anger and to defuse the meaning of these feelings, facing hurtful words from one you are applying consequences to, etc., are all issues that are faced in life even without children. Granted, children make such issues come up a lot more often, but the song remains the same (something tells me I will look back at this when I'm actually a parent and lament the folly of my youthful thinking, though!). Perhaps an exercise like the 'file-drawer' exercise (for example)--where you start with a painful experience your parents have been having with their children, then flip back through the file drawer to find connected experiences that may speak volumes about the literal meanings they attach to those experiences--might help parents provide some painful, longstanding thoughts that prove to be great candidates for defusion. Of course, this is all anecdotal--my data isn't in yet, and even when it is, it wasn't designed to do a serious assessment of changes in parenting effectiveness. One of the cool things about ACT + parenting is that it explicitly calls for skills training to be integrated with the ACT stuff. It explicitly calls for clinical behavior analysis at its finest....
CHILD & ADOLESCENT Parenting - ACT interventions; barriers [cont'd] Kelly Wilson	I have never met a behavior analyst who is as good a behavior analyst with his/her own children. There is a really good RFT/ACT reason why this is so. It goes like this.... Question: What is the sound of one hand clapping? Answer: The sound of one hand clapping is the sound of one hand clapping. Question: What is the sound of one child misbehaving? Answer: The sound of one child misbehaving. Question: What is the sound of *my* child misbehaving? Answer: The sound of my failure, the sound of my lack of control, the sound of "I should have control," the sound of "I can't take another second of this," the sound of "I hate this child," the sound of "I shouldn't hate this child," the sound of "what is wrong with me," the sound of "anyone would feel this way though," the sound of "yeah, but you are *the parent*!, you are supposed to love them," the sound of "but I do love them," the sound of "doesn't sound like it to me," the sound of #$%$%#, the sound of "they would be better off without me," the sound of ..., the sound of ..., the sound of .... I ask you, how can anyone be expected to be an effective parent with all that racket going on?

	To be a parent is one of the least Zen experiences one can possibly have, except maybe being a son, or daughter, or wife, or husband. The higher the stakes, the tougher the job (less Zen). Why? More meanings, more fusion, more verbal regulation, more insensitivity, less flexibility, more narrow, more stuck. Hey are we about to drive off a cliff? Yes, but I don't know what else to do. Man, it is really hard to be with people, especially the ones that count. Look around at divorce rates, family discord, family violence. It's tough. We simply must make room for the centrality of this difficulty in human existence. It just won't do to pathologize it, to blame the culture, to blame ourselves. We have to do better than that. We have to get at the root of it. That's what makes it radical behaviorism.
CHILD & ADOLESCENT **Parenting inc. experiential avoidance/ cognitive fusion [4-28-05]** Laurie Greco	William Kordonski wrote: I wonder whether any work has been done on experiential avoidance and parenting. Lisa Coyne and Kelly wrote a really cool paper on using RFT and ACT to extend traditional behavioral parent training models - talks about sensitivity to context, role of verbal processes in parenting, experiential avoidance and cognitive fusion etc., and gives some really rich kiddie examples. Highly recommended! ... We also have a paper coming out in Behavior Therapy showing that experiential avoidance mediates the relation between parental stress during preterm birth and post-discharge adjustment outcomes (post-traumatic stress, parental distress). And Kris Berlin and colleagues have done some neat work on the effects of experiential avoidance on parenting practices and child outcomes. On our clinical team, we will at some point work with parents on their own stuff. We try to give them as close to a full dose of ACT as possible, which includes helping them face the futility of their own efforts at control and putting this up against their parenting and parent-child relationship values (among others). Commitments in therapy and in life are often made in the service of being the kind of parent and having the kind of relationship with their children that they truly want. My experience is that this work can be very scary and also validating and empowering for parents.... Sometimes there are lots of stories and resistance ("But this is the way I was raised"; "I'm not the one with the problem," etc.) but putting ourselves in the same screwy human boat, validating current and past parenting efforts and pointing to the "unworkable system" as opposed to the unworkable person and deficient parenting, and doing creative hopelessness in combination with values work often seems to be a good entry point.
CHILD & ADOLESCENT Parenting inc. experiential avoidance/ cognitive fusion [cont'd] Kelly Wilson	... if interested in the paper, it is out. You can download a PDF version from my webpage. Just scan down towards the bottom of the page to publications and look for this one. Coyne, L. W., & Wilson, K. G. (2004). The Role of Cognitive Fusion in Impaired Parenting: An RFT Analysis. *International Journal of Psychology and Psychological Therapy, 4*, 469-486.
CHILD & ADOLESCENT Parenting inc. experiential avoidance/ cognitive fusion [cont'd] John Blackledge	My dissertation was comprised of ACT workshops for parents of children diagnosed with autism. While the role of EA in parenting was not empirically examined in the study, prior research on parenting practices was reviewed through an EA lens in the introduction, and potential roles of ACT in enhancing parenting are in the discussion. Also have a set of PowerPoint slides on ACT-enhanced parent training I presented at the last ACT Conference....
CHILD & ADOLESCENT Parenting inc. experiential avoidance/ cognitive fusion [cont'd] Kristoffer Berlin	With regards to recent posts about experiential avoidance and parenting, myself and others here at UWM (Amy Sato, Kristen Jastrowski, Doug Woods, & Hobey Davies) have collected some data looking at how these factors influence adolescent behavior problems. Using path analysis and parent questionnaires we found that parental EA significantly predicted inconsistent discipline, poor monitoring, and less parental involvement, which in turn predicted parent reported adolescent behavior problems. Pretty neat from an ACT perspective. Should these results hold with other measures and methods, there are implications that fit well with ACT. If parents are "unwilling to set up house rules or consistently deliver consequences," experiential avoidance and cognitive fusion may be playing a role. For those particular families, ACT may give parents an opportunity to look at the workability of their current parenting practices in the context of what they value. As behavior analysts we have tons of techniques and empirically supported interventions that have a proven track record to help parents and kids. ACT in the front end of treatment may get them ready to tackle all that is involved with these treatments and move them toward what matters in their lives. There are some important caveats. These are preliminary findings. Path analysis is essentially a bunch of fancy correlations so we can't say anything about causation. I think using ACT first is a great idea for future research with parents; however, clinically I would be very careful. A big part of my training is to use treatments with empirical support first (treatments by Patterson, Barkley, Eyberg etc.-- http://www.effectivechildtherapy.com is a good site for specific info). If parents are struggling or not progressing well using these treatments, then ACT may be indicated. If ACT is implemented in the front end clinically, I would argue for a detailed informed consent about the empirical status of ACT with this

population. For those who are curious, below is the abstract for a talk we submitted for an ABCT symposium put together by Laurie Greco and Lisa Coyne.

Effects of Experiential Avoidance on Parenting Practices and Adolescent Outcomes

Kristoffer S. Berlin, Amy F. Sato, Kristen E. Jastrowski, Douglas W. Woods, & W. Hobart Davies

The success of behavioral parent training (BPT) programs has been well documented. These empirically supported treatments yield both short- and long-term benefits for the majority of families who complete training (Brestan & Eyberg, 1998; Lonigan, Elbert, & Johnson, 1998). However, evaluation of the literature consistently reveals negative outcomes of BPT programs among a sizeable minority of families (e.g., Eyberg & Boggs, 1998; Webster-Stratton & Hammond, 1997). These negative outcomes include high rates of premature family dropout, parental failure to engage in the treatment process, and failure of the child and parents to maintain positive changes at follow-up (Miller & Prinz, 1990).

Recently, Greco & Eifert (in press) have suggested that acceptance-based approaches may enhance outcomes of BPT. They argue that parental experiential avoidance (EA) may contribute to and/or exacerbate the presenting problems of these families by directly affecting parenting practices which in turn influence their children's behavior. For example, parents may be inconsistent in use of the disciplinary techniques of BPT or lessen the severity of consequences in an attempt to assuage their guilt or discomfort occasioned by setting firm limits or enforcing behavior plans. EA may also decrease adequate parental involvement and monitoring of their children in an attempt to avoid stressful situations or conflict. These aforementioned parenting practices have previously been linked to adjustment problems in children and adolescents.

Given the paucity of empirical investigations exploring these linkages, the goal of this study was to test three models in which parenting practices such as inconsistent discipline (model 1), poor monitoring (model 2), and parental involvement (model 3) mediate the path between parent's ability to take action in the face of unwanted internal events (EA) and adolescent behavior problems. Parents (N = 171) of children age 12 - 17 (m = 14.17, SD = 1.9) completed the Alabama Parenting Questionnaire (APQ), Acceptance & Action Questionnaire-16 (AAQ-16, Action subscale), and the Pediatric Symptom Checklist (PSC). The three hypothesized models were tested using path analysis and all provided an excellent fit to the data (Chi Square range = .58 to .94, p range = .33 to .45; NNFI/CFI/NFI ranges = .97 to 1.0; indirect effect z range = 2.95 to 3.17). More specifically it was found that the parental EA significantly predicted inconsistent discipline (model 1: beta = -28, t = -3.80, p = <.05), poor monitoring (model 2: beta = -.28, t = -3.84, p = <.05), and parental involvement (model 3: beta = .29, t = 3.90, p = <.05), which in turn predicted adolescent behavior problems (model 1: beta = .39, t = 5.56, p = <.05; model 2: beta = .40, t = 5.61, p = <.05; and model 3: beta = -.33, t = -4.50, p = <.05). Three alternative models were also tested. Results showed that the relationship between parent EA and parenting practices were mediated by adolescent behavior problems. All three of these models provided an inadequate fit to the data (Chi Square range 9.97 to 10.75, p >.05; NNFI range = .09 to .34; NFI & CFI ranges = .70 to .78), providing further evidence for the viability of the hypothesized models. These results provide preliminary evidence linking EA to ineffective parenting practices, which in turn, may contribute to adjustment difficulties in adolescents. Acceptance-based approaches may be a useful adjunct for families experiencing negative outcomes or minimal benefits from BPT. Additional implications and limitations will be discussed.

CHILD & ADOLESCENT

Phobia - intervention considerations with 6 yr. old [7-19-03]

Steve Hayes

Kirrilie Smout wrote:

Early next week I am going to see a 6 year old with a choking phobia (he choked on a piece of candy last week) who is now refusing to swallow anything hard. It is taking him up to an hour or more to eat even things like scrambled eggs, and he has become anxious and withdrawn. I'm wondering what ideas the ACT list server people might have for analogies/metaphors to use with a six year old to help start an exposure process?

Does he have any scary or homely stuffed toys that he likes to play with? Any cartoon characters like that? (Wasn't there a Disney movie recently about a scary monster who turned out to be OK? The recent movie Ice Age has some characters like that.) Bugs? Animals?

If you have something like that that the kid feels somewhat protective of, you could let them stand for scary feelings / bodily sensations. Pushing them away would be like banishing the toys to the cold closet or lonely outside. Exposure could be like going to find them. Acceptance would be like giving them a place to stay.

If that doesn't fit, you might find rebellious images and do much the same thing. The feelings could be like excessively bossy people or bossy friends (again, there are movies or cartoon shows that have such characters ... Rug Rats comes to mind). Exposure would be like not being bossed around. Acceptance would be like still letting bossy friends be friends. Just ideas....

CHILD & ADOLESCENT Phobia - intervention considerations with 6 yr. old [cont'd] Laurie Greco	... I'm not sure if I'd necessarily use ACT (per se) in this case, particularly given the child's age and the sudden-onset (?), circumscribed (?) nature of the problem. Like, is this really a choking 'phobia' or more of an age-appropriate, probably temporary reaction? The response you described, for example, is not that uncommon among preschoolers who have had an aversive feeding experience (e.g., choking). In which case, a very circumscribed and time-limited parent-child feeding intervention could be just what the doctor ordered. Whether and how to integrate ACT? I guess it would be easier to make some suggestions if we knew what feeding was like prior to the choking incident and how the parents/others are responding to the child's mealtime behavior. If the feeding difficulties started only one week ago in response to an identifiable trigger, I might start by doing brief functional analyses during mealtime - probably lunch with the primary caregiver(s) feeding. If this is a "clean-cut" feeding case, then good suggestions/clinical examples can be found in the Kedesdy & Budd book, "Childhood Feeding Disorders: Bio-behavioral Assessment and Intervention." If this is a more complex, ongoing, and/or bigger family systems issue, I'd be thinking about how to use ACT functionally with this little one and his family, too....
CHILD & ADOLESCENT Phobia - intervention considerations with 6 yr. old [cont'd] Steve Hayes	Laurie is right about all of this. I hope it's obvious that my earlier post was addressing the content of the question asked, not the appropriateness of ACT for any specific case. ACT is not a primary, empirically supported intervention for much of anything yet, so you'd want to have some good reason to go in that direction in most situations (like existing empirically supported interventions had been tried and failed; client rejected better empirically supported alternatives; fit with specific functional analysis; special case characteristics; etc.).
CHILD & ADOLESCENT **Self-harm - need for functional analysis** **SELF-HARM** **Functional analysis, need for - child case [5-2-04]** Amy Murrell	Nelly Vanzetti wrote: I have recently started working with a 10-year-old boy who scratches his forearms up when he encounters certain situations. Specifically, situations in which he has done something wrong, sometimes when there is some unfair thing going on (a teacher yelling at a student -- not even him), or if he feels he has made someone feel bad. He is a very bright child who is always characterized by teachers as a "model" student and citizen. He has excellent social skills and lots of friends.... Any suggestions will be welcome. I would say that this particular SIB [self-injurious behavior] does appear/sound different than the SIBs that are sometimes typical in children who have MR [mental retardation]. It does appear more indirectly conditioned for example; however, I would also guess that it certainly has become self-reinforcing. The two are not necessarily exclusive. The scratching quite probably has multiple functions, and I would say that a thorough functional analysis would be required before making any case conceptualization or treatment formulation. I would think ... that avoidance of uncomfortable private experiences is quite probable, but I think that we need to be clear that an ACT approach would advocate for assessment rather than assuming….
CHILD & ADOLESCENT **Values taught in school vs. values in ACT** **Experiential exercise re values (school group)** **VALUES** **Community values (school taught) vs. values in ACT [3-16-03]** Amy Murrell	I have been doing ACT with children and adolescents, ages 6 to 18, for about two years. Much of the work that I have done has been in a school setting...many schools "teach" values by focusing on moral issues ... the schools' intentions are different but certainly overlap with ACT's view and values-directed focus.... Basically, in treatment we can talk about the same things that the teachers and guidance counselor are talking about; we just do it in relation to consistency with the child's values, usually about education or family relationships. For example (just one), one month's virtue [school-taught value] was respect. In a group session, I had children make collages depicting the way that they interact with the people that they value the most. I did this by saying something like, "I want you to show me all the ways that you act when you are with the people who are the most important to you." You can do it with thoughts and feelings too, but this time we focused on actions when with others. Without further explanation, I asked the kids to do an exercise for me. "Close your eyes. Now, I want you to pretend that your life is a movie. See if you can see yourself. Look at your face, your body. Rewind to a time that you acted one of those ways that you put on your collage. Who are you with? See if you can let yourself feel what was going on for you then? Did you feel anything in your body? What does your face look like? What about the other person? What does their face look like? How did the other person react? Do you feel close to them or far away from them? Ok, rewind again to the first time that you can remember doing that thing...." We talked about whether those things were consistent with ("acting so that you and the people who are most important to you know that they are important and that you care about them") or inconsistent with valuing our loved ones. By the way, the kids had already all said that their relationships with their families were important values. Then we specifically talked about the lessons that they had gotten from class on

	respect, how the ways that they act were either respectful or not, and how that was either consistent or inconsistent with their values of family relationships. One little boy, who was ten, said, "I talk-back to my mom a lot. It is not respectful. It makes me feel far away from her. Then I feel guilty and sad, very alone."...
CHILD & ADOLESCENT Values taught in school vs. values in ACT [cont'd] **VALUES** Community values (school taught) vs. values in ACT [cont'd] Patty Bach	It seems to me that the school goal is not *necessarily* at odds with the ACT goal. Williard Quine has a nice treatment of "morals" as being prescribed and prohibited behaviors established through 'truth by consensus.' That is, members of a community agree that, say, 'people should not harm each other.' This can only be established by consensus, it can't be established empirically, or derived mathematically in the way I can "prove" that 'if you consume more calories than you burn, you will gain weight' or that if X = 2 and Y = X, then Y = 2. (No longer Quine here) It seems that the ACT and cultural perspective work in opposite directions. The ACT perspective works backward to behavior from the perspective of desired outcomes, "here is the outcome I desire, what behaviors will take me in that direction?", while the cultural perspective works in the opposite direction of "here is the behavior you should/shouldn't do and these are the consequences we will impose if you do/don't behave that way." In other words, from the cultural perspective 'morals' are about desired behavior, and socially-mediated consequences are implemented to establish social control over 'moral behavior.' If you do that you will go to jail (or go to hell!), if you don't do that then you will pay a fine. While in ACT, values help one choose among behavioral options. Values influence behavior, versus values determine/prescribe behavior. Once the community establishes 'morals' they then establish socially-mediated consequences in relation to the morals. If the 'moral' is "people should not hurt each other," you are praised if you follow the rule and do not harm others. If you do harm others, then you are labeled a "bully," and may be arrested and fined or jailed. In ACT, suppose someone comes in saying "I value hitting people." However, this is focused on a behavior, not a desired outcome, so the therapist might shape thinking about values in terms of desired outcomes. The person might eventually conclude that "I value getting people to do what I want them to do." This 'outcome' focus allows more behavioral flexibility. I may still harm others, but I may now also decide to offer rewards, or become a persuasive speaker, join the military, etc. If I also value staying out of jail, I may give up hitting OR I may get better at a 'hit and run' strategy. If I also value "Obeying the law" or "being kind to others" or "not harming others" I may choose the non-hitting ways to get people to do what I want. So the cultural values are not necessarily at odds with ACT. There will be problems when "my values" and "cultural values" are in conflict, and there may be aversive socially-mediated consequences for choosing my value over the cultural value, say the dilemma faced by 'conscientious objectors' to war. On the other hand, there will be aversive personal consequences for doing that which I don't value. I might decide that I value changing the cultural value, avoiding jail, avoiding war, avoiding war *and* jail (flee to Canada), etc. From an ACT values perspective I think I have more choices about my behavior than from the cultural perspective of Do's and Don'ts. And they are not necessarily at odds in terms of the effect they have on my behavior, so long as I 'freely choose' the cultural values.
CLIENT **Concentration/ attention/ impulse-control difficulties [9-24-03]** Patty Bach	Matthew Smout wrote: I'd be very grateful to any clinicians out there who might offer some pearls of wisdom from their experience in dealing with people (other than the therapists) who have difficulty concentrating, attending, or have impulse-control difficulties that are evident within psychotherapy sessions. I think that if poor concentration, attention, or impulse control are in the service of avoidance that might be material to import into the session content. In other cases, where these problems reflect cognitive and/or behavioral skills deficits I think we have to merely accommodate limitations and/or shape up increased attention, concentration, and impulse control. (For example, in leading psychiatric rehabilitation skills training groups I have observed that there is a percentage of consumers who seem to benefit very little in terms of learning the content of the skills training group. However, many of those same clients seem to fare well the second or third time around, and I believe that the first time around they do learn "how to be in a group," and learn to increase attending, listening, focusing, responding, and generally "how to be in a group" skills.) In ACT work with persons with schizophrenia and other psychotic disorders where poor attention and concentration are common, I have used many strategies including: to have shorter (and sometimes shorter and more frequent) sessions; to move at a slower pace primarily by lots of within and between session repetition; where possible to occasionally have a session while going for a walk or sitting outdoors; to use simpler metaphors (e.g., "tug of war with a monster" or "Chinese handcuffs" instead of "man in the hole"); to spend a good portion - around 25% or more - of each session reviewing the previous session. In inpatient settings in particular I have also used good old reinforcers such as a coffee outing in a common area or a walk on the grounds after the session to encourage engagement.

CLIENT **Homeless [7-10-03]** Zamir Korn	Mark Webster wrote: I have an involvement with a homeless project and wanted to consider the use of ACT with these people. Is there any research in the area or any tweaks to ACT that I would have to consider? Coming more from a clinical perspective where the population is transient, does ACT need to be adapted? I haven't come across any relevant literature about homelessness. Here are my comments on ACT as applied to homeless individuals from my own experience: - There is little stability for families living in homeless shelters in that on any given day they may be transferred or discharged out of the facility and for all intents and purposes the therapeutic work ends without completion or closure. I look therefore to keep sessions very "here-and-now." Instead of a more traditional, progressive ACT protocol week to week, I engage residents in experiential work and tie it in loosely to an emotional acceptance theme. Yalom's book on brief inpatient psychotherapy may be helpful for you as a guide to structuring the sessions. - The number one presenting problem is extreme stress. I'll often begin with relaxation strategies influenced by Tai Chi, Chi Gung, the healing form of Tai Chi. It's contextual, and can be combined with movement meditation to ground excess mental energy. A good reference for this is: *The Inner Structure of Tai Chi* by Mantak Chia & Juan Li, 1996, Healing Tao Books, PO Box 1194, Huntington, New York. The microcosmic orbit described on page 2 is especially useful. The entire form need not be learned, only a few simple movements done mindfully. - Hyperactivity and hypervigilance are also observed much in this setting, the latter due in part to the extreme level of physical danger people experience themselves to be in. I find Tai Chi especially helpful for hyperactive/aggressive children and adolescents. In addition to the Tai Chi form, we play board games and speak ultra-slowly and mindfully via a Chi flow. In a similar vein, ACT deliteralization techniques can also be used to achieve desired outcomes. Incidentally, I find these latter strategies effective for people with borderline autism as well.
CLIENT **Inarticulate - fusion with verbal events** **CAUSE** **Contingencies "cause" behavior [6-4-04]** John Blackledge *Cross Reference:* *See 3-104 for a later post in the thread:* *CLIENT* *Inarticulate - fusion with verbal events*	Theresa Glaser wrote: It has been my experience that, while clients appear "fused" to a lot of different ideas/contents, a great share of them come to my office without having specific terms/language to describe their experience. In fact they come ONLY with experience, which they have a difficult time describing in words. For example, an extremely anxious patient I had (with Posttraumatic Stress Disorder) wouldn't ever label herself as "anxious," rather she just knows she feels bad. Even though a client may have some very marked deficits when it comes to specifically identifying how they feel and what they think, he/she may still be demonstrating some serious and problematic fusion. I think all that is necessary for verbal fusion to cause difficulty is that the client be able to verbally identify some general state of affairs, negatively evaluate aspects of their experience, and remain constricted by ineffective verbal rules (whether explicitly articulated or implicitly derived) about how she must and can't behave in such situations. The client you mentioned may not need to "know" she is anxious in order for fusion with verbalizations about this aspect of her experience to cause trouble. She need only know that she feels bad, that feeling bad indicates there's something wrong with her or her world, and that feeling bad means she has to do certain things and can't do others. [TG] I don't know if behavior patterns follow from the premise that one does not make a distinction between the process of thinking and actual thought, and becomes fused with actual thought content, thereby leading directly to ingrained behavior patterns. I suppose one could explain this as troublesome behavior patterns becoming automatic due to conditioning (i.e., not being aware of the interaction pattern itself); however, I'm not sure if this is because one is fused to a verbal event. If I'm reading this right, I agree. The notion that fusion with verbal events causes behavior actually serves as kind of a shorthand notation for some broader contingencies. From an ACT/RFT perspective, language has power because we are reinforced and punished for using it in certain ways. For example, we're reinforced for things like doing what we say we'll do, accurately describing publicly observed events, and for following rules laid down for us. Similarly, we're punished for doing the opposite and for talking about things in disapproved ways. It is these contingencies that 'cause' behavior--whether the behavior in question is verbal or otherwise.
CLIENT **Involuntary/ semi-voluntary (substance abuse)**	Matthew Smout wrote: Suppose a client comes to therapy - maybe out of a sense of obligation to their family, as mandated by the court, or something. Or, suppose a client comes to therapy not relating to any of the hallmarks of the creative hopelessness phase - they say their life is working fine (ok if you press them they'll admit it's not fine, but they're not about to talk about that). Can ACT begin yet? How would experienced ACT therapists respond to these kinds of "classic" presentations? Do you get creative hopelessness on the

SUBSTANCE ABUSE

Involuntary/ semi-voluntary client [10-2-03]

Kelly Wilson

agenda? Or values on the agenda - if so how? I used to adopt a motivational interviewing stance in this situation. Clients often didn't come back, but I wasn't bothered by that. Now I've been trying to take an ACT stance. Clients still aren't coming back and now it's bothering me. I get fine retention rates with clients who do not present as I've described above. Any suggestions would be great (BTW - I am showering regularly).

This is long--and underdeveloped, but all I have time to do.

However, I and Michelle Byrd are working on an ACT chapter right now for substance abuse. When folks are coerced, and many substance abusers are coerced by someone, they push off. In these cases, the first thing you need is to find a place where you and they can meet and work together.

Typically clients come in with some vulnerability--some substance clients do also. With these, I tend to work, as I do with most, going from creative hopelessness (CH) to a very preliminary values contract around their sense of loss and their desire for "more." If they are open in this way, I have two worksheets I use. The worksheets are essentially CH/values pieces. They help the client make contact with their own sense of loss and with the areas of their life in which they have let go of important things in the service of getting high. Sometimes these losses are insidious. Sometimes there is a slow progression of losses and narrowing of life--I have seen clients quite stunned when they lay their pattern of use and their pattern of losses out all in one place and in writing. There is a kind of willingness/ exposure/ defusion involved in these worksheets that can be quite powerful.

That said, many substance abuse clients come in pissed off. They don't want to be there. They don't see the problem, or if it is a problem, why are people meddling in it. It is their problem after all. I really think you have to join the client and if this is where they are, you have to go there and get what it is like to walk in their shoes. If you can't get how much it sucks to be there, from the inside, the phenomenology of a life where you are the goat, you will be impaired in your ability to work. Here, I would tend to start with the complaint, dissatisfaction, gripe, anger. If you move too quickly to values with someone who is mad, it will be experienced as (1) intrusive (without permission), or (2) as just another judgment on them, or (3) you will get pissed off pseudo-compliance (as opposed to non-pissed off pseudo-compliance).

Values work is intimate business and you can only get intimate with permission. Try getting intimate with the person next to you in line at the grocery and see what I mean. Second thought, don't do that. You'll probably get arrested and your wife will be pissed. Anyhow, my guess is that you are moving too quickly into an area without permission. With folks in pain, you should get permission too, but there is some implied permission in the vulnerability they put in front of you (though I like it to be explicit and make it so). So start with the aggravation they have about being there. Start with what brought them in. How is it going? is the wife mad? the boss? how much does that suck? A complaint is always a great place to start, because a complaint followed out will lead ultimately to a vulnerability and a vulnerability to a value (or there would be no complaint). In a sense this is a standard ACT piece--you can start anywhere as long as it is where the client is. Go where they are. Let yourself climb into that place. Reflect it back and check to see if that is right.

The portion of the chapter I refer you to …--the client profile is the substance abuse client who is non-pissed off pseudo-compliant. I am sure you see some of these folks. No time this morning for the sullen client--which is probably another important pattern. And a little tougher than the pseudo compliant client....

Bottom line--first get where they are. You have to get to a vulnerability in order to do the values piece. These folks you are struggling with are massively defended. First you have to get where they are--*then* you can go on a trip with them.

There are frequently some coercive events surrounding a person's entry into treatment. In the most extreme cases clients are ordered to treatment under threat of incarceration. Even with these extreme cases, a solid therapeutic relationship and therapeutic contract is typically possible. In order to forge the contract, all that is needed is a shared value between the therapist and the client that can dignify the work of treatment. Very often, the ability of the client to make their own decisions about what they would do in their lives is a value that the therapist and client can agree upon. It is ironic, but not inconsistent, that I as a therapist could work very hard with a client towards their having the freedom to terminate treatment. (Here Matthew--I would ask you--how would you like it? even if you knew you needed help, how would you like being threatened and coerced into treatment?)…

[Editor's note: For further text cited in this post, see pp. 157-161 of the following chapter.]

Wilson, K. G., & Byrd, M. R. (2004). ACT for Substance Abuse and Dependence. In Hayes, S. C., & Strosahl, K. D. (Eds.), *A Practical Guide to Acceptance and Commitment Therapy* (153-184). New York: Springer.

CLIENT **Modifying ACT - young/ indifferent/ hostile clients** **CHILD & ADOLESCENT** **ACT interventions; research [3-4-05]** Laurie Greco	Jason Gosnell wrote: Are people who are working with teens basically using the ACT approach the same as with adults--I don't mean the details--but the same basic goals ... defusion, contact with self as context, values clarification, etc.? We're working primarily with teens (and parents) and have seen children as young as six on our practicum team. Functionally speaking, the purposes, goals, and processes are the same. Many of the clinical methods are the same, too. We use metaphor, paradox, experiential exercises and target excessive, at-the-end-of-the-day unworkable, experiential avoidance, fusion, and rigid rule governed behavior, as it shows up both in the therapy room and in the child's/parent's life. What *might* differ, particularly with younger kids, is our language as therapists and the content or form of particular ACT interventions (although, I don't think this is unique to ACT or to work with children). My students and I are working on an "ACT for Teens" manual that incorporates language and exercises we've found particularly useful in working with teens.... There are now quite a few people doing this work with children and teens and many more who are interested in extending third-wave behavior therapies to young people, which is so exciting. My thought is that doing acceptance and values work with children (say at age 8, rather than age 18) will prevent a whole lot of unnecessary suffering. We submitted a few symposia and posters to ABCT this year and hope to demonstrate the relevance of this stuff to mainstream child-clinical folks now that the data are starting to roll in. Seems to be picking up a bit more slowly in this crowd... I'll attach a few of those abstracts to show some of the neat work that's being done in different labs. [Titles of Abstracts: Third-Wave Behavior Therapies for Children, Adolescents, and Families: Clinical Applications, Empirical Findings, and Future Directions Dialectical Behavior Therapy with Adolescents: Treatment Development and Pilot Study in a Community Outpatient Clinic ACT for Adolescents with Chronic Health Conditions: Feasibility and Pilot Data from an Uncontrolled Clinical Trial Acceptance and Commitment Therapy with Young Children and their Families Values-based Behavioral Activation with Adolescents Mindfulness-Based Stress Reduction (MBSR) for Adolescents with Insomnia, Daytime Sleepiness, and a History of Drug Abuse Extending Acceptance and Mindfulness Research to Child and Adolescent Populations: Empirical Findings, Clinical Implications, and Future Directions Effects of Experiential Avoidance on Parenting Practices and Adolescent Outcomes The Impact of Acceptance-Based Parent Communication on Adolescent Emotion Regulation Role of Maternal Mindfulness in Parenting Behaviors, Maternal Depression, and Child Outcomes Acceptance, Experiential Avoidance, and Cognitive Fusion among Youth: Are these "Third-Wave" Processes Relevant to Child and Adolescent Behavior Therapists?]
CLIENT Modifying ACT - young/ indifferent/ hostile clients [cont'd] Leslie Rogers	Your post raised an interesting issue about modifying language and devising a workable form of ACT to work with different populations. My colleague, Catherine Adams and I have developed a protocol that addresses ways to do ACT with differing populations in particular those that may not be ACT friendly (or even hostile). It is a more process-oriented protocol which calls for modifications in order to facilitate an alliance with the client/individual in training/hostile person. Initially we made this to increase receptivity of the ACT message in residential facilities and educational settings. Oftentimes we found that we were not being heard. Behavior plans would go unimplemented. People hated us and rolled their eyes at us. But what we found was instead of working to make this go away we made the space for it. Then we used this space to get with them and incredible things happened. They began working with us, listening to us and doing what we suggested more oftentimes than not. We have been tempted to get caught in the form and when we have been it has been counterproductive. We think it's because you end up working from two separate contexts. On the one hand the therapist is trying to look right, be smart, help and follow the protocol. While the trainee, teacher, hostile person is in the context of trying to be heard (beyond the complaints), and be given credit for their incredibly hard job as well as looking right, and being smart. We made this protocol to put us in the same context as them....

CLIENT	Kristina Cole wrote:
Older adult/ carer - modifying intervention [10-20-04] Mary Politi	I am in the process of putting together a group intervention to help caregivers of people with dementia. I anticipate difficulties in several areas ... for example, what many caregivers seem to 'value' is their relative returning to health; and I have found that many older adults find working with metaphors confusing either because their capacity for abstract thinking is limited or they have been brought up in a medical model generation which assumes medication is the answer to suffering.
	Something I have used when working with cancer patients or older adults is exploring the workability of their strategies. Sometimes control works very well with regard to external aspects of their medical illness (i.e., taking meds regularly, adhering to treatment, changing diet, exercise, other things that could improve medical outcomes). However, the internal and emotional control tends to leave clients feeling helpless and frustrated. Also, there are many aspects of medical illness that no one can "change," so focusing on a change agenda can be unproductive, anxiety-producing, and depressing.
	You mention in the case of the caregivers, they often want to get rid of their relative's dementia-- how is that working for them? Are there ways they can help their relative live the best possible life without trying to change the impossible? What is the value underlying the desire to change the dementia? I suspect it is their relationship with their relative and their love of their relative.
	With regard to the medication issue, medication could work for their medical condition/suffering, but focus on their internal suffering when bringing in the ACT concepts. The medical model can be compatible with ACT in these different contexts.
CLIENT Older adult/ carer -- modifying intervention [cont'd] Patty Bach	While my work is primarily with persons with serious mental illness rather than elder adults, many persons with schizophrenia have cognitive deficits and difficulty understanding complicated metaphors. I use a combination of three different strategies for simplifying the metaphors in ACT.
	The first, and most obvious if you are using ACT books/articles, is to use the simplest metaphor whenever more than one is available to address the same concern; e.g., the Man in the hole metaphor is very lengthy. The Chinese handcuffs and Feeding a baby tiger metaphors are much shorter and also to get at the futility of an unworkable strategy/agenda.
	Metaphors are easier for some clients to understand when you use physical props: e.g., use actual Chinese handcuffs while presenting that metaphor; have a cup on hand and hold and point to it while describing the "Bad cup" metaphor; have a pair of socks for "Argyle socks"; use a box or wastepaper basket for the "Box full of stuff," etc. Some of the exercises are already fairly 'concretized,' e.g., in 'Taking your mind for a walk' the therapist supplies the 'mind chatter' to the client.
	Finally, modify some of the existent metaphors and exercises, or make up your own. I've modified the Observer exercise using physical props to make it more concrete, and I've made up some simple exercises that are both brief and fairly concrete; e.g., to address 'reason giving' I have the client brainstorm and generate a list of reasons why someone who likes cake might turn down a piece of chocolate cake that is offered to her (and I sometimes return to this exercise later in therapy in the context of choice, committed action, values).
	The chapter on ACT with serious mental illness in the forthcoming *A Practical Guide To ACT* addresses this topic and provides some specific examples.
CLIENT **Stuck** **DEPRESSION** **Anti-depressants - use during therapy** [2-24-05] Matthew Smout	I would be most grateful for any suggestions regarding the following case:
	I have been working with this man in private practice on and off for about 6 years. He initially presented with panic attacks and generalised anxiety. In early work the panic attacks ceased and as time went on, we reconceptualised the generalised anxiety as essentially anxiety of anxiety -experiential avoidance in ACT terms. About 3 years ago, I switched from what was predominantly a traditional CBT mode of working to predominantly ACT (i.e., dropped any cognitive restructuring, retained exposure components though in an ACT-consistent way). He was fascinated by the different approach, and embraced the "if you can't have it, you've got it" ethos and for about 2 years I heard no more from him. He is quite a high functioning man who "read up" on ACT from the internet, purchased the book and now has a fairly intellectual understanding of the approach.
	He has begun presenting again recently. Now he tends to present with "I know I have to be willing to have this, and I know I can't say I'm willing to have this to get rid of it, and I know this is just a thought and I know I should just notice this - and I know this is just a thought too, and I don't care and I can't keep doing this!" There's no comedy in this either - this is in tears and desperate. (BTW - his "outside the skin life" is value-laden - a further source of angst in the midst of his rumination - "I should be happy I have no reason to be unhappy.")
	I have tried some sessions where I might spend an hour or so with him, gently inviting him to be with these

	feelings. Lately the spiral of anxiety has escalated past the point where he can get any defusion - if anything he seems to fuse more with his evaluations that "this is a real and DANGEROUS feeling that I can't keep on experiencing regularly for the rest of my life." I have resorted to distraction (talking about not-so-related things) in these circumstances, and often he can calm and start to entertain a less fused perspective on the struggle.
	I guess I'm not sure the best way to proceed. I feel I can't shed any more light on his struggle - I can't be willing for him. He is now contemplating antidepressants and I'm not sure what to say about that to him. I am not wanting to buy into his appraisal of the situation. I am very conscious that even being reluctant to engage in dialogue about antidepressants could be seen as invalidating to him. At this stage I see myself doing less in-session exposure work (asking him do that at home) and using the less fused space to talk about things like workability, scheduling mindfulness practice and reinforcing ACT-based psychoeducation. But I'm not at all sure if there would be a better way to go. Not sure if my defusion/exposure work was too hands off? Need to throw something else in to shake up the network? Would love some thoughts.
CLIENT Stuck [cont'd] DEPRESSION Anti-depressants - use during therapy [cont'd] John Forsyth	Sounds like he is now using some of what he has learned in a rigid and inflexible fashion. What you describe has lots of rule-based statements in there. He has worked to become the expert at ACT -- does he see this as a quick fix, a tool to run from his pain?, guided by the idea that "because he knows so much about ACT, he should be better … he should be happy... he should feel better (less anxious)." His statement that "I should be happy and I have no reason to be unhappy" rings on this theme. Can you clarify what he meant by "I can't keep doing this?" Is he chasing happiness (the feeling) using ACT concepts? At a basic level, it sounds like he is having a set back -- getting back on the rollercoaster of fusion, struggle, and control. Turning to antidepressants may be one outcome of this too, and he could certainly do that. You could explore this as a choice on par with many other choices he could make. What does he want here? -- the outcome with antidepressants, the outcome with his life?
CLIENT Stuck [cont'd] COPING STRATEGIES **Distraction, function of [cont'd]** **EXPOSURE** **General inc. consent seeking, "distraction"/ defusion [cont'd]** Matthew Smout *Cross References:* *See 2-75 and 6-260 for earlier posts in the thread:* *COPING STRATEGIES* *Distraction, function of* *See 2-74 and 6-260 for earlier posts in the thread:* *EXPOSURE* *General inc. consent seeking, "distraction"/ defusion*	Yeah he is very verbal - he has abstracted the rules from ACT and swings between following these and rejecting/arguing with them. I have been trying in my work to spend a lot of time *experiencing / exposing* to the distress, and thoughts like "I may have this for the rest of my life." OK, from a traditional CBT point of view, he isn't habituating in session, or between sessions. And from an ACT point of view he isn't getting any more accepting. Maybe either of these goals would be too simplistic?
	It is not straightforward to me how to bring values into this situation. All the big lifestyle stuff is happening - intimate relations, family, work, health etc. His only gripe is having his day constantly interrupted by intrusive feelings of free-floating anxiety which he then starts ruminating about. He can get on with his work/childcare and sometimes loses himself back in those moments and other times has the experience of working, childrearing *with* anxious thoughts and feelings and he hates that! When he says "I can't keep doing this" he means I don't want to keep having anxiety interrupt my life. However, I don't know what to say here because if I say any of the usual ACT responses - he goes "I know," (I suspect feels invalidated) and then retreats into his mind, whereupon I try to get him back out of his head into the moment of the present environment and being with me. The only vaguely value-related thing I can think of is pointing out that he is currently engaging in rumination, what is this in the service of? What else could you do? What would you choose to do in this moment?
	If I try to apply ACT thinking to my own therapeutic behaviour, I come up with "this isn't working!" meaning he is neither habituating nor is he becoming more willing from our exposure/willingness exercises. I admit clients like this rock me a little and I start wondering whether I'm being unnecessarily cruel in persisting to encourage them to pursue anxiety acceptance when maybe it would work to pursue anxiety reduction. I can pull myself out of this.
	Kelly - the way you described how you do exposure makes sense. It falls between the published literature I have seen which has either had participants focus exclusively on phobic stimuli and avoid distraction, or engage in a distracting activity which is not related to anything about the moment (e.g., slides, spelling). Incidentally, while the literature is somewhat mixed, people who distract within exposure sessions usually experience greater subjective fear reduction (but not physiological arousal) and despite much conventional wisdom focusing exclusively on the phobic stimulus is often less effective in reducing within-session subjective fear particularly if the stimulus arouses high levels of fear rather than lower levels . The long-term effects of distraction during exposure appear more equivocal, and there is plenty of room for much more detailed study. Kelly, your description sounds pretty win-win: the person can break attention from the most horrific aspects of their present experience but remain in contact with other aspects of their present environment which ought to promote flexible responding to the fear-engendering situation - sounds more adaptive than a retreat into 'mindville.'

CLIENT Stuck [cont'd] **DEPRESSION** Anti-depressants - use during therapy [cont'd] Steve Hayes	Any ACT clinician will hit this - in fact most ACT clinicians who apply ACT to him or herself will probably at least nibble at it enough to know the process if not step into it fully. I sure have. It involves a cycle of "success" (defined by feeling BETTER); an unnoticed resurgence in fusion (using resurgence technically); entanglement of ACT related concepts into this new network with the same functional end as the old one; and finally the functional impact being replicated. The pivot points are creative hopelessness and defusion. They are harder to do second time around, but if you are unable to do them, this will be an ACT failure. [At some point we should have a discussion about facing failure while fully present, and sharing that with your client without blame or shame.] If you can get that far, staying present and conscious as a goalless goal - as a process without purpose beyond the process - should cement it. Then just make sure the value work retains these qualities so that motivation is motivation to be present and live, not motivation to behave and get rid of one's history. BTW if he says he's doing values great, I wonder. How can you devote so much energy to struggle and actually be present while doing these behaviors? I think what he means is that he is forcing the motor behavior out - but what is that motor behavior ABOUT? I'd bet that what it is about requires more psychological flexibility than he has been giving to it. He is probably compromising a lot there. Suggestions: Do creative hopelessness in a very affiliative way. Be compassionate. Cry a little together. And face the void together. This is hard. This is easy to do in your state because you can bring the hopelessness of not knowing what to do into the room and let it be part of it. I say things like "if there was any way I could do what you are asking, I probably would. For me too. Maybe it's good that there isn't a way - because I'm not sure that move would really be the healthy or growing thing to do. AND my experience tells me that this is a trap, and that truly I have nothing healthy to give that will take away your pain as the beginning step of a vital life journey. If your experience doesn't tell you that, then maybe more struggle is needed. Who knows, maybe there is a way. You can come back if or when life teaches you there isn't. It's scary for me to say that - and everything I know about you and your situation tells me that to move ahead we need to face what your experience -- your actual experience -- tells you about how struggle actually works in your life." Agreement is not the issue here. Letting go and facing the void is the issue. Defusion from "First I must have" is the issue. Be relentless in defusion but give up logic. Apply defusion even to ACT talk. The loop that ensnared this client is why we say "don't believe a word I'm saying." He's turned ACT into a belief system and look at what it bought him. Mindfulness meditation -- harnessed to being present -- can be helpful. Substitute practice for understanding. Be very behavioral. But do not give any rope to the idea that meditation will lead to less anxiety. The goal has to be to be present - period and end of story. The goal is to be here with his history. His anxiety is his history showing up in the present -- to commit to avoiding anxiety is to commit to living on the basis that one should have a different history in order to live. It is a commitment to start from where you are not, which is why it cannot work. Then bring that sensibility into the values work. Personally, I wouldn't care much if the person used anti-depressants (etc.) for a while. I'd just be neutral on that. Eventually, if things move on, they would probably fall away anyway. And sure, they are a compromise - a thread tied back to avoidance - but learning to let go of avoidance is a life process that is never finished so if we demand absolutes today we are demanding failure today. Let's do progress today. There is no speedometer on our foreheads. As long as it is not reformulated into more rigidity ("I must have this in order to do that") it will eventually fall away. This situation is hard.
CLIENT **"Understanding" ACT not necessary [7-19-03]** Steve Hayes	Amy Murrell wrote: > I know that a few people have done ACT with [individuals with mild to moderate mental retardation] ... it is my belief ... that ACT can be adapted to be useful in this population. The ACT - retardation connection is a long one. Chris McCurry started this work perhaps a dozen or more years ago.... This issue is important because the usual take on ACT (that it is "oh so hard to understand") is radically irrelevant. And its irrelevance is very revealing. Understanding is the booby prize. It is the brainiacs on lists like this that have the hard time -- because they are so understanding-oriented. My sense is that ACT is easy to connect with and easy to make use of. Kids. Retarded folks. Psychotic folks. You name it. ACT *is* hard to understand, but that is not what it was clinically about anyway. Scientifically that is another matter ... that is one reason we scientists have a hard road. We can't completely abandon understanding as an issue.

COMPONENT SEQUENCING **Values or pain first?** **TRAUMA/ ABUSE** **Component sequencing; group/ individual work** **GROUP** **Individual work, combination with [2-25-03]** Sue Orsillo	ACT Listserv Member wrote: Has anyone done ACT with CSA [childhood sexual abuse]? What has worked? What hasn't? I have done ACT-like groups with mixed trauma female veterans (most have CSA, adult SA, domestic violence, etc.). I have billed the groups as "commitment to action" groups with a very heavy focus on values and action first, looked at control efforts as barriers and of course the trauma stuff comes up in that context. I have also put in a lot more mindfulness practice to help with the defusion piece. I have not done the forgiveness stuff in group. My population is pretty tough and I would say the groups were mixed in their success. I like doing values in a group because of the stand up and commit with others, but sometimes it is hard to really get in there with someone in group. So I now think a combination approach might be best.
GROUP Individual work, combination with [cont'd] Kelly Wilson	We are also liking the mixed model here (group and individual mixed). We are currently using it in our college risk project and wish we would have used it in our high school risk project. The groups can focus on core ACT pieces -- how minds work -- and give folks a little glimpse that they are not alone. Groups are also a great place to do stand-up commitments and to get other people in the group standing for the person making the commitment. Individual sessions can be used for really careful, intensive exposure/defusion work and can be used to leverage full participation in the group.
COMPONENT SEQUENCING Values or pain first? [cont'd] Steve Hayes	The sequencing of components itself needs to be worked out conceptually and empirically. Kel is known for the values first approach. Personally, I've been supportive of that as a conceptually sensible thing to do (when folks come visit Reno and look at old tapes, they often comment on how component sequencing is quite flexible and indeed the values early example is usually the most obvious). The technological advances Kel is making help make that move more possible more often. In my own therapy work I tend to go into pain first and then loop up into values after people begin to see that how they've handled pain is itself an issue ... the values are in the pain anyway. We hurt about things because of what we want. If we hurt about a betrayal it is because we value trust. If we hurt about fear, it is because we value involvement and participation. Variability, a process focus, and good data will work all of this out if we keep our eyes open and we test the alternatives....
COMPONENT SEQUENCING Values or pain first? [cont'd] **CLIENT** **Involuntary/ semi-voluntary - "values first" approach** **PSYCHOSIS** **"Values first" approach** **ACT cf.** **Motivational Interviewing - values work [2-26-03]** Patty Bach	I also value the flexibility of the component sequencing in ACT. I have found a 'values first' approach useful in ACT with clients with serious mental illness (SMI), e.g., schizophrenia, schizoaffective disorder. I suspect there are two related reasons that a values first approach has been useful with this population. Personally, I have seen most of these clients in involuntary and 'semi-voluntary' settings, such as inpatient hospitals or outpatient settings where the client has little involvement in their own treatment planning and was referred to therapy by a case manager or treatment team. Persons with SMI are often in mental health systems where their goals and values are identified for them by others on a treatment team. Many cannot or are reluctant to identify goals and values at all. Starting with values is a useful way to get these clients thinking about what is important to them, rather than what others have told them should be important to them. When they see goals and values as their own, there may be more motivation for treatment, or any behavior in the service of goal attainment. Also, I've noticed that the values component seems to share some features with Miller and Rollnick's "Motivational Interviewing" approach, and especially in terms of 'stages of change' and moving from pre-contemplation to contemplation via 'raising consciousness.' Like motivational interviewing, the values component in ACT may facilitate motivation for treatment through addressing values and goals and raising consciousness so the client makes the link between present behavior and goal attainment (or lack thereof). Values may be a useful place to start with other 'involuntary' or otherwise unmotivated clients, such as those in the legal system, or some substance abusers, etc. While starting with pain may be more useful with clients who are more willing to be in treatment.

COMPONENT SEQUENCING Values or pain first? [cont'd] ACT cf. Motivational Interviewing - values work [cont'd] **ACT** **Core components/ discriminations [2-27-03]** Kelly Wilson	I think Steve is right. Go into pain--you find values, go into values-- you find pain. Of course, we are integrated organisms--there are really no "parts," except conceptualized parts, so this makes sense. Part of what has driven this stuff, as Steve said, is technology (well, and that old worn out copy of Man's Search for Meaning and Camus' Myth of Sisyphus I have been packing around for the past 30 years). I think that some of the technologies around values are less tricky to train than some of the defusion strategies--though I have no hard data on this contention.... There are a couple issues afoot that bear analysis. One is at the level of technology and training--are some things easier to train than others? Another is the theoretical sensibility of the ordering of pieces. I have argued for the theoretical sensibility of putting the values piece early and argue for this in the [Values chapter with Amy Murrell in the *Mindfulness and Acceptance* book] as a way to direct other interventions. I know for a fact though that one can work it in the other direction--have done so and have seen it done. After all, Steve trained me, so I know the other route (well he had some help, I am hard to train---special ed). There may also be matching issues to be considered--what is the most salient thing the client presents (as Pat suggests). Another consideration - on the issue of order - is a matter Niklas Törneke mentioned on one visit after watching a long series of tapes of me doing therapy with a tough substance abuse client. Niklas commented that I do all session in all sessions. I hadn't really noticed until then, but I think he is right and have since tried to train it that way. The focus of a session may change, but I have my hand on a small set of principles in every session. I am either addressing them directly, or at least touching them and preparing the ground for later sessions. There are also a core set of discriminations we train in ACT: chosen/ coerced (by this I mean experienced as coerced or not), vital/ nonvital, self-as-context/ self-as-content, mind/ experience, struggle-control/ acceptance. Each session provides many opportunities for discrimination training trials. I have put in a few recent pieces that if you hang onto values, exposure, defusion, and empowerment, you are doing ACT. There are probably many ways to cast it, but this is a small set that can keep you on point. Values (what is the therapy for), exposure-defusion (building broad and flexible repertoires), empowerment (keeping clear about the relationship between the therapist and client--their sense of direction, their willingness, their choice--not ours). BTW on the relationship to motivational interviewing--Pat is right on point. In fact, I remember treating a substance abuse case from an ACT perspective back in '90 or '91 maybe. Niloo Afari got a hold of a copy of Miller's MI book and told me--you are doing MI. (Niloo--are you out there? Seems like this is how it went--but early onset Alzheimer's and all). Anyhow, I think that ACT contains a lot of attention to motivation--it's all about establishing operations--check out Mike Dougher on this. The values stuff is definitely EO stuff. I think that Miller's MI stuff is very nice. Look how well just a little touch of MI did in Project Match. Since MI was shorter, and did just as well, I think that you could conclude that a little client-centered motivational interviewing (as opposed to motivation by threat) can go a long way.
COMPONENT SEQUENCING Values or pain first? [cont'd] **CLIENT** Involuntary/ semi-voluntary - "values first" approach [cont'd] David Hubbard	I would agree with Kelly's statement that when one goes into pain one discovers what one values, etc. I had the opportunity to study Morita therapy in Canada and Japan. Morita would say that anxiety (any feeling) is like a coin. On one side there is fear and the other side there is desire. You can't have one without the other. My co-worker and I have been working with the offender population for over a decade and have found it necessary to integrate principles of Morita and ACT with its emphasis on a purpose/value-centered and behavior-centered approach to life. We found that just providing the standard CBT/RP approach was ineffective. In addition to acquiring certain skills, these clients (everyone, eh?) need a reason (value, meaning, etc.) to actually utilize the skills and move in a different direction (prosocial). What Existentialists said "if one has a why they can find a how"? I like to place values first in the therapeutic sequence in order to invite the client to invest in the tx. As you can imagine this is even more important for people who are court-ordered....
COMPONENT SEQUENCING Values or pain first? [cont'd] **TRAUMA/ ABUSE** Component sequencing; group/ individual work [cont'd] Sonja Batten	In my experience, especially that with trauma survivors, I have at times actually found it difficult to begin the therapy with values work explicitly. I think especially those who come to therapy in great pain and are able to express that, often seem to do better by starting with the pain, creative hopelessness, idea that there's a way out of the hole, etc. For those folks, I feel like sometimes it can be experienced almost as if the therapist doesn't get what they're coming to therapy for if you jump right into values. Of course, I think it's also totally in how you frame it, and I'm sure that Kelly and Sue do a good job with linking the values stuff up front with a client's stated goals, for example. But in general, starting with values is not the way I would go with CSA survivors. Overall, this whole thread has gotten me thinking a bit more about this issue again. I know we've struggled with it when trying to put together therapy protocols. In the heroin grant, the compromise we came to was to do the first set of sessions in the standard order as they're laid out in the ACT book, and then, once that

	groundwork has been done, allow the therapist to choose where to go next. One of those places was then values.
	But I wonder about 2 larger issues:
	1) What if it's the case that some clients respond better to values up front (maybe those who are more defended and less willing to access emotions at first), and others do better with the gung ho creative hopelessness, exploring change efforts, etc.? Wouldn't it be interesting to generate some hypotheses about what would predispose someone to respond to one ordering of components or another, test people on those characteristics at the beginning of treatment, and then run a bunch of people through in both ways? It really is an empirical question.
	2) And since these are all empirical questions, but we have some pretty divergent thoughts on what works and why, I also found myself wondering about how the role of therapist style/ personality factors into this. What if it's no more complicated than that some of us like to do things one way, or it fits with our therapeutic style/ personality better, so we see evidence that fits our heuristics, etc. How could we sort that out?
	Finally, I totally agree with the point that Kelly made that experienced therapists who are competent rather than just adherent are working in every session with all of the components in an integrative manner. But that's really hard to operationalize and disseminate, so I think this idea of testing the order that components go in, so that we can give the technology away for people who aren't yet "experts" is extremely important.
COMPONENT SEQUENCING Values or pain first? [cont'd] ACT Core components/ discriminations [cont'd] Steve Hayes	On the components: I would say acceptance in addition to exposure. Properly defined, exposure is the same thing (a method of establishing new response functions in the presence of repertoire-narrowing events), but 99% of the folks out there think of exposure as a way to decrease arousal, and that agenda IS the main repertoire-narrowing event out there. I would also want something in there on committed action. Values define (verbally) the reinforcers. Action produces them. If you want to simplify the components, I think you could replace most of them with these words (if we had time to define them): Love and Be On the values front end: I've sometimes said I do ACT like an anxiety-disordered person does ACT. Kel does it like someone with a history of drug problems does ACT (Kel and I talk about these personal histories openly, so I'm pretty sure I'm not outing anything to say this). If you can't breathe, the issue of values hardly seems to be an issue (hold your breath for a minute or more and see). That very difference suggests that matching may be an issue. But regardless, you have to have enough values work on the front end to get a powerful therapeutic contract. That was always true, which is why those old tapes often have a lot of value like stuff in the front. Even if you are doing acceptance and defusion nominally as a front end, you will need a commitment to living a vital life, aside and apart from the issue of whatever you've been struggling with. Talk of "having your life work" and "stepping out of the war so you can get about living, not putting your life on hold while you try to win it" is right up against the issue of values, which after all is simply vitality. I do think also that defusion can be a protector against excessive pliance inside values work, though true values work does defusion anyway and some of the technical advances are diminishing this problem. I've seen it be a problem though, and anyone doing ACT for very long will have examples. Pliance in the implementation of values is fine, but that is different. Usually you can sense the difference and take corrective action, but that can be a hard discrimination, so it is not clear to me which is a slam dunk on the issue of simplicity. In the grand scheme of things these issues are very small, precisely because ACT is process focused, not technology focused. We will work all of this out over a period of years.
COUPLES **ACT-oriented interventions [2-26-05]** James Monroe	Joanne Steinwachs wrote: I'd like to know if anyone's done any work using ACT with couples. I have found that there are various models for couples work out there that have an ACT quality to them ... e.g., Christensen and Jacobsons' Integrative Couples Therapy ("unified detachment"), Daniel Wiles' "After the Fight" ("The Platform"), etc. Basically these interventions have to do with "observing" vs. getting enmeshed in the struggle. I have also conceptualized the concept of "differentiation" (e.g., David Shnarchs' "Passionate Marriage") to be essentially ACT oriented ... i.e., there is no way I can see that one can

"differentiate" in a couples' situation without being "the observer". I also speak to couples about how it may be possible to "have" their respective agitated, troubled thoughts and feelings about one another and yet respond in ways that are perhaps more workable in service to their relationship (and in service to their mental health!). The thing is, there are tons of "workable" relationship dynamics/skills out there (compromise, Gottman's "repair" mechanisms, problem-solving, increasing positive events, "leaning towards" vs. "leaning away," (also Gottman) etc.,etc.,etc.) ... 5 decades plus of research and marital intervention literature on all of this but it all can easily go to-hell-and-a hand basket (or at least not be durable) unless couples learn to observe, not respond so reflexively to their thoughts and feelings and do something, anything (!) that is more workable in any given situation than to repeat the same old unworkable, conflictual stuff. Sometimes I say to couples ... "Are you in this to prove who is right or wrong, or are you in this to have a relationship?"

CULTURAL DIFFERENCES **Applicability of ACT [11-23-04]** Niklas Törneke	Rhiannon Patterson wrote: RFT, if it is correct, would seem to be a universal, transcultural theory of psychology. All humans have language and use language similarly, so RFT should apply to all cultures. This seems to imply that ACT should be a universally applicable form of psychotherapy, since it is based on RFT. Yet ACT seems so very applicable to the specific forms of psychopathology found in modern, industrialized countries, that I find it hard to imagine that it is also a universally useful psychotherapeutic approach. There is that existentialist quality to ACT that seems so modern -- the idea that one creates a meaningful life by creating or discovering one's own personal values, and then engaging in behavior consistent with these personal values. This understanding of how a meaningful life is formed seems very accurate in modern industrialized societies, which do indeed permit tremendous individual freedom and flexibility, and give people access to an amazingly wide set of economic, personal, and social choices. Yet, I can't help thinking that this existentialist approach to the meaningful life is, surely, not applicable to people in traditional cultures that aren't characterized by extensive individual choice. It seems then that RFT may be universal, but ACT is culturally specific, because any therapeutic approach must be very responsive to the particular cultural constraints of the patient. Any disagreements on either point? Well, I think I vote for disagreement on the second point (ACT being only for problems in the modern, industrialized countries). Of course there are ways ACT is done that would be restricted to the specific therapist, and the culture she/he is part of. Specific metaphors, exercises, the way things are put forward. Even the setting with a therapist meeting a client once/twice a week etc. But the basics I would guess are universal exactly because human language is universal and the side effects of language also should be, more or less. The basics then would be helping people to gain psychological flexibility by disrupting dysfunctional language-control (that is, defusion) and supporting action towards valued ends. That is the core of ACT. As for valuing I do not think that is restricted to modern, individualized society. The act of valuing is action towards verbally constructed, over all desirable consequences. All human cultures are full of that. As I understand it all humans make choices (in the ACT sense), regardless of culture. There is mainly a difference of topography. And, of course, the verbal constructions we do regarding this behavior differs. We call it "choice," "free will" etc. Other cultures might not construct it verbally this way. But the behavior is there ... I live in Sweden, which I guess is an example of modern society. But I have also lived several years in the Middle East and in Africa, that is in mainly traditional Moslem culture. I would say the basics of ACT would make sense there and psychological problems (what is usually called psychopathology) were everywhere.
CULTURAL DIFFERENCES Applicability of ACT [cont'd] Nico van der Meijden	Here in Holland we have a large community of Muslims originating from rural areas of Turkey and Morocco, who form an important part of the clients of the outpatient mental health care center where I work. The people coming from these areas come as a rule from group cultures where the interests of the individual are subordinate to those of the group/family. Saving the honour of the family is very important. In these traditional milieus arranged marriages are customary. When a marriage goes awry, as you say in English I believe, the position of the woman is often not enviable. For many women divorce is no option because the consequences are too severe. It means a breach not only with the family, but also with the community; a divorced woman is more or less considered as a whore. When you are brought up in such a context the best option is often making concessions and trying to make the best of an (unhappy) situation, sometimes with the help of family members who are invoked to mediate. For many of those women the step of divorce and of individual autonomy is just one step too far. In a more general sense I believe that even if you're raised in a modern industrialized society life amounts to making concessions, because personal values often conflict with each other.

CULTURAL DIFFERENCES Applicability of ACT [cont'd] Steve Hayes	Everything verbal is contaminated by culture, virtually by definition. Indeed RFT helps explain that very process. And ACT was developed in a western industrialized culture. But it was also deliberately linked to basic processes derived from an understanding of human language. So is it "universal"? ACT has been around long enough to have surprised many of us. Every attempt so far to put it in a small box has proven not to be correct. Some ACT folk assumed early on that ACT applied more to educated or high IQ folks (for somewhat analogous reasons to those listed here) and then the data began to beat that down. It was said not to apply to severe disorders such as psychosis ... it was more for "neurotic disorders." That turned out to be wrong. (A lot of us got that one wrong! Thanks Patty for helping to beat down the wall.) It supposedly required many sessions to have an impact so it would not apply unless folks could afford the time and effort of an extensive course of psychotherapy. Not so. The core message is useful even in greatly abbreviated form. Maybe it will even be useful in book form (the self-help folks in ACT need to do the evaluations of their books to see...). It supposedly would not apply to African Americans or Asians or Hispanics or Native Americans because the group was too important or the culture was very different or the SES was different or ACT was supposedly too individualistic. But now there are Japanese studies on ACT procedures and the data look just like US data; and there are studies with high minority percentages and the data look the same. And workshops with Native Americans and those are very well received. Supposedly ACT was only for adults because kids can't do metaphors and they can't really make choices and so on and on ... and then the kid data started to come in. And, yes, maybe it only applies to industrialized societies. We shall see. But just look at JoAnne Dahl / Tobias Lundgren's epilepsy workshop in India and Africa. These folks are quite literally dirt poor; uneducated. But ACT work there not only seems to be well received -- the data that result look like ACT data from studies in the industrialized world.... Sure there are huge differences in culture. Rural Muslims from Turkey and Morocco may be different than native Dutch, say, but these differences you describe could well be cast as values issues ... not core differences in processes of empowerment and change. There is nothing in ACT that says "don't participate in an arranged marriage." If "saving the honor of the family is very important" this will likely show up as a values issue. Values do not occur in a vacuum. Treating them as choices does not mean they are a-social or unconditioned when viewed from the outside; it means allowing globally desired life consequences to be sensitive to factors that go beyond literal, evaluative language as seen from the inside. If industrialized societies encourage different values than non-industrialized societies, that does not contradict the importance of empowering humans to seek what they value and transforming the emotional and cognitive barriers to doing that. Of course, if someone wants to subjugate women as a value ... well that is not a problem with the ACT model. That is a values conflict. And yes, I would not participate in that. But nothing in the ACT model tells you what values to have. That is why ACT and religion will never be one and the same -- ACT may empower religious values but it does not contain them. If you say "but in these societies it is not really the individual who behaves ... it is the group so individual values are irrelevant." Well, if one truly means that, then they've left psychology entirely. In that case, I'd just say "show me the data that the psychological level does not apply to ALL organisms ... including all human beings." As for me, I prefer to operate on the basis (held lightly but vigorously pursued) that the core issues ACT targets are core issues that come from language itself and thus apply to all verbal humans. I am worried that buying thoughts about how "what I have found useful for me does not apply to you" may not really be a matter of being humble and respectful of others (after all these thoughts about others are OUR thoughts ABOUT others) but may instead be a subtle form of social distancing and stigmatization. Instruction about other cultures contain these seeds of stigmatization inside them (see this month's issue of *Behavior Therapy* for data we've generated on ACT compared to training in cultural diversity on reduction of stigma). I think we need information about other cultures but we also need enough defusion / acceptance / etc. to hold even that information lightly (and it looks as though we may get the $$ to test that idea in a large grant that looks at the separate and combined impact of ACT and multicultural training - keep our toes crossed on the NIH budget). We just need to stay open and look at the data as they come in. Assumptions one way or the other can be incorrect. "Beginner's mind" is needed. So far I know of no actual data that would comport with the "it does not apply" idea - and we have at least *some* data from several sources that contradict that possibility.

CULTURAL DIFFERENCES **Applicability of ACT [4-26-05]** Steve Hayes	Sarah Dew wrote: ACT seems like an excellent therapy for "multicultural" use. I ... was wondering if anyone has focused on ACT and ... cultural issues (e.g., using ACT with diverse client populations, ACT as "culturally competent" approach, etc.)? Haven't seen that said but it makes sense. This issue has been covered in previous posts, but in brief: Datawise: some of the ACT studies have most of their Ss from minority groups (e.g., Jen Gregg's dissertation) and have good outcomes. JoAnne and Tobias have good data from India and South Africa. There are good data from Japan, Sweden, Spain, etc. ACT compares well with multicultural training in reducing bias (see study in BT two issues ago). We may have that grant looking at ACT in combo with multicultural training in a multi-site study ... if we get it we will have several hundred therapists doing ACT workshops either alone or in combo with multicultural training so we will have a lot of data on this. Jason Lillis has some new and nice data on the impact of ACT on racial bias. Kel has done training with Native Americans with good buzz. I think there are a lot of reasons to think that ACT is well suited in this area.
CULTURAL DIFFERENCES Applicability of ACT [cont'd] **COMPONENT SEQUENCING** **Culturally diverse clients [4-26-05]** Mary Politi	[In using ACT with culturally diverse client populations] focusing on values and workability before focusing on emotional acceptance can be effective--only emphasize emotional acceptance in the context of what is working (which we do anyway, but it is even more important with individuals from different cultural backgrounds). Many people from non-European cultures use higher levels of emotional control, and this can be adaptive in some settings. Emphasizing values and workability can let the client test for him/herself when it is beneficial to use EA vs. control.
CULTURAL DIFFERENCES **Control of emotions - effect on cancer survivors [12-6-04]** Mary Politi	There has been some discussion about emotional acceptance in different cultures. It's a particular interest of mine, so I've been keeping my eye out for articles on the subject. There's a great one in this month's Psycho-oncology, Ho, Chan, & Ho. (2004). Emotional control in Chinese female cancer survivors. *Psycho-oncology, 13*(11), 808-817. I'll paste the abstract below if anyone is interested. It's a good example of how emotional control might be more common among certain cultural groups, but it is not necessarily beneficial just because it has persisted as a cultural norm. Chinese persons are not known as strong in expressing emotions, especially negative ones. However, being diagnosed with cancer and going through treatment can be an emotionally traumatic experience and cancer patients are supposed to have a stronger need to express these negative feelings. The control of expression of negative emotions such as anger, anxiety and depression in Chinese female cancer survivors (n=139) was examined in the present study using the Chinese version of the Courtauld Emotional Control Scale (CECS).... Correlation analyses suggested that cancer survivors with higher emotional control tended to have higher stress, anxiety and depression levels and to adopt negative coping with cancer. Regression analysis showed that emotional control would positively predict stress level even after the effect of depressed mood was under control....
CULTURAL DIFFERENCES **Response to ACT interventions** **PHYSICAL ILLNESS** **Diabetes [7-20-04]** Steve Hayes	Mary Politi wrote: I was wondering if anyone has done a study using ACT as an intervention (or even just measuring emotional acceptance) in ethnically-diverse samples. Most or all of the studies I've seen have included samples in which 95% of the participants or more identify as Caucasian. The reason I think this is important is that there is some evidence that African-Americans, for instance, rely more on emotional control strategies than on those requiring emotional acceptance. I also found this in my dissertation--the scale I used to measure emotional control was highly related to ethnicity. African-Americans endorsed these items much more frequently than European-Americans. Theorists believe control strategies have been adaptive for some cultural groups in the past, particularly in settings where there is a lot of discrimination (i.e., expression of anger can lead to more discrimination or prejudice). If this is true, there might be more resistance to ACT within certain ethnic groups. Has anyone looked at ethnic differences in response to ACT interventions either in a research study or just clinically?

	There are a few.
	Jennifer Gregg's marvellous study on diabetes management is the best one on this front so far. It was done in a health clinic that served the poor and only 25% of the subjects were Caucasian.... Super outcomes.
	As far as ethnicity and experiential avoidance, the critical question is not the level or reliance on EA strategies w/in group ... it is their function. It would be a big mistake to assume that higher levels within ethnic groups means that it would be ethnically insensitive to intervene on it ... any more than higher levels of cycle cell anemia in AA populations means that we should not intervene with CCA. It depends on the relationship to health within that group. There, so far, it seems that the concept holds up. For example Dosheen Toarmino's dissertation shows that Asian Americans have higher levels of EA than Caucasians ... but the EA - health relationship was the same in each group.... Same with women v men as I recall.
	Based on what we know so far it seems most likely that if you have a tougher situation to face you will rely on EA more because that is what is in our general culture... but it is equally toxic to all. If that is what is going on you will find higher EA levels among any disadvantaged group but it will still predict poor outcomes group by group.
CULTURAL DIFFERENCES Response to ACT interventions [cont'd] **PHYSICAL ILLNESS** **Epilepsy [7-20-04]** Steve Hayes	There is also a nice study on the use of ACT with epilepsy done in both South Africa and India. Good outcomes and the process model works. It is Tobias Lundgren's thesis done with JoAnne Dahl. [available at http://www.contextualpsychology.org]
DEPRESSION **Post-natal - protocol [3-29-05]** ACT Listserv Member	For my clinical product (in place of preliminary examination) I wrote a treatment manual using ACT to prevent post partum depression. Today it was formally approved. If anyone is interested in a copy please contact me back channel.
EATING DISORDER **Literature [2-28-03]** Steve Hayes	Frank Gardner wrote: Would anyone happen to know of any references discussing efficacy/use of either ACT or DBT in the treatment of Bulimia? Yes, there was an ACT and eating disorders case recently: Heffner, M., Sperry, J., Eifert, G. H., & Detweiler, M. (2002). Acceptance and Commitment Therapy in the treatment of an adolescent female with anorexia nervosa: A case example. *Cognitive and Behavioral Practice, 9*, 232-236. It describes the use of ACT in anorexia and shows resulting data. The case study is followed by discussion articles: Wilson, K. G., & Roberts, M. (2002). Core principles in Acceptance and Commitment Therapy: An application to anorexia. *Cognitive and Behavioral Practice, 9*, 237-243. Hayes, S. C., & Pankey, J. (2002). Experiential avoidance, cognitive fusion, and an ACT approach to anorexia nervosa. *Cognitive and Behavioral Practice, 9*, 243-247. Orsillo, S. M., & Batten, S. J. (2002). ACT as treatment of a disorder of excessive control: Anorexia. *Cognitive and Behavioral Practice, 9*, 253-259. There is also a cognitive paper that is nominally a response to the case, but it mentions ACT only in passing, focusing instead on the traditional CBT model.
EATING DISORDER **Obesity, morbid, ACT formulation of [9-2-03]** Jeremy Gauntlett-Gilbert	I'm working with morbidly obese people, and would like to swap ideas about how to treat them with ACT. I'm starting from a couple of premises here: (1) that normal CBT for obesity isn't terribly effective in the short or long run (10% weight loss relapsing to 5%); (2) normal CBT isn't based on a particularly psychologically sophisticated model of what makes obesity persist; (3) and there's no evidence base for people with BMI > 40 anyway (the very, very big). Here's some thoughts for an ACT formulation of chronic, morbid obesity.... Unworkable agendas: Most clients can lose weight. They generally use a drastic [approach], low calorie diets, Slimfast, etc.

	Currently treating a guy who lost 8 stones by eating a bean burrito a day. As a generalisation, my clients are addicted to rapid weight-loss extreme methods. As these fail and they get bigger they opt for more extreme methods. A target for 'creative hopelessness.'
	Avoidance:
	Clients are avoiding feeling deprived, feeling hungry (both of which may be genuine when cutting down from a massive baseline). They are also avoiding the desperate preoccupation and cognitive impairment associated with dieting (which they shouldn't experience if they do it right). Also avoiding emotions through food (though many overeat when in a good mood). Clients also avoid by going into 'not thinking about food' states in which they manage total avoidance of the topic.
	Fusion:
	With ideas that behavioural change will be horrible, futile, lead to awful deprivation and not work. (Classic CBT challenges are often tricky here as there is often no evidence whatsoever to the contrary.) Also there is a sticky fusion between emotions and eating / activity, though this can go in both directions (eat when miserable, eat when happy and with friends).
	Reasons:
	"I've got a metabolic condition, people don't understand that it's different when you're this size, it's not fair - I don't eat that much, I eat chocolate but so does everybody else, I had a deprived post-war childhood, I shouldn't have to do this - all I'm doing is eating what I want and I'm getting punished," etc.
EATING DISORDER **Values, conflict of - verbal cf. non-verbal [3-1-05]** Audrey Lowrie	... If, for instance, I am working with a bulimic client, ... I would explore pliance possibilities, wondering 'what does this client really want when s/he reflects on the matter in a supportive, reflective, client centred space,' if s/he decides that s/he really wants to stop binging and purging, I would discuss the tunnel vision that s/he experiences *at times* that promotes a focus on the immediate 'preference' (a non-verbal value based in their sensuality), to over-eat and purge, and contrast this with the preference that is his/her (consciously chosen) goal that exists in the wider perspective, that is, to maintain a basically healthy eating lifestyle. I would then assist the client to increase their power to consistently 'choose' their (conscious, verbal) preference. One way that I would do this is by encouraging the client to create a large, bright, colourful, collage depicting 'the "who" that they want to be,' to keep in an appropriate place, by the fridge, or food cupboard perhaps. I find images most useful for such goals.
FORENSIC PSYCHOLOGY **Exhibitionism (case example) [10-4-02]** Sonja Batten	ACT Listserv Member wrote: Does anyone know of any research or literature on using ACT with offenders, such as sex offenders, prison inmates, or in community-based treatment for offenders? You might try: Paul, R. H., Marx, B. P., & Orsillo, S. M. (1999). Acceptance-based psychotherapy in the treatment of an adjudicated exhibitionist: A case example. *Behavior Therapy, 30*, 149-162.
GROUP **Bus metaphor, Passengers on** **METAPHOR** **Bus, Passengers on - group use [2-19-05]** ACT Listserv Member	I've been running an ACT group at the Honolulu VA for the last two months. The group includes folks with PTSD, bipolar, substance use, severe depression, anger and chronic pain; the usual VA mix. The group was slow to warm up at first and by now some of the initial hostility has mostly dissolved. What was an amazing experience for me is how the group responded to Passengers on the bus. It really got to all of them, although in different ways. The whole group transformed and became energized (or agitated). The depressives wanted to park the bus and walk away; the angry ones wanted to slam on the brakes and hurt the passengers; some of the substance users wanted to medicate the passengers. One PTSD guy needed to watch over everybody else's bus to make sure they're OK. It was great to see how they all at first attempted to deal logically with the dilemma inherent in the choices and could not get very far. A few got the idea and led the group into a valued direction. After a while the rest started to get the idea of the control agenda vs. valued living tension in different ways and to different degrees. For me it was so interesting to see how experiential avoidance and the control agenda manifested across conditions, yet with such commonality. Too bad we're stuck with so called homogenous samples in our research work.
GROUP **Experiential exercises/ metaphors [9-1-02]** Chad Emrick	ACT Listserv Member wrote: Recently I used the soldier-parade exercise within a psychotherapy group. It worked quite well. ...There are other metaphors and exercises which seem to be suitable for group-work (e.g., awareness exercise). Who else uses ACT interventions within groups? What are your experiences? Did you create new ideas as to groups, which go beyond the pool of methods as described in the ACT "bible"? In my groups of substance-dependent veterans (most of whom are dual-diagnosis patients), my graduate students and I have used virtually all of the experiential exercises found in the ACT "bible." The only exception is that of "taking your mind for a walk." However, I have demonstrated this exercise with one of the patients being my "mind." While my "mind" was talking to me, I focused on making eye and hand

	contact with every member of the group. To my surprise, I did not listen AT ALL to my "mind" despite the fact that my mind was saying things that engaged the members of the group. This experience taught me the value of focusing outside of myself (in the direction of having genuine encounters with others) in helping me get some distance from my "mind."
	In our groups, we have done what amounts to a psychodrama with the "passengers on the bus" metaphor. After getting some history from a patient, other group members play various "passengers" while the patient, who is driving the bus, is encouraged to stay focused on moving his/her life in a valued direction (in most cases, in our groups, the direction is identified as living a life that is free of alcohol and drug abuse).
	I consider group to be an excellent forum for helping patients get into experiential contact with deliteralization, acceptance, and commitment.
GROUP Experiential exercises/ metaphors [cont'd] Steve Hayes	Almost everything in the ACT book can be used in groups and several studies have tested ACT in groups. [See contextualpsychology.org for a list.] There are several exercises not in the book that we use in group ACT training. The easiest way to get next to these is to come do a 2-3 day training.
	... The problem with the "bible" deal is that bibles do not change and ACT is a dynamic, open system. I think ACT should be what the world ACT community creates it to be.
	On an external focus and distance from one's "mind": that will have that effect so long as one doesn't use such a focus **in order to** create that distance. In that case, the volume of self evaluative (etc.) talk will go right back up because the volume will be important and thus focused on in a second-order fashion. Committed, valued action works that way in day-to-day life -- there is no quicker way to decrease cognitive fusion with the normal chatter ... unless that is the purpose.
GROUP Experiential exercises/ metaphors [cont'd] Robyn Walser	I have used a number of exercises in groups...including most of those contained in the book. We have also generated several other exercises based on group make-up. For instance, in one group, where the members were having a difficult time seeing themselves as separate from that which they experience - specifically thoughts - we wrote thoughts out on 3x5 cards and taped them to the individuals (they had thoughts taped all over the place). We made the thoughts as specific to each individual as possible - although many had several of the same thoughts. (We had them say a thought that they struggled with, then the response to that thought, then the response to that thought, etc.) Once they had 20-30 thoughts taped to them, we had them participate in other activities such as walking around, interacting with each other, describing each other (with their thoughts - most describers, by the way, did not describe the thoughts that they saw, but rather the person). This was a nice demonstration of carrying your thoughts and doing what works. We also do many mindfulness exercises with an ACT twist....
	I have generally found that ACT exercises work just as well in group as in individual format.
GROUP **Non-clinical (police) - homework** **HOMEWORK** **Group, non-clinical (police) [4-28-03]** ACT Listserv Member	Joseph Ciarrochi wrote: We are about to start the pilot work on a major acceptance-based intervention with the police force.... I am just wondering what sort of homework one might give during the two week interval between the workshops?
	We have been conducting ACT groups with non-pathological population for performance enhancement. It sounds like a similar population, in which you are trying to train the police to act based on their values, rather than their particular thoughts and emotions at the time.
	One thing that we have done with a "normal" population is begin with mindfulness homework exercises. For a police force this may be for them to notice the details of their thoughts and emotions while performing a mundane or automatic aspect of their job, such as sitting in their cruiser, reading someone their rights, or other things which they may not normally attend to. This has worked for us in helping people identify their thoughts and emotions in particular situations, which lays the foundation for the rest of the ACT work.
	As you mentioned, we have also used Linehan's conveyor belt homework, or the cloud homework, to help people understand the way in which they judge and categorize their thoughts and emotions.
	We have then focused our homework on behavioral activities. It is hard to give particular suggestions for your work, because I think that the best homeworks are specifically tailored to the population. I think the trick is to understand the situations in which your population relies on their specific thoughts and emotions to act, and then develop exercises to accept their thoughts in these situations and act in a different manner. Exposure seems to be a very powerful tool in helping people understand that the rules they have developed based on their own specific cognitions and feelings may be accepted without adverse consequences (or may result in beneficial consequences). This also provides individual data and experiences to work with for increased skill building and further theoretical explanation. It may be helpful to think of it as a graded exposure, where you set up situations in which it is easy to act in a new manner and accept, and then build up to situations in which thoughts, emotions and behaviors are more ingrained and it is difficult to commit to alternative behaviors....

GROUP **Panic disorder - ACT cf. CBT** **ACT cf.** **CBT - panic disorder group [12-10-03]** Nico van der Meijden	I'm a psychologist working in a Dutch outpatient mental health care center. Last September a colleague and I started a group for people with a panic disorder. The center used an old protocol consisting of a mixture of conventional cognitive techniques (identifying negative thoughts and replacing them by positive ones), relaxation training and exposure in vivo. We decided to rewrite the protocol completely and make it an ACT group, using the panic protocol Steve Hayes has sent to this Yahoo-group, the old Zettle group protocol for depressed people (on the ACT website) and the ACT book. We've done 9 sessions by now and though this approach needs getting used to, our overall experience is positive. The attendance is high and some clients really have improved. The participants seem to like the metaphors and they also seem to work (after the driver-in-the-bus metaphor a very defensive client unwittingly started to talk of 'they' when she talked about her thoughts). The experiential exercises make the meetings much more lively. I also have the impression that this approach gives you a much sharper impression of the dynamics of individual clients; it's somehow 'more in the open.' Compared with ACT the old approach was much more 'softening' or subdued....
GROUP **Smoking cessation; ACT/CBT [2-19-05]** Mary Politi	ACT Listserv Member wrote: Does anybody have an ACT protocol for smoking cessation? I am about to start a CBT group and would like to bring in ACT. I did a smoking group at a cancer center that I considered a tailored CBT intervention with acceptance components. The main ACT related parts that I included were acceptance of "slips" (vs. abstinence only groups), and acceptance of thoughts and feelings associated with a desire to smoke/difficulty quitting. Hank once posted that "Quitting is not hard...lifting up a car is hard. Quitting is just uncomfortable" (thank you Hank!). I used this concept a lot, getting them to recognize that they can quit smoking even in the presence of cravings, uncomfortable thoughts, emotions, and physiological sensations. They just have to be willing to sit with the discomfort. I can send you the protocol if you want. I didn't collect data, but did find that the acceptance parts were helpful.
GROUP Smoking cessation; ACT/CBT [cont'd] Steve Hayes	The smoking article published in *Behavior Therapy* is Liz Gifford's NCI funded dissertation.... The outcomes in that study were pretty good. It's interesting because that treatment group is straight-ahead ACT and it's not combined with anything. Of course you have to add targeted behavioral components as you would with any ACT manual (e.g., mindful smoking; or smoke holding; or scheduled smoking etc. etc.). Rick Brown is doing a large NIDA funded ACT smoking study right now.... There is a second NIDA funded study that is in the can (good outcomes) that combines ACT and FAP. The manual is a little different than the NCI one, but not that much. Liz, Barbara Kohlenberg, myself and a few others had a hand in that version.... This study also added Zyban to the ACT / FAP combo and compared it to Zyban alone, so the design is more complicated. The outcomes were better than Zyban and worked according to the model (acceptance etc. predicted outcomes). They seemed to be about the same as the outcomes in the ACT group in the NCI study though, maybe a little weaker (probably from the mixed message from the Zyban + ACT/FAP).
OBSESSIVE-COMPULSIVE DISORDER **Religious obsessions** **RELIGION** **Obsessions, religious [3-12-05]** Rainer Sonntag	Casey Capps wrote: I would like to help [an OCD client] see what 'stuff' is coming from her mind and what her experience tells her. For example, the thoughts tell her, "If I don't pray five times daily, I will go to hell." However, she'll never be able to come into the natural contingency of going to hell while alive. I have observed myself that under the cover of "what does your experience tell you?" I rather worked for changing cognitive content (cognitive restructuring) than to foster the client making discriminations when to follow rules and when not. One of the difficult things for me again and again is not to be drawn into the games of rational discourse. I wonder whether this rational logic might be undermined by asking, for example, "Well, and now that you are praying five times daily, what happens to your anxiety of going to hell?" Maybe this could help the client to shift from "going to hell - then and there" to "my anxiety of going to hell - here and now." [CC] What do folks think about saying the following to the client, "My guess is that, and see what your experience tells you about this, God himself/herself could come down and say, 'you don't have to pray five times a day to get into heaven,' and, after he/she left, your mind could come up with some new and obscure reason why you still have to pray five times a day to go to heaven. Could you see your mind doing that? If you can, let me ask you, is your mind on your side here, does it really have your best interests in mind?" Is the thing to do here to continue to reinforce the fact that her mind is not her friend? This also sounds too familiar to me. If I observe me doing something like this I often notice that I am struggling with the client and her mind, trying to convince her to think and act in other ways and be more rational. There are many different things one could do at this point. One that comes to my mind is to "make room" for her fears and hopes. For example, "What comes up when you imagine going to hell? Why is this

so bad?" and things like this; or "What do you think about heaven? How will life be in heaven?" Hell and heaven are very abstract notions; I would like to get them more concrete and experiential, and eventually get a foot in the door to turn to talking about values.

Another move might be to have her pray in-session if she is willing to do so; this could help to get in experiential contact with her kind of praying rather than talking about it and might promote defusion and the therapeutic relationship.

[CC] How do I get her to risk something so absolute (eternal bliss) to have a life here? A move I made was something like this, "If all you want is to make it to heaven, it sounds like you've got a handle on that. You just need to keep doing what you're doing. But you want more than that, you're here. You've said that your life is crippled. Yes, you're alive, you're not in jail, you're pretty sure that you're headed for heaven, you don't have any diseases. But is that all you want for your life? It doesn't seem like it."

This seems to be about motivation. There are two ways to motivation: suffering and values. Again there will be many ways to move forward from here; I think I could do the following. Asking "How does this life feel, day to day struggling for heaven?" - "Do you have the experience that you got closer to heaven, say, within the last couple of years?" If her answer to this last question should be "yes," I might ask "Is this your experience or a belief?" (This question would not have the purpose to get a concrete answer but to do some tiny bit of discrimination training by introducing the difference between experience and belief.)

Another question at this point might address the costs of struggling towards heaven and avoiding hell: "How does this struggle (e.g., praying) affect your life, work, relationship etc.?" Again these questions not only (or even mainly) call for a concrete answer (the rational discourse game); rather they may help to work out the change agenda and point to the function of praying as one way of struggling and they may open up the client to distinguish between praying-as-struggling and praying-as-loving - not on the basis of a rational analysis but her experience ("How does it feel to pray this way or that way?").

A final question that my mind comes up with now is "Imagine that you get a clear sign from God that your praying has been and is heard. Let's even say that God's message is that you can be sure that when you pray, say for ten minutes, five times a day you will go to heaven. What then would you do with the rest of your day, with those many hours left?"

OBSESSIVE-COMPULSIVE DISORDER Religious obsessions [cont'd] **RELIGION** Obsessions, religious [cont'd] John McNeill	First of all, I don't know if you're going to be able to out duel her mind with more words about its process. As one possible intervention for your OCD client: you could record your client's entire stream of obsessional thinking [the complete storyline] aloud via an open-end audio-recording and have her listen to it using stereo headphones for 10-15 minutes non-stop several times per day [this could be done weekly in-session if the storyline alters from week-to-week]. This exercise provides repeated direct exposure to the entire storyline and may help to undercut verbal functions inherent therein. The exercise could be followed up with an expressive writing task for added effect. Worrisome thoughts outside the exposure periods are simply noted in a diary; once recorded, she is instructed to mindfully immerse herself within the present moment. You could also set up established prayer-periods at specific times daily. These two tactics may help to establish some stimulus narrowing on occurrence episodes. Additionally, you might work on (1) various mindfulness practices, (2) defusion exercises aimed at 'knowing selves,' and (3) exercises that help contrast "don't know mind" with the mind that naturally "adds" to one's direct experiencing of things. Pragmatically, she must create space for both the obsessional thinking while also wedging out space for other valued-direction as one whole life experienced, so that one feature doesn't have to be cancelled out in order to realize the other.
OBSESSIVE-COMPULSIVE DISORDER Religious obsessions [cont'd] **RELIGION** Obsessions, religious [cont'd] **EXERCISE** **Milk, milk, milk [3-15-05]** Patty Bach	It sounds like your client is in hell already. She said that saying the word evil would bring evil into the room - it seems to me that there might be some room to do work on the difference between milk being in the room and the stimulus functions of milk (evil) being in the room. E.g., when you say milk or lemon they don't show up in the room - evil isn't in the room and some responses that might show up if evil were in the room might be present, e.g., fear, thoughts of going to hell. What would evil 'look like'? How would she know it when she sees it? Isn't 'evil' an evaluation of something rather than a 'thing'? I.e., it's more like 'cold and creamy' showing up when we say 'milk' rather than milk showing up when we say milk. If she said "good" or "love" or "mother" over and over would they show up in the room? If so, what is their effect? Is it powerful enough to make her good and more loving, or to make her unable to stop thinking about evaluations of her mother? I'm not suggesting this as a way to logically convince her of anything, and as a way to experience what shows up when we say words, and beginning with benign words and then perhaps moving to more 'powerful'/loaded words.

OBSESSIVE-COMPULSIVE DISORDER Religious obsessions [cont'd] **RELIGION** Obsessions, religious [cont'd] Steve Hayes	One thing I've done with religious obsessives, just to create enough wiggle room to do acceptance/defusion/exposure, is to arrange a joint meeting with their minister. Find out who it is, ask permission from the client to meet with him / her (on the ground of wanting to understand their religious beliefs), and go have a conversation first. If it goes well, get permission to bring that person into session. The goal is not to convince the client to change their obsessive views - the goal is to distinguish religious faith from thoughts. Once we have it in the realm of thoughts and fears, we are able to work. I do the same with fear of contamination etc. First we make sure we know the facts (e.g., will touching a bottle of Draino contaminate you, etc.), all the while emphasizing that we do NOT expect this to change anything psychologically. Then we move in on the fears. Factually mistaken beliefs and OCD are two different things, by definition. Religious obsessions are tricky in part because it seems as though making this distinction is anti-faith. It is not. Religious obsession is ALWAYS bad theology. It helps if you've had extensive religious training yourself and have worked some on how to fit ACT ideas into it. A key distinction that often applies: in Judeo-Christian theology sin requires an act of the will, just as faith does. That is, it requires a choice. That is why a wet dream is not a sin in any theology I know of. In the same way, automatic thoughts are not sins. Choosing to operate on the basis of thoughts can be, however (that idea makes good sense from an ACT perspective). Thus, defusion / acceptance is a way to reduce the actual capability of thoughts to lead to "sin" (if we were to use that language). It is off point re OCD but it is related re religion: There are some Mormon ACT folk who have used ACT to help gay Mormons notice their attraction to same sex others while choosing not to operate on the basis of that attraction. (Some on the list may find this an offensive idea - after working it through I did not. If we can allow monks to choose celibacy on religious grounds we can allow gay Mormons to choose the same. I emphasize the word choose.) Anyway, some of the church elders were concerned about the idea of acceptance being applied to gay attraction and asked for an explanation. The therapist ... came back with a cool example: the temptation of Christ. By definition, temptation involves attraction. If mere attraction is a sin, then Christ is a sinner. But that is bad theology within the Judeo-Christian tradition. If there is no act of the will, there is no sin. And acceptance and defusion help teach folks how to apply behavioral choices to values instead of to whatever language programming we happen to have (what are the numbers?). Same with the word "evil." Repeating it is not the same as choosing what it refers to. The exact opposite in this case.
PERSONALITY DISORDER **Avoidant - ACT treatment approach** **AVOIDANCE** **Severe - ACT treatment approach [8-4-03]** Brandon Gaudiano	Archana Jajodia wrote: I have been trying to use ACT with a client who meets criteria for Avoidant Personality Disorder (after having tried and failed with CBT). The client is heavily invested in avoiding unpleasant feelings at all costs and even after over 6 months of using ACT with him, his (un)willingness has not changed. Are there particular ACT interventions that might work better with such a client? ... interpersonal exposures (both in vivo and role played in the session) based on the person's individualized fear hierarchy would still be the crucial element of effective tx for someone with APD. We know that the APD dx is rather redundant with generalized social phobia or social anxiety disorder (almost everyone who meets DSM criteria for APD also meets criteria for SAD) and that this supposed "personality disorder" tends to "remit" in most with as little as 6-12 weeks of CBT. I have found ACT to be useful in this population, but exposure is still the basis of the treatment. I simply modify the CBT exposure protocol so that it is done within the context of ACT instead. Anecdotally, when working with one socially phobic client (meeting criteria for severe APD and SAD) whose avoidance behaviors were making for a slow tx response and producing much ambivalence in session, I focused more on the values clarification component with much success. After a few weeks of this approach, the client was much more willing to do the exposures and was moving toward his goals quicker.
PERSONALITY DISORDER Avoidant - ACT treatment approach [cont'd] AVOIDANCE Severe - ACT treatment approach [cont'd] Mary Politi	I used ACT with a client with Avoidant PD, and I found the "control is the problem" interventions to work best for his situation. Also, if you say your client is unwilling to feel emotions, you can try the "if you're not willing to feel it, you have it" examples with him. It would be helpful to think about what brought him into therapy, and what he was seeking from the start. Can he achieve whatever goals he set while avoiding his emotions?

PERSONALITY DISORDER **Narcissistic/ Anti-social - values work** **VALUES** **Anti-social/ harmful** **[4-28-05]** Patty Bach	Amanda Johnson wrote: Does anyone have any ideas about using ACT with clients with Narcissistic or Antisocial Personality Disorders? … Specifically, their values are usually very self-serving, frequently to the point of harming others in the process of helping themselves. Is harming others a value, or is it a behavior in the service of some other value? I would suggest that even most of those with APD or NPD (excepting perhaps the case of psychopathy) are not likely to say that "I value harming others," and instead would be more likely to endorse that "harming others is okay in the service of value X." If that's the case, then you might be able to make a move around workability. The fact that these clients are being seen in a forensic/correctional setting is one indicator that something about their behavior isn't working. On another note, as "verbally construed global desirable outcomes" there is a sense in which all values are self-serving. This might be another way in.
PERSONALITY DISORDER Narcissistic/ Anti-social - values work [cont'd] VALUES Anti-social/ harmful [cont'd] John Blackledge	I'd suggest remaining alert to situations where a relatively narcissistic pursuit of such a client's personal values actually negatively affects his movement toward that or other values, then examine these behaviors collaboratively and try to get the client's honest take on whether they are serving him well. For example, a 'narcissistic' client might value close relationships, and his perennial focus on himself and disregard for the other person's preferences during conversations with that person might adversely affect pursuit of this value.
PHYSICAL ILLNESS **Pain, chronic - ACT-based programs** **[11-4-03]** Lance McCracken	Jill Sloan wrote: I am a psychologist working in a multidisciplinary pain team. Our patients all have a chronic pain condition, usually comorbid with a range of other conditions - depression, anxiety, anger regulation difficulties, trauma, etc.... I would like to implement a more ACT-oriented therapy with this patient group, instead of a predominantly CBT approach. I feel that CBT approaches, particularly the cognitive restructuring, fail to address some of the real needs of these patients, particularly in relation to acceptance and their avoidance of experience. We have been developing an acceptance-based approach to chronic pain for a number of years. It started in 1995 when Steve H. put me in touch with a dissertation by David Geiser from Reno. We adopted a chronic pain acceptance measure (based on the AAQ at the time) from the appendices of that dissertation and started to study and think about the area. At this point I am in Bath, UK, working in a multidisciplinary treatment center, possibly not different from yours. We are group-based and primarily residential (3 or 4 week). We use some of the stuff from Geiser, some material from the ACT book, and other methods we have developed over the years. Our physiotherapists are on board with the exposure and willingness material - so physical exercises on the program form an important part of treatment. As you mentioned we don't do any cognitive restructuring at all - it seems less confusing to treat all private experiences in the same way, including thoughts, sensations, and moods. In the psychology stream of the program we do quite a bit on undermining the pain control agenda, exposure sessions of various sorts, and various awareness and mindfulness exercises. We also use some traditional methods like a sensate focus exercise, habit reversal, and relaxation. We do something fun with the relaxation in that we don't use it as any type of "analgesic" strategy but more as a method that includes being aware of everything that is present when sitting quiet and focused and for the goodness of the overt behavioral pieces of appearing relaxed (regardless of how one feels). We (Kevin Vowles, Chris Eccleston, and me) actually have a study under review. It includes 108 consecutive patients in treatment from our center here in Bath. Our patients are generally quite complex and long term cases. We have data at pre-, post treatment, and 3-month follow-up. The results are unanimously quite good including such things as reduced medication consumption and health care visits, improved working rates, and large reductions in depression, anxiety, etc.. Remarkably, this treatment process seems quite powerful - everything we touch with treatment changes just about as we would hope.... I have to say that it is an interesting challenge in this type of complex treatment environment. We have nurses, physicians, occupational therapists, psychologists, and physiotherapists. It requires that we constantly tend to a sort of culture shift, basically maintaining the spirit that one doesn't have to feel good (or be pain free) to live good.

PHYSICAL ILLNESS Pain, chronic - ACT-based programs [cont'd] **Pain, chronic - child and adolescent** **CHILD & ADOLESCENT** **Pain, chronic [11-4-03]** Rikard Wicksell	At the Astrid Lindgren Children's Hospital (Karolinska Hospital) in Stockholm, we are developing an intervention program that we label as "behavioral medicine" and that is exclusively based on ACT. We are focusing on the "idiopathic" pain syndromes, which constitute a rather big part of the chronic pain group (including low back pain, whiplash, fibromyalgia, headache and diffuse abdominal pain etc.). So far we have seen dramatic improvements across the patients and we are currently running a RCT, comparing the ACT-based approach with the standard pharmacological treatment (amitriptylin), and have so far included about 8 patients. Currently we are working with children and adolescents although we are planning to conduct similar studies on adults (as soon as we get time/money to hire another psychologist). To an important extent, Lance's list of interventions count for us too. In some aspects, our model is different. We run this as an outpatient facility (which limits our possibilities to work with patients outside Stockholm) and see them about once a week. Although we have physiotherapists at the hospital (that are sometimes involved with the chronic pain kids) they are not involved in the ACT treatment. Instead this is run by a psychologist and anaesthesiologist only. Although there are advantages with having a multidisciplinary team as Lance and Chris have set up, my experience is that it is possible to achieve very good results with a much smaller organisation too. I agree with you and with Lance in that this approach has tremendously exciting potential (and promising...) for this type of patient (with "chronic" symptoms resulting in a very dangerous pattern of avoidance). I also agree that this approach is suitable (attractive) across disciplines (it's not a shrink-thing). As some of you know, Gunnar Olsson (the anaesthesiologist) lectured at the world congress and has during this last two years learned and adopted an ACT orientation. I think this is vital for the treatment program and crucial in the development of a new approach to treatment as well as new theories about the etiology, maintenance and "treatment" for longstanding debilitating pain....
PHYSICAL ILLNESS **Pain, chronic - child and adolescent** **CHILD & ADOLESCENT** **Pain, chronic [10-21-02]** Rikard Wicksell	Rainer Sonntag wrote: Has anyone experiences (or even outcome data) on the application of ACT with somatic symptoms. In particular, I would like to see if anyone has experience with exposure and defusion with somatic symptoms, e.g., taking the metaphors clients use themselves to describe their experiences and experientially exploring them by physicalizing the symptoms and going into the sensory images and scenes related to them; e.g., "burning" pain, a headache that feels like "the skull would burst" (can you imagine that?). At Astrid Lindgren Children's Hospital in Stockholm, Sweden, we are currently developing a rehabilitation programme for children and adolescents with longstanding pain, using a behavioral medicine perspective. Although we initially talked about CBT (emphasizing B), we are today using an ACT-oriented approach. Even if we don't discuss in terms of diagnostic labels, this includes fibromyalgia, juvenile rheumatoid arthritis, musculosceletal pain syndromes, CRPS, migraine/chronic daily headache, functional gastrointestinal disorders, Chrohn's disease, etc. The analysis is based on learning theory. Subsequently, our main intervention is thus exposure. Exposure to pain-related stimuli is difficult, partly because - as you mention - it is an obvious and unpleasant somatic experience that "communicates" (to both the client and parents, friends etc.) a threat to the client's organism. This threat, of course, is justifying avoidance as a strategy used by the client him/herself to reduce pain. (Avoidance, as a means to reduce pain, is logical and is many times in line with injections, medications, TENS etc. used by doctors and other health care professionals, emphasizing pain reduction as the ultimate goal of treatment.) Nevertheless, it seems possible to work with exposure to conditioned pain stimuli. Clinically, this means that we are initially working with a shift in perspective. The client has, for several years, strived towards a "pain-free" life, using interventions such as medications, injections, relaxation exercises as well as avoidance of pain stimuli and "following body signals." We spend some important time finding out how successful this has been, and more important, whether this has brought them closer to things they value in life. Establishing important goals (in life) and finding out that these are not coherent with a life free of risks (for pain, fear, failure, worrying, anxiety etc. - we emphasize that this is not just about pain), in addition to the initial "reassurance" that the pain is not dangerous, facilitates exposure to the goals of life/values. It gets to be "ok" to do things that hurt a bit. Defusing is a very important part of this process. Thoughts ("I can't handle pain," "I can't do it because I have a pain syndrome," "I can't go with them next weekend, I don't know how I'll feel then") have created big and important obstacles that need to be "defused." Your point of exposing to/ defusing sensory images in themselves is interesting. I haven't done it, and even if this might be an important defusing process I think I might consider this a "symptom focus" that might be a bit inconsistent with working towards, and focusing on, values. (I have to contemplate this for a while, though. Anyone else?)

Sometimes when I talk to the client about the process of working towards the goals/ important stuff, I describe it as "we are walking, using two legs - one is finding and questioning thoughts and the other is training/practising our body and pain system / increasing the strength of the system (desensitization)."

The functional analysis is particularly important since our intervention program involves the parents. It seems vital to success, especially with the younger children, that the operant mechanisms are understood. However, I think that the most important reinforcer is reduction of pain/ fear/ "threat." This goes along with the shift in perspective, focusing on the avoidance of important values, activities and situations.

We started up with a group of patients this spring, and some of them are now through a successful rehabilitation with a dramatic increase in functioning (school, physical activities, social life), an optimistic attitude with regards to the future and also reductions in reported pain. So, the clinical impression and reports by the clients and parents are promising (although we have difficulties finding appropriate instruments), suggesting this approach might have potential when assisting these kids in accomplishing something great in life.

So, if anyone has worked through this ... rather long ... note - my hypothesis is that an application of ACT is powerful in working with clients suffering from severe and disabling somatic symptoms and that exposure, defusion (as well as values and empowerment) will bring these clients further down the road towards a truly meaningful life.

PHYSICAL ILLNESS Pain, chronic - literature [5-31-05] Kevin Vowles	ACT Listserv Member wrote: I would like anyone's feedback on using ACT for chronic pain. There is a growing literature regarding chronic pain and ACT. Here are a few references. There are two books out this year on the topic as well, which I listed at the bottom of the list. McCracken, L. M. (1998). Learning to live with the pain: Acceptance of pain predicts adjustment in persons with chronic pain. *Pain, 74*, 21-27. McCracken, L. M., Carson, J. W., Eccleston, C., & Keefe, F. J. (2004). Acceptance and change in the context of chronic pain. *Pain, 109*, 4-7. McCracken, L. M., Vowles, K. E., & Eccleston, C. (2004). Acceptance of chronic pain: Component analysis and a revised assessment method. *Pain, 107*, 159-166. McCracken, L. M., Vowles, K. E., & Eccleston, C. (in press). Acceptance-based treatment for persons with complex chronic pain: A preliminary analysis of treatment outcome in comparison to a waiting phase. *Behaviour Research and Therapy*. Dahl, J., Wilson, K. G., Luciano, C., & Hayes, S. C. (2005). *Acceptance and commitment therapy for chronic pain*. Reno, Context Press. McCracken, L. M. (2005). *Contextual cognitive-behavioral therapy for chronic pain*. Seattle, IASP Press.
PHYSICAL ILLNESS Pain, chronic - seeking comfort **COPING STRATEGIES** Comforting activities - forestalling avoidance agenda [6-22-05] Steve Hayes	Kevin Vowles wrote: I generally spend some time with [chronic pain] patients talking about methods of achieving "momentary comfort" - this can be a variety of things from watching a TV show, taking a bath, reading, shopping, prayer/ meditation/ relaxation, etc. Finding some time to enjoy oneself is, in my opinion at least, pretty important, especially with chronic diseases/conditions. The problem arises when I consider how easily all of these "momentary comfort" things can become problematic avoidance behaviors and I have struggled to address this with patients. All too often, it essentially comes down to "do these things a little, but watch out because if you do it too much, it can cause problems." Needless to say, that's a pretty lame intervention . . . I have also discussed some mindfulness concepts - e.g., remain aware of the effects of your actions with regard to values/goals, etc., but this too seems to fall a bit short. It seems that there is a fine line between seeking comfort in an adaptive manner and seeking comfort for the purpose of avoiding negative feelings/sensations. I suppose a parallel is the use of alcohol - a little might be adaptive/comforting, but too much can be maladaptive; I'm just not sure where the line should be. I've noticed that many times. Have you tried it without the comfort component? I'd do that for a while and bring comfort in later ... then rearrange the rationale and structure. There is another way than: "do these things a little, but watch out because if you do it too much, it can cause problems." You do all of these behavioral things more as additions than subtractions; more as exercises in mindfulness than in methods of producing emotions - e.g., the orientation would be something like this: If you have done your work in acceptance and letting go from attachment and valued action (but only then) it is safe to engage in some of these other behaviors that life affords ... but be careful to do them

	with an openness to all thoughts and feelings that might come up; do them to broaden the range of things you can do, not as yet another secret method of experiential control; and stay mindful throughout. When you take a bath really notice what it feels like to take a bath: what the water feels like; what the soap smells like; and so on.
	These are "Get With Your Comfort" exercises. They are NOT "Get Comfortable" exercises.
	"Getting with Your Comfort" literally means what the etymology of the word says: get with ("com") your strength ("fort" from the Latin "fortis" or strength). In order to get with our strength we need to let go of control of the content of what our history gives us and instead focus on being present, aware, and linked to our values and purposes with our actual behavior. You tell me, which is a stronger place to stand: that place or "I only want to feel X" or (worse) "I must not feel Y"? Looking at these different ways of being, when do you feel bigger; more alive; more connected; more solid? [clients nearly always see that "I only want to feel X" or (worse) "I must not feel Y"? is a weak, deadening place to stand] OK. So we will do these behaviors not as a means of self-manipulation but as a means of being present and expanding the range of things we are working on from pain and pain coping to living itself. If they become methods of "getting comfortable" it means now we are turning them into means of self-manipulation; as means of avoiding, controlling, and regulating ... as if our history is our own enemy. As if pain is an enemy. That is where you were when we started. Haven't you suffered enough? So, be cautious as you try these things.
	Then I would include mindfulness assignments and let them start small and make sure the goal is to be present, open etc. We see this same thing with virtually every ACT protocol ... you can add all of these skills methods etc., but you have to be careful of starting yet another round of psychological infighting.

PHYSICAL ILLNESS
 	
Pain, chronic - seeking comfort [cont'd]
 	
BOOK
    ACT and treatment of chronic pain [6-22-05]
 	
    Joanne Dahl
	I don't know if you have used our book about ACT and chronic pain but there are step-by-step protocols there with examples of how you could apply each component of ACT to persons with chronic pain. I find that it is using the values by means of developing the "life compass" and exercises like the funeral exercise that help to "clear the path" to getting active in valued activities. The second major principle is acceptance of pain as it is. This is a tricky part and requires much more than talking about it. We have developed exercises using role play of the metaphors so that the client can experience the difference between resistance and acceptance of pain. Also showing that nursing pain leads to more pain. Differing between clean and dirty pain. I have never included "finding comfort"; rather we have "looked for Mister Discomfort."

	By discriminating the value in all activities and the vitality, the discomfort of pain that has been avoided gets exposed. In my experience, it is often the fear of pain rather than the pain itself that is the barrier. Therefore, I have not seen the need for any "comfort." On the other hand self-care issues, like eating properly and exercising and taking time to reflect are often neglected areas which need to be attended to.
	In the more traditional CBT programs for pain there was a focus on "comforting = avoiding" pain in the form of some cognitive mental training and coping strategies. I can see the value of teaching some of these "coping" techniques to use towards the end of treatment for the client to use when sudden pain, in fact, occurs. The danger of teaching them at the start prior to acceptance is that they may be just added to the list of avoidance strategies. And here we are talking about avoidance not of pain but fear of pain.
	I think the use of ACT with chronic illness is a fascinating area. The area of behavior medicine was big in the 70's but somewhere lost its pace. I think we should pick it up again, do research and write about it!
PHYSICAL ILLNESS Pain, chronic - seeking comfort [cont'd] Jim Hegarty	I work a lot with chronic pain, and finding comfort is not something I even consider. We openly talk about, and notice the difference between, how when doing something interesting the pain can seem to disappear for a while, and how distraction does not work. We also get into heavy doses of mindfulness. Analyse the pain: where is it, how wide is it, how deep, what sensations are in it etc. One client, at a follow-up group, told us that the sharp throbbing, burning, gnawing sensation was still there, but the pain was gone. She had discovered that Pain was an evaluation. She also managed to increase her activity, and started to live a more satisfying life.
	Our approach is to try to use ACT principles towards helping people to "live life well." I am generally pretty confident that most clients are good at finding their own comfort.
	As an aside, one of our medical consultants got really worried about the idea that pain doesn't exist. The International Association for the Study of Pain says it does after all. I am pleased to say that he is now much happier with the meta-cognitive stance of mindfulness among our clients, and is also becoming distinctly ACT friendly.
PHYSICAL ILLNESS Pain, chronic - seeking comfort [cont'd] Carl Graham	I agree. The more one is comfortable IN pain rather than seeking comfort in the absence of pain, the more likely valued life goals can be approached. Once a patient is actively trying to be in the centre of their pain the more the evaluative changes you mention become apparent.

PHYSICAL ILLNESS **Tinnitus [2-28-05]** Jennifer Gregg	ACT Listserv Member wrote: Does anyone have any ACT-oriented approaches to tinnitus? I have done some work with tinnitus (in behavioral medicine at a VA) and have found an ACT approach to be very helpful. My experience has been that focusing on values has been especially useful, particularly at the beginning of treatment when many patients are still focused on eliminating the sound.
PSYCHOSIS **Delusions - anomalous experiences/ reasoning bias [6-18-05]** Audrey Lowrie	... I spent about seven years of my life working consistently with this group of people [those with psychotic delusions] in an acute psychiatric hospital some years ago. My argument was always "you can't look at 'Schizophrenia,' you have to look at and understand the possible etiology of the 'symptoms' or experiences of the individuals." I completed many neurological assessments, as well as spending a lot of time just talking/listening with the people. There is a lot of hard evidence that in laboratory settings (not my working environment) people with delusions in Schizophrenia have 'loose relational frames,' that is, they do not hold the 'A=B=C therefore A=C' frame for as long as people without schizophrenia do *after the reinforcement for A=C changes*. I argued in a number of papers at the time that the people with delusions that I worked with were trying to explain to themselves 'anomalous experiences' of their minds (for instance, intermittent misfirings would make 'a look' from somebody else seem unusually prolonged or intense, or thoughts were often being analysed via the networks dedicated to 'hearing from outside,' and were experienced as exactly the same as sounds that were being correctly analysed via that channel, etc.). And they were using (what I might now term) '*loose frames of reference*' to do so. Quite consistently, the 'frames' that they chose to use could be understood as 'frames' that were easily accessed by the individual. They were 'frames' that had been used in a 'spiritual' book that was being broadly and highly publicised in the city that we lived in (a book that itself had very loose frames of reference, and was easily applicable to 'strange' phenomena), or they were 'frames' that were well known, such as the Mafia, or 'frames' that appeared on a specifically impactful TV commercial at the time. Once the 'frame' had been established it was difficult to shift. I believed that: (a) the individual experienced no need to shift the established 'frame' because it was so loose that it didn't come into 'conflict' with any other 'frame' - that is, the 'boundaries' at which this frame could be 'found wanting' were not accessible; and (b) the individual rapidly processed information within a specific area of the left hemisphere which, research has found, promotes in all of us a 'sense' of the correctness of an idea when it is processing that idea. I consistently found that people that I worked with (with Schizophrenia and delusions) had great difficulty in interpreting metaphors while in an acute phase of the illness. In fact they could not do this. Their level of analysis during that time was very loose but also very concrete regardless of their previously achieved educational level.
PSYCHOSIS Delusions - anomalous experiences/ reasoning bias [cont'd] Gerhard Kugler	Audrey, many years ago I worked with "schizophrenics" and can confirm your observations. At that time there was a test that showed the weak relational frames (by Bannister & Fransella?). The weakness was observable in times also, which were relatively free of productive symptoms. My work with severe personality disorders today lets me ask whether there is a distinct solidness of connections which is necessary for a well-functioning personality.
PSYCHOSIS Delusions - anomalous experiences/ reasoning bias [cont'd] Audrey Lowrie	... My position was that psychologists working with this group of people need to have a good acquaintance with the literature on the anomalous perceptual experiences of people with head injury, stroke, epilepsy, and partial-epileptic like signs and symptoms, as delusions are so often attempts by the person to explain, or 'frame linguistically' the same forms of anomalous perceptions as those experienced by patients with ABI, particularly those with right hemisphere damage. The model that I presented in two conferences way back in 1998 was: 1) First, be aware of the anomalous perception that the individual is trying to explain to him or herself (I would now probably say 'linguistically frame'). 2) Be aware of the form/extent of a language-based impairment that is resulting in the person not being able to come up with a more 'culturally viable' 'frame for the experience.' (I suggested that this was a right-hemisphere language-processing impairment). 3) Be aware of what stressors in daily life resulted in these cognitive impairments rising above the sub-clinical threshold such that they are now apparent and disruptive in their daily functioning. 4) Be aware of what the person is trying to achieve in their life right now, and how they might do that despite the sub-clinical and episodically acute cognitive impairments. (I would now say identify their values, and help the person to move towards these by helping in the acceptance and management of the sub-clinical cognitive difficulties and episodic acute episodes.) I specifically differentiated between personality disorders and schizophrenia. The last paper that I wrote on this model was for the 5th Annual International Schizophrenia Conference held in Hobart, Tasmania in 1998, and was called Assessment and Intervention Between the Processes of

	Perception and Belief: Working with Delusions in the Schizophrenia Spectrum Disorders. Quite RFT-ish I think now.
PSYCHOSIS Delusions - anomalous experiences/ reasoning bias [cont'd] Eric Morris	Interesting post re recasting models of delusional belief within RFT. To introduce myself: I work within an early intervention for psychosis service in London, primarily engaging clients using a CBT for psychosis approach. As you no doubt are aware, there is now an extensive literature on the formation and maintenance of delusional beliefs, at least from a cognitive perspective. In the UK there has been a lot of fruitful research in this vein which has influenced the development of CBT approaches to psychosis. There are now cognitive models about positive symptoms that consider an "emotional pathway" route in addition to the anomalous experience one, such that some people may not need to have cognitive dysfunction to experience positive symptoms (e.g., the model described by: Garety, P., Kuipers, E., Fowler, D., Freeman, D., & Bebbington, P. (2001). A cognitive model of the positive symptoms of psychosis. *Psychological Medicine, 31*, 189-195.). These models consider the effects of how appraisal is influenced by reasoning biases, the individual's history, adverse environments, as well as emotional processes and metacognitive beliefs. There is also a literature about how common certain anomalies of experience are within the general population. The interesting thing is (from my ACT perspective) that whenever clinicians talk about anomalous experiences, it is hard to describe them without using an appraisal - it is anomalous *experience* which is then *made sense of*. In supervision noticing the role of language (with even trying to describe a person's experience) helps clinicians to get in contact with how we live within constructed meaning, and that watching the process of construction is interesting and useful. Also IMHO, I think that the CBT approach to delusions de-emphasises cognitive dysfunction as an "alternative explanation" of psychosis to the client and their family. Part of this is because the function is to not provide a stigmatising view of psychosis (many clients find the "schizophrenia is a brain disease" stance invalidating and not that helpful in dealing with their lives). In contrast it involves a normalisation agenda about anomalies of experience and validates the process of how people come up with the conclusions they have, while also focusing on how the delusional beliefs affect decision-making now, actions, goals, values, and the dilemmas that come with that. Perhaps this can be thought of as an approach that while using a lot of Crel moves, tries to come up with alternative meanings that are at least more functional for the client (explanations that work, rather than what is the "right" way to see things).
PSYCHOSIS Delusions - anomalous experiences/ reasoning bias [cont'd] Audrey Lowrie	... In my papers I commented extensively on the research done in England, Melger and Freeman, Frith, Garety, Coulthart, etc. I accepted a reasoning bias as central, but believed that understanding the anomalous experiences *that were being reasoned about* was also vitally important (I thought Hoffman and McGlashan, John Cutting, McGrath, etc.'s work in USA an important adjunct to the reasoning bias stuff). I wrote about why I thought a reasoning bias alone was insufficient to cause the outlandish ideas that are 'delusions,' just as anomalous experiences without a reasoning bias were also insufficient. I found that families found it harder to understand a 'reasoning bias' explanation if they didn't also understand the repetitive anomalous experience that the patient was trying to understand/ frame/ reason about. And that without this extra understanding they still continued to try (often angrily) to convince the patient of their 'faulty' reasoning. I also found that the patients experienced considerable relief if I could say to them ... "yes, I think I know what you are talking about, I was speaking to somebody else recently who also perceived the clock changing shape in line with the different sounds coming from it" or "'hearing' many different unfamiliar people repeating the same phrase as she walked past" or "what seemed like the same person walking one way wearing women's clothes, and then the other way wearing men's clothes" (this person had a facial recognition deficit which was also in evidence in her reaction to hospital staff). These anomalous experiences were sensory perceptions that needed explaining ... not appraisals, the explanation (delusion) was the appraisal of the sensory experience....
PSYCHOSIS Delusions - anomalous experiences/ reasoning bias [cont'd] Steve Mahorney	... I would comment that [Audrey's] perspective seems a little focused on the brain injury thing as an analogy when I'm used to thinking from the perspective provided by a comprehensive evaluation and probably further observation and evaluation to determine what elements in the presentation might reflect thought process disorder and which might be serving interpersonal purposes that might be subject to a functional analysis (of sorts). There might be a large differential in a case like this. Anyway, it's hard for me, in a case like this to jump to ideas like how to advise the family until I'm clearer on the diagnostic picture as well as the functional behavioral components.

PSYCHOSIS **Group intervention** **GROUP** **Psychotic/ schizophrenic clients [10-3-03]** Rainer Sonntag	Brandon Gaudiano wrote: I would be interested in hearing from others who have tried ACT in a group format with [a Schizophrenic] population. I think that would be the most "user-friendly" format for inpatients. I am a front line psychiatrist in a private, general psychiatric practice since 1989. Already before I began to reorganize my work around an ACT perspective, I had been running a weekly open group for severely mentally ill, i.e., mainly schizophrenic patients, that is attended by about 5-12 patients once a week for 1 hour. Since 1998 I have begun gradually to infuse more and more ACT moves into the sessions. The structure is very simple. The sessions begin with each patient telling what is important for him to tell or what happened since last week. Sometimes a theme a patient brings up, is taken for a "deeper treatment" after every participant has spoken. Most often the sessions end with talking about something taken from the daily local newspaper to connect patients to what happens in our community and in the world (this is the only point where I take responsibility for the content of sessions). Every theme is welcome. And what is really wonderful about ACT is that every theme opens up opportunities for talk that can make a difference. For example, symptoms or feelings about a political event may be used to target emotional avoidance maneuvers, how they worked and their further effects. BTW, this was where I started to introduce ACT into my work. Furthermore, we talk about values, which has brought more than one patient to go to a sheltered workplace instead of just hanging around at home. The most difficult for me was to flexibly introduce cognitive defusion. However, as it seems to me, this makes the other components much more powerful. It has brought a lot of humor and laughing into the sessions because of the often unexpected ways of responding to what patients say. Medication is also treated in an ACT-consistent way, leaving it up to patients to make their experiences and share them with each other. I only tell them what the literature says. With regard to results, I can only tell that attendance is very stable and patients generally say they like to come. Those who attend regularly have had no major psychotic exacerbation for years. One patient who after several years developed another episode of persecutory delusions talked about this freely in the group, used only a few additional single sessions for more intense work, and had only a 3 week period of hospitalization. He once said what he liked most in the group was that he can tell everything without that being medically judged or interpreted with respect to the illness. However, having a history of psychiatric training it was and is not always easy for me to stay non-judgemental in this respect. Generally, it is my experience that talk about symptoms gradually fades away, being more and more replaced by talking about life circumstances, stressful events and "normal" feelings. Medication compliance is very high in the group; over time most patients reduced their drug dosages to comparably low levels. I like this group format. Much of the work is done by the patients themselves and for each other. Unfortunately, it is often difficult to get patients into groups. Furthermore, I think it is useful to run a group over years with a relatively stable membership. Finally, I must shamefully admit that it was only from the ACT perspective that I really learned that persons with schizophrenia are really normal people and can be dealt with as such without any paternalistic attitude. Maybe they suffer some biologically-based disturbance of derived relational responding; however, in my view that will not explain the devastating course of the illness in so many of them....
SELF-ESTEEM, LOW **Reinforcing factors [9-30-04]** Steve Hayes	ACT Listserv Member wrote: I've read in a chapter on FAP (functional analytic psychotherapy), I think it was a chapter in the book *Clinical Behavior Analysis* ed. by Dougher, that self statements like "I'm useless" and so forth perhaps might be reinforced by the avoidance of hearing it from someone else (which is of course much worse). And my guess is that having learnt that self blame prevents others from blaming You (and sometimes even providing you with comfort and opposite statements) are enough to keep you going at it for a life time. I think the most immediately available and pervasive reinforcer for things verbal is "being right." Relational coherence predicts the utility of verbal networks. It also predicts arbitrary social consequences that specifically target it. You can detect the coherence of a relational network immediately as you derive it. Those are the perfect conditions for conditioned reinforcement: events that very reliably predict other highly desirable events. Once you have being right as a conditioned reinforcer, it can be quite reinforcing to dive into how awful things are; how screwed up you are; how your screwed-up-ness is caused by Mom, or Dad, or your biology, or trauma, or a mental disease, etc. You get to be right.

	Plus it has secondary effects: it coerces comfort, help, reassurance, etc. Try this: when talking to a friend tell them in a serious tone "I think I'm probably the biggest, stupidest, most useless idiot on the planet. I can't think of anything I do right." Then pause. Watch what happens.
SELF-ESTEEM, LOW Reinforcing factors [cont'd] Kelly Wilson	As far as reinforcers go, it is always good to keep in mind the notion of relativity of reinforcement. Consider worry as a solid example. Worry sucks, the only thing worse is what shows up psychologically when you stop worrying. Thinking that you are a piece of crap sucks, but what would show up if you stopped? Well ... just maybe ... response-ability. And, that is some very scary business.
SELF-ESTEEM, LOW Reinforcing factors [cont'd] Sven Rydberg	A more simple[-minded] answer to the question "How is low self-esteem (believing) reinforced?": For the moment at least, *you need not make an effort*. Great reinforcement, at times, for at least some of us.
SELF-ESTEEM, LOW Reinforcing factors [cont'd] ACT Listserv Member	First, in my opinion, self-concept is not an operant response. Therefore, I am not sure if the thoughts I am having about myself obey to the principles of operant conditioning (e.g., a thought will extinguish if the consequences are punishing, or a thought will remain if it leads to positive consequence). Thoughts are not voluntary (we don't choose to have them). Skinner will even argue in his book "Beyond freedom and dignity" that nothing is really voluntary. But I do think that we can't escape our thoughts about who we are, and we can't voluntary change them. On the other hand, we can escape from external aversive conditions.
	Nevertheless, as previously said there can be some secondary gains for having low self-esteem/self concept. When you are fuse with the thought "I am useless," you assign yourself a role. This can exempt you from taking responsibility, and protect you from failing. You might say "I am useless, so I better not try" and if you don't try you will never fail. Another secondary gain is to receive attention and reassurance from others. If you verbally state that you are useless, it invites other to comfort you.
	From systemic view, low self-concept can be very functional for the system (e.g., couple, family). In a complementary relationship, if one of the partners is up, the second one must be down (otherwise the relationship won't hold). So in this case, if one partner has high self-concept, it is very functional for the second partner to adopt a low self-concept.
	In families, a child with low self-concept can reinforce his/her father/mother. If the child has low self-concept it can empower the parents. Each will have a different role. The parents will be "care-givers" and the child will be dependent on them. The parents will also be assigned the role of the "comforter." Sometimes, saying to someone "You are useless" can function as a way to establish more power and control in the relationship. If I tell you "you are useless," and you fuse with the thoughts, then I establish power and control over you.
	Why do we fuse with these thoughts even after our parents are out of the picture? Well, I don't believe that our parents can be ever out of the picture. But these figures were apparently very important in forming our identity, and identity can't be easily changed.
SELF-ESTEEM, LOW Reinforcing factors [cont'd] Steve Hayes	From an RFT point of view all self-talk is operant, but it is in a second contingency stream and once the relational repertoire is established, many other consequences (functional control over the environment; sense-making) overwhelm the role of the arbitrary social consequences that largely established the repertoire in the first place. It is virtually impossible to extinguish for that reason: you can't remove the consequences. One might imagine that long periods of absolute, unpredictable, intense chaos in which nothing can or does make sense might do it, but (fortunately) that experiment will never be done and the natural experiments (twin towers; war) are not really very close to what you might imagine would do it.
	But you might get the excesses of the repertoire (esp. the Cfunc excesses) under relative contextual control in a gentler way. It is a step toward extinction but focused more narrowly and more relatively. More like differential reinforcement, by trying to reduce the immediate utility of sense making, problem solving, prediction, reason giving, etc. etc. That is what acceptance, defusion, mindfulness, meditation is about.
SELF-HARM **ACT/DBT group for self-harming BPD clients**	ACT Listserv Member wrote: I am looking for any work done with using ACT with "cutters"? You might want to look at Kim Gratz's protocol. She ran an ACT / DBT combo group with self-harming BPD clients and got great results. The protocol seemed pretty well done. It is under review. ...at the level of technology my sense was that it had a pretty big ACT chunk (perhaps 60-70% of the protocol appears to be ACT derived) and at the level of theory/model it fitted the overall ACT approach really well. I like how she brought together traditional behavioral methods; a little bit of Greensburg's stuff (which I've always liked ... Les has a quote on the back of the ACT book for a reason); a good chunk of DBT, and ACT methods,

PERSONALITY DISORDER **ACT/DBT group for self-harming BPD clients** **GROUP** **ACT/DBT - for self-harming BPD clients [4-28-05]** Steve Hayes	though she gives some of these things her own labels. Part of what is most exciting about it is that this was extremely efficient ... a small amount of input in group form for a big output -- not what we've come to expect with this population. The shocking phrase in the abstract is this one: "and reached normative levels of functioning on most." Pretty cool. Here is the abstract: Preliminary Data on an Acceptance-Based Emotion Regulation Group Intervention for Deliberate Self-Harm among Women with Borderline Personality Disorder Kim L. Gratz and John G. Gunderson, McLean Hospital and Harvard Medical School Abstract: Borderline personality disorder (BPD) and deliberate self-harm are clinically-important conditions for which additional economically and clinically feasible interventions are needed. Literature on both the emotion regulating and experientially avoidant function of self-harm and the role of emotional dysfunction in BPD provided the rationale for developing a group intervention targeting emotion dysregulation among self-harming women with BPD. This study provides preliminary data on the efficacy of this new, 14-week, emotion regulation group intervention, designed to teach self-harming women with BPD more adaptive ways of responding to their emotions so as to reduce the frequency of their self-harm behavior. Participants were matched on level of emotion dysregulation and lifetime frequency of self-harm and randomly assigned to receive this group in addition to their current outpatient therapy (N=12), or to continue with their current outpatient therapy alone for 14 weeks (N=10). Results indicate that the group intervention had positive effects on self-harm, emotion dysregulation, experiential avoidance, and BPD-specific symptoms, as well as symptoms of depression, anxiety, and stress. Participants in the group treatment condition evidenced significant changes over time on all measures, and reached normative levels of functioning on most. While these preliminary results are promising, the study's limitations require their replication in a larger-scale randomized controlled trial.
SELF-HARM ACT/DBT group for self-harming BPD clients [cont'd] **PERSONALITY DISORDER** ACT/DBT group for self-harming BPD clients [cont'd] **GROUP** ACT/DBT - for self-harming BPD clients [cont'd] Kim Gratz	The manuscript on that group is now in press at Behavior Therapy.... As Steve mentioned, the group (developed to target self-harm among women with BPD) combined aspects from a few different treatments, drawing most heavily from ACT and DBT. It was based on the assumption that teaching folks with self-harm different ways of responding to their emotions (i.e., increasing emotional acceptance and willingness, decreasing experiential avoidance) would decrease urges to self-harm. Results were actually fairly promising. We saw significant reductions in self-harm (as well as emotion dysregulation and experiential avoidance), and my sense, clinically, is that the active ingredients of the treatment responsible for this reduction in self-harm were the modules on willingness and valued actions -- these really seemed to resonate with the clients. Of course, we also taught basic behavioral strategies for impulse control, etc., and I am sure these helped as well ... the interesting thing, though, was that none of the behavioral change strategies were introduced until quite far into the group, as the emphasis initially was on emotional acceptance, awareness, and clarity. Given its premise, my sense is that this group should be most useful for self-harm that serves an emotionally avoidant function ... probably less useful for folks whose self-harm serves an interpersonal function (although self-harm rarely serves only one function, and may in fact be reinforced by both intra- and inter-personal consequences ... an empirical question...). The other interesting thing is that the benefits we observed seem to continue -- and improve -- after the group ends. A non-behavioral colleague had once expressed a concern that initial improvements may not continue following the end of the group if the changes clients had made in their response to/stance toward their emotions had not been internalized ... initial follow-up data, however, suggest that not only do the observed treatment effects remain 4 months after the group, they continue to improve, with further decreases in self-harm and AAQ scores, etc. (although keep in mind that these data are incredibly preliminary and based on a very small N at this point ... suggestive nonetheless, though...).
SELF-HARM **Adolescent - use of ACT** **CHILD & ADOLESCENT** **Self-harm - use of ACT [10-3-03]** ACT Listserv Member	Brenna Tindall wrote: Does anyone know anyone who has done ACT with adolescents who are involved with self-harm, specifically cutting? I worked with a 14 yr old boy who had literally thousands of scars from cutting on his arms, legs, stomach, everywhere. I was only one member of a treatment team, so I cannot say for certain the ACT components were helpful or reduced his SIB, but I did use a lot of the exposure and defusion components of ACT and he seemed to improve. A really helpful way to get him to open up was looking at his art work, asking him to read his poetry, and using photographs from his childhood to stimulate discussion about his feelings and to meet him where he was when he created those works. My belief is that being present with him while he was expressing his pain allowed him to experience them as emotions and to see that it was okay to have them. One of the most powerful sessions we had, was looking at his photo from admission to the program and having him look at himself in the mirror near discharge and notice the differences, both physical and

	behavioral changes; and then my reinforcing/validating his observations. The photographs can be used as a tool to assist in the observer exercises when they have trouble doing it, asking about memories from the photo, noticing there is a part of them that was there then and is here now ... etc.
SELF-HARM **Suicidality - contracts; ACT approach [3-10-05]** ACT Listserv Member	Casey Capps wrote: Does anyone know of any data on the effectiveness or ineffectiveness of suicide safety plans? I think a difficulty here is that too much focus often is put on the "written contract," while much of the content often fits well within the therapy anyway. I have found myself, when discovering that a client is suicidal, drop out of my usual therapeutic framework in order to complete the suicide contract. I realize, however, that in most cases I do not need to leave behind my general approach and that the contracting can fit within it. From an ACT perspective I see the behavioral contracting as one of those cases where rule-governed behavior is actually good and hopefully the client will develop the rule that when feeling suicidal then call X and do Y. It also fits within a framework of valuing and goals. To me the contract becomes about the client retaining a modicum of distance despite a generally high level of fusion (which I believe suicide almost invariably is) - enough distance to realize that these thoughts and feelings are pushing for a course of action that is not consistent with what the client cares about. Indeed, a couple suicidal clients I have talked with have appeared to respond very well to some brief valuing.
SELF-HARM Suicidality - contracts; ACT approach [cont'd] Steve Hayes	Minu Aghevli wrote: I am interested in the strategic use of suicide in therapy. In a non-suicidal person, it may sound defensible (though you would certainly chip away at it) to say "well, I want to try out X, but I am afraid to because of getting hurt, having this consequence, etc., and I would have to live with it, possibly forever." However, in someone that plans to kill themselves, this logic really breaks down. Is there any way, therefore, where suicide can be almost freeing, in that for chronically suicidal people the constant spectre of it removes the threat of consequences most of us use to limit our ability to try the things we want - kind of like a credit card you are not going to have to stick around to pay off? Of course, the only way you get to enter into this is by accepting that the person will likely kill themselves. The gamble would be that if you do, and they start engaging in the things they have wanted to try, they may not feel suicidal anymore. I know Erickson did some of this, but I would be interested to get people's views on how this would fit into an ACT perspective. You will find a lot of ACT in Kirk Strosahl and John Chiles recent book on suicide (published by American Psychiatric Association press). Kirk is great at using suicidal thoughts somewhat in the way you are suggesting. The book is worth having if you want to explore this area.... What I worry about with suicidal contracts is that, done wrong, they convey the idea that suicidal thoughts and impulses are somehow wrong and indicate that the person is disturbed. That's just not so. What people are facing are issues of meaninglessness and the pull of the ultimate avoidance move. The former has to be walked through to get to values as a choice; the latter needs to be faced to see why avoidance can't work as a source of living. I don't think you have to accept that people are likely to kill themselves to use suicidality for good in therapy ... it is a matter of seeing that if the "final solution" is on the table you've played out the logic of this string and you might as well play for life with all your heart. It is probably obvious but it is worth noting that this thread connects with an earlier one last week. In one sense the "final solution" is not only on the table but is certain to reach us all, willing or not. That recent story posted on the list about the man dying had the same message in it. The bottom line message is the same: Might as well play for life with all your heart. Seen in that way, suicidal thoughts could be a gift not a source of oppression. Depends on what you do with them and learn from them. This is not the whole of the issue with suicidal thoughts but it is one strand of the issue and it shows why merely "managing" suicide per se is a mistake, just as merely "managing" symptoms is a mistake. Acceptance of finitude is at the core of human vitality. That's one reason why funeral exercises (etc.) find their way into ACT protocols. Avoidance of finitude means attachment to it which means the present moment is never fully present and there you are ... back to human suffering. Suicidal thoughts contain a lesson, if we are willing to learn it.
SELF-HARM Suicidality - contracts; ACT approach [cont'd]	ACT Listserv Member wrote: Steve, can you expand upon your comment that "merely 'managing' symptoms is a mistake," as it applies more broadly? Supporting self-management of symptoms is a major focus in clinical health psychology at present and I find it sits well with ACT approaches, i.e., 'manage' or allow as opposed to trying to control internal experiences. Just concerned I was missing something subtle. What I meant is that behaviors have functions, and you need to understand these and address these.

BEHAVIOR ANALYSIS **Function cf. topography of behavior [3-22-05]** Steve Hayes	Suppose a child is not doing very well in school and is constantly disrupting the classroom. You put in a strong contingency and disruptions go down. But merely managing disruptions is not enough. What was the function of the disruptions? Suppose it was to avoid difficult academic tasks, or it was elicited by the aversive properties of failing to do well in academic tasks. Shutting down the disruption will not be likely to have much effect on these things: being *still* does not make you *studious.* But if you improve the academic performance you might get reduced disruption for "free." (In fact, most of this has been worked out empirically long ago - my example is not an arbitrary one). To get at function you need a good theory (to know where to look); good assessment technology (to see what is going on); and good intervention technology (to know how to change any of it). If you have all of this, there is nothing wrong with managing symptoms because they are then functional entities. When you are flying blind the "structural error" is much more likely: you can mistake topography for function in an undesirable way. Physical health problems are more the former, but look at the sad examples of things like anxiety and you see the danger. Eating benzos is maybe "managing anxiety" but it is not very effective in coming to terms with anxiety in a broader sense. Or take prejudice. Learning not to say prejudicial thoughts out loud has turned us into a nation of liars, suppressors, and avoiders -- because we thought (mistakenly) that it was the thought that was harmful and we thought (mistakenly) that not saying them aloud removed their harmful functions. Meanwhile, steps to alter the functions of these thoughts are not yet on the radar screen (the ACT community will change that!).
SELF-HARM Suicidality - contracts; ACT approach [cont'd] Kirk Strosahl	First thing to realize is that in the entire area of mental health, there is no area where there is LESS evidence based practice than in the assessment and treatment of suicidal patients. So many of the things we are taught as "fact" actually have no factual basis and, often, are contradicted by the clinical evidence. So, that being said, no-suicide contracting, which is a generally accepted standard of practice, has some problems. Re: the use of no-suicide contracting, in two different standard of care books on treating the suicidal patient (one in 1995 and one this year), we have recommended against the use of this strategy. There is no data to indicate that it has an ameliorative impact on suicidal behavior and, in fact, functions as an anxiety management tool for the clinician, but is of little value to the patient. In fact, the best way to look at this is an example we use in the basic ACT workshops: "Don't think of X" or "Don't do behavior Y," always places a problematic and paradoxical frame around the instruction. If you are going to do any type of behavioral intervention, try to create a positive behavior action plan with the patient. This is getting the patient to commit to engaging in behaviors that are the antithesis of suicidal behavior. In other words, if the patient is engaging in social behavior with a friend, it is highly unlikely that he/she will be thinking about and/or planning suicidal behaviors at the same time. Plus, I find this much more consistent with the ACT perspective on committed action. I like committed actions to have a positive, proactive valence that are consistent with core values. What is the action, "not committing suicide" in the service of? So, you can see how some believe that no suicide contracts may actually have a counter-instructional property that may actually increase suicidal risk. As for dealing with suicidal thoughts and urges, we of course know that suicidal behaviors are a form of emotional avoidance. They represent an attempt to regulate, eliminate or control undesirable private experiences. In that sense, they function as a self-reinforcing behavior because once you conclude that you can always kill yourself if things don't get better, some of the affective pressure dissipates. This reinforces thinking about suicide (or engaging in self-destructive behaviors) as a form of emotional control. Just as with other forms of emotional control, there is a paradoxical effect. The more you use suicidal thinking for one purpose, the more suicidal you get. But the main point a patient has to hear is that suicide is a LEGITIMATE solution, and it may not be the only solution available. And it does function to solve problems. As Kierkegaard once stated, "Thoughts of suicide have gotten me through many a dark night." From the ACT point of view, what makes a suicidal "crisis" is the attempt to suppress suicidal thoughts and urges in the name of social pliance. So, I often talk with patients about their willingness to simply have suicidal thoughts, just like they would have other thoughts. They have no more level of reality than any other private experience. It is the attempt to evaluate, categorize, suppress or eliminate them that make the associated urges seem unmanageable. At the same time, you can talk with the patient about that fact that thinking about suicide as a solution indicates that there may be things in life that are not working to promote the client's sense of vitality, purpose and meaning. If we were to simply let those thoughts be there without attachment or struggle, AND, at the same time, engage in valued actions that would serve to solve life problems that are detracting from a positive life direction, we might have an opportunity to create positive momentum. So, what you folks are touching on is actually close to the zone I work in. Suicidal ideation, suicidal urges, even making a suicide attempt present an opportunity to accept what is there to be accepted and to engage

in what I call "value based problem solving." Suicidal behavior as a class of responses generally has a problem solving function associated with it. It usually involves an attempt to regulate arousal associated with fusion to emotions, thoughts, memories, etc. It may also function as a form of social problem solving because it does elicit a very strong reaction from the social surround (just think about how freaked out therapists get at the mere mention of suicidal thoughts!).

BTW, if anyone on the listserv wants to read more about an evidence-based, ACT consistent approach to assessment and treatment of suicidal patients, here is the reference: Chiles, J., & Strosahl, K. (2005). *Clinical manual for assessment and treatment of suicidal patients.* Washington, DC: American Psychiatric Publishing Inc.

SEXUALITY **Gender identity -** **acceptance vs. change** **[10-10-02]** John Blackledge	Barbara Kohlenberg wrote: I am struggling with trying to conceptualize Gender Identity Disorder. From an ACT perspective, do you all see it as a "content" issue, much like anxiety or depression, that we would relegate to something that very likely will never be solved but will be a continued source of feelings for the person and then help that person proceed in other valued directions, or is solving the GID the value itself? We would push a client to consider if they really wanted on their tombstone "I got rid of anxiety"; is a similar push reasonable if the person (who has a penis) enters therapy wanting to be able to write on their tombstone "I died a woman"? GID does strike me solely as fusion with content, though with some rather atypical content. I would hazard a guess that clients diagnosable with GID have their gender identity tied to a rigidly-held rule about what state of affairs is necessary for them to live a good or vital life, to move forward --in the same way that clients hold the absence of anxiety, for example, as a necessary precursor for a good or vital life. I would guess that the topography of this particular fusion (i.e., with the thought that one must be a different gender for life to go relatively well) would be particularly distracting and disorienting for client and therapist alike (I know it would spin me). But I'm still left with the thought that it looks and quacks like a duck, even if the duck has some particularly unusual and colorful feathers. I suspect that, if such a client did endorse an epitaph like "I died a woman", some gentle probing around what the client feels he would be able to do as a woman that he couldn't do as a man, would be in order--followed by some defusion and acceptance work to see if the client actually could do those things as a man. I wonder how many clients diagnosable with GID actually would endorse an epitaph like "I died a woman" after going through an experiential exercise like the 'witnessing your own funeral' one. It seems that clients generally endorse more vital, 'bottom line' values during such exercises, rather than "values" that center around supposed preconditions (like the absence of anxiety or being a different gender) to a richer and more vital life. If they did endorse it, and stuck to it rigidly, I would still likely conceptualize it as cognitive fusion. But the operational issue would then become, is this fusion that can be lived with and that won't drastically interfere with the pursuit of potentially more envitalizing values?
SEXUALITY Gender identity - acceptance vs. change [cont'd] John Blackledge	[Responding to a post pointing to the availability of surgical options in relation to gender identity, as an alternative to acceptance] Thanks for providing balance to a short e-mail that understandably appears to endorse acceptance over change. Let me clarify a bit where I was coming from. As with any issue conceptualized from an ACT perspective, I definitely agree that change/control strategies are called for when they are viable and can make a positive, value-consistent difference, and I can definitely see this happening for a person diagnosable with GID who follows through with a sex-change operation. However, I suspect it would be wise (when realistically possible) to do some defusion and acceptance work in advance of an operation to try to cut through any potential erroneous assumptions about what kinds of values-consistent behavior are not possible given one's current gender. The client (and therapist) might be surprised, and what is found might make the client better informed regarding how he wants to proceed. Either way, I imagine some acceptance and defusion work on both sides of an operation would be a bonus. And either way, if the final decision (whether it is to have an operation or not) turns out to be sub-optimal, the sun will continue to rise and acceptance and defusion strategies will still be available. Actually, I don't think GID is a "mere content issue"-- I think it's a content issue just like virtually everything we struggle with as verbally-capable human beings. A person diagnosable with GID would essentially assume, in my mind, that (1) a verbal label (in this case, gender) accurately captures a set of experiences/stimuli; and (2) that this verbal label necessitates certain experiences and courses of action and prohibits others. This 2-step process establishes verbal content that can then be fused with (as it most often is) or defused from. This 2-step process is also no different from what the rest of us do every minute of our lives when we apply verbal labels to our experience and these labels unnecessarily limit what we do next....

SEXUALITY Gender identity - acceptance vs. change [cont'd] Barbara Kohlenberg	All of these comments have been so interesting and helpful. But the issue continues to be unresolved. Maybe that is in part because we are looking for "rules" when there really are none--when the function of the request needs to be considered on an individual basis. For example, if a client complains of anxiety, and we recommend that they take a hot bath at night, call their best friend and have a good talk, and then take a walk in the morning, and they do so and then feel much better and the issue resolves, haven't we done a good job? I think we have. Let's hope we all have such skills and resources in our repertoires. It seems that we only would recommend acceptance strategies when change strategies don't work or do work but are too costly in terms of creating additional suffering. In other words, our behavior of identifying something as "content" is functionally related to experienced unworkability manifest by the increased misery and suffering of our client and maybe our own increased misery and suffering if we have been trying to help them do something that does not work. But the issues do get more complex when the content themes of identity emerge. Think about homosexuality, and the person coming to therapy wanting to work on figuring out, or on accepting who they "really are." Then, given what we know today, we would accept this readily as a valid journey (and a valued direction), and if on one's tombstone was "I lived being true to myself", well, that would seem just fine to me. I'd be proud to have helped a person be able to say that. Other identity themes--finding birth parents or birth children, going back to your "homeland," searching out part of your history, being around people of your own religion, ethnicity or sexual orientation, are other examples of times the function of the requested content would determine our response. But this would not always be very easy to be sure of. If the issue became more clear than not clear, then we would have several options: we could jump on board and help; orient toward a different, "larger" value first and then help; or encourage embracing a "larger" value and maybe not engaging in the search. So too with the GID person, when do we help them achieve what they say they want or think they want (given that we may be able to help them with that), and when do they (and we) conclude that what they want is not workable, thus opening up the value of acceptance and values work. I now think that we would be remiss (and pretty mean) to label anyone's search for identity as verbal chatter or fusion or say "thank your mind for that thought that you are a girl," or anything like that, as a working assumption. Though these issues certainly may recede in importance or may even turn into "content" to be accepted, not changed, as other material emerges in the therapy. I guess, as we do with any presenting problem, we must proceed to do a good old-fashioned functional analysis and let that guide our intervention strategy.
SEXUALITY Gender identity - acceptance vs. change [cont'd] **CHOICE** **Brink of [10-13-02]** Kelly Wilson	Just one comment on issues where a client struggles with a should I, shouldn't I ... a most recent one involved a should I, shouldn't I divorce. My posture on this was-- "I believe that you could divorce with integrity, or divorce without integrity, or stay with integrity, or stay without integrity. My commitment is to coach you in doing whatever you do with integrity." Integrity is not to be found in the properties of the response. It is in the functional relation between the response and deeply-held values--or conversely, a functional relation to deeply-held fears. I expect little benefit for someone who has lived without integrity in a marriage if they *leave* the marriage blaming their partner for a screwed-up life. That will function in ways similar to *staying* and blaming the partner for a screwed-up life (and will be equally non-vital). Now, that said, there is suffering inherent in every choice, including the choice not to choose. We may cut off something of extraordinary value in a choice. We may feel that we are making a values-driven choice and find later that we were completely blind and acting in a self-righteous and mean-spirited way (I sweat as I recollect such events in my own history). The possibility of one of these negative outcomes is psychologically inherent in the choice--it is why the choice is hard (and avoided). Now the issue of living with integrity falls back a step and we need to examine the integrity of not choosing in the service of fear-- is that what we want our life to stand for? We need to do exposure and defusion within this frightening region where delightful and tragic possibilities dance--that place on the brink of choice. It is a hard place to stay. Two inclinations predominate. One is to back up from choosing and dwell in the land of should I/shouldn't I, making little lists in our head of the reasons we should and reasons we shouldn't in vain hope that the scales will finally tip decisively and will tell us the truth about the choice we should make. A second option is to just choose--but in the service of ending the burden this frightening psychological space engenders. But, is that what we want our life to stand for? I explore both of these with clients. Roll in them. Take imaginal trips where we walk up to the edge of choice, feel the anxiety, the pressure, then back up into rumination, worry and adding up pluses and minuses. We examine the vitality of that act. Then, again, we walk in an experiential exercise to the edge of

choice. Again, feel the anxiety, notice the memories, how the body feels, this time, at the peak of anxiety, we choose a direction--but explicitly in the service of ending the anxiety. And then notice what happens. Relief, but also, the thought, what if I would have chosen the other way.

In both of these scenarios, the choice occurs psychologically as a "must" and as a "must do correctly"-- these are both psychological aspects of the choice that beg for defusion and exposure. They occur psychologically as a lack of freedom.

There is a third path. Camus describes it best in The Absurd Reasoning: "The real effort is to stay there, rather, in so far as that is possible, and to examine closely the odd vegetation of those distant regions. Tenacity and acumen are privileged spectators of this inhuman show in which absurdity, hope, and death carry on their dialogue."

What if we can, by defusion and exposure, create a space where the client can stand rather than *have to* jump forward or backward? To me, that is the place from which choices with the most vitality emerge. That place where even *whether* to choose occurs psychologically as a choice.

STIGMA

> **Study re; applicability of ACT concepts**

EVIDENCE

> **Stigma study (re drug and alcohol counselors) [8-31-02]**
>
> Steve Hayes

We have now pretty well analyzed our ACT / RFT intervention with stigma. I presented our preliminary analyses last week at APA. Thought you might like to see them.

I have [co-written] a paper [*Prejudice, Terrorism, and Behavior Therapy*] that explains how ACT might apply to prejudice. It was inspired by 9-11, as will be obvious if you read it. I gave it as an oral talk at AABT (now ABCT) -- thus the oral tone.

Following that connection, we tried to find a way to test out these ideas. As part of the Nevada "Practice Improvement Collaborative" (a SAMHSA funded project) our team did a one day ACT / RFT group workshop (Barbara Kohlenberg and I actually ran the groups ...) and compared it to a control condition and to a pretty well developed form of multicultural training (also done in a one day workshop). The three were compared in a randomized controlled trial -- about 30 per condition. The target group was drug and alcohol counselors. Our idea was that counselors have to struggle with stigmatizing attitudes about their own clients, and that this would result in client disengagement and burnout. The intervention essentially taught participants to accept the presence of stigmatizing and disengaging thoughts; to defuse from them; to connect "board level" with the folks they are treating (i.e., connect with them as human beings); to reconnect with their values in doing this work; and to move ahead helping others. There were a few RFT things in there too ... for example we had someone introduce themselves in a sentence or two and then we noticed all of the categorical and evaluative thoughts that these statements kicked off in all of us in the group. Then we started asking our volunteer questions -- things like "when did you last cry?" or "what most worries you about your family?" As these were answered you could almost physically feel how a human being showed up and the narrow, evaluative chatter became increasingly irrelevant. In essence we used an overload of cross cutting categories as a kind of defusion technique.

Here are the data.... Follow-up is at 3 months.

The first data are a measure of the presence of stigmatizing attitudes. ACT and multi are better than control at post; only ACT is better than control at F-up (using ANACOVAR).

["Stigmatizing Attitudes" data chart]

These are believability in stigmatizing and disengaging attitudes (when they occur to you, do you buy into them). Similar effects as with the presence or absence of these thoughts.

["Believability of Stigmatising Attitudes" data chart]

On the AAQ only ACT differs from the control but washes out by F-up.

["Acceptance and Action Questionnaire" data chart]

You get an effect on general mental health but it too goes away at F-up, most because the control group improves.

["GHQ" data chart]

Here is a measure of a sense of personal accomplishment at work. Both ACT and multi are better at post; only ACT at F-up (actually on this one I think ACT is better than multi as well at F-up).

["Personal Accomplishment" data chart]

And here is a measure of disengagement and depersonalization at work. On this one ACT and multi are better than the control at post but by F-up the control is better than multi (and ACT is better than multi).

["Depersonalization" data chart]

Anyway... the bottom line message is that stigmatizing and prejudiced thoughts and feelings in work settings are very similar to depressogenic thoughts and feelings; anxiety-related thoughts and feelings; hallucinations and delusions; pain; stress-related thoughts at work; and just about every other kind of negative private event ACT-competent folks have looked at so far. Some of these are called "signs of mental illness" -- some are not -- but the basic issue seems to be the same. This should embolden the ACT community a bit more to push these ideas out into various nooks and crannies that have not been the focus of intervention by behavior therapists. We may have something to contribute if the issue involves experiential avoidance, cognitive entanglement, lack of clarity about values, or a failure to act consistently with values.

I think we are seeing that the range of issues that have these features is very large indeed....

Editor's Note: This study was published in 2004 in *Behavior Therapy*, 35, 821-835. Please see the original for the data charts.

SUBSTANCE ABUSE

Comprehensive Substance Involvement Worksheets [9-6-04]

Matthew Smout
(Kelly Wilson)

For anyone doing work in the drug and alcohol field, Kelly's responses to some of my questions about the Comprehensive Substance Involvement Worksheets (CSIWs) [see *A Practical Guide to ACT* pp. 160-161] should be of interest. Thanks Kelly - very helpful.

[KW] Hi Matthew- I think that variability is often the case.

With the CSIW-I, I've had some clients with extensive drug histories - changes from drug to drug, ROA changes etc. - whose reactions to making contact with their history are things like: pride, that they've reduced from some of the drugs, indifference - "that's all in the past."

[KW] I doubt that these presentations are as simple as they appear. The client may be indifferent, but I doubt they are merely indifferent. They may be proud, but I doubt they are merely proud. The question becomes, what to do with my concerns/suspicions.

I could see how the therapist might say something where the underlying message is "ah, but it's not all in the past is it? because what you're doing now is really more of the same."

[KW] I would bet on this response blowing up in your face. It is too conventional--they have heard it before and you are likely to activate well worn defenses.

or "you wouldn't be indifferent if you REALLY stopped to look at how much you've used in the past."

[KW] The better strategy is to be interested in collecting minute detailed account--in short "really" look. The response above implies that they have not "really" looked, even though you asked them to. This is to accuse them of bad faith/ lying/ denial/ laziness/ lack of motivation/ stupidity (you pick) and will likely activate defenses/avoidance. There is an accusation in it; the client's history will select which one they think you are up to. It may be that they detect you *trolling* for reactions. This may generate counterpliance.

I've tended to err on the side of non-judgementalism and not pressed either of these hypotheses, which is all very well, but I often end up sitting there nodding along "yeah, drinking 6 days a week is definitely a reduction from 7." Not that satisfying and can leave both myself and client wondering why we went through it.

[KW] The statement in quotes above seems a bit like an endorsement. I don't endorse or condemn. I am hands off. I think your nonjudgement is not an error. The purpose of the exercise is to map the ground, if you press into the costs too early, you may activate avoidance around the costs. I can almost guarantee that they have not experienced a detailed, entirely nonjudgmental cataloguing of drug use patterns. People who have collected these histories, including them flip flop back and forth between endorsement and condemnation (the client too) depending on the moment by moment goodness or badness of the properties of the history. Drinking down ... mmmm good ... uh oh ... drinking back up bad...

I feel like I'm missing something here - any thoughts?

[KW] Nope, I don't think there is anything missing except perhaps cataloguing a process note on how your reactions ebb and flow as you collect the hx. Notice also how anxious you are to cut to problem solving. It's cool man. Just hang in there and watch the show. Watch the history unwind, and watch your own reactions to it. And the client's.

Some drug use pattern changes are in line with relapse prevention skills training (RPST) approaches / harm reduction approaches - cutting down, switching ROA, reducing times/situations used in. An RPST therapist would praise these kinds of efforts and try and build on them. With ACT hats on, are we making something different of these changes?

[KW] As I said above, I would be unlikely to praise or blame. Drinking is not good or bad in and of itself. It simply is.

The CSIW-II nearly always gets to the nub of the matter. I guess I've been underwhelmed by my clients' reactions to their CSIW-I. I don't get much sense of wonderment from them or painful avoidance to introduce other ACT work. How common is this?

[KW] Really depends on the client. Sometimes this history will really spin them. Sometimes not. Depends on the history, damage caused, level of avoidance, etc. If it leaves you a little perplexed, be perplexed. Notice that.

Would you suggest just accept these reactions and wait for the CSIW-II to stir things up? Or would you spend some time working some angles to get a reaction from clients to the exercise?

[KW] Depends what you mean by work more angles. I would say that if you see hesitation, things that make you suspicious, just slow down and get more detail. Ask about reactions to the history. But be damned careful about cheering on one sort of reaction and disdaining others. It is a trap. I would say that it is an empirical matter, whether to just skip the CSIW-I and go straight to the II, but absent deconstructing it experimentally, I would say, theoretically, the CSIW-I maps the ground upon which the CSIW-II is played out. Once you get into the costs (if there are perceived costs) there is little way to retreat from the pervasiveness, since the use patterns have been laid out in detail. There is less chance that the client can turn a bad event into something very discrete and therefore more easily dodged, since it is embedded in a well mapped hx of use. The kinds of questions you posed above, about "really" looking at the history may actually be possible. Kind of hard to detail this too much in an email, but my sense is that it is important. There is a bit of defusion in the wholly nonjudgemental history taking. It is a process. My sense is that the I lays the ground work for the II. The two is really the important part, because who cares how much someone drinks or uses if it never interferes with important valued domains. But, we want to create a context where retreat from the pervasiveness is tough, once the costs become apparent. It is also a good faith effort on your part. As an ACT therapist, you are saying, well? if drug use is a problem, we will see that. You don't need me to tell you whether it is or not. So, what we will do is look at it very carefully and then you will tell me.

SUBSTANCE ABUSE

Motivation to change [4-10-05]

Steve Hayes

Gijs Jansen wrote:

I'm having a lot of trouble with clients who are not really open to the long-term benefits of behaviour based on values. Even though they know their behaviour is counter-productive, they cannot seem to let go. Especially drug-addicts seem to have this problem. And, I think they have a point. What can we offer those who want to quit destructive behavioural patterns on short term?

I think we might need to know a bit more about your work circumstance and what you are trying to produce in order to respond. It might be a mistaken reading but in between the lines it sounds as though you are bargaining with them ("well if you won't quit drinking will you at least cut down?" etc.). If that is the situation, things will not go well -- there is no real therapeutic contract. It could be that you had a formal goal before therapy started - if that is the case, you will get resistance.

It can help to walk through the substance involvement worksheet (Kel can send it to you) and really look at what has been happening - but no matter what is on that sheet it is up to the client what happens next.

This issue usually shows up when:

a) the cost of experiential avoidance has not been faced, or

b) the cost is not yet high enough and the actual contingencies are not yet powerful enough to compete with the benefits of the pattern being targeted.

You can work through the first, but the second is up to the individual. If there are no costs, why change?

And if there are no costs who are you to say they should? If it *really* is the second issue, I usually just say "well, come back when you've suffered enough." We are not cops. We are not God. We do not dole out punishment or absolution.

If, as you say, "they know their behaviour is counter-productive" -- then how do they know that? If it is really something they view as counter productive - what do they want to produce that is being countered? Go into that pain and you will find the values. (Or go into the values and you will find the pain.) If you mean they know their behavior is disapproved of by others but they themselves do not view it as counter productive, then in fact they do NOT know it is counter productive.

In order to do this properly, you need an absolute posture of openness and a radical respect for the ability of human beings to make choices. You are not there to make them behave; to make them stop using drugs; to make them clean up. You work for the client -- it truly has to be up to them what they want in their life. That does not mean you have to enable bad behavior. You can respectfully withdraw from witnessing a tragedy.

I usually tell addicted folks:

We are not here to make you stop using.

We are here to empower your life ... we are employees ... we work for you.

We care about that role too much to feed you bullshit so we are not here to applaud if you do self-deceptive or self-destructive things, despite our employee status. We need to look at what has been happening in great detail, but YOU need to say whether there is a cost to drug use; and whether this life as you've been living it is *really* what you want. If it really IS then therapy is over. If it ISN'T and folks want to bargain, well you

	aren't someone who can deliver whatever it is folks want to bargain for. If it ISN'T and folks want to work to make things different ... say what that is and we have a contract.
SUBSTANCE ABUSE Motivation to change [cont'd] **MIND** **Voice, internal - "How about doing something stupid?"** **CONTROL** **External behavior, of - hands, feet etc.** **COMMITMENT** **Keeping - need for practice [4-11-05]** Hank Robb	Just a few thoughts to add on to Steve's. I'm fond of, "The trouble with a philosophy of 'Eat, drink, and be merry for tomorrow we die' is tomorrow comes and we aren't dead. So, if you plan to be around tomorrow it's best to act like it today!" Additionally, everybody has a voice inside his or her head that says, "How about doing something stupid?" The "stupid thing" varies from person to person, place to place, and time to time. This is not something you get over. It is not something that is "wrong" with you. It is one of the symptoms of being a child, including an "adult child," of humans. The main thing is learning to recognize that voice, refusing to go along with it, and, instead, doing stuff that is most important. In the substance abuse field, people have developed what is called a "Decisional Balance Sheet." Don't worry about "deciding," that's just what the form is called. It's a 2x2 - the "top" 2 are the positives and negatives of maintaining the current pattern of use. The bottom two are the positives and negatives of changing to some other pattern of use, including no use. Fill out the positives of using first because there are some or folks wouldn't be doing it. Sometimes the positives of using are just the negatives of changing and similarly for the negatives of the current use pattern and the positives of changing, but not always. So, once you have all the boxes filled in, a person can go back and see how long term each of the positives and negatives are. For example, there may be ten positives to the current pattern and only three negatives, but the ten positives are all fairly short term and the three negatives are fairly long term. Then look at how important each thing in each of the four boxes is. Again there may be ten positives of using but they are all + 1 and the three negatives are all -10. Note, the results of all this is not to "make a decision." It is to show where the current pattern of behavior, in this case using, leads, and where a different pattern of using is likely to lead. In other words, it helps establish VALUES as lived. Now I want to underline an agreement I especially have with Steve. If a person's most important value is getting loaded, then who am I, or anyone else, to get in their way. The thing is, I've yet to run into anyone who really finds this the most important thing. I suspect those who do are not seeing any of us. Most folks I've run into want the advantages of using and the advantages of not using at the same time and I don't know anyone who knows how to accomplish this. Unfortunately, one has to stick with one or the other. "Digging," in this case, is, "I can have the advantages of both if I just 'do it right.'" Great! How's it been working and, by the way, I'll bet your mind provided you with that insight - huh?! The next problem is "loss of control." Many people have gotten this funny idea that when they strongly want to do something or strongly don't want to do something, they lose control of their hands, arms, feet and mouth. Granted, it often seems like that but just before you used, check and see if it wasn't YOU who acted. Using, or not using, is a choice - not something that "happens to you." "Happens to you" is a fun story, and an important story for avoiding a lot of bad stuff if you dare to admit you did it, but while thoughts, images and sensations about using do often just "happen," moving your hands, arms, feet, and mouth don't - unless you have a seizure or a stroke. I'm sure once this is recognized we will get a boatload of temporal lobe epilepsy for using or some other "chemical imbalance" but we are home free on this score for the moment. I would suggest that one of the big problems here is practicing keeping a commitment when one doesn't feel like it. If one is not well practiced at something, including keeping a commitment, then all the things that go along with any behavior that is not well practiced apply, namely a lot of non-target behavior. So, work on practicing commitment, especially the one that has to do with changing the pattern of use if, indeed, that is what the person has CHOSEN to do. The more you practice doing what's important, whether you feel like it at the moment or not, the better you will get at it. Not everybody who practices the piano goes to Carnegie Hall but everybody gets better. At least that's the way it seems to me.
TOURETTE'S SYNDROME **Behavior Therapy (habit reversal) - integrating ACT** **ACT cf.** **Behavior Therapy - compatibility; ACT as BT [2-15-04]** Mike Twohig	Thomas Gustavsson wrote: I'm about to start a treatment with a 15 year old boy with Tourette's syndrome.... My question is if there is anything written (or any data) on Tourette's/tics and acceptance/ACT? Doug Woods and I (as well as others) have been integrating ACT into the treatment of many repetitive behaviors. We have a paper on the treatment of Trichotillomania with ACT and habit reversal coming out in the special issue of BT. (To toot my horn a little more, I have data on ACT with skin picking and OCD as well.) Habit reversal is an effective, well-validated intervention for tics and other habit behaviors. Information on habit reversal is generally easy to find. We have found that ACT can easily be integrated into the treatment of these types of repetitive behaviors.... Habit reversal is a validated treatment for TS whereas ACT is not, and I can only assume that ACT will help. I will explain why. Tics generally occur to reduce a premonitory urge: a feeling of tension in a particular area of the body. If a kid has an arm tic, he or she will likely report tension somewhere in the arm that is reduced by ticking. Habit reversal (an overt behavior control strategy) is likely effective because it does not allow the tic to

	occur, and instead forces the child to sit there with the feeling of tension. After enough trials like this, the urge habituates, thus, the rate of tics begins to decrease.
	Verbal processes seem to exacerbate this urge and make it more painful and annoying than it actually is. Acceptance and defusion work can be done around this urge to tic, thus making it easier to have around. Values work can be useful to change the context of the urge to something that can be experienced in the service of something worthwhile.
	I would do it like this. Teach the kid habit reversal. If the tics go away that quickly, lucky for you. If the kid is having difficulty doing the competing response (that is, the behavior that does not allow the tic to occur) you can begin to integrate ACT. I would focus ACT on the urge to tic. Don't forget that the control strategies in behavioral interventions are usually around overt behavior. Control over overt behavior works well. Control over private events such as urges to tic is difficult. As you can see I am focusing on the tics; I think that there is enough data that they can be decreased with behavioral interventions.
TOURETTE'S SYNDROME Behavior Therapy (habit reversal) - integrating ACT [cont'd] ACT cf. Behavior Therapy - compatibility; ACT as BT [cont'd] Doug Woods	I agree with Mike Twohig's assessment and recommendations. I think this is a good example of how people can get easily confused with what ACT does or is intended to do. I think people who start with ACT often get confused and think the target of acceptance should be the overt problem, and this stance, in turn, seems very confusing to the outside observer. As I understand it, ACT is only designed to indirectly treat behaviors that are somehow functionally related to a language-based process. Having people accept their verbal processes related to tic occurrence will have a number of positive features including an increased self-evaluation and social functioning. ACT may also provide a benefit of decreasing tics indirectly by decreasing the likelihood of stressful situations, which could exacerbate tics. However, tics are not primarily verbally controlled, and as such, I seriously doubt that ACT alone would be effective in eliminating tics. Thus, if a person desires a reduction in tics, traditional behavior therapy procedures would be necessary.
TOURETTE'S SYNDROME Behavior Therapy (habit reversal) - integrating ACT [cont'd] ACT cf. Behavior Therapy - compatibility; ACT as BT [cont'd] Steve Hayes	Doug makes an awfully important point, which is worth reiterating. ACT is a behavior therapy. Almost every ACT protocol will have and should have specific behavioral components, homework, etc. to fit the specific problems being dealt with. If values and commitment work doesn't show up in the world of behavior it's just not real. I doubt that ACT for depression will work without changing behaviors and engaging life (i.e., without behavioral activation), or that ACT for anxiety will work without exposure, or ACT for diabetes will work without education about self-management and commitment to the medical regimen ... etc.
TOURETTE'S SYNDROME **Treatment - contingency management/ ACT [4-19-04]** Mike Twohig	Ann Bailey-Ciarrochi wrote: I was wondering if anyone has used ACT with Tourette's Disorder? I do not think that anyone has done ACT work with T.S., at least nothing has been shared. Contingency management procedures are very effective for managing T.S. Look up habit reversal if you are not familiar. ACT would only be useful if the tics are produced or exacerbated through verbal processes, and that makes the contingency management procedure insufficient. I believe this is the case with some people. People with TS will sometimes report the urge to ticking being too strong that they cannot handle it. They will report needing to get rid of the urge. When a person is verbally entangled like that, it might be useful to increase the client's willingness to experience that urge to tic. I would teach the client habit reversal and see what level of decrease you get with the tics. If the decease is not sufficient, and the urge to tic is an issue, then handle that with ACT procedures. ACT and more basic contingency management procedures fit together very nicely.
TRAUMA/ ABUSE **Road accidents [2-27-05]** Hank Robb	Alan McAllister wrote: I would like some pointers to work done by ACT-oriented therapists on grief and guilt associated with automobile accidents. Be present with the heartbreak long enough that the impression that you will die from it passes just enough to notice that you haven't and can ask where it is important to go from here.

TRAUMA/ ABUSE Road accidents [cont'd] Kelly Wilson	On fatal car accidents: In the deep, dark, damp evergreen forests of western Washington, where I spent my time as a boy, sometimes a big evergreen would fall. It is sad when you see a big beautiful cedar fall. It would lay in the woods for years decomposing, and out of it a neat little row of 8 or 10 new trees would grow all along that decomposing trunk. Slowly, over decades, the trunk is taken up into this new growth. We called them nurse logs. I wonder, if something new could grow out of this tragedy, what that might be. There are places in life where new grows from things fallen, not away from them. I might wonder about this with the client. I might wonder--if you could grow something new and beautiful, that could honor what has fallen, what might that be?
TRAUMA/ ABUSE Road accidents [cont'd] Madelon Bolling	I would emphasize that there is time inherent in this story: little cedar trees don't start growing the day after a tree falls. Or the week after, or the month after.... It takes time for the tree to soften after its fall, time and rain weeping onto its fallen body, passing seasons of ice and heat to encourage the small life forms that consume wood to transform it into nurturant substrate.
	Too often people want grief and guilt to go away instantly--in a week, in a month. DSM says more than 2 months is diagnosable, but there is a long human tradition of allowing a year for grieving. The latter is based on the experience of untold generations. It's up to the clinician to sense whether the quality of grief is of the transformative, nurturant variety, or if it is tightly fused.... Another case of learning to FEEL well.
	Guilt in the case of an auto mortality also carries aspects of grief that need to be honored. If nothing else, one's record of having caused no significant harm is gone forever.
TRAUMA/ ABUSE Road accidents [cont'd] Steve Hayes	Julieann Pankey has some nice AAQ data showing that complicated grieving is associated with experiential avoidance.
	If you aren't willing to grieve you may grieve for a long time.

Chapter 6
<u>Clinical Issues and Barriers in ACT</u>

This chapter comprises material relating to a variety of factors implicated in problems encountered in therapy. The concept of control and the use of coping strategies, both closely linked with the client's unworkable agenda, are debated, as is creative hopelessness, the phase of therapy in which such issues commonly arise. Avoidance, being perhaps the prime example of a maladaptive coping strategy adopted by humans, and also identified in ACT as a barrier to progress towards a values-directed life, is also discussed, as are other of the barrier components of the FEAR acronym in ACT, namely Evaluation and Reason giving. (The missing barrier - Fusion - is covered in Chapter 3.) Other topic areas addressed include those of the mind and its works: thoughts, memories, emotions and pain - the private experiences that often exert unhelpful influences on behavior, to the detriment of progress in therapy.

AVOIDANCE **Experiential - cf. existing concepts [5-10-05]** Steve Hayes	Rhiannon Patterson wrote: Could someone explain a bit further the distinction between experiential avoidance (EA) (or psychological flexibility, if that is a preferred term) and related concepts that have already been defined by behavioral psychologists, particularly distress tolerance (but also impulsivity and sensitivity to punishment)? A lot of folks are working on those interconnections ... It is going to be pretty hard work. The whole ACT / RFT agenda is about the basic issue that underlies this question (and many more) -- how and why do language and cognition processes interact with direct experience to produce these kinds of phenomena? Once you get started you will find a couple of dozen obviously related concepts. Many of these are also fairly low level concepts or just names for empirical phenomena (e.g., delay discounting) with unknown sources of control over them. But there is a cast in the question that seems incorrect. You are talking about the relation between EA "and related concepts that have already been defined by behavioral psychologists, particularly distress tolerance." The word "already" suggests that distress tolerance is a well worked out idea and that it was around first and EA was sort of added to the mix lately without carefully distinguishing the new idea from the old. That isn't right. The 1996 JCCP paper was a fairly comprehensive take on EA. That take is not adequate theoretically (thus, we are starting to talk more about "psychological flexibility" not as a matter of preference for terms but as a matter of digging more deeply into the processes underlying EA, defusion, values etc.) but it was a pretty good start. Conversely, even today there is no decent theoretical account of distress tolerance that I know of. It is a relatively common sense term for a set of phenomena. That's it. I'd answer your question this way: even before getting into content, the biggest and most obvious difference is metatheoretical. EA is part of a research program designed to produce a comprehensive theoretical account of how language processes work. It is not merely an empirical phenomenon; and it is not merely an isolated "concept." As for the substantive difference -- we do not yet know. There is no comprehensive theory of distress tolerance so we can't compare the theories. We know they are related empirically -- both correlationally and experimentally. When you target EA through ACT you get improvements in DT. But some DT performances may be controlled by other processes (e.g., I'd bet some pretty big suppressors can hold their breath for a very long time). It will need to be worked out empirically. It is not a simple matter of "definition." There are ACT grants right now working on distress intolerant folks (Rick Brown's smoking grant). We are doing distress tolerance research in my lab. A lot of the ACT pain studies (etc.) going on world wide bear on this issue. So the ACT / RFT community is onto the connection.
AVOIDANCE Experiential - cf. existing concepts [cont'd] Steve Hayes	Amanda Adcock wrote: What does this term (EA) add to traditional avoidance, as discussed in the behavior analytic literature? Traditional avoidance is focused on stimuli. There is no evidence that I know of that non-verbal organisms avoid private events in reaction to these stimuli. Humans avoid thoughts, feelings, bodily sensations and so on. RFT explains why. These loose sets become verbally organized as they enter into relational frames; they become temporally and causally predicted and analyzed; and evaluated and compared. Avoidance is then regulated by a mix of direct contingencies and verbal processes. None of the traditional behavior analytic models of avoidance deal with this because verbal / cognitive processes are not part of the traditional analysis. So, if you control for amount of exposure to aversive events; amount of unreinforced exposure; etc. that won't tell you as much as it will if you know whether the avoidance patterns include experiential avoidance. The data on EA is growing rapidly and seems to do more in picking up the variance that you would without the concept. The technical behavior analytic answer comes down to understanding RFT so if this seems vague that is where to go. An example: Train A < B < C ; Shock in the presence of B. C is now avoided more than B because 'C will even be worse' (or more technically because of the person's history with comparative frames; the Crel contextual control that evoked B < C; and the Cfunc contextual control .. e.g., a context of literality; emotional control; reason giving ... that elicited high arousal and avoidance). That last part is experiential avoidance. Nothing in direct contingency control gives you such effects.
AVOIDANCE Experiential - cf. existing concepts [cont'd]	Take Mike Dougher's data: Train: A < B < C. Train: B as a CS. Testing result: C is a bigger "CS" than B ("CS" in quotes because it is not really a traditional CS ... it is a relational CS). Analog: Panic person goes into corner store - nothing bad happens except experiencing anxiety (this is like an extinction trial in an animal model). Person relates the store to other things due to Crels present (e.g., "I almost lost it. The mall will be much worse!") [i.e., store < mall]. Now Mall elicits more anxiety than the store given the right Cfuncs [Mall is a bigger "CS" than the store]. Furthermore "anxiety" is now related to

ANXIETY
 	
    Panic - RFT account of
 	
RFT
 	
    Anxiety/ panic -
    account of [5-17-05]
 	
       Steve Hayes
	"almost lost it" which is related to "and if I did I would just die" or whatever. So anxiety predicts huge aversives in a temporal /causal frame. The emotional arousal from "just die" now transfers to the detection of this fuzzy set called "anxiety" and the temporal / causal frame makes it appear imminent. Given the right Cfuncs that relation will lead to anxiety occasioning even more anxiety. When the person goes in the corner store the next time a small amount of anxiety seems to predict huge aversives -- voila, panic.
	
	But note that all of this started with a panic disordered person going into a corner store and having nothing bad happen except experiencing anxiety. The "extinction" trial has become a training trial because of the interaction between relational operants and the direct contingency stream. This simply does not happen in animal models of anxiety. Extinction does not magically become reconditioning ... because the animal does not fear fear and has no mechanism to do that. The animal fears shock. No shock + exposure = improvement. In humans that formula does not always work unless something else happens during exposure.
	
	An RFT account puts the causal control here into the contextual cues that regulate relational frames and into their history, not into the behavior of relating itself. That is why RFT leads to odd contextual interventions like defusion. If the theory is right defusion/ acceptance/ self as context/ contact with the present moment should super-charge exposure because it promotes response flexibility and undercuts the kinds of interactions that lead to the process above (mostly by arranging for unusual social/verbal Cfuncs). In essence you are moving humans closer to non-humans with regard to the healthy impact of extinction.

AVOIDANCE
 	
    Experiential - evidence
    of link with anxiety
    pathology
 	
EVIDENCE
 	
    Experiential avoidance
    - link with anxiety
    pathology [3-4-05]
 	
       John Forsyth
	I think the experiential avoidance and RFT stuff jibbes really well with the emerging work coming out of the emotion regulation area. EA seems to capture numerous self, emotion, and behavior regulation processes. This literature is converging in showing that flexibility/rigidity seems to be a core dimension that discriminates healthy forms of self-regulation from less functional forms of self-regulation (see Psych Science Article on the Importance of Being Flexible).
	
	We just had a look at some data on coping processes as predictors of anxiety pathology for an ABCT submission. I am stoked by some of the findings. Basically, many of the so-called problematic coping strategies predicted negative anxiety outcomes (anxiety sensitivity, trait anxiety, etc.). Yet, when we plugged experiential avoidance in as a mediator, all of them dropped out. In fact, the coping processes to anxiety disturbance was completely mediated by EA. The blurb from the abstract appears below.
	
	    The current study investigated the effects of coping and emotional responses styles on anxiety-related distress, and whether these effects were mediated by experiential avoidance. Eighty-five healthy undergraduates completed the Acceptance and Action Questionnaire as a measure of experiential avoidance, the Coping Styles Questionnaire (CSQ) and Emotional Control Questionnaire (ECQ) as indices of adaptive and maladaptive coping with emotion and the tendency to inhibit the expression of emotional responses, and several other measures known to assess anxiety-related pathology (e.g., anxiety sensitivity, suffocation fear, number of fears, body sensation fear, body vigilance). The results, based on the approach to mediation outlined by Baron and Kenney (1986), showed that experiential avoidance mediates the effects of coping and emotional responses styles on anxiety-related distress. Severity of fears and anxiety was influenced by tendencies to (a) ruminate on emotionally upsetting events, (b) be more impulsive, (c) feel more involved with stressful events, and (d) a predisposition to be more irrational and avoidant. Yet, the relation between these individual styles and anxiety-related distress was completely mediated by experiential avoidance.

AVOIDANCE
 	
    Experiential - potential
    misconceptions [5-3-05]
 	
       Steve Hayes
	Monica Pignotti wrote:
	
	    I wonder about the idea of experiential avoidance and whether it is always a bad thing, especially for people who do not have any particular psychological diagnosis.... While experiential avoidance is detrimental to the small percentage of people who go on to develop PTSD following a trauma, this is not necessarily the case for most people who experience a trauma, who are resilient and recover on their own without therapy and could be engaging in "experiential avoidance" in a way that is healthy.
	
	The data on experiential avoidance defined the way we do in ACT is extensive with normal populations. Thousands of normal subjects have been examined in scores of studies in normal environments including performance in the workplace. Frank Bond recently did a meta-analysis which will be part of an upcoming paper in BRAT we are doing.
	
	You have to be careful with words ... when you ask if experiential avoidance is always a bad thing, and then point to specific moments of emotional expression, you are almost certainly using EA in a lay fashion. "Debriefings" could easily *increase* experiential avoidance, for example, and casting it as the flip side of the term functionally refines the concept as used in ACT. If the alternative to experiential avoidance was just feeling emotions we could throw our patients into burning buildings and expect positive outcomes because we are undermining experiential avoidance. An ACT protocol will have acceptance, defusion, self-as-context, contact with the present moment, and values work -- all of which will support healthy changes in

the area of EA. Emotionally evocative moments are not necessarily positive ... the same applies to exposure in all forms. Something has to happen in those moments for good things to happen. That is what is missing from debriefing work -- it went sideways because it was based on weak theory. ACT says what has to happen: acceptance / defusion / etc.

EA does not mean fully experiencing all emotions available in every moment. It depends on what that moment affords and what is needed for effective action. Emotional regulation skills are not the flip side of EA either -- we had an extensive discussion on distraction on the list recently that focused on that very point. The goal is psychological flexibility -- not tears.

You have to climb into the theory and the data, or these concepts become dangerous cartoons. Even then, every step needs to be studied and validated.

AVOIDANCE **Functional term in ACT [8-3-03]** Steve Hayes	Jonathan Kandell wrote: I hope this isn't too naive a question, but why does ACT concentrate so much on avoidance mechanisms and so little on compensation (e.g., projection, acting out, etc.)? The same dynamics underlie both types of responses, and many of the ACT therapy moves would seem to apply to both (since compensation also serves to avoid unpleasant internal experience). Or am I misrepresenting ACT? You are mixing terms from different traditions. Avoidance is a functional term in ACT. If "compensation also serves to avoid unpleasant internal experience" then it is avoidance functionally speaking. That probably explains why your intuition is that the ACT therapy moves would apply to both: they should if they are the same functional entities. The technical distinctions made within other traditions don't precisely map onto ACT because the functional contextual behavioral features of ACT have their own philosophy and theory. But ACT is dealing with relatively deep clinical issues, so there is a notable overlap in terms of issues. I think it is fine to use whatever seems to be valuable within ACT, but to see it from the inside, so to speak, the theory and philosophy is needed....
AVOIDANCE **Verbally established vs. directly acquired [4-17-04]** Steve Hayes	Nico van der Meijden wrote: As a practitioner originally trained to detect and change dysfunctional belief structures of clients, I found that it's not the theory that underlies ACT (or the RFT book) that's most difficult to understand, but the contextual-functionalistic way of thinking. But once you've grasped this way of thinking ('once the coin has dropped') you suddenly start to see a lot of 'obvious' things you somehow overlooked before. One of those obvious things is the extent to which disorders can be considered as reactions to preceding stressful events. As a conventional cognitive therapist I noted these events but didn't pay much attention to them, because it was changing the thinking I was after. (Recently I interviewed 9 people in connection with our upcoming panic group and with all of them it was possible to identify stressful events preceding the onset of the disorder.) Another 'obvious' fact I started to notice is the extent to which ACT itself is rooted in this functionalistic 'Skinnerian' way of thinking. When you, e.g., ask a client in the 'Creative Hopelessness' phase of the therapy: "What have you tried?", "How did it work?", "How did it work in the long run?", what are you doing other than letting the client perform a functional analysis on his own behavior? (though the link with functional analysis isn't explicitly made in the ACT book). What the client does is mentioning negatively reinforced avoidance behaviors that are in the long run followed by aversive consequences. A classical Skinnerian therapist would immediately start to 'poison' the negative reinforcers and emphasize the aversive punishing consequences. ACT of course differs from other contextual theories in that it distinguishes two behavioral systems, language and its rule governed behavior (of which it has developed an impressive theory) and the contingency-shaped 'experiential' system. The way in which these two systems operate next to each other and influence each other is what makes practicing ACT complicated. The ACT book explicitly states that the above-mentioned avoidance behaviors are rule-governed (see Chapter 4 on "Creative Hopelessness"); they are the result of overexpansive 'control' tracks which we acquire during our socialization. But I wondered, how can you ever know which of the two systems dominates in a given situation? Doesn't immediate negative reinforcement strengthen contingency shaped behavior, despite long-term aversive consequences? When I drink alcohol to reduce my anxiety, can I tell for sure if I do this mostly under the control of an overexpansive track or mostly under the control of the immediate negatively reinforcing effect of alcohol? And in the latter case, what's then the most efficient treatment? One way you can tell that experiential avoidance is verbally entangled and rule governed is that without language emotions per se are not the targets of avoidance. Emotions are qualities of responses to situations. Nonhumans don't avoid responses -- they avoid situations that evoke certain responses. More precisely, it buys you nothing (indeed it costs) in the world of prediction and influence to assume that non humans avoid anxiety (etc.) as distinct from avoiding painful stimulation. Humans verbally categorize these responses and then avoid these very categories. More precisely, it buys

	you something in the world of prediction and influence to assume that there are two contingency streams with humans -- directly acquired avoidance of negative situations, and verbally established avoidance of anxiety (etc.) itself.
	People are not purely verbal creatures and in humans both types of avoidance overlap, so some of what may look like experiential avoidance can be directly shaped -- and for sure you can shape unhealthy behaviors, whether or not it fits the experiential avoidance category. Much like the distinction between "clean and dirty" emotion (or what others have spoken of as "clear and muddy") it tends to be what we add by language that most causes us trouble however.
	That's not always so, of course ... one reason ACT is part of behavior therapy writ large ... not a substitute for it.
CONTROL **Appetitive vs. aversive; Skinner's view of "freedom" [4-14-04]** Kelly Wilson	There is plenty wrong with Skinner's book Beyond Freedom and Dignity and with Walden II, but there is a central concern of his that I think is terribly important in my world. Freedom for Skinner meant free from aversive control. This is a tricky topic and not enough time to nuance thoroughly, but the values stuff is, IMO, about altering the therapeutic work from work that is under aversive control--done to make something bad stop, or to keep something bad from happening-- and to move it into the world work under appetitive control--in Skinner's terms--positive reinforcement. I want the work to occur for the client as being *for* something they would choose in a world without limits. A formally identical act can be utterly transformed if we shift the context from aversive to appetitive control. In the latter instance you will feel free. This, I think was the whole point of Walden II and really an entirely central concern for Skinner throughout his life. A cool calling I think.
CONTROL **Approach (cf. avoidance) behavior; narcissism [10-22-04]** Patty Bach	Joseph Ciarrochi wrote: I propose that there are two classes of behaving in RFT that are relevant to clinicians: 1) relational framing in the service of avoiding aversive private experiences; 2) relational framing in the service of approaching, or creating, positive private experiences. Whether characterized as seeking to increase positively evaluated private experiences or to decrease negatively evaluated private experiences, the individual's behavior is in the service of controlling private experience, which may lead to similar negative outcomes if accompanied by insensitivity to other contingencies - and insensitivity to social and other contingencies is diagnostic of 'narcissism.' I'm reminded of a listserv discussion some time ago contrasting, "if you're not willing to have it you've got it" with "if you're not willing to lose it, you've lost it."
CONTROL Approach (cf. avoidance) behavior; narcissism [cont'd] Rainer Sonntag	I agree with Patty. Positive self-concepts can be as problematic as negative ones; both are often accompanied by context insensitivity. Furthermore, isn't emotional avoidance always related to emotional approach? We want to get rid of bad feelings and approach good feelings. This reminds me of the tricky distinction between positive and negative reinforcement. When we leave the cold outside and go into a warm room, is this negative or positive reinforcement? Do we avoid the cold or approach the warm?
CONTROL Approach (cf. avoidance) behavior; narcissism [cont'd] Steve Hayes	The approach / avoid distinction is inherently tricky but it does at times seem to tap into something important. Rainer is right ... it is like the positive / negative reinforcement issue. But just as with that issue, even though people like Jack Michael seem technically correct that they are flip sides of the same coin, there are typically important parametric differences. In broad generalities: Positive events tend to come on slower; last longer; peak less dramatically; dominate the repertoire less; be more sensitive to context // Negative ones can have that fast/high/dominant quality that produces particularly obvious forms of disruption and rigidity. Shock someone and the need to stop it eliminates virtually all other aspects of the repertoire. Few positives are like that except things like injectable drugs and they too are pretty disruptive. There is more to ACT / RFT models of psychopathology than experiential avoidance: fusion, lack of clear values, poor contact with the present moment / weak "self as process," weak contact with "self as context"; attachment to the conceptualized self, lack of committed action; etc. Narcissism clearly can involve emotional avoidance, but sometimes it does not seem to. When narcissism is an approach issue the problem usually seems to be more in the fusion / attachment to the conceptualized self area (among others above). "I'm special / better / right" when fused with is pretty dangerous. People will fight to protect a relational network as if their lives depended on it -- and when we are talking about a conceptualized self in a sense one's "life" DOES depend on it. The almost animalistic rage that comes when that concept is threatened is more understandable in that context -- narcissistic rage has the look and feel of

	a cornered animal fighting for his life.
	I don't think there is anything in an ACT model that says that all problems are experiential avoidance problems. I'm pretty sure that has never been said. The take is that virtually all human problems involve language (and even there, there are exceptions such as simple skills deficits linked to impoverished environments and things of that kind). But there are many ways language can create mischief. Experiential avoidance is a very common one. It's not the only one.
CONTROL **Self-control - evidence from animal research [7-12-03]** Steve Hayes	Joseph Ciarrochi wrote: I am looking to animal-experimental models to get a better understanding of avoidance and getting stuck. Are there any animal experiments examining the following: Scenario A: animal presses lever to reduce punishment at time 1, but receives greater punishment at time 2. (similar to classic avoidance scenario) Scenario B: animal presses lever to increase punishment at time 1, but receives less punishment at time 2. (similar to exposure) Do animals ever stop pressing the lever in scenario A, and keep pressing the lever in scenario B? Check out Howard Rachlin's work on "self control." He has an article recently out (or upcoming, but I read it in prepublication form a couple of years ago) in *Behavioral and Brain Science* which summarizes some of it. He shows that if you build larger units of behavior over many trials you can establish patterns of animal behavior that are more resistant to the short term / long term conflicts (etc.) that are characteristic of a self-control problem. It's a profound point ... in fact, I used it plus an ACT-based analysis to lose about 45 pounds and I've kept it off for over 2 years. Unfortunately for Howie's theory, he can't explain why his article had that impact on me (but RFT can). If you just throw an animal into the fray, they will always succumb to the scenarios you describe (the aversive now/less aversive later scenario is called a "behavioral fence" and the good now/bad later one a "behavioral trap"). Humans solve the problem (to a degree) through the bidirectionality of language, which enables the category/time/evaluation frames to bring the derived functions of the conceptualized better or worse "future" into the current difficult or pleasing (respectively) present.
CONTROL **Workability of** **METAPHOR** **Control, workability - alchemy [4-20-04]** Leslie Telfer	I have had a patient insist that the control strategies that he'd been using do work, to a level of 60%, e.g., which is less than he would like, but "better than I was before." He wanted my help making them work the other 40% of the time. (We never resolved this, but he has made a lot of progress in ACT, and it became a non-issue.) Some strategies do work pretty well for a limited purpose, such as alcohol or avoidance, but not in the larger scheme. I've had a few other patients insist that control strategies will and even must work even though they haven't so far. I have had 2 patients drop out over this issue, which I attribute to my lack of expertise with this approach. A metaphor for unworkability I've tried, with some success, has to do with alchemy. I ask patients if they know what alchemy was, and if not I explain. We talk about why alchemy failed (because it's not possible to turn base metal into gold), and how alchemists believed wholeheartedly that it *was* possible. Then I wonder if this may be a similar case. It can illustrate how cultural consensus is not infallible.
CONTROL Workability of [cont'd] Susan Orsillo	Leslie, I have to say I believe (based on research and my personal experience) that control strategies do work in changing internal experiences some percentage of the time. Look at the efficacy of PMR, breathing during labor, etc. The thought suppression literature is compelling, but the reality is there are definitely mixed findings (control efforts do not always yield more thoughts and distress). And, there are sure times I stop myself from thinking or feeling something (or at least it seems like I am able to). The problem is sometimes when I really need control to work, it doesn't. Or it works for a time, then quits. Or (most critically) I lose something big along the way. I really, really try to hold on to workability over truth and not debate with my clients about whether control does or doesn't work. I tell supervisees over and over again (and I hope that I really mean this) - if it does turn out that my client is right - and control works (and by works I mean the client really watches their experiences, whether or not they use control, whether it works, and what the consequences are) I will go with control working. I guess that is how I got here. I believed control worked (as a CT therapist). Then I looked at my experience, and my clients' experiences, and decided to go another way.

CONTROL Workability of [cont'd] Kelly Wilson	Sue is right on topic. Workability of control is an empirical matter and best settled in the laboratory of experience. And, of course, in the context of works *for* what. Control is great where it's great. And it is great some places. We have never said otherwise. On the issue Leslie raised - on what control sometimes "wins" you--two of my favorite quotations to share: One quoted by William James in Varieties of Religious Experience: "When the half gods go, the gods arrive." (Here James is quoting Emerson without saying he is--I suppose any classically educated person of the time would have immediately recognized Emerson--I had to hunt when I read it--pre Google and much harder--Give All to Love is the poem.) The other is Bill Wilson in the Alcoholics Anonymous 12 steps and 12 traditions book: "The good is oft times the worst enemy of the best." I think this is what Leslie is pointing to and has been right often in my own self-as-laboratory. I can think of a few half gods I let go of to marvelous good effect.
CONTROL Workability of [cont'd] Steve Mahorney	Leslie, That's interesting. This is very similar to medical situations. Patients who have been taking benzodiazepines (such as Xanax) as a treatment strategy and want to involve physicians in a further pursuit of this approach, will invariably respond, "a little bit" or "some" when asked if the Xanax helped. This, in spite of that fact that neutral observers can detect no difference in symptoms once tolerance is developed to the medication. It's a tricky situation because the response implies that a little of this approach has been good and more will, therefore, be better. Rather than continue this agenda, I've always taken the position that if the approach hasn't worked completely, it hasn't worked at all. This meets with various levels of success depending on the chronicity and multiplicity of problems.
CONTROL Workability of [cont'd] **METAPHOR** **Control, workability of - desert island [4-21-04]** Lisa Coyne	As far as control strategies, I recently muddled through this with a client of mine, and I used the metaphor of that Tom Hanks movie, "Castaway." Control strategies, and I agree with Kelly on this one, are good for what they are good for. The character Tom plays is marooned on this beautiful little island - and at first, he's pretty terrible at living there. But after years, he's gotten to be an expert: he can make fire, he has a nice cave to live in, and he can spear a fish at 20 yards. And that's great, if you want to live marooned on a little island. You might think you have enough - and maybe that is enough for some - at least some of the time. But nothing he learned there would be necessarily useful in the larger world - not did it really help him get off the island. I love the ending of this film - where we are left not with certainty, but possibility, and the choice of direction (I won't describe it in case folks want to watch it who haven't). It makes me very sad when clients choose the island - and I try to be respectful of that choice, and I recognize the enormity and terror of that other choice of launching into the sea. And I stand with and for a client's desire for the possibility of a larger world.
CONTROL Workability of [cont'd] **METAPHOR** **Control, workability of - pre-Copernican astronomy [5-1-04]** Joanne Steinwachs	Quoting Francis De Groot: "We start by asking people what they've tried and how that worked out, with the only intention of discovering the unworkability." I'm a brand new ACT-er, so take this for what it's worth. I find it useful to begin the questioning with 'beginner's mind.' Perhaps what they tried did work out, in some way for them. Of course, if they're stuck in a framework of unworkable rules, then in the larger picture, it doesn't work, but sometimes talking to people about what they do and how it works in their idiosyncratic rule system illuminates the rule system both for them and for me. If I start with the agenda of discovering unworkability, then I can miss a lot of the nuances of trappedness, both for them and for me, and I feel like I move into a place of expert rather than co-explorer. I also feel that using "discovering unworkability" as my guide, respect and curiosity are harder to maintain as my base feelings towards the client. I can't do this if I've got the agenda of discovering unworkability. I have to hold the idea that the system DOES work for the client as a possibility. Usually, in my experience, clients have worked hard and creatively, their shtick does work in some way and it's often an elegant and creative adaptation to some crazy rule. I talk to people about the pre-Copernican world, and how astronomers were trying to describe the path of the planets, starting from the wrong assumption that the earth was the center of the universe. They came up with elegant and complex theories that sometimes could predict the position of the planet. Men spent their entire lives on these theories. To let them go took enormous courage and great pain. That conversation comes after I and the client understand the complex rules that govern their "planetary movement" and we've paid tribute to the fact that the rules can in some ways predict and control their experiences.

COPING STRATEGIES **Avoidance - workability of** **AVOIDANCE** **Coping strategy, as - workability of [12-19-03]** Steve Hayes	Rob Unruh wrote: In reference to the FEAR algorithm, this one youth I work with would rather call Avoidance, 'coping.' The Reason is that Avoidance has a negative connotation. For instance, instead of talking about drug use as an example of avoidance this youth would rather it be termed coping.... One factor is that avoidance behaviors are prevalent and are a key issue. This leads me to believe that terming avoidance 'coping' is just another example of avoidance. I'd appeal to the etymology. I often do that because it helps us see why we choose the words we do and what baggage is coming along for the ride. Etymologically coping is fighting. Nothing wrong with fighting if fighting works, but often it doesn't. If drug use is fighting, what is one fighting against? 99.9% of the time the answer will loop back to regulating one's insides: if so, well, that's what experiential avoidance is all about. In broad brush strokes, emotion-focused and passive coping styles predict poorer outcomes; active coping predicts better outcomes. Easy to see why from an ACT perspective. Fighting with one's insides is just bad business. Sure "avoidance" is negative: that's why it is in that algorithm, which after all is meant to lay out what usually doesn't work. Of course workability is always the ultimate arbiter, but ACT theory and practice has a model of what is and is not likely to work.
COPING STRATEGIES Avoidance - workability of [cont'd] **Substance abuse - workability of** AVOIDANCE Coping strategy, as - workability of [cont'd] **SUBSTANCE ABUSE** **Coping strategy, as - workability of** **THERAPIST** **Experiencing same "psychological space" as client [1-3-04]** Kelly Wilson	I wouldn't worry much about what to call it. It is, in fact, a way of coping. Getting high does work. But only for what it works for. The problem with these coping strategies is that they are often unworkable for lots of other things. If you pit yourself against the experienced fact that they help the person to manage, you will find yourself in trouble. The issue from an ACT perspective is workability. You are right in your reluctance to directly challenge the behavior, because the person likely has a very well-developed set of stories that justify the drug use--some of them are even true. Why activate them? You just end up putting them and you into a set of social/verbal interactions that are both well worn and wholly unproductive. ACT is about upsetting the verbal apple cart. I am typically very sympathetic in these matters. I often think that we are too quick to create drug use as a demon for our clients. Don't get me wrong, they often are demons, but they are not *merely* demons. They are sometimes also the only psychological space the person has in which it feels ok to be inside their own skin. If you want to provide yourself with the right psychological space to understand what you are asking of a serious substance abuser, try this: Think about what offers this to you. In my life, right now, I can think of a few. Here's one. Sitting in my easy chair with one of my school age kids curled up in my lap. My nose in their hair, theirs nuzzled into my neck. Sometimes, briefly, they will just sit there, very still. In those moments, all is right with the world. There is nowhere I need to be, no deadline that matters, no upcoming evaluation that concerns me. Imagine that there is only one place in your whole life that is like that, *and* it turns out that going to that place is also killing you. The fact that it is killing you does not take away from the *other* fact that it is your only source of solace. We have to recognize this or we put ourselves and our clients in peril. Departing drug use, fully experienced, is often as the poets say, sweet sorrow. Sadly, as Bill Wilson, the author of the main AA texts says "the good is oft times the worst enemy of the best." Drugs are good--heck I came of age in the 60's--problem is that they got in the way of the best. If you can keep hold of what it would be like to voluntarily walk away from something you yourself hold very dear, you will interact with greater compassion. The other issue is that clients must make experiential contact with the unworkability. Our telling them that it doesn't work won't cut it--just sets in motion a well-established counterpliant repertoire. I think that if we have a good sense of what the client values, including feeling good, then we can explore the workability of their substance involvement without prejudice. After all, probably most folks on the list use some drug or another in part because of how it makes them feel. I have a near religious experience with coffee every morning--some Ethiopian Horse Harrar blended with an equal part Indian Monsooned Malobar this morning, home roasted just about 20 seconds into second crack, brewed in my press pot after degassing for 12 hours … ahhhh. But no downside (well I take up a bit more counterspace than my wife would like with beans roaster, grinder, pot, 8 kinds of beans, etc.--but little downside). We need to find out about workability long term, short term, and for what precisely (and at what cost) in the client's experience.

COPING STRATEGIES Substance abuse - workability of [cont'd] SUBSTANCE ABUSE Workability of [cont'd] THERAPIST Experiencing same "psychological space" as client [cont'd] **METAPHOR** **Substance abuse, workability of - drugs as employee [1-4-04]** ACT Listserv Member	I would like to reinforce and echo Kelly's post; I really like the example of the feeling he gets when his child is snuggled close - it is a great illustration of what a substance user is looking for in the high. Most drug treatment programs, including some AA based programs, demonize the drug, point out the negative consequences of drug use on both the physical and psychological self, and emphasize the direct legal consequences of usage. This approach rarely takes into account the positive effects of drugs, however temporary and deleterious they may be…. It may be useful to focus on helping the client discover what the drugs are doing for them (the function of drug use), to then evaluate the drug's performance, both short and long term, of this job (I have used a group exercise that utilizes the metaphor of being a boss at work giving an employee evaluation, where the drugs are the employee, the job is what the clients want the drugs to do for them, and they of course are the boss), then start working from there on values and goals etc. You can focus on the typical consequences of drugs, but be aware that most users are more than aware of them and may have even tried to use them to motivate themselves to stop using. Highlighting the costs of drug use during values work can be more effective, because it may be less likely to activate counterpliance and you can directly connect a relationship between the value and how continued drug use will affect moving towards it.
COPING STRATEGIES Substance abuse - workability of [cont'd] SUBSTANCE ABUSE Workability of [cont'd] THERAPIST Experiencing same "psychological space" as client [cont'd] Niklas Törneke *Cross Reference:* *See 3-142 for a later post in a related thread*	I think Kelly's point is extremely important to any work with psychotherapy, regardless of what is the problem in focus. What a human being does always works--for something.... To see that is important for validation of the client's position and experience. But it is also important for the possibility of change, as you get to the question: and what do you really want your actions to work for?
COPING STRATEGIES **Avoidance, distraction etc. - non-clinical populations** **METAPHOR** **Experiential avoidance - bear trap in living room [3-12-03]** Steve Hayes	Francis De Groot wrote: > I think a differentiation has to be made between clinical and non-clinical populations. Probably for clinical populations avoidance is part of the problem. For non-clinical populations avoidance might be part of the solution. It seems likely to me that some forms of distraction, avoidance, and so on are relatively harmless in non-clinical populations. A person who does not know that anxiety can be a problem can relax to control anxiety without an overarching rule backed up by relationally framed aversive consequences (or at least not intense ones). The control effort thus does not elicit the outcome that is being controlled. Said another way, anxiety is not yet something to be anxious about. However, this same pattern, in other contexts, is probably not helpful even for our imagined "non-clinical" person. For example, relationships may be detuned on the same basis. Furthermore, when our imagined person falls into some real hole, these same coping strategies lie in wait to rip up their life. That is probably why experiential avoidance is predictive of poorer quality of life indicators later on, even in the absence of a current struggle. Metaphorically, it is like leaving a bear trap in the corner of the living room, cocked and ready to clamp on a leg that happens to activate it. If you don't step in it, it won't hurt you. But it will if you do. The culture gives such poor instruction in how to defuse and accept (with the possible exception of some aspects of our spiritual and religious traditions), that we leave vast majorities needlessly vulnerable to psychological harm.

	Some forms of distraction (e.g., positive distraction that never attempts to subtract from experience but only to add to it) are probably safe in most contexts. Some are safe only in some contexts. If we had more flexible repertoires, we could learn what works in what contexts, but to do that we need broader skills. That is what is a bit upsetting about the "repression is good" message -- it misses the larger issue. The culture already gives us lots of suppression and avoidance skills. Who will teach us the value of a willingness to experience things we don't like? Who will show us how to do it, in the context of an evaluative verbal repertoire that makes it very difficult?
COPING STRATEGIES **Distraction [3-2-04]** Steve Hayes	Matthew Smout wrote: Just came across a study (and apparently there are a couple of others that have also found this) showing distraction during exposure led to greater anxiety reduction within sessions and between sessions (and greater progress on the BAT) than exposure where the individual focuses on the phobic stimulus. (Attention to phobic stimuli during exposure: The effect of distraction on anxiety reduction, self-efficacy and perceived control, Kristy A. Johnstone and Andrew C. Page).... My impression of ACT is that we are trying to facilitate clients engaging in focused exposure - we wouldn't be instructing distraction would we? Distraction is a very complex issue. Distraction can mean: - attraction to other things - response variability and flexibility - contact with other aspects of the current context - avoidance among other things. It is sometimes said that ACT is against distraction, but it is not so simple. In the ACT book we say (near the section on "Looking for Mr. Discomfort"): In the exposure session, ask the client to look for emotional discomfort and disturbing thoughts. If client begins to experience discomfort, get a description of what the discomfort is in great detail. Look for specific components: bodily sensations, emotions, memories, thoughts, and so on. For each element, ask the client "Just see if you can let go of the struggle with [disquieting thought, feeling, memory, physical symptom] for just a moment, if you can be willing to have it, exactly as it is, not as it says it is or as it is threatening to become." If the client begins to sink into panic, sadness, or some other negative state, suggest that the client direct attention back into the external environment. Ask the client to remain aware of the negative private experiences, but also to notice the other things happening in the external environment. We are obviously talking about distraction ... but I think we show a sensitivity in that last sentence to its functions. The top three senses of distraction can be very positive (attraction to other things, response variability and flexibility, contact with other aspects of the current context) -- if the last (avoidance) is not fed. One thing that happens with that kind of "distraction" is that effective contact with anxiety itself is promoted. When we "sink into panic" only a small range of behavioral functions of these events are activated (e.g., escape). If you watch clients you will almost see their eyes almost roll up into their heads as they disappear into a fused focus on these evaluated experiences. Nothing else can happen in that posture. Knock that off center (e.g., "open your eyes ... look around the room") and something else *can* happen. Kel's rap on extinction mechanisms fits here. I always emphasize that this move is to *add* to what the current moment affords, not to *subtract* anything.
COPING STRATEGIES Distraction [cont'd] **ACT cf.** **DBT [2-3-04]** Jacqueline Pistorello	In terms of the thread on distraction... I thought the following excerpt from a manuscript comparing ACT and DBT might be helpful. The context is discussing similarities and differences between ACT and DBT in terms of control vs. acceptance of private events, after pretty much saying that ACT is acceptance based and DBT relies on both strategies. I'm only pasting a section pertaining to ACT. (From Pistorello & Fruzzetti) In ACT, experiential acceptance of private events is not the target, living a valued life is. The prohibition against experiential avoidance is pragmatic, not philosophical and not absolute. For example, the relentless attack on the control agenda in ACT sessions comes from the fact that undermining excessive literality and experiential avoidance is a difficult task, one which often goes against the mainstream thought. This approach is not maintained by dogma, but rather by workability. ACT authors describe five conditions that make control of private events troublesome, such as when the process of deliberate control contradicts the outcome, and conclude that "If all five contraindications for deliberate control -

are added together, most clinical situations are not likely to be those in which experiential avoidance will succeed (Hayes et al., p.68). Thus, even at a conceptual level, acceptance of private events is not absolute.

Although in terms of intervention ACT does not promote change efforts towards private events as DBT does, it might not necessarily attack such efforts in situations where deliberate change in the private domain is *additive, not subtractive.* For example, in an in-vivo exposure session with an agoraphobic client, the therapist may draw the client's attention to interesting things in the environment in an effort to increase contact with valued living, and not <u>away</u> from the anxiety itself. Similarly, ACT interventions in depression promote behavioral activation, partly to increase contact with reinforcers and perhaps even increase positively-evaluated emotions, but not in <u>opposition</u> to negative ones. Basically, acceptance of private events is always subsumed under workability, and not for its own sake.

Having said that, a word of caution is warranted. There are pragmatic reasons for attacking the control agenda in ACT sessions on a regular basis. In ACT, encouragement of any strategy targeting control of private events might undermine the goal of changing the social-verbal context in which aversive private events come to occasion avoidance behaviors. It might also inadvertently actually reinforce responses that are thought to maintain the excessive literalization of thoughts (Hayes et al., 1999; Hayes & Wilson, 1994)."

COPING STRATEGIES **Distraction, context of - acceptance cf. avoidance [11-23-04]** John Forsyth	Russ Harris wrote: [Do others agree that] if defusion is practised from an agenda of acceptance, distraction may occur (especially if you then become mindfully engaged in a valued activity) but this is not problematic because it's not about intentional experiential avoidance. However if defusion is practised from an agenda of control, then the resulting distraction may well be problematic because it is really just another form of experiential avoidance? I like the breakdown Russ. Distraction in the context of acceptance can mean attraction -- approach -- toward valued ends. Not buying into the painful content may look like distraction from an acceptance posture, when it may be about running into reality and in a direction that one cares about. Distraction, as you point out, can function as experiential avoidance. I think distraction here would operate much like benzos do in the context of exposure -- blunts contact with the direct functions of events. So, when the distraction is not on board, those events will come back with a bite again, and again, and again. Distraction is rarely a workable lasting solution. Imagine living with distraction 24/7 so as to avoid painful content. That would be tough to do.
COPING STRATEGIES Distraction, context of - acceptance cf. avoidance [cont'd] Steve Hayes	Distraction is often subtractive. It is a way to "dis" something that is present and thus has "traction." That kind of distraction is dominantly under aversive control. It can also be additive and appetitive, however. When you do distraction to amplify the number of things that are present and not to get rid of any one thing, then you are no longer "dis"-ing something. You are with something else. That's "A"- "traction," not really distraction. The guess would be that distraction in the service of flexibility is not dangerous and the long term effects are probably positive. In the service of avoidance, it probably is dangerous and the long term effects are likely not positive. The contradictory data on the effects of distraction (the data are messy as heck) I think may come because these two very different functions are mixed together. It matters exactly how questions about it are asked and the contexts it is applied to. For example, with truly unavoidable things distraction is probably more functionally appetitive since the event is not removed. With things that vary (e.g., anxiety) the short term impact of distraction can have negative reinforcement effects, which will lock it in as functionally avoidance. This is why with anxiety exposure work (etc.) when we try to amplify flexibility (e.g., "in addition to noticing your anxiety, look around and see if you can find who has the worst hairdo" etc.) you have to be very careful to prevent this move from becoming part of a functional avoidance class (e.g., by deliberately looping back to awareness of the anxiety; by verbally cautioning that this is in addition to what is present emotionally; etc.). A recent study on tinnitus (which I have, so it jumps out as of interest) showed that ANY coping efforts predict bad outcomes. The best outcomes were associated simply with getting on with living. Moving on is not a matter of "dis"ing, though it can look topographically like distraction. [you can find the tinnitus study with Google Scholar, which is how I found it] It should be said though that all of this could be wrong. In my lab Adam Grundt tried to distinguish these two kinds of distraction in a laboratory task (in his dissertation ... you can order it on the internet) and had limited success. So nailing this down empirically is still out there to be done.

COPING STRATEGIES Distraction, context of - acceptance cf. avoidance [cont'd] Thomas Gustavsson	I think this is a very important point, to detect the shift in any and all behavior, from positive to aversive control. Our days with Kelly in Sweden made this clearer and suddenly I started to notice new small things in therapy that made a difference (in the clients' AND my own behavior...). A psychotic client with some anxiety problems that participate in a group based on acceptance and behavioral activation, told me today about the similarity between what he experienced during exercising mindfulness and piano playing. "I become so absorbed by it that I suddenly found my mind all quiet, it was like the voices wasn't there for a while." I asked him where his psychosis was right then and he started to laugh.... An example of distraction under positive control that he could very clearly distinguish from all of the avoidant ones (drinking, OCD, aggressive behaviors etc. etc.).
COPING STRATEGIES **Distraction, function of [cont'd]** Dermot Barnes-Holmes *Cross Reference:* *See 2-75 for an earlier post in this thread*	Been doing some experimental analog work on acceptance and distraction with pain recently and we've come around to the idea that distraction is NOT ipso facto avoidant if it is used to help achieve some valued goal, rather than simply remove negative content. If we'd thought functionally, rather than topographically, we'd have seen this immediately! But this is a tough one to parse out experimentally (as it seems to be clinically, from the emails I've seen). But it's cool that clinicians and nerdy experimentalists are struggling with the same issue here....
COPING STRATEGIES Distraction, function of [cont'd] **EXPOSURE** **General inc. consent seeking, "distraction"/ defusion [cont'd]** Kelly Wilson *Cross References:* *See 5-213 for a later post in the thread:* *COPING STRATEGIES* *Distraction, function of* *See 2-74 for an earlier post, and 5-213 for a later post in the thread:* *EXPOSURE* *General inc. consent seeking, "distraction"/ defusion*	Even calling it distraction may be problematic. Distraction is a loaded term--it is not descriptive, it carries a functional load--i.e., it implies what the behavior is *for*. Let me give an example: when you are out doing in vivo with an OCD client--a checker, say, they will often spin off into their head; they get locked onto one thing and everything else goes away psychologically. So, what do I do? I might say, as I walk along beside them, notice the sensations on your skin right now. Can you feel the cool of the air conditioning? Where do you feel it the most? Look around, which person in the store is the prettiest? Who looks like they are most tired? etc., etc. You could say that I am distracting them, or you could say that I am bringing them into richer contact with the environment. I am clear about what I am doing, and it is not distraction. I will bring the point home experientially by coming back to the thing they were obsessing on (obsess as hard as you can), then off to other thing, then back. Why? A couple things I am working on. I am working to fatten their interaction with the environment. I want to build fluency in shifting from obsession to rich contact and back, etc. This is all defusion work-- moving from narrow inflexible patterns of behavior to broad and flexible--including the flexibility to get off inflexibility. Even actual distraction, that is, asking the same questions as I asked, but doing it *for* the elimination of the disturbing thought may be somewhat helpful in that it disrupts a high strength stream of behavior (and may make other behavior momentarily more probable). However, as a strategy it has a potential dark side. To the extent that you count on it, to the extent that you *need* it to work, it will likely fail over the long run as you begin to check on how well it is working, bam--you are off into "if you aren't willing to have it you've got it" land. We definitely need to keep our eye on the ball in terms of function. And note that in this example, events can be functionally complex. Their function may look different depending on how molar or molecular our analysis is. Connecting back to what Sonjarita was saying [see 2-75], a BPD client's ability to engage in distraction (even meant functionally) may well represent a broadening of repertoire. My ability to choose a hot bath versus a self-inflicted burn is not an unimportant bit of flexibility. Staying clear on the purpose of such activities from the outset, as Sonja suggested, may help both you and your client recognize things like distraction and self-soothing as steps along the path to flexibility and choice.
COPING STRATEGIES **Suppression/ reappraisal - role of EA/ acceptance**	Ben Shachar wrote: Gross's research on emotion regulation has focused on suppression and reappraisal, showing positive consequences for reappraisal and negative consequences for suppression. Do you think both suppression and reappraisal are forms of experiential avoidance?

COGNITIVE RESTRUCTURING **Cognitive reappraisal, acceptance and [7-7-05]** John Forsyth	I don't think either of these are necessarily forms of experiential avoidance. You need to know for what purposes a person is using either strategy. If it's to run from feelings and related thoughts, then reappraisal may be a form of experiential avoidance. Even so, I would caution all of us to not see this as a problem. We are all avoidant to some degree -- it is hard to escape this fact. It's the rigidity stuff that makes emotion regulation, experiential avoidance, fusion, etc. potentially problematic because it tends to be rule-based where the rules are largely unworkable and ineffective in the present context. In fact, you could argue that acceptance is a broad-band reappraisal strategy that affects both antecedent and consequent forms of emotion regulation. Reappraisal, in the emotion regulation literature, is not simply about thinking differently (i.e., replacing cognitive content with "newer, better, different" cognitive content). It is mostly about developing new relations with cognitive content. In fact, I would say that reappraisal is about flexibility -- same with suppression. So, you may still be scared about something but also say "I am scared and I can get through this" in a particular context and for a given purpose. At other times, reappraisal would make no sense (e.g., staying in a traumatic situation) and the more reasonable approach would simply be to run like hell. If you get into this emotion regulation literature, and know something about the ACT and RFT literature, you ought to start seeing a connection. The emotion regulation literature has largely retained its affinity with functional accounts -- mostly socio-developmental. Acceptance is a broad-band emotion regulation strategy. It transforms approach-avoidance relations into approach-approach relations. The conflict goes away when this happens. With acceptance, the very need to regulate first in order to take effective action second weakens. What you get then is behavioral action -- movement forward (approach) in important life areas and with a range of psychological content (approach). If anyone is interested, we have a chapter that banged some of this out in the context of fear learning and with some inspiration from a largely ignored paper by Steve that appeared in BT many moons ago.
COPING STRATEGIES Suppression/ reappraisal - role of EA/ acceptance [cont'd] COGNITIVE RESTRUCTURING Cognitive reappraisal, acceptance and [cont'd] **EVIDENCE** **Experiential avoidance/ acceptance - mediating factor [7-7-05]** Todd Kashdan	With some colleagues, we just submitted a paper demonstrating that the negative consequences of emotion suppression and the positive consequences of cognitive reappraisal are mediated (or partially mediated in the case of reappraisal relationships) by experiential avoidance/ acceptance. Emotion suppression appears to be a component process of experiential avoidance. As for cognitive reappraisal, it seems intuitive that tendencies to reflectively search for pathways to solve problems may be related to more adaptive outcomes as a function of low experiential avoidance (or high acceptance). In a given situation, there are a variety of meanings and features to focus on. Cognitive reappraisal involves strategically selecting ways in which situations are construed to reduce their negative emotional impact. The benefits of reappraisal appear to be a function of adapting a non-judgmental, accepting stance to the personal meaning assigned to a situation, and the triggered emotional consequences. However, our line of work is merely a starting point in disentangling these processes....
COPING STRATEGIES Suppression/ reappraisal - role of EA/ acceptance [cont'd] COGNITIVE RESTRUCTURING Cognitive reappraisal, acceptance and [cont'd] EVIDENCE Experiential avoidance/ acceptance - mediating factor [cont'd]	Ah, this is so cool. Exactly what one might expect. I've had that "cognitive reappraisal" finding almost thrown at me once or twice lately ... as if it proved that cognitive disputation and challenging is therefore necessary. How poorly understood correlational data overwhelms actual experimental analysis escapes me. It seems to be driven by the label, not the actual questions asked and possible mechanisms to explain the data. ... There was an item [in the original AAQ] that said something like "You can't control what you think and feel." As I recall, particularly successful ACT patients actually sometimes changed in the "wrong direction." They experienced directly that they have enormous control over what thoughts and feelings DO ... which almost immediately gave them more "control" where it REALLY counts. And -- irony of ironies -- they often saw directly that this move quickly even had an impact on form and frequency. In effect you even can control the form, just by letting go of all suppressive and avoidant attempts to control the form. This is the sense in which we've always said things like "you can control panic ... you just can't control anxiety." People should remember that this talk of lack of control is clinical talk, not scientific talk. We warn of that in the book and I always warn of it both in therapy and in workshops. By the way, there was a thread on this recently and I said nothing but no one has yet responded. I would like to say just this given the late hour -- there is nothing in ACT or RFT that literally says that emotional change or cognitive change is impossible. Hell, RFT is all about cognitive change ... which is why its biggest ultimate application (if it all works according to plan) will probably be education, not therapy. And

CONTROL **Content change - scientific cf. clinical talk [7-7-05]** Steve Hayes	acceptance / defusion is about the biggest change you can think of. "You can't change it" talk literally means something more like "you can't first have another history in order to succeed, and trying to suppress or avoid your own history is dangerous." Said in another way -- it is talk that produces changes in the social / verbal context (control and reason-giving) and that in turn can change the functions of private events. The scientific rules are something more like: 1. If you want to change existing emotions and thoughts, change their functions. 2. If you want to change their functions, help clients let go of changing their forms. 3. If you want new forms, go for it, provided it does not violate step 2. 4. If you want to change the form of existing emotions and thoughts, see step 1. But you can't quite DO that clinically because folks so want "4" that they try to DO 1-2-3 (what are the numbers?) in order to do 4, and voila, they are no longer doing 1-2-3! So we have funny talk in ACT to get around that problem. We use language to attack normal language functions. But SCIENTIFICALLY it is obviously wrong that systematic cognitive and emotional change is impossible. If that were not true ACT would have a much higher hill to climb because we would have to argue for "success" using entirely new measures since almost all of the measures are based on cognitive and emotional change. Shockingly (to me anyway), we don't. I used to think we would HAVE TO invent new quality of life measures etc. before we could even have a chance to compete. Not so. Regularly ACT does well using existing cheeseball measures that never anticipated the indirect "second order" agenda of ACT folk. Anyway, this is very twisty and very exciting Todd....
COPING STRATEGIES Suppression/ reappraisal - role of EA/ acceptance [cont'd] **COGNITIVE RESTRUCTURING** Cognitive reappraisal, acceptance and [cont'd] **EVIDENCE** Experiential avoidance/ acceptance - mediating factor [cont'd] **ACT cf.** **CBT - cognitive restructuring/ acceptance [7-7-05]** Todd Kashdan	With an emphasis on cognitive reappraisal/ restructuring, I recently had a long discussion with a colleague about the similarities and differences of CBT and ACT/ Mindfulness techniques. Of note, I was strictly trained in the Barlow, Craske, Heimberg, Clark, Foa, etc. incarnation of CBT. In my experience, many clients have inordinate difficulty integrating techniques such as cognitive disputation and replacement (although many can and I have seen very impressive gains!)... it simply is not a natural, easily integrative approach to dealing with one's spontaneous private experiences alone and in social contexts (e.g., disrupting and challenging oneself in the midst of conversing with others). In contrast, being fully aware of one's values, private experiences, and actions, and actively exploring (with as little judgment as possible) the ways in which one's values and actions ebb and flow with one another, is a much more natural, spontaneous way of being oneself in important life domains. From a social perspective, awareness and acceptance leads to some of the most rewarding and memorable conversations whereas filtering and challenging are remembered as excessively effortful endeavors with little pay-off (from a cost-benefit perspective). To me, one of the most satisfying ways of living is one of authenticity... being in more and more situations, with and without other people, in which one is naturally and effortlessly oneself in tandem with core values... Now what is interesting is that if you go back to the origins of CBT, Beck and Emery (1985) explicitly discuss the importance of helping clients accept their thoughts and behaviors, and then, working with them to minimize the suffering they cause. I could be mistaken, but this non-judgmental view was never elaborated and appears to have been abandoned in the current, dominant incarnation of CBT. Sure, CBT has exposure-based therapies to enhance contact with unwanted events. From a somewhat different orientation, acceptance-based models focus on the tyranny of excessive evaluations and the deliberate efforts to evaluate and control these events as opposed to changing the content ... in essence, the goal is not to modify the content of an individual's cognitions, behaviors, and emotions as it is to change the relationship one has with these cognitions, behaviors, and emotions while the content remains the same. While some proponents of CBT are successfully integrating acceptance-based components, others want to claim these components without attending to the philosophical underpinnings that are often diametrical to CBT theories, tools, strategies, and exercises.... I think that cognitive restructuring really hits the jackpot when people are accepting of personal events and experiences, yet, work to align their choice of interpretation with their values. With the advent of more sophisticated assessment tools, perhaps this process may differentiate responders and non-responders to CBT over and above symptom reduction. What do others think? Anyway, here is the current citation and abstract of my findings on experiential avoidance, suppression, and cognitive reappraisal: Kashdan, T. B., Barrios, V., Forsyth, J. P., & Steger, M. F. (2005). Experiential avoidance as a generalized psychological vulnerability: Comparisons with coping and emotion regulation strategies. (Manuscript submitted for review)

Chronic and pervasive experiential avoidance was targeted as a core mechanism in the development and maintenance of psychological distress, and disruption of pleasant, engaging, and spontaneous activity. Extending previous work, we conducted two studies to test hypotheses concerning the toxic influences of experiential avoidance. Of particular interest was whether experiential avoidance accounted for relationships between coping and emotion regulation strategies on anxiety-related pathology (Study 1) and psychological distress and hedonic functioning over the course of a 21-day monitoring period (Study 2). In Study 1, experiential avoidance mediated the effects of maladaptive coping, emotional responses styles, and uncontrollability on anxiety-related distress (e.g., anxiety sensitivity, trait anxiety, suffocation fears, and body sensation fears). In Study 2, experiential avoidance was associated with diminished daily positive affective experiences and healthy life appraisals, and less frequent positive events, and greater negative affective experiences and more frequent negative events. Experiential avoidance completely mediated the effects of the emotion regulation strategies of suppression and reappraisal on daily negative and positive experiences. Further consideration of experiential avoidance as a generalized diathesis and toxic process will be useful in improving our understanding of the etiology, phenomenology, and treatment of anxiety conditions, general human suffering, and disruptions in hedonic capacity....

CREATIVE HOPELESSNESS
General [4-15-04]
Kelly Wilson

Sven Rydberg wrote:

I remember two clients who on their own--before they even contacted me--had worked out the unworkability of previous experiential avoidance. I found it unnecessary and even potentially counterproductive to again immerse them in "hopelessness." With them, I used relaxation procedures ... and went directly towards values--with very quick and good results.

I don't think I ever use the term creative hopelessness with clients. It is a weird term; I personally like it because it has an ambiguity to it, a juxtaposition that appeals to me. But then I like, really like, Camus' essay An Absurd Reasoning. Probably diagnostic, but I have had to cultivate a deep appreciation for ambiguity in order to stay alive (really alive). There is something at the heart of dense ambiguity and our capacity to sit with it, to appreciate it, to savor it; that seems very important to me. Don't have it worked out entirely. (gotta get that damned Camus paper written!) So using the term - no incredible need there.

As to procedurally--well therapists do not like the CH work. Psychology selects for people who are troubled by the suffering of others, and want to ease it. So I always want people to check their motives - are we skipping it because we don't like how we feel when they feel how they feel? Or, is it not indicated? Or both? (could be)

Here is the test. The content one is hopeless about is very likely to show up for a client when pursuing a value. So, a concrete example. Say I am hopeless about relationships. Well, that sense of hopelessness will very likely show up when I am engaged in activities that could create a relationship. If thoughts of hopelessness generate strong antecedent stimulus control (increase arousal, generally suppress operant responding--except escape), then just when I need to *be there* in order to make the relationship possible, I will be off in my head or off down the road.

So, if that is the case, if I have no behavioral flexibility in the presence of these thoughts--there is work to be done. What kind, well it is not merely getting the person to "understand" that control doesn't work--that's not creative hopelessness anyway. I want to generate flexibility--at the level of process, creative hopelessness really works the respondent end of the behavioral equation (strong antecedent stimulus control). At the level of procedure--I will get them interacting with hopelessness in new and varied ways. Like what happens if we touch that darkness and then say "What if there is something of tremendous value, right at the center of all that pain? What if there were a way of beholding that pain that could cause you to say-- 'there is life here'? What if there is something in your pain that can allow you to hear your fellows? Allow you to be fully human with your children, your wife?" And now I ask *you* (yes you) this about your own pain--what if it is not the enemy? What if it could allow you to really hear your clients? What if it is not something to neatly package up before you go into session, but instead the thing that can make you an instrument? Would you build a room on the house for it? Would you set a place at the dinner table? Would you honor it? Hmmmm? Could it be? Me thinks so?

What just happened? The client interacted in a different way with their hopelessness, with their pain. Perhaps they were curious. Before they were certain. Where there was certainty (and the absence of vitality and flexibility) now there is possibility, a little spark of life. Now we are getting somewhere. Woo hoo!

In a more straightforward way, no you absolutely don't need to do CH like it says in the book. If it needs to be done, you will end up doing it. Why? Well as you pursue values, it will appear as an obstacle--then you will do defusion of hopelessness, and the emergence of what we like to call creative hopelessness.

CREATIVE HOPELESSNESS
General [cont'd]

Re when to introduce creative hopelessness ...

I often begin with values and goals and then shift later to creative hopelessness when working with involuntary or semi-voluntary clients with 'low motivation' for treatment such as those involuntarily

COMPONENT SEQUENCING **Low motivation clients [4-19-04]** Patty Bach	committed to inpatient treatment, some substance abusing clients, and those attending therapy primarily at the urging of someone else. You can sort of go into the system through the back door by starting with exploration of goals and values, whether behavior is consistent with stated goals and values; barriers to attaining desired outcomes; "what stands between you and X?"; "How has that worked for you?", etc. - then onto CH.
CREATIVE HOPELESSNESS General [cont'd] James Herbert	For what it's worth, a brief comment re CH. I generally use it pretty much "by the book" with one exception. When asked the inevitable question, "So, doc, then what do I do?" I don't respond "I don't know" for two reasons. First, it would not be entirely genuine, as (hopefully) I do have some ideas about what is likely to be helpful. Second, it risks coming across as dismissive of the client's suffering. I suppose one could argue that it's technically true that the therapist never really does know exactly what will work for any particular client, but that strikes me as splitting hairs. On the other hand, the last thing I'd want to do is to give a simplistic rule like, "well, perhaps you can learn to accept unpleasant experiences and move forward with life, etc. etc." What I do instead is to say something like (paraphrasing), "There's no simple answer as to what exactly is going to work for you. I'm optimistic that by working together we can come up with a whole new way of approaching the problem that is very likely to help." I then resist saying anything more specific at that stage. In my experience, this approach achieves the goals of CH while simultaneously providing a (non-specific) glimmer of hope and while allowing me to maintain genuineness.
CREATIVE HOPELESSNESS General [cont'd] **METAPHOR** **ACT, introduction to - kids in car; boat in ocean [4-20-04]** Matthew Smout	In my experience, creative hopelessness is less contrived and works better if you remain very sensitive to what the client has been through. If the client has been struggling with a control agenda for a long time, it will come through in your assessment with them if you are sure to ask how long they've had the problem, and what they've done to try and deal with it. There may be fatigue from struggling, fear that they will never find a way to make the pain go away, or the beginning of resignation - something that indicates they have been trying hard and unsuccessfully to control private experience. On the other hand, a client who is presenting for the first time with a problem that has emerged recently with a change in life circumstances and is looking for a couple of strategies to deal with it, may be less likely to have had the same experience of unworkable control attempts and a lot of the creative hopelessness material may not resonate with them at all. I've found it's pretty safe to start with the assessment - what does the client want, what have they done to try and get that, and how has it worked? If that's done in detail, you'll know whether there are unhelpful habits (attempts to control the uncontrollable) that need to be eroded before the client can engage in something new (defusion, acceptance, valued activity scheduling). In terms of sequencing, it would make sense to give the overview of therapy / informed consent after this kind of assessment had been done - you can then tailor your forecast of therapy a bit to each client. In terms of rationale, I have found it helpful to use one or two metaphors that describe the therapy in very general terms. The first works for most situations, the second mainly for more chronic clients: Screaming kids in the car: "It's like you're driving along with screaming kids in the back seat and passenger seat. And they tantrum until you turn the wheel their way. Sometimes you just let them grab the wheel. Sometimes you just want to kick them out of the car. Mostly you wish they'd just shut up. This therapy is about helping you to drive where you want, no matter whether the kids are screaming or silent. It's not about kicking the kids out of the car - we don't want to kill the kids, they're part of you. But you are the driver. So this therapy is about helping you be clear where you want to drive, and learning to drive with screaming kids." Boat in the ocean: "It's like you've been in the ocean. Sometimes you've been swimming against the tide, sometimes you've been engulfed in waves, and sometimes you've given up swimming - and been pushed out to sea wherever the waters take you. This therapy is about giving you a motorboat - you will still be in touch with the water - it will still crash into you and swish around you, but you have a motor and can steer. This therapy is about helping you decide where to travel and to keep you travelling in that direction, even when the weather is rough."
CREATIVE HOPELESSNESS General [cont'd] Steve Hayes	If you want to pick a pivot point about CH it is this: if you are talking *about* it, it isn't it. I find CH work uplifting, real, validating, and most of all human. To me it means embracing your experience unvarnished, straight on, no dodges. It is not criticism; it is not from the outside; the emotion it induces is not hopelessness. The emotion is bittersweet -- both sad and hopeful. Painful and empowering. It feels open, spent, sober, humble, and courageous. My advice: forget the words; go for the experience. Don't tell the client what to experience -- get with that experience. All you have to do is to stand with it. If CH isn't there, it isn't anywhere. I'm reading a cool article on ACT and negative schizophrenia comparing ACT and existentialism. If the authors are willing and are on the list, I'd ask that they post the section on CH from that article (or what they call "creative despair"). It did a better job than I have in creating a picture of what it might mean to simply validate the client's experience, even when that experience is frightening.

CREATIVE HOPELESSNESS General [cont'd] John Forsyth	I see creative hopelessness as part of the process of unfolding layers of unworkability with the client. Former solutions to problems are not solutions, but dead ends to living a life. By making contact with creative unworkability (hopelessness), clients are likely to become more open to creative workability as an alternative way of living.
CREATIVE HOPELESSNESS General [cont'd] **EMOTION** **"Negative", healthiness of; creative hopelessness [4-29-04]** Steve Hayes	Hope Jackson wrote: In many cases, hopelessness seems like it might create more pain. Hopelessness "bought" is what is unhealthy. Guilt, anxiety, etc. are the same way. They aren't just emotions: they contain a fused thought (I am bad; nothing can ever change; there is something fundamentally wrong with me). It is the fusion and avoidance that is the problem, not the emotion. All those emotions, felt as a feeling, can be healthy. They are just the past being brought into the present by the current situation. Guilt held that way is a warning about possible values violations; hopelessness is a warning about unworkable strategies; etc. But good old CH is not an emotion anyway ... most often the emotion is quickly light or even hopeful ... if it is a so called negative emotion that shows up it is more likely to be sadness or anger or guilt, not the emotion of hopelessness. Sometimes ... but not the majority of times and certainly not always.
CREATIVE HOPELESSNESS **Hope, and - use/ meaning of terms; hope as avoidance [8-28-03]** Steve Hayes	Joseph Ciarrochi wrote: Steve H. et al. no longer seem overly happy with using the term creative hopelessness. They strongly recommend not using it in therapy. How about "creative letting-go"? I actually like the term for what it is *about*. I caution against using it in therapy as a term, though not as a prohibition, primarily because it often seems to be misunderstood to refer to a feeling, not a process of abandoning a destructive agenda and being open to something truly new. Weird fact #72: Martha Beck (a bit of an ACT fan) used "embrace creative hopelessness" in her latest column in Oprah's magazine. I was OK with how she used it, from the brief moment I had to look at the column. Maybe if she can get away with it, we can. So I guess you can use it in therapy if it works to do so ... but be careful (and the term was not really designed for that originally). The reason I'm not always happy with it in general ACT training is that some folks learning ACT get spun by it. It was meant to be almost an oxymoron that would leave an open space behind. And often it works that way, but sometimes it seems to lead astray. So, I'm not 100% sure it was worth it, but I actually haven't abandoned it ... I'm just more cautious about it. "Facing one's experience," "abandoning an agenda that hasn't worked," "giving up on what hasn't paid off," "radically validating one's actual experience" etc. are what this weird term is about. If that is how it is used, I'm still OK with it. "Feel hopeless and you will be saved" is NOT what the term ever was about.
CREATIVE HOPELESSNESS Hope, and - use/ meaning of terms; hope as avoidance [cont'd] John Bush	I don't use the *term* in talking to clients, but I often deploy the concept. Example: "Well, it looks like no matter how much you need and deserve X and how hard you try, things just don't come out the way they're supposed to."
CREATIVE HOPELESSNESS Hope, and - use/ meaning of terms; hope as avoidance [cont'd] Patty Bach	I can't recall the source, and I remember reading that instead of hope or hopelessness one should cultivate "no hope." Along those lines, Pema Chodron (and probably others) uses hopelessness as 'abandoning hope,' because hope, like wanting, is about what isn't present. She likens hope and fear in that both are about what is missing and are in the future and rob us of the present moment. In a more humorous light she suggests that "Abandon hope is the beginning of the beginning. You could even put 'Abandon hope' on your refrigerator door instead of more conventional aspirations like 'Every day in every way I'm getting better and better.'"
CREATIVE HOPELESSNESS Hope, and - use/ meaning of terms; hope as avoidance [cont'd] Kelly Wilson	Joseph Ciarrochi wrote: I wonder if people can use "hope" as a kind of avoidance move? Hope has tremendous potential as an avoidance move. This is why we have to attend to the functional properties of behavior--not its form. Hoping can be something done as an alternative to living. It can be, need not, but can be exactly as you say--excessively future oriented at the expense of the present. Values involve a constructed "later," but they are wholly non-vital unless they are lived in the present moment.

CREATIVE HOPELESSNESS Hope, and - use/ meaning of terms; hope as avoidance [cont'd] Steve Hayes	ACT Listserv Member wrote: I think "abandoning hope" should really be clarified before it's used. As discussed, "hope" can be pretty significant for some people, just as "faith" can be significant. In the proper context. "Abandon false hope," or "abandon hope that has no grounding in reality," seems more appropriate than just "abandoning hope" altogether. Dante places "abandon all hope" over the entry gate to Hell because in (some forms of) Christianity the final "destination of the soul" is fixed. There's no hope your "soul" will ever leave.... It is a bit creepy to link creative hopelessness to "hope" in the sense of "faith, hope, and charity." At least it is for this Catholic / Jew (I practice neither, by the way, but I have that background). Fortunately you don't have to. "Hope" in a biblical context is different than our current lay usage of the term. The OED tells me that in biblical terms "hope" generally means "to trust, have confidence"; e.g., Psalms 49 "The word upon which thou hast caused me to hope." ["Confidence," as many ACT folk will know since it is discussed in the book, essentially means "with self-fidelity" etymologically. Trust is linked to the concept of "strength" and "comfort" in the original Latin sense of "with strength."] I think hope in a biblical sense fits very much with ACT at the level of philosophy and process. Considered as a kind of trust or strength, the hope we are standing in is in the present. It can include a future too ... as kind of extension and fulfillment of the present. If I hope/trust that my beloved loves me, I am standing in the extended present that includes that she will love me tomorrow. If that is not so, "hope" devolves into "maybe she will" which soon becomes "now I fear she doesn't." You can see why that more common sense of hope does not fit Biblically (nor would it in relationships ... "I hope you love me" is very unlikely to be very intimacy enhancing). Biblically, "hope" was not about "maybe something will change tomorrow." God's love included a tomorrow but it was here today. In a Biblical sense, "Abandon all hope" over the gates of hell means something like "abandon trust in God and yourself; you are apart from God's strength or love." In more common terms "hope" means "expectation of something desired." You can see why the Buddhists go after it (attachment and desire being a chief source of suffering in their view). "Expect" etymologically means something like "deprived of seeing." It is quite similar to "want" actually. Living life on the basis of what is NOT present is just not very empowering, which is why leading with change as the basis of being able to really live sometime in the future (whether that be in the language of motivation, achievement, removal of pain, successful psychotherapy, etc.) is so troublesome. ACT is change focused, but on the basis of radical acceptance of the experience of the current moment. So the Buddhist view of hope makes sense from an ACT perspective. However, when in China one speaks Chinese. The hidden trap in the common sense concept of "hope" is hard to detect in our culture. On this listserv is one thing, in therapy is another. I might go after "hope" in a normal clinical context if I detected its entanglement with avoidance or with trying to live your life in a state of fusion with an imagined future that is not here yet ... but if that happened I would tread a bit carefully for the reasons this listserv dialogue makes clear. "Hope" just has a lot of connotations....
CREATIVE HOPELESSNESS Hope, and - use/ meaning of terms; hope as avoidance [cont'd] Patty Bach	The distinction between talking about hope/hopelessness in this sort of listserv discussion versus hopelessness in clinical work is nicely said in the ACT book (p. 107): 'This phase of ACT does not involve talking *about* hopelessness. It involves facing the *experienced* hopelessness of the client. If there is a lot of dialogue *about* the issue of hopelessness, chances are the therapist is trying to "convince" the client, which is a certain route to trouble.' ACT never calls for the client to "abandon ALL hope ye who enter here"; in 'creative hopelessness,' hopelessness is limited to 'abandoning hope' in the workability of the old change agenda. The therapist makes clear that the client is not hopeless - only that the old change agenda is 'hopeless' in that it hasn't 'worked' - this conclusion is reached based upon the experience/history of the client and the futility of past change efforts. In the metaphor of letting go of the rope, one lets go - abandons hope - because it is necessary to make room for something else. The ACT therapist at this time makes statements such as "don't believe a word I am saying" or "I don't expect that what we've done here will be of any help," because to do otherwise would most likely create more of the same kind of unworkable hope. This is the 'leap of faith' - one abandons hope in the old agenda and for a time one is 'hopeless' - there is no agenda. This absence of a change agenda may be experienced as unsettling and it is 'creative' because, rather than abandoning all hope/trust/fidelity, it creates space for the emergence of a different kind of hope in relation to the presenting problems. I'm not so certain (hopeful?) about this, and I make a functional link between 'creative hopelessness' and acceptance - and maybe a counterpart, say 'creative hope' could be functionally linked to commitment?

EMOTION **Anger - clinical issues [10-5-04]** Steve Hayes	Luke Moynahan wrote: Does anyone have any thoughts about and/or experiences with (possible) RFT/ACT approaches to "anger problems"? From an ACT perspective it would seem that the first thing to try is straight-ahead acceptance, defusion, self stuff with values focused on the issue of acting angrily / aggression etc. This seems esp. worth trying given that a lot of the bad health effects from anger are from suppressed anger, the bad social effects are from bad behavior, not the feeling. From an RFT perspective the thing that seems most interesting to me is the whole issue of right and wrong. Over and over when I dig into anger I find hurt or anxiety that is being avoided by anger -- but the glue that prevents exposure is the verbal behavior about how what was done was not right, fair, proper etc. I think we need to really dig into this on the RFT side. It bears on detected relational coherence as a reinforcer for relational framing in verbally mature individuals, but goes beyond that into the arbitrary social consequences occasioned by relational coherence, and the say-do correspondence that then follows. That combo can be poisonous in the case of angry and aggressive individuals: I've had clients say that they "had to" hit because some given behavior was "not right" - as if the lack of correspondence would be some kind of sin.
EMOTION Anger - clinical issues [cont'd] Niklas Törneke	Patty Bach wrote: I've recently encountered a few clients in individual and group treatment who live primarily in violent neighborhoods in Chicago's infamous Southside, and who use the "I had to hit/shoot him" argument and frame it as "he disrespected me and I had to do it to show others that they have to respect me and/or if I didn't do it then everyone would disrespect me." When I make a move to address the workability of aggression as a strategy for responding to 'disrespect' clients insist that it works. These same clients are often involved with the criminal justice system because of their history of violence and want to stay out of prison, be good fathers, and have been shot, have seen loved ones maimed and killed, etc. and so have no shortage of experiences of the negative consequences of aggression. I'm not sure where to go in treatment when, in response to asking about workability, the client insists that "violence works." I think part of the issue is confusing being feared with being respected, and/or not acknowledging that one is responding to *feeling* 'disrespected' - a la the example in the ACT book of the person who says "I need more confidence" - and the client who insists that 'aggression works' is not likely to go there. It seems to me that the classical ACT intervention in a situation like this is "works for what?" Aggression does work for something, of course. Ultimately, if it really works for what they want (all over) what's the problem for them? If not, then there is an experience of "not working." Go for that. But that is maybe too basic for your situation?
EMOTION Anger - clinical issues [cont'd] Rainer Sonntag	Another move in addition to that suggested by Niklas may be to go right into the moment of the session, for example, by asking the client "What thoughts, feelings, bodily sensations come up with you while we are talking about whether aggression works or not?" or "Do you hear me saying that I say that you are doing wrong?" or "Let's go into a recent violent encounter you had. What comes up when you remember it right now?" (and then going through the remembered events and the reactions to them as they appear in session very detailed) or "Imagine that I would act in a disrespectful way against you, how do you feel about that as you hear me saying this? And then imagine that you would hit and hurt me, how do you feel about that?" In my experience, when clients insist that whatever problematic behaviors work it often turns out that the issue on the table in session is that right/wrong thing. I then work to make this issue explicit and target it directly. With some clients this may happen very early in treatment.
EMOTION **Anger - general inc. possible functions of [12-21-04]** Jonathan Weinstein	Mike Kirkeberg wrote: Is anger always a dirty emotion/discomfort/feeling? In my experience, anger tends to show up as a reaction to another feeling, thought etc. that is less tolerable than anger. Most of the time it happens so quickly that anger functions to help me avoid feeling some variation of hurt or scared. Clinically, I have found it difficult to get clients to talk about times when they were angry because it generally ends up in the land of regret, a place where an avoidance strategy like anger is just another way of digging one's hole. Instead, I have asked clients to discuss resentments (something Kelly has adapted from the 4th step of AA). As hw or in session if need be, I'll have the client fill out a chart with some version of the following topics:

	I'm resentful at... (what they did) It affects my... (what it hurt) What I did or didn't do... What it cost me... My fear was... (what I was protecting). Sometimes I will do one for myself with the client just to humanize and dignify the process of accepting parts of our behavior that we don't like. I think this exercise can open up avenues for exposure and defusion and allow the client to see how their anger functions to limit one's possibilities. It can also present an opportunity for the client to clarify what they value. For example, if feeling hurt and scared did not have to be chased off by getting angry, what would you do instead?
EMOTION Anger - general inc. possible functions of [cont'd] Patty Bach	When would anger be "bad"? I can't imagine suggesting that "this fear/sadness/happiness is okay while that other fear/sadness/happiness is bad" and I don't think anger is fundamentally different. What does seem different is that people seem more likely to see the actions of another as a "cause" of anger and feel they must do something "about" the anger and usually something in relation to someone else - e.g., if that bad driver "scares" someone they may drive away or stop driving - if the same driver angers someone road rage might ensue and they feel a need to get back at the driver. Put another way, anger seems to be more outwardly directed while anxiety and depression often seem more inner-directed (perhaps thereby the oft used description of depression as "anger turned inward"?). No feeling is ever "bad"; feelings, including anger, are what show up given one's history. What is relevant to ACT is what one does when anger shows up. And mindfulness might decrease the intensity or duration of anger and even if it does not, what is one doing with their feet (or mouth) when angry? The anger management client who feels unable to focus or to "move in a valued direction" does not strike me especially different from the anxiety client feeling the same when anxious, or the depressed client when feeling depressed. Even when anger looks like avoidance, e.g., feeling anger in relation to anxiety, is the anger functionally in the service of "avoiding" anxiety, or is anger what shows up when one feels anxious or sad and attributes that state of affairs to the actions of another (anxiety + evaluation of anxiety → anger)? I suspect that sometimes formally, anger might 'mask' anxiety (or whatever), and functionally it is another feeling that shows up as a consequence of an evaluation of some event. In some cases it looks more like it is in the service of avoiding negative evaluation (by self or another) than in the service of avoiding anxiety or some other feeling per se, e.g., I'm mad because you scared me, not because I avoid fear, but because scaring people is a "bad" thing to do. A different kind of "anger management" problem, seen more often in women than in men, is in the case of someone who denies ever feeling angry or who feels anxious or sad or depressed in situations that would tend to make others angry - anger + evaluation (anger = bad) → anxiety/depression/guilt?? And this client might deny that "I'm mad because you scared me" and focus on the fear while 'avoiding' the anger... Ultimately, there is no universal sense in which anger is "good" or "bad"; it depends on how the individual relates to it and how that relating to it "works" in context.
EMOTION Anger - general inc. possible functions of [cont'd] John Bush	To unconfuse: anger is anger. It might be avoidance behavior or it might not. It also might or might not be an appetitive behavior. Our job is to try to suss out just what its function is in a given instance. No amount of definitional (verbal) behavior on our part will eliminate the need for that.
EMOTION Anger - general inc. possible functions of [cont'd] John McNeill	Distinguishing anger vs. aggression: I agree that anger is neither a 'problem' nor a 'dirty' anything, and that for some it may be hierarchically arranged as less threatening relative to other unwelcome experience. We need to be reminded that anger is a construct, not a self-existent *thing*. *Anger* exists nowhere. Contextually speaking, anger is not a *state of possession* but rather a *way of becoming* - and being so-of-itself, is inseparable from the world of contingencies. More specifically, anger denotes a particular contingent phase of private experience, often occasioned by loss, aversive events, other changing life circumstances, or by verbal-abstractive construal of such events. Some in the behavioral community have described anger as 'frustrated non-reward.' In any case, resentment, blame, and unforgiveness are often correlative features. The 'problem of anger' [or any other unwelcome experience] reflects the unwillingness to *presence* the edginess of bodily manifestations once they have come to dominate our experience. In running away from the immediacy of our experience, we may habitually 'spin off' harshness as a kind of mindless-acting in the world. For some, anger and aggression coincide as 'fused' partners. Anger is so-of-itself, but aggressive responding in humans is a choice-act, at least under most conditions. Aggression as a form of social control owes to communities that reinforce its functions - those cultures that affirm aggression get more of it. And its spillover may come to affect non-violent others. So-called 'dirtiness' is <u>not</u> reflected in the experience of anger per se, but rather in the reasons used to justify harshness in the world.

	Anger and fear are opposed-sides of one experience; likewise harshness and compassion oppose each other. Perhaps if we were less fearfully concerned with affirming *who we are* through positional standings [rightness/wrongness] or coercive action, but instead affirmed ourselves through our choices - *what we want to matter about*, we would pursue a non-aggressive path. By listening to what anger says, we may even be convinced by what anger says, but by not doing as anger says, we cultivate a new life-practice. In this way, we *learn to stay* [Pema Chödrön], thus *relating to* rather than *relating from* the immediacy of our angry moments. But then one would have to be mindful of the totality of the situation. Insofar as the hopeless logic of avoidant coping is reversed, psychological acceptance embraced, and value-based commitments pursued, we may begin to chip away at the harshness that hardens our experience of others, the world, and ourselves. The behavioral exercise outlined by Jonathan is a step in the right direction.
EMOTION Anger - general inc. possible functions of [cont'd] John Forsyth	Feeling or thinking angry need not be about acting angry or acting on anger. I've been thinking quite a bit lately of the processes involved when we talk about "pushing someone's buttons" and the outcome of that being anger. I imagine that most of us know what this experience is like. The buttons seem to be about aspects of our history, sense of self, and so on that we would otherwise not want to have in our face. When our buttons are pushed, that history is right there in our face and not by our own doing. So, we react to defend it, to push it away. And, who is at fault? Often with anger the button pusher is to blame -- "you did this on purpose." The buttons are verbal and function like sticks and stones.
EMOTION Anger - general inc. possible functions of [cont'd] John Forsyth	My intent in the post about pushing buttons wasn't to use it as a justification for anger. It was instead about acknowledging common actions and real processes. Button pushing happens and folks tend to act on it. It nicely illustrates verbal processes, fusion, etc. It wasn't meant to be a technical account, though I think we could provide one. There is anger the feeling and anger the action. Both can be fused or defused from. There is a hell of a lot of verbal behavior entangled in anger the feeling and anger the action. There is certainly a huge narrowing of behavioral and psychological flexibility with anger, as you'll see when someone is in the middle of a panic attack, extremely depressed, and so on. Additionally, angry persons tend to act on anger as one would in self-defense. These actions, in turn, can get people into trouble, with the trouble being about not living a valued life.
EMOTION Anger - general inc. possible functions of [cont'd] **METAPHOR** **Anger - gasoline [12-22-04]** ACT Listserv Member	In my work with patients I tell them anger just is, neither good nor bad, just is. I then describe anger as energy, like gasoline. It is what we do with it that is important. To use the analogy of gasoline, we can pour it over ourselves and light it off, or we can put it in our vehicles and drive. Either way the energy will be used, destructive or not, that is up to us. Anger, like any explosive fuel, needs to be treated with respect and responsibility. I also point out to my patients that most people have heard of anger management, but never heard of anger denial or anger extinction. We then often go to the constructive functions of anger (getting things done, getting out of an old, ineffective way of being, etc.). Ending with one of my favorite questions "Well, what are you going to do?"
EMOTION Anger - general inc. possible functions of [cont'd] Scott Temple	I've found some useful material regarding emotions, generally, and specifically anger, in the work of Paul Gilbert, who writes about CBT and evolutionary psychology. If I can venture a comment here, 'clean' anger strikes me as a quick, visceral, perhaps midbrain-mediated, response to threat. As such, it doesn't necessarily have a moral valence one way or the other. To me, the issue with patients is: 1) normalizing the somatic and emotional experience of anger (it's one response available to mammals under threat), while 2) examining the threat estimate 3) helping the person tolerate the emotion (as if there's a really good alternative) while behaving in ways that are appropriately responsive to the situation. I have been interested in wolves since seeing them when I lived in Northern Minnesota. I read a story recently about a Bengal tiger that got loose in an Indian zoo and made its way into the wolf pen. Guess what happened? The alpha male wolf, weighing perhaps 100 lbs., went straight for the throat of the 600 lb. Bengal tiger. Now I'm not assuming that wolves consciously process threat, or relationally frame tigers, self, etc. But I see that as the prototype of mammalian anger ... by the way, the animals were sedated before anyone could discover who'd 'win.' Frankly, sometimes it's appropriate to go at the tiger. Often, it's not a tiger at all. It's useful to know the difference, and to have choices about how to respond.
EMOTION Anger - general inc. possible functions of [cont'd] Chad Drake	This topic is of such personal interest to me that I want to contribute even though I probably don't have anything new to add to the wisdom that has already been provided. I have done the list of resentments detailed by Jonathan. I can honestly say it changed my life. I spent years being supremely pissed at a lot of people who, by my own self-righteous reckoning, had completely and totally wronged me. I had a great story for myself about it - so bittersweet it was practically addictive, all the more so because it was so True. And it was the bane of my existence. I was angry at just about everybody for something. Strange how I

	always managed to find people who didn't just do things, but did things to me. Hmm!
	By the time I made my list, I was pretty spent and willing to do anything. Hitting that low point probably helped me. I listed everyone for everything. I listed who I resented, what they did to me, how it affected me, how my own behavior contributed to it, and what was threatening about the experience. That last one is really important - getting into contact with the vulnerability my anger was protecting. I was struck - and amused - by how repetitive and boring it all was. It was almost always the same thing - someone did something that set an occasion for me to feel unimportant or unwanted (or something in that general vicinity), and I reacted to the hurt in that by defending myself with anger and resentment. I had spent years of my life investing myself in these feelings and the story that justified it, and afterward I had to ask myself, "That's it?!?" It was a massively defusing exercise. I agree that anger is a means of avoiding something that feels worse - it seems like it certainly was for me.
	I still get angry about things, don't get me wrong, but I have gotten fairly good at seeking out the vulnerability that I want to protect when anger shows up. There is this odd serenity about the experience (well... except when there isn't - can't do it perfectly all the time). It has become more than just the one shitty thing it used to be. I have also made amends with a lot of the people on my list. Woooo, that has been and continues to be hard. And very scary. And sometimes it makes that hurt I want to protect much more present than I have previously allowed. And I have absolutely no regrets. It has been a very liberating and vitalizing experience for me. It has pushed me further into the life I care about living. I cannot recommend it enough.
	I'm not sure what to make of the discussion about clean and dirty anger, other than that I think it's interesting. It seems to me anger is always in the service of protecting something one is attached to, and unless the threat involves an actual threat to one's life, then that attachment is probably verbally constructed. And in every scenario I can imagine involving a threat to my life, it seems like I'd be more likely to feel afraid than angry. I'm not sure if that clarifies anything or even if determining what makes anger clean or dirty is a useful distinction. Personally, what matters to me is having some elbow room with the experience.
	I like the gasoline metaphor.
EMOTION Anger - general inc. possible functions of [cont'd] Kelly Wilson	The thing about humans and anger is that we *stay* mad for a very very long time--sometimes forever. The sort of activation that goes with mad, the narrowing of repertoire, the focus and intensity are all to the good in an immediately hostile environment. Good stuff in a world where we are trying to keep from being eaten. But ... do the sort of resentment list that Chad is talking about (from Alcoholics Anonymous AA Big Book) and what you will not find is lions tigers and bears. Even where you find a resentment connected to a genuine physical danger, the danger is typically long since past. But we stay mad and as the health psychologists have revealed, we are not built to stay mad for fifty years--it chews away at a system that evolution designed to get mad, get safe, and get on to the next thing. If you poke a dog with a stick, it will bite you and may be wary around you for a time. If you poke a human with a stick, she will spend the next 50 years grumbling about how unfair it was, how it shouldn't have happened, how they should have known better, what they might have done otherwise, how "the other" was a subhuman species for poking them, blah, blah, blah. This stream of activity will continue unabated even if the person who did the poking is dead.
	Setting aside the often contentious spiritual aspects of AA, I think that AA's insight into the incredibly corrosive nature of resentments is the most potent, liberating and surprising aspect of their 12 steps to recovery. The amazing thing, described by Chad, is how incredibly repetitive and pervasive resentments can be. I have sometimes thought about doing a weekend advanced experiential workshop where people would bring their single most potent resentment and we would spend the entire weekend on it. Blast it with defusion, examine workability. Look closely at issues of right and wrong, fair/unfair, vitality. Ask the old ACT question: who would be made wrong if you were to forgive? Blowing up resentments can have an extraordinary effect psychologically. I guarantee that it would be a rocking weekend. You would be shocked. I promise.
	An old loon I knew back when I was crawling out of the bottle used to say "Resentments are like taking poison and waiting for the other guy to die." There is something to this me thinks.
EMOTION Anger - general inc. possible functions of [cont'd] Scott Temple	So wouldn't it be reasonable, then, to say that resentment is to anger as depressive rumination is to sadness? Intense emotions have no 'bad' or 'good' valence, in and of themselves; they are built into the system via evolution, and they will continue to be visitors in all our lives for the duration ... rumination that stokes intense emotion, but provides no way out is another matter.

EMOTION Anger - general inc. possible functions of [cont'd] John Forsyth	There are some intense human responses that are aversive. There are also intense human responses that are aversive to nonverbal organisms. We call these unpleasant, bad. The rat simply responds by running away or avoiding in any way that it can. The issue, in my view, is that humans (unlike our nonverbal counterparts) can take the pain to another level. Why? Because of our capacity for language and derived verbal relations (speaking to the choir here). We too are masterful at avoiding even when it does not look like we are avoiding. And, this tends to get we "happy" humans into trouble.
EMOTION Anger - general inc. possible functions of [cont'd] Russ Harris	Kelly quoted: "Resentments are like taking poison and waiting for the other guy to die." On the same subject, Buddha said resentment is like grasping a red hot coal in one hand in order to throw it at someone else. And Swami Chadvilasinanda describes holding onto anger as akin to burning down your house to try and get rid of a rat.
EMOTION **Anger - general inc.** **possible functions of** **[6-30-05]** Rainer Sonntag	Joseph Ciarrochi wrote: It seems like the kid with poor attributional style blames him/herself for bad things. But don't hostile people tend to blame other people for bad things? Don't they tend to think that the problem lies outside of them (e.g., I would be fine, if everybody at school would stop picking on me). Or do they secretly blame themselves for things? ... But if they blame themselves, why are they getting so angry? Wouldn't they get sad or depressed? I think anger can serve several different functions. To begin broadly, anger can be a defence or it can be an attempt to get something (people might have learned that they can get things more easily by behaving aggressively). Of course, an anger response may be selected in order to avoid or escape from private experiences. Another option may be that angry behavior is selected because it is coherent with a corresponding self-image. Self-verification theory (e.g., Swann, W.B. Jr. (1992). Why people self-verify. *J Pers Soc Psychology, 62*, 392-401.) seems to show that self-images are very powerful in governing behavior - as long as they are taken literally - we might add from an ACT/RFT perspective. Quite close to our ACT/RFT perspective, I think, Swann theorizes that it is a "need" for coherence which causes the correspondence; from an ACT/RFT perspective we might say that this kind of cognitive fusion is reinforced by generating coherence within relational networks (verbal descriptions of what I am doing and verbal descriptions of who I am). There may be different routes how people acquire and learn to adhere to even self-damaging self-images. RFT seems very useful to study this. For example, many positive outcomes may be framed in coordination with angry behavior: power, get money, be the big boss, have beautiful women, be respected, not being cheated etc.; others may imitate an angry model and are reinforced in some ways for doing this; others may have needed aggressive defences some time in their life and generated a self-image of an angry person by way of self-observation or listening to others who described their behavior. One could also turn your question around: Do people who blame themselves really blame themselves? I do not think this is always the case. Secretly they often blame others, too. But they avoid interpersonal conflict when blaming themselves. We all know the clinically-rich descriptions of depressed people who turn out to be quite angry when you know them closer and they become more open to say what they really think and feel. And doesn't the verbal construct of blame entail hostility. Even in self-blame we may take a perspective on some aspects of our conceptualized self as if we were looking towards another person (e.g., "I hate ME" is grammatically indistinguishable from "I hate JACK"). Besides this question of how to define blame, I think there is no mechanic link between self-blame/blame and sadness or hostility. These are behavior-behavior relations and they have to be examined individually in order to construct a useful model that sets the occasion to change them in a helpful direction. Some loosely connected thoughts. Not very coherent. Therefore not very comfortable to send this email. May it be so.
EMOTION Anger - general inc. possible functions of [cont'd] Patty Bach	How about an emotional control agenda as one possible function of aggression/hostility? ... Even if the evaluation "I am bad" is global, is "I am bad" always psychologically present? It probably IS psychologically present when YOU pick on ME - and then I feel bad in that context. If you pick on me because "I am bad" (globally) and you picking on me causes me to 'feel bad' (momentarily), even if I can't change 'being bad,' maybe I can avoid/control feeling bad in some contexts if I can get you to stop picking on me - and one way to get you to stop picking on me is to "be mean" - so I try to control YOUR behavior in the service of controlling MY feelings/evaluations....

	If I am mean, you'll be so intimidated you will stop picking on me and I won't have to feel bad about being picked on - of course you will stop hanging out with me altogether, which reinforces both "I am bad" and that I can control your behavior by 'being mean' and control my feelings by controlling your behavior - and then the solution becomes part of the problem.
EMOTION Anger - general inc. possible functions of [cont'd] **BOOK** **ACT on Life, Not on Anger [7-5-05]** John Forsyth	We (Georg Eifert, Matt McKay, & John Forsyth) just wrapped up an ACT book on anger -- *ACT on Life, Not on Anger* (2006). Anger is typically thought of as a secondary emotion, and problematic anger typically has more to do with acting on anger (i.e., anger behavior) not the experience of anger "the emotion." Most conceptualizations that I have come across -- and I am certainly not an anger expert -- view anger as a means of defending against hurt and pain. I learned from Matt (CBT expert on anger) that virtually all anger starts with an evaluation -- blame (a verbal process). That is, "I hurt, and you or someone else did it to me." This blame puts the anger person in the role of victim. Having your buttons pushed is a simple example of this process. Typically, when we have our buttons pushed, we experience painful aspects of our history. They are right in our face and not by our own doing. So, the tendency is to fight back -- act in anger. This pushes the pain out of view, at least temporarily, and creates a host of other problems. The alternative, of course, is to have the emotional hurt for what it is and take responsibility for how one responds to it. Anyway, we really could use a good RFT analysis here.
EMOTION Anger - general inc. possible functions of [cont'd] ACT Listserv Member	In my experiences as a clinician, I would say that anger can function for just about anything. I have seen it used to redirect self blaming to an external target; it often gives someone the feelings of power because of the adrenaline; I have even seen it as an antecedent for sexual arousal in a male patient. In theory, true anger (anger that is accompanied by all the behavioral and physiologic symptoms) would work wonderfully to facilitate avoidance of private experiences; it energizes, facilitates focus of thoughts on to a group or single target, raises pulse, etc. Chronic anger though is different - often chronically angry folks will not be aware of how angry they appear to others. I have had many deny that they feel angry even after gestures or verbal behavior that are consistent with anger are emitted and brought to their attention. Anger is powerful, and functions are always contextually derived and idiosyncratic....
EMOTION Anger - general inc. possible functions of [cont'd] Steve Hayes	I think of anger as an active form of hurt / fear, but chronic anger seems to require fusion with an evaluative relation (right / wrong etc.) that justifies attack. I know in working with anger patients defusion from right / wrong and focus on values and workability is usually the linchpin that holds chronic anger together ... once you get that far you usually then find hurt (and sometimes anxiety / fear) surfacing prominently. Often folks are quite uncomfortable with hurt (and / or anxiety) ... and sometimes there is another level of fusion (e.g., this is "weak"). That makes me suspect that the right / wrong fusion is functionally sustained in part by its emotional avoidance functions, but these are all doubled-headed arrows so it will not disentangle easily. Could be done though. The social reinforcement for the coherence of relational networks is huge -- needs to be to get language working properly. For its problem-solving functions to work, being able to detect relational coherence is critical. Plus we then link relational networks to socially-established archetypes -- we train folks to detect whether their conceptualized actions are consistent with other relational networks (e.g., moral standards, etc.). That seems key to proper socialization. Seems likely since we do it very early. Have you ever watched children on this front? Five year olds will talk about what is "fair" like it is the most important thing in the world. First and second graders will torture each other over who is right about this or that. Being right about what is fair (etc.) -- which looks to me like a core of chronic anger -- could thus just be a side effect of the social / verbal community setting up language to have its desired functional and social effects. I don't think this is a very high level process. But run amuck it will literally kill folks.
EMOTION Anger - general inc. possible functions of [cont'd] Steve Hayes	At some level anger probably involves hurt or threat ... how do you get a dog angry? Opening up to that is not with the goal of eliminating the anger, however ... it just expands the context and creates more options. That doesn't mean anger is reducible to hurt or fear either ... it just has some of these participants. Some folks suppress anger because it is so closely linked to actions they fear -- they would rather be afraid or hurt than angry. Bad idea. For them "getting in touch with anger" can expand the context and give more options. For them, there may be no immediate utility in connecting anger to hurt etc. -- it is far more important just to feel angry and to know you are feeling angry.... All emotions can be an adaption and inform effective action. You can tell if you can't afford to feel. That's why acceptance is so important. I think of defusion as more related to thoughts than emotions per se. The defusion stuff in my note [above] applied to the possible verbal components of some types of chronic anger. But defusion is also not with the goal of reducing an emotion ... it is designed to create more behavioral flexibility when rules are getting in the way.

EMOTION Anger - general inc. possible functions of [cont'd] Steve Hayes	Tony Biglan wrote: Are you saying that anger is justified by the unfairness that is experienced when things are perceived as not right, but that the insistence on being right is in the service of justifying the anger, which is the preferred alternative to feeling hurt? I think I'd say it this way. Chronic anger seems commonly to be evoked by the combination of aversive events and fusion with relational frames of "fair/unfair" and "right/wrong." The insistence on being right seems also to have a common set of functions: it achieves social approval and influence; it maintains a consistent story; and it avoids other experiences (e.g., feeling hurt or afraid; thinking one is weak; feeling vulnerable; admitting that you care about others; crying in front of others; etc.).
EMOTION **Anger, components of; threat to health [5-18-04]** Steve Hayes	As I recall the data (e.g., Charlie Speilberger's) the big impact of anger on health comes from chronic suppressed anger, not angry feelings per se. Chronic anger is not just an emotion IMHO ... it is a combination of another (avoided) emotion or two (usually hurt, anxiety, or shame), and a fused evaluation (usually with a heavy right and wrong component). If you feel it without acting on it, and more importantly, feel what else was there right before you got angry and notice what came up in the world of cognition without taking it literally, anger comes and goes very quickly. Nothing harmful about it. Anger looks different because the emotion-action link is so tight as to seem to be nearly the same thing ... and people know for sure that they can't "be" angry if that means impulsively acting angrily.
EMOTION Anger, components of; threat to health [cont'd] Joseph Ciarrochi	Yes, my memory of that finding agrees with Steve's. It is chronic anger that is problematic. Importantly, it is not just any kind of hostility and anger that bodes poorly for the health of one's heart, but rather, a particular kind: cynical hostility. It is characterized by suspiciousness, resentment, florid displays of anger, antagonism, and distrust. Cynical hostility creates excessive cardiovascular reactivity. The heart and vascular system tend to over-react to minor stressors (Siegman & Snow, 1997), and this is especially true in situations involving other people (Suls & Wan, 1993). The emotional arousal often experienced by cynically hostile people is associated with lipids being shunted to the bloodstream (perhaps to provide "fuel" for the ensuing fight that the body is expecting). This increase in blood cholesterol and triglycerides creates a risk for the build up of plaques, which can block arteries feeding heart muscle and result in a heart attack (Dujovne & Houston, 1991)....
EMOTION **Feeling "good" - therapist response [1-21-05]** Daniel Moran	David Chantry wrote: I'd like to ask how others respond when clients are feeling *good* - whether because they've just had a good week, or maybe because they feel therapy is "working." My concern is that having got (albeit perhaps temporarily) what they originally wanted (before I explained that our work is really about *feeling* good), they may forget about process and go straight back to fusing with content, perhaps undoing some of our hard work. And yet I don't want to be a killjoy, which I seem to be if I suggest that they remember to observe feeling good as another feeling - seems like I am depriving them of enjoying their present experience. I wrestle with David's question a lot when considering the progress of some of my clients. I think it takes an awful lot of sophistication with mindfulness to observe the good mood and not lose the lustre. I often cringe before going into that area because I too don't want to seem like a killjoy. Personally, I doubt the passing fusion is too detrimental during happiness. Saying to oneself: "This is great!" and then experiencing the greatness seems perfectly sound ... it's another story when the "This is great" occasions "and great things end" or "but not as great as the other time that I felt x" and the person gets fused to those evaluations. That's when good mindfulnessing can help. I like to check where the "good mood" is coming from, and try to time the mindfulness discussion in this regard. If the client is coming in feeling great because of passing gratuitous events, like winning an argument with their spouse, that might be a good time to check how their "good feelings" might be running counter to values. So I think you need to assess the client's level of sophistication with their mindfulness before having them notice good private events as EVENTS, and also check the influences on the new good mood.... This is reminding me of some quote I heard somewhere.... Most people look at things as either a blessing or a curse, the samurai looks at these things as a challenge.... That little phrase was REALLY impactful with a tough-guy biker dealing with black-and-white anger issues. He seemed ready to examine good thoughts/ events/ feelings from the observer position, and it led to measurable change in his behavior.

EMOTION	Francis De Groot wrote:
Grief (human cf. animal) - role of verbal behavior [2-25-04] Nico van der Meijden	Years ago I did some chimpanzee observation in a Dutch zoo. I remember a chimpanzee mother "mourning" for days after her baby drowned in a pool (sitting quiet by the pool, no more playing, no more fighting, no more grooming ...). Is this the result of verbal processing? (Was it mourning? - always have to be careful with the interpretation of animal behavior.)
	I don't know if you can compare the mourning of a chimp who has lost a baby chimp with the mourning of a human who has lost a child. In the case of the baby chimp, I believe a behavior analyst would say the chimp is showing signs of 'extinction'; the chimp has lost something which was very reinforcing for her. Of course humans show signs of extinction too when they've lost something that's very reinforcing and (because of that) dear to them. But as I understand it from the [ACT] book, the difference between chimps and humans is that because of language (symbols acquiring the stimulus functions of the referent and vice versa) the loss of a child can 'haunt' a human the rest of its life. In every situation there can be stimuli which can remind a human of the loss. Lots of stimuli in the world are connected with words (symbols) which are in several ways connected to the death of the child (for example, seeing a young child walk on the street). I wonder if a chimp is 'reminded' of the death of her baby chimp the same way.
EMOTION	Jason Gosnell wrote:
Guilt, general discussion of [9-1-04] Steve Hayes	So, does guilt have any function any use for the human being--or is it completely unnecessary? How do other ACT people view guilt?
	Definitions quickly become an issue, so it depends. I can't see any positive value from buying into "I'm bad." I can see lots of value for acknowledging and taking responsibility for cleaning up actions that were "bad" in the sense that they violated one's values / faith / choices / commitments. All of the major religions make the distinction: hate the sin / love the sinner etc.
	The emotion that is associated with seeing one's failures could be called guilt and if that is what we mean, I see a positive role for it. But in the book we were talking specifically about that emotion plus fusion with "I'm bad." Sometimes people also call that "guilt" (or shame, etc.). If you look at what happens over time that emotion/fused thought combo -- whatever you call it -- seems just to grease the wheels of more unworkable action ("Of course I'm doing more of the same. I'm bad - what do you expect?").
	In religious traditions one tries to solve this by accepting the person 100% (as a gift - or as it is usually said, by the "grace" [from gratis -- gift] of God). It is a gift (unearned / not conditional), but it still needs to be accepted by choice to make a difference. As a psychotherapy matter in ACT we try to solve this issue by acceptance, defusion, a transcendent sense of self, chosen values, and workability. Same basic territory. Still a gift (unearned / not conditional). Still needs to be accepted by choice to make a difference.
	Pull out the fusion and avoidance I know of NO emotion that is ipso facto harmful. Emotions are only indications that certain aspects of the past are relevant to the present - how could seeing the relevance of your history be ipso facto harmful?
EMOTION Guilt, general discussion of [cont'd] Victoria Follette	This is not really in disagreement with Steve but a slight twist. I think that guilt as it commonly exists and is considered is not useful in that it does lead to shame and other negative cycles that make it very hard to change behavior. A tricky distinction with clients ... but I really try to focus on taking responsibility, changing behavior, sometimes making amends … and moving away from guilt...
	I think guilt is used a lot to control people, esp. children. And it works at times but the side effects can kill you.
EMOTION Guilt, general discussion of [cont'd] **PAIN** **Ally, as - signaling system [9-1-04]** ACT Listserv Member	I tend to use pain as a metaphor for guilt in that it serves a useful purpose in notifying us that there is a problem, but that either too much or too little is in itself another problem. For example, take a broken leg (something with which I am way too familiar). Too much pain, and all you do is lie there and scream, and may start thrashing about doing further damage, and at best failing to do anything useful. Too little pain, and you are likely to get up and try to walk on it, causing further damage such as compound fractures, loss of limb, death, etc. Pain, like guilt, serves a useful purpose in notifying us that a problem exists. If we simply accept pain, or guilt, for what it is, a signaling system, we are then able to make decisions regarding how we plan to respond to the signal, and then do so.
	Ever noticed how sitting alone in a dark room focusing on how much something hurts, a headache for example, only makes it worse? Guilt is the same way. Spending time dwelling on the pain, or guilt, is a means of self distraction, and self abuse, to no useful purpose. Kind of like dwelling on how terrible the gas gauge being on empty looks, instead of getting out and filling the tank (yes, I did just metaphor my metaphor - tends to catch their attention).
	So, we are best served by neither ignoring pain, or guilt, nor obsessing on pain, or guilt. My suggestion is to accept that the pain, or guilt, exists and then take appropriate action.

EMOTION Guilt, general discussion of [cont'd] John Billig	I think often the problem is not guilt, but the effort to control or be excused from guilt that gets people trapped in negative cycles that are hard to change. Patients can do lots of reason-giving in an effort to avoid feeling badly about things they have done, but this usually does not work. I think moving in close, being willing to experience guilt that arises will allow for defusion from the literality of the feelings and the associated fused ideas ("I'm bad").
EMOTION Guilt, general discussion of [cont'd] Scott Temple	Your very interesting postings reminded me of an essay by the philosopher Martin Buber which has stayed with me for a long time. Buber gave a series of talks in 1957 at the Washington School of Psychiatry, one of which was published as "Guilt and Guilt Feelings," in the book The Knowledge of Man. Buber believed that there exists 'real' guilt, which arises through violating one's values, faith, etc., as you describe. He took psychiatry at the time to task for being dismissive of the concept of guilt; he thought it was a big mistake to minimize or deny a person's own experience of guilt. But he never encouraged wallowing in guilt ("I'm bad, I'm bad"). Instead, he saw guilt as an opportunity for meaningful, heartfelt change (repentance in Hebrew essentially means 'turning'): behavior change based on seeing one's failures, as you note, with acceptance, compassion, and commitment to turning toward one's values. Sounds a bit like ACT to me.
EMOTION Guilt, general discussion of [cont'd] ACT Listserv Member	The function of guilt can be a productive enquiry. I might ask a client if we could look at some of the ideas about why guilt has evolved with us humans. We seem to be wired up to feel a noxious emotional state we learn to label guilt. This feeling tends to turn up after we have transgressed in some way. There is an idea that the unpleasant noxious emotion promotes behaviours related to making-good, putting things right, etc. Following such behaviours, there can be a felt reduction in discomfort. If our attempts to put things right are blocked, or impossible for some reason, we can be stuck with the wretched feeling. Clients are very interested in looking at function, and it can help them see that 'there but for the grace...etc.' We would then move on to examine the question 'who benefits from your guilt now? Is there anyone on the entire planet who might benefit from you sticking close to this noxious emotion?' Usually this leads to a real curiosity about the possibility of moving on, or accepting that the guilt emotion may be there, but we don't need to suppress it or amplify it. Just notice it and expand behaviours.
EMOTION Guilt, general discussion of [cont'd] Mark Webster	Another way to look at guilt is to explore how the world would be without it. Our clients often 'get it' from this angle. And understand the social functions of the emotion.
EMOTION Guilt, general discussion of [cont'd] **PAIN** **Values, link with; response to [9-2-04]** Steve Hayes	OK. I'm off into pontification mode (uh oh ... "I'm bad!"). Whether he [client in clinical example re guilt in the ACT book] shares with the family or not is not the big issue and not the first issue. If sharing is part of furthering a valued relationship then share. Sometimes sharing is not that path, though usually it is. The biggest issue is whether he is open to the clean experience of pain that comes from stepping away from what you value and is willing to then pour that back into doing what he values (not to undo the pain but because that is what he wants to be about). The deep message of "I screwed up" is "I care about...." Let the pain be about that. First you have to feel it. Feel it, fully and without defense. As it is and not as what it says it is. Then you carry it. The question is this: in what direction do you carry it? Do the inside work well and the outside work will be a lot easier. Do the outside work as a way around the inside work and you are asking for trouble. Sharing is not a substitute for acceptance. It can be an empowering manifestation of it but for that to be so, it has to BE so. As a formula: Defuse from all the verbal categorization and evaluations wrapped around the pain. Get with the pain fully. Embrace it. Connect with the values that are inside the pain. Behave effectively in accord with those values, carrying your history with you. No guarantees on social outcomes from this -- but there is a psychological guarantee: you are moving toward wholeness. [Etymological fact of the day stolen from Barbara Kohlenberg: the root of the word "heal" is "whole."]
EMOTION Guilt, general discussion of [cont'd] Julian McNally	Yes, like the ACT Listserv Member and Steve, I recognise and suggest to clients that the pain of guilt, like any painful emotion, is just information or feedback about what has happened (historical and observable fact) and what is so (your current experience). Like Scott, I differentiate the immediate shame-like emotion ("I see you see I did something that 'violated one's [my] values / faith / choices / commitments'" Steve) from the fused, entrapping version - guilt ("I did bad so I AM bad" ...). The former may give rise to expressions of remorse and new commitments to re-align

	behaviors with values e.g., by compensating those injured or reconciling with others/faith. What the latter does can be uncovered by asking "What is that in service of?" or "This fulfils your values/commitments how exactly?" As well as the social control ..., notice how guilt serves a useful purpose of helping the 'sinner' avoid the challenging, responsible work of owning up (attendant shame), making amends/recompense (being vulnerable to humiliation or exploitation, or perceived as weak), committing not to re-offend (fear of failing, limiting one's freedom to be 'bad,' 'lazy,' etc.), asking forgiveness (humiliation again) and forgiving self (freedom). Everything in brackets is something to fear or avoid. What I would 'hear' in the professions of guilt of some offenders I used to work with was something like, "Hey! Waddya mean I have to ask for forgiveness, make amends and all that crap. I already feel guilty! Isn't that enough?" Clearly guilt is anything but 'clean' pain! It's arbitrary, but could we say for our purposes: shame = clean, guilt = fused, remorse = behavior?
EMOTION Guilt, general discussion of [cont'd] Patty Bach	For many clients rather than changing behaviors that make them 'feel guilty,' they benefit from changing their evaluations of which behaviors and in what contexts constitute 'bad behavior.' It seems that willingness to be present with guilt and 'do it anyway' is often useful work. A common clinical example is the person who stays in an unsatisfying relationship or job because, "I would feel guilty if I left," and the behavior of 'staying' is in the service of avoiding guilt even while 'staying' is inconsistent with other valued goals. The work is defusing from the evaluation "doing X is bad" and seeing it as just a thought that shows up. Can I be present with feeling bad when my actions might be followed by someone else feeling bad? If someone else feels bad and the thought "if they feel bad, then I have done bad" shows up, and guilt shows up, then does that mean that I have been bad - nope - it may merely be an evaluation that shows up given one's history.
EMOTION Guilt, general discussion of [cont'd] Greg Schramka	Reinforcement history of clients who express self-flagellating guilt over past behavior may also need to be considered. For example, self-deprecating remarks such as "I'm bad" may have been followed by reassurance and comforting behavior from others. Conversely, the same verbal behavior may function as avoidance of aversive reactions from others. That is, a child saying "I'm bad" after doing something "wrong" may have deterred a parent or caregiver from levelling similar damning remarks or from punishing the child.
EMOTION **Hatred, psychology of [9-18-04]** Rhiannon Patterson	I just read a really interesting summary of Robert Sternberg's (and his colleagues') current work on the psychology of hate.[1] The work strikes me as very complementary to and consistent with ACT, and I would love to hear what ACT psychologists think of it. According to the summary, a key part of Sternberg's theory of why humans can and do hate (as opposed to just acting out acts of spontaneous or instrumental aggression like animals do) is that "humans hate in narrative. We cannot hate without a tale to tell." The same summary describes the work of political theorist Alford, who says that we are particularly attached to our hate stories. A fascinating quote from Alford: "The history of one's hatreds constitutes the single most important, most comprehensible, and most stable sense of identity for many people. [Hatred is] a self-chosen bondage to another, serving to structure the psyche." Love can bring attachment and meaning; hatred is "a cheap imitation of love." The reason we need to be given meaning in the first place, Alford thinks, is that at the core of every human heart lives a crushing sense of dread. To that dread, hatred sings its siren song. "Hatred makes hopelessness meaningful, and so bearable" says Alford. "'You, my enemy, are going to become the coffin for my feelings.'" Wow, I found this to be fascinating stuff. For one thing, it resonates strongly with the existential element of ACT, as well as the emphasis in ACT on the self-inflicted bondage we can get into with our attachment to particular narratives about ourselves and the world. It also really rang true to me. I found especially striking that part about hatred being a cheap imitation of love. I think we can all recognize the feeling of being really attached to our hatreds (well at least I can), even though we may know that these attachments aren't getting us where we really want to go, and aren't the way we truly want to structure and motivate our lives. Sternberg, according to the article, argues that the antidote for our attachment to hate narratives is to cultivate wisdom. He defines wisdom as "striving towards the common good, a good that transcends just the groups of which one is a member." I don't know whether Sternberg has anything to say about the ACT approach, which I assume would involve attacking the power of narrative itself, hence giving the hating person more psychological space in which to decide if this hatred is truly a value he or she wishes to live by. [1] William Speed Weed (Sept./Oct., 2004). Why we hate. *Yale Alumni Magazine*.

EMOTION **Hope - as feeling cf. quality of action [4-2-05]** JoAnne Dahl	Patty Bach wrote: I am reminded of the discussion about "confidence" in the ACT book: What if we regard hope as both a feeling state and as a quality of an action - then moving in a valued direction is hopeful action even in the absence of feelings of hope. Creative hopelessness can be the birthplace of radical hope? Does moving in a valued direction entail hope? I liked your way of looking at 'Hope' Pat. As I have been writing in our new self help book for ACT and chronic pain, we have been trying to define vitality in a similar way. It is a feeling and a quality. Before you take a step or enter into an activity, you might take a moment to re-connect to your values and reflect on if this activity is consistent to my valued intentions and as you take the step, you can "feel" the vitality or consistency. I think the words we are using here like hope or vitality reflect the quality of the positive reinforcement, or what gives us meaning in life. Just taking steps would reflect more traditional CBT, but mindfully reflecting over if the quality of these steps is consistent with my valued intentions is an ACT development.
EMOTION Hope - as feeling cf. quality of action [cont'd] Niklas Törneke	We are trying to assist people in acting towards what they value, regardless of the inner state of the moment, when that could help them out of traps they are in. If an inner state is assumed to be needed, you are in a vicious circle. That is so even if the wanted inner state is called hope or vitality. Of course words can be used differently and if hope is used as a word for a certain kind of action then you can use it in an ACT-consistent way. It is good, though, to beware of how easily the "control-inner states-agenda" slips in and the fact that "good ACT language" is no ultimate protection from that. One related clinical question is how to talk about the fact that inner states will in fact be affected, in the long run, [as a result] of valued (as of any) action. If you do things that work for what you want, of course that will give inner states of vitality, hope, joy, satisfaction etc., in the long run. More or less. This is so and, at the same time, the temptation of "control inner states" can always use this. On the other hand I think that it would be a mistake to give the impression that ACT therapists don't give a shit about what inner state they are in and that that is what ACT stands for. As I see it that is simply not true and no human being really takes that position in the long run. Not regarding him or herself, anyway. So one challenge is how to talk about the effect valued action has on inner states in a way that minimizes the risk of falling into the trap. Not so easy....
EMOTION Hope - as feeling cf. quality of action [cont'd] Steve Hayes	Faith / hope / and charity are more important as actions, not emotions, and I like how ACT fits with them all. Faith because we promote a leap of self-fidelity (e.g., through acceptance; defusion). Charity because we promote connection with a sense of self that is inherently connected to others. And hope because we support the creation of valuable, meaningful lives NOW. Hope as an action can be trusted. Hope as an emotion cannot. Radical hope is a nice way to say it. The usual emotional results of "creative hopelessness" are confusion, interest, relief, and hope, but all of these come and go.
EMOTION Hope - as feeling cf. quality of action [cont'd] Barbara Kohlenberg	For me, hope is kind of an implicit ingredient that occurs in the context of relationships with others. In therapy, when you are helping people acquire the skills to move in valued directions, you do so in the context of your relationship with that person. In a way, simply by being present with their pain, their hopes, their wants, and by offering to meet again next week, we are offering hope without ever uttering that word. Not necessarily hope that they will feel better (though they may), but hope that there is meaning, dignity, and value in their struggle, and that what they value and cherish in life also has worth. In addition, by doing what we do, and accepting money for it, or donating our time for it, we are presumably offering something that we believe or hope to be of value. This "contract" implies hope. Unless we (or they) believe it is only for financial gain or some other personal gain or is exploitive in some way. Other thoughts on hope ... I think hope is transmitted when we offer a combination of empathy and perspective. Empathy "I know how you feel," would not be sufficient, and perspective "you won't always feel this way about your break up with so and so...," wouldn't be sufficient, but a sensitive intermingling of these perspectives, along with a nice dose of appreciation for the tenderness of the person sitting with us, might be what we are experiencing when we feel hope. In a more diluted way, or perhaps not, this kind of hope is transmitted in written materials, be they ACT materials or other self help materials, or literature or poetry; I think that reading these materials can offer perspective on one's current struggles, perspective that these struggles are a part of a journey. Maybe the experience that struggling has meaning beyond its face value may be what we mean by "hope."

EMOTION **"Marinating" in grief etc. - avoidance/ fusion? [3-5-05]** Casey Capps	Audrey Lowrie wrote: We are parsing out our ideas about emotional avoidance, but I get more perturbed by clients who want to stay 'marinating' in one painful experience in their history, an emotion associated with grief and/or trauma. Not only those who feel guilty if they consider giving up being continually mindful of a lost loved one, but those whose identity is tied up with being a sufferer, and (it seems to me) are coming to the therapist as a maintenance and elaboration of that identity.... My belief is that "marinating in emotions" is just another avoidance move. The wallowing and fusion with the continued remembering and with the belief that I am a "sufferer" is just another way to avoid/stay out of contact with what would show up if he/she began living his/her life in a valued direction, with his/her history in tow.
EMOTION "Marinating" in grief etc. - avoidance/ fusion? [cont'd] Nico van der Meijden	I think ACT would say they're 'fusing' with their life story; I think the best you can do as a therapist in this case is to pay the life story its due respect and not challenge or dispute its content; it often amounts to entering a mine-field. You could try to 'defuse' by taking a more functional stance and pointing to the costs of identifying with the story: e.g., 'if you believe the thought he ruined your life ... where does it lead to?'
EMOTION "Marinating" in grief etc. - avoidance/ fusion? [cont'd] John McNeill	Try this: Have 'em count their heart beats while they sit there 'marinating' HERE-NOW. Then say, "Feel that? That's your life ticking away. It's your choice!" An experiential exercise for both a personal and clinical practice.
EMOTION "Marinating" in grief etc. - avoidance/ fusion? [cont'd] John McNeill	My posted comments were more directed at choice-values work [not the message to escape experience, but rather having history exactly as is, and the possibility of moving with it relative to other life-directions]. Clearly we should be careful not to convey any message to the client that there is something 'wrong' with being exactly where one is. Moving to one's 'heart beating' often entails that correlative experience can then be exposed, attuned, and transformed by ongoing awareness in this moment. I might add that perhaps if we understood the act of 'marinating' to mean context, behavior, and function, we might find some compassion for the person who experiences it as they do.
EMOTION "Marinating" in grief etc. - avoidance/ fusion? [cont'd] David Fresco	When I read your post, I was thinking about marinating in a painful experience quite differently than you and the others who responded. The connotation of marinating for me is coming into "full contact" with this painful experience and allowing a maximal amount of your surface area to come into this contact. The metaphor of marinating after all, comes from cooking, and in most cases results in a more seasoned and delectable meal through the penetration and transformative properties of the marinade. Interestingly, in some of his guided meditations, Jon Kabat-Zinn talks about noticing thoughts and stirring them in the big pot of mindfulness, not quite marinating, but a cooking metaphor alluding to transforming with the heat of cooking and stirring. It is not clear whether marinating was your word or a particular client's word, but it strikes me that you have an opportunity to reframe what marinating is so that it promotes defusion and approach both for yourself and for a client.
EMOTION "Marinating" in grief etc. - avoidance/ fusion? [cont'd] Steve Hayes	There are data in support of what Casey is saying in the areas of trauma (several studies ... Marx, Orsillo, Roemer, Follette and others); and complicated grieving (Pankey). Probably the best example is complicated grieving. When grief leads to chronic grief it superficially does not look like emotional avoidance since it seemingly involves people experiencing grief. But like people holding on to anger; or people cutting on themselves; etc. you have to ask the question that is always applicable when speaking of avoidance: what would be there if this was not there? The complicated griever often has yet to face loss and finitude. They are fused with the idea that there is something wrong, invalid, impossible, and so on about their loss. What is not yet being felt is actual, permanent, undefended, loss and the emotions that go with that. They are using grief to prevent facing it ... as if someone cares (God? The fates?) and will rescue them from having to face the situation as it is ... like a kid holding their breath until they turn blue or somebody changes their ways. Experiential acceptance is not wallowing. It is a matter of being present to your history and current situation, in the service of living a vital life -- one that comports with your chosen values. I suspect the reason that therapists feel perturbed by "marinating" is that they feel the coercive qualities of this move; and they resent being forced into what feels invalidating. Valuing, and workability linked to valuing, pops the illusion and reveals the avoidant / fused purpose of the coercion. That can make it easier

	to compassionately confront the avoidance and fusion that is showing up as defended stewing in negative emotions.
EVALUATION **ACT interventions [9-24-04]** Joseph Ciarrochi	(the E. in F.E.A.R.) We often evaluate our private experiences as good or bad (and this, in the right context, can lead to avoidance). We also evaluate our entire "selves" as good or bad. One way to undermine the power of unhelpful evaluations is via defusion exercises (e.g., Bad cup metaphor). You basically create a context where people become aware of the evaluations (looking at them, rather than through them), and can then choose to act or not act according to the evaluations. A second kind of intervention involves targeting the frequency of the evaluations. This seems to be a point in which ACT differs from other third wave therapies. ACT does not seem to directly target the frequency of judgments. In contrast, DBT and other approaches encourage people to take a nonjudgmental stance, or to not judge whilst practicing mindfulness. Ok, first, am I right that ACT rarely tells people to practice "not judging" (sounds like an avoidance frame)? Second, would it be useful for us as a community to make explicit the ways in which ACT indirectly seeks to reduce excessive, ineffective evaluating? Here is a starting list: 1) Defusion - evaluations seen as less powerful and meaningful. People become less motivated to engage in evaluating. 2) Paradox, confusion - people are helped to directly experience the traps of reasoning/evaluating. This discourages future evaluating (in a specific context, etc.). 3) Mindfulness exercises and other interventions that encourage acceptance of private experiences (being mode), as opposed to the "doing mode" in which you feel like you have to evaluate experiences and do something about them....
EVALUATION ACT interventions [cont'd] **FUSION/ DEFUSION** **Meaning, debate re [9-24-04]** John Blackledge *Cross Reference:* *See 3-110 to 3-113 for later posts in the thread:* *FUSION/ DEFUSION* *Meaning, debate re*	Very interesting points. I think defusion/acceptance strategies like those used in ACT may be very likely to reduce the frequency of negative evaluations, whether explicitly 'intended' or not. Since these strategies (at least when used in an ACT context) are antithetical to suppression attempts (and the paradoxical increase in frequency such attempts generally result in), they would logically be expected to decrease frequency. Also, I think defusion can be thought of (in part) as a type of response prevention, as defusion strategies disrupt the context of literality that leads to endless verbal response chains--so using defusion strategies in the midst of an 'evaluation-fest' might be expected to reduce the frequency of those evaluative responses. I realize this may be a point of departure from the way many on the listserv think about defusion, but I would consider both of the latter strategies you mention in your post (mindfulness exercises and paradox/ confusion) as sub-categories of defusion--that is, as specific defusion techniques or components. I think anything that either focuses on direct and immediate experience (i.e., formal or sensory stimulation occurring right now) and/or significantly violates the 'rules of discourse' that make language function meaningfully and logically (or at least pseudo-logically) qualifies as defusion, as it violates the key features of the context of literality that give rise to verbal transformations of function (i.e., language only has meaning when you play by the rules when using it--and when you don't notice the difference between the black and white feel of abstract thought and the immediate vitality of full-color direct experiencing). So, from this perspective, every technique that serves a defusive function might be expected to contribute to a decrease in the frequency of thoughts affected by that defusion (whether explicitly intended or not--but perhaps more likely if not intended, as this would circumvent the paradoxical problems of using defusion as a suppression strategy).
EVALUATION ACT interventions [cont'd] Steve Hayes	As an empirical fact defusion and acceptance leads to lower frequency. Makes sense. If you remove the functions of behaviors they tend to occur less over time since behavior is regulated by its function. Often if you try to make them occur less you paradoxically increase their functions. Furthermore, being judgmental requires more than occurrence so in no way does an interest in a non-judgmental stance mean adoption of a frequency target. If in meditation you had a judgmental thought and merely observed it would you still be following the "non-judgmental" maxim of mediation? Sure. If you judged the judgmental thought and tried to make it leave would you still be following the "non-judgmental" maxim? No, because now you are DOING judgment in the name of non-judgment. As JT just posted meditation and mindfulness is in part defusion. It seems likely that you can get to a "non-judgmental" stance more quickly and with greater certainty through defusion than through self-censorship of content -- for the paradoxical reason just described. Bottom line: why target mere occurrence? It is safer, quicker, and more direct to target function. The added benefit: occurrence moves anyway and nothing in mindfulness etc. requires that you target occurrence.

EVALUATION
 	
   **Automatic,
   pervasiveness of; cf.
   deliberate judgment**
 	
FUSION/ DEFUSION
 	
   **Verbal functions,
   dominance of**
 	
EXERCISE
 	
   Saliva [8-20-03]
 	
     Kelly Wilson
	Niklas Grebäck wrote:
	
	   [Mindfulness] is non-judgemental (i.e., describing without evaluating). According to Kelly W. every experience being verbalized is automatically evaluated. The outcome of that would be that the easier we can describe our experience, the more judgements have been made. I detect a possible incoherence here, or have I got it all wrong?
	
	When I say this I am being a bit of a provocateur. I am trying to make folks notice the pervasiveness and persistence of the application of comparative and evaluative frames (coupled with a bias towards dangerous interpretations). I do think that we can get little breathers in this endless stream--and, things like mindfulness are one way to defuse a stream of evaluations. Flexibility and stability are conditionable properties of responding. It can be demonstrated with lever presses and key pecks. Certain histories can make behavior very persistent or very flexible. Derived relational responding (including the application of comparatives) is itself operant responding, so I expect that there are means by which we can alter the flexibility of this behavior too.
	
	I have said that--at least my most current thinking (Wilson & Murrell, in press) is that fusion is the domination of particular verbal functions over other potentially available nonverbal functions *and* other verbal functions. It is a narrowing of stimulus control. (I use the term "stimulus control" broadly meant--following Charlie Catania.)
	
	I use Ellen Langer's little experiential exercise with saliva to make this point, and have added a bit to make the above point about the domination of specific verbal functions over other verbal functions, besides domination over direct sensory functions.
	
	So for those who have not had the pleasure?--take a moment and notice the feel of the saliva in your mouth, notice its qualities, how it feels smooth on the backs of your teeth, notice the places in your mouth where there is more and less of it, notice if there are any tiny differences in the temperature in your mouth in places where there is more and less. Now, think about some of the things your saliva does for you in eating and digestion. Think about the role it plays in that process. Take a moment and get present to the things you know about saliva and digestion. Let yourself be curious about that. Now, imagine that you have a clean glass in front of you, and you gather the saliva up and spit it into the glass.
	
	Now imagine drinking that.
	
	This little exercise will reliably precipitate disgust among at least some members of an audience. At the moment I suggest drinking spit, the "dirty," "germy," "nasty" functions of spit dominate. All of that stuff having to do with the tactile properties of saliva *and* the entirely verbal functions such as "aids in digestion" are gone. Disgust dominates over all other functions. Now this isn't universal, except insofar as our conditioning histories are universal.
	
	I have said that defusion is the process whereby domination of that particular verbal function lessens and other functions become available. So, imagine an exercise where you describe all of the aspects of some event, and you stayed on that task. Try it with the saliva example: sit quietly, close your eyes, and go through all of the different aspects of saliva--everything you "know" about saliva, directly and indirectly. I will bet you anything that in that process, the domination of the disgust functions would diminish. If you persisted for half an hour, a more and more nuanced contact with saliva would emerge. Voila--defusion....

EVALUATION
 	
   Automatic,
   pervasiveness of; cf.
   deliberate judgment
   [cont'd]
 	
     Rainer Sonntag
	Could it be useful to make a distinction between automatic evaluation that inherently goes with description and judgement as a deliberate action?
	
	In mindfulness we may describe things and our automatic evaluations of them. The verbal self-report about the latter allows us to recognize that automatic evaluations are there. It may function like a safeguard against buying these evaluations and by taking them literally to have transformed them into what might be called "judgements" which then transform the stimulus functions of a thing.
	
	For example, looking out when it's raining may go like this:
	
	1. Mindless: "Oh, it is raining. This is bad. I will not go for a walk with my dog." Person not going for a walk; evaluation works as a formative augmental for avoidance.
	
	2. Mindful: "Oh, it is raining. This is bad. Oh, I notice I have the thought that the rain is bad. Well, I will take that thought with me and go for a walk with my dog." Person going for a walk; evaluation does not work as a formative augmental for avoidance.
	
	So "judging" may be viewed as a process that involves choosing to follow rules which come from automatic evaluations taken literally, whereas "not-judging" may be viewed as a process that involves choosing to do what one wants to do in the presence of automatic evaluations (e.g., within a mindfulness exercise to let the mind wander instead of hanging on to evaluations).

EVALUATION **Good/ bad - attributed properties of events [7-24-03]** Steve Hayes	Good and bad are not primary properties of events, they are secondary or attributed properties that emerge from organisms (especially verbal ones) interacting with events. Linguistically, abstracted and attributed properties are identical, which helps create the problem. Evaluative frames are too useful to abandon (problem solving would falter without them), but we are doing the framing....
EVALUATION **Quotation - Beyond fields of right-doing (Rumi) [8-5-03]** John Blackledge	Here's a great ACT-relevant saying by Rumi: "Out beyond fields of right-doing and wrong-doing there is a field. I will meet you there."
FORGIVENESS **One-time event vs. continuous process [10-29-03]** Steve Hayes	Rob Unruh wrote: Is forgiveness … a behavior that can be repeated ... or is it a sort of one-shot deal? It seems that in the book it is spoken of as more of a one-time event.... Forgiveness is like values: it sets a direction but you still have to walk the walk. Walking the walk in this case is a continuous process of letting go of an attachment to "right and wrong" (i.e., defusing from verbal evaluations) when it interferes with valued actions. In that sense, forgiving is anything but a one time thing.... A bottom line suggestion: focus on the personal costs of playing the right and wrong game.
MEMORY **Aversiveness, possible sources of increases in** **AVOIDANCE** **Aversiveness, possible sources of increases in [5-16-03]** Steve Hayes	Joseph Ciarrochi wrote: It seems to me that there are at least two important dimensions of aversive memories. Both these dimensions might be influenced by avoidance. 1) Accessibility. This dimension is influenced by two factors: (i) How activated the thought is ... (ii) How many "routes" there are to the memory.... 2) Intensity or level of aversiveness.... Possible sources of the increase in aversiveness: It's OK to talk in terms of "accessibility" (though the implicit "storage" metaphor may not be helpful) and the analysis of that seems good, but then add to that: increased behavioral functions for avoided events so they begin to become dominant events (as you avoid more and more, these events have more and more behavioral functions, by definition); decreased life success and the repertoire-narrowing effects of avoidance (as you avoid more, you do less and you succeed in whatever you value less, because avoidance and some kinds of approach are incompatible); the loss of social reinforcers as people around you begin to back off; the greater likelihood of larger negative self-evaluative frames ("I'm failing; my life is out of control; I'm weak"); greater surveillance of aversives in general; and direct aversive properties of any unsuccessful control attempt; elicited effects of dire conceptualized futures; -- and a few more such processes, and when you've done all that the increased aversiveness of avoided events seems very understandable. Cioffi & Holloway showed that even neutral events will assume aversive properties under conditions in which you are suppressing something, so you don't need much of this to prime that pump.
MEMORY **Change, possibility of [8-13-04]** Patty Bach	Steve Mahorney wrote: There is emerging evidence from neurobiology that each time a memory is recalled, key elements of the biochemical process by which they were originally "stored" are reactivated. What is "a memory"? A storage/retrieval model gives "memories" thing-like status. Another view is that you can't separate "the memory" from "the recalling"; the memory IS the recalling and is in the present.... Another part of content is emotional and evaluations of a past event. "I was attacked and it was frightening and awful." We can't change past functions - they are in the past. E.g., I doubt the trauma survivor would be encouraged to remember, "I was attacked and it wasn't frightening and awful." We don't change the content of a remembered event, its functions in the present are changed - e.g., "the past event was frightening and awful, and recalling it in the present is frightening and awful" might become "the past event was frightening and awful, and I don't have to avoid talking about it today," or "I felt frightened then and the event was awful, and I can recall that - and today I can choose to take action when I feel

	frightened or have the thought that 'something awful is going to happen.'" This is also addition of verbal content not a subtraction of "content." And in light of new content - which could also be called new experience - behavior/responding is 'different' (and not 'subtracted').
MEMORY Change, possibility of [cont'd] Steve Hayes	We got this string going with the issue of whether anything is ever removed. Several reasons have been given for a "no" answer but there is a more basic philosophical reason: Since the past is gone and no longer exists it is not possible to remove it. The issue then shifted to "is it possible to change a memory?" It is a trick of mind to think that this is the same question. A memory is not in the past and it is not a thing: remembering is happening now. Memories are historically situated, of course, as are all psychological events, but they are dynamic events sensitive to the current context. Each time you "remember" you have now added to the history of this stream of action you call a "memory." But the fact that the "memory changes" provides no support for the idea that anything is eliminated -- the exact opposite is true. It only reaffirms the point that new things are always being added -- even to remembering which is supposedly (but only in a literal sense) "about" the past, or (worse) *in* the past. …[The illusion] is that memories are somehow in the past or at least are faithful representations of it. The idea that nothing is eliminated does not mean that nothing changes. ACT is all about change. Extinction is change. But extinction and every other psychological process builds on the present, which is another name for a point in the evolution of what we call the past. When you add functions in a RELATIVE sense you subtract functions ... as one response function increases another HAS TO decrease because time is finite and there are only so many moments in a day. That is the deep message of the matching law. But we never LITERALLY subtract anything because the past is forever gone and no longer exists except in the present. To say that the "functions of the past are changed" is identical to saying "there are now new functions." The literal past has no functions ... it is gone. Events with histories have functions, but they occur in the present. The joyful message in this: Since it is only the past in the present that we ever deal with, and since new functions are always possible in the present, we do not need to be captives to that illusion called "the past." That is why ACT is a transformational technology. Change truly key aspects of the present and the world is now new.
MIND **Dominance of - Tolle quotation [5-7-05]** ACT Listserv Member	From Eckhart Tolle, in *The Power of Now*: "This incessant mental noise (of the thinking mind) prevents you from finding that realm of inner stillness that is inseparable from Being. (p.15) ...It also creates a false mind-made self that casts a shadow of fear and suffering ... it is not so much that you use your mind wrongly, - you usually don't use it at all. It uses you. This is the disease. You believe that you are your (thinking) mind. This is the delusion. The instrument has taken over...you are its slave...(p.16)... Emotion arises at the place where mind and body meet. It is the body's reaction to your mind (p.25)."
MIND **"Monkey mind" - origin/ meaning of [4-29-03]** Tuna Townsend	Joseph Ciarrochi wrote: Can any of you Buddhists tell me the origin of "monkey brain"? I can't find any text that refers to it, but I am pretty sure it is a Buddhist idea. I think it refers to this mindless bouncing around from one thing to the next. I've read/heard many references in vajrayana and vipassana meditation to comparisons of the undisciplined mind to "a tree full of chattering monkeys" ... usually in the context of developing observer perspective in meditation practice.
MIND "Monkey mind" - origin/ meaning of [cont'd] Patty Bach	I did a little research to satisfy my curiosity (or my monkey mind?) and found that the concept 'monkey mind,' is widely referred to in Buddhism (and less so in some other approaches that emphasize meditation/mindfulness), seems to have originated in Chinese Taoism, and refers generally to the tendency of the mind 'to run and jump from one thought to another like an excited monkey,' and especially, as Tuna suggested, to the tendency of the mind to wander and generate 'noise' when one attempts to be still and meditate.
PAIN **Ally, as [3-8-04]** Niklas Törneke	Mary Politi wrote: We had our second discussion group today, and we came up with a question about the quote on pg. 35 of the 1999 book, *Acceptance and Commitment Therapy* --"'Your pain is your greatest ally' is a common ACT phrase." We were wondering when a clinician would use that quote. Does it have to do with exploring the function of a person's pain? What the pain is saying to the client? What the pain means as far as the workability of the client's solution(s)? There are several points that an ACT-therapist could try to convey by that comment. One is the one you

	mention and has to do with workability. In work with creative hopelessness, pain is assumed to be the problem, it has to be taken away (according to the old agenda). But what if it has a message of importance to the client, "this is not working"? That could be a message of an ally.

Another area is when working with values, with what is really important. When something is painful, often something important is close at hand. Why be sad to the point of pain if nothing important is at stake? Why be painfully angry if there is nothing important around? So pain often points to values in one way or another. Also a message from an ally... |
| PAIN

Ally, as [cont'd]

Sonja Batten | I'll say something like "what if your pain is your greatest ally?" for a number of reasons, some of which are:

1) the reason that you point out about helping people realize that sometimes pain points out what the person values;

2) trying to change the function of the word/abstract concept "pain" by shaking up the evaluations that go along with it … what if "pain" is neither an intrinsically "good" or "bad" thing?; and

3) I truly believe that going through painful things in an open and courageous way can make people stronger, so I suggest to them that being in touch with this difficult thing that they carry around with them anyway can actually be one of their greatest strengths. |
| PAIN

Ally, as [cont'd]

Steve Hayes | And without pain ... maybe even a lot of it ... why would you ever question life inside a literal box? The poisonous message that feeling good = living good is built in ... it is only pain that prepares us to back up and look again. |
| PAIN

Ally, as [cont'd]

Andy Santanello | Avoiding pain is usually what gets people into trouble. This is another paradox that ACT plays with I think. You have to be willing to accept the fact that you are in pain, to make contact with the "stuckness," in order to actually move toward goals/values. In a sense, getting in touch with pain is the first step in changing one's habit of moving away from aversive internal events and toward the things that will allow him or her to live a vital, fulfilling life. |
| PAIN

Ally, as [cont'd]

BUDDHISM

Meditation practice (tonglen) - breathing in pain [3-10-04]

Aaron Murray-Swank | This thread about pain reminds me of a meditation practice in Buddhism called tonglen. The basic concept/technique of tonglen is to "breathe in" pain and suffering (of self/others) on the in breath, and to breathe out/send out "positive" feelings that create spaciousness (peace, joy, well-being). On the in breath, a conscious effort is made to focus on particular instances and experiences of pain and suffering, evoking the texture of the emotions and sensations. For me, the practice is a "wake up call" towards connecting with the pain of being human, not as an end in itself, but as a means towards valued spiritual ends.

Although I am a beginner in this practice (and in ACT), my experience tells me that there is something similar going on - the normative "poisonous message" of feeling good = living good is short circuited through a direct connection with experience in the pursuit of valued directions.

I wonder if there is a place for the use of tonglen in ACT interventions? |
| PAIN

Ally, as [cont'd]

BUDDHISM

Meditation practice (tonglen) - breathing in pain [cont'd]

EXERCISE

Acceptance/ defusion - breathing in pain [3-11-04]

John Blackledge | I used a variant of tonglen as a homework exercise for clients in a recent ACT outcome study. My intention was to give clients a way to practice acceptance and defusion during idle times with mildly-moderately unpleasant emotions involved (e.g., when stuck in a traffic jam or standing in a long line). I think the notion of trying to hold on to unpleasant feelings and let go of pleasant ones is completely antithetical to a context of literality that pervasively involves just the opposite--so it seems to serve a defusing function. Don't know if any clients used it or if it actually helped--just know it helps me and seems ACT-consistent. For what it's worth, here it is:

One of the conditions required for you to believe your mind is the assumption that "bad" or painful feelings need to be gotten rid of, and "good" or pleasant feelings need to be held on to. One way to break up the conditions that lead you to believe your thoughts involves reversing this tendency. Try the following exercise when you find yourself struggling with your pain:

A. Focus on the difficult feeling or feelings involved with that pain. Once you've found that feeling, willingly focus on it as you breathe in. Breathe the feeling into your body, expanding your openness and willingness to carry that feeling just as your lungs expand to take in more air. Drop the physical tension that you feel toward that feeling - drop the struggle against it. Just as relaxing your body gives more room for air to fill your lungs, relaxing your struggle against your feelings gives the feelings more room. It's like easing your fingers into those Chinese handcuffs - creating some space around your pain rather than constricting it. Focus on breathing in the feeling(s) for several inbreaths.

B. Imagine the "antidote" to the feeling(s) you are feeling. In other words, find the pleasant feeling or experience that is the opposite of that feeling. It may be an image, or a thought, or just the feeling itself. For example, if you were stuck in rush hour traffic and felt angry and resentful, the "antidote" to this |

feeling might be an image of you sitting comfortably at home in your favorite chair, watching television and drinking a cup of coffee. Once you've found the "antidote" to your unpleasant experience, don't do anything with it yet. Just "file it away" for the moment.

C. If you're willing, imagine that everyone around you is feeling the same unpleasant feeling(s) as you are. As you breathe in, imagine you are taking in that feeling for you and everyone around you. Remember, you're not doing this as a "martyr" or a "hero," you're just doing this to exercise your willingness muscle and see what happens.

D. Continue breathing in the unpleasant feeling(s) for you and everyone around you. On the outbreath, imagine you are breathing out the "antidote" feeling or image you located earlier, giving it away to everyone around you. So, on each inbreath, you breathe in your unpleasant experience for you and everyone around you, and on each outbreath you give away your "antidote" to everyone else. Continue this until at least several breaths after you find yourself completely willing to "breathe in the bad air and breathe out the good."

Your mind will probably tell you this exercise is a "bad idea," that it's "crazy" to give away your "good" feelings and try to hold on to and amplify your "bad" feelings. You are encouraged to thank your mind for this thought and try it anyway.

PAIN **Clean vs. dirty pain/ discomfort - alternative terms [5-25-04]** Jonathan Kandell	ACT Listserv Member wrote: I have had some difficulty with the 'clean' vs. 'dirty' terminology.... Has anyone come up with alternative terms that describe this distinction in less value-laden (for me) terms? I also don't like the term "dirty" discomfort because of its connotations that the client is dirty/ stained/ tainted/ sinned. It's too evaluative. With patients I use the terms "base" and "amplified" discomfort.
PAIN Clean vs. dirty pain/ discomfort - alternative terms [cont'd] Carl Graham	I have responded to clients on this issue in terms of what is a pain signal in their body (clean) and what is distress that they have about having the pain (dirty). I have also found Steve's 'what is' vs. what stuff is 'added or subtracted' to-from the 'what is,' helps people see what we would term as the clean-dirty difference. From there I suggest that the more they are in deliberate accepting contact with their pain, the less of them there is available to be in contact with the distress. Given that they are in pain either way, the pragmatic nature of the approach is easily made apparent.
PAIN Clean vs. dirty pain/ discomfort - alternative terms [cont'd] Steve Hayes	ACT Listserv Member wrote: So, the general consensus seems to be (Steve included - as per his comments at the Southampton, UK workshop) that we need a different form of words other than clean v dirty. My initial thoughts are in the semantic domain of: automatic v controlled (or effortful); spontaneous v laboured; natural v distorted; simple v complex; as it is v what you make it become. I would welcome suggestions, because this is a key concept and we need a neat 'X v Y' that feels just right, to use clinically without the unintended pejorative of 'clean v dirty.' Naw, I wouldn't say that. Sometimes clean and dirty seem to fit. They are evaluative of course ... but hey, who is looking for consistency here? Use those relational frames when it works to use them. I'm not sure the pejorative aspect is fully unintended. I'm pretty darn sure it was intended actually ... how to parse the sources of control over language choices. And in some cases it might even be helpful (think of times when irreverence might work). I think we can use variability on this point. Sometimes with extremely self-evaluative, guilty types using a term that has a strong evaluative aspect is just not wise. Using "dirty" with some obsessives may not be wise. Some therapists don't like how it feels ... it doesn't fit their style. It is the function that matters. All of your distinctions could work in some cases. Orsillo and Roemer's clear and muddy fits. Natural and artificial might work. Direct and indirect. Acquired and manufactured. This can go on for a long time.
PAIN Clean vs. dirty pain/ discomfort - alternative terms [cont'd] ACT Listserv Member	No matter what pairing of words used in the X v Y format, all are wrought with the same pitfalls of creating evaluations and the capacity to be endowed by the client with negative connotative powers. This is due to two important factors: first, most X v Y pairings are comparisons, and a good portion of those are good versus bad/evil; secondly, words are not pure, they come with idiosyncratic variations in meaning and function (for example, the word "dog," for most is neutral or positive, but for someone phobic of dog bites

	it functions differently), so any pairing you come up with could be problematic. All aspects of any therapy can be problematic if they become dogma...it is important to watch for clients utilizing any tool in the service of the old change agenda. It is also key not to overemphasize any one aspect of the therapy ... find balance and use functionality as your guide.
PAIN **Quality of life [12-5-04]** Steve Hayes	Russ Harris wrote: I've been pondering this comment that Steve wrote in a recent posting: 'There is as much life in an embraced moment of anxiety/ sadness/ pain etc. as in joy.' I agree that there is 'as much life.' What I'm pondering is: is there as much 'quality of life'? This is hard to answer because both the question and the answer is verbal and we are dancing at the edge of what literal language can do. The question demands application of evaluative relational frames. Answering inside that literalized set may eliminate some forms of answering. Is it OK to answer this cheesy way? As an exercise: a) imagine that the answer is "potentially yes." b) a serious question: what would have to happen for the answer in a given moment as it is revealed by living itself to be the functional equivalent of a simple "yes"? This Q is worded funny, I know. Back to the problem noted ... above.
PAIN Quality of life [cont'd] **EVALUATION** **Quality of life [12-17-04]** Casey Capps	I also wonder about the usefulness of the higher/lower evaluation, which is essentially 'my life is good' (or 'like I want it to be')/ 'my life is bad' ('not like I'd like it to be'). I guess I think of this evaluation as problematic because any evaluation naturally entails its opposite. When a person evaluates his/her life as of 'high quality,' the fact that life could easily become of 'lower quality' is ever present also. If a person evaluates his/her life as of 'poor quality,' then he/she is always grasping/hoping for the opposite, to have it be of 'high quality.' This makes it hard for the person to be exactly where they are. These are both places to suffer. The key is not to get rid of the evaluations, but to see them for what they are, nothing more, nothing less.
PAIN Quality of life [cont'd] EVALUATION Quality of life [cont'd] Patty Bach	Russ Harris wrote: Pain can take up a significant proportion of awareness/attention - thus reducing the ability to engage in the valued process, and reducing the inherent satisfaction therein. Pain patients tend to report the highest pain ratings while they are "inactive" and often when "relaxing" such as just before falling asleep; this is thought to be because they are then more focused on pain rather than attending to some other activity. People who are engaged in valued activities pay less attention to pain; this is not 'distraction' because it is not in the service of decreasing pain and is rather in the service of engaging in something else. Perhaps we're operationalizing "quality of life" differently. Experiencing pain strikes me as more ongoing self-awareness then as "self-as-content." "Quality of life" is an evaluation and therefore verbal content. "I am feeling pain" seems ongoing self-awareness; "I am in pain and therefore I have a bad quality of life" seems more evaluation/content - Is "the quality of this moment sucks" the same as "I have a poor quality of life"? Is the time frame of 'quality of life' "ME/HERE/NOW" or a larger perspective/time frame? It seems that "quality of life," is largely contextually determined. If the relevant context for a positive quality of life is the absence of pain/discomfort in any moment, then who would learn to walk, much less choose to bear children, go to the dentist, get vaccinated, start exercise programs, quit smoking, go to graduate school, get involved in another romantic relationship after the pain of a break-up, ride a bike after falling off of one, etc. And even where one might evaluate that "my quality of life NOW is not as good as it was THEN", does that then mean that the quality of one's life is "bad"? And if so, then "bad," compared to what? given that we do not know the subjective quality of another's life or the quality of not living. I don't think anything in ACT suggests that pain (and I mean 'pain' broadly) is not real or that pain is not painful - and I think it might suggest that one can learn to relate to private events differently in contexts where pain is offered as the major "reason" for a poor quality of life.
PAIN Quality of life [cont'd]	The issue comes back to truth in the form of workability not truth in the form of correspondence. But workability requires a statement of "truth for what." So I'd like that put on the table: truth for what? You [Russ Harris] are arguing this in terms of pain, which is so powerful a term that the structure of what is being said and the grounds being appealed to slip away. Note that you can put in "does not have legs" or

EVALUATION Quality of life [cont'd] **THOUGHT** **Workability cf. truth [12-19-04]** Steve Hayes	"lost hearing" or "gets too old to play basketball" and you can structure precisely the same sentences. If you did you would end up with statements like: *For example, a client can accept their lack of legs and go to a basketball game - and the clean discomfort they are left with (i.e., the level of inability to dribble down the court that remains after full acceptance of their lack of legs) will to some degree diminish their ability to play basketball and thus the inherent satisfaction thereof.* Ergo: a loss of legs logically entails a diminished quality of life. (and surely all rational folks just have to accept that) Hmmm, are you comfortable with where this leads? It leads to: age, even fully accepted, can interfere with 'engaging' lack of legs, even fully accepted, can interfere with 'engaging' lost hearing, even fully accepted, can interfere with 'engaging' But it does not end with pain, or legs, or age, or hearing. The mind marches on endlessly, firm in its belief that its thoughts are true because they are logical and because they correspond with the evidence. Meanwhile something is being missed. What is creating this list in the service of? Truth for what? I am NOT saying that lack of legs (etc.) make no difference (despite my students' teasing on this front). Inside literal language if you disagree that something entails a necessary diminishment of life quality, then seemingly you must be arguing that this something makes no difference. Not so. It is also possible to argue that literal language is itself creating an illusion and it is our job to watch the process in the moment and then move on. That "argument" (if it be called that) is orthogonal to the evaluative issues that occur in normal language. Acceptance and defusion are such orthogonal moves. For example, you say *There is no problem in acknowledging this, as long as it is accepted rather than becoming something else to be upset about.* That sounds soothing enough but I'd like to know the assumptive basis of the statement. If it is a statement about workability I'd still like to know "works toward what?" and then I'd like a little more evidence that there is "no problem" in workability. I know that depends on the moment and the person. Yet that is what I'd look for. If it is a statement grounded in correspondence-based truth then I worry. It could mean that if someone were to say "there is no problem with taking the thought literally that age (etc.) necessarily interferes with quality of life" the basis of the "no problem" claim could be that, say, age actually DOES interfere with engaging in various things you might like and you might as well acknowledge it. There you've lost me. This looks like another variant on "surely you must fuse with this because it corresponds with the world." The problem there is that it is being argued along a single dimension inside literal language (right / wrong; good / bad; True / False) and meanwhile that whole ball of wax resides inside a single end of another continuum (present / not present; fused / not fused; literal / nonliteral). If I detected that kind of move in therapy I would go back to values, defusion, acceptance etc. and want to know "- and what is saying *that* in the service of." The German edition of the ACT book put what my students call "the razor blade of life" graphic (the weird flying wing graphic inside the ACT book) on the cover. I thought that was cool. That graphic could be what we are speaking about. Time for another slide on the razor blade. Weee
EVALUATION Quality of life [cont'd] John McNeill	The notion of 'quality of life' exists as a consensus reality; *it* has no onto-status in the world.... For *Zhuangzi*, 'the fundamental error is to suppose that life presents us with issues which must be formulated in words so that we can envisage alternatives and find reasons for preferring one to the other' (Graham, 2001, p. 6). Grasping for 'quality of life' is a prescription for misery. Hovering in wait for one's life to begin anew as it once was [past] or could be [future] is a certain way to have it *dead-as-it-is.*
PAIN **Suffering, vs. [11-28-04]** Steve Hayes	Russ Harris wrote: I'm seeking clarification on the ACT definition of the word 'suffering.' Some parties use the formulation that pain is the primary (physical or emotional) distressing sensation that occurs in relation to a distressing stimulus, whereas suffering is the psychological reaction to the pain (i.e., the non-acceptance of it and consequences thereof). Re: suffering = dirty discomfort, pain = clean discomfort. (Thus pain is inevitable, suffering is optional.) vs. suffering = clean discomfort + dirty discomfort?

	There is no official deal on this, and I've seen folks in ACT say "suffering is inevitable," but I personally think it is clearer to distinguish pain and suffering - i.e., without struggle you have pain, not suffering per se. However we need to remember that *inside* struggle the two formulae above are indistinguishable for the person struggling. As pain itself becomes the enemy, suffering expands for 2 reasons: There is now second order pain, AND the target of struggle now (unknowingly) includes both sources of pain - leading to an even stronger inducement to struggling.

That is why struggling amplifies suffering so.

Said another way: the upper formula I take to be consistent with an ACT model, but ironically when a person struggles the lower formula becomes functionally (unnecessarily, but still functionally) true. |
| PAIN

Suffering, vs. [cont'd]

Madelon Bolling | I've always been a little conflicted about the "suffering is optional" piece because of the root origins of the word, roughly, "to bear up under," to carry or experience one's pain, in which case suffering is required. Avoidance means I don't suffer enough (or well enough), in this context! (Actually had a therapist tell me I had to suffer more, once.) Accordingly, ACT's mandate to FEEL well fits this picture of suffering as carrying, experiencing.

On the other hand, tradition and usages bring in "dirty" suffering, the unending pain of effort to avoid the inevitable, and this is the basis for the translation of "dukkha" as "suffering" in Buddhist terms. I don't think dukkha has the same (in)felicitous connotation of "bearing consciously."

So we're kinda stuck with the confusing meanings. The great part about this is that it mirrors experience and the confusion when hurt continues and transforms into massive, smoggy, inescapable dirty suffering, vs. bearing it consciously and openly.

So now, "suffering is optional" takes on another meaning (I hadn't seen this before): if you don't (choose to) carry your pain consciously, it will dog you forever. |
| PAIN

Suffering, vs. [cont'd]

Steve Hayes | The etymology of suffering seems more complex.

The "fer" part means "to bear" alright. Same root as reference and relation actually ... L. ferre.

The "suf" part is the same as "sub" which has 29 meanings in the OED. It means "up" in this use but there is a subtlety to it.

The OED says it this way: "from below, up (hence) away."

Thus some of the words using "sub" in that sense do indeed have the connotation "to take up; to include" (e.g., subsume) in which case your etymology ("to bear up under") would be unambiguously correct. But some words using the word "sub" in that same sense have the connotation of "away." "Subduce" for example means "to take away" and comes from the combination of "sub" and a word (L. ducere) that means "to bring; to lead."

This distinction linked to "sub" colors the meaning of suffer: I think the word (in modern usage anyway) goes beyond "to bear up" or "to allow" to include a flavor of "up (hence) away." Note that in the explanation of the primary meaning in the OED it speaks of being "imposed upon" or "inflicted" or "wronged."

I think of suffering as a kind of "carrying" and "enduring" that has a link to "away" ... as in "carrying what I wish would go away."

It's like the distinction between tolerance and acceptance. In ACT, we target the "away" part. |
| **PAIN**

Verbal activity, "contamination" by
[6-22-05]

Steve Mahorney | I once had a patient who wished to have a baby but was avoiding the experience because of her fear of the "pain." It turned out the "pain" also was contaminated by ideas of humiliation, loss of control, fear of bodily damage, and abandonment by others. "Pain" seemed to be a more tolerable phenomenon when it was separated from and experienced in the absence of this relational baggage. I always think about the "baggage" being avoided in pain cases. |
| **REASON**

Excuse for inaction
[5-15-04]

John Bush | Hank Robb wrote:

> I think this "understanding" issue is best categorized under reason giving. "As soon as I have the 'right reasons,' namely the ones that 'explain' what is happening, then I can get acceptance/ willingness with regard to what is in front of me and start dealing effectively with it. No explanatory reason - no action."

Other popular cop-outs:

"I can't do it because I'm not MOTIVATED."

"I can't do it because it would be so HARD."

The need in both cases of course is to take well-chosen action, as a result of which something useful or even enjoyable may get done. As a bonus, the actor may become motivated after the fact or discover that it |

	wasn't as hard as he thought.
	As the Pushmi-Pullyu knows, there's more than one way to make things happen.
REASON **Reason giving, ACT stance on [2-8-03]** ACT Listserv Member	Jonathan Kandell wrote: Can someone explain the ACT aversion to client "reason giving" as a central part of the method (it's the R in FEAR)? From the book (p. 163), the idea seems to be to circumvent client excuses for lack of action on valued action. ("Ok, you're right, now what?") The ACT [stance] sounds more like a criticism of *rationalization* or *excuses* as barriers to action, not reason-giving per se. Maybe I'm just getting too caught up in the terminology, but I don't see reason-giving itself as part of any problem or even an example of avoidance. I think ACT would focus on the watching of the flow of reason giving from the observer self realizing that one becomes fused with language, and then intervention could be as simple as an exercise making that awareness obvious to the reason giver/observer. One would then be able to detach from this literalization, get some flexibility and based on valuing, act [pun intended] differently. So, there is the aspect of distancing, observing the self, getting flexibility by deliteralization and then the ability to take action commensurate with valued goals.
REASON Reason giving, ACT stance on [cont'd] Niklas Törneke	I think it is important to see that ACT is not opposed to reason giving "as a principle" or not even opposed to avoidance "as a principle." Everything is based on a functional analysis. What function does this particular "reason giving" have for this client, in this context? ACT interventions in this regard are based, though, on repeated experience (and research) showing that reason giving very often is a trap of language and as that, is a central process of a lot of human suffering. One example, I believe, is the condition we call depression. In this respect the most problematic reasons are very often the "good" or "true" ones.
REASON **Reason giving/ reasoning/ sense making, helpfulness of [3-23-04]** Steve Hayes	Joseph Ciarrochi wrote: Pennybaker and his colleagues find that talking about a traumatic event leads to improvements in physical health. Pennybaker has his participants write about the traumatic event in a diary for 15 minutes a day for four straight days. They then observe all kinds of health benefits several months later (fewer hospital visits, better immune function, etc.). This kind of research sits pretty well with ACT in general (because it involves getting people to lean towards their private experiences, undermining experiential avoidance, etc.). However, there is one finding that perhaps does not sit as well. Pennybaker analyzed the content of what people wrote about, and found that the more people used causal and insight words in their diaries, the more they showed physical improvements. It looked like they were reasoning through and making sense of their trauma, and this was beneficial. ACT often, but not always, views reason giving as problematic. Indeed, there is good evidence that reason giving can interfere with behavioral activation (Addis & Jacobson, 1996). So it looks like sense making and reasoning can sometimes be good and sometimes be bad. I wonder if you folks have some ideas about when, in an ACT framework, it might be ok to encourage a client to "reason" or make sense of their past traumas. I thought his findings were more complex: The emotions had to be negative but not too extreme. The talk had to be initially disorganized. Then it had to become more organized. Is my memory off? If my memory is not off, that pattern tells me: - you are dealing with difficult emotions but not so horrible as to overwhelm people; - they are not things the person has thought about a lot; - organizational talk emerges as the person exposes themself to these events and tries to do something with them. If that is so, the organizational talk changes may be a proxy variable for a) not avoiding, and b) doing something new. Psychological flexibility in other words. If so, you could probably get the opposite results with well-worn stories. There you get a lot of organized talk from the beginning -- I believe Pennybaker's methods do not work in this case. If you did an ACT deal and blew up well-worn traumatic stories, journaling might show the opposite pattern ... letting go of organized talk (in this case) might be an indicator of a) not avoiding, and b) doing something new.
REASON Reason giving/ reasoning/ sense making, helpfulness of [cont'd] John Forsyth	Humans engage in reason giving all the time, and much of it is quite functional. Good and bad are evaluative judgments, not properties of the reasons themselves. My take is that the value of reason giving ought to be understood in relation to other behaviors and context.

REASON Reason giving/ reasoning/ sense making, helpfulness of [cont'd] ACT Listserv Member	On the subject of giving reasons as a way to encourage/motivate clients to come in contact with negative emotional content, a couple of questions come to mind. First, reasons have three basic (with subcategories I am sure) functions: making sense/ordering the world, which in turn allows rules to be formed; to avoid negative consequences of bx (making excuses for behavior, to justify behavior either a priori or post hoc, etc.); and reasons can be used as attempts to motivate (e.g., staying together in a relationship for the kids, sacrifices made for a greater good, etc.). All three of these categories can be good; values, especially how they are utilized in ACT, fall into #3. All three of these can be bad also: #1 can create insensitivity to actual contingencies; #2 is obvious, WMD's, for example as an excuse to kill thousands; #3 I sort of gave one already, staying in bad relationships; charities also do this and sometimes con men and politicians utilize reasons this way too. So if there is this fine line between helpful and harmful, is it ethical to encourage clients to utilize reason giving as a step towards "mental health"? (and really the clients we see will most of the time, have been engaged in reason/causal talk for a long time before coming in, so workability really becomes an issue - if it worked they wouldn't be sitting in our office). Secondly, assuming that you could establish tight contextual control over causal talk/reason giving, how would you maintain it outside of therapy to avoid the pitfalls of reason giving? Wouldn't that be more than a little unethical? The great thing about Values work is that it is difficult to take it to the extreme and cause harm. Establishing behavioral flexibility and goals that move toward improving quality of life, should be self maintaining - in other words if it is creating improvements in living/vitality, that would continue to motivate after the initial motivation utilized in therapy of identifying values (which is when they sort of act as reasons in my opinion).
RELIGION **Compatibility with ACT - thought/ deed distinction [10-9-02]** James Herbert	Not all Judeo-Christian perspectives make sharp distinctions between an individual's responsibility for private experiences versus overt action. In fact, some traditions (at least implicitly) equate the two, as in "the thought equals the deed," resulting in extremely damaging attempts to keep a "clean" mind. ACT is clearly much more compatible with some spiritual traditions than others.
RELIGION Compatibility with ACT - thought/ deed distinction [cont'd] James Herbert	Kirk Dougher wrote: Often you must illustrate the difference between religious cultures and religious doctrine. It is certainly imbedded in many religious cultures that the thought equals the deed. However, it is often an artifact of social convention rather than cannon. Further, defining what temptation or impulse might mean with reference to history and current context often liberates clients into having a choice for the first time. Kirk, interesting point about the culture/doctrine distinction. Even if confounding the thought-deed distinction reflects culture rather than doctrine, however, it may be an academic point, as people are embedded in cultures (including religious ones), and it is at that level that we meet them.
RELIGION Compatibility with ACT - thought/ deed distinction [cont'd] James Herbert	ACT Listserv Member wrote: Fantasizing about homosexuality is a deed. Having an automatic thought about homosexuality is not a deed. I think you're on shaky ground, however, in marking such a sharp distinction between a "fantasy" and an "automatic thought." When does one become the other? Imagine if I told myself that it was okay if an image of chocolate cake "involuntarily" popped into my head, as long as I didn't fantasize about eating it, which would be a sin. Guess what would happen? (rhetorical question!) According to your example, I assume that a homosexual thought experienced as intrusive and involuntary would be okay, but lingering on that thought too long would be verboten, right?
RELIGION Compatibility with ACT - thought/ deed distinction [cont'd] Kirk Dougher	We do meet people at the level of being embedded in their culture. However, to let them reside there in the face of conflicting evidence within their own religion would be difficult. Rather, I would suggest they grapple with the issue from within that context. That is, check it out with their ecclesiastical leader. Study their doctrine and examine the implications in their culture. Many people within a religious culture not only recognize but are disturbed by doctrinal shifting within the culture. I would have to agree with the ACT Listserv Member in making a distinction between what was labeled an automatic thought and what was called fantasy. A line of cleavage must be established between reactions to context and history and behavior. To move it to a less cognitive example, I would expect individuals confronted by the physically-threatening stance of another to react by ducking, running, or assuming a defensive posture. However, I would separate that movement, especially the latter, from a combination one-two delivered to the chin of physical threat. This situation again is historically dependent because if the person confronted has a boxing history, the one-two may be of the automatic type rather than the volitional one. Yet, the differing backgrounds do not change the fact that at somewhere along the way events become more deliberate rather than responsive. In the world of thoughts, clients are also able to mark a difference in that which is impulsive from that

which is volitional. For many this demarcation is different. For some, the thoughts of sex with another, regardless of gender, may be both volitional and outside their value system. For others, the same thought may be historically and contextually so entrenched that they have that thought as a response to the stimuli. My experience in working with ACT in the context of many sexual behavioral excesses, is that this line shifts for clients over time. The difficulty for the therapist is to not get caught up drawing the line. Rather, to have the client examine the possibility of its existence. It is when we engage in debate over where the line is that clients can revert into the stance of trying to force themselves into not having fantasy. Which, as James points out, would be an exercise in futility. With only a slight window to operate in, the client can let go of much of the guilt and shame associated with the thoughts and move west rather than expecting to have already been there.

Within the Christian traditions much emphasis is placed on thought as sinful. However, much like trying not to think of something requires thought of the issue one is trying to avoid, being tempted requires a desire for the behavior that cuts against a value system. To take Christian clients and illustrate this through having them consider the probability of Jesus' desire for the bread he was tempted with, puts them in the sacrilegious position of considering their savior as committing sin or freeing themselves up to have automatic thoughts that are not sinful.

Just for the record, it is kind of fun to use this in session to put the client in contact with previously avoided emotion, regardless of the therapist's own spiritual stance.

THOUGHT **Feeling, and - link between [1-15-05]** J. A. García-Higuera	For me, many times, thoughts and feelings are inextricably linked. I explain to my clients that, when we produce a thought preceding an act, immediately our body reacts preparing the behaviour, then a set of feelings appears; and generally, when we perceive a feeling, a thought accompanies it. When we produce a thought many times, we summarize it successively, until the extreme that a word or an image produces the same reaction in our bodies, and, finally, we may only perceive the reaction, it is said, our feelings. These are our automatic thoughts. The problem is to follow the inverse way and disautomate the thought. Under the phrase "I am feeling…," most of the times there is a thought. The problem is to find it, but normally is very easy, because we may ask it directly to the client. Monsters in the bus say two things, one catastrophic prediction and a suggestion of the behaviour to avoid it. Usually we first eliminate of our conscious thought one of the two parts. Our client may say "I feel as this is going to be a catastrophe" or "I feel as if I must do that," but we, with the client, must search the other part. Problems with clients are that they find some feeling because they avoid and substitute them by thoughts, and other times they have feelings linked to automatic and unconscious thoughts.
THOUGHT **Self-acceptance affirmations, caution re [1-7-05]** John McNeill	Russ Harris wrote: Saying to yourself, "Even though I have this problem, I deeply and completely accept myself" can be very powerful. A word of caution regarding use of self-acceptance affirmations: I have made this point elsewhere on the ACT discussion list, and in response to other topics like the 'quality of life' and 'anger as a non-dirty anything.' My point is this: Distinctions occasion their opposites, and where social and egological divisions are emphasized, 'thorns and briars may grow' [from the *Daodejing*]. In regard to self-acceptance affirmations, a self that seeks acceptance is at odds with itself during times when unacceptance dominates experience. The experience designated by one pole expresses psychological 'tensionality' with the other, and a double-sided mind divided against itself generates needless suffering. I believe that RFT explains and demonstrates how this can be so - on the basis of verbal relational framing processes [opposition, distinction, comparison, hierarchy, so on] and the stimulus functions transformed therein. Self-affirmation content becomes vulnerable in the face of <u>threats to</u> self-identifying concepts and group status, and there is a growing literature demonstrating that identity-threats increase to the extent that we more firmly fix and attempt to secure ourselves through essentialist conceptions [affirmations] of self. The real insidious trap is this: Increasing personal identity affirmation does artificially enhance a sense of self-worth, but it then becomes the very source that creates our greatest vulnerability in an impermanent world. As hope for personal affirmation in the world increases, so does the fear of it being lost. So we defend our personal and social inventions as a way to keep our self-views about others, the world, and ourselves intact. However, self-identity concepts that serve as an index of one's 'okayness' - self-esteem, pride, and confidence - are easily eroded when achievement environments become challenging or when coping attempts fail. [Thus, the Daoist and Buddhist emphasis on selflessness.] Moreover, verbal formulations of truth are open to *either-or* debate, and so I can regard myself as *either* worthy of *or* unworthy of acceptance depending upon my particular moment. No amount of verbal convincing can convert a verbal truth into a nonverbal truth [though the reverse may be possible, they are not the same]. The self that lives undivided with itself, just as an inbreath exists in harmony with its opposed outbreath, finds no duality, and thus finds

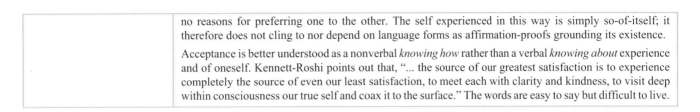

no reasons for preferring one to the other. The self experienced in this way is simply so-of-itself; it therefore does not cling to nor depend on language forms as affirmation-proofs grounding its existence.

Acceptance is better understood as a nonverbal *knowing how* rather than a verbal *knowing about* experience and of oneself. Kennett-Roshi points out that, "... the source of our greatest satisfaction is to experience completely the source of even our least satisfaction, to meet each with clarity and kindness, to visit deep within consciousness our true self and coax it to the surface." The words are easy to say but difficult to live.

Chapter 7
<u>ACT: The Therapeutic Process and Clinical Resources</u>

This final chapter contains posts concerning the process of therapy, including discussion of the therapist's role and the therapeutic relationship. Suggestions for ACT clinical and reference resources, such as books, measures and materials for use in therapy are also to be found here. Comments on exercises and metaphors used in ACT, along with proposed new (or borrowed) exercises and metaphors, constitute a major part of the chapter.

BOOK

   Acceptance and change: Content and context in psychotherapy

   Mindfulness and acceptance: Expanding the cognitive-behavioral tradition [6-11-04]

   Steve Hayes

The "new paradigm" deal is starting to get out there. It will be laid out very clearly in the ACT special issue of Behavior Therapy (by the way, you can see it coming also in Barlow's lead article in the current issue). But the book length idea you [Darin Cairns] have is a good one. So good we've actually tried to do it.

There are two books that try. The 1994 book was the first shot across the bow: Hayes, S. C., Jacobson, N. S., Follette, V. M., & Dougher, M. J. (Eds.) (1994). *Acceptance and change: Content and context in psychotherapy*. Reno, NV: Context Press. It is still available. It came out of the first Reno conference we organized on this topic, and it has chapters from an interesting group of folks:

Hayes - domains of acceptance
Dougher - acceptance as action
Greenburg - humanistic approaches
Linehan - dialectics
Biglan - culture practices
Jacobson & Christensen - marital
Follette - abuse
LoPiccolo - paraphilias
McCurry - caregivers to the elderly
Marlatt - substance abuse
Wulfert - relation to AA
Auguston - family context
Robb / Ellis - REBT
Cordova and Kohlenberg - therapeutic relationship

The "third wave" is really more addressed in the newer volume of this kind, though ironically I could not beat the 3rd wave drum TOO hard because some of the 3rd wavers are not yet comfortable calling themselves that. The new book is Hayes, S. C., Follette, V. M., & Linehan, M. (2004) (Eds.), *Mindfulness and acceptance: Expanding the cognitive-behavioral tradition*. New York: Guilford Press. Guilford already has it on their website ... may be out by APA in August. It also came from a Reno conference. The chapters in it are:

Chapter 1. Acceptance and Commitment Therapy and the New Behavior Therapies: Mindfulness, Acceptance, and Relationship. Steven C. Hayes
Chapter 2. Dialectical Behavior Therapy: Synthesizing Radical Acceptance with Skillful Means. Marsha Linehan, Clive Robbins and Henry Schmidt III
Chapter 3. Mindfulness-Based Cognitive Therapy: An Integrative Approach for Prevention of Relapse in Depression. Zindel V. Segal, John D. Teasdale, and J. Mark G. Williams
Chapter 4. Acceptance, Mindfulness, and CBT: Comparisons, Contrasts and Application to Anxiety. Susan Orsillo, Lizabeth Roemer, Jennifer Block Lerner, & Matthew T. Tull
Chapter 5. Functional Analytic Psychotherapy, Cognitive Therapy, and Acceptance. Robert J. Kohlenberg, Jonathan W. Kanter, Madelon Bolling, Reo Wexner, Chauncey Parker, & Mavis Tsai
Chapter 6. Values Work in Acceptance and Commitment Therapy: Setting a Course for Behavioral Treatment. Kelly Wilson and Amy R. Murrell
Chapter 7. Finding the Action in Behavioral Activation: The Search for Empirically-Supported Interventions and Mechanisms of Change. Christopher Martell, Michael Addis, & Sona Dimidjian
Chapter 8. Mindfulness, Acceptance, Validation and "Individual" Psychopathology in Couples. Alan E. Fruzzetti and Kate M. Iverson
Chapter 9. Acceptance, Mindfulness, and Trauma. Victoria M. Follette, Kathleen M. Palm, and Mandra L. Rasmussen-Hall
Chapter 10. Generalized Anxiety Disorder: Bringing Cognitive Behavioral Therapy into the Valued Present. T. D. Borkovec and Brian Sharpless
Chapter 11. Acceptance and Change in the Treatment of Eating Disorders: The Evolution of Manual-Based Cognitive Behavioral Therapy (CBT). G. Terence Wilson
Chapter 12. Vipassana Meditation as a Treatment for Alcohol and Drug Use Disorders. G. Alan Marlatt, Katie Witkiewitz, Tiara M. Dillworth, Sarah W. Bowen, George A. Parks, Laura Marie Macpherson, Heather S. Lonczak, Mary E. Larimer, Tracy Simpson, Arthur W. Blume, and Rick Crutcher
Chapter 13. Acceptance, Mindfulness, and Change in Couple Therapy. Andy Christensen, Mia Sevier, Lorelei Simpson, & Krista Gattis

We did ask authors to keep a focus not just on their technologies but on how it linked to these larger changes in the field.

My guess: if what we are doing hits as it should, there will eventually be a number of books on this topic looking backward. We are in the middle of creating change, and the full description of what the change is comes as much after the change as before it....

BOOK **ACT - recommended for clients? [12-12-03]** Steve Hayes	Mark Taylor wrote: Has anyone suggested a patient/client read the ACT book? Or, would you? The only time I've mentioned the ACT book to a client is toward the end of successful treatment, and then only for folks with substantial education. More for fun than clinical utility at that point. Folks do find it on the web though, so occasionally you get clients coming in who have it. They rarely get through it.
BOOK **ACT and treatment of chronic pain [4-29-05]** JoAnne Dahl	Our new book on ACT and treatment of chronic pain that was released just a couple of days ago deals with using ACT not only with the person with pain and on sick leave but also using ACT as a consultant at the workplace.... Dahl, J. C., Wilson, K. G., Luciano, C., & Hayes, S. C. (2005). *Acceptance and Commitment Therapy for Chronic Pain*. Reno, NV: Context Press.
BOOK ACT and treatment of chronic pain [cont'd] Steve Hayes	JoAnne's new *Acceptance and Commitment Therapy for Chronic Pain* book is indeed finally out. Definitely worth having ... check it out at the CP website, www.contextpress.com. If you are an ACT person, it is one of those books that needs to be in your possession. Kel, Carmen, and I helped out as well with this project.
BOOK **Mindfulness - recommended text** **MINDFULNESS** **Recommended text [8-23-03]** Niklas Törneke	As there is so much interest on the list on definition etc. of mindfulness I want to recommend a very nice text on that subject, for those who have not already read it. It is a chapter in the book *A small matter of proof: The legacy of Donald M. Baer* from Context Press. Chapter 15 is written by Ruth Baer; the title is "Mindfulness and Behavior Analysis." This is one of the best texts on mindfulness, from a scientific point of view, that I have read. It is simple (in the good sense of that word!) and it hits at the core of the process, as I understand it. It is a beautiful illustration of Skinner's classic line: "A person who has been made 'aware of himself' is in a better position to predict and control his own behavior." The text gives a good base for the kind of "functional talk" that is so important in psychotherapy. There are also parallels to what is called "self as context" in ACT ("Organism as host"). This is a pre-RFT analysis. To my thinking that does not lessen its value. Good behavior analysis can always be done on different "levels." A step "down," of course, would need RFT. As a matter of fact the author ends the article with important questions on the origin of stimulus-functions of thoughts and feelings and that is exactly the point where RFT provides important answers. Highly recommended reading for anyone who wants to understand mindfulness from a scientific perspective!
BOOK **Philosophical writings (re suffering; avoidance) [6-2-03]** Graham Taylor	Couldn't resist sharing these gems. They come from a recent book, *The Consolations of Philosophy* by Alain de Botton. The book was put out last year, at the same time as a 6 part BBC series of the same name, looking at how philosophers have tackled the problems of everyday life. Montaigne: "We must suffer whatever we cannot avoid. Our life is composed, like the harmony of the world, of discords as well as of different tones, sweet and harsh, sharp and flat, soft and loud. If a musician liked only some of them, what could he sing? He has got to know how to use them all and blend them together. So too must we with good and ill, which are of one substance with our life." And a couple from Nietzsche, anticipating experiential avoidance: "The worst sickness of men has originated in the way they have combatted their sicknesses. What seemed a cure has in the long run produced something worse than what it was supposed to overcome. The means which worked immediately, anaesthetizing and intoxicating, the so-called consolations, were ignorantly supposed to be actual cures. The fact was not noticed ... that these instantaneous alleviations often had to be paid for with a general and profound worsening of the complaint." "To regard states of distress in general as an objection, as something that must be abolished, is the [supreme idiocy], in a general sense a real disaster in its consequences ... almost as stupid as the will to abolish bad weather." East or west, the message is an old one....

BOOK **Tuesdays with Morrie** [8-22-03] Eric Fox	I read a good book that may be of interest to some on the list. It is entitled "Tuesdays with Morrie" written by Mitch Albom, and it's about a journalist who is reunited (and it feels so good) with a former professor and mentor who he has not seen in 20 years. The mentor is dying of Lou Gehrig's disease, and as his body slowly withers away, he meets with his former student every Tuesday during the last couple weeks of his life. They discuss issues such as the meaning of life, the importance of values and family, and dealing with death.
	Those involved with ACT may find the book interesting because themes such as valuing and acceptance are central throughout. Other Buddhist principles are espoused at various points, as well (actually, at the airport I saw a copy of the book sitting in the "eastern religion/philosophy" section of the bookstore). It's also a very quick and easy read; perhaps something to be suggested for clients?
BOOK **Tuesdays with Morrie** [3-4-04] Jennifer Block Lerner	This comes from Mitch Albom's *Tuesdays with Morrie: An old man, a young man, and life's greatest lesson*. It is an excerpt from the chapter entitled, "The Sixth Tuesday: We Talk about Emotions." It is a chronicle of Mitch Albom's reunion (and subsequent "class sessions") with a beloved college professor who has recently been diagnosed with ALS/Lou Gehrig's disease.
	On a particularly challenging day, Mitch sat down with Morrie in the midst of a violent coughing spell. When Morrie subsequently closed his eyes and sat quietly, Mitch waited expectantly. Morrie then explained that what he was doing was "detaching" himself. Given his previous admonitions to Mitch to experience life and emotions fully, this didn't seem to fit. Upon further questioning, Morrie continued:
	Ah. You're thinking, Mitch. But detachment doesn't mean you don't let the experience penetrate you. On the contrary, you let it penetrate you fully. That's how you are able to leave it…. Take any emotion - love for a woman, or grief for a loved one, or what I'm going through, fear and pain from a deadly illness. If you hold back on the emotions - if you don't allow yourself to go all the way through them - you can never get to being detached, you're too busy being afraid. You're afraid of the pain, you're afraid of the grief. You're afraid of the vulnerability that loving entails. But by throwing yourself into these emotions, by allowing yourself to dive in, all the way, over your head even, you experience them fully and completely. You know what pain is. You know what love is. You know what grief is. And only then can you say, 'All right. I have experienced that emotion. I recognize that emotion. Now I need to detach from that emotion for a moment' (Albom, 1997, pp. 103-104).
	Mitch thought about how different Morrie's approach was from how most people dealt with their emotions. "How we feel lonely, sometimes to the point of tears, but we don't let those tears come because we are not supposed to cry. Or how we feel a surge of love for a partner but we don't say anything because we're frozen with the fear of what those words might do to the relationship" (Albom, 1997, p. 105). Furthermore, Mitch recognized the wisdom inherent in Morrie's seemingly paradoxical method: "It won't hurt you. It will only help. If you let the fear inside, if you pull it on like a familiar shirt, then you can say to yourself, 'All right, it's just fear, I don't have to let it control me. I see it for what it is'" (p. 105).
	ACT-related interpretation: Morrie's stance toward his emotions, bodily sensations, and other private experiences is obviously consistent with ACT's emphasis on defusion and willingness. For example, his description of his "most fearful moments" in the same chapter (i.e., "…but once he recognized the feel of those emotions, their texture, their moisture…"; Albom, 1997, p. 104) bears some similarity to the process of participating in the *Physicalizing* and *Tin Can Monster* exercises. What I find most compelling about the book, however, is the portrayal of Morrie Schwartz (late professor at Brandeis Univ. as someone who has clearly asked himself some hard questions about what matters and who has lived a full life (post and pre diagnosis) in accordance with these values. Thus, all of the above (wading through the swamp of at-times intensely painful physical and emotional experiences) is in the service of this valued action.
CONSENT **Experiential exercises** [4-13-04] ACT Listserv Member	[Re the importance of 'voluntary exposure' - p.85 of the ACT book - when conducting experiential exercises] On my practicum team with Kelly, we focus on asking for permission a lot. In asking for permission connected to their value, it seems that individuals are more willing. But more importantly, it is a choice of their own. Experiential exercises are incredibly difficult for the client (and therapist too:)), and I think it's important when we're in the room to get with how hard it is for the client to experience these private events. And making this task a choice attached to their values is of incredible value to the client. And it makes your work together about something that is chosen instead of something that must be done.
EXERCISE **Defusion - cinema screen (NLP); ACT/ RFT perspective** [5-14-05] Niklas Törneke	Paul Woodcraft wrote:
	I wonder what people's views are of an NLP technique I came across for PTSD? The technique involves people observing the traumatic event in imagination from a point prior to the start as though viewing on a cinema screen.
	I have used the particular exercise mentioned many times in doing ACT. As a typical defusion exercise, both with memories and with thoughts: With thoughts, for example having clients change the color or kinds

	of typing of particular thoughts, as the client sees them written out on the screen. You can also have clients change position in relation to what they see, as in the classical NLP exercise.... Why this would be helpful can be understood from an RFT perspective.
EXERCISE Defusion - cinema screen (NLP); ACT/ RFT perspective [cont'd] Niklas Törneke	Monica Pignotti wrote: Would it be possible for you to explain this further -- that is, how it works from an RFT perspective? The RFT perspective on this exercise would be similar to other typical defusion work. It could be described as work with content (whatever is put out on the screen) and helping the client to experience that as separate (at least in part) from "me," that is self as context. A simple RFT perspective (I have a preference for simplicity, when it works...) could be to see a typical problem for clients (read: humans) to be this. Aversive experiences (thoughts, memories, negative affect) easily enter into frames of coordination with self. Defusion exercises like this one, using the experience of spatiality (is that the English word?) or distance establish a different context. What is there (on the screen, for example) is not here. Here/there is in a frame of opposition, or at least difference. (This could be conceptualized as a frame of perspective, but for the present discussion that does not matter.) So a context is established that cues a relational framing of the aversive experience (negative affect, thoughts, whatever) as different from self. The purpose in treatment, of course, would be to change the way this experience controls action. This work then should be done together with work on valued action. The classical NLP exercise (as I learned it and use it) has two steps. First you sit in the cinema, watching whatever you want to work with on the screen, changing it in different ways (color, speed, running it backwards etc.). Then you imagine yourself going back to where the camera is, watching both the screen and yourself sitting in the cinema. I am not sure what the latter move would be from an RFT perspective. Maybe just "further away," or maybe something more (?). The first move would be a more typical ACT defusion exercise, I guess. An excellent article that expands on this whole topic (rather than this specific NLP-thing) is: Luciano, C., et al. (2004). A proposal for synthesizing verbal contexts in experiential avoidance disorder and Acceptance and Commitment Therapy. *International Journal of Psychology and Psychological Treatment, 4*, 377-394.
EXERCISE Defusion - cinema screen (NLP); ACT/ RFT perspective [cont'd] Niklas Törneke	Thinking a bit more about it I have a hard time seeing the difference between the two parts of the exercise, on the level of process or action. There is a difference in content of course ... (what is seen, or watched) but from an ACT perspective that is probably not essential. It is the "stepping back" that is the heart of defusion, the action that is encouraged. If that is so, the point of the second part is doing it again, with a somewhat different content. Like in the typical ACT exercise of watching thoughts floating on leaves. Whatever turns up, you put it out there. Something new turns up, you put it out there again. And the same, once again, and again... I think this makes sense as doing this over and over is usually needed for defusion to make a difference. From a behavioral perspective what is needed is discrimination of this very behavior, which of course is easier as it is repeated. That it is repeated with different content is also essential. That selects *the action, the way of behaving* as the thing to discriminate.
EXERCISE **Defusion - programming re Santa Claus etc. [2-23-05]** Graham Taylor	This story isn't a metaphor in the conventionally presented sense, rather a metaphorical conversational piece that varies in nature with each client, but the basic structure is common. I can illustrate it with a recent session transcript between me (T - therapist) and C (client, a female client, 33 y.o., with lifelong issues around the theme (early maladaptive schema for all the lurking cognitive therapists) of never being good enough. Origins were parents who set unrealistic standards and were overly critical, even of excellent performance, e.g., if she got 95% for maths; "What did you get wrong?" was a typical parental response. This woman is a high achiever, driven, and came to therapy because she was burning out (depression) and having marital problems due to work taking up potential couple and family time). This is how it went: T: Tell me Susan (not her real name), as a child did you believe in Santa Claus? C: Yes, we used to put out a carrot for the reindeer and a beer for Santa. They were always gone the next morning. (both laugh) T: Still believe? C: 'Course not, but it's great for the kids. T: Yeah. And when you see a rainbow reaching the ground (T arcs hand) - what's over there? (pointing to end of arc) C: (chuckles) A pot of gold. T: Strange - everyone says that. Not a BAR of gold, or a CHEST of gold, but a "POT of gold." (pause) Ever gone digging? C: (laughs) No. T: Back to Santa for a moment. When you walk through the children's toys section at Myers (an Australian

wide department store) in mid December, what do you see?

C: Santa, all the Christmas stuff, my kids post their letters [to Santa] in the box.

T: Great. Hope you know what's in them. And when you picture that now - just close your eyes - (pause) what comes up?

C: (smiles) Santa's toy factory at the North Pole - the elves.

T: Now you don't believe in this stuff, right, (C affirms with nod) but it still comes up. And when you see a rainbow, what pops up in your mind?

C: A pot of gold. (smiles)

T: Wow, that's some programming. Just as well we don't actually believe what our minds say, or we'd both be chasing rainbows with a shovel. Where did these thoughts come from?

C: What we learnt as a child I suppose, stories.

T: And this idea, you haven't done well enough, you've failed. Where did that come from?

C: Same place I guess - lots of those stories.

T: So when a rainbow comes along, along comes a pot of gold, and at Christmas it's thoughts and images of the elves, ... and when you don't get something exactly right, what's going to show up?

C: I'm not good enough.

T: Yeah. And tell me, how would we get rid of the thought of a pot of gold, or the elves?

C: Don't know, I guess we don't.

T: So what about this other stuff ... I've failed ... I'm not good enough ... nothing I do is ever quite good enough ... and all the dozens of variations?

C: You're saying it's like that?

T: Could be - what would it be like for you if it was?

The session moved towards how thoughts (believed) drove compensatory behaviour (working longer hours, taking work home), and what would show up if she broke the old behavioural Rules of Living, e.g., left home when others did rather than staying late, not taking the laptop home, etc. Such examples of increased behavioural flexibility emerged over the next weeks, and the believability of the old thoughts went down (just like Zettle & Hayes showed many years ago).

Comment: This is one of many ways of doing cognitive defusion, or as I prefer to write it, de-fusion. It also introduces the notion that images, thoughts, beliefs will show up given (1) our history / programming, and (2) the current context (Christmas, a rainbow, a mistake, etc.). It's an illustration of Relational Frames. I use examples I can reasonably guess have been a part of their history. The "could be" in the last T statement is a suggestion to hold what we have worked out lightly; it introduces another possible way to respond to the stuff that keeps coming up.

EXERCISE **Eye contact - purpose of [5-5-05]** Patty Bach	Monica Pignotti wrote: To clarify regarding Scientology's eye contact exercise, the purpose of the exercise as stated by Scientology was very much the same as that stated in the ACT book ... to train a person to comfortably be in the presence of another person -- to just "be there" without feeling the compulsion to do anything else. The purpose of the ACT exercise is not training to be comfortable or be present without feeling the compulsion to do something. It is partially to notice just how uncomfortable merely being present with another can feel; to learn to be present with another person while simultaneously being present with compulsions to do something else, to avoid, to laugh, etc.; to let go of trying to do the exercise "right" and notice how you tend to drift in and out of being fully present; to notice how amazing it is to be fully present with another. To point out that barriers to willingness and commitment - such as discomfort - show up in all kinds of activities, even in something as simple as making eye contact with someone for a minute or two. The exercise is a good example of how an exercise might have different purposes in therapy versus in training. The above description applies to both therapy clients and trainees, and I like it in training as an example of "the stance of the therapist" - that we are in the same boat as the client. Describing it without doing it definitely does not have the same impact. I've done the exercise numerous times and I still can't do it "right," i.e., be fully present without some discomfort or compulsion to do something else showing up. And I find it always powerful. Sometimes - when mindful, I suppose - even thinking about it, "the incredible fact that there is another person here, another human being, looking back at you" moves me to soften my stance with almost anyone I experience as difficult.
EXERCISE **Milk, milk, milk [6-4-04]** ACT Listserv Member	Francis De Groot wrote: Can deliteralization exercises be seen as a kind of skill training? Sure, it is a skill. Deliteralizing teaches people to see words as words, and therefore not harmful (in the physical sense of the word harmful) although they are hurtful (have an emotional impact). This process can be used to create a space that allows for more flexible responses to both internal words (our cognitions) and

external words that normally accompany psychological suffering, and behaviors that may not be socially acceptable (violent actions being connected to anger which may be connected to both internal and external words that are connected to some idiosyncratic experience...etc. etc. (btw "connected to" could easily be restated as "relationally framed")). So in a sense, deliteralizing language is teaching clients to see words as just words, that have power because of their connection to our history and to current perceived consequences or contingencies (e.g., someone calls you an asshole and you "have" to respond or you will be seen as weak).

[FDG] The milk, milk, milk exercise: one can do it with other negative thoughts. Is it wise to try this immediately with personally relevant thoughts (I tried it but it wasn't very successful; maybe not long enough); or is it better to start with the more neutral milk, milk, milk?

Starting with more "neutral" words like milk, makes it easier for the client to experience the loss of meaning through the repetition for two reasons: 1) milk has physical properties that most westerners have experienced on a semi-regular basis; 2) milk for most people is "neutral" (meaning it doesn't usually carry any negative connotations, though it is certainly possible that for some it will (e.g., vegan clients)); this "neutrality" is a farce because it actually has for most Americans a positive connotation, and therefore it is easy to get a client to do the exercise.

A note on my use of quotes around neutral - as I alluded to with milk, neutrality of words is not attainable (at least not for any sustainable time period); in fact the exercise is meant to give the client that experience of a word becoming relatively neutral and/or meaningless. All words have meaning, that is part of their function, in fact all words have multiple meanings (even outside the dictionary's multiple definitions). They are derived from our experiences with the words or words and concepts used in connection with them, that will alter how those words function for each individual. I have alluded to this before in the discussion on clean vs. dirty - we cannot ever be sure that words we use in sessions will be received the way we intended; this is where our basic clinical skills come in to play (using clarification statements, questions, being present and watching for changes in client verbalizations or body language) to help us choose our words or at least restrict their meaning in session by clarifying our usage (although I like to promote clients coming up with their own descriptors for certain concepts, so I use clarifying the intended meaning of the words as a way to elicit "better," functionally synonymous, words that the client connects with the meaning of, that I then use in session).

By repeating this exercise with more clinically relevant words (and you may, for some, have to build your way up to the more difficult words somewhat like a SUDS scale), you allow the client to see it works with all kinds of words, and hopefully will promote some generalization of the process.

EXERCISE **Milk, milk, milk - French philosopher version** **Reciting the telephone directory [9-7-03]** Graham Taylor	There are several ACT relevant exercises in a fascinating little book by a French philosopher, including a variation milk, milk, milk. The translation from the original French is itself a joy to read. *Empty a word of its meaning* This can take place anywhere, and at any time. Simply make sure, once again, that no one can hear you. Best to avoid the tear of being ridiculed while you're doing it. Speaking to oneself is nothing. But to be spied upon and teased would spoil the desired result. So, choose a place where no one will hear you. Take what comes to hand, the most ordinary object - a pen, a watch, a glass - or even a piece of your own clothing: a button, a belt, a pocket, a shoelace. Whatever. Just let it be ordinary. Its name is known, its presence familiar. You have always called this object by the same word. Consistent, natural, normal. Now take this inoffensive, familiar, safe little object in your hand. Repeat its name, in a low voice, as you look at it. Stare at the watch in your hand and repeat: watch; watch; watch; watch; watch; watch; watch. You can keep going. It shouldn't take long. In a few seconds the familiar word detaches itself, and hardens. You find yourself repeating a series of strange sounds. A series of absurd and meaningless noises, that denote nothing, indicate nothing, and remain insensate, formless or harsh. You probably experimented like this as a child. Nearly all of us have felt the extreme fragility of the link between words and things. As soon as it is twisted, or pulled, or distended, that link becomes problematic. It becomes contorted, or it breaks. The word dries out and crumbles. A scattered shell of sonorous inanity. And what happens to the object is no less startling. It's as though its substance becomes thicker, denser, cruder. The object is somehow more present, and differently so, the moment it escapes the fine net of recognizable syllables. You should repeat this old game of dissociation. Try to observe the moment when meaning dissolves, and how a new, raw reality emerges outside of words. Glimpse the hard scale beneath the prose. Repeat the same word several times, for the same object, and dissipate all meaning. Is it not marvellous? Terrifying? Funny? Just a few seconds are enough to tear that fine film within which we make sense of

things, smug with the power of giving things a name.

There are other fascinating exercises in this book such as ritually reciting the telephone directory on your knees at the same time each day for 15 minutes and noticing "A sense of the extreme force inherent in these absurd constraints, the strange fascination they exert, and the power with which, confusedly, one cannot help investing them. There is a strong likelihood that you won't be able to go on without furnishing some explanation. You will probably start by constructing a reason for your behaviour. You will elaborate, if only for a joke, a myth that can incorporate your recitation, its meaning and its goal. ... If you find you can't stop, found a sect."

From Roger-Pol Droit (2002). *101 Experiments in the Philosophy of Everyday Life*. London: Faber & Faber. (Translation by Stephen Romer, pages 5 & 187).

EXERCISE **Physicalizing - effect on distress level** **EXPOSURE** **Distress level, effect on [10-27-03]** Niklas Törneke	Mark Taylor wrote: I tried a distancing exercise in which I had the client think of a distressing thought (his past) and notice the sensations associated with it (feeling in gut). I then had him describe the sensation (size, shape, color, texture). When I asked if he felt more or less distressed, he responded "more." I then went on to have him describe some other thoughts and sensations in the same manner. However, he reported feeling more distressed. Certainly, this isn't what I expected. He really bought into the stingerless bee idea of thoughts not being able to harm him, so I thought he would do well with this exercise also. This is quite common, I would say. Remember, this kind of exercise (if it is a part of ACT) is not done with the purpose of having the client "feel less distressed." Some feel less, some feel more distressed. If feeling "more distressed" is between this client and valued action, going there with him might be an important step in therapy. This is not the enemy. Is he willing to go there, if that is what it takes to do what is really important to him? If so, going there in different ways (more of the same exercise, other similar ones) with an open, observant attitude (mindfulness...) might make a difference to him. What if this "distress" is not what it says it is?
EXERCISE Physicalizing - effect on distress level [cont'd] **EXPOSURE** Distress level, effect on [cont'd] Steve Hayes	Not uncommon, however: I usually don't ask about distress at least initially. Too tempting to the client to cast what we are doing as a new, tricky way to mount the old agenda. I use the metaphor of size, shape, color, texture to communicate that to me. I keep focused on a specific psychological item ... if the item is too complicated it sustains itself. So the item might be "the feelings associated with your divorce" not "your divorce" since that will pull in the story, not the psychology of it. I assume that it is stuck so after looking at it for a while, I look for other reactions that are less obvious. E.g., if I've had the person "place the thought on the floor: and describe its size, shape, color, texture," I have them find what they feel *about* this object ("this big, black, heavy, powerful" item etc. ... use the client's own words). Then I have them move the first one to the side and put THAT thought or feeling on the floor and I do the whole thing over. After some time on that second order reaction I take a peek at the first one. 8 times out of ten the answers (metaphorically) show some reduction in distress ... e.g., it is smaller, or lighter, etc. I never say I expected that and I show no disappointment if it is still unchanged. However I will sometimes use it (unchanged functions) as a cue to look for still other reactions that the client is fused with that is holding the whole system in place.
EXERCISE Physicalizing - effect on distress level [cont'd] **Defusion - repeating description of distress [10-29-03]** **EXPOSURE** Distress level, effect on [cont'd] Jonathan Kandell	I have had that experience with "physicalizing" exercises too--I think it is more iffy because it's a relatively indirect method of achieving defusion. I tend to use other methods. For instance I find one of the quickest ways to get to distancing is to have clients immediately describe to me what I can see is distressing them (say during a flashback), then repeat the description again, and then again. I ask them if they are as distressed (or other internal discomfort) right now at this moment as much as they were when they first "experienced" it a few minutes ago. After they say "no," I point out how they have spontaneously defused from the words, thoughts, feelings, and sensations --in fact, even their initial experiencing (which was pretty fused) was less disturbing than the original event itself, which was non-verbal and "real." I congratulate them on this achievement, and on their being willing to experience the internal state a few times, and how, ironically, by being open to it, it actually lost its power. Of course the theoretical background needs to be in place before you do this, but it works for me. It's kind of a variation of the milk, milk, milk exercise but using their own experience as the vehicle. I like it because it points out how defusion is not a hard chore (unless you make it by forcing) but a spontaneous part of healing within all of us.

EXERCISE **Tombstone/ funeral eulogy - concern re pliance [9-3-03]** John Billig	Joseph Ciarrochi wrote: Is anybody else concerned that the value-funeral induction will elicit pliance in clients? (Recall that you ask people what they would like their loved ones to remember them for.) Will people think, "Well, what do other people want from me?" Yes, the funeral induction can elicit pliance, but with a recent patient of mine, it was helpful. I have a patient who has recently been working on values identification. He used the funeral metaphor to help identify values in various domains, coming up with a long list in each domain. He recognized that some of the values were HIS and some were values he had learned or thought that he SHOULD hold. It was a very useful exercise for him to help distinguish and let go of pliance-related values, while clarifying, owning, and reinforcing his own values.
EXERCISE **Walk, taking an existential [3-31-04]** Steve Hayes	[Taking an existential walk] is not described in detail in the 1999 ACT book. The mention in the second paragraph below is as close as we get: "Other exercises with the cards may be helpful depending on what sort of struggles the client is having with avoided thoughts. For example, a particularly disturbing thought can be written on a card. The therapist holds the card up on the palm of their hand and asks the client to push against the card. The therapist tells the client to hold the thought away, then pushes the card towards the client. After a few seconds the therapist can ask the client how much effort this takes. Then hand the card to the client, ask them to hold it, and ask them to notice the difference in effort. Ask the client to notice that in both instances they are equally in contact with the card. This provides a physical metaphor showing how avoidance increases effort without delivering on the promise of reducing contact. Yet another card exercise has the client carry several cards with disturbing thoughts on them in their back pocket. Sometimes this is combined with a walk outside, with the client choosing where to go while also periodically being given difficult cards to carry by the therapist." I usually do it sort of like Hank described a while ago. Spontaneously go for a walk with a client. Claim it is a nice day or you'd like to stretch your legs as your justification. As you get to choice points step back just a half step. When the person notices and asks "where should we go?" say something like "I don't know. Where do you choose to go?" If they want reassurance, stay in that passive stance. As they start to go in a direction say something like "but there may be robbers down that way" or something like that. If they go in the other direction say "and they may be that way too." If they begin to walk, say out loud or write down some things that are issues for them on card (like "I need to know that I will be successful" or "I can't stand any more loss in my life"). If on cards ask them to read them and carry them in their pocket. Focus on choice as you come to each fork in the road. Debrief when you get back to the office. You can do this in groups by having the members of the groups be doubts, fears etc. You can do in groups as an overt version of the bus metaphor.
EXERCISE **What are the numbers? [5-19-04]** Steve Hayes	Everdien Tromp wrote: I have a little problem with the arbitrariness of the "irrelevant and nonfunctional private responses." Clients often mention that their inner evaluations etcetera are not very random or arbitrary to them. These specific thoughts can be very special to people because they are part of the socialization or education patterns their beloved (or hated, or both) parents intentionally laid down on them. This is an over extension of what was said and what was meant. The book says "Experiential exercises are particularly useful for demonstrating how easy it is to condition a irrelevant and nonfunctional private response." An example is "what are the numbers?" in which you ask the person to remember 3 numbers. Just make up anything, present it to anyone, and you can very easily get them to remember it. Once in, it is in (even if they forget it they will probably learn it later more readily etc.) because we are historical and developmental organisms. If you try just minutes later to suppress the 3 numbers you learned and change them, you remember the 3 and say 3 more -- now you have 6 and the first 3 were not subtracted. The book doesn't say that most private events are irrelevant and nonfunctional -- the point is that their mere presence does not say how one should deal with them or what they mean. For example, if you have the thought "I am mean" you could be dealing with the equivalent of something like the 3 numbers (Mom's voice?). Of course this "point" in ACT is probably not going to be drawn out literally -- it is an experiential "point" that is being made. I've found it quite useful personally and as a therapist to come into direct experiential contact with how easy it is to condition a irrelevant private response -- it creates a bit of skepticism about minds and how they work. Minds do what minds do. They are not the whole person and they are not necessarily friend or foe. They are tools.

HOMEWORK **Assigning homework practice [1-13-05]** John Forsyth	Archana Jajodia wrote: Where does ACT stand with respect to any kind of daily homework in therapy? I think homework is crucial -- we want clients to get well (i.e., live better) outside of therapy. This requires practice and doing. I never liked the BT term "homework." It tends to bring up all kinds of relations -- someone is making me do it, I have to do it, and if I don't do it I will get in trouble. Georg Eifert and I have reframed homework as "experiential life enhancement exercises" in the ACT and Anxiety Book we've put together. This move was strategic. We tried to focus the homework on living, and to make it about that. I think it is good not to force homework/out of session exercises on clients -- "you must do this, or I want you to do this or that." Try asking the client if they are willing to do the exercises, if they are willing to make a commitment to them in the process of co-creating the life they want because working to have that life matters to them.
HOMEWORK Assigning homework practice [cont'd] John Bush	I agree that it is better to present homework as voluntary. And that for a few, calling it "homework" will backfire. But the editor in me bridles at the phrase "experiential life enhancement exercises." I preface discussion of the first homework task with the observation that the therapy is not about what we do in my office, but about the other 167 hours of the week. That way I never have to use a category label, but simply describe concretely on each occasion what I'm proposing the client do between sessions.
HOMEWORK Assigning homework practice [cont'd] John Forsyth	I like how you frame out of session exercises John. As far as your editorial side goes ... the homework is homework regardless of what we may call it, right? How it -- the out of session work -- is presented and framed will likely matter to clients and may, in turn, influence whether they do it or not.
HOMEWORK Assigning homework practice [cont'd] Eric McCollum	Something I have taken from some of my solution-focused friends is asking clients to "assign" their own homework. I am amazed at how creative they can be and how it removes me from the study hall monitor role that seems to breed rebellion. I end the session by saying something like, "What, if anything, do you think you would like to do between now and next week to keep your work here moving forward?" If they decide to do nothing, that's fine. And I don't find people coming up with things that are all that inappropriate - I'm better at assigning inappropriate homework than my clients seem to be.
HOMEWORK Assigning homework practice [cont'd] Russ Harris	Practice is an essential part of improving any skill, so it makes sense to encourage it. ACT and mindfulness can be thought of - at least, to some degree - as skills to increase response flexibility. In using these approaches, we are creating new neural pathways in our brain that allow us to broaden our repertoire of responses to salient stimuli. In neuroscience, there is a principle known as Hebb's law: 'neurons that fire together, wire together.' Following Hebb's law, it makes sense that the more we rehearse these new neural pathways, the more established they become; therefore the more likely we are to use them. So rather than use the term 'homework,' I talk about 'practice' - using the concept that they are learning a useful skill.
HOMEWORK **Form, homework/ values** **VALUES** **Form, homework/ values [4-14-04]** Joseph Ciarrochi	We find that having people complete the homework/values form below greatly increases the chance that they will actually do the homework (sorry about the formatting problems. The fonts and nice formatting disappear when I insert the form). Essentially, we have people explicitly state what value their homework is in the service of...then we have them set concrete, achievable goals, etc. etc. This homework format has been designed and evaluated in the lab of a colleague and friend, Frank Deane. (Kazantzis, N., & Deane, F.P. (1999). Psychologists' use of homework assignments in clinical practice. Professional Psychology: *Research & Practice, 30*, 581-585.) Please cite him if you use. Having people "discuss" the values related to homework does not seem to be as effective as having them write the values down on a piece of paper ... at least not in my experience.... p.s. Of course we avoid the word "homework" at all costs. ** Practice description (e.g., Tin can monster exercise. Tape side A. 10 minute exercise) Relevant values (For you, what is this practice in the service of?) How often (e.g., times per day/hour/week)

	When (e.g., 11.45 am before lunch)
	Where (e.g., in the bedroom; on the train; at work)
	Confidence rating (circle one). How confident are you that you will achieve this practice goal?
	0 20 40 60 80 100 Not at all confident Moderately confident Totally confident *Circle the days you practiced* Monday Tuesday Wednesday Thursday Friday Saturday Sunday
	Comments. Did anything come up during the practice that you would like to discuss?
HOMEWORK **Non-compliance [9-15-02]** Kelly Wilson	ACT Listserv Member wrote: I noticed that self-monitoring is difficult for some ACT clients. Failing to complete self-monitoring can be a form of experiential avoidance because the client avoids documenting and sharing their emotions/thoughts. Understandably, the client needs to complete homework to get the full exposure experience and practice approaching (not avoiding) the negative emotions. How should an ACT therapist address homework non-compliance? Aside from being curious about the nature of the homework you are assigning, I would say that it depends on the meaning of not doing the homework. Not doing homework is an act in context. Don't get hooked on the idea that doing the homework is necessary for treatment--it is likely the case that not doing the homework *is* doing the homework--just not the homework you had in mind. What to do? Get inside not doing the homework. Tell the client ... cool, there may be something really important here. Maybe not, but let's go into it and check it out. I would want to get a sense of what shows up for the client when you assign it, when you ask for it, when they say they haven't got it. Also, what shows up for you on your side of the relationship? What do you feel like doing? lecturing? insisting? how do you feel? mad? like giving up? powerless? If so, how do you like those feelings, and what do you do with them? do you manage them? if so how? It is almost a certainty that whatever shows up for you as a behavioral predisposition will be unproductive if this is a standard way of operating in the world for this client. Is there anything familiar in the interaction? for you? for the client? One really must go into this like an explorer I think--meaning is to be found in the context? Right now, I don't know what not doing homework means ... I don't have enough context. Rest assured though, the client is doing exactly the right thing. You just need to figure out what it is right for. Could be a million things, but here are a couple ... client is living a story about how they never do anything right. Client could be telling you that you are a jerk for insulting them by pretending that their problem could be solved by doing some little homework assignment. Client could be refusing to eat their vegetables (that's mine), or, maybe they just forget, or maybe they have done homework for some other therapist that was shoved in a file and forgotten. Check out context by asking questions or with an exercise ... for example, put them in an eyes closed exercise and ask them to imagine coming into the treatment room and telling you "here it is, I did all of it." Really let that show up and ask, "how does your body feel right now, what thoughts show up? what memories? what images? what emotions? ok, now imagine coming in again, imagine that this is the 5th time you have not brought in your homework, you know you will be asked for it, how do you feel going in body, emotion, thoughts, memory, images, ok, now I ask for the homework (really ask the client in the exercise 'Do you have your homework?'), now what shows up? thoughts, memories, images, body, emotions." Play with iterations on the story of not doing or doing homework. There is defusion and exposure all over in this exercise. I would expect that the client's response to the simple question "do you have your homework?" would be "no, I forgot" or "no I was too busy." Exercises like the above are a context for a much richer, broader set of response functions to emerge. If it is avoidance, as you imagine it is, such an exercise might illuminate it. May put the not-doing in a context. Just an idea.
HOMEWORK Non-compliance [cont'd]	John Bush wrote: Local linguistic conventions aside, this sounds remarkably like exploring and analyzing the countertransference. Do you see any important differences? Within dynamic thinking it would be both transference and countertransference. Both are their attempts to

ACT cf. **Psychoanalysis - interest in function [9-16-02]** Steve Hayes	get beyond form to function. Behavior analysts have the same interest. Kelly's answer is a very nice statement of why it is important to explore and analyze the function of any event.
	The difference between behavior analysis and psychoanalysis is the theory, the scientific basis for the theory, the technological implications of it, and how the data that follow are examined. The functional strategy, however, is shared.
	Personally, I'm reassured by these connections. Clinicians are not idiots. No clinical tradition of note is stupid. That a scientifically-based clinical theory touches on other, less scientific traditions just tells me that we are dealing with some real clinical issues. ACT / RFT did not add these elements in order to create overlap -- rather, a bottom-up approach produced them.
	At its deepest level ACT / RFT is about creating a new, more progressive paradigm that allows the best of the clinical past to be carried forward. Those who think that function is more important than topography -- which includes some old time clinical traditions -- have a new, more scientifically viable place to go. The same applies to those interested in cognition / emotion / values / behavior change / spirituality / experience / etc. Winning breadth without giving up precision, depth, or coherence is the game. Overlap-with-a-scientifically-viable-difference is one small indication that the game is a progressive one. In the case of this comment, it looks progressive to my eyes. Note, for example, how precise and focused Kelly's comment is -- he is not just searching for ANY function, but for specific ones that we know have a good data base and clear treatment implications.
HOMEWORK Non-compliance [cont'd] ACT cf. Psychoanalysis - interest in function [cont'd] Kelly Wilson	I was supervised for three years by a psychodynamic person (a Reno adjunct). I also hung out with the wonderful folks over at the Mt Zion psychotherapy research group in San Fran for a bit in grad school. What fascinated me about that tradition was this interest in function. One can roughly think of form vs. function as similar to manifest vs. latent content. No surprise to a behavior analyst that two formally dissimilar behaviors could be functionally identical. Identity is found in the context--if pressing the lever, pulling the chain, and stepping on the treadle all produce a food pellet in the context of the house light being on--they are the same behavior.
	I would tell my psychodynamic supervisor what happened with my very, very, difficult client (yes Steve knew about it, and approved). She would say: "Yes, Yes, but what does it mean? What does it mean?" I would do the functional analysis (but not in behavioralese) and we got along great. I learned a lot--about therapy and about translating.
	What I am looking for is 1) whether not doing homework is a member of a functional class of behavior (experiential avoidance); and 2) what would show up if you took "I forgot" off the table (possible avoided content?). I do so by tinkering with different aspects of the context in exercises, with questions, etc.
	I look at what is happening with the therapist because that behavior (not keeping commitments), if common for the client, has interpersonal implications. The implication may be idiosyncratic to the therapist (a countertransference issue to work on in supervision--another story) or they may be pretty conventional--in the latter instance, your reactions are great data on what the person gets in the world. Reacting in the way your dispositions suggest is likely the treatment the world is already giving to the client. If that were going to work, it already would have. So, if I felt mad and hurt and like rejecting the client--like, "I have worked my ass off here, and they aren't doing a damn thing!" I might open up an interesting line of inquiry by exploring whether the client experiences people liking them for a while, but ultimately growing distant. I might even say that I notice this showing up for me, while at the same time committing to stay in the work--and I mean a well-communicated commitment here. I find myself wondering what would show up if we had this issue on the table *and* worked in a committed way. Usually people say that they are feeling like pushing you away in the context of being just about to push you away. What shows up when you have it and stay close and committed? Could be interesting.
	Note that in saying this and staying close, I am also modeling having thoughts and dispositions as thoughts and dispositions, while staying on a commitment. I smell defusion.
HOMEWORK Non-compliance [cont'd] ACT Listserv Member	Another possible angle to approach the incompleted homework issue is to look at the possibility that the homework symbolizes change, and change may scare your patient. A question I often ask a patient unwilling to do homework, especially when they have been making good progress, is 'what would doing "x" cost you? In other words, what would you be giving up by doing the homework?' It is possible that the homework, especially if it is the values assessment, may symbolize giving up a way of life that is familiar, or it may relate back to something similar to the discussion of "I don't know." [Cross Reference: see 3-142 - VALUES Difficulty accessing - "don't know" clients] Doing the values assessment may bring up some anxiety about making choices about directions/paths in life, something the client may not be comfortable with and thus be trying to avoid. I know that I have had difficulty working with an eating disorder girl when it comes to values work because it symbolizes giving up an old friend, her bulimia.

HOMEWORK Non-compliance [cont'd] Kelly Wilson	Definitely so, and well said. Now that's a functional analysis of experiential avoidance. And what is called for (one possibility) … generate the anxiety in an exercise--do exposure to all aspects of the experience of anxiety in the presence of potential change ... the product ... increased flexibility around anxiety, change.
IMAGE **Ideas for ACT pictures [5-20-03]** Steve Hayes *Cross Reference:* *See 5-203 for a later post in this thread*	... Some images that come to mind: Someone sitting in the middle of a relatively barren field with interesting things in all directions saying "I can't choose, so I choose to sit"; A person struggling and sinking in quicksand with others nearby safely laying out flat on it; A person nailing him or herself to a cross, saying "I was treated so badly -- see the evidence"; Digging like mad in a hole, with a big pile of dirt up on the edge; someone up at the edge hollering "dig harder -- you are to blame";  Scary (but also slightly airy) monsters on the bus harassing the driver;  A person driving on a road with an "emotional avoidance" detour sign tempting them off the main road into a crazy loop that dumps back near where they started; Two folks sitting in front of keyboards and computer screens saying "deep down there is something wrong with you" -- one of them nose on the screen, lost in it, terrified; the other sitting back, smiling, calling a friend over to look; A chessboard without edges with a terrified fellow on the back of the smiling but insecure white queen (and similar ally pieces) fighting a load of frightening-looking black pieces; A person with a compass facing a swamp going off as far as one can see in side directions but with a beautiful meadow on the other side;

A person hanging over a cliff hanging on to a small shrub growing into the side looking up in terror screaming "I *can't* let go" and because he/she is not looking down is not noticing that the "cliff" is only 8-10 feet high and their feet are only a couple of feet from the bottom [old Zen story];

Two craps tables -- one you play for vitality and pay with self-righteousness; one you play for self-righteousness and pay with vitality (don't have a clear image of how to set this up yet) [Chris McCurry came up with this one years ago];

A person looking at a picture of a mountain, holding it up so close that nothing else can be seen, meanwhile covering the ability to see an actual mountain not far away ... the caption "I see the mountain!";

A person with a hook though them first and then through their parents, saying "I want off this thing ... but not if it lets them off first" [Kel came up with this one years ago] ...

MEASURE **AAQ - 16 item version [8-2-02]** Frank Bond	Kelly Wilson wrote: ... measures of experiential avoidance are often very disorder specific (fear of fear), or specific to emotions, or specific to cognition. Is there anything that covers more ground. I think of experiential avoidance as encompassing thought, emotion, bodily states, behavioral predispositions, memories, imaginings and all other manner of private experience. I am considering using a version of the AAQ, though not the short version for sure. Frank, others? What is your best bet right now? My best bet right now, on a measure of experiential avoidance, is the AAQ-16. Using several large samples, I have found this to be more psychometrically sound than the 9-item version. In particular, alpha is far better (I can never get an alpha of above .60 on the latter); and the factor structure (using both exploratory and confirmatory factor analysis) of the 16-item version is more interpretable and of a better fit (in my experience). Furthermore, the predictive validity of it is pretty good. In particular, I found that, in a two wave panel design study, the 16-item version predicted mental health (GHQ, Depression Anxiety Stress Scales) one year on, but that these measures of mental health did not predict the AAQ one year on, which is what I would expect. In this same study, I found that the AAQ-16 also predicted the number of computer input errors that call centre operators made over the course of one year. Interestingly, I can never find that the AAQ predicts job satisfaction (which is interesting for Occupational Health Psychology people). I think that these findings show that it is useful to have an easily completed, self-report measure of experiential avoidance, as very important information can be gained from this assessment method. I think that John [Forsyth]'s advocacy for a test battery that is more idiographic in nature is excellent for certain clinical purposes, but would be impractical in the organisational and hospital settings in which some work. Therefore, I think that the ACT community does need to work on improving a self-report measure of acceptance, in conjunction with the development of a more behaviourally-based assessment battery....
MEASURE **AAQ - 8 item version [10-10-03]** Frank Bond	I wanted to share with everyone the most psychometrically sound version of the AAQ that we currently have. ...We have tested it on over 800 people over the past few months, and the items load convincingly onto one factor. Its alpha is also good as it hovers around .77. Its predictive validity (over time) for mental health and job performance is also very good. 8-item AAQ The following items are attached to the same 7 point Likert type scale that the AAQ typically uses (i.e., 1 (never true) to 7 (always true)). We score it such that higher scores indicate greater acceptance. I choose to get on with my life, rather than struggle with my worries or unhappiness. Despite doubts, I feel as though I can set a course in my life and then stick to it. I'm not afraid of my feelings. I am in control of my life. If I get bored of a task, I can still complete it. When I feel depressed or anxious, I am unable to take care of my responsibilities. I rarely worry about getting my anxieties, worries, and feelings under control. When I compare myself to other people, it seems that most of them are handling their lives better than I do.
MEASURE **AAQ meta-analysis; other measures/ need for [5-5-05]** Frank Bond	Steve noted in a posting that I conducted an AAQ meta-analysis for a paper that will appear in *Behaviour Research and Therapy*. Here is the headline finding (for a very dull newspaper): We found 21 studies that correlated the AAQ with some relevant psychological or behavioural outcome measure. These individual findings were integrated into a meta-analysis in which correlations established with a greater number of people were given more weight in calculating an average, or overall, effect size using the Pearson product-moment correlation coefficient (r) as the effect size metric. These 21 studies, involving 4,721 participants, investigated the relationship between the AAQ and various

	quality of life outcomes, including psychopathology (e.g., depression, anxiety, post-traumatic stress, trichotillomania), stress, pain, job performance, and negative affectivity. These studies produced 52 correlations between the AAQ and these outcomes. The overall effect size (or magnitude) of these relations was 0.30 (95% confidence interval: 0.29 - 0.32) showing that this measure of ACT processes had a moderate relationship with psychological outcomes, generally. Finding a medium sized effect here is pretty good. It shows that psychological flexibility (i.e., acceptance/mindfulness and values-based action components) predicts a fairly wide range of psychological/behavioural outcomes (amongst people with and without diagnosable psychological problems) to a very meaningful extent. This is good news for the ACT community....
MEASURE AAQ meta-analysis; other measures/ need for [cont'd] Steve Hayes	Andy Santanello wrote: Does anyone know of any non-self-report measures of experiential avoidance? I think that the AAQ is fantastic, but I wonder if there aren't other ways to measure things like willingness and action. This needs to be worked out. One on the website is scoring of actual in session behavior. Hard to do but there is a process posted there (Khorakiwala's "Acceptance Process Measure"). Delay discounting measures seem to correlate. Distress tolerance measures seem to correlate ... (see that piece Dermot just posted [Cross Reference: see 1-36 - EVIDENCE Normal population - avoidance/ acceptance/ defusion] and all of those pain / CO2 etc. studies). The AAQ is actually a broader measure than experiential avoidance narrowly defined since the original item pool was made up of just about everything ACT targets. We called it experiential avoidance because at the time that was what we were focusing on as the core of the theory of psychopathology ... but that has elaborated. Long run we may have to rename it (psychological flexibility?). There is some discussion about this as it applies to the AAQ-II. I mention it here because all of these ACT processes need to be measured more specifically ... but if the theory is right they all interrelate with some sort of general process we are now calling psychological flexibility. If you get that far there are a number of overt measures that might bear on that process.
MEASURE **Therapist adherence to treatment** **THERAPIST** **Adherence to treatment, measuring [10-2-03]** Steve Hayes	Joseph Ciarrochi wrote: Has anybody written something on how one might measure the extent that a therapist is adhering to ACT? I am really interested in observational-type measures, which appear to be more valid. The only real *observational* measure we've ever successfully developed is Durriyah Khorakiwala's "Acceptance Process Measure." She developed it using Willard Day's "Reno methodology" (a qualitative method leading to a quantitative measure). With effort (and a LOT of transcribing) you can get reliability and it does seem to characterize the flow of ACT treatment regimens. But we have not yet published it. Long story. Still, feel free to play with it. ...It measures both therapist and client ACT-relevant behaviors in session. If you use it and get to publishing something check with me ... maybe we will get it out in the meantime. As far as more usual adherence measures, we developed one for the heroin study that worked. Liz headed up the team ... the smoking study is tweaking it further. Others around the world have developed various things.... Obviously, the worldwide ACT/RFT community has a long way to go in this area. But we are making progress ...
METAPHOR **Acceptance - Aikido; throwing hot coals/ dog poo [3-26-04]** Malcolm Huxter	Aikido is a martial art where practitioners often get out of the road of aggressive blows or, if contact is made, force is deflected so that the opponent's weight is used against themselves. In therapy I sometimes describe this martial art by getting up and actually moving my body. I describe being centred and dodging blows and working with powerful physical energies. Teenage boys, in particular, seem to appreciate these descriptions. Then, I discuss emotional Aikido. That is, we discuss working with powerful emotions by being balanced with them. The term "equanimity" is sometimes equated with this. The philosophical background of Aikido is Buddhist and in Buddhism equanimity refers to being emotionally centred and unshaken by the vicissitudes of life. Equanimity is not detached disinterest but more like engaged acceptance. Equanimity can be used in our relationships with aggressive people. There is a traditional Buddhist simile of the hot coals. Those who pick up and throw hot burning coals at you are, in fact, burning their own hands in the process. In a way to encourage emotional Aikido with young people I have changed the hot burning coals simile to the simile of throwing dog poo. When an aggressor throws verbal and/or emotional abuse at someone, the person who is the target can either jump into its pathway or skilfully, with emotional balance, step to the side and let it fly by. Just like throwing dog poo, the foul smell remains on the hands of the

	person throwing. I like Linehan's Teflon mind. Emotional Aikido is like having a Teflon mind.
METAPHOR **Avoidance/ choices/ feelings - road sign [8-22-04]** Niklas Grebäck	This is of course about avoidance, choices and feelings as your best friends. The Road Sign Metaphor When you're out on the road driving along, headed somewhere you want to go, you often come across road signs. They can sometimes be hard to understand, especially if you're in a foreign land. Some of them tell you how fast you can drive, some tell where to drive and some tell you that there's a danger ahead. These signs are sometimes disturbing and they can restrict your driving, but they have a purpose and that is to help you get to where you want to go in a way that is safe for you as well as other drivers. Although sometimes irritating they're your friends on the road. If you don't pay any attention to these signs you might be in trouble. Some you may ignore without anything particularly happening, but others are more crucial to follow. If you don't read any signs of direction you're lost, if you ignore speed limits and warnings of sharp turns you're soon off road and hurt and so on. There is of course one way of ridding yourself from all this and that is to stay home, but then you aren't going anywhere so you're stuck, right? Another way is to just drive where there are no signs, brilliant! Every time a sign shows up, you turn away. But then again you're kind of restricted in possible destinations for the ride so you have to limit those to fit signposts. You can also spend your time ruminating over the fact that there are a lot of these signposts in your neighbourhood and how it would be if they were gone or you were living somewhere else or didn't have the urge to go somewhere or could let someone else drive or… The question of how to get from here to there is maybe not about how to get the safest ride, but more about how to use what actually is out there in order to reach your destination.
METAPHOR **Change agenda, workability of - slate, trying to erase [6-16-04]** John Billig	Here is a new metaphor that a patient of mine provided. The metaphor is similar to the chess board and illustrates the unworkability of the patient's change agenda.... He stated to me ... : "It's like I keep trying to wipe my slate clean." We used this metaphor of a slate on which all of his life history is written. He looked at the various ways and all the effort he had put into trying to erase his history of abuse. As he said, "I have rubbed my knuckles raw trying to erase the slate." He was able to experience a deep sense of creative hopelessness, realizing the unworkability of erasing the slate. He started making choices of what he wanted his life to be about, trying to erase the slate or moving the slate (i.e., his life) along with everything on it in a valued direction. He made great progress, committing to changes that are tied to his values rather than about changing his history.
METAPHOR **Chessboard - mind's responses are more pieces** **EXERCISE** **Tombstone/ funeral eulogy - nihilist response** **ACCEPTANCE** **Not effortful cf. avoidance - clinical illustration [8-28-03]** Steve Hayes	Leslie Telfer wrote: [A client] said that as a chessboard, he wouldn't want to move with the pieces, he would want to move without any of them. That's just another piece. It's the piece that says "hey, I don't like pieces." Thank your mind for that one. Wanting to move *with* the pieces is also a piece. We don't need that either, and it is important not to turn these moves into yet another search for what is missing. The question is not "what you want." We are not talking about what is missing (the literal meaning of want). We are talking about what is present, when it is present, thus the question life asks is "are you willing to have THIS" and THIS and THIS ad infinitum. Even values questions are not about what is missing. When you choose values you have them now, not later. I usually do something concrete in these situations. For example, I touch the person's knee with the tip of my finger and ask how much effort it takes to feel this. Then I ask him or her to buy into the thought that s/he doesn't want that feeling and then try hard NOT to feel it. I touch his or her knee again. It becomes very clear that board level there is no effort. It is simply being present with what is present. That's what board level means. The effort comes from trying to only have certain things be present, even when they are already present. Not feeling what you feel is hard. Feeling what you feel is easy (in an effort sense) ... though tricky (in a "mind field" sense). [LT] I also tried, at different points, the eulogy and the headstone exercises, and he said he didn't want to be remembered for anything by anyone. More wants. This "what would you want to be remembered for?" question is a common sense way to get at "what do you stand for?" It doesn't literally mean that we should want to be remembered for anything. If the answer to "what do you stand for?" is "nothing," fine. Own it. Have him stand up and say "my life is about standing for nothing." I betcha a million bucks there are tears and pain behind that ... and if you sniff that out, go for it. How much life and vitality is in the room when he says "my life is about standing for nothing"? Traumatic deflection happens right inside ACT sessions, like it does everywhere else.

METAPHOR	Adapted from: Bach, Richard (1977). *Illusions: The adventures of a reluctant Messiah*. New York: Delacorte Press.
Control agenda, abandoning - clinging creatures [10-22-04] Claire Godsell	Once there lived a village of creatures along the bottom of a great crystal river. Each creature in its own manner clung tightly to the twigs and rocks of the river bottom, for clinging was their way of life, and resisting the current was what each had learned from birth. But one creature said at last: "I trust that the current knows where it is going. I shall let go, and let it take me where it will, rather than die clinging." The other creatures laughed and said: "Fool! Let go, and that current you worship will throw you tumbled and smashed across the rocks, and you will die a worse death than from clinging!" But the one heeded them not, and taking a breath did let go, and at once was tumbled and smashed by the current across the rocks. Yet, in time, as the creature refused to cling again, the current lifted him free from the bottom. I think there are several ways this story could be used to illustrate ACT related concepts. Firstly, 'clinging' can be seen as a metaphor for trying to control private experience. In the story it is acknowledged that 'clinging' is what we learn from birth. This reflects ACT-related concepts about how control efforts are verbally transmitted and supported within our social context, and that humans universally experience control as an unworkable agenda. 'Clinging' parallels 'digging' in the 'man in the hole' metaphor. In contrast, "letting go" in the story can be seen as a metaphor for willingness, and an alternative to control (like putting down the shovel). There is a clear message in the story that letting go will certainly not facilitate an easy ride down the current (i.e., one will still get 'tumbled' and 'smashed'), but nonetheless it has the potential to free us from clinging. The last sentence also suggests that willingness (or letting go) is a choice that we are faced with repeatedly, and that practicing the choice 'not to cling' increases our engagement with the current instead of the bottom of the river (i.e., valued living vs. fusion). Additionally, the warnings of the other creatures about what 'might' happen if the creature were to let go, illustrate the 'mindiness' that comes up for humans when they think about moving toward their valued direction. The metaphor could also be used in conjunction with values work (e.g., are you willing to have all that shows up and still commit/step into the current?).
METAPHOR	A client of ours came up with this helpful metaphor when we were discussing digging and creative hopelessness:
Control, workability of - smelly lagoon [3-11-05] Ann Bailey	Every day I go walking on the beach near our home. I always enjoyed these walks, except for one thing. In one section of the beach a lagoon had formed, separated from the ocean by only a sandbar that was a metre or so in width. This lagoon would have been fine, except it has no flow to the ocean (due to the sandbar) and has become putrid and smelly and very unpleasant to walk past. Every day, on my walks I used to look at the sandbar that separated the lagoon from the ocean and wished it could be removed so that the clean fresh sea water could wash out the unpleasant smell. So one day I decide that I have had enough. I arrive at the beach with my shovel and start to dig the sandbar away. It took hours, and my muscles were aching and sore by the time it was done. I stood back, pleased with my effort at seeing the lagoon's stinking water meet the sea. I walk home, and allow a few hours to pass before I am lured back, muscles still aching, to look again at my handiwork. I am dismayed to find that any trace of my efforts had vanished, the sandbar was back in place as if I had never touched it, and the stinking lagoon was unchanged. The tide had come in and replaced the sand bar entirely. All my work was in vain, and all I was left with were sore muscles and a stinky smell. This metaphor can sum up a number of ACT concepts: Creative hopelessness: the fact that unpleasant (stinky) emotions are a part of us all and distressing, and our impulse is to get rid of them or avoid them as much as possible. The reality is we can spend a lot of energy and time in this endeavour, only to find that the emotions come back and we are never rid of them. Our lives have become about getting rid of the stinky stuff, instead of being about walking at the beach. Often our avoidance attempts can add to our original distress, in the form of sore muscles, or dirty discomfort.
METAPHOR	I work in a psychiatric unit in a maximum security state prison. Here is a metaphor that seemed to resonate with a chronically mentally ill inmate who was very hesitant to take medication:
Medication non-compliance - football protective gear [5-12-04] Hans Van Laake	It seems from what you have been telling us that for you, living life has been like being on a football field, in the middle of a game, without a helmet or any protective padding. Every time you try to join in the game, you end up getting bruised and hurt, so eventually you found that you could either sit on the sidelines and stay away from everyone, or you could get really mad and frighten people away from you. Taking medications that work might be like putting on a helmet and padding, they would enable you to

	play and practice your skills without getting totally beat up. You still might hurt at times, football is a rough game, but at least you wouldn't have to fear for your life anymore...
	We were able to find a medication regimen for this inmate that did not give him side effects, and he has continued to take (and benefit from) meds. In addition we were able to start him in some skill training groups as well. I'm sure many factors were at play, but I'd like to think that the metaphor played a little part in his decision to give medications another try.
METAPHOR **Memorability/ impact of - evidence re [4-20-05]** Steve Hayes	Niklas Törneke wrote: As I understand it, in a situation when a metaphor is experienced as rich, or fitting, is when it brings in essential nonverbal stimulus functions. The same is true for stories, anecdotes, etc. There are data showing that more sensory metaphors are better remembered and have more impact (provided they are apt ... meaning provided that the dominant relations in the vehicle lead to new but well fitted relations in the target). That would fit with what you are saying here. An old article that reviews that literature is McCurry, S., & Hayes, S. C. (1992). Clinical and experimental perspectives on metaphorical talk. *Clinical Psychology Review, 12*, 763-785.
METAPHOR **Mind - Bad news radio [5-17-04]** ACT Listserv Member	... [This metaphor] seems to have been so rich with both depression and anxiety patients. We check on what's been broadcasting this week, and how helpful all that stuff was - and what was playing on the other channel. [as "tweaked" by Steve Hayes] BAD NEWS RADIO: 'This is bad news radio, broadcasting inside your head 24 hours a day. Wherever you are, the signal will reach you. When you wake in the early hours, we'll be there to make you aware of all the unhappy aspects of your life, even before you get out of bed. Let us take over and control your life.' 'Bad news radio is compelling listening, and guess why! It's the news station you've grown up with, and now it comes to you automatically, 24/7.' 'Pay attention, Bad News Radio knows what's best for you. So don't forget that, and remember, if you should forget us and ACT without seeking permission, then we'll broadcast all the louder.' 'Remember, what you feel inside your skin can be so awful, so you should stay tuned to this station to know what to think and how to control it.' JUST SO RADIO: 'Wake Up! Bad News Radio is just a station - you can tune in, or you can tune out! One thing is guaranteed though, whatever the time of day, you'll hear the same old stuff.' 'If that's been really helpful to you, then go ahead, tune in and stay tuned. That would make sense.' 'If not, then tune in more often to JUST SO RADIO - we bring you the news of actual experience, in the moment -- all live, all the time. ACTUALITY IS OUR BUSINESS!' 'We give it to you straight -- as it is, not as what it says it is. In contact with the world and even inside beneath the skin, you can experience what it is to be human, and it's entirely free!' 'We can guarantee that experiencing what's inside the skin - exactly as it is - will never damage you, but it just might bring you joy.' 'Just So Radio brings you information about how things are - not how you fear they might be.' 'Just So Radio invites you to step forward and touch the world - just as it is, and to touch your life - just as it is.' 'Stay tuned - give us a fair trial, and if not convinced by your own experience (please don't take our word for it) then Bad News Radio is still there on the dial.'
METAPHOR Mind - Bad news radio [cont'd] Julian McNally	I've used something similar with clients with low self-esteem - or any intrusive thoughts: It's like having talkback radio on in the background - it's only when you tune into/turn up what they're saying that you notice what nonsense they're talking. Convincing nonsense some of it. Now you can't turn this radio off, but you can acknowledge that there are going to be many opinions expressed on it - some may be useful (cf. contribute to workability) some may not. For now just recognise that it's background noise you can't get rid of.
METAPHOR **Mindfulness - melting frozen emotion/thought blockage** **BUDDHISM** **Mindfulness - melting frozen emotion/thought metaphor [7-12-04]** Jason Gosnell	I read over the weekend a quote by a Zen teacher, Charlotte Joko Beck, in the book *Everyday Zen*. She said that Zen practice is to "melt the frozen blockage of emotion-thought." I think that this doesn't mean to do away with these things, but allowing them to flow more freely. I think that Hahn might say that mindfulness is the heat to melt the frozen blockage.

METAPHOR Misunderstanding; when to use literal talk [8-11-04] Steve Hayes	Francis De Groot wrote:
	What's the use of metaphors when clients understand them the wrong way? Doesn't one have to talk about it?
	If someone misunderstands a metaphor I usually try to get at the issue another way. That can include other metaphors. It can include lots of talk but not so much in the way of logical, linear talk.
	Once someone is on to the issue, talk about it is different. It is fine to state things literally once the issue is seen ... as long as you don't overdo it. The worry in stating it before then is that you have a harder time discriminating pliance from other forms of behavior and you may even block out progress because sensitivity to pliance easily produces insensitivity to other things.
METAPHOR Skiing - acceptance, defusion, creative hopelessness ACCEPTANCE Difficulty of, when fused [5-9-05] Philippe Vuille	... I like the skiing metaphor. It seems to apply to therapy in particular and to life in general. The slope is time. Being able to verbally construct time, we have to live with a special kind of fear of heights. If we want to live, there is only one way: down (and if we don't want, it is the same...). There are a lot of technical details that are interesting if you want to learn skiing. But if you want to boil it down to one sentence, this is it: Always put your weight on the downhill ski, i.e., lean your body towards the frightening abyss. I was twelve when I learned this skill and never was tempted again to search for security by leaning the wrong way. I must say it is much more difficult to apply this skill to therapy and life issues and I ever again find myself being unwilling to experience what happens to me. This seems to be the case for my patients too. So, creative hopelessness is something we have to address again and again. Many people already commented that the neat separated aspects of ACT as they are presented in a didactic way in the ACT Book often have to be treated simultaneously in therapy. Defusion helps to find a safe place from which you can lean. Willingness without defusion is very difficult. As long as there is a lot of fusion, to be willing is equivalent to accepting to lie down on the chessboard, fallen from the white tower, with broken bones and a bunch of swords of the black pieces on one's throat....
METAPHOR Suffering/ acceptance - rock blocking path [11-29-04] Steve Hayes	[Re: rock blocking path as a metaphor for suffering] About that rock. The goal is not to get over it, get through it, get beyond it, get rid of it - the goal is to get with it. If so, inside this metaphor, do what plants do (not to get rid of the rock but as a matter of sustenance and being): eat the rock. Take it in. Willingly. After all, there is as much life in an embraced moment of anxiety / sadness / pain etc. as in joy. Ironically, if you do it fully, you are already up where you can see. Without all of the effort. From there lots of other journeys are possible.
METAPHOR Values and vulnerability - boy in the bubble [6-12-04] Amy Murrell	One of the first things that I can actually remember watching on TV was "The Boy in the Plastic Bubble." The movie starred John Travolta, and his character was a teenager struggling to choose between being protected in his bubble and leaving it, risking his life, to be with the beautiful girl next door (or somewhere in the neighborhood, anyway). It is pretty clear that artistic license was involved here; David Vetter, the person on whom the character was based, died at age 12. He had to live all of his life in an extremely sheltered environment - one that was completely sterile, because the smallest germ could have killed him. Another circulating story is that David, when he knew for certain he was dying, asked to reach outside his bubble and touch his father. Whether this story is any more true than the Hollywood version, I am not certain - of course, the "real" truth isn't important here anyway. Whether the receiver of the touch was a romantic love interest or a parent, we can learn a lot and it can be useful.
	Our lives are filled with moments in which we feel compelled to step out of our safe places, all the while feeling a strong pull to stay put. This place, the one that is full of contradiction and ambiguity, for many of us somehow feels uncomfortable and comfortably familiar at the same time. These are the instances when valued-choices and committed action are on the line.
	In our work group, we often talk about values and vulnerability being connected. I think that the story of the boy in the bubble is a perfect metaphor to illustrate how those are intimately related. For David Vetter, reaching out to others (literally and figuratively) meant the ultimate vulnerability - his own death - and yet in either version you choose, his value of close connection with others was related to him behaving in a way that would allow him to experience that.
	Each time we reach out to another person, we, like David, are exposing ourselves to potential hurt. Each time we show a weakness, or admit a fault aloud, we risk being hammered. Every time we take a chance, but especially when social interaction is involved, we strip ourselves of our safety and put ourselves in a position where there are equally great possibilities of love and disappointment. For so many of us, close connection to others is an important value. When we who genuinely value such relationships find ourselves in "the bubble," it doesn't feel very vital - safe, maybe even good for a while, but not life-giving - not "what

	you want your life to stand for"-meaningful. Of course, with clients, we would want to check out workability not assume anything. I believe this story is a good lead-in to that.
POEM **Birgitta Ederyd poems [12-29-02]** Birgitta Ederyd	*Poem For The New Year* I met a torchbearer in-between the past and the future A soft shimmer around his lonely being still wandering still on the move through suffering hearts with a ray of hope Glimpses of light from the torch transfers far beyond frames of absent mind and priming Opens up hidden doors to humanity and compassion I rub my eyes hum a tune a new glance, it is still there like eyes soft with sorrow and love reflection from the moon a mirror of my heart Breath sweeps like a wind into glowing hearts I can see a formation of igniting sparks in the dark night from a torchlight procession.
POEM Birgitta Ederyd poems [cont'd] Birgitta Ederyd	*Impermanence and openness* (read at the 2003 World Conference) There is a door, there is a key, there is openness Where non-action is the core of action The open door is you in this present moment In awareness and acceptance, The problem is not thoughts, perceptions, emotions It is the attachment to some parts and the struggle against others. Awareness includes everything and flows through openness and impermanence. It is not knowledge about some thing, it's you - opening up for what is here and now, your action will flow through the open door in your heart. In compassion and faith, the spirituality of imperfection will heal you And the new breath in --follows by breathing out-- as long as you live. Life is short, taste it, open your senses, have some joy.
POEM Birgitta Ederyd poems [cont'd] Birgitta Ederyd	*Prison of Words* (June 2002) I have been sitting in prison of language I'm out now I found a strange key now I can walk into the cell and out from it

Sometimes I find myself "waking up"
in that old stinky cell
not knowing how in hell I got there again

I only know it has something to do
with the old apple
with my fusion with thoughts and feelings
and words words, a scattered brain stream

Walls of words around me
back in prison
Just a little light
I have the key in my pocket

I want to learn to use language as a tool
So I can be just the human I am
Meeting you as the human you are
In our struggle for vital life

The key in my pocket is a magic key
Small and functional for my purposes
when I pay a soft and
eagle eye attention to it
When I'm not aware
it can be absorbed by conditioned words
In a rapid chain with tremendous
hypnotizing snake eyed power

I'm a human, I do have the language
I will pay attention.

ACT-related interpretation:

To sit in the "prison of words" is to be fused within/into the content of the language. The conditioned words have a kind of power over the present moment and influences my responses. The "key" is mindful attention to what is happening to attention. When I "take a step back" and just see what's going on, observing the process I "defuse" from content and I can see the content in the context. To just bring attention back to the present moment, is like finding a key (one eye in, one eye out). Mindful attention.

To be back into "prison" also means a cycle of responding to the content (like words reinforcing themselves, or a priming process). To "wake up" in the "cell" is to remember to be aware of the process again. Like climbing up from the water one was half drowned in. To get up on the shore and observe the thoughts as thoughts again. First a bit confused (like a wet dog) but to have the key, the possibility to observe the process and not blindly believe in the content of the words or thoughts. To rub the eyes and shake away the water...

We have evolved to use words and language and it has an important function. How to let the language serve us, not enslave us? It is no way back, we have been eating the "apple" off of the tree of knowledge. Language is like a "tool." I can learn to use it, not let the language use me. To be human is not to just have words. How can I live a "vital life" (not just as an automatic "puppet on a string") and at the same time in acceptance of all feelings and reactions that I cannot control (ACT - "Control is the problem, not the solution")? How can I live with a compass and in a direction of my values? Perhaps there is no answer. I have to find out through my own experiences and learn from my own life and what "works."

The "key" of mindful attention can be a small invisible friend helping me to pay attention to "what's going on inside and outside my skin." "When I'm not aware" about how my attention shifts and absorbs into "contents of chain-reactions," then this absorbed attention fuses into "conditioned words in a rapid chain" and I get "hypnotized" by it. And verbal behavior can reinforce this process. "Prison of words."

... oh, I am not used to analyzing my own poems like this. In a way it is a bit confusing. A poem for me is best when the reader can "walk into it" in a free way and interpret it in his/her own way. A poem can be more like a concentrate and the explanation/interpretation is to dilute it. At the same time I found this process of "ACT-interpretation" funny and interesting, like "dissecting" the poem and taking a step back. (In this process I did in fact also change some words to make the message clearer.) It is not a question of "right or wrong," it is to look. It is also a kind of paradox to use words about words and trying to say something about it.

	Perhaps the nature of attention is to "jump like a monkey," continuously shifting. And through mindfulness practice we can be a little bit more aware of this process and learn more about how and what happens when we shift between content and context. We can also learn how to focus attention and from that "point of view" it can be more obvious how moveable attention is and how fast it can shift. This is an interesting perspective.
	I can finish up with a second little story. It is about a Zen disciple asking his master about how to get peace in mind. The master sat silent and after a while he just said one word - "attention." The disciple asked again "but how shall I practice." The master repeated - "attention." Then the disciple begs him "please show me" and the master looked at him ... and again he said "..........".
POEM Birgitta Ederyd poems [cont'd] Birgitta Ederyd	*Gaps in the warp* (January 2003) In the ashes of innocence we started to build the tower of evaluated knowledge You looked at me in a strange way I reflected dread Spinning minds create yarns Building up a warp a net of thoughts and any chain of conclusion grows into a weave an inner landscape We perceive each other through an invisible veil struggling with effort to change the weave with new yarns Life and death in our breath silence is broken we still ask who are my brothers A breezy wind dancing through inborn gaps in the warp leaving us craving
RESOURCES **Discomfort Diary [5-24-04]** Jonathan Weinstein	Kelly Wilson wrote: I expect that all of the creatures of the earth suffer, but only humans suffer *that* they suffer. The latter half of the sentence seems to me a concise account for 'dirty discomfort.' I like to use the discomfort diary (from the ACT book) with most of my clients. Helps me to organize my assessment into a functional analysis of classes of avoided events and behavioral repertoires that promote and support the avoidance of unwanted experiences, while enabling the client to see in their own experience whether their current strategies for solving problems are working.
RESOURCES **Willingness and Commitment Worksheet [3-2-04]** Joseph Ciarrochi	I've been trying to break the fundamental ACT question into parts and squeeze it onto a single sheet of paper. I think I've done it (though I excluded the defusing the self part). Take a gander at this. People seem to find it quite useful (by the way, it is derived from one of the exercises in the ACT book that is intended for the therapist). <u>Willingness and Commitment Worksheet</u> What value do you want to put into (more) play in your life? Values are like guiding stars. You set your course by them, but you never actually reach them, or permanently realize them. Now pick a goal that you would like to achieve, with respect to the value, that would let you know that you are "on track." Now pick an action(s) that will lead you to accomplish that goal. What private stuff is likely to arise as a result of your committed action? Emotions and sensations? Unhelpful and/or negative thoughts and self-evaluations? Memories and images?

	The key here is to look at this private stuff as what it is (just stuff), not what it says it is. Private stuff seems more powerful than reality sometimes. It often says it is something that is dangerous, or something that is literally true. Take anxiety. It says it is powerful, like you have to run away from it or listen to what it says. Notice how "anxiety" is just a word that describes a bunch of fleeting thoughts and feelings. Notice how you can have those thoughts and feelings and still do what you value. Are you willing to make room for the thoughts and feelings that show up as a result of your committed action? Yes (Go forward with your journey and experience it!) No (Go back and choose a different valued action, and repeat this exercise.)
BOOK **Anorexia Workbook** **EATING DISORDER** **Anorexia Workbook** **[5-25-04]** Joseph Ciarrochi	I reviewed *The Anorexia Workbook* (Heffner and Eifert) published by New Harbinger, and I think these folks have done a spectacular job. I mean, the book is really accessible and interactive. It is compassionate ... it supports claims with evidence ... the ethical implications of the book have been well thought out, and laid out in the book (discussing alternatives to the self-help approach) ... it is quite different from your typical self-help book. ... I suspect that the workbook may be quite useful if used in a therapy context, with the guidance of a good therapist ... but that needs to be evaluated too. Ultimately, I think it will be shown to be useful as a self-help intervention ... but we must wait for the evidence.
BOOK **Self-help books, cautionary notes re** **[5-24-04]** Steve Hayes	I agree with Gerry [Rosen] that we need to be mindful of the importance of evaluating self help books linked to ACT. Done as an adjunct to therapy I see no real issue since written materials of this kind have been in most of our studies and you have the protection of a therapist who can alter things to make sure good outcomes occur. And I don't worry too much about excessive claims made by authors because I think the culture we've created is careful on that part and it seems unlikely ... but people do need to realize that publishers have control over titles and covers -- look at your contracts -- and in the self help area they often get a bit grandiose. You need to do the best you can to keep them reasonable but your control is limited there. The biggest issue comes when books are cast as help. If it is cast as help you'd like to know that it helps ... in that format. Even good information can hurt. The recent disaster with the drug czar's TV ads are a good (or perhaps bad) example. Some suggest that we shouldn't publish self-help books that haven't themselves gone thru the filter of outcome research, but even that standard does not solve the issue. Even if you do a study showing good outcomes you have no assurance that other populations will show the same effect and when you publish a book you let go of which populations use it. Even if the "same" population uses it, the problem is not solved because we virtually never randomly sample from a known population -- we randomly assign from a conceptual population gathered by methods of convenience ... and that is simply not the same thing. So, truth is, we could still be doing harm even if we did a *lot* of front end work. ACT is in a better position than many since several studies have been done that have used highly focused micro interventions and shown good effects, and the underlying theoretical model is both tighter and better tested than most. Some of these studies have used audiotapes or very simple metaphors presented on a computer screen or by script etc. It does not seem to be a big step from this to the written word. Most of these are in press or recently out .. but I am very gratified by the data and the fact that they are being done. But of course these studies cover only a fraction of the total ACT stuff out there ... and again, you have no idea who will try to apply this study to what so even if you are, say, using an acceptance script virtually the same as one that was successfully tested, it could blow up for some folks who are different than in the original study and who knows who is different? My own resolution of this is five fold: say what you know about what the data show; give reasonable guidance about how to use the materials; let folks know that there are other options to pursue esp. if the response is not positive; try to stay linked to tested principles and techniques, and test the resulting volume fairly quickly with at least a plausible target population (ideally before it is published, but if not then, then soon). ACT will get more and more scrutiny as we move in this direction, but it will also get more as it becomes more popular, as more research is done, etc. etc. Such is the way of the world. When the shit hits the fan -- and it will -- we will only have our values, integrity, and data to fall back on. All those little things in the ACT / RFT culture -- like lack of centralization, openness, sharing protocols, sharing measures, basic research, process research, component analyses, testable hypotheses, etc. etc. will all be important. Even then you can count on some rough sledding (e.g., from a reporter or a politician or a fellow scientist with a hostile angle). What we are hoping to do with ACT and RFT is just too bold for that not to happen. As long as they don't find out about the tattoos and the secret chicken rituals, though, it will all be OK ...

STORY **Conditioning - tiger "trapped" by former cage [5-8-05]** John McNeill	Once there was a magnificent Bengal tiger. In its natural range it roamed freely over 150 square miles. The tiger was happy and free, and hunted only when hungry. Then one day, a trapping team caught the tiger and sold him to a very prestigious Asian zoo. The zoo had planned to build a very special enclosure for the tiger where it would be free to hunt live game on its own. But the construction project took two years longer than expected. During that time, the tiger lived constrained within an 8 x 8 cage, and it was fed in one particular location. For two years, the animal traced the perimeter of its cage and was made dependent on humans for food.
	Finally the day arrived when the tiger was released into the zoo's holding enclosure, but the tiger refused to leave its cage, and had to be forced out into the open. Finding itself in an unfamiliar situation, the tiger began to pace 'as if' still caged; it refused to go beyond its conditioned limits, it refused to hunt on its own, and it refused to eat unless fed by humans.
	One can see the narrowing effects of aversive contingencies on a once beautifully variable behavioral repertoire. The tiger could not make its 'condition' go away, thus it seemed unable to free itself or to extend its range beyond what conditioning had established. Its response to the new situation was rigidly fixed and inflexible to an extreme. The tiger now had but one understanding of its situation.
	We all live in conditioned enclosures of one kind or another, the professor cage, the attorney cage, the plumber cage, the family cage, and so on. We may be making our cages stronger and more difficult to free our minds from, to the extent that our conditioning history is allowed to rigidly fix our views. We understand the domain of the conceptualizing mind, the realm of narrow understanding within the cage, but all too often we fail to see the rest of the world that ranges beyond our conditioned awareness. Anais Nin observes, "We don't see things as they are, we see them as we are."
STORY **Negative self-evaluation - successful actors [9-11-04]** ACT Listserv Member	Dustin Hoffman: "At the conclusion of the shoot Gene said to me 'I don't know about you' he says 'but you know what I feel immediately after a film is wrapped?' And I said, 'I think I know what you are going to say.' And he said 'that I'm never going to get a job again.' And I said, 'yeah, I think any actor that has put in all those years feels that...'"
	I think a lot of people can relate to the "mindiness" in this story. What Gene Hackman is saying is that even with the Oscars he has won for Best Actor as Popeye Doyle in the French Connection, and Best Supporting Actor in Unforgiven, his mind still tells him that he is not good enough to work again. And Dustin Hoffman, with his multiple Academy Awards (The Graduate, and Kramer vs. Kramer) and Oscar for Best Actor (Rainman), concurs about his own mind's reactions.
	I think this vignette is good for a few different issues in therapy. A good number of my clients have a real strong tendency to grind over things in their heads. I like to "unpack" (as Kelly would put it) these reactions, which a good deal of the time comes down to "I'm not good enough," as if the fraud police (as one of my clients put it) are going to come and haul you away. And this feeling is almost never seen as a good thing to have. I've used this type vignette for a couple different things in therapy:
	- control as the problem - "how long have you been trying to get the feeling that you are not good enough to go away?"
	- acceptance - your mind's reaction doesn't need to go away before you live the kind of life you value.
	- values - especially if one of those values is a deep and intimate connection with people, "What if everyone has a secret, and what if it's the same secret?"- this "mindiness" that is seen as something that needs to go away, can be the thing that connects us to people.
THERAPEUTIC RELATIONSHIP **Intimacy vs. boundaries [9-12-03]** ACT Listserv Member	Claire Godsell wrote:
	Just wondering if other ACT therapists have had the same experience that I have, of making deep human contact in the moment within session with clients, and then fearing that client has placed sexual/romantic connotations on the therapeutic relationship? I'm struggling with wanting to be fully engaged in the moment with clients but at the same time feeling concerned that this blurs boundaries with certain clients. I would love to hear other people's ideas on how to maintain intimacy AND boundaries.
	Go there, be there and model how to have the feelings, not act on them if acting on them would be destructive, which in therapy it would. It is okay to have the feelings, it is not okay (in this situation) to act on them, should be the message you send through your acknowledgement and validation of the feelings...
THERAPEUTIC RELATIONSHIP Intimacy vs. boundaries [cont'd] Barbara Kohlenberg	We have been sensitive to this issue of intimacy and ACT and have used guidelines out of FAP [Kohlenberg, R., & Tsai, M. (1991). *Functional analytic psychotherapy: Creating intense and curative therapeutic relationships.* Plenum.] to help guide us in focusing ACT interventions on the intimacy that can arise in a therapeutic interaction.
	... helping the client feel how they feel about you (let's say sexual attraction, the feeling that they are in love, the feeling that you really should be friends), all the while being mindful and clear about boundaries,

	actually can open up really meaningful areas.
	I have found this to be the place to talk about how it feels to want something and not be able to have it, to have a relationship that gives you so much but not everything, to experience both love and sorrow intermingling right there, in front of you, in your office. This can be hard for the client, and hard for you, but then it is about appealing to ACT as a way to feel your feelings, help the client feel their feelings, and move together in a valued direction which might be simply to acknowledge that love is worth having even when it is full of longing and pain.
THERAPEUTIC RELATIONSHIP Intimacy vs. boundaries [cont'd] Barbara Kohlenberg	Hank Robb wrote: I want to echo Barbara's comment. "You desire this from me and I am not going to give it to you. Now let's have that experience fully and without defense while moving in a valued direction." or "I desire this from you but I am not going to ask it of you and will reject it even if you offer it. Now let's have that experience fully and without defense while moving in a valued direction." are really very powerful for everyone involved. Just a note of caution. Moving in a valued direction does not have to mean moving away from the interaction in the therapy room. Moving in a direction is sometimes read as moving "forward," or "toward somewhere else." Sometimes the direction is actually to stay where you are, but more deeply so.
THERAPEUTIC RELATIONSHIP **Silence; storytelling - avoidance or intimacy?** [4-14-05] Barbara Kohlenberg	Philippe Vuille wrote: ... What about silence in ACT? I just felt the only thing to do was to stay with [a client] and to stay with the images, feelings and thoughts that went through my mind.... I for one appreciate the value of silence in a psychotherapy session. Because silence, I hope, is really about listening. And listening is something that can be deeply meaningful, and can be an experience of acceptance. And sometimes having listened well potentiates more direct intervention. One thing I struggle with about the quest for etiology, is understanding the difference between the quest being about avoidance, and the quest being about intimacy. I think when we call something "storytelling," we are responding to a description of history that functions as avoidance of the present moment. However, telling someone about one's past, one's joys and heartaches, one's regrets and shame, is one way that we begin to feel intimate with another person.
THERAPEUTIC RELATIONSHIP **Various aspects - comments on ACT book pp. 271-275** **SELF-AS-CONTEXT** **Transcendence, experience of** [9-7-04] Joanne Steinwachs	Contradiction and uncertainty: the willingness to entertain contradictory themes of uncertainties without feeling compelled to use verbal behavior or verbal reasoning to resolve them. Two things come to mind: The test of a first-rate intelligence is the ability to hold two opposed ideas in mind at the same time and still retain the ability to function. One should, for example, be able to see that things are hopeless and yet be determined to make them otherwise. - *F. Scott Fitzgerald* And Alice laughed: "There's no use trying," she said; "one can't believe impossible things." "I daresay you haven't had much practice," said the Queen. "When I was younger, I always did it for half an hour a day. Why, sometimes I've believed as many as six impossible things before breakfast." The phrase "field of play" seems apt to me. When I am in ACT mode with a client, it does feel like play, even if we're working on heavy painful stuff. Field of possibility is another way I think of it. No guarantees, no warranties - just living. My clients and I have a bus metaphor when we talk about the impermanence of life. Years ago, when I was making another appointment with a client, he told me he planned to be there, but as John Lennon said, "Life is what happens when you're busy making plans," and that either of us could be hit by a bus. He was right and I try to remember it. It seems to me that this awareness leads right into values work. If you have no guarantee that you will survive the day, how does that affect what you're doing right now? Tolerate paradox, ambiguity, confusion and irony. I suppose you'd have to be a fan of Monty Python, then, hey? I still find the rescuing bit hard not to buy. Getting older helps. I'm beginning to realize on a gut level that I have no idea what happens next. Some days that's really hard. One woman and I were discussing the whole uncertainty thing and I got rescue-y. I suggested to her that it was like being a trapeze artist, and you just let go of one trapeze, fly through the air for a while and grab the next. She replied, "Right. Except for a few things: you've never seen a trapeze before, you're blind, all of your enemies are watching, your hair's on fire, and you're naked." Point taken. Identification with the client: "We are not cut from different cloth, but from the same cloth." This, to me, is perhaps the most precious thing about doing ACT. Being trained in the psychodynamic camp, I always felt like a fraud. I knew that I wasn't necessarily stronger or more psychologically healthy,

but the work seemed to need me to put on my therapist suit and pretend that I was. So the client would be wearing their client suit and I'd be wearing my therapist suit and we'd sit in the room and pretend not to notice when the suits slipped. Not as much fun as you might imagine.

Normal reassurance vs. soft reassurance. How I make this distinction is this - normal reassurance has the flavor of the tense pat on the back and the underlying desire for them to stop talking. "It will be all right," is usually for me. I can feel the tenseness in my face when I'm being normally reassuring, and I can find myself wandering, thinking about grocery shopping and whatnot. When I'm doing soft reassurance, I'm often more uncomfortable, tending to see how close their suffering is to mine and I'm rivetted. I can't hold anything else, just the awareness of how hard it is sometimes to be human. Often, I get teary, especially when I get in touch with the amazing courage it takes for some of my clients to just get out of bed in the morning.

Self-disclosure: An essential aspect of developing a human relationship. Where I still struggle is with the workability of the self-disclosure. If I'm having a terrible day, I think the client can tell, but they're paying me to be present for them, although some of them would love to caretake me in the session, if only to avoid their stuff. It's messy, this edge, and I like precision. But I think the messiness is where the life is. Perhaps.

Therapeutic Use of Spirituality. "A view of the world that recognizes a transcendent quality to human experience, acknowledges the universal aspects of the human condition, and respects the client's values and choices."

Stepping back from a personal struggle and examining it openly and non-defensively. Easier said than done. This is where the observer exercise comes in, for me. I've had the experience of transcendence with this exercise, and clients had described the same. When they can dip into that open-hearted space and observe themselves from there, their faces and bodies soften. It's really wonderful to watch. This observer position is the most fluid position I can take in the session as well. That being said, it takes repeated effort and intention to come to this place. But when someone--myself or client--has had the experience of this observer self, they know that it's possible. There's a there there for them, if you will. Until the experience happens, there's no there for them to go to. At least as I see it.

Radical respect: "There is no right or wrong way to live one's life. There are only consequences that follow from specific human behaviors."

Another quote I've stolen from a client. "So the way I look at it, there's six billion and counting humans on the planet. There's probably not one right way to be a human being, so my job is to find the way I want to be a human being and choose things that get me there."

In my experience, this defining of valued direction tends to evolve over time. Not many of the people I work with can immediately describe what matters to them. We tend to do successive approximation, and look for a non-verbal response, sort of an aha experience. Values work is the part of ACT I struggle with the most.

Clinical use of humor and irreverence: "The therapist's irreverence comes from an appreciation of the craziness and verbal entanglements that surround human living." It seems to me that this can backfire if I'm not in radical respect. Radical respect seems to infuse all of the work with a client from the ACT perspective. RR for their values, RR for their history, RR for their choices. RR for how they show up in the room. Is RR the same as acceptance? It's great when the client begins using humor and irreverence with their stuff. Another steal: Client's doing a lot of reason giving, catches themself and says, "Anyway, that's my story and I'm sticking with it." Then laughs. Very cool stuff.

Hopefully this is of some use to the list. Rank beginner here. Remember, I am only an egg.

THERAPIST

Acceptance/ respect, attitude of [7-23-04]

Patty Bach

This discussion [Cross Reference: see 5-220 - CULTURAL DIFFERENCES Response to ACT interventions] has made me think of how often we treatment providers use control rather than acceptance strategies in the context of working with our clients. I'm not speaking of any individual therapist, and more about the field as a whole... And that perhaps clients "know" this about psychotherapy and are thus not so willing to engage in treatment. For example, admonitions that one must be abstinent to participate in this substance abuse treatment; or must follow this diet to be in the weight management group; etc. As one of my colleagues put it (in the context of discussing harm reduction strategies in the treatment of substance abuse) "substance abuse is the only field where we demand that the client first recover and only then do we agree to provide treatment"; e.g., many SA treatment programs require abstinence as a condition of treatment - as if someone who could so readily abstain would seek treatment in the first place! I think this is a challenge in using manualized treatments generally and especially those that prescribe very specific behaviors such as in the areas of substance abuse, compulsive behaviors, and behavioral medicine in particular.

When I've done staff training and presentations on acceptance and on harm reduction behavior change strategies I often find largely African-American treatment provider audiences somewhat more receptive

	than largely Caucasian audiences, and I have noticed that the enthusiasm is most visible only after I discuss the "radical respect/acceptance" stance of the therapist. (And some treatment providers from all cultural backgrounds are horrified by this stance seeing it as tantamount to endorsing "bad" behavior and giving the client the message that anything goes.)
	I think the stance of the therapist is an important component of ACT. This stance of radical respect/acceptance is also present in motivational interviewing, which is of course all about increasing motivation to change behavior.
	The data on harm reduction and substance abuse show that in the European countries where more harm reduction strategies are used more members of the target population are engaged in treatment as compared to countries such as the USA that use more abstinence based (my way or the highway) treatment...the difference in treatment engagement is tremendous - for example in the Netherlands 80% of substance abusers are actively engaged in some form of treatment while in the United States the number is more like 10%. I can describe all kinds of personal experience with 'treatment failure' in sharing my experience of trying to apply group treatment on social and conflict management skills that 'worked' with clients in Reno Nevada to clients from Chicago's impoverished and violent South side...
	In short, I wonder if making the therapist stance more clear at the outset of ACTherapy might not increase engagement in treatment. As always I am reminded of the utility and power of the statement in ACT that "outcome is the process through which process becomes the outcome." We may have a sense of what works and data to back it up, and it doesn't hurt to let the client know explicitly that we ACT therapists know and respect that the ultimate expert on what works for the client is the client. I learn this lesson again and again each time I catch myself thinking I know what is best for a client.
	Some clients come to therapy hoping we will tell them what to do and how to do it, and some dread therapy fearing we will tell them what to do and how to do it. Maybe making the ACT stance clear, that we will engage in the journey of facilitating the client's discovery of what works and what doesn't work in this or that context and helping the client set a course rather than a destination can increase treatment engagement - making clear that we are about changing process in the service of outcome rather than dictating outcomes. I think this is important in the context of culture. Though the paradox that outcome and process are linked remains, at least we are acknowledging it up front....
THERAPIST Acceptance/ respect, attitude of [cont'd] **ACT cf.** **Motivational Interviewing** **DBT [7-23-04]** Jonathan Kandell	You mention Motivational Interviewing, which shares with ACT being radically client centered but also directive (which is not a contradiction). In this sense ACT is a strategic therapy. In my opinion it is a given that ACT therapists use a motivational interviewing style.... We strategically arrange things to get clients to give up their control strategies *but we let the client provide their own motivation.* Everything in ACT is about "workability"--which is always defined by the client and their life in context. Standard MI techniques such as developing the discrepancy, amplifying, Columbo are the bread-and-butter of successful ACT, especially in the creative hopelessness stage (which may be one reason some prefer to bring values in early). And then later with "values" on one end of the pole and FEAR on the other.... The Prochazka "stages of change" model fits nicely with ACT too.
	[As an aside, I think this is one of the key differences between ACT and DBT. DBT like ACT aims at increased flexibility by skillful use of acceptance and control strategies in different contexts. But DBT is not client centered. While DBT also emphasizes workability, it frequently "pulls rank" on the client by confrontation. "OK, so what skill did you use when that happened?" is a DBT mantra.... For Borderline clients this works well; but for clients in general it can backfire. Of course DBT can be done in a non-directive manner as well ... but then it starts to look a lot like ACT.]
THERAPIST **Advice/ reassurance/ rescuing client [8-21-04]** Mary Politi	Marcelo Mombelli wrote: I gave [a client] the advice to wait and to stick to his choice, because he asked me what to do with his girlfriend: Should I go back with her or should I keep my decision?
	I frequently feel the urge to "rescue" my clients when they are feeling badly about something through reassurance, advice, etc. It's not clear to me that you did that here with your advice, as that would look something like "you did the right thing," or some variant of "it will be ok." I would try to be aware of that, though, when you are working with your clients in case you have the same tendency I do. It's important in ACT to be comfortable yourself with the same emotions you are trying to get the clients to feel. It's not about "defending the ACT stance," as you put it, but helping the client get comfortable with both unpleasant and pleasant emotions. You can't do that as effectively if you're not comfortable with those feelings yourself. (I hope that makes sense.)
	In this case, maybe values work would help the client understand why he made the choice he did and you can help him feel whatever he feels with regard to his choice about the girlfriend.

THERAPIST	Tony Balazs wrote:
Burnout/ stigmatizing fusion process [11-28-04] Steve Hayes	At the center where I used to work, some labels, "borderline" for instance, were used in a somewhat derogatory way by some therapists, as if to say "Lord save me from my borderline clients." Would this, and would this kind of labeling in general, be examples of fusion? It surely is. If you replaced the words we as therapists use about difficult clients with similar words that are linked to racial or sexual stereotypes, we'd all have to put bags over our heads in shame. It is a big source of the burnout therapists often feel. There is a study on using ACT to reduce this stigmatizing fusion/burnout process in therapists in the next issue of *Behavior Therapy*. I suspect this will eventually be an enormous goad to growth in ACT: we now have several data sets showing that the model is helpful to therapists, quite apart from the use they put it to with clients.
THERAPIST **Compassion; experiential workshops** [6-22-04] Steve Hayes	Eric McCollum wrote: I have been struggling with the issue of where compassion fits in ACT. In my understanding of Buddhism, the two "wings" of mindfulness are clear seeing (aka wisdom) and compassion. ACT seems to be right on target with the clear seeing part - helping clients to see the operation of the mind, how one can not hold thoughts so tightly, etc. I wonder, however, if the discussion about therapists' problems and therapy is a nod to the need, as well, for compassion. With only clear seeing, it might be too easy to create an "us vs. them" mindset, to see people's problems as intellectual knots that need to be untied, etc. and to miss the pain involved and the struggle that accompanies changing one's view of, and relationship to, one's own experience. So, maybe it is not the necessity of therapy *per se*, but is the need to balance wisdom with compassion in our work. One vital source of compassion, it seems to me, is to realize that we have much the same struggle as do our clients (sometimes more, in fact). Therapy may certainly be one route to compassion but there may be others - meditation practice, life experience, etc. This post seems so right on. This is why we have settled on training ACT the way we have: intense experiential workshops that go into this space of pain, avoidance, and values. More typical skills-based training comes later. It's not to "fix" the therapists or "treat" them or get them "clear." It is to ground the work in the reality of being human a) so that ACT work can be functional rather than topographical (so that you can "hear the note" when a client is fused or defused; vital or deadened; avoiding or accepting ... because you've learned more about that "note" in your own experience), and b) so that the therapeutic relationship can be equal, intimate, and compassionate.
THERAPIST Compassion; experiential workshops [cont'd] Jim Bastien	One way to view the wisdom and compassion dialectic is to re-cast it as acceptance and change. From this perspective compassion is akin to acceptance and willingness and wisdom are related to change techniques. Wisdom is knowing what works and developing the skill to employ what works clinically. Compassion and acceptance is the ability to be present in the moment and be willing to experience life as it is just now. Wisdom and compassion work together as two aspects of caring. Wisdom is the "head" aspect and compassion is the "heart" aspect. They are like two sides of a coin. The coin is caring and wisdom and compassion are the heads and tails. When caring for clients it is important to know what works (wisdom) but understand and accept that we must remain open and accepting of whatever happens with the client in the moment because it is the truth of his/her experience.
THERAPIST **"Don't believe a word I'm saying"** [11-5-04] Kelly Wilson	Sven Rydberg wrote: Here is one more who has felt hesitant about the phrase: "Don't believe a word I'm saying." (It may feel like fun to say or write it. But it causes confusion, and confusion is not an end in itself.) I will NOT use that phrase. At times, I have said: "If you question something I am saying, feel free to tell me." "Don't believe a word I am saying" can, but need not, sound like some kind of mind game. Typically when I say this, it is in the context of a relationship with a client in which I am unmistakably on their side and in a context in which I am appealing to their own sense of workability (believe your own experience). Nothing head trippy about it said in that context.
THERAPIST "Don't believe a word I'm saying" [cont'd] Mary Englert	I get into the 'Don't believe a word ...' arena when encouraging clients to compare their experience with their thoughts. In encouraging experimenting with behaviors that are more consistent with values, data gathered is more reliable than anything I could ever say.

THERAPIST "Don't believe a word I'm saying" [cont'd] Steve Hayes	The only time I've run into problems using it is in groups. The reason is simple. It is not a literal formula… and it is used in context, as Kelly describes. Used properly it is irreverent, edgy, challenging, affiliative, and compassionate. It is not cutesy, psychobabble, one-up, or literal. Of course it is confusing. All paradox is confusing. But ACT is inherently paradoxical and confusing because it is challenging the excesses of normal language processes. The GOAL is not confusion - it is just that we will not back away from confusion as if confusion is ipso facto harmful, anymore than we would back away from removing the chains off of a prisoner merely because it would at first lead to a lot of unpredictable limb movements. Unpredictability is not the goal: liberation is the goal. In the same way confusion is not the goal: liberation is the goal. It would be idiotic to have an entire theory of how language works and then turn around and attack the general utility of belief. If that was the issue, whacks to the head until we were all non-verbal would be therapeutic. But I'm a bit surprised by the capitalized NOT Sven. If it doesn't fit your style, don't use it. But the core of that sentence is important and "If you question something I am saying, feel free to tell me." is not in touch with it. Consider a client struggling mightily to figure it all out, practically killing themselves to understand it, and sinking ever deeper into despair as a result. Could you imagine saying compassionately "maybe you will not find the solution to your struggle inside literal belief."? And might you say "and believing me may not be the answer -- as if I have THE ANSWERS and others don't." If so, this is just a way to do that. If not, then what is the LITERAL belief that will help that person? What concrete understanding is the "over-understander" missing? Clients want you to know all the answers. So do you. So do I. Our minds all want what any human mind wants: a formula based on literal understanding. But the whole analysis of psychopathology on which ACT depends says that it is the excesses of that very repertoire that is at the core of human suffering. That does not mean that we would do better by blowing up all literal understanding. When "know how" is established it is sometimes safe and helpful to create an instance of "know that." Note that in the ACT book, creative hopelessness is followed immediately by "control is the problem" - which is a sequence in which response opportunities that come from defusion are followed by a strategic rule. And sometimes "know that" establishes "know how." That is why we use metaphors that show in a common sense way that "sometimes it works like that." And we have and are working hard to further develop a whole (literal) theory of language and psychopathology that is all about "knowing that." Best I can figure out, what is happening here is that verbalizations that are not meant to be literal are being looked at as if they are. The "voice" in these writings changes, as the ACT book itself warns. If you want literal, read the RFT book. When we do science we do literal. But when we do therapy we do what works. That means saying things in different voices for different purposes. Sometimes literal. Sometimes not. But always workability is the bottom line. We warn clients of that too. That is another aspect of the message in "don't believe a word I'm saying." We literally say "sometimes we are a reporter; sometimes a coach; and in here I'm mostly a coach -- the measure of success is not consistency or Truth -- it is serving you; it is workability." Doing a literal analysis of paradox is fine with our science hats on. It is not fine with our therapy hats on - not if the point is to do what paradox does in a therapeutic context. A scientific analysis of dancing is not dancing.
THERAPIST "Don't believe a word I'm saying" [cont'd] Russ Harris	This echoes what Buddha repeatedly said to his disciples: "Don't believe something just because I say it. Trust what your experience teaches you."
THERAPIST "Don't believe a word I'm saying" [cont'd] Steve Hayes	... Everything has to be contextually situated in the relationship and it all has to fit your style. Neither of those can be expressed in an email but I doubt if that is a problem here. Brainstorming other ways of getting at the core issue: "Your mind is not necessarily your friend here..." seems like a softer version. A funny version (stolen from a comedian - I forget who) is "Well, I used to think my mind was the most important organ I had - until I realized what was telling me that." If you want the language of belief retained, you can roll it into a positive direction with "Well, which do you believe here - your mind or your experience?" Or "I can see you are trying hard to understand me. And of course that's what minds do. But let me just ask this: how has understanding and figuring out worked for you so far in this area?" If the person says it has had limited benefit, a follow up might be "well, then would it be OK to look at

	what we are doing through other lens? Maybe having the "right belief" - even about what I'm saying - is not as important as finding more effective ways to move forward. Would you be willing to do that even if it meant not being able to figure it all out moment by moment?"
	If they are on board with that, a slightly softer version of the sentence that bothered you now fits easily: "so maybe BELIEVING what I'm saying is not really helpful here - especially if some of what we need to create together is beyond word, and rules, and simple logical formulations. Experience and workability is the real bottom line - not belief as such." etc.
	The bottom line is this: is it OK to let go of belief when it seems to get in the way? How can you help the person do that given that minds CAN'T do that since minds are just a way of speaking about collections of temporal, causal, and evaluative relational frames and letting go of the domination of that repertoire ("Belief" is just another way of speaking about that same collection of actions) is what we are trying to do. The repertoire that can find more flexible ways of responding is defused, accepting, in the moment, conscious, valuing, and non-evaluative.
THERAPIST **Openness** **ACT cf.** **CBT - therapist openness** **DBT - therapist openness [5-31-05]** Jonathan Kandell	Martin Cernvall wrote: As I understand it, one of the great virtues of the CBT-therapist is the absence of a hidden agenda (as opposed to more insight-oriented therapies) and a total openness about purpose, technique and rationale to the client. Does the ACT therapist have a hidden agenda or not, and if so, how would this be defended.... What I'm thinking is, would it be possible to show the client the model early in therapy (as perhaps would be advocated by a more traditional CBT-posture) or would this hurt our purpose? In my opinion you're correct that relative to CBT, ACT "hides" more from the client. The part of ACT which resembles Zen (you can't talk your way out of language's limitations but have to see) often involves manipulation by the therapist to prove their point, amounting to what are essentially noble tricks. But ACT isn't alone in this: any kind of strategic therapy faces the same ethical issues. Is using paradoxical intervention, therapeutic double-binds, or avoiding colluding with maladaptive personality traits any different? Any theory, really, tries to "mold" the client, no matter how much one claims otherwise. Since in ACT the client and you agree on the larger goal, and you're not moving too far ahead of where they're at, there are hopefully no ethical problems with some things you don't disclose along the way. (Even the best marriage has secrets.) Since ACT's specific techniques are based on efficacy, there is no inherent reason one couldn't be more or less hidden-- there is no inherent reason you couldn't very openly tell the client what you intend to do and why you are doing it, as does CBT. The ACT group protocols I've seen, for instance, have been much more out-on-the-table. In my ACT groups I often just argue for the points rather than engage in esoteric exercises which "show" the points, and sometimes it works. It's interesting to compare DBT with ACT in this regard. DBT is much more "open" (in your sense) since the whole agenda is on the table from the beginning with the client simply needing to learn the "skills." DBT doesn't question language however, so has an easier time with this.
THERAPIST Openness [cont'd] **"Don't believe a word I'm saying" [cont'd]** Steve Hayes *Cross Reference:* *See 2-60 for an earlier post in the thread:* *THERAPIST* *"Don't believe a word I'm saying"*	I don't think anything is hidden. It is just that we have to take responsibility for what is heard not just what is said. The literal truth said in a way that absolutely cannot be understood is a functional lie and pointless. They hired a therapist not a textbook. Personally I say all I can - which is virtually everything and by the end is everything. Ironically, some of the things cited earlier in this string as evidence of "hiding" are also literally true and, if timed well and done from compassion and connection are also functionally true ("don't believe what I'm saying" - which I usually follow with something like "I mean that the value of this will not be found in the domain of belief"). How is that hiding?
THERAPIST **Logical talk/ contradiction [2-24-05]** Julian McNally	By the way when I 'contradict' myself I usually notice it first, but whether or not I notice it or the client does, my response is the same: "I know that seems illogical or contradictory, but we're not trying to provide you with a set of rules for living your life. We're just looking for what works. And that's all it has to do - work, not make sense or be logical, or even be explainable to someone else. So listen to your experience, not to your mind's opinion about whether it is logical."

THERAPIST **Novice - need for experiential contact with ACT** **METAPHOR** **Experiential contact with ACT - swimming [10-3-03]** Kelly Wilson	Mark Taylor wrote: I had the privilege of hearing Steve Hayes speak at Lackland AFB (two 1.5 hour talks) during my residency last year. I have also read most of the ACT book and have been on this listserv for a while. I just met with a client who seems perfect for this type of therapy. However, since I have not attended any workshops and have no supervisors trained in ACT, would it be ethical to try these techniques and head down the ACT road? Is a workshop necessary for the stamp of approval? I don't know about necessary. I don't think we have the science available to make any big claims about necessary and sufficient conditions. I do think there are things that are important about ACT that are hard to write down. The metaphor I use is swimming. I can tell you all about swimming--in perfect detail. In the end, you would still not know how it feels to slip into the water, to glide through it, or that swimming is as close to flying as humans get. That is to say--I recommend the workshops to help you integrate a principled understanding of ACT with the experience you will have "in the room." I am sure others on the list who have attended will have opinions. Perhaps before too long, we will have data.
THERAPIST **Reassurance giving** **EXERCISE** **Child, making contact with self as [6-25-05]** Steve Hayes	Russ Harris wrote: When clients are beating themselves up about the past, therapists often say 'You did the best you could, given the level of awareness/ knowledge/ life experience you had at the time.' ... From the ACT perspective, should we avoid statements like this altogether? My first thought is that they mainly serve the function of reassurance, which is often intended to avoid painful emotions. Therefore the more useful approach is to ask how we can learn from these memories (or in some instances, how we can honour them). On the other hand, I think that such statements can be very useful in promoting self-acceptance. Just a thought. The problem with reassurance / rescue is not the emotional impact on the reassuree so much as it is the impact on the reassurer. After all it is the reassurer who is behaving and whose behavior might be reinforced by any avoidance agenda ... Plus it has verbal implications. Reassurance often implicitly suggests that the reassurer is strong / right / wise and the reassuree is weak / needs to be guided. So the therapist gets to be wise and strong (at the cost of the client) and the therapist gets to feel better seeing the client feel better. And it gets justified by a philosophy (e.g., "we are all always doing the best we can") and there you are with another rule with its area of rigidity built in (as you noted: "Well, no, I didn't do my homework. But hey, isn't that a natural response?"). You can do the same work without as much danger more experientially -- and acceptance and defusion is right there inside this work. For example, in the little kid exercise the person is guided to meeting himself / herself when younger. Looking into the eyes of that child it is obvious to the client that she or he was doing what she or he knew to do. In this set, acceptance now = love = forgiveness = reassurance. Control = criticism = invalidation = suffering. No need for philosophy or lots of words from on high (i.e., from the therapist). Just a little support / guidance / experience. You might even still say "you were doing the best you could with what you knew" (or not) but if you time it right it will just express an obvious experiential reality after the work has been done -- the functional equivalent of "it is OK to be me" or even "I am." When a client is beating themselves up and you sit with that; defuse from that; accept that, feel that (as it is, not as what it says it is) you are giving the client the tools to do something different while you yourself are doing what you are asking the client to do. Seems safer for the client. Especially seems safer for you. PS I wonder if some of the worry about true belief / skepticism [a separate thread] comes from the clinical voice of the list. For example, if I write a post like the one I just wrote, at every point I could be writing about functional analysis; the basic principles that might lead to this possible direction etc. but instead I'm just putting out content ideas, as if it is the content of the ideas that is alone important (and why? Because I said so? Because it is logical? Hmmm Troublesome). All of these ideas are based on a history of much more than what is said (principles; seeing contingencies; etc.) and some of these are not shared; some are pointed to in the formal analysis, but others are implicit and not yet worked out. All should be held lightly and tested as hypotheses, but they are presented more in the voice of "how about this." This is a big problem ... though I'm not sure how to solve it. It seems to be pulled by the implicit purpose of the list and the difficulty of sharing some aspects of one's history on the list.
THERAPIST **Values**	... Here are the first 4 of Thich Nhat Hanh's 14 precepts. With apologies to the good monk, I've tweaked them to fit ACT. Do not be idolatrous about or bound to any doctrine, theory, or ideology, even behavioral ones. All

VALUES **Therapist [3-17-04]** Steve Hayes	systems of thought, including ACT and RFT, are guiding means; they are not absolute truth. Do not think that the knowledge you presently possess is changeless, absolute truth. Avoid being narrow-minded and bound to present views. Learn and practice non-attachment from views in order to be open to receive others' viewpoints. Truth is found in life and not merely in conceptual knowledge. Be ready to learn throughout your entire life and to observe what works in yourself and in the world at all times. Do not force others, by any means whatsoever, to adopt your views, whether by authority, threat, money, propaganda, or even education. However, through compassionate dialogue, help others renounce fanaticism and narrowness. Do not avoid contact with suffering or close your eyes before suffering. Do not lose awareness of the existence of suffering in the life of the world. Find ways to be with those who are suffering by all means, including personal contact and visits, images, sound. By such means, awaken yourself and others to the reality of suffering in the world. Those are some of the values we are trying to protect....
THERAPY **Goals - Og Lindsley's dead man rule [3-24-04]** Kelly Wilson	... ACT is all about Og Lindsley's dead man rule. This is a variant of Og Lindsley's dead man rule for behavioral targets--someone reminded me of it at ABA a year or so ago and I have used it in training a lot. The dead man rule is basically that you shouldn't pick a behavioral target that a dead person could do better. So, and Og cared about kids, you might say not to pick a target like "stay in seat," pick one like "get 3 math problems done per minute." The idea--a dead man could do the former, but not the latter. For ACTers: not feeling anxious, depressed, etc. no matter how successful treatment, could be bettered by a dead person. Here is a bit of transcript from a chapter Michelle Byrd and I just completed. In it we are speaking to an addict about treatment and its purpose--Olivia, referred to in the transcript, is the client's 9 y.o. daughter: Therapist: Yes. OK Tim, so here is the deal. What if this therapy could be about making a rich, meaningful relationship with Olivia possible? Not certain. I don't know the future Tim. But possible. What if this could make it *possible*. Let's have the therapy be about something you'd want on your tombstone Tim. Tell me this: if you could have on your tombstone "he dedicated his life to not using drugs" or "he dedicated his life to not feeling bad" or "he dedicated his life to being a father to his daughter," which would you choose? There is a guy in my tradition Tim, named Og Lindsley. Og had a saying about working with people. Never choose a goal that could be done better by a dead person. So something like "not using drugs" or "not feeling bad"- well a dead person could do that - perfectly in fact. Dead people never get high; they never feel bad. But a dead person couldn't be a Dad. No way! Can you be a dad? Maybe? Maybe? You don't think so, but have you ever thought something, and later found out you were just wrong? Ever believe, really believe, there was a Santa? We can't be certain how this will turn out Tim, but we can decide what this treatment will be about. Is Olivia worth betting your time on, worth betting your pain? Which will you choose Tim? Client: I choose Olivia. Therapist: Yeah man. I think we have a contract here. Here is what I will promise you Tim. If we do this, really do this it will be painful, I mean painful like detox will look like a picnic. But let me promise this too. We will not do anything painful that is not *for* something *you* value. For something that *you* would say is worthy of your pain. And, one last thing Tim. I promise you that I am going to hang in there with you through this. Can you hear me Tim? Do you get that this matters to me? I have not taken your path Tim, but I know that showing up for life is hard. I get how important this is to you and I am committed to working on your behalf. Wilson, K. G., & Byrd, M. R. (2004). Acceptance and Commitment Therapy for Substance Abuse and Dependence. In S. C. Hayes & K. Strosahl, (Eds.), *A Practical Guide to Acceptance and Commitment Therapy* (pp. 153-184). New York: Springer Press.
THERAPY **Instruction, use of [6-17-03]** Kelly Wilson *Cross Reference:* *See 3-124 for a later post in this thread*	Joseph Ciarrochi wrote: Does ACT exclude the more vigorous style? I know it discourages disputing, but is there such a thing as vigorous defusing? Or vigorously encouraging people to make contact with certain experiences? Can you possibly say, "Don't believe a word I am saying, but here is something I think...." and then express your position with passion and conviction (e.g., You tell me you value X but when you get drunk every day, you seem to be throwing X away. Look at your life. Is this what you want?)? It seems like in the above example, by your tone and passion, you are implying that one alternative (getting drunk every day) is less acceptable than the other, which I think is an ACT-inconsistent move. Not sure if this is official ACT either, but, hell, I have been known to jump up and down, climb on the

	table, lay on the floor, weep openly, etc. - whatever breaks up the log jam. That said, it is no coincidence that we are prone to instruct--it is damn efficient, but a slippery slope. Plus, the clients that most activate our urge to instruct are probably already activating plenty of instruction in others. Consider the drinking example--the daily drinker has heard it from everyone, including themselves, at one time or another.
	I say ACT with flexibility and sensitivity and beware verbal control of behavior, not evil, just is what it is, always contains a compelling, intoxicating dark side. Almost by definition, you get more than you bargained for.
	We wouldn't want to say instruction is a priori wrong - when I say "notice your thoughts, and, if judgments show up, see if you can notice those judgments as thoughts too," we may coach this observing posture--it is certainly instruction and quite direct.
	Notice the backside too--the person doing it will start a stream of evaluation about how they are doing-- oh I am really doing this now (and that is good), or what's wrong with me, I am not doing this right (and that's bad), or I wonder if I am doing this right (and that must be settled), or ... this is stupid, why should I do this (and that is bad), or I wonder why he is having me do this ... and if you told them why beforehand, they would be evaluating the effects ... and on.
	As soon as we instruct there is the instruction and the social contingency of following (or not), and the meaning of following (or not). So even using instruction in these pretty benign ways, we need to be mindful of the buzz that will be occurring, and notice that, and the next thing. And use the mind's own process as exemplars in a bit of discrimination training in which we learn to notice our own mind doing its job ... everywhere, all the time, and on.
THERAPY **Setbacks [8-2-04]** Theresa Glaser	[Re: committed action] I think it's crucial in *any* behavior change undertaken by humans to realize (intellectually and experientially) that it is a process, and one will *inevitably* "fall off the wagon." I attribute this to "stress inoculation" or the Zen meditative notion of guiding one's wandering mind back to task.

Index

All page numbers refer to the page on which the relevant post begins; for posts with multiple headings, the indexed heading/ sub-heading may sometimes be found on the subsequent page.

MINDFULNESS

OBSESSIVE-COMPULSIVE DISORDER

PAIN

PERSONALITY DISORDER

PHYSICAL ILLNESS

POEM

POLITICS

PRESENT MOMENT

WORK